CRIMINAL TRIALS

First Edition	2007
Second Edition	2014
Third Edition	**2017**

CRIMINAL TRIALS

Third Edition

Universal
Law Publishing
an imprint of LexisNexis

LexisNexis®

This book is a publication of LexisNexis
(A Division of RELX India Pvt Ltd)
14th floor, Building No 10, Tower-B, DLF Cyber City, Phase-II,
Gurgaon-122002, Haryana, India.
Tel : + 91 124 4774444 Fax: + 91 124 4774100
Website : www.lexisnexis.co.in / E-mail : help.in@lexisnexis.com

---

Kakde : *Criminal Trials*, Third Edition 2017

ISBN: 978-81-3125-235-2

Printed by: Shree Maitrey Printech Pvt. Ltd., A-84, Sector 2, Noida

Printed and bound in India.

DEDICATED TO

Great legendary revolutionary Bhagat Singh
and all Human rights activists
who have sacrificed their lives
for our better tomorrow.

PREFACE TO THE THIRD EDITION

In this edition I have added latest and significant judgments of various High Courts and the Apex Court touching the subject. I have also included significant judgments of Supreme Court of United Kingdom, United States, South Africa and European Court of Justice, etc. The book has been revised thoroughly and new chapters have been added. I hope the book would be of immense value to students and young entrants of the Bar.

I am grateful to Adv. Surendra Gadling, Adv. Viplav Teltumbade, Adv. Pravin Puri, Adv. Ganesh P. Neet, Adv. Anil R. Kapse who have rendered help to me in revision of the book. I am also grateful to LexisNexis which has published the third edition of the book within a short span of time.

Wani

Dated 14/07/2017

Adv. Vinayak D. Kakde,

R/o Wani, Dist-Yavatmal (Maharashtra)

Residence:

R/o Vitthal Wadi, Ward No. 3, Wani,

Tq. Wani, Dist - Yavatmal (MS)

Pin No. 445 304

Cell Phone:- 9420046230, 7709719292

PREFACE TO THE SECOND EDITION

In this edition I have added latest and significant judgments of various High Courts and the Apex Court touching the subject. The book has been revised thoroughly and ten new chapters have been added. I hope the book would be of immense value to students and young entrants of the Bar.

Wani
July 2014

Vinayak D. Kakde

PREFACE TO THE FIRST EDITION

Philip to writing this book was given by my friend Mr. Surendra Gadling (Practising Lawyer, Nagpur) and I am thankful to him for the same.

In this edition I have endeavoured to include latest and significant judgments of various High Courts and the Apex Court touching the subject. The purpose of this book is not to write the section-wise commentary but to show the students the judicial process at work and how a Judge arrives at his conclusions.

Neither I do claim this book to be a legal classic nor do I claim to have discovered anything new. Only arrangement is mine. Healthy criticism is welcomed but the same should be done keeping in view the purpose and scope of this book.

I am grateful to Adv. D.P. Kale, Wani who allowed me to use his library for this purpose. I am also grateful to Adv. Viplav Teltumbde, Mr. Sudhir Andraskar and Mr. Ganesh Neet (Typist).

I am indeed grateful to Universal Law Publishing Company Pvt. Ltd. for publishing this book.

I hope this book would be of immense value particularly to students and young entrants of the Bar.

Wani

Dated 31/12/2007

Adv. Vinayak D. Kakde,

Vice-President, Indian
Association of Peoples Lawyers,
Maharashtra Committee

CONTENTS

TABLE OF CASES

A

B

D

H

I

J

L

M

N

S

W

Y

Z

CHAPTER I

RIGHTS OF ARRESTED PERSONS, UNDERTRIALS AND PRISONERS

SYNOPSIS

"... when this organisation of politics and commerce, whose other name is the Nation, becomes all powerful at the cost of the harmony of higher social life, then it is an evil day for humanity"—***Rabindranath Tagore***

The Constitution of India guarantees human rights and fundamental rights to every citizen. However, it should be remembered that the Constitution does not confer fundamental rights. It only confirms their existence and gives them protection; *M. Nagaraj* v. *Union of India,* 2007 All SCR 91:

M.C. Mehta v. *Union of India,* (1987) 1 SCR 819 (Constitution Bench). In this case, the Apex Court held that public-spirited individual or social action group can bring an action by filing regular writ petition under Article 226 in High Court and under Article 32 in Supreme Court and also by addressing a letter to the Supreme Court, if there is violation of fundamental or other legal right of a person or class of persons.

Despite the constitutional protection and safeguards for human rights, the police machinery acts in flagrant violation of the same and therefore the Supreme Court of India and various High Courts in India have rendered various judgements from time to time for the protection of human rights. Few such judgements are given below under different heads for the readers.

(i) Freedom of Speech and Expression

Mohd. Jafar v. *Union of India,* (1994) 3 SCR 111. In this case, by a notification dated 10th December, 1992, the Central Government declared the *Jamaat-e-Islami Hind* (JEIH), an unlawful association under sub-section (1) of section 3 of the Unlawful Activities (Prevention) Act, 1967 . One of demands made by JEIH was that the Government should hold plebiscite on Kashmir. Part of Notification, *viz,* "and directs, in exercise of the powers conferred by the proviso to sub-section

(3) of that section, that this notification shall have the effect from the date of its publication in the official gazette" was held to be bad in law and was struck down by the court. Further, the court held that even temporary suspension of fundamental right is invalid unless covered by article 19(4).

In *Prabha Dutt* v. *Union of India,* (1982) 1 SCR 1184, petition under article 32 was filed by the Chief Reporter of the *'Hindustan Times'*, asking for a writ of *Mandamus* or any other appropriate writ or direction directing the respondents, particularly the Delhi Administration and the Superintendent of Tihar Jail, to allow her to interview convicts Billa and Ranga who were under a sentence of death. The apex court held that (a) The right conferred by article 19(1)(a) which includes the freedom of the press, is not an absolute right. The press in entitled to exercise its freedom of speech and expression by publishing a matter which does not invade the rights of others citizens and which does not violate the sovereignty and integrity of India, the security of the state, public order, decency and morality. (b) The right to means of information through the medium of an interview cannot be claimed by the press unless in the first instance, the person sought to interviewed is willing to be interviewed.

In *Gajanan Visheshwar Birjur* v. *Union of India,* (1994) Supp 1 SCR 466, the petitioner challenged the validity of confiscation of books by the Customs authority in this writ petition. Books imported contained writings, speeches and works of Mao, besides works of Marx, Engels and Lenin. Quoting Robert Jackson, J. who said "thought control is a copyright of totalitarianism" and allowing the appeal, the court observed—".... *we must express our unhappiness with attempts at thought control in a democratic society like ours. Human history is witness to the fact that all evolution and all progress is because of thought and that every attempt at thought control is doomed to failure. An idea can never be killed. Suppression can never be a successful permanent policy. Any surface serenity it creates is a false one. It will erupt one day. Our Constitution permits a free trade, if we can use the expression, in ideas and ideologies. It guarantees freedom of thought and expression – the only limitation being a law in terms of clause (2) of Article 19 of the Constitution. Thought control is alien to our Constitutional scheme*".

Sanskar Marathe v. *State of Maharashtra,* 2015 All MR (Cri) 4637: 2015 (2) ABR (Cri) 478. In this case, one Assem Trivedi was arrested on 8th September, 2012 on the basis of registration of FIR on 30th January, 2012 alleging, *inter alia,* commission of offence of sedition under section 124A of IPC, leading to filing of PIL which was registered as Criminal PIL. It was alleged that said cartoonist published cartoons on website which insulted and defamed the Parliament and the Government. While allowing the petition and quashing the FIR, the Bombay High Court held that provisions of section 124A of IPC cannot be invoked to penalise criticism of the persons who used strong words to express disapprobation of the measures of the Government with a view to their improvement or alternation by lawful means.

Himat Lal K. Shah v. *Commissioner of Police Ahmadabad,* (1973) 2 SCR 266: AIR 1973 SC 87. Here, the Constitution Bench of five judges has held that, "the right to hold public meeting in a public street is a fundamental rights of citizens.... freedom of assembly is an essential element of a democratic system".

Vishwa Hindu Parishad v. *Collector and DM Machilipatnam,* AIR 2001 AP 173, In this case, the Andhra Pradesh High Court has held that permission to hold public meeting in a public place cannot be denied simply because the proposed meeting was a religious meeting.

The Full Bench of the Bombay High Court has held that right to information is a part of cherished fundamental right of freedom of speech and expression. The Court further held that fundamental freedom should not be kept in wraps by using outdated tool of *locus standi; Sangharaj Damodhar Rupwate* v. *Nitin Gadre,* 2007 (5) AIR Bom R 166 (FB): 2007 (2) Mah LR 433 (FB).

Chief Information Commissioner v. *State of Manipur,* AIR 2012 SC 864, In this case, the Honourable Apex Court held that right to information is intrinsic part of fundamental right to free speech and expression guaranteed under Article 19(1)(a) of the Constitution. However, such right is subject to reasonable restrictions under Article 19(2) of the Constitution. *Maria Monica Susairaj* v. *State of Maharashtra,* 2009 (3) AIR Bom R 1: 2009 (1) Mh LJ (Cri) 264: 2009 Cr LJ 2075: 2008 All MR (Cri) 3343. Here, the Honourable Bombay High Court has held that police have responsibility to ensure that any information given to media was accurate. Police department would lay down norms for its officers regarding sharing of information to press.

(ii) Right Against Self-Incrimination (Right of Silence)

One Miranda was arrested at his home and taken in custody to a police station where he was identified by the complaining witness. He was then interrogated by two police officers for two hours, which resulted in a signed, written confession. At trial, the oral and written confessions were presented to the jury. He was found guilty of kidnapping and rape and was sentenced to 20-30 years imprisonment on each count. On appeal, the Supreme Court of Arizona held that Miranda's constitutional rights were not violated in obtaining the confession. He filed appeal before the Supreme Court of United States. The issue before the Court was whether statements obtained from an individual who is subjected to custodial police interrogation are admissible against him in a criminal trial and whether procedures which assure that the individual is accorded his privilege, under the Fifth Amendment to the US Constitution, not to be compelled to incriminate himself are necessary? The Supreme Court of United States held that a defendant must be warned prior to any questioning that he has the right to remain silent and he has the right to the presence of an attorney. If he cannot afford an attorney, one will be appointed for him prior to any questioning, if he so desires. This case came to be known as "Miranda Warning" and is cited throughout the world as a landmark judgment on custodial interrogation and right to silence; *Miranda* v. *State of Arizona,* 384 US 436 (1966).

Nandini Satpathy (Smt.) v. *P.L. Dani,* 1978 Cr LJ 968: AIR 1978 SC 1025. In this case, the apex Court has held that the accused persons cannot be forced to answer questions.....he is entitled to keep his mouth shut if the answer sought has a reasonable prospect of exposing him to guilt in some other accusation actual and imminent. However, fanciful claim, unreasonable apprehension and vague possibilities cannot be the hiding ground for an accused person. He is bound to answer where there is no clear tendency to incriminate.

However the Constitution Bench of 11 judges in *The State of Bombay* v. *Kathi Kalu Oghad*, AIR 1961 SC 1808: (1961) 2 Cr LJ 856: (1962) 3 SCR 10 has held that in compelling an accused person to give his specimen handwriting or signature, or impressions of his thumb, fingers, palm or foot to the investigating officer or under orders of a Court for the purpose of comparison is not violative of Article 20(3) of the Constitution. Further, the Honourable Court held that the provisions of section 27 of the Indian Evidence Act did not offend Article 20(3) unless compulsion was used in obtaining the information. In a landmark judgment, the Apex Court held that compulsory administration of certain scientific techniques, such as narco-analysis, polygraph examination and Brain Electrical Activation Profile (BEAP) test violate the right against self-incrimination and it would also amount to cruel, inhuman or degrading treatment. The Court further held that results obtained from such tests amount to testimonial compulsion thereby attracting the bar of Article 20(3) of the Constitution of India; *Selvi* v. *State of Karnataka*, 2010 (2) Crimes 241 (SC).

Amrit Singh v. *State of Punjab*, 2006 (4) Crimes 380 (SC). This is a case of rape and murder of a six years old girl. The investigation officer claimed that some human hair were found in the hands of the deceased and therefore he filed an application in Court for obtaining specimen of hair of accused. However, accused refused to give such specimen hair. The Honourable Apex Court held that appellant had the right to give or not to give sample of his hair. He could not be made a witness against himself against his will.

State of Uttar Pradesh v. *Sunil*, Criminal Appeal 1432-1434 of 2011 decided on 2nd May, 2017. In this case, the Honourable Apex Court held that compelling an accused to provide footprint specimen is not in violation of the protection guaranteed under Article 20(3) of the Constitution and non-compliance by accused to give footprints cannot be the sole basis of conviction.

(iii) Double Jeopardy

The provisions relating to double jeopardy are as follows:

Article 20(2) of the Constitution of India – No person shall be prosecuted and punished for the same offence more than once.

Section 300(1), Cr.P.C. – A person who has once been tried by a Court of competent jurisdiction for an offence and convicted or acquitted of such offence shall, while such conviction or acquittal remains in force, not be liable to be tried again for the same offence, nor on the same facts for any other offence for which a different charge from the one made against him might have been made under sub-section (1) of section 221, or for which he might have been convicted under sub-section (2) thereof.

Section 26 of The General Clauses Act, 1897 – Where an act or omission constitutes an offence under two or more enactments, then the offender shall be liable to be prosecuted and punished under either or any of those enactments, but shall not be liable to be punished twice for the same offence.

Section 71 of IPC – Where anything which is an offence is made up of parts, any of which parts is itself an offence, the offender shall not be punished with the imprisonment of more than one of such his offences, unless it be so expressly provided. The principle is based on the maxim *"nemo debet bis vexari, si constat curice quod sit pro una iti eadem causa"* which means that no man shall be punished twice, if it appears to the Court that it is for one and the same cause.

The doctrine of *'autrefois convict'* (former conviction) and *'autrefois acquit'* (former acquittal) applies only when the offence for which the accused was tried and the offence for which he is again tried must be identical and based on the same set of facts. This principle does not apply if the later charge is civil rather than criminal in nature.

Maqbool Hussain v. *State of Bombay,* AIR 1953 SC 325. In this case, the Constitution Bench held that Article 20(2) incorporates within its scope the plea of *'autrefois convict'* as known to the British jurisprudence or the plea of double jeopardy as known to the American Constitution but circumscribes it by providing that there should be not only a prosecution but also a punishment in the first instance in order to operate as a bar to a second prosecution and punishment for the same offence; *Jitendra Panchal* v. *The Intelligence Officer,* NCB, 2007 All MR (Cri) 3127 (Bom).

In this case, the Bombay High Court held that Article 20(2) undoubtedly prohibits prosecution and punishment to a person for the same offence more than once. It incorporates the rules against double jeopardy, but it is different from the one found in USA and UK in the sense that it restricts to the principle of *'autrefois convict'* and does not extend to that of *'autrefois acquit'*. The Article 20(2) to be operative, both prosecution and punishment must co-exist. In other words, Article 20(2) would become operative in a case when the second prosecution and punishment is for the identical offence for which the person concerned had already been prosecuted and punished earlier. The Apex Court dismissed the appeal of the appellant and upheld the above decision of the Bombay High Court, which is reported in 2009 All MR (Cri) 902 (SC): AIR 2009 SC 1938: 2009 (3) SCC 57: 2009 (2) SCALE 202.

The State of Bombay v. *S.L. Apte,* (1961) 3 SCR 107: AIR 1961 SC 578. Here, the Constitution Bench held that the crucial requirement to attract Article 20(2) is that the two offences should be identical. It is, therefore, necessary to analyse and compare the ingredients of the two offences and not the allegations made in the two complaints, to see whether their identity is established.

Monica Bedi v. *State of Andhra Pradesh,* 2010 All SCR 2794: (2011) 1 SCC 284. Here, the appellant was tried and convicted at Lisbon in Portugal for being in possession of fake passport. However, she was again prosecuted and tried in India for the offences punishable under sections 120B, 419, 420 of IPC. The Appellant raised the plea of double jeopardy and prayed for setting aside the conviction. The Apex Court held that plea of double jeopardy is wholly untenable and unsustainable. The Court further held that protection against double jeopardy is in the nature of an injunction against the state but initial burden is upon accused to take necessary plea and establish the same. *Mumbai Municipal Corporation* v. *Haji B. Choudhary,* 2009 All MR (Cri) 2052. This case relates to complaint regarding unauthorised construction, where one complaint was filed with police under MRTP Act and second complaint in respect of the same subject-matter was filed by the Municipal Corporation. The complaint filed with police under MRTP Act was already dismissed. The Court held that principle of double jeopardy would be applicable to the present case.

(iv) Right to Privacy

PUCL v. *Union of India,* (1996) Supp 10 SCR 321. In this case, the petitioner filed the Public Interest Litigation (PIL) in the wake of the report on "tapping of politicians' phones" by the CBI and challenged the Constitutional validity of section 5(2) of the India Telegraph Act, 1885. Upholding the right to privacy as the human right, the apex Court held that (1.2) *"Right to privacy would certainly include telephone – conversation in the privacy of one's home or office. Telephone - tapping would, thus, infact Article 21 unless it is permitted under the procedure establish by law."* Further, the Apex Court held that (2.2) *"when a person is talking on telephone, he is exercising his right to freedom of speech and expression which is guaranteed under Article 19(1)(a) of the Constitution."* And issued orders and directions that *"An order of telephone tapping in terms of section 5(2) of the Indian Telegraph Act, 1885 shall not be issued except by the Home Secretary, Government of India and Home Secretaries of the State Government.*

Number of persons raised concerns about sharing of bio-metric data in Aadhaar Card, alleging that such exercise infringes the right of privacy. In one of the petitions, filed by Retired Justice K.S. Puttaswami, numbered as W.P. (Civil) 494/2012: *Justice K.S. Puttaswamy (Retd.)* v. *Union of India,* 2015 (5) All MR 970 (SC), the Honourable Apex Court has passed an interim order directing the Union of India that no person should suffer for not getting the Aadhaar Card, inspite of the fact that some authority had issued a circular making it mandatory. In the related matters regarding the Aadhaar Card issue, the honourable Apex Court has directed the Union of India and held that the Aadhaar Card Scheme is purely voluntary and it cannot be made mandatory till the matter is finally decided by the Supreme Court.

While hearing WP (Civil) No. 494/2012, the Honourable Apex Court observed that doubt has been created by the judgement in *M.P. Sharma* v. *Satish Chandra,* AIR 1954 SC 300 and *Kharak Singh* v. *State of Uttar Pradesh,* AIR 1963 SC 1295, the matter has been referred to larger bench. But the bench has passed an interim order directing that UIN *i.e.,* Aadhaar Card will not be used by the Government for any purpose other than PDS scheme and in particular for distribution of food grains, cooking fuel and LPG distribution scheme; *Google Spain SL, Google Inc* v. *Agencia Espanola de Proteccion de Datos (AEPD), & Mario Costeja Gonzalez,* decided on 13th May, 2014.

The right to be forgotten is of recent origin and this concept was put into practise in the European Union and Argentina since 2006. Though the right to be forgotten is not strictly right to privacy, nevertheless it is a human right. Right to privacy includes "the right to be forgotten" or "right to be erased" or "right to de-link". The right to be forgotten or right to be erased allows an individual to request for removal of his/her personal information/data online. The origin of this right can be traced back to the French jurisprudence on the 'right to oblivion' or 'droit a l'oubli'. In this case, Mario Costeja Gonzalez filed a complaint in 2010 with the Spanish Data Protection Agency (the AEPD) against a local newspaper and Google Spain for claims relating to auction notices mentioning Gonzalez published in 1998. The notices concerned real estate auctions held to secure repayment of Gonzalez's social security debts. He contended that these pages were no longer necessary because the attachment proceedings concerning him had been fully resolved. He sought removal of the pages from local newspaper and also sought removal of the links from Google. The AEDP dismissed the plaintiff's claim against the newspaper, but allowed those against Google. Google appealed to Spain's High Court, which in turn referred the matter to European Court of Justice. In appeal, the Grand Chamber of the European Court of Justice held that the European citizens have a right to request that commercial search firms, such as Google, that gather personal information for profit should remove links to private information when asked, provided the information is no longer relevant. The Court observed that the fundamental right to privacy is greater than the economic interest of the commercial firm. However, Google won the right to be forgotten case in Japan where a man who brought suit had been found guilty years ago of child pornography charges and wanted articles about his arrest removed from Google searches. The Supreme Court of Japan rejected his demand for removal of news search results of his arrest on sex charges and further held that to do so would violate freedom of expression. However, the Court held that if the legal interests for non-disclosure clearly outweigh the reasons for providing information, search engine providers can be requested to remove the relevant URLs from search results.

(v) Right to Life (Right to Dignity)

The Supreme Court of India in its various judgements has held that handcuffing or chaining a person is violative of basic right to dignity. The Supreme Court of India has held in *Prem Shankar Shukla* v. *Delhi Administration*, (1980) 3 SCR 855 that *"handcuffing is* prima facie *inhuman and therefore, unreasonable, is over harsh and at the first blush, arbitrary. Absent fair procedure and objective monitoring to inflict "irons" is to resort to zoological strategies repugnant to Article 21..... But to bind a man hand and foot, fetter his limbs with hoops of steel, shuffle him along in the streets and stand him for hours in the Courts is to torture him, defile his dignity, vulgarise society and foul the sole of Constitutional culture. Iron straps are insult and pain writ large, animalising victim and keepers"*. Further the Court held that the escorting authority must record contemporaneously the reasons for doing so.

In *Citizens for Democracy* v. *The State of Assam*, (1995) 3 SCR 943 the Apex Court has held that *"handcuffs or other fetters shall not be forced on a prisoner-convicted or undertrial while lodged in a jail any where in the country or while transporting or in transit from one jail to another or from jail to court and back. The police and the jail authorities, on their own, shall have no authority to direct the handcuffing of any inmate of a jail in the country or during transport from one jail to another jail or to Court and back"*. Further, the Court has held that in all cases of arrest by police, the persons arrested shall not be handcuffed unless special orders in that respect are obtained from the Magistrate at the time of the grant of the remand. The apex Court has warned all police and prison authorities that if they violate any of the direction issued by the Court, they shall be summarily punishable under the Contempt of Courts Act apart from other penal consequences under law.

In *Shabnam* v. *Union of India,* 2015 All SCR 2136 it was held by the Apex Court held that Article 21 of the Constitution has its traces in dignity of human being. It does not end with confirmation of death sentence, but goes beyond and remains valid still such convict meets his/her destiny. Even condemned prisoners have a right to dignity.

In *Umesh Kumar* v. *State of Andhra Pradesh,* 2014 All SCR 661 the Apex Court held that right of reputation is a necessary element in regard to life of a citizen under Article 21. Even international covenant on Civil and Political Rights, 1996 recognises the right to have opinions. The right of freedom of expression under article 19 is subject to the right of reputation of others. Reputation is not only a salt of life but the purest treasure and the most precious perfume of life.

In a landmark judgment in *D.K. Basu* v. *State of West Bengal,* AIR 1997 SC 610: (1996) Supp 10 SCR 284, the Supreme Court directed that the following requirements shall be followed in all cases of arrests or detention till legal provisions are made in the behalf as preventive measures:

(i) The police personnel carrying out the arrest and handling the interrogation of the arrestee should bear accurate, visible and clear identification and name tags with their designations. The particulars of all such police personnel who handle interrogation of the arrestee must be recorded in a register.

(ii) That the police officer carrying out the arrest of the arrestee shall prepare a memo of arrest at the time of arrest and such memo shall be attested by at least one witness, who may be either a member of the family of the arrestee or a respectable person of the locality from where the arrest is made. It shall be counter signed by the arrestee and shall contain the time and date of arrest.

(iii) A person who has been arrested or detained and is being held in a police station or interrogation centre or other lock-up, shall be entitled to have one friend or relative or other person known to him or having interest in his welfare being informed, as soon as practicable, that he has been arrested and is being detained at the particular place, unless the attesting witness of the memo of arrest is himself such a friend or a relative of the arrestee.

(iv) The time, place of arrest and venue of custody of an arrestee must be notified by the police, where the next friend or relative of the arrestee lives outside the district of town, through the Legal Aid Organisation in the district and the police station of the area concerned, telegraphically within a period of 8 to 12 hours after the arrest.

(v) The person arrested must be made aware of this right to have someone informed of his arrest or detention as soon as he is put under arrest or is detained.

(vi) An entry must be made in the diary at the place of detention, regarding the arrest of the person which shall also disclose the name of the next friend of the person who has been informed of the arrest and the names and particulars of the police officials in whose custody the arrestee is.

(vii) The arrestee should, where he so requests, be also examined at the time of his arrest and major and minor injuries, if any present on his/her body, must be recorded at that time. The "Inspection Memo" must be signed both by the arrestee and the police officer effecting the arrest and its copy provided to arrestee.

(viii) The arrestee should be subjected to medical examination by a trained doctor every 48 hours during his detention in custody by a doctor on the panel of approved doctors appointed by Directors, Health Services of the concerned State or Union Territory. Directors, Health Services should prepare such a panel for all Tehsils and Districts as well.

(ix) Copies of all the documents including the memo of arrest, referred to above, should be sent to *Illaqua* Magistrate, for his record.

(x) The arrestee may be permitted to meet his lawyer during interrogation, though not throughout the interrogation.

(xi) A police control room should be provided at all districts and state headquarters, where information regarding the arrest and the place of custody of the arrestee shall be communicated by the officer causing the arrest, within 12 hours of effecting the arrest and at the police control room it should be displayed on a conspicuous notice board.

Further, the Court has held that failure to comply with the requirements hereinabove mentioned shall apart from rendering the concerned officials liable for departmental action, also render him liable to be punished for contempt of Court and the proceedings for contempt of Court may be instituted in High Court of the Country, having territorial jurisdiction over the matter. Further, the Court has held that monetary compensation can be granted for the infringement of right to life of the citizen or to the family of deceased.

Even the Bombay High Court has directed the Magistrates to take steps against police officer who handcuff the persons in violation of the rules framed under Bombay Police Manual, 1959; *Bhimrao A. Mhaske* v. *State of Maharashtra*, 1990 Mh LJ 838.

In *Kashinath Laxmanrao Marwalikar* v. *State of Maharashtra*, 2002 All MR (Cri) 1791, the Bombay High Court has held that, "act of giving third degree treatment to person in police custody cannot be said to be an act done in discharge or purported discharge of duty or in excess of duty. Protection under section 161 of Bombay Police Act, 1951 and section 197(2) of Cr. P.C. cannot be extended to the accused".

In later part of the book, we shall see the effect of violation of human rights and the directions and guidelines issued by the Honourable Supreme Court and various High Courts in India.

(vi) Rights of Suspected Accused

The accused or the person suspected to have committed crime, has right to be heard, whether the order under challenge is at pre-process stage or at post-process stage is unconsequential; *Manharbhai Kakade* v. *Shaileshbhai Patel,* 2013 Cri LJ 144 (SC).

(vii) Rights of Woman

The Apex Court, in *Nandini Satpathy (Smt.)* v. *P.L. Dani,* 1978 Cri LJ 968, has held that the act of a police officer directing a woman to appear in police station is violative of section 160(1) of Cr. P.C.

In *Rekha M. Kholkar* v. *State of Goa,* 1996 (1) Mh LJ 430, the Division Bench directed I.G. to instruct all officers in writing, to strictly comply with the provisions of section 160(1), Cr. P.C. in all cases involving interrogation of woman.

In *State of Maharashtra* v. *Christian Community Welfare Council of India,* AIR 2004 SC 7, the Supreme Court has directed the arresting authorities to make all efforts to keep a lady constable present while arresting a female person.

In *Delhi Domestic Working Women's Forum* v. *Union of India,* (1994) Supp 4 SCR 528: (1995) 1 Bom Cri Cases 194, where six women were raped by seven army personnel in Muri express on way from Ranchi to Delhi, on petition filed by the petitioner under Articles 21 and 32 of the Constitution, the Court has indicated the following broad parameters in assisting the victims of rape—

(a) The complainant of sexual assault cases should be provided with legal representation. It is important to have some one who is well acquainted with the criminal justice system. The role of the victim's advocate would not only be to explain to the victim the nature of the proceeding, to prepare her for the case and to assist her in the police station and in the court but to provide her with guidance as to how she might obtain help of a different nature from other agencies, for example, mind counselling or medical assistance. It is important to secure continuity of assistance by ensuring that the same person who looked after the complainant's interests in the police station, represent her till the end of the case.

(b) Legal assistance will have to be provided at the police station to the victim of rape.

(c) The police should be under a duty to inform the victim of her right to representation before any questions were asked of her and that the police report should state that the victim was so informed.

(d) A list of advocates willing to act in these cases should be kept at the police station for victims who did not have a particular lawyer in mind or whose own lawyer was unavailable.

(e) The advocate shall be appointed by the Court, upon application by? the police at the earliest convenient moment, but in order to ensure that victims were questioned without undue delay, advocates would be authorised to act at the police station before leave of the Court was sought or obtained.

(f) In all rape trials anonymity of the victim must be maintained, as far as possible.

(g) To setup Criminal Injuries Compensation Board.

(h) Compensation for victims shall be awarded by the Court on conviction of the offender and by the Criminal Injuries Compensation Board whether or not a conviction has taken place.

The Apex Court in its landmark judgment in *State of Maharashtra* v. *Madhukar Narayan Mardikar,* AIR 1991 SC 207 has held that *"woman, even of easy virtue, is entitled to privacy and it cannot be invaded by any person."*

In *Surjit Singh Thind* v. *Kanwaljit Kaur,* AIR 2003 P&H 353, the High Court held that *"allowing medical examination of a woman to prove her virginity violates her right to privacy and personal liberty"*. Keeping in view the social object of section 228A of IPC, the Apex Court in *Bhupinder Sharma* v. *State of Himachal Pradesh,* AIR 2003 SC 4684 has directed the lower Courts and High Courts not to mention the name of victim of sexual offence in judgment.

The Apex Court in *Apparel Export Promotion Council* v. *A.K. Chopra,* AIR 1999 SC 625 has held that *"sexual harassment of woman at the places of work is violative of Articles 21 and 24"*. The Court further observed that, Courts must remain alive to International covenants and instruments and apply the same to a given case when there is no inconsistency between the international norms and the domestic law occupying the field.

In *Sheela Barse* v. *State of Maharashtra,* (1983) 2 SCR 337 the Apex Court has given following direction to protect females:

(a) Four or five police lock ups should be selected in reasonably good localities where only female suspects should be kept and they should be guarded by female constables. Female suspect should not be kept in a police lock up in which male suspects are detained.

(b) Interrogation of females should be carried out only in the presence of female police officers/constables.

(c) A person arrested must be immediately informed of the grounds of his arrest.

(d) Whenever a person is arrested by the police and takes to the police lock up, the police should immediately give intimation of the fact of such arrest to the nearest Legal Aid Committee which should take immediate steps to provide legal assistance to him at State cost provided he is willing to accept such legal assistance.

(e) In the city of Bombay a City Sessions Judge, nominated by the Principal Judge of the City Civil Court, preferably a lady Judge if there is one, shall make surprise visits to police lock ups in the city, periodically, with a view to providing the arrested persons an opportunity to air their grievances and for ascertaining the conditions in the police lock ups.

(f) As soon as a person is arrested, the police must immediately obtain from him the name of any relative or friend whom he would like to be informed about his arrest and the police should get in touch with such relative or friend and inform him about the arrest.

(g) The Magistrate before whom an arrested person is produced shall enquire from him whether he has any complaint of torture or maltreatment in police custody and inform him that he has a right under section 54 of Cr. P.C. to be medically examined.

While dealing with a case under NDPS Act, 1985, the Constitution Bench of the Apex Court in *The State of Punjab* v. *Baldev Singh,* (1999) 3 SCR 977 has held that *"no female shall be searched by any one excepting female.... The document prepared by the Investigation Officer at the spot must invariably disclose that the search was conducted in the aforesaid manner and the name of the female official who carried out the personal search of the concerned female should be disclosed.... The personal search memo of the female concerned should indicate compliance with the aforesaid provisions. ....Failure to do so may not only affect the credibility of the prosecution case but may also be found as violative of the basic right of a female to be treated with decency and proper dignity".*

In a celebrated judgment of *Vishaka* v. *State of Rajasthan,* AIR 1997 SC 3011, the Apex Court held that sexual harassment of working woman amounts to violation of rights and gender equality and right to life and liberty and issued guidelines to ensure the prevention of sexual harassment of women at work places. The Apex Court further held that victim is entitled to remedy of Article 32 of the Constitution.

Protection of Women from Domestic Violence Act, 2005 is a welcome legislation looking into the fact that domestic violence on women is on rise not only in India but in other parts of the world. Recent survey has shown that domestic violence on women is also on rise in China and 40,000-50,000 complaints are received annually. It seems that China needs a Act like Protection of Women from Domestic Violence Act, 2005 very urgently.

In PIL 10 of 2007 *(Surekha Kailash Mote* v. *The State of Maharashtra)* the Bombay High Court has issued direction that all Magistrates should entertain applications made under section 12 of Protection of Women from Domestic Violence Act, 2005 in keeping with the authority conferred to them to pass interim and *ex parte* orders and to exercise this powers according to law under section 23 of the Act.

Pre-natal Diagnostic Techniques (Regulation and Prevention of Misuse) Amendment Act, 2002 is also a welcome legislation which protects the dignity of women. In *Vijay Sharma* v. *Union of India,* 2007 (6) All MR 336 the Division Bench of the Bombay High Court has observed as regards pre-natal diagnosis and determination of sex that *"such sex selection prior to conception is as bad as foeticide. Same offends dignity of women. It undermines their importance. It violates woman's right to life. It violates Article 39(e) .....It ignores Article 51A(e) .... Sex-selection is therefore against the spirit of the Constitution.... It insults and humiliates womanhood".* *Sabu Mathew George* v. *Microsoft, 2016.* This case pertains to advertisements of pre-natal sex determination flooding the internet after the Act came into force in 1994 to crack down on female foeticide. In this case, the Honourable Apex Court held that Internet search engines Microsoft, Google and Yahoo are under obligation to see that 'doctrine of autoblock' is applied within a reasonable period of time to prohibit any attempt to search any keyword pertaining to pre-natal sex determination.

(viii) Rights of Juveniles and Children

In *Gopi Nath Ghosh* v. *State of West Bengal,* (1984) 1 SCR 803, the Apex Court has held that:

(a) where a juvenile delinquent is arrested, he/she has to be produced before a juvenile Court, and if no juvenile Court is established for the area amongst others, the Court of Sessions will have powers of a juvenile Court and

(b) Such juvenile ordinarily has to be released on bail irrespective of the nature of the offence alleged to have been committed. Further, the Court issued practice directions that whenever accused appears to be aged 21 years or below, an enquiry must be made about the age of the accused on the date of occurrence. And the Court further directed that, Magistrate may refer him to Medical Board or Civil Surgeon or The Magistrate may direct accused to lead evidence about his age.

The Apex Court, in *Sheela Barse* v. *Union of India,* (1986) 3 SCR 562 has held that the children accused of having committed offences should not be kept in jail. They should be kept in Remand Homes or released on bail. Further, the Court directed the investigating agencies to complete the investigation of offences within three months of lodging complaint/FIR The Court further directed the juvenile Courts to complete the trial within six months from the filing of charge sheet.

The Apex Court in *Sanjay Suri* v. *Delhi Administration,* AIR 1988 SC 414: 1988 Cri LJ 705: 1988 (Supp) SCC 160 has directed that juvenile delinquents should not be assigned work in the same area where regular prisoners are made to work and care should be taken to ensure that there is no scope for their meeting and having contacts with regular adult prisoners.

In addition to the directions given in *State of Punjab* v. *Gurmit Singh,* 1996 (2) SCC 384, the Apex Court has given following directions in *Sakshi* v. *Union of India,* 2004 All MR (Cri) 2520 (SC) to protect children who are victims of sex abuse or rape:—

(i) The provisions of sub-section (2) of section 327 of Cr. P.C. shall, in addition to the offences mentioned in the sub-section, would also apply in inquiry or trial of offences under sections 354 and 377, IPC

(ii) In holding trial of child sex abuse or rape:

- (a) a screen or some such arrangements may be made where the victim or witnesses (who may be equally vulnerable like the victim) do not see the body or face of the accused;
- (b) the questions put in cross-examination on behalf of the accused, in so far as they relate directly to the incident, should be given in writing to the Presiding Officer of the Court who may put them to the victim or witnesses in a language which is clear and is not embarrassing;

(c) the victim of child abuse or rape, while giving testimony in Court, should be allowed sufficient breaks as and when required.

(ix) Right to Medical Aid

In *Sheela Barse* v. *State of Maharashtra*, AIR 1983 SC 378: 1983 (1) Crimes 602 (SC), the Supreme Court has held that, the accused or arrested persons have a right of medical examination and duty is cast on Court to inform the arrested person that he has right under section 54 of Cr. P.C. to be medically examined.

In *State of Karnataka* v. *Manjanna*, AIR 2000 SC 2231, the Supreme Court has held that the doctors cannot refuse to conduct medical examination of victim of rape on the ground that case was not referred to them by police.

In the landmark judgment, *Paschim Banga Khet Mazdoor Samiti* v. *State of West Bengal*, AIR 1996 SC 2426: (1996) Supp 2 SCR 331, the Apex Court has held that failure on the part of Government Hospitals to provide timely and immediate medical assistance to a person sustaining serious injuries results in violation of his right to life guaranteed under Article 21 of the Constitution and awarded compensation to the family of deceased. The Court further issued following directions—

(a) Adequate facilities are made available at the Primary Health Centres where the patient can be given immediate primary treatment so as to stabilise his condition.

(b) Hospitals at the district level and sub-division level should be upgraded so that serious cases can be treated there.

(c) Facilities for giving specialist treatment should be increased and made available at the hospitals at district level and sub-division level having regard to the growing needs.

(d) A centralised communication system be established so that the patient can be sent immediately to the hospital where bed is available in respect of the treatment which is required.

(e) Proper arrangement of ambulance is made for transport of a patient from the Primary Health Centre to the District Hospital or Sub-division Hospital and from the District Hospital or Sub-divisional Hospital to the State Hospital.

(f) The ambulance is provided with necessary equipment and medical personnel.

(g) The Health Centres and Hospitals and the Medical Personnel are geared to deal with larger number of patients needing emergency treatment on account of higher risk of accidents on certain occasions and in certain seasons.

In the instant case, *Sujata Mukunda Manerao* v. *State of Maharashtra*, 2003 All MR (Cri) 2285 (Bom), there has been negligence and lapses on the part of jail authorities in providing adequate, effective, proper and immediate treatment to the deceased, resulting in his death. The Division Bench of the Bombay High

Court held that proper medical aid to inmates is a right available under Article 21 of the Constitution and State is liable to pay compensation to the family of deceased who died in custody.)

The Bombay High Court in *Rekha M. Kholkar* v. *State of Goa,* 1996 (1) Mh LJ 430 has held that detenues, undertrials and prisoners, affected in cases of police violence, have right to obtain copies of medical reports and directed Superintendents of all Government Hospitals to give the same when so requested by such persons.

In *Ragunath G. Raheja* v. *Maharashtra Medical Council,* 1996 (1) Mh LJ 687, the Bombay High Court held that Hospitals and Doctors cannot claim any secrecy or any confidentiality in matters of copies of case paper and relevant documents relating to patients and are bound to give such copies to the relatives or friends of the deceased or injured. The Court further directed the medical council to issue such direction to all Doctors and Hospital and also to issue a Press-note.

In this case, the Apex Court directed the central and state Governments to give proper medical facilities and maintain appropriate hygienic conditions in jails; *Rama Murthy* v. *State of Karnataka,* AIR 1997 SC 1739: 1997 Cri LJ 1508.

(x) Right to Free Legal Aid

The accused has a right of free legal assistance at the State's cost. The Supreme Court has held in *Ranchod Mathur Wasawa* v. *State of Gujarat,* (1974) 2 SCR 72 that "*indigence should never be a ground for denying a fair trial or equal justice. Therefore, particular attention should be paid to appoint competent advocates equal to handling the complex cases – not patronising gestures to raw entrants to the Bar*".

The Supreme Court in *Khatri* v. *State of Bihar,* AIR 1981 SC 928: 1981 Cri LJ 470 has held that State's duty to provide legal aid to the arrested persons also arises when accused is first produced before Magistrate.

In serious and heinous offences, the Bombay High Court has directed the subordinate Courts to appoint only those advocates who have experience of actual conducting of minimum three cases under NDPS Act or five cases in serious and heinous offences; *Fulkumar S. Sighrahwav.State of Maharashtra,* 2004 ALL MR (Cri) 3029.

This was a case of murder, where a junior lawyer of three years standing was engaged to defend the accused under legal aid. There was no effective cross-examination on material points. Neither omissions were brought to the notice of witnesses nor contradictions were put to witnesses. The Court set aside conviction and sentence holding that poor lawyering of defence lawyer can be taken as a ground vitiating the trial; *Abdul Razak* v. *State of Kerala,* 2010 (1) Crimes 551 (SN) (DB) (Ker).

(xi) Right of Lunatics

The Punjab and Haryana High Court in *Dial Singh* v. *I.G. of Prisons, Punjab,* 1988 Cri LJ 661 has observed as regards the detention of persons in mental asylum and duty of Court that "*a person might conceivably have all kinds of delusions, but if his conduct remains normal, there does not appear to be any power to deal with him under the Act.... What appears material for purposes of the Act is the conduct exhibited by the alleged lunatic. It is the test which is to be kept in view by the Court while assuming jurisdiction under the Act.... The Court is duty-bound to determine judicially keeping in view the distinction between mere weakness of intellect and lunacy as defined in section 3(5) of the Act as to whether the person alleged to be lunatic deserves to be confined within the four walls of an asylum".*

In Re: Death of 25 Chained Inmates in Asylum Fire in Tamil Nadu, (2002) 1 SCR 839, the Apex Court has directed the Central and State Governments to undertake a comprehensive awareness campaign, with a special rural focus, to educate people as to provisions of law relating to mental health, rights of mentally challenged persons, the fact that chaining of mentally challenged persons is illegal and that mental patients should be sent to doctors and not to religious places such as Temples or Dargahs.

(xii) Right of Undertrials, Satyagrahis, Detenues, etc.

The Supreme Court of India in *Kadra Pehadiya* v. *State of Bihar,* AIR 1981 SC 939: 1981 Cri LJ 481 has held that *"undertrial prisoners cannot be kept in leg irons nor can he be asked to work outside the jail wall".*

In *Sunil Batra* v. *Delhi Administration,* AIR 1980 SC 1579: 1980 Cri LJ 1099: (1980) 2 SCR 557 the Apex Court has held that *"practice of keeping under trials with convicts offends Article 21".* The Division Bench of the Bombay High Court in *Asgar Y. Mukadam* v. *State of Maharashtra,* 2004 All MR (Cri) 3010, has held that *"unconvicted prisoners, detenues and Satyagrahis have right to have their own food, clothing, etc and the Magistrate concerned can grant permission for the same on an application moved by such persons".*

The Constitution Bench of the Apex Court, in *State of Maharashtra* v. *Prabhaka Pandurang Sanzgiri,* AIR 1966 SC 424: (1966) 1 SCR 702 has held that *"prohibiting a detenu from writing a book or sending it for publication infringed the personal liberty of the respondent."*

In *Francis Coralie Mulin* v. *The Administrator, Union Territory of Delhi,* (1981) 2 SCR 516, the Apex Court has held that (a) the prisoner or detenu has all the fundamental rights and other legal rights available to a free person, save those which are incapable of enjoyment by reason of incarceration. A prisoner or detenu is not stripped of his fundamental or other legal rights, save those which are inconsistent with is incarceration, and if any of these rights are violated, the Court will immediately spring into action and run to his rescue. (b) .... any act which damages or injures or interferes with the use of any limb or faculty of a person either permanently or even temporarily would be within the inhibition of Article 21(c) the right to life includes right to live with human dignity and all that goes along with it, namely, the bare necessaries of life such as adequate nutrition, clothing and shelter and facilities for reading, writing and expressing oneself in diverse forms, freely moving about and mixing and commingling with fellow human beings. (d) He would be entitled to have interviews with the members of his family and friends and no prison regulation or procedure laid down by prison regulation regulating the right to have interviews with the members of the family and friends can be upheld as constitutionally valid under Articles 14 and 21, unless it is reasonable, fair and just. (e) the right of a detenu to consult a legal advisor of his choice for any purpose not necessarily limited to defence in a criminal proceeding but also for securing release from preventive detention or filing a writ petition or prosecuting any claim or proceeding, civil or criminal is obviously included in the right to live with human dignity and is also part of personal liberty and the detenu cannot be deprived of this right nor can this right of the detenu be interfered with except in accordance with reasonable, fair and just procedure established by a valid law.

(xiii) Rights of Prisoners

In *Sunil Batra* v. *Delhi Administration*, (1979) 1 SCR 392 the Constitution Bench of the Apex Court has held that *"section 30(2) of Prisons Act, 1894 does not empower the prison authority to impose solitary confinement upon a prisoner under sentence of death... Even a convict is entitled to the precious right guaranteed by Article 21.... Prisoners under sentence of death shall not be denied any of the amenities including games, newspapers, books, moving around and meeting prisoners and visitors. ..If the prisoner desires loneliness for reflection and remorse, for prayers and making peace with his maker or opportunities for meeting family or friends, such facilities shall be liberally granted."*

In *Charles Sobraj* v. *The Superintendent, Central Jail, Tihar, New Delhi*, (1979) 1 SCR 512, the Apex Court has held that though the petitioner being a foreigner cannot claim rights under Article 19, the prisoners retain all rights enjoyed by free citizen except those lost necessarily as an incident of confinement.

In *Quasi-Habeas Corpus* Petition filed by the petitioner complaining prison torture, the Apex Court in *Ramesh Kaushik* v. *B.L. Vig, Superintendent*, (1980) 3 SCR 929 has held that "prison torture is not beyond the reach of the Supreme Court in its Constitutional Jurisdiction" and warned the prison authorities, observing that "if vengeance is the spirit of punishment, violence will be the prison way of life".

In *Sunil Batra* v. *Delhi Administration*, (1980) 2 SCR 557, Batra, a prisoner, wrote a letter to a Judge of Supreme Court complaining of a brutal assault by the Head Warder on another prisoner, Prem Chand. The letter was treated as a Habeas Corpus Petition. The Apex Court has held that (i) A prisoner wears the armour of basic freedom even behind bars and on breach thereof by lawless officials, the law will respond to his distress signals through writ aid. (ii) The prisoners' rights shall be protected by? the Court by its writ Jurisdiction plus contempt power. (iii) Visit to prisoners by family and friends are a solace in insulation and only a dehumanised system can derive vicarious delight in depriving prison inmates of this humane amenity.

The Division Bench of the Bombay High Court, in *Madhukar Bhagwan Jambhale* v. *State of Maharashtra*, 1987 Mh LJ 68, overlooking all formalities, treated the letter sent by the petitioner as an application under Article 226 of the Constitution and directed the respondents to implement the following procedure:

(i) Grievance Deposit Box – In addition to complaint boxes which are presently kept in different cells in the prison, a sealed Grievance Deposit Box shall be kept at a conspicuous place inside the prison under lock and key. The key of said box shall remain exclusively with the District Judge.

Access to the complaint box shall be accorded to the prisoners. The said box shall be opened by the Sessions Judge within whose jurisdiction the prison falls, at regular intervals. In case of jails which are rendered impracticable for the Sessions Judge to visit, Additional District Judge or a Senior most Assistant Judge, nominated by the Sessions Judge should perform the aforesaid task. A concerned Sessions Judge, who will also investigate into the complaints, and if found necessary and expedient shall take appropriate action. The records of complaints shall also contain the particulars of the action taken.

(ii) Complaint Register – The District and Sessions Judge shall maintain a Complaint Register in prison office in such manner as may be directed by him in respect of the complaints found in the Grievance Deposit Box. He shall also record the appropriate action taken in respect of the said complaints.

(iii) Visits by District and Sessions Judge/District Magistrate – The District Magistrate and the Sessions Judge shall personally visit prisons in their jurisdiction and offer effective opportunities for ventilating the legal grievances of the prisoners and shall make expeditious enquiries and take suitable remedial action. They shall also ascertain the conditions prevailing in the prison, and ascertain whether the prisoners are provided with all the necessary facilities as set out in the Maharashtra (Facilities to Prisoners) Rules, 1962. In the appropriate case, report shall be made to the High Court by a letter to initiate, if necessary, habeas action.

(iv) Visit by Lawyers – The Sessions Judge shall nominate lawyers to make separate visits to the prison within his jurisdiction. The lawyers so appointed, in their visit shall be afforded by the prison administration, facilities and opportunities to inspect the prison premises and the record relating to complaints from the prisoners and to interview and receive confidential communications from the inmates of the prison subject to disciplinary and security conditions. The lawyers so nominated shall carry out periodical visits and report to the concerned Court results which have relevance to legal grievances.

The Apex Court has condemned the practice of keeping young inmates with adult prisoners and directed that they should be separated and freed from exploitation by adult prisoners; *Sunil Batra* v. *Delhi Administration,* AIR 1980 SC 1579: 1980 Cri LJ 1099: (1980) 3 SCC 488: (1980) 2 SCR 557.

The Apex Court in *Sanjay Suri* v. *Delhi Administration,* AIR 1988 SC 414: 1988 Cri LJ 705: 1988 (Supp) SCC 160 has directed that the visitor's Board should consist of cross-section of society, people with good background, social activists, people connected with the news media, lady social workers, Jurists, retired public officers from the judiciary as also the executive. The Sessions Judge should be given an acknowledged position as a visitor.

Inhuman Conditions in 1382 Prisons, (in re:), 2016 All SCR 640; (2016) 3 SCC 700 In this case, the honourable Apex Court held that due importance needs to be given to the rights of prisoners and undertrials in various prisons across the country and issued guidelines on prison reforms.

Even the Bombay High Court has expressed its anguish over the poor facilities in jails and directed the state to make sufficient arrangement of toilets and bathrooms in jails and separate bathrooms for women to maintain their dignity. In *Jan Adalat* v. *State of Maharashtra,* 2017 All MR (Cri) 1166 the Court issued following directions—

(a) The State Government shall frame a time bound programme for completing construction of additional Jails or additional construction in existing Jails;

(b) The State Government shall ensure that separate bathrooms are made available to the women prisoners for taking bath in privacy. The State Government shall maintain the dignity of women prisoners by providing privacy to individual women prisoners;

(c) Immediate arrangements shall be made for providing bathrooms in all the Jails in the State. This exercise shall be completed within a period of six months from the date of order;

(d) The State Government shall construct sufficient number of additional toilets in all the Jails in the State within a period of 6 months from the date of order;

(e) The State Government shall undertake repairs and renovation of the toilets and bathrooms in all jails in the State and it shall be completed within a period of six month from the date of order;

(f) The State Government shall provide modern facilities to enable family members/relatives to meet the prisoners in all the Jails. Instead of fixing a metal grill for separating the prisoners and the persons interviewing the prisoners, glass windows or transparent acrylic windows shall be provided to ensure that the prisoner and visitor are clearly visible to each other. Modern audio system shall be provided so that the prisoners and the persons interviewing the prisoners are clearly audible to each other. An arrangement shall also be made to provide adequate number of windows in all the jails in the State so that all inmates can get an opportunity to meet their family members and lawyers as provided in the rules. The State Government shall provide electronic clock for the benefit of the visitors in the hall/room where interviews are conducted. Compliance with these directions shall be made within 6 months from the date of order;

(g) The State Government shall appoint a permanent Committee of Social Workers and Dieticians to make surprise visits to all Jails for testing the quality and quantity of food served to the prisoners as well as the cleanliness and hygiene in the kitchens in the Jails. The State Government shall appoint such committees for every district. The Committees shall make surprise visits (without prior intimation to the Jail Officers) at least once in a month and regularly and punctually submit a report to the

Inspector General of Prisons or to any senior officer appointed by him. Immediate remedial measures shall be taken on the basis of the report including action against erring Jail staff;

(h) As regards the children staying with their respective mothers in Jail, necessary arrangement for their benefit shall be made in terms of the directions of the Apex Court and as observed in paragraph No. 23 of the Judgement within a period of six months from the date of order;

(i) The State Government shall evolve a scheme for ensuring that women prisoners are able to meet their minor children (who are not staying with them) at frequent intervals. If necessary, amendment may be proposed to the Maharashtra Prisons (Facilities to the Prisoners) Rules, 1962.

(xiv) Right to Speedy Trial

In *Kadra Pehadiya* v. *State of Bihar,* AIR 1981 SC 939: 1981 Cri LJ 481, the Apex Court has held that a speedy trial is a fundamental right implicit in the guarantee of life and person liberty enshrined in Article 21 of the Constitution. Any accused who is denied this right of speedy trial is entitled to approach the Supreme Court and Supreme Court has the power to give necessary directions to the State Government and other appropriate authorities for securing this right to the accused.

In *A.R. Antulay* v. *R.S. Naik,* (1991) Supp 3 SCR 325 the Constitution Bench has also held that right to speedy trial is the fundamental right of every person accused of a crime as implicit in Article 21.

However, the Constitution Bench has held that no time limit can be prescribed or fixed for conclusion of trial. The law laid down in this case has been approved and followed by Constitution Bench of seven Judges in *P. Ramchandra Rao* v. *State of Karnatka,* (2002) 3 SCR 60: 2002 (3) Mh LJ 145.

(xv) Right to documents

An accused is entitled to copies of all the documents/statements brought on record of case, even though not relied on by the prosecution; *Ramesh* v. *State of Maharashtra,* 1995 Cri LJ 3424 (Bom).

An accused is entitled to get a certified copy of the FIR at an earlier stage than as prescribed under section 207 of the Cr. P.C. and the same shall be given within 24 hours; *Arun Kumar Budhia* v. *State of Orissa,* 2013 (2) Crimes 186 (Ori).

In *Jessica Lal Murder* case, the honourable Apex Court held that right of accused to receive documents/statements submitted before Court is absolute. Mandate under section 207 of Cr. P.C. is in contradistinction to section 173, where legislature has used expression "documents on which prosecution relies", which words are not used in section 207. Hence, section 207 needs to be given liberal and relevant meaning to achieve its object; *Manu Sharma* v. *State (NCT of Delhi),* (2010) 6 SCC 1: 2010 (2) Crimes 154 (SC).

In this case Honourable Apex Court held that doctrine of free and fair trial demands that accused is entitled to documents submitted in Court along with report under section 173 of Cr. P.C., though the said documents are unexhibited or unmarked; *V.K. Sasikala* v. *State*, AIR 2013 SC 613.

In this case, appellant filed application for production of documents pertaining to scientific tests conducted on persons who at one time were suspected accused in *Arushi Murder* case. The High Court rejected the application on the ground that application was filed after about two months of passing impugned order. The Honourable Apex Court rejected the application of the appellant holding that no interference is required in the order of the High Court; *Dr. Rajesh Talwar* v. *C.B.I.*, 2013 All SCR 3416.

It is submitted with respect that both the High Court and Apex Court took narrow and technical view thereby denying fullest opportunity to the appellant to prepare his defence.

In *Manjeet Singh Khera* v. *State of Maharashtra*, 2013 All SCR 3067 complaint was filed by unknown person to Anti-Corruption Bureau which triggered an investigation in the matter. The appellant contended that he was not furnished the copy of complaint and that non-supply of complaint violates principle of fair trial enshrined in Article 21 of The Constitution. The Apex Court held that non-supply of complaint or contents thereof does not violate principle of fair trial. The Court observed that it is not a case where some materials/documents were collected by the investigation officer which are in favour of prosecution and prosecution is suppressing those documents. Therefore the Apex Court negatived the contention of the appellant.

In *Sujoy Mitra* v. *State of West Bengal*, 2016 All SCR (Cri) 146 questions arose as to whether supply of video graphic testimony of witness to accused is proper. The Honourable Apex Court held that furnishing of such recorded video graphic testimony is a cumbersome process and it is likely to lead to more record, to be maintained for its safe custody. Therefore, accused allowed to what an ordinary accused would be entitled to have, had the statement been recorded by trial Court itself.

In *Omprakash R. Aggrawal* v. *State of Gujarat*, 2017 (1) Crimes 712 (Guj) the Honourable Gujarat High Court has set aside the impugned order of the subordinate court which denied copy of roznama/daily order and held that an accused or litigant is entitled to apply for copy of order sheet (roznama) which has to be provided by Court.

CHAPTER II
ARREST AND PREVENTIVE DETENTION

SYNOPSIS

(i) Judicial Pronouncement on Arrest
(ii) Preventive Detention
(iii) Detention under Chapter VIII of Cr.P.C.
(iv) Writ of *Habeas Corpus*

The word "arrest" in section 41 of Cr.P.C. is derived from the French word "arrater" which means to stop or stay. It signifies a restraint of a person. "Arrest" is thus a restraint of a man's person, obliging him to be obedient to law. Thus "arrest" can be defined as the execution of the command of a Court of law or of a duly authorised officer; *Union of India* v. *Padam Narain Aggarwal,* 2009 All MR (Cri) 1835 SC.

The difference between 'arrest' and 'custody' has been explained by the Apex Court in *Directorate of Enforcement* v. *Deepak Mahajan,* AIR 1994 SC 1775: (1994) 1 SCR 445. The Court held that *"The Code gives power of arrest not only to a police officer and a Magistrate but also under certain circumstances or given situations to private persons. Further, when an accused person appears before a Magistrate or surrender voluntarily, the Magistrate is empowered to take that accused person into custody and deal with him according to law. Needless to emphasize that the arrest of a person is a condition precedent for taking him into judicial custody thereof. To put it differently, the taking of the person into judicial custody is followed after the arrest of the person concerned by the Magistrate on appearance or surrender. In every arrest, there is custody but not vice versa and that both the words 'custody' and 'arrest' are not synonymous terms. Though 'custody' may amount to an arrest in certain circumstances but not under all circumstances. If these two terms are interpreted as synonymous, it is nothing but an ultra legalist interpretation which if under all circumstances accepted and adopted, would lead to a startling anomaly resulting in serious consequences."*

The Bombay High Court has given a note of caution to all Criminal Courts in Chapter I of the Criminal Manual regarding the attitude of police. The Bombay High Court observed: *"Attempts are sometimes made to evade the law by describing custody or detention of any kind as 'nazarkaid' or surveillance. Surveillance is one thing, and detention in any kind of custody is another. It is a mere evasion of the law to keep a suspected person in any kind of custody and then by calling such detention 'nazarkaid', to say that he is not under arrest. The system is still more objectionable when applied to witnesses."*

(i) Judicial Pronouncement on Arrest

The belief that a police officer is entitled to detain every arrested person in custody, at all events for 24 hours is quite unwarranted by the Court; *Queen* v. *Suprosunno Ghosaul,* 6 WR 88.

Section 57 of the Cr.P.C. does not give the police officer a right to keep the arrested person in custody for at least 24 hours; *R.K. Naba Chandra Singh* v. *Manipur Administration*, AIR 1964 Mani 39: 1964 (2) Cri LJ 307.

Though the police has power to arrest a person, this power is not unfettered or unlimited. The Supreme Court of India in *Jogindar Kumar's* case, AIR 1994 SC 1349: (1994) 3 SCR 661: 1994 Cri LJ 1981 has held that *"except in heinous offences, an arrest must be avoided.... No arrest can be made merely because it is lawful for the police officer to do so..... The police officer must be able to justify the arrest apart from his power to do so..... It would be prudent for police officer in the interest of protection of the Constitutional rights of a citizen and perhaps in his own interest that no arrest should be made without a reasonable satisfaction reached after some investigation as to genuineness and bona fide of a complaint and a reasonable belief as to the person's complicity and even so, as to the need to effect arrest."*

In *Amarwati's* case, 2005 (1) Crimes 44, the Full Bench of Allahabad High Court has held that, even if cognizable offence is disclosed in FIR, arrest of accused is not a must and police should be guided by Supreme Court Judgement in *Jogindar Kumar's* case (*supra*).

To safeguard the interest of arrested person and for the protection of human rights, the Apex Court has issued guidelines in all cases of arrest or detention in *D.K. Basu's* case, AIR 1997 SC 610: (1996) Supp 10 SCR 284. In this landmark Judgment, the Supreme Court has ruled that the concerned official failing to comply with the requirements mentioned in the judgement shall be liable not only for departmental action but also render him liable to be punished for contempt of Court.

In this case, the Apex Court held that a police officer can arrest a person if he has come to know of a design of the person concerned to commit any cognizable offence. A further condition for the exercise of such power, which must also be fulfilled is that the arrest should be made only if it appears to the police officer concerned that the commission of the offence cannot be otherwise prevented. If these conditions are not fulfilled and a person is arrested under section 151 of Cr.P.C., the arresting authority may be exposed to proceedings under the law for violating the fundamental rights inherent in Articles 21 and 22 of the Constitution of India; *Rajender Singh Pathania* v. *State of NCT of Delhi*, 2011 All MR (Cri) 3287 (SC).

The Apex Court has held that even in cognizable case, investigation officer is not obliged to arrest accused as soon as report is lodged. Exercise of his discretion would depend upon nature of offence and type of person who are accused to have committed offence; *M.C. Abraham* v. *State of Maharashtra*, 2003 Bom CR (Cri) 650 (SC).

As regards arrest of female, the Apex Court has held that it may not be always possible and practical to have a lady constable present. In such a case arresting officer may arrest a female person for lawful reasons at any time of day or night even without presence of lady constable. However, he should record reasons either before arrest or immediately after arrest for adopting such a course; *State of Maharashtra* v. *Christian Community Welfare Council of India*, 2004 All MR (Cri) 301 SC.

Recently, the Apex Court clarified that directions given in Para 52 of *Jacob Mathew* case, (2005) 6 SCC 1: AIR 2005 SC 3180: 2005 (2) BCr C 703 (SC) (*i.e.*, requirement to obtain independent medical opinion before investigation is initiated against a doctor) is meant for criminal cases and not for civil cases filed in Consumer Fora for the purpose of determining civil liability. The Court further held that general directions given in para 106 of *Martin F. D'Souza* case, (2009) 3 SCC 1: AIR 2009 SC 2049: 2009 AIR Bom R 242 (SC): 2009 (3) Civ LJ 137 (SC) extending the same to civil cases, are *per incuriam* and not binding; *V. Kishan Rao* v. *Nikhil Super Speciality Hospital,* (2010) 5 SCC 513.

In this case, the Apex Court held that indiscriminate prosecution of medical professionals for criminal medical negligence is counterproductive and does no service or good to society; *Ins. Malhotra* v. *Dr. A. Kriplani,* (2009) 4 SCC 705.

In *Riyaz* alias *Ahemad* v. *State of Maharashtra.,* 2006 (1) AIR Bom R 955, the division Bench of Bombay High Court has observed that *"police officer must be able to justify the arrest apart from his power to do so."*

In *Hariharanand* v. *Jailer,* AIR 1954 All 601: 1954 Cri LJ 1317 the Court has held that *"a Magistrate directing an arrest under section 44 of Cr.P.C. does not act as a Court. The person arrested must be produced before another competent Magistrate within 24 hours. The Magistrate directing the arrest cannot himself pass an order under section 167 of Cr.P.C. Detention under an order of remand passed by him is illegal."*

In *Pawan Kumar* v. *Delhi Admn.,* 1989 Cri. LJ 127 (Del): (1988) 1 Crimes 172 has held that it is not enough to arrest a person under section 41 of Cr. P.C. that there was likelihood of a cognizable offence being committed in future.

The Gauhati High Court in *Kajal Dey* v. *State of Assam,* 1989 Cri LJ 1209 (Gau) has held that on mere suspicion police must not arrest a person unless suspicion is well founded.

In a celebrated case of *Udai Chand* v. *Shaik Mohd. Abdullah,* 1983 SCC (Cri) 529: (1983) 2 SCC 417, the Apex Court has held that if, after an accused is enlarged on bail by the Court, the authorities consider it fit to arrest that person for any other offence committed by? him prior to the date of granting bail to him by the Court, it is their duty to apprise the Court before taking the concerned person in custody, especially when no disclosure was made to the Court, when it passed the order of bail that any case or cases were under investigation against that person. Such an arrest without informing the Court was held to be illegal.

In this landmark judgment, Hon'ble Apex Court condemned the attitude of police to arrest first and then proceed to investigate. The Court held that the police officer is required to issue notice directing the accused to appear before him at a specified place and time. Law obliges such an accused to appear before the police officer and it further mandates that if such an accused complies with the terms of notice he shall not be arrested, unless for reasons to be recorded, the police officer is of the opinion that the arrest is necessary. The Court expected that police officers do not arrest accused unnecessarily and Magistrate do not authorise detention casually and mechanically. The Court issued following directions (a) all the State Governments to instruct its police officers not to automatically arrest when a case under section 498A of the IPC is registered but to satisfy themselves about the necessity for arrest under the parameters laid down above flowing from section 41, Cr.P.C. (b) All police officers be provided with a check list containing specified sub-clauses under section 41(I)(b)(ii). (c) The Police officer shall forward the check list duly filed and furnish the reasons and materials which necessitated the arrest, while forwarding/producing the accused before the Magistrate for further detention. (d) The Magistrate while authorising detention of the accused shall peruse the report furnished by the police officer in terms aforesaid and only after recording its satisfaction, the Magistrate will authorise detention. (e) The decision not to arrest an accused, be forwarded to the Magistrate within two weeks from the date of the institution of the case with a copy to the Magistrate which may be extended by the Superintendent of Police of the district for the reasons to be recorded in writing. (f) Notice of appearance in terms of section 41 A of Cr.P.C. be served on the accused within two weeks from the date of institution of the case, which may be extended by the Superintendent of Police of the district for the reasons to be recorded in writing.

The Apex Court warned that failure to comply with the directions aforesaid shall, apart from rendering the police officer concerned liable for departmental action, shall also be liable to be punished for contempt of court to be instituted before High Court having territorial jurisdiction. Authorising detention without recording reasons as aforesaid by the Judicial Magistrate concerned shall be liable for departmental action by the appropriate High Court.

The Hon'ble Apex Court clarified that the directions aforesaid shall not only apply to the cases under section 498A of the IPC or section 4 of the Dowry Prohibition Act, but also to such cases where offence is punishable with imprisonment for a term which may be less than 7 years or which may extend 7 years, whether with or without fine; *Arnesh Kumar* v. *State of Bihar*, 2014 (3) Crimes 206 (SC).

In this case also, the Hon'ble Apex Court held that arrest in cognizable offences is not mandatory in offences for which maximum sentence is 7 years. Section 41 and 41A of Cr.P.C. place check on arbitrary, unwarranted exercise of power of arrest; *Hema Mishra (Km.)* v. *State of Uttar Pradesh*, AIR 2014 SC 1066.

In this case, question arose as to whether police has power to arrest a person in the course of making report under section 202 of Cr.P.C. The hon'ble Apex Court held that under section 202 of Cr.P.C. Magistrate is in seisin of the matter and has yet to decide whether there is ground to proceed further. Therefore, at such premature stage police of its own, cannot exercise its power of arrest; *Ramdev Food Products Pvt. Ltd.* v. *State of Gujarat*, 2015 All SCR 1577: 2015 SAR (Criminal) 688.

In this case, police suspected petitioner to be a *Maoist* and he was taken into custody for questioning. However petitioner was released next day without registering any crime. It was contended on behalf of police that petitioner was taken to a safe place to protect him from agitated people. The High Court negatived the claim of the police and held that it was deprivation of movement of a person for purpose of answering any criminal charge potentially capable for conviction. The Court further held that flouting any norm under section 41 of Cr.P.C. would itself result in deprivation of liberty and directed State to pay Rs. 1,00,000 to the petitioner; *Shyam Balakrishnan* v. *State of Kerala,* 2015 (4) Crimes 191 (Ker).

In this case, petitioners were arrested and put in the compartment of a train without being produce before local magistrate from Pune to Bhopal. Procedure under section 41A of Cr.P.C. was not followed while making the arrest. The Hon'ble Apex Court held that the arrest is illegal and awarded compensation of Rs. 5,00,000 each to be paid by the Government of MP; *Rini Johar (Dr.)* v. *State of Madhya Pradesh,* 2016 ALL SCR (Cri) 3113 (SC).

In this case, about 40 hearings were given to the contemnors but they remained adamant and did not deposit or pay the amount to the investors. Due to this attitude of the contemnors, payable amount increased to more than Rs. 36,000 crores. The Hon'ble Apex Court justified the order of arrest holding that arrest or detention of accused is permissible means for enforcement of financial liability. The Court further held that Supreme Court is vested with the powers to enforce compliance with the judicial orders and also the power to punish for contempt of Court; *Subrata Roy Sahara* v. *Union of India,* 2014 ALL SCR 2133.

In this case, Chief Judicial Magistrate at Nadiad (Gujarat) was arrested, forced to consume liquor and on his refusal he was assaulted, handcuffed and tied with rope by police officials. A photographer was arranged to take his photograph which was published in the newspaper. As the incident undermined the dignity of courts in the country, Judicial Officers, Judges and Magistrates all over the country were in a state of shock, felt insecure and humiliated. The petitioner and others approached the Apex Court by means of telegrams and petition under Article 32 for saving the dignity and honour of the judiciary. The Apex Court took cognizance of the matter and awarded punishment to police officers concerned including District Superintendent of Police holding them guilty of criminal contempt. The Hon'ble Apex Court issued following guidelines in case a judicial officer is to be arrested: (a) if a judicial officer is to be arrested for some offence, it should be done under intimation to the District Judge or The High Court. (b) if facts and circumstances necessitate the immediate arrest of a judicial officer of the subordinate judiciary, a technical or formal arrest may be effected. (c) the fact of such arrest should be immediately communicated to the District and Sessions Judge of the concern district and the Chief Justice of the High Court. (d) the judicial officer so arrested shall not be taken to a police station, without the prior order or directions of the District and Sessions Judge of the concerned district, if available. (e) immediate facilities shall be provided to the Judicial Officer for communication with his family members, legal advisors and Judicial Officers, including the District and Sessions Judge. (f) No statement of a Judicial Officer who is under arrest be recorded nor any *panchanama* be drawn up nor any medical test be conducted except in the presence of the Legal Advisor of the Judicial Officer concerned or another Judicial Officer of equal or higher rank, if available; *Delhi Judicial Service Association Tis Hazari Court, Delhi,* v. *State of Gujarat,* (1991) 3 SCR 936.

(ii) Preventive Detention

Though the Apex Court has termed preventive detention as a "jurisdiction of suspicion" and directed the States to exercise the same under strict constitutional restrictions, experience has shown that number of orders for preventive detention are being passed by the State every day assuming itself to be the sole arbiter. One of the leading cases that figured in the media was that of *Ram Manohar Lohia (Dr.)*, (1966) 1 SCR 709. This case figured in the backdrop of proclamation of emergency by the president of India under Article 352 of Constitution. This presumably was done in view of China's attack on the North Eastern frontiers of India in September 1962. The petitioner was detained under rule 30(1)(b) of Defence of India Rules, 1962. The petitioner moved the Supreme Court under Article 32 and challenged his detention and suspension of rights under Articles 21 and 22 by The Presidential order under Article 359(1) of the Constitution. The Apex Court allowing the writ of habeas corpus held that the detention order is bad in law and the petitioner was set at liberty. In this landmark decision, the Apex Court observed that *"the contravention of law always affects order but before it can be said to affect public order, it must affect the community or the public at large. One has to imagine three concentric circles, the largest representing "Law & Order", the next representing "Public Order" and the smallest representing "Security of the State". An act may affect "Law & Order" but not "Public Order", just as an act may affect "Public Order" but not "Security of the State". Therefore, by using the expression "maintenance of law & order", the district Magistrate widening his own field of action and was adding a clause to the Defence of India Rules."*

This is a case under Maintenance of Internal Security Act, 1971 (MISA). Majority of the Bench held that in view of the Presidential Order dated 27th June, 1975 no person has any *locus standi* to move any writ petition under Article 226 before a High Court for habeas corpus or any other writ or order or direction to challenge the legality of an order of detention on the ground that the order is not under or in compliance with the Act or is illegal or is vitiated by *mala fide* factual or legal or is based on extraneous considerations. The Majority held section 16A(9) of the Act constitutionally valid and the appeals were accepted. This majority judgment was criticised by eminent jurists and alleged that the Supreme Court failed to protect the Constitution of India and the role of *parens patriae*. However there was a silver lining to the above view in the form of dissenting judgment by Justice H.R. Khanna who held that: Law of preventative detention, of detention without trial is an anathema to all those who love personal liberty. Article 21 cannot be considered to be the sole repository of the right to life and personal liberty. Even in absence of Article 21, State has got no power to deprive a person of his life or personal liberty without the authority of law. No power has been conferred upon any authority in the Constitution for suspending the power of the High Court to issue writs in the nature of *habeas corpus* during the period of emergency; *Additional District Magistrate, Jabalpur* v. *S.S. Shukla*, (1976) Supp SCR 172 (Constitution Bench).

In this case, the Apex Court held that non-placement of relevant materials before detaining authority vitiates the detention order. Five grounds for entertaining petition at pre-execution stage mentioned in *Smt. Alka Subhash*

Gadhia's case *Additional Secretary, Govt. of India* v. *Alka Subhash Gadhia,* 1992 (Suppl 1) SCC 496, are illustrative and not exhaustive. The Court further held that liberty of a person is a precious fundamental right under Article 21 and should not be lightly transgressed; *Deepak Bajaj* v. *State of Maharashtra,* (2009) ACR 82.

In this case *Shri Mukhtar* alias *Pappu Abdul* v. *Shri M.N. Singh,* 2002 All MR (Cri) 1334 (Bom) detention order against co-detenues revoked on ground that incidents referred to in grounds of detention had no nexus with maintenance of public order but the detention order against the petitioner detenue was confirmed on the ground that 12 criminal cases are pending against him. The Division Bench of Bombay High Court has held that, *"circumstance of 12 cases being pending against the detenue does not place him in a separate class because they have no nexus with the detention order....... failure of State Government to revoke the detention order against the petitioner detenue is discriminatory and in violation of the fundamental right guaranteed by Article 14 of the Constitution."*

In *Nritendra Chakravarty* v. *District Magistrate,* AIR 1969 Tri 44, the Court has held that, *"detention under Preventive Detention Act, 1950 should be sought only when the ordinary laws of the land and their application to any particular person are found not enough to meet the situation."*

In this case *Ajjy* alias *Hajidali Sabdarali Mirza Baig* v. *R. Mendonca, Commissioner of Police, Greater Bombay,* 2000 All MR (Cri) 535 (Bom), copy of bail application supplied to the petitioner detenue was wholly illegible. The Division Bench of Bombay High Court quashed the order of detention and ordered the release of the detenue forthwith on the ground that illegible copy of bail application supplied to the petitioner rendered his right to make representation illusory.

In this case, the petitioner was apprehending detention under section 3 of A.P. Prevention of Dangerous Activities of Bootleggers, Dacoits, Drug Offenders, Goondas, Immoral Traffic Offenders and Land Grabbers Act (1 of 1986). He filed *Habeas Corpus* petition in the High Court for seeking direction to State to refrain from making order of detention. But the High Court dismissed the petition on the ground that no special reason existed to depart from normal rule and prayer in the writ became infructuous. On petition being filed by the petitioner, the Supreme Court held that, "order dismissing writ by the High Court was not justified." It further held that writ was maintainable for protection against imminent violation of fundamental right to liberty; *S.M.D. Kiran Pasha* v. *Govt. of Andhra Pradesh,* (1990) 1 SCC 328: 1989 (4) JT 366.

In this case the Hon'ble Apex Court held that obligation of Central Government to forward representation of detenu before the Advisory Board is mandatory. Where there is non-compliance of the same, detention of the detenu is constitutionally invalid; *Golam Biswas* v. *Union of India,* 2015 All SCR 3779.

(iii) Detention under Chapter VIII of Cr.P.C.

It is the universal practice of police to arrest persons under section 151 read with 107 of Cr.P.C. for trivial matters though there is no necessity of arrest. The Apex Court in *Balraj Madhok* v. *Union of India,* AIR 1967 SC 31, has dealt with the said provisions and observed that, *"what is required under section 151 of the Code is that the officer concerned must know that the person to be arrested is designing to commit a cognizable offence. An "apprehension" that he may commit an offence in not sufficient under the provision. Apprehension is not the same thing as knowledge. The former is a mere feeling, later is a definite conclusion. Further, even mere knowledge that the person concerned would endanger peace or tranquillity need not result in a cognizable offence. Again, the possibility of the commission of a cognizable offence does not mean that he is designing to commit such an offence. Lastly, it is not said that it appears to the officer concerned that the commission of the offence could not be otherwise prevented."*

When attempt to arrest or detain a person fails, the police adopts a notorious tactics of arresting the person under Chapter VIII of the Code of Criminal Procedure (Sections 106 to 110) and the Executive Magistrates and Sub-Divisional Magistrates who belong to the Executive are ever ready to oblige the police by passing orders & remanding persons to custody and that too without following the procedure contemplated in sections 111 to 117 of Cr.P.C. This phenomenon is universal which is sanctified by the Executive. Thus, no rule or law and settled procedure is applicable to the Executive Magistrates and Sub-Divisional Magistrates invested with the power under the Code. Therefore the learned authors of Criminal Procedure Code namely Mr. Ratanlal and Dhirajlal have termed these sections as "Badmashi Sections".

In landmark decision the Division Bench of Bombay High Court in *Surendra S/o Ramchandra Taori* v. *State of Maharashtra,* 2001 All MR (Cri) 2079 has held that vesting of powers of Executive Magistrate to Police Inspectors is improper and the Court expected that the State Government. Should resort section 478 of Cr.P.C. and power and functions allocated to Police officers may be allocated to Judicial Magistrate of the First Class or Metropolitan Magistrate, as the case may be.

Though there are number of Judgments of various High Courts and the Apex Court condemning the orders passed by the Magistrates under Chapter VIII of the Code, situation has not changed yet and innocent persons are being arrested and detained under the said chapter.

The Constitution Bench consisting of seven Judges in *Madhu Limaye* v. *SDM, Monghyr* AIR 1971 SC 2486: (1971) 2 SCR 711, has held that it is not open to a Magistrate to adjourn the case without entering upon an inquiry and in the interval send the person to jail if he fails to furnish a bond. Further the Court held that in proceedings under section 107 of Cr.P.C., the Magistrate must proceed under sections 117(1) and (2) to inquire into the truth of the information that the person brought before him is likely to commit a breach of peace or disturb the tranquillity and only after prima facie satisfying himself about the truth of the information and after recording his reasons in writing can the interim bond be asked for.

Where the petitioner was arrested in chapter proceedings, the Hon'ble Bombay High Court held that arrest of the petitioner is illegal as there is no provision to arrest a person on initiation of chapter proceedings. The High Court awarded compensation to the petitioner; *Rafiq M. Gowli* v. *State of Maharashtra,* 2015 All MR (Cri) 2677.

The Bombay High Court in *Christalin Costa (Smt.)* v. *State of Goa,* 1992 Cri LJ 3608, had held that quarrels between two private individuals do not attract provisions of sections 107 and 111 of Cr.P.C. and initiation of proceedings under section 107 Cr.P.C. is bad in Law.

In *Jayant D. Shah* v. *State of Maharashtra,* 1986 (1) Crimes 405, the Bombay High Court has held that initiation of proceedings under the provisions of sections 107 to 110 of Cr.P.C. on the basis of incidents involving trivial quarrels without application of mind would amount to gross abuse of the process of law.

In yet another decision [*Indravadan Killawala* v. *State of Maharashtra,* 1989 Cri LJ 1253] the Bombay High Court has held that the provisions of sections 107 and 110 show that the powers vested in an Executive Magistrate under these sections have to be exercised only in cases of a serious nature, not in cases involving trivial quarrels and certainly not to be used as a vehicle of private vendetta.

The Andhra Pradesh High Court in *Aluva Balaiahgari Chandra Reddy* v. *The Revenue Inspector, Rajampet,* 1980 Cri LJ 1169 (AP), has held that, *"when police investigation was in progress in the case of offence under section 353 of IPC, initiation of simultaneous proceedings under section 107 of Cr.P.C. for the same act is not proper."*

In recent landmark judgment *Riyaz alias Ahmad* v. *State of Maharashtra,* (2006) 1 AIR Bom R 955, the Bombay High Court has condemned the action of police for arresting and initiating preventive action against minor under section 107 of Cr.P.C. and awarded compensation of Rs. 5,000 to the minor.

The Bombay High Court in *Chandrabhan Rama Dhengle* v. *Indirabai Chandrabhan Dhengle,* 1998 (1) Mh LJ 234, has held that provision of section 107 of Cr.P.C. is preventive and as it confers wide and unusual powers interfering with the liberty of the subject who is not found guilty of offence, it must the exercised strictly in accordance with law.

In a landmark decision the Bombay High Court in *Mohd. Salam Mohd. Sakir Ansari* v. *L.S. Danekar,* 1999 (3) Mh LJ 864, has held that passing interim order and requiring accused to furnish two sureties for two years one from Hindu Community and other from Muslim Community is illegal and improper and therefore quashed the order.

(iv) Writ of *Habeas Corpus*

Habeas Corpus is a Latin phrase which means literally "that you have the body". It is a recourse in law through which a person can report an unlawful detention or imprisonment to a Court and request that the Court order the custodian of a person, usually a prison official, to bring the prisoner to Court to determine if the detention is lawful.

Any High Court under Article 226 and the Supreme Court under Article 32 of the Constitution of India has power to issue directions or orders or writs in the nature of *Habeas Corpus.*

Where there is a violation of a fundamental or other legal right of a person or class of persons, he/she can file not only regular writ petition under Article 226 in the High Court and under Article 32 in the Supreme Court, but also by addressing a letter to the Court; *M.C. Mehta* v. *Union of India*, (1987) 1 SCR 819.

In this case, the Apex Court held that it is incorrect to say that writ of *Habeas Corpus* lies only when there is illegal detention. The words 'in the nature of' imply that the powers of Supreme Court or the High Court are not subject to the traditional restrictions on the powers of the British Courts to issue writs. Thus the powers of Supreme Court and the High Courts are much wider that those of the British Courts. The celebrated writ of *Habeas Corpus* has been described as 'a great constitutional privilege of the citizen' or 'the first security of civil liberty'. The writ provides a prompt and effective remedy against illegal detention and its purpose is to safeguard the liberty of the citizen which is a precious right not to be lightly transgressed by anyone. The Court further held that writ petition against the order of preventive detention at pre-execution stage can be entertained only in exceptional circumstances. However, powers of the Court, are not limited to the grounds mentioned in *Alka Subhash Gadia's* case; *Deepak Bajaj* v. *State of Maharashtra*, 2008 AIR SCW 7788: AIR 2009 SC 628.

In this case, the High Court held that writ of *Habeas Corpus* can be invoked not only against State but also against any individual who is holding any person in unlawful custody or a detention. It is the duty of police in such circumstances to make necessary efforts to see that detenue got released; *Jayamma (Smt.)* v. *State of Karnataka*, Writ Petition (HC) No. 158/2007.

In this case, the Apex Court held that if fresh grounds are involved, successive writ petition of *Habeas Corpus* is not barred. Principles of constructive *res judicata* are not applicable in such proceedings; *Srikant* v. *District Magistrate*, (2007) 1 SCC 486: 2007 All SCR 368.

In this case, the Apex Court held that the Courts have the necessary power to entertain grievances against any detention order prior to its execution if *Habeas Corpus* petition is filed, where the Courts are prima facie satisfied that (i) the order is not passed under the Act under which it is purported to have been passed, (ii) it is sought to be executed against a wrong person, (iii) it is passed for a wrong purpose, (iv) it is passed on vague, extraneous and irrelevant grounds or (v) the authority which passed it had no authority to do so; *Additional Secretary* v. *Alka Subhash Gadia (Smt.)*, (1990) Supp 3 SCR 583: 1992 (Suppl) 1 SCC 496.

In this case, the Apex Court held that ordinarily, the basis for issuance of a writ of *Habeas Corpus* is an illegal detention. But in the case of such a writ sued out for the detention of a child, the law is concerned not so much with the illegality of the detention as with the welfare of the child. Therefore writ of *Habeas Corpus* can be entertained where the custody of minor child is sought; *Gaurav Nagpal* v. *Sumedha Nagpal*, 2009 (1) All MR 925 (SC).

CHAPTER III

HUMAN RIGHTS VIOLATION AND REMEDIAL JURISPRUDENCE

"He who would put security before liberty deserves neither"

—Benjamin Franklin

"Human Rights should be placed higher than the laws of the Country"

—Shiv Khera

Human rights means the rights relating to life, liberty, equality and dignity of the individual guaranteed by the Constitution or embodied in International covenants and enforceable by Courts in India.

The *Magna Carta* first issued by King John of England in 1215 AD was an agreement between an unpopular King and rebel barons which is supposed to be implemented by the council of 25 barons. It was a potent international rallying cry against the arbitrary use of power. The right to petition is the first ever human right recognised by *Magna Carta*. The *Magna Carta* outlined the response when petitions for redress were ignored. This also includes about rebellion. The right to rebellion defined in 1215 was exercised in 1776 and explained in 4th July, 1776 declaration under the supervision of Thomas Jefferson. The *Magna Carta* was followed by Great Charter of 1216 and 1217. Lord Denning called it the foundation of the freedom of the individual against the arbitrary authority of the despot.

The International Covenant on Civil and Political Rights (ICCPR), 1966 is a multilateral treaty adopted by United Nations General Assembly on 16th December, 1966. It commits its parties to respect civil and political rights of individuals, including the right to life, freedom of religion, freedom of speech, freedom of assembly, electoral rights and rights to due process and a fair trial.

Despite there being International Covenants and the Constitution of India for the protection of human rights, police machinery does not seem to respect the same. National Human Rights Commission (NHRC) has held that 16 out of 19 police encounter with the suspected maoists in Guntur and Karnool districts of Andhra Pradesh, prior to 2002 were fake and recommended to the government payment of compensation of Rs. 5,00,000 each to kin of the families *vide* its Order dated 13th July, 2012.

Misuse of the powers vested in the Army by the draconian Armed Forces (Special Powers) Act, 1958 has led to the killings of many persons in fake encounters in the state of Manipur. Extra-Judicial Execution of Victims' Families Association (EEVFAM) has filed petition before the Apex Court under Article

32 of the Constitution of India praying for enquiries into the fake encounters. EEVFAM has culled out 1528 possible encounters, for the assistance of the Court, out of which 37 are judicial enquiry cases, 35 commission of enquiry cases and 23 NHRC cases. Apart from these cases, there are 170 cases with written complaints. This petition has been admitted by the Hon'ble Apex Court. However the Union of India filed review petition challenging the order of the Apex Court. But, the Hon'ble Apex Court has dismissed the review petition filed by Union of India. Now the Union of India has to mandatorily register FIR and investigate the said matters.

During the counter insurgency period (1984 to 1995) in Punjab, there were arbitrary detentions, tortures, extra-judicial executions, and enforced disappearance of thousands of Sikhs. Investigations by human rights activists Jaswant Singh Khalra and Jaspal Singh Dhillon conducted in 1994 and early 1995 revealed that there were six thousand secret cremations by the Punjab Police in just one of then 13 districts in Punjab. Based on the information gathered by the duo, the Committee for Information and Initiative on Punjab (CIIP) moved the Supreme Court in April 1995 to demand a comprehensive inquiry into extra – judicial executions ending in secret cremations. The Supreme Court of India ordered NHRC in 1996 to address all the issues raised in the petition filed by CIIP. But NHRC failed to address civil liability and accountability issues by refusing to independently investigate a single abuse or allow a single victim family to testify even after ten years of proceedings. NHRC failed to investigate a single within a decade and refused to identify any official responsible for the abuses. It rejected cases from other districts and ignored violations of human rights by security forces. Though Indian Government admitted that it illegally cremated 2,097 individuals in Amritsar, yet no official had been held accountable for the same. However in 1999, CBI registered only 30 regular cases out of which 12 cases have been finalised and 18 cases are pending in investigations. (Lateron, Punjab Police killed Jaswant Singh Khalra in October 1995 and the trial Court convicted six police officers for his murder.

In 2011, there were reports that mass graves were found in North Kashmir containing 2,900 unmarked bodies. After investigations 2,700 unknown, unmarked and mass graves containing 2,900 bodies, in 55 villages in 3 districts-Bandipura, Baramulla and Kupwara of North Kashmir were found. International People's Tribunal on Human Right and Justice demanded an independent probe. According to the Shrinagar-based Association of Parents of Displaced person (APDA), at least 8,000 people have disappeared since the insurgency began. Various Human Rights Organisations have found that violence and militarization in Kashmir, between 1989-2009 have resulted in over 70,000 deaths, including through extra-judicial or fake encounter executions, custodial brutality and other means. Culprits behind killings are yet to be brought to justice.

Bhopal Jail Break and murders of 8 SIMI activists in alleged encounter in the wee hours on 31st October, 2016 is another classic example of misuse of political power. Human Rights activists and members of slain SIMI members have alleged that it is staged shootout and cold blooded murders. Claim of the police that accused escaped from the jail after killing the guard at Bhopal

Central Jail was dismissed by many human rights activists on the ground that it is rather impossible to climb the 32 feet boundary wall of the jail and use of tooth brush to open the lock which has earned an ISO certificate. Mehmooba Bi, mother of a slain alleged SIMI member, has filed a PIL in Jabalpur High Court and the Court has issued notices to the State Government.

India does not have any legislation that defines the expression "torture" or "custodial torture". The Prevention of Torture Bill, 2010 was presented in Rajya Sabha on 6th December, 2010 but Union of India does not seem to be in hurry to pass the said bill. In such circumstances, a PIL has been filed in the Apex Court by former Union Law Minister Ashwani Kumar seeking the Court's intervention to ensure an effective and purposeful legislative framework/laws and its enforcement to fulfil the constitutional promise of human dignity and prevention of custodial torture at all levels. Final decision is yet to come.

National Human Rights Commission is a failed institution. Its recommendations are just advisory and not binding in nature. It cannot investigate a case if complaint is made more than one year after the incident. It has no right to penalise authorities which do not implement its orders. As the protection of Human Rights Act, 1993 does not extend to the State of Jammu and Kashmir, NHRC cannot investigate the human rights violation cases in Jammu and Kashmir. In June 2016, NHRC Chairman Justice H.L. Dattu said that NHRC is a toothless tiger.

An organisation affiliated to the UN High Commissioner for Human Rights has deferred NHRC's re-accreditation until November 2017. The Global Alliance for National Human Rights Institutions (GANHRI) has cited appointment of political representatives as one of the reasons for it. It has referred to the NHRC's failure in ensuring gender balance and pluralism in its staff, among other reasons for the deferment. The GANHRI has noted that panel's selection process was not sufficiently broad and transparent. It has criticised NHRC for its practice of having police officers and former police officers involved in the investigation of human rights violations, particularly in circumstances where the alleged perpetrators are the police. [*November 2016 Report*]. In view of the decision of the UN High Commissioner for Human Rights for deferment of NHRC's re-accreditation until November 2017, NHRC will be unable to represent India at UN Human Rights Council.

In this case, the Court held that human rights are rights of humans relating to life, liberty, equality and dignity. However, the said term would not apply to individual rights of parties even against State arising under contract; *MHADA* v. *Maharashtra State Human Rights Commission*, AIR 2010 Bom 104.

The Center and the States are finding hard to combat terrorism. Instead of initiating dialogue and solving basic problems, they are indulging in easy option of eliminating the people who are fighting for their civil and democratic rights. This has often led to armed clashes between people and the police. Number of persons are killed every day by police and military forces in fake encounters. This has resulted in filing of number of petitions before various High Courts and the Apex Court. Such petitions have helped in the development of remedial jurisprudence which has become boon for the families of deceased persons who died in such fake encounters.

After investigating complaint of fake encounter deaths, the National Human Rights Commission held that 16 out of 19 police encounters with the suspected maoists in Guntur and Kurnool districts of Andhra Pradesh, prior to 2002, were fake and recommended to government payment of compensation of Rs. 5,00,000 each to kin of the families. [*Source*: National Human Rights Website]

This case relates to killings of number of persons by the State Police and Paramilitary Forces in Manipur. In this case, the Apex Court held that where petition alleges human rights violation, Court is bound to directly step in and examine the matter. Plea that such matter should be first examine though Human Rights Commission is not tenable. The Court further observed that State is infested by insurgency and lives of many policemen and members of security forces are lost in fight against insurgency, can be a valid defence to fake encounters. The Court appointed high powered commission to investigate the matter; *Extra-Judicial Execution Victim Families Association* v. *Union of India*, AIR 2013 SC 818: 2013 All SCR 821.

In a landmark judgment while condemning the policy of State of Chhattisgarh to use tribal youths in counter insurgency activity, the Apex Court held that state policy of employing them as Special Police Officers in counter insurgency activity against Maoists and Naxalites is irrational, arbitrary and capricious. It is also denigration of their dignity as human beings. The Court directed the State to cease and desist from using Special Police Officers in controlling, countering, or eliminating Maoists, Naxalites activities in State and also to take measures to prevent operation of any such group including but not limited to *salwa judum and koya commands*. The Apex Court also directed Union Government not to use its funds in supporting or in engaging Special Police Officers in counter insurgency activities; *Nandini Sundar* v. *State of Chhattisgarh*, AIR 2011 SC 2839.

In a landmark judgment the Hon'ble Apex Court issued following directions to all the states and union territories to prevent custodial torture: (a) installation of CCTV cameras in prisons; (b) appointment of non-official visitors to prisons; (c) deployment of women constables in each police station; (d) all states to set up human rights commission for their respective territories and also for setting up of Human Rights Courts; *Dilip K. Basu* v. *State of West Bengal*, 2015 All SCR 3091.

Before discussing the remedial jurisprudence, let us see the guidelines issued by the Bombay High Court in cases of encounter deaths.

Three writ petitions were filed by PUCL before the Bombay High Court in which the issue of genuineness or otherwise of nearly 99 encounters between the Mumbai police and the alleged criminals resulting in death of about 135 persons between 1995 and 1997 was raised. In response to the said petitions, the Division Bench of the Bombay High Court has issued certain guidelines in cases of encounter death in case of *PUCL* v. *The State of Maharashtra*, 1999 All MR (Cri) 877 which are as under—

(i) The police must produce such of the materials and the important witnesses before the Court of law, particularly in the encounter case and examine them for the purpose of recording evidence so as to substantiate their case.

(ii) Whenever the respondents – police are on receipt of intelligence or a tip off about the criminal movements and activities pertaining to the commission of grave crimes, it shall be entered into a case diary. If the receiving authority is the police officer of a particular police station, the relevant entry has to be made in the General Diary and if the receiving authority is the higher police officer, the relevant entry to the said effect has to be made by a separate diary kept and provided therefore and then pursue further in accordance with the procedural law.

(iii) Regarding any encounter operation is over and persons are killed or injured and the same is reported to either orally or in writing to the police in furtherance of section 154 of Cr. P.C., it shall be registered in Crime Register of that particular police station and that further the said First Information Report along with copies to the higher officials and the Court in original shall be sent with immediately without any delay whatsoever through proper channel so as to reach to the Court without any delay at all. A report, as enjoined under section 157(1) of Cr. P.C., shall also be followed necessarily by the concerned police station.

(iv) After setting the law in motion by registering the FIR in the Crime Register by the concerned police officer of the particular police station, the investigating staff of the police shall take such steps by deputing the man or men to get the scene of crime guarded so as to avoid or obliterate or disfigure the existing physical features of the scene of occurrence or the operation encounter. The guarding of the scene of the occurrence shall continue till the inspection of occurrence takes place by the investigating staff of the police and preparation of spot *panchanama* and the recovery *panchanama*.

(v) The Police officer who takes part in the operation encounter or the investigating office of the concerned police station, shall take all necessary efforts and arrangements to preserve fingerprints of the criminals or the dreaded gangsters of the weapons who handled immediately after the said criminal was brought down to the ground and incapacitated and that the said fingerprints, if properly taken and preserved, must be sent to the Chemical Analyzer for comparison of the fingerprints of the dead body to be taken.

(vi) The material which are found on the scene of occurrence or the operation encounter and such of the materials including the blood stained earth and blood stained materials and the sample earth and other moveable physical features, shall also be recovered by the investigating staff under the cover of recovery *panchanama* attested by the independent witnesses.

(vii) To fix the exact date and actual place of occurrence in which operation encounter has taken place, a rough sketch regarding the topography of the existing physical features of the said place shall be drawn by the police or the investigating staff of the police either by themselves or by the help of the staff of the Survey Department even during the spot *panchanama* is prepared.

(viii) The inquest examination shall be conducted by the investigating staff of the police on the spot itself without any delay and statements of the inquest witnesses are to be recorded under section 161 of Cr.P.C. and the inquest *panchanama* shall also be sent along with the above case record prepared along with the FIR without any delay whatsoever to the Court.

(ix) If the injured criminals during the operating encounter are found alive, not only that they should be provided medical aid immediately but also arrangements and attempts shall be taken by the police to record their statements under section 164 of Cr.P.C. either by a Magistrate, if possible and if not, by the medical officer concerned duly attested by the hospital staff mentioning the time and factum that while recording such statement the injured were in a state of position that they will be able to give statements and the connected certificates by the doctors appended thereto.

(x) After the examination of further witnesses and completing the investigation inclusive of securing the accused or accused persons, the concerned police is directed to send final report to the Court of competent jurisdiction as required under section 173 of Cr.P.C. for further proceeding.

(xi) Either in sending the first information report or sending with the general diary entry referred in the guideline Nos. 1 and 2, the concerned police shall avoid any iota of delay under any circumstances whatsoever so also rough sketch showing the topography of the scene and the recovery of the materials and the blood stained materials with the sample earth with the other documents *viz.*, the spot *panchanama*, recovery *panchanama* – all seems very vital documents – the respondants – police are also directed to send them to the Court of concerned Jurisdiction without any delay.

PUCL was not satisfied with the adequacy of the reliefs granted by the Bombay High Court and , consequently, it filed three SLP's against the judgment and order dated 22nd February, 1999 to 25th February. The Supreme Court of India has lamented the absence of structured guidelines and procedures where police officer is involved in shooting. The Hon'ble Apex Court has framed the guidelines and directed all the States to follow the same. Having regard to the directions issued by the Bombay High Court, guidelines issued by NHRC, suggestions of appellant-PUCL, amicus curiae and others, the Apex Court issued following guidelines:

(i) Whenever the police is in receipt of any intelligence or tip-off regarding criminal movements or activities pertaining to the commission of grave criminal offence, it shall be reduced into writing in some form (preferably into case diary) or in some electronic form. Such recording need not reveal details of the suspect or the location to which the party is headed.

If such intelligence or tip-off is received by a higher authority, the same may be noted in some form without revealing details of the suspect or the location.

(ii) If pursuant to the tip-off or receipt of any intelligence, as above, encounter takes place and firearm is used by the police party and as a result of that, death occurs, an FIR to that effect shall be registered and the same shall be forwarded to the Court under section 157 of the Code without any delay. While forwarding the report under section 157 of the Code, the procedure prescribed under section 158 of the Code shall be followed.

(iii) an independent investigation into the incident/encounter shall be conducted by the CID or police team of another police station under the supervision of a senior officer (at least a level above the head of the police party engaged in encounter). The team conducting inquiry/ investigation shall, at a minimum, seek:

(a) To identify the victim; colour photographs of the victim should be taken;

(b) To recover and preserve evidentiary material, including blood-stained earth, hair, fibers and threads, etc., related to the death;

(c) To identify scene witnesses with complete names, addresses and telephone numbers and obtain their statements (including the statement of police personnel involved) concerning the death;

(d) To determine the cause, manner, location (including preparation of rough sketch of topography of the scene and, if possible, photo/ video of the scene and any physical evidence) and time of death as well as any pattern or practice that may have brought about the death;

(e) It must be ensured that intact fingerprints of deceased are sent for chemical analysis. Any other fingerprints should be located, developed, lifted and sent for chemical analysis;

(f) Post-mortem must be conducted by two doctors in the District Hospital, one of them, as far as possible, should be Incharge/Head of the District Hospital. Post-mortem shall be videographed and preserved;

(g) Any evidence of weapons, such as guns, projectiles, bullets and cartridge cases, should be taken and preserved. Where ever applicable tests for gunshot residue and trace metal detection should be performed;

(h) The cause of death should be found out, whether it was natural death, accidental death, suicide or homicide.

(iv) A Magisterial inquiry under section 176 of the Code must invariably be held in all cases of death which occur in the course of police firing and a report thereof must be sent to Judicial Magistrate having jurisdiction under section 190 of the Code.

(v) The involvement of NHRC is not necessary unless there is serious doubt about independent and impartial investigation. However, the information of the incident without any delay must be sent to NHRC or the State Human Rights Commission as the case may be.

(vi) The injured criminal/victim should be provided medical aid and his/her statement recorded by the Magistrate or Medical officer with certificate of fitness.

(vii) It should be ensured that there is no delay in sending FIR, diary entries, *panchanamas*, sketch, etc., to the concerned court.

(viii) After full investigation into the incident, the report should be sent to the competent court under section 173 of the Code. The trial, pursuant to the charge-sheet submitted by the Investigating Officer, must be concluded expeditiously.

(ix) In the event of death, the next of kin of the alleged criminal/victim must be informed at the earliest.

(x) Six monthly statements of all cases where deaths have occurred in police firing must be sent to NHRC by DGP's. It must be ensured that the six monthly statements reached to NHRC by 15th day of January and July, respectively. The statement may be sent in the following format along with post-mortem, inquest and, where ever available, the inquiry reports:

- (i) date and place of occurrence.
- (ii) Police Station, District.
- (iii) circumstances leading to deaths:
  - (a) Self defence in encounter.
  - (b) In the course of dispersal of unlawful assembly.
  - (c) In the course of affecting arrest.
- (iv) Brief facts of the incident.
- (v) Criminal case number.
- (vi) Investigating Agency.
- (vii) Findings of the Magisterial Inquiry Inquiry by Senior Officers:
  - (a) disclosing, in particular, names and designation of police officials, if found responsible for the death; and
  - (b) whether use of force were justified and action taken was lawful.

(xi) If on the conclusion of investigation the materials/evidence having come on record show that death had occurred by use of firearm amounting to offence under the IPC, disciplinary action against such officer must be promptly initiated and he be placed under suspension.

(xii) As regards compensation to be granted to the dependants of the victim who suffered death in a police encounter, the scheme provided under section 357A of the Code must be applied.

(xiii) The police officer(s) concerned must surrender his/her weapons for forensic and ballistic analysis, including any other material, as required by the investigating team, subject to rights under Article 20 of the Constitution.

(xiv) An intimation about the incident must also be sent to the police officer's family and should the family need services of a lawyer/ counselling, same must be offered.

(xv) No out-of-term promotion or instant gallantry rewards shall be bestowed on the concerned officers soon after the occurrence. It must be ensured at all costs that such rewards are given/recommended only when the gallantry of the concerned officers is established beyond doubt.

(xvi) If the family of the victim finds that the above procedure has not been followed or there exists a pattern of abuse or lack of independent investigation or impartiality by any of the functionaries as above mentioned, it may make a complaint to the Sessions Judge having territorial jurisdiction over the place of incident. Upon such complaint being made, the concerned sessions judge shall look into the merits of the complaint and address the grievances raised therein.

The Hon'ble Apex Court directed that the above guidelines will also be applicable to grievous injury cases in police encounter, as far as possible. The Court further directed that the above requirements/norms must be strictly observed in all cases of death and grievous injury in police encounters by treating them as law declared under Article 141 of the Constitution of India; *PUCL* v. *State of Maharashtra*, (2014) 10 SCC 635: 2014 All SCR 3842.

This was a case *Nilabati Behera (Smt.)* v. *State of Orissa*, (1993) 2 SCR 581 of custodial death of the petitioner's son who was taken from his home to police custody. The petitioner alleged in her letter which was treated as a writ petition under Article 32 of the Constitution that it was a case of custodial death and prayed for compensation. Repelling the defence of sovereign immunity and allowing the petition, the Court held that, "award of compensation in a proceeding under Article 32 by Supreme Court or by the High Court under Article 226 of the Constitution is a remedy available in Public Law based on strict liability for contravention of fundamental rights to which the principle of sovereign immunity does not apply even though it may be available as a defence in Private Law in an action based on tort. This is a distinction between the two remedy to be borne in mind which also indicates the basis on which compensation is awarded in such proceedings."

In the writ petitions filed on behalf of two woman *Saheli, A Women's Resources Center* v. *Commissioner of Police, Delhi*, AIR 1990 SC 513: (1989) Supp 2 SCR 488 who were severely beaten by the alleged landlord, in collusion with the local police, in their attempts to get the rooms occupied by them vacated, the petitioners prayed for directions to the respondents to pay exemplary charges to one of the women for the death of her son but to injuries inflicted on him by the police. Allowing the writ petitions, the Apex Court held that, "An action for damages lies for bodily harm which includes battery, assault, false imprisonment, physical injuries and death. In cases of assault, battery and false imprisonment, the damages are large and represent a solatium for the mental pain, distress, indignity, loss of liberty and death..... ... It is well settled that the State is responsible for the tortious acts of its employees."

This was a case of a Bangladeshi national who was gang raped by many including employees of the Railways in a room at Yatri Niwas at Howrah Station of the Eastern Railway and thereafter at a rented flat. The public interest litigation was filed by the practising advocate of High Court for various reliefs including the relief for compensation for the victim of rape. Allowing the petition the Apex Court held that the contention that the liability under the Law of Torts would arise only when the act complained of was performed in the course of official duty and since rape cannot be said to be an official act, the Central Government would not be liable even under the Law of Torts, is, wholly bad and is contrary to the settled legal position. .... Foreign nationals can be granted relief of compensation under Public Law for violation of fundamental rights on ground of Domestic Jurisprudence based on constitutional provisions and Human Rights Jurisprudence; *The Chairman, Railway Board* v. *Mrs. Chandrima Das*, AIR 2000 SC 988: (2000) 1 SCR 480.

This case pertains to Ramlila Maidan incident of 4th June, 2011 where supporters of Yoga Guru Baba Ramdeo were gathered for the agitation against black money and corruption. Police crackdown at midnight on members of public sleeping in enclosed public ground and were asked to leave Ramlila Maidan at midnight itself. This confrontation led to caning and tear gas shelling from police side and stone-pelting from public side. Several persons including police personal were injured and one woman succumbed to injuries later on. The Apex Court held that police action is unconstitutional inasmuch as there was no justification to compel sleeping public to leave at night when there was no immediate danger of peace being disturbed. The Court awarded compensation of Rs. 5,00,000 to legal heirs of lady who died as a result of this incident and Rs. 50000 to the persons who sustained serious injuries. The Apex Court held the organisers of Yoga Camp to be negligent and for their contributory negligence, they were directed to pay monetary compensation. The liability to pay monetary compensation was apportioned between State and Yoga Guru in the ration of 3:1; *Ramlila Maidan Incident, (in re:)*, Suo Motu WP (Crl.) No. 122 of 2011, decided on February 23, 2012 and reported in (2012) 5 SCC 1.

This was a case where minor was arrested and preventive action under section 107 of Cr.P.C. was initiated against him. The Division Bench of the Bombay High Court has held that provisions of Chapter VIII of Cr.P.C. are not applicable to Juvenils. And awarded compensation of Rs. 5,00,000 to the minor; *Riyaz* alias *Ahemad* v. *State of Maharashtra*, 2006 (1) AIR Bom R 955.

In this case *P.E. Arifa* v. *State Kerla*, AIR 2006 NOC 238 (Ker) innocent woman was forcibly detained in police station without registering crime against her. The Court held that this amounts to curtailment of her personal liberty and subjecting her to mental torture of immeasurable proportions. And compensation of Rs. 50,000 was awarded to the victim.

This was a case *Sau. Sharda Narayan Bhongade* v. *Surendra Jagmohan Patil,* 2003 All MR (Cri) 17(DB) (Bom) where petitioner's name was included in charge sheet by Investigation Officer without any kind of investigation or verification. Petitioner had sent a letter to High Court alleging that he suffered mental agony and financial loss due to the action of Investigation Officer. This letter was converted into a Criminal Writ Petition. The Court directed the State Government to pay compensation of Rs. 25,000 to the petitioner with liberty to recover half of the amount of compensation from the concerned police officer.

This was a case *Raju* alias *Narsingh Kulkarni* v. *The Suptd. of Prisons,* where Lathi Charge was resorted to without first taking inmates into confidence and explaining them purpose of surprise inspection on the ground that inmates refused to co-operate during surprise inspection of jails. The Court observed that the officers failed in their duties to explain them the purpose of surprise inspection and therefore directed the State Government to pay token compensation of Rs. 1,000 to the inmates who receive injuries.

In this case *Dinkarrao Rajaram Pole* v. *State of Maharashtra.,* 2003 All MR (Cri) 1096 (Bom) (DB), a practising lawyer who was a senior citizen was arrested by the police without any justification. The Court held that the State is liable for tortious act committed by it servant within the scope of his employment and awarded monetary compensation to the petitioner.

In *Bhim Singh, MLA* v. *State of Jammu and Kashmir,* AIR 1986 SC 494, the Apex Court awarded compensation of Rs. 50,000 to petitioner MLA whose arrest was mischievous and malicious.

In this case, appellant who was a doctor by profession was arrested and compelled to hold a placard with his photograph on which it was written, "I, Dr. M.N. Azam, am a cheat, fraud, thief and rascal." The placard was then circulated in general public and in revenue proceedings. The Hon'ble Apex Court took a serious note of mental torture of the appellant at the hands of insensible police officials and directed the State government to pay a sum of Rs. 5,00,000 to the appellant and directed the State to recover the same from erring police officers from deducting it from their salaries; *Dr. Mehmood Nayyar Azam* v. *State of Chattisgarh,* 2012 All SCR 2401.

In this case *Walmik S/o Deorao Bobde* v. *State of Maharashtra,* 2001 All MR (Cri) 1731 (Bom) (DB), the petitioner was arrested after his acquittal under the non-bailable warrant issued by JMFC 3rd Court, Wardha and taken in MCR. The Division Bench of the Bombay High Court while allowing the compensation to the petitioner has held that (i) Non-bailable warrant for arrest should not ordinarily be issued in the first instance. Such a stringent measure is applied only as a last resort. Magistrate before signing such a warrant should satisfy himself whether such a warrant is really required to be issued to procure presence of accused facing trial before it. (ii) Even though arrest is by competent Court it violates not only his fundamental rights but such action deserves to be condemned being taken in utter disregard to human rights of an individual citizen.

Recently the Division Bench of the Bombay High Court has condemned practice of stripping accused persons in police lock ups in the State of

Maharashtra. The Court observed that "prisoner does not cease to have basic human rights merely because he was put up in police lock ups" and directed the Director General of Police to issue necessary direction; *Rahul S. Thakur* v. *Commissioner of Police,* 2006 AIR Bom R 551 (Bom) (DB).

In this case *Kalpana D/o Nilaram Harinkhede* v. *State of Maharashtra,* (1999) 3 Mh LJ 483, the accused/respondent was prosecuted for the offences punishable under section 354 read with section 34 of IPC. However, he was discharged for non-prosecution. The petitioner filed a petition under Articles 226 and 227 and section 482 of Cr.P.C. for quashing the order of discharge. The petition was dismissed. However the Bombay High Court held that "dismissal of petition does not deprive the petitioner to press for compensation in review application. .... The petitioner/victim is entitled to compensation under section 357 of Cr.P.C. from State."

In a landmark judgement the Apex Court considered problems faced by *Hijras,* Eunuchs and transgender persons and issued directions to safeguard their constitutional right as persons belonging to transgender community. The Court held that discrimination on ground of sexual orientation or gender identity is illegal. The Court further held that treating these persons as male or female is denial of their Constitutional rights and directed that they must be recognised as "third gender" in law; *National Legal Services Authority* v. *Union of India,* 2014 ALL SCR 2022.

Due to scientific research, problems have arisen in the field of human rights and world is in dilemma on human cloning. Recently *Mr. A.H. Zakri,* Head of the Institute of Advanced Studies, Yokohama, Japan has said that "which ever path the international community chooses it will have to act soon either to prevent reproductive cloning or to defend the human rights of cloned individuals."

Other Landmark Cases on Human Rights

1. *P.T. Munichikkanna Reddy.* v. *Revamma,* 2007 All SCR 1582: 2007 (6) Mh LJ 336 (SC): Claim of adverse possession (Article 64 & 65 of The Limitation Act) falls within the new dimension of Human Rights.
2. *Dilip S. Dahanukar* v. *Kotak Mahindra Co. Ltd.,* 2007 (4) CRJ 258 (SC): Right of appeal from a judgement of conviction affecting the liberty of a person keeping in view the expansive definition of Article 21 is also a fundamental right.
3. *Bhagubai Dhanabhai Khalasi* v. *State of Gujarat ,* 2007 (6) All MR 472 (SC): Access to justice is a human right.
4. *Dwarka Prasad Agarwal (Dead) by LR's.* v. *B.D. Agarwal,* (2003) 6 SCC 230: 2003 (3) All MR 1158 (SC): The right to get a fair trial is a basic fundamental/human right. Any procedure which comes in the way of a party in getting a fair trial would be violative of Article 14 of The Constitution.
5. *Moti Lal Saraf* v. *State of Jammu and Kashmir,* 2007 All SCR 162: Speedy trial is an essential part of right to life and liberty. Delay at every stage from the actual restraint imposed till final decision must be avoided.

CHAPTER IV

PROFESSIONAL ETHICS, MISCONDUCT AND CONTEMPT OF COURT

* "The only thing that stands between the crime for extortion and a solicitor's fee is a practising certificate."
* A lawyer, a priest and a doctor are the only survivors of a tourist cruise wreck. After the ship went down they held on to a raft for hours hoping to be rescued. To their horror they were suddenly surrounded by hungry sharks who immediately ate the doctor and the priest, but refused to touch the lawyer. A few hours later the lawyer was saved. When he was interviewed he was asked: "How did you survive such a vicious shark attack?" The lawyer answered: "Professional courtesy".
* "Q: How can you tell there's an afterlife for lawyers?

  A: Because after they die, they lie still."

Can we change the above perceptions of a common man about the lawyers? Answer to this question lies in knowing professional ethics. Therefore there is a detailed discussion in this chapter.

The Advocates joining the bar must know the professional ethics and the standard expected from them by the Bench and the Society. Without knowing the same, one may get himself entangled in the cobweb of the contempt of Court and also may have to face the disciplinary proceedings. Your noviceness will not be a defence in contempt proceedings. Therefore, certain cases are given to let the readers know the judicial views on this topic.

In *R.D. Saxena* v. *Balram Prasad Sharma,* 2001 (1) Mh LJ 23, the Apex Court has held that Advocates are not entitled to withhold the papers of client on the ground that his fees were outstanding.

In *John D'Souza* v. *Edward,* (1993) Supp 3 SCR 1016, the Apex Court has held that, the Advocate who did not return will drafted by him and kept in his safe custody despite written request by the Client is guilty of professional misconduct and the Court further held that Advocate is duty bound to return the documents to client.

In *Lt. Co. S.J. Chaudhary* v. *State (Delhi Admin.),* (1984) 2 SCR 438, the Apex Court has held that, *"It is the duty of every Advocate who accept the briefs in a criminal case to attend the trials from day-to-day... .... Having accepted the brief, he will be committing a breach of his professional duty if he fails to attend the Court."*

---

* From the Book titled "The Joke's on Lawyers" by Stan Ross and Published by – Universal Law Publishing Co. Pvt. Ltd. Delhi.

In *State of Maharashtra* v. *Prakashchand B. Kankaria*, 2004 (1) Mh LJ 806, the Bombay High Court has held that, once appearance is filed by Advocate in Court by filing *Vakalatnama* signed by his client, the Advocate cannot later on withdrew his appearance for non-payment of fees for final hearing.

In this case (*C.S. Venkatsubramaniam* v. *State Bank of India*, (1996) Supp 9 SCR 67) the client asked for "no objection certificate" to engage another Lawyer. But the Advocate insisted on payment of fee and refused to give consent. The Court held that counsel cannot insist on fees as a condition to give consent. ..... Client is entitled to change the counsel where he looses confidence in him.

In *N.G. Dastane* v. *Shrikant S. Shivde*, AIR 2001 SC 2028, the Apex Court has held that seeking repeated adjournments by Advocate for postponing the examination of witnesses who are present in Court even without making other arrangement for examining such witnesses is a dereliction of advocate's duty to the Court, as that would cause much harassment and hardship to the witnesses. Such dereliction if repeated would amount to misconduct.

The Bombay High Court has condemned the practice of Courts to discharge advocates on mere filing of no instruction *pursis* and held that advocate cannot withdraw his *Vakalatnama* without obtaining leave of the Court (*Govinda Kamble* v. *Sadu Kamble*, 2005 (1) Mh LJ 651: 2005 (1) All MR 272 and *Dattusingh G. Rajput* v. *Bhagwant Devasthan, Barshi*, 2005 (2) Mh LJ 743).

In *Rajinder Singh* v. *Union of India*, 1993 Cri LJ 1968 (P&H), the Court has held that, Advocate appearing in Court but not recording his presence and not arguing case is unprofessional and unethical.

In *M.Y. Sherif* v. *Hon'ble Judges of High Court of Nagpur*, AIR 1955 SC 19: (1955) 1 SCR 757, the Constitution Bench has held that Counsel who sign applications or pleadings containing matters scandalizing the Court without reasonably satisfying themselves about the *prima facie* existence of adequate grounds therefore, with a view to prevent or delay the course of justice are themselves guilty of contempt of Court.

In *Chetak Construction Ltd.* v. *Om Prakash*, (1998) 2 SCR 1016, the Apex Court has held that Lawyers and litigants cannot be permitted to browbeat the Court or malign the Presiding Officer with a view to getting a favourable order... ... Lawyers and litigants cannot be allowed to "terrorise" or "intimidate" "Judges" with a view to secure orders, which they want..... .. A litigant cannot be permitted 'choice' of the 'forum' and every attempt at 'forum shopping' must be crushed with a heavy hand.

In *Radha Mohan Lal* v. *High Court of Rajasthan*, AIR 2003 SC 1467, the Apex Court while holding the contemner guilty of contempt of Court has held that freedom of expression guaranteed under Article 19(1)(a) of the Constitution cannot be equated or confused with a licence to make unfounded and irresponsible allegations against the judiciary. *Vinay Chandra Mishra (the alleged contemner), (in re:)*, (1995) 2 SCR 638, the Apex Court has held that, "every member of the Bench has a right to ask whatever questions he wants to, to appreciate the merits or demerits of the case ..... No Lawyer or third party can have any right or say in the matter and can make either an issue of it or refuse to answer the questions on ground of juniorship of the member of Bench .. . ... The Lawyers or the litigants concerned have to answer the questions put to him by any member of the Bench.

In the Matter of Rustom C. Cooper v. *Union of India,* (1971) 1 SCR 512, the Constitution Bench of the Apex Court has held that *"while fair and temperate criticism of this Court or any other Court even if strong may not be actionable, attributing improper motives or tending to bring Judges or Courts into hatred and contempt or obstructing directly or indirectly the functioning of Courts is serious contempt of which notice must and will be taken."*

However the Division Bench of the Madhya Pradesh High Court in *Indrani Dutta* v. *Baldeo Sharma.,* 1994 Cri LJ 1958, has held that publication against judicial officer in personal capacity is not a criminal contempt.

In *State of Orissa* v. *Nalinikanta Muduli,* 2004 All MR (Cri) 3421, the Apex Court expressed anguish at the falling standards of professional conduct when Bar cited judgement overruled by Higher Court nearly quarter of a century back. But unfortunately the Apex Court did not rap the High Court Judge for relying on a judgment overruled by the Apex Court. It is respectfully submitted that a judge is not expected to follow mechanically the judgements cited by the bar and it is his duty to see whether judgement cited by the bar has been overruled or not , particularly when all facilities have been provided to the judges.

However, the Punjab and Haryana High Court in *Balbir Singh Wasu* v. *Parbandhak Committee, Gurudwara Sahib Patsahi,* AIR 2001 P&H 49 has held that citing overruled decision of Court does not amount to contempt of Court.

In *POTA Review* case *(PUCL* v. *Union of India,* AIR 2004 SC 456) the Apex Court has held that, Lawyers have no right to withhold information under a guise of professional ethics.

In *U.P. Sales Tax Association* v. *Taxation Bar Association,* (1995) Supp 3 SCR 228, and *State of Uttar Pradesh* v. *Ramsevak,* 2003 AIR SCW 161: 2002 (9) SCALE 619, the Apex Court has held that *"Advocates have no right to go on strike or give a call of boycott."*

In *C.R. Iyer* v. *A.M. Bhattacharjee, Justice,* (1995) Supp 3 SCR 319, the Apex Court has held that, *"... No other forum or fora or a platform is available for discussion of the conduct of a Judge in the discharge of his duties as a Judge of the Supreme Court or the High Court, much less a Bar Council or group of practising advocates .... They are prohibited to discuss the conduct of a Judge in the discharge of his duties or to pass any resolution in that behalf."* However, the Apex Court has devised a scheme to take up the matters to higher Court regarding the conduct of a Judge which is futile and ineffective. The Apex Court has held that where the complaint relates to the Judge of the High Court, the Chief Justice of that High Court, after verification, and if necessary, after confidential enquiry from his independent source, satisfy himself about the truth of the imputation made by the Bar Association through it office bearers against the judge and consult the Chief Justice of India, where deemed necessary, by placing all the information with him. When the Chief Justice of India is seized of the matter to avoid embarrassment to him and to allow fairness in the procedure to be adopted in furtherance thereof, the

Bar should suspend all further actions to enable the Chief Justice of India to appropriately deal with the matter...... On the decision being taken by the Chief Justice of India, the matter should rest at that and await his response for the action taken thereunder for a reasonable period. .... In case the allegations are against Chief Justice of a High Court, the Bar should bring them directly to the notice of the Chief Justice of India. On receipt of such complaint, the Chief Justice of India would in the same way act as stated qua complaint against a Judge of the High Court, and the Bar should await for a reasonable period the response of the Chief Justice of India. *"It is respectfully submitted that the observations of the Apex Court are not correct as they do not appeal to logic and reason of a prudent man. It is emphatically and most respectfully submitted that the lawyers are the best persons to know the behaviour and conduct of the judges as they are part and parcel of the judiciary. It is necessary to do away with such thinking to have more transparency in the administration of justice."*

In *Satyendra Narain Singh* v. *Ram Nath Singh,* (1985) 1 SCR 609, the Apex Court held that Justice S.K. Jha acted in the best traditions of the Judiciary in seeing that his Advocate son withdrew from the case and expected that the Advocate son, rather than the Judge father withdraws from the case.

In *Pandurang Dattatreya Khandekar* v. *The Bar Council of Maharashtra, Bombay,* (1984) 1 SCR 414: AIR 1984 SC 110, the Apex Court held that there is a distinction between the giving of improper legal advice and the giving of wrong legal advice. Giving improper legal advice may amount to professional misconduct. However, mere negligence unaccompanied by any moral delinquency on the part of an advocate in the exercise of his profession does not amount to professional misconduct. The Court further held that it is professionally improper for a member of the Bar to prepare false documents or to draw pleadings knowingly that the allegations made are untrue to his knowledge.

Similarly the Apex Court has held in *V.P. Kumaravelu* v. *Bar Council of India,* AIR 1997 SC 1014 that, conduct with amongst to the dereliction of duty by an advocate towards his client or towards his case, would amount to professional misconduct. But, negligence without moral turpitude or delinquency may not amount to professional misconduct.

In *P.D. Gupta* v. *Rammurti,* AIR 1998 SC 283 the Apex Court has held that *"where the advocate purchased from his client property which it was the subject matter of dispute pending in the Court, he was held guilty of professional misconduct and a sentence of debarring from practice for one year was affirmed."*

In *V.C. Rangadurai* v. *D. Gopalan,* AIR 1979 SC 281: (1979) 1 SCR 1054, the Apex Court has held that it is not in accordance with professional etiquette for an Advocate to hand over his brief to another to take his place at hearing and conduct the case as if the latter had himself been briefed, unless the client consents to this course being taken.

The Apex Court has expected that the lawyers should maintain a sense of detachment and non-identification with the causes espoused by them and deprecated the practice of making reckless allegations and aspersions in the pleadings against the order of the Supreme Court. *(T.V. Choudary, (in re:),* AIR 1987 SC 1550).

The Apex Court has held in *John D'Souza* v. *Edward Ani*, AIR 1994 SC 975, that where privilege of cross examination conferred on advocate exceeded the legitimate bounds, the advocate was held guilty of misconduct and a punishment of six months suspension from practice was imposed. Therefore, trial Court advocates must not abuse the privilege during examination and cross examination of witness.

In *Damayanti G. Chandiramani (Mrs.)* v. *S. Vaney*, AIR 1966 Bom 19: 1965 Mh LJ 541, the Bombay High Court has held that, disrespect or disregard to an advocate in certain circumstances so as to deter him from discharging his duties would amount to contempt of Court and that would amount to a direct interference with the administration of justice.

The Division Bench of the Bombay High Court in *Vasanta Rajaram Rathod* v. *State of Maharashtra*, 2006 (6) Mh LJ 374 has warned the authorities not to disregard the precedents of the Higher Courts and held that *"disregard of precedent may amount to contempt."*

However it must not be understood that judges are exempted from prosecution under The Contempt of Courts Act, 1971. There are few judicial pronouncements holding the judges guilty of contempt of Court. Few such decisions are given.

In *Anantalal* v. *A.H. Walter*, AIR 1981 Cal. 257, the Court has held that any comment upon the advocate which has reference to the conduct of his case, may amount to contempt of Court.

In *Telhara Cotton Co.* v. *Kashinath Gangadhar*, AIR 1940 Nag 110, the Bombay High Court has held that threat to an advocate interferes with the due performance of his duty and therefore, amounts to contempt of Court.

In *P.D. Shamdasani* v. *King-Emperor*, AIR 1945 PC 134, the Privy Council has observed that abuses, insults or aspersions cast upon counsel in the course of discharge of his duties and tending to deter them from duty amount to contempt of Court. A judge or a Magistrate who insults or intimidates a counsel in the course of something done by him legitimately is guilty of contempt. But the words or actions must be such as to interfere with the course of justice.

In *Bar Association of Moradabad* v. *Kothari*, 1966 All WR (HC) 197, a Magistrate got unnecessarily agitated and ordered an advocate out of the Court. The Bar association took up the action of contempt wherein it was held that *"If the Presiding Officer acts in such an outrageous and undignified manner he can verily be held guilty of contempt of his own Court, for he is only one of the component parts which constitute the comprehensive and manifold concept of a Court."*

In this case, accused managed to stay in hospital for 527 days to evade arrest. The Hon'ble Apex Court held two medical professionals guilty of contempt for granting medical asylum to an accused, without there being any reason or medical condition justifying his prolonged admission as an indoor patient; *Sita Ram* v. *Balbir @ Bali*, Jan 2017 All SCR (Cri) 86.

The students and trial Court advocates are requested to read the article titled 'The Unprotected Lawyer' written by Miss. Phiroza Ankoesabia. The author writes "*Any undue or unwarranted interference with the advocate's duty amounts to criminal intimidation on principles analogous to those contained in section 503 of IPC...... When an advocate is habitually insulted and thereby justifiably provoked into answering in a manner gravely injurious to the dignity and the decorum of the Court, which is the advocate's first duty to preserve, he is induced thereby to commit an offence at the instance of the Judge*". The observations of the author would make it clear that a Judge can render himself open to grave criminal charge if he is by habitually adopting a discourteous or otherwise rude and insulting behaviour towards an advocate whilst the latter is pleading a cause. Therefore the advocates should defend the cause of his client without fear and while conducting a case if the Judge insults or intimidate him, initiate contempt proceeding against the Judge concerned.

Other cases

Supreme Court Bar Association v. *Union of India*, (1998) 4 SCC 409: An advocate could be debarred from appearing before the Court even if the disciplinary jurisdiction for misconduct was vested with the Bar Council.

Central Coal Fields Limited v. *Sanjay Mahto*, AIR 2007 (NOC) 1077 (Jhar): 2007 (1) AIR Bom R 730: The High Court set aside the order reprimanding advocate as his client filed forged documents in Court holding that advocates are not entrusted with the duty to verify documents as may be produced into Court.

R.K. Anand v. *Registrar, Delhi High Court*, AIR 2013 SC 670: Appellant senior Advocate was held guilty of contempt of Court for suborning court witnesses in criminal trial.

Narain Pandey v. *Pannalal Pandey*, 2013 All SCR 73: The Court suspended the advocate from practice for three years as he was held guilty for filing vakalatnamas without authority and later on filing fictitious compromises.

High Court On Its Own Motion v. *N.B. Deshmukh*, 2011 (2) Mh LJ 273: Advocate espousing his own cause in the proceedings before the Court or facing contempt of court action cannot appear as an advocate before the Court but may appear as any other ordinary litigant in-person.

Vitusah Oberoi v. *Court of its Own Motion*, 2016/2017 SC: Supreme Court quashed the Delhi High Court order finding Mid-Day Editor, Publisher and Cartoonist for contempt of court for publishing materials against former Chief Justice of India Mr. Sabharwal holding that a High Court cannot initiate contempt proceedings or punish for contempt of the Supreme Court.

Ram Kishan v. *Tarun Bajaj*, 2014 All SCR 678: The proceedings under the Contempt of Courts Act, 1971 are *quasi*-judicial in nature. Therefore proof beyond all reasonable doubt is necessary to prove the charge. Court cannot act on probabilities. Disobedience of order has to wilful. Disobedience of order must involve a degree of default and misconduct.

CHAPTER V

RIGHTS AND DUTIES OF THE PUBLIC PROSECUTOR

The role of Public Prosecutor is very important from the point of view of the State and the society. The Public Prosecutor is expected to be fair to the Court and honest to the society as he conducts prosecution on behalf of the State.

A Public Prosecutor is not the agent of the police but is a man associated with the holy mission of assisting the Court in arriving at the correct decision and it is his duty to act fairly; *Madhav* v. *State,* (1977) 18 Guj LR 896.

The Public Prosecutor is supposed to use evidence reasonably believed to have been obtained through recourse to unlawful methods. He should scrupulously avoid suppression of material capable of establishing the innocence of the accused; *Deepak Aggarwal* v. *Keshav Kaushik,* 2013 All SCR 952: 2013 AIR SCW 1190: (2013) 5 SCC 277.

It has been held in *Sarla R.* v. *T.S. Velu,* AIR 2000 SC 1731, that, *"the role of Public Prosecutor is inside the Court. It commences after investigating agency presents the case in Court after completion of investigation ...... Involving Public Prosecutor in investigation is injudicious ...... An investigation Officer cannot be directed to consult the Public Prosecutor before filing his report."*

Where the complaint was filed against Police Officer, it was held that the Public Prosecutor ought not to defend the officer against whom the allegations of acts of commission or omission are made. [*Sudhir M. Vora* v. *Commissioner of Police,* 2004 All MR (Cri) 2745 (DB) (Bom)].

In *Sushil Hiralal Chokhani* v. *State of Maharashtra,* 2005 All MR (Cri) 2673, the Bombay High Court has held that it is the primary duty of the Public Prosecutor to place before Court all evidence collected by investigating agency whether it be in favour or against accused for proper consideration thereof.

It has been held in *State of Uttar Pradesh* v. *Iftikhar Khan,* (1973) 3 SCR 328, the Apex Court has held that *"ordinarily it is the duty of the prosecution to examine all material witnesses essential to the unfolding of the narrative on which the prosecution is based, whether in the result the effect of that testimony is for or against the case of the prosecution."*

Where there are two categories of witnesses, one related to victim and other not so related, the Apex Court in *Banti* alias *Guddu* v. *State of Madhya Pradesh,* 2004 All MR (Cri) 288, has held that the Public Prosecutor's duty is to produce witnesses from the later category, also subject to his discretion to limit to one or two among them. ...... But if the Public Prosecutor gets reliable information that any witness would not support the prosecution he is free to state in Court about that fact and skip the witness from being examined as a prosecution witness.

In this case (*Sakharam* v. *State of Madhya Pradesh,* (1992) 1 SCR 638) accused/ appellant and deceased were 'children' as defined under the Children Act, 1960. The trial Court convicted appellant for murder and sentenced him to imprisonment for life. High Court also confirmed the conviction. The Apex Court while pointing out the duty of prosecution has held that when presumption of juvenile-innocence is sought to be displaced by the prosecution on basis of circumstantial evidence the circumstances must unmistakably prove the guilt beyond doubt.

In *Rajendra Kumar Jain* v. *State through Special Police Establishment,* (1980) 3 SCR 982, the Apex Court while considering the scope of section 321 of Cr.P.C. and the rights of Public Prosecutor, has laid down following propositions:

"*(i) Under the scheme of the Code Prosecution of an offender for a serious offence is primarily the responsibility of the Executive.*

(ii) The withdrawal from the Prosecution is an executive function of the Public Prosecutor.

(iii) The discretion to withdraw from the Prosecution is that of the Public Prosecutor and non else, and so, he cannot surrender that discretion to some one else.

(iv) The Government may suggest to the Public Prosecutor that he may withdraw from the Prosecution but none can compel him to do so.

(v) The Public Prosecutor may withdraw from the Prosecution not merely on the ground of paucity of evidence but on other relevant grounds as well in order to further broad ends of public justice, public order and peace. The broad ends of public justice will certainly include appropriate social, economic and, political purposes Sans Tammany Hall enterprises.

(vi) The Public Prosecutor is an officer of the Court and responsible to the Court.

(vii) The Court performs a supervisory function in granting it consent to the withdrawal.

(viii) The Court's duty is not to re-appreciate the grounds which led the Public Prosecutor to request withdrawal from the Prosecution but to consider whether the Public Prosecutor applied his mind as a free agent, uninfluenced by irrelevant and extraneous considerations..... .

It shall be the duty of the Public Prosecutor to inform the Court and it shall be the duty of the Court to apprise itself of the reasons which prompt the Public Prosecutor to withdraw from the Prosecution......Once the case has travelled to the Court, the Court and its Officers alone must have control over the case and decide what is to be done in each case."

Where the prosecution cited two categories of witnesses to the occurrence, one consisting of persons closely related to the victim and the other consisting of witnesses who have no such relation, it is the duty of the public prosecutor also to produce witnesses from the latter category, subject to his discretion to limit to one or two among them. If prosecutor gets reliable information that any one among the category would not support the prosecution version he is free to State in court about that fact and skip the witness from being examined as a prosecution witness; *Banti @ Guddu* v. *State of Madhya Pradesh*, 2004 All MR (Cri) 288 (SC): AIR 2004 SC 261: 2004 Cri LJ 372 (SC): (2004) 1 SCC 414.

Where a case is transferred from one State of another State, transferor State loses control over the prosecution. The transferee State has the prerogative to appoint a public prosecutor. The public prosecutor appointed by one State is not answerable to the government of another State; *K. Anbazhagan* v. *State of Karnataka*, 2015 (2) Crimes 268 (SC).

Where the articles are recovered and seized from the spot of incident, it is the duty of public prosecutor to show such articles to the accused during the trial or at the time of recording of statement of accused under section 313, Cr.P.C.; *Varun Chaudhary* v. *State of Rajasthan*, (2012) 1 SCC (Cri) 616.

The Constitution Bench of five Judges in *Mohd. Mumtaz* v. *Nandini Satpathy*, (1987) 1 SCR 680 has also held that consent can be given for withdrawal from the prosecution of a case, not only when the charge is not framed, but even after the charge is framed and at any time before the judgment and relied on *R.K. Jain's* case (*supra*).

This was a case [*Abdul Karim* v. *State of Karnataka*, AIR 2001 SC 116] where Veerappan, a sandalwood smuggler, abducted film star Raj Kumar and three others from Gajanoor in Karnataka. The State Government conceded to the illegal demands of Veerappan which included *inter alia*, the withdrawal of cases under TADA and other criminal cases against him and his associates in lieu of safe release of the film star. Special public prosecutor moved an application for withdrawal of cases and the same was allowed by the Court. Condemning the act of public prosecutor and the State, the Apex Court held that "*Criminal Cases cannot be withdrawn from prosecution to concede to the illegal demands of a deal.*"

CHAPTER VI

RIGHTS AND PRIVILEGES OF DEFENCE LAWYER

Celebrated author of the book "Legal & Professional Ethics" Mr. P. Ramanath Aiyar has enumerated rules of conduct of an advocate some of which are given below:

(i) Under no circumstances an advocate should be a party to a breach of law.

(ii) An advocate must be careful and honest with regard to money or other property held on behalf of his client.

(iii) An advocate should not vary his fee according to the success or failure of the case. But an advocate may conduct the case of a poor client with a *bona fide* case on the basis that his costs will be met out of what is recovered in the event of success.

(iv) An advocate must not be a party to fabrication of documents or false evidence. If he knows that his client has given false evidence he should withdraw from the case.

(v) An advocate should not present a dishonest claim or defence on behalf of his client.

(vi) An advocate should see that the client discloses true facts. But if the client refuses, he should retire from the case.

(vii) An advocate must not solicit business nor should he advertise himself either directly or indirectly.

(viii) An advocate must not disclose at any time confidential information except with the client's consent or use it otherwise than for the benefit of the client.

(ix) He must disclose to his client any personal interest in consistent with the client's interests.

(x) An advocate cannot represent two or more clients whose interests conflict.

(xi) An advocate should give his opinion about the hopes of success in the litigation; where it is doubtful, he should clearly tell him.

(xii) An advocate must devote himself entirely to his client's interests.

(xiii) An advocate should not use unfair methods against his opponents.

(xiv) An advocate should not certify the fees without receiving the same or receive a post-dated cheque.

Apart from this, the Bar Council of India has framed rules for the conduct of advocates. Important rules are given below in brief:

(1) **Rule 36** – An advocate shall not solicit work or advertise, either directly or indirectly, whether by circulars, advertisement, touts personal communications, interviews not warranted by personal relations, furnishing or inspiring newspaper comments or producing his photograph to be published in connection with cases in which he has been engaged or concerned. His sign-board or name-plate should be of a reasonable size. The sign-board or name-plate or stationery should not indicate that he is or has been President or Member of a Bar Council or of any Association or with any particular cause or matter or that he is specialises in any particular type of work or that he has been a Judge or an Advocate General.

(2) **Rule 39** – An advocate shall not enter appearance in any case in which there is already *Vakalatnama* or memo of appearance filed by an advocate engaged for a party except with his consent; in case such consent is not produced he shall apply to the Court stating reasons why the said consent should not be produced and he shall appear only after obtaining the permission of the Court.

The defence Lawyer plays an important role in the administration of justice. He should conduct his case without any fear from inside or outside the Court. It is very difficult to discharge the duty of a defence Lawyer particularly when judge is prejudiced or predisposed against him. The trial Court advocates also face a problem of Court's undue interference while cross-examining the witnesses. In such circumstances the advocate should insist upon his question being taken down or his objection noted in the deposition itself. If the judge refuses to note down the objection in deposition, the advocate should file written application.

Though the Court has power to ask any question to any witness at any stage of the proceeding to elicit the truth, it is expected that Courts should not encroach on the rights of cross-examiner. If a Court frequently asks questions to the witness during cross-examination, the advocate should boldly protest and insist on to take down the question asked by the Court as the "Court Question".

In *Ahmad Khan Ali Khan Deshmukh* v. *State of Maharashtra,* (1999) 1 Mh LJ 401, the Bombay High Court has warned the trial Courts not to assume the role of Prosecutor or Defence Lawyer and observed that, power under section 165 of the Evidence Act should be used sparingly and only when circumstances justify its use.

It has been observed that, the trial Courts some times direct the advocate to disclose the questions which he desires to put in cross-examination. But it has been held in *Harnam Singh* v. *Emperor,* AIR 1931 Sind 38: 32 Cr LJ 666 (DB) that the Court cannot compel a counsel to disclose the questions which he desires to put in cross examination.

In this case, wrong date and time of lodging FIR was mentioned in the inquest report. But the said discrepancy was neither pointed out nor was any explanation sought from the author of the inquest report by the defence counsel during cross-examination. The Court held that no argument on the basis of an alleged discrepancy, overwriting, omission or contradiction in the inquest report can be entertained; *Radha Mohan Singh @ Lal Saheb* v. *State of Uttar Pradesh,* 2006 All MR (Cri) 1172 (SC).

Subject to the proviso to section 126 of The Indian Evidence Act, 1872, advocates cannot be compelled to disclose any communication made to him in the course and for the purpose of his employment.

CHAPTER VII

POWERS AND DUTIES OF THE COURT

SYNOPSIS

Eminent lawyer Mr. F.S. Nariman in *'A Presentation made to the International Commission of Jurists' has cited the remarks of late Arthur Koestler who had a conversation with Sir Osbert Sitwell. In a conversation with him, Sir Osbert Sitwell once admitted – rather casually – that he did not know about Hitler's treatment of the Jews. Arthur Koestler replied *"it was your duty to know and be haunted by your knowledge. As long as you didn't feel ashamed to be alive while others were put to death, you will remain what you are, an accomplice of omission."* This story explains the importance of study and knowledge and it is expected that judges and lawyers would strive hard to gain knowledge.

The Judge plays an important role in the administration of justice. And it is expected from him that, he should function as a neutral umpire. It should be seen that a fair trial is being conducted. Otherwise the society will loose confidence and faith in the judiciary.

It is the duty of the Judge to maintain high standards of conduct. A Judge must be a man of high integrity and honesty. He should respect privileges of the Bar.

It has been held in *Ibrahim Husen* v. *State,* AIR 1969 Goa 68: 1969 Cri LJ 739, that the Presiding Judge has to be careful so as not to identify himself with any party.

The Judge should not be a mute spectator and he should actively participate in the proceedings of the Court while a witness is under examination. The Judge has the power to ask any question to any witness at any stage of the proceeding to elicit the truth.

However he should not question the witnesses so as to render the cross-examination of the defence counsel to a great extent ineffective by assisting

* From the Book titled "Expanding Governmental Lawlessness and Organised Struggles" Published by – Popular Books (First Edition 1991) and Edited by A.R. Desai.

the witnesses to explain away, in anticipation, the points which might have afforded proper grounds for useful cross-examination. Such a procedure is apt to be embarrassing to counsel and would take him away from the trend of his questions. [*Sivasubbu Nadar, (in re:),* AIR 1951 Mad 772: 52 Cr LJ 844: (1951) 1 MLJ 207.]

In *Annu Beg* v. *Emperor,* AIR 1944 Nag 320: 1944 NLJ 396, the Bombay High Court has held that *"Courts questions should not be intermixed with the cross-examination an any attempt on the part of the Court to get at the real meaning of the witnesses statement must be separate and not fused with the answers in cross-examination. It is a practice most unfair to the cross-examiner."*

In *Salag Ram* v. *Emperor,* AIR 1937 All 171, the Court has held that *"while it is the duty of every Court to keep the cross-examination of a witness within the legitimate limits, it must be careful in the discharge of that duty to avoid too much interruption and undue interference, the result of which would be to rob the cross-examination of its efficacy."*

In *Ram Chander* v. *State of Haryana,* (1981) 3 SCR 12, the Apex Court held that, *"it is the duty of a Judge to discover the truth and for that purpose he may ask any question in any form, at any time, of any witness ...... But this he must do without unduly trespassing upon the functions of the Public Prosecutor and the defence Counsel, without any hint of partisanship and without appearing to frighten, coerce, confuse, intimidate or bully witnesses."*

In this case, it has been held by the Hon'ble Delhi High Court that Judge should take care not to allow defence counsel to ask conflex or confusing questions and questions containing a negative or double negative meaning during cross-examination; *Sudeshjhaku (Smt.)* v. *K.C.J.,* 1998 Cri LJ 2428 (Del).

Where final report was submitted by the investigating agency under section 173 of Cr.P.C. and the learned Magistrate accepted report and passed the order of dropping proceedings without issuing notice to the informant, it was held that the order of the Magistrate is illegal. *U.P.S.C.* v. *S. Papaiah,* AIR 1997 SC 3876: 1997 (7) SCC 614: 1997 Cri LJ 4636 (SC). Thus, it is the duty of the Magistrate to issue notice to informant where he decides to drop proceedings.

Where the Magistrate granted summary without hearing complainant, it was held that order of the Magistrate is illegal; *Khamgaon Urban Co-op. Bank Ltd.* v. *State of Maharashtra,* 2007 (6) Mh LJ 424 (Bom).

In *State of Kerala* v. *Babu,* (1999) 2 SCR 978 the Apex Court held that the Court has power to summon the case diary of a different case not pertaining to case in hand and this power emanates from section 91(1) of The Evidence Act.

In *Shree Bhagwan Samardha Sreepada Vallabha Venkata Vishwandadha Maharaj* v. *State of Andhra Pradesh,* AIR 1999 SC 2332: 1999 Cri LJ 3661: 1995 (5) SCC 740 the Apex Court held that the Magistrate has power to order re-investigation without affording opportunity of hearing to accused even after receipt of first report of police.

Where the accused is not represented by a Counsel, the Apex Court has issued direction to all Courts to appoint *amicus curiae; Dilawar Singh* v. *State of Delhi,* AIR 2007 SC 3234.

The Apex Court in *Anil Rai* v. *State of Bihar,* AIR 2001 SC 3173: 2001 All MR (Cri) 1930, has taken serious note of the delays in pronouncement of judgment and directed the judges to deliver judgment within two months in any case and observed that "justice withheld is worst than justice denied".

(i) Powers of Magistrate Under Section 156(3) of Cr.P.C.

Any Magistrate empowered under section 190 of Cr.P.C. has power to order police officer to investigate any cognizable case brought to his notice. This power has been conferred upon the Magistrate under section 156(3) of Cr.P.C.

Application under section 156(3) of Cr.P.C. should be filed after availing recourse to section 154(1) and 154(3) of Cr.P.C. It has been directed that application under section 156(3) of Cr.P.C. must be supported by an affidavit giving details of availing provisions of section 154(1) and 154(3) of Cr.P.C. The Court also directed Magistrates to mandatorily verify veracity of the affidavit filed with application under section 156(3); *Priyanka Srivastava (Mrs.)* v. *State of Uttar Pradesh,* 2015 (2) Crimes 179 (209) (SC): 2015 Cri LJ 2396 (SC).

In *State of Bihar* v. *J.A.C. Saldanha,* AIR 1980 SC 1883: (1980) 2 SCR 16, the Apex Court has held that the power of the Magistrate under section 156(3) of Cr.P.C. to direct further investigation is clearly an independent power and does not stand in conflict with the power of the State Government. The power conferred upon the Magistrate under section 156(3) can be exercised by the Magistrate even after submission of a report by the investigating officer which would mean that it would be open to the Magistrate not to accept the conclusion of the investigating officer and direct further investigation.

The Apex Court in *Suresh Chand Jain* v. *State of Madhya Pradesh,* AIR 2001 SC 571 has held that any Judicial Magistrate, before taking cognizance of the offence, may order investigation under section 156(3) of the Code.

In this case, the Hon'ble Apex Court held that if the complaint discloses cognizable offence, it would be conducive to forward the complaint to police under section 156(3) of Cr.P.C. for enquiring into the matter; *Srinivas Gundluri* v. *M/s. SPECO Electric Power Construction Corporation,* 2010 Cri LJ 4457 (SC): 2010 All MR (Cri) 2982 (SC).

In *Rajwati* v. *State of Uttar Pradesh,* 2007 (2) CRJ 104 (All), the Allahabad High Court has held that if the Magistrate *prima facie* found that a cognizable offence is made out from the contents of application, he is bound to order police to register the case and investigate the same.

The Apex Court in *Madhu Bala* v. *Suresh Kumar,* AIR 1997 SC 3104: 1997 (4) All MR 738 (SC): 1998 SCC (Cri) 111 has held that when an order for investigation under section 156(3) of the Code is to be made, the proper direction to the police would be to register a case at the police station treating the complaint as the FIR and investigate into the same.

However it has been held that petitioner has no right to challenge an order passed under section 156(3) at a pre-cognizance stage in a petition filed under section 482/397 of Cr.P.C.; *Rakesh Puri* v. *State of Uttar Pradesh,* 2007 (1) CRJ 79 (AP).

In this case police submitted report under section 169 of Cr.P.C. that no case is made out for sending up accused for trial. The Apex Court held that Magistrate has no power to call upon police to submit a charge-sheet but he may order further investigation under section 156(3) of Cr.P.C.; *Abhinandan Zha* v. *Dinesh Mishra,* AIR 1968 SC 117.

In this case, the Apex Court held that Magistrate can direct registration of FIR and recommend to the SSP/SP to change the investigation officer if necessary; *Mohd. Yusuf* v. *Afaq Jahan (Smt.),* (2006) 1 SCC 627: AIR 2006 SC 705.

(ii) Power to Order further Investigation

Further investigation cannot be directed by Magistrate after cognizance is taken on the basis of earlier report, process issued and accused has entered appearance in response thereto. Direction by Magistrate for investigation under section 202, Cr.P.C., though is at a post-cognizance stage, is not in the nature of further investigation, as contemplated under section 173(8), Cr.P.C.; *Ram Lal Narang* v. *State (Delhi Administration),* (1979) 2 SCC 322 and *Amrutbhai Shambhubhai Patel* v. *Sumanbhai Kantibhai Patel,* 2017 All SCR (Cri) 369.

Where a Magistrate orders investigation by the police before taking cognizance under section 156(3), Cr.P.C. and receives the final report from the police, he has power to issue notice to the complainant, record his statement and the statements of other witnesses and issue process under section 204, Cr.P.C.; *Tula Ram* v. *Kishor Singh,* AIR 1977 SC 2401: 1978 Cri LJ 8 (SC): (1978) 1 SCR 615.

First Proviso to section 201(1), Cr.P.C. does not debar Magistrate to send complaint to police for investigation under section 156(3), Cr.P.C. even though complaint discloses offence exclusively triable by the Court of Sessions; *Devarapalli Lakshminarayana* v. *Narayana Reddy,* AIR 1976 SC 1672: (1976) SCR 524.

However Magistrate cannot direct the police the course of investigation or to submit a charge-sheet when it had already submitted a final report; *Abhinandan Jha* v. *Dinesh Mishra,* AIR 1968 SC 117.

Magistrate cannot order investigation by SHO of police station outside his territorial jurisdiction; *Nishu Wadhva* v. *Sidharth Wadhva,* W.P. (Crl) 1253/2016.

(iii) Power to Order Re-investigation

In this case investigation report was submitted to the Magistrate and thereafter protest petition was filed by *de facto* complainant. On the basis of same, statement of the complainant was recorded by the Court. After recording reasons, the Magistrate directed the investigation officer to examine complainant with reference to relevant documents under section 156(3), Cr.P.C. and also directed to conduct proper investigation again by another police officer. The Apex Court justified the order of the Magistrate holding that the same is in tune with the principles laid down in *Bhagwant Singh's* case, (1985) 2 SCC 537 and therefore refused to interfere; *B. Jayaraman* v. *Anandaraj,* 2017 All SCR (Cri) 388.

(iv) Powers of Judge to put Questions to Witness (Section 165 of Evidence Act)

The Judge has power to put questions to any witness in order to discover or to obtain proper proof of relevant facts at any time. However it has been held that this power should not be exercised in a manner which would give the impression that the Judge is acting as a prosecutor; *Dami @ Damini* v. *State*, 1993 (3) Crimes 91 (Ker).

Though Judge has power and also a duty to question witnesses to elicit relevant material, Courts shall not put a leading question or put words into mouth of witness; *Md. Noor Ahmed* v. *State of Assam*, 2010 (4) Crimes 158 (Gau).

It has been held by the Apex Court that Court has unfettered powers under section 165 of the Evidence Act and party cannot tell the Court that question is irrelevant or not in issue; *Ritesh Tewari* v. *State of Uttar Pradesh*, 2010 All SCR 2398.

In this case, the Court observed that although the Judge can put any question at any time, the time generally considered proper for an extended examination is when the lawyers have finished their questions or at least when the lawyer examining at the time is passing on to a new subject. But, if he does more and stops counsel again and again to put a long series of his own questions, he makes an effective examination or cross-examination impossible; *Sunil* v. *State*, AIR 1954 Cal 305: 57 CWN 962.

In this case, the Court observed that it frequently happens that the persons actually appointed to conduct defence at Crown's expense do their work very badly and conspicuous opportunities for cross-examination, and obvious arguments are entirely ignored. In such circumstances the Judge should remember that he has the duty not only to the prosecution but to the defence, and he should use his greater experience to cross-examine the witness when the sees that the defence lawyer is incompetent; *Dikson* v. *R.*, AIR 1942 Punj 90.

(v) Powers of Court to Use Any Former Statement (Section 157 of Evidence Act)

Section 157 of the Evidence Act permits the Court to use any former statements made by a witness before any person relating to a fact if it was made "at or about the time when the fact took place." The interval between the occurrence and the time of witness's reporting to his father, did not cross the boundaries envisaged by the words "at or about the time when the fact took place" in section 157 of the Evidence Act; *Mahabir Singh* v. *State of Haryana*, AIR 2001 SC 2503: 2001 (3) Crimes 366 (SC): 2001 Cri LJ 3945 (SC).

It has been held by the Apex Court that the mere fact that there was an intervening period of a few days, in a given case, may not be sufficient to exclude the statement from the use envisaged in section 157. The test to be adopted, therefore, is this: Did the witness have the opportunity to concoct or to have been tutored; *State of Tamil Nadu* v. *Suresh (A-2)*, AIR 1998 SC 1044: 1998 Cri LJ 1416 (SC): 1997 (4) Crimes 414 (SC).

(vi) Duties of Magistrate to commit case to Court of Sessions (Section 209 Cr.P.C)

If the materials filed along with the charge-sheet disclose that the offence is exclusively triable by the court of sessions, the Magistrate is duty bound to commit the case to the court of sessions. The Magistrate is required to follow the provisions of section 202 and section 208 of Cr.P.C., it he decides to commit the case to the Court of Sessions. At the stage of commitment of case to the Court of Sessions, the Magistrate has no power to discharge the accused. However the scope of enquiry during committal proceedings is very limited and narrow.

In this case, the Hon'ble Apex Court held that the Magistrate at the stage of section 209 of Cr.P.C. is forbidden to apply his mind to the merit of the matter and determine as to whether any accused needed to be added or subtracted to face trial before the Court of Session. Such proceedings did not fall within the ambit of "inquiry" as defined in section 2(g) of the Cr.P.C. which defines that " inquiry means every enquiry, other than a trial conducted under this Code by a Magistrate or a Court", because of the prelude of its being "subject to the context otherwise requiring". The context required the proceedings before a Magistrate to be formal, barely committal in that sense, and that any notion based upon the old state of law of its being an inquiry to which section 319 could get attracted, had been done away with; *Raj Kishore Prasad* v. *State of Bihar*, (1996) Supp 2 SCR 125.

Where the offence is exclusively cognizable and triable by the Court of Sessions, Magistrate cannot probe into the matter and discharge accused; *Ajay K. Parmar* v. *State of Rajasthan*, 2012 All MR (Cri) 3792 (SC): 2012 AIR SCW 5492: AIR 2013 SC 633.

(vii) Powers of Magistrate to Postpone or Adjourn Proceedings (Section 309 Cr.P.C)

The Central Government amended section 309 by adding new sub-section (1) *vide* Criminal Law (Amendment) Act, 2013 (13 of 2013) with effect from 3-2-2013. This newly inserted provision makes it mandatory to conduct trial from day-to-day until all the witnesses have been examined. The purpose of introduction of provisions of section 309 is expeditious disposal of the trial. It is an integral and essential part of the fundamental rights guaranteed under Article 21 of the Constitution.

Section 309 mandates that enquiry or trial of a case shall be continued from day-to-day until all the witnesses in attendance have been examined. This section also mandates that when witnesses are in attendance, no adjournment or postponement shall be granted, without examining them. It has been held that once sessions trial commences, the Court shall proceed *de die in diem* until the trial is concluded and adjournment should not be granted except on very special reasons; *Lt. Col. S.J. Choudhary* v. *State (Delhi Administration)*, AIR 1984 SC 618: 1984 Cri LJ 340 (SC): (1984) (2) SCR 438.

In this case, it has been held that when a witness is available and his examination-in-Chief is over, unless compelling reasons are there, the trial Court should not adjourn the matter on the mere asking; *Mohd. Khalid* v. *State of West Bengal*, (2002) 7 SCC 334: 2002 SCC (Cri) 1734.

However, there is one exception to the above rule. This has been embodied in proviso to sub-section 3 of section 242 of Cr.P.C. The proviso permits the Magistrate to defer the cross-examination of any witness until any other witness or witnesses have been examined. The use of this proviso can be made when prosecution acts unfairly and does not examine a material witness on the first day of the trial along with other material witnesses; *State of Karnataka* v. *Anngowda,* 2006 All MR (Cri) 3230 (SC).

In this case, trial was closed after examination of a formal witness. It was said that summons were issued to the witnesses. However trial judge did not even try to verify whether warrants were executed or not and he mechanically recorded that witnesses were not present. The Hon'ble Apex Court uphold the order of the High Court directing retrial and observed that it is the duty of the court to see that neither the prosecution nor the accused play truancy with the criminal trial or corrode the sanctity of the proceedings. Court is duty bound to see that neither the prosecution nor the defence takes unnecessary adjournments and take the trial under their control. If the Court is of the opinion that the material witnesses have not been examined, it should not allow the prosecution to close the evidence; *Bablu Kumar* v. *State of Bihar,* 2015 All SCR 3199.

(viii) Power of Court to Disallow Closure of Case

In this case, the Apex Court held that the Court is under the legal obligation to see that the witnesses who have been cited by the prosecution are produced by it or if summons are issued, they are actually served on the witnesses. If the Court is of the opinion that the material witnesses have not been examined, it should not allow the prosecution to close the evidence; *Bablu Kumar* v. *State of Bihar,* Criminal Appeal No. 914 of 2015 (Arising out of SLP (Crl) No. 3187 of 2013), decided on 20 July, 2015 By SC.

CHAPTER VIII
RIGHTS AND DUTIES OF MEDIA

Press is regarded as the "forth estate" as it is one of the important institutions of any democratic nation. The term "forth estate" comes from the Reporter's gallery in the House of Commons of the British Parliament. Researchers have traced the origin of the term to Edmund Burke, a British orator, writer and statesman. He used the term in parliamentary debate in 1787 on the opening of the House of Commons of Great Britain. However said expression is currently used to mean the journalistic profession and the news media.

Trial by media is a recent phrase which came into existence after the advent of electronic media. The words 'trial by media' are often used to denote an exercise undertaken by the media virtually taking up the role of a judicial forum. In India, electronic and print media is owned by big corporate houses and they have made huge investments in the said industry. This has led to the misuse of power of media. *ISRO Espionage* case, *Aarushi Talwar Murder* case are few examples of media excesses and trial by media.

However there are positive aspects of the Media Trial too. It is due to the media trial that the victims got justice in *Priyadarshini Mattoo Murder* case, *Jessica Lal Murder* case and *Nitish Katara Murder* case.

Nevertheless, the importance and role of free press in a democratic country cannot be denied. The freedom of press has always been regarded as an essential pre-requisite of a democracy. It is said that without the freedom of press truth cannot be unearthed. But this freedom of press is not absolute and unfettered. If a newspaper publishes what is improper, mischievously false or illegal and abuses its liberty, it can be punished by Court of law. The press has right to publish fair and accurate report of what takes place in a Court of Law.

In a case where CNN-IBN English News Channel was sought to be prosecuted for defaming a police officer, the Hon'ble Apex Court rejected the defence taken as to freedom of press under Article 19 and 21 of the Constitution and held that reputation of an individual is equally important; *Rajdeep Sardesai* v. *State of Andhra Pradesh,* 2015 All MR (Cri) 3250 (SC).

In this case article titled 'Doomed by Dowry' was published in a magazine based on interview of family of deceased giving their version of tragedy when the matter was subjudiced. Facts narrated in the article showed all materials that may be used in forthcoming trial of that case. The Apex Court deprecated such practice of holding trial by media when the issue was subjudiced and held that this amounts to interference with the administration of justice. The Apex Court cautioned publisher, editor and journalist of the said magazine; *M.P. Lohia* v. *State of West Bengal,* AIR 2005 SC 790.

In *R.K. Anand* v. *Delhi High Court,* (2009) 8 SCC 106, the Apex Court stated that it would be sad day for the court to employ the media for setting its own house in order and the media too would not relish the role of being the snoopers for the Court. Media should perform the acts of journalism and not as a special agency for the Court. The impact of television and newspaper coverage on a person's reputation by creating a widespread perception of guilt, regardless of any verdict in a Court of law, will not be fair.

Recently, the Apex Court warned the media and observed that presumption of innocence of an accused is a legal presumption and should not be destroyed at the very threshold through the process of media trial and that too when the investigation is pending. In that event, it will be opposed to the very basic rule of law and would impinge upon the protection granted to an accused under Article 21 of the Constitution. .... The criticism or even the reporting particularly in subjudiced matters must be subjected to check and balances so as not to interfere with the administration of justice; *Sidhartha Vashisht @ Manu Sharma* v. *State (NCT of Delhi),* 2010 (2) Crimes 154 (SC).

In *Maria Monica Susairaj* v. *State of Maharashtra,* 2008 All MR (Cri) 3343, the Bombay High Court has held that it will be too risky to permit media to have a wide and sweeping pre-trial publicity of any case, whether criminal or civil, virtually developing a trial by Court into a trial by media especially on the basis of undisclosed source of information. The Court directed that press while reporting a crime or an investigation should not tilt its report either towards the guilt of an accused or towards his innocence. The Court further directed that if the reports that have appeared in the newspaper attributing various statements to the accused supposedly made by her during the course of her alleged confession, if are not correct, the investigating agency was duty bound to clarify the same by issuing requisite public statement.

In this case, accused was allegedly beaten up by police during his custodial interrogation. Thereafter, he was treated at hospital. While in hospital he spoke to a local television channel, complaining about the third-degree treatment meted out him by police. During the interview he inadvertently said something that showed his involvement in the murder. During the course of trial, prosecution requested the trial Court to include his TV interview footage as evidence against him. The Apex Court held that TV interview is an evidence against the accused and can be admitted in evidence; *Sajidbeg Asifbeg Mirza* v. *State of Gujarat,* CRA No. 694 of 2006.

The role of TV channels and electronic media came for consideration before the Hon'ble Apex Court while hearing appeal of Mohd. Kasab in Mumbai Terror Attack dated 26th November, 2008. The terrorists attacks at all the places, in the goriest details, were shown live on the Indian TV from beginning to end almost non-stop. All the channels were competing with each other in showing the latest developments on a minute to minute basis, including the positions and the movements of the security forces engaged in flushing out the terrorists.

The reckless coverage of the terrorist attack by the channels thus gave rise to a situation were on the one hand the terrorists were completely hidden from the security forces and they had no means to know their exact position or even the kind of firearms and explosives they possessed and on the other hand the positions of the security forces, their weapons and all their operational movements were being watched by the collaborators across the border on TV screens and being communicated to the terrorists. The Apex Court observed that any attempt to justify the conduct of the TV channels by citing the right to freedom of speech and expression would be totally wrong and unacceptable in such a situation. The freedom of expression, like all other freedoms under Article 19, is subject to reasonable restrictions. An action tending to violate another person's right to life guaranteed under Article 21 or putting the national security in jeopardy can never be justified by taking the plea of freedom of speech and expression. The shots and visuals that were shown a live by the TV channels could have also been shown after all the terrorists were neutralized and the security operations were over. But, in that case the TV programmes would not have had the same shrill, scintillating and chilling effect and would not have shot up the TRP ratings of the channels. It must, therefore, be held that by covering live the terrorists attack on Mumbai in the way it was done, the Indian TV channels were not serving any national interest or social cause. On the contrary they were acting in their own commercial interests putting the national security in jeopardy. It is in such extreme cases that the credibility of an institution is tested. The coverage of the Mumbai terror attack by the mainstream electronic media has done much harm to the argument that any regulatory mechanism for the media must only come from within; *Mohammed Ajmal Mohammed Amir Kasab @ Abu Mujahid* v. *State of Maharashtra,* 2012 All MR (Cri) 3303 (SC).

Trial by media of the *Arushi Murder* case has not only done harm to the accused in their defence but also resulted in character assassination of the victim. The investigation carried out by two teams of CBI and different stories put forth by them finally resulted into submitting of closure report in Court. This has been shown in a movie "Talwar" directed by Meghna Gulzar.

However, Investigative journalism by Tehalka magazine and other news papers have exposed corruptions in government departments and public life. A sting operation carried out in public interest has been approved by the Hon'ble Apex Court in *R.K. Anand's* case; *R.K. Anand* v. *Registrar, Delhi High Court,* (2009) 8 SCC 106.

On 16th November, 2003 in the Delhi edition of the Indian Express a news item under the caption "Caught on Tape: Union Minister Taking Cash Saying Money is No Less Than God" had appeared showing visuals of one Dilip Singh Ju Dev, the then Union Minister of State for Environment and Forest, receiving illegal gratification from one Rahul @ Bupinder Singh Patel in the presence of the Additional Private Secretary to the Minister. Immediately on publication of the above said news item a preliminary enquiry was registered by the ACU-II of CBI, New Delhi and on conclusion of the said preliminary enquiry, FIR dated 19th December, 2013 was filed against the appellants alleging commission of offence under section 12 of the Prevention of Corruption Act, 1988 read with section 120B of IPC. The Appellants filed application before the Delhi High Court for quashing of FIR but the same was dismissed. The Appellants challenged the order of Delhi High Court before the Apex Court by filing criminal appeals. The Hon'ble Apex Court dismissed the criminal appeals filed by the appellants and affirmed the order of Delhi High Court. As regards sting operation, the Apex Court observed that a sting operation essentially is a deceptive operation, though designed to nab a criminal. It raises certain moral and ethical questions. The victim, who is otherwise innocent, is lured into committing a crime on the assurance of absolute secrecy and confidentiality of the circumstances raising the potential question as to how such a victim can be held responsible for the crime which he would not have committed but for the enticement. Another issue that arises from such an operation is the fact that the means deployed to establish the commission of the crime itself involves a culpable Act. However a crime does not stand obliterated or extinguished merely because its commission is claimed to be in public interest. Any such principle would be abhorrent to our criminal jurisprudence. At the same time the criminal intent behind the commission of the act which is alleged to have occasioned the crime will have to be established before the liability of a person charged with the commission of crime can be adjudged. The doctrine of *mens rea,* though a salient feature of the India criminal justice system, finds expressions in different statutory provisions requiring proof of either intention or knowledge on the part of the accused. Such proof is to be gathered from the surrounding facts established by the evidence and materials before the court and not by a process of probe of the mental state of the accused which the law does not contemplate...... A journalist or any other citizen who has no connection, even remotely, with the favour that is allegedly sought in exchange for the bribe offered, cannot be imputed with the necessary intent to commit the offence of abatement under section 12 of the Prevention of Corruption Act, 1988 or that of conspiracy under section 120B of IPC. Non-applicability of the aforesaid provisions of law in such situations, therefore, may be *ex facie* apparent. The cause of journalism and its role and responsibility in spreading information and awareness will stand sub served. ..... Whether the sting operation was really a journalistic exercise and the giving of bribe to accused (A-1) was a mere sham or pretence or whether the giving of the bribe was with expectation of favours in connection with mining projects, are questions that can only be answered by the evidence of the parties which is yet to come. Such facts cannot be a matter of an assumption. The inherent possibilities of abuse of the operation as videographed, namely, retention and use thereof to ensure delivery of the favours assured by the receiver of the bribe has to be excluded before liability can be attributed or excluded; *Rajat Prasad* v. *C.B.I.*, 2014 (2) Crimes 281 (SC): 2015 ALL SCR 233.

In the instant case *Life Insurance Corporation of India* v. *Manubhai D. Shah*, AIR 1993 SC 171 views propagated by a person where criticised in a magazine but his counter was not published. The Apex Court has held that it is the duty of the print media to publish his counter view in the magazine.

CHAPTER IX

RIGHTS AND DUTIES OF POLICE

Police Officer has no right to investigate into the report which discloses the commission of non-cognizable offence without the order of a Magistrate having power to try such case or commit the case for trial as provided in section 155 of Cr.P.C. However, any Police Officer-in-charge of a police station may investigate any cognizable case without the order of a Magistrate as provided in section 156 of Cr.P.C. But this power is not unlimited or unfettered as has been held in *State of West Bengal* v. *Swapan Kumar Guha,* AIR 1982 SC 949: 1982 Cri LJ 819: (1982) 3 SCR 121. The Apex Court in *Swapan Kumar's* case (*supra*) has held that *"the condition precedent to the commencement of investigation under section 157 of Cr.P.C. is that FIR must disclose, prima facie, that a cognizable offence has been committed. It is wrong to suppose that the police have an unfettered discretion to commence investigation under section 157 of the Code. Their right of inquiry is conditioned by the existence of reason to suspect the commission of a cognizable offence and they cannot, reasonable, have reason so to suspect unless the FIR prima facie, discloses the commission such offence...... If that condition is satisfied the investigation must go on. The Court has no power to stop investigation..... On the other hand if the FIR does not disclose the commission of a cognizable offence, the Court would be justified in quashing the investigation on the basis of the information as laid or received."*

However in *Apren Josef* v. *State of Kerala,* AIR 1973 SC 1: 1973 Cri LJ 185, the Apex Court has held that, *"the receipt and recording of information report by the police is not a condition precedent to the setting in motion of a criminal investigation nor does the statute provide that such information report can only be made by eye witness."*

In *State of Uttar Pradesh* v. *Bhagwant Kishore Joshi,* AIR 1964 SC 221: 1964 (1) Cri LJ 140 also the Apex Court has held that, *"the receipt of information is not a condition precedent for investigation."*

In *State of Haryana* v. *Ch. Bhajan Lal,* AIR 1992 SC 604: 1992 Cri LJ 527 the Apex Court has held that *"the commencement of investigation in a cognizable offence by a police officer is subject to two conditions, firstly, the police officer should have reason to suspect the commission of a cognizable offence as required by section 157(1) and secondly, the Police Officer should subjectively satisfy himself as to whether there is sufficient ground for entering on an investigation even before he starts an investigation in to the facts and circumstances of the case as contemplated under clause (b) of the proviso to section 157(1). Further, as clause (b) of the proviso permits the Police Officer to satisfy himself about the sufficiency of the ground even before entering on an investigation, it postulates that the Police Officer as to draw his satisfaction only on the materials which were placed before him at that stage, namely, the first information together with the documents, if any, enclosed. In other words, the police officer has to satisfy himself only on the allegation mentioned in the first information before he enters on an investigation as to whether those allegations do constitute a cognizable offence warranting an investigation."*

In this regard reference can be given of the case [*Sau. Sharda Narayan Bhongade* v. *Surendra Jagmohan Patil,* 2003 All MR (Cri) 17 (DB) (Bom)] where petitioner's name was included in charge-sheet by investigation office without any kind of investigation or verification, and on the letter sent by the petitioner to the High Court which was treated as a criminal writ petition, the Court directed the State Government to pay compensation of Rs. 25000 to the petitioner.

In *Jamuna Choudhary* v. *State of Bihar,* AIR 1974 SC 1822, the Apex Court while pointing out the duty of the investigation officer observed that, *"the duty of the investigation officer is not merely to bolster up a prosecution case with such evidence as may enable the Court to record a conviction but to bring out the real unvarnished truth."*

In *Bhagwan Singh* v. *State of Rajasthan,* AIR 1976 SC 895, the Apex Court expressed its displeasure and held that, *"investigation by the complainant/informant himself is an infirmity which is bound to reflect on the credibility of the prosecution case."*

Concerned with the misuse of section 167 of the Code by police officers/ investigation officers, the Bombay High Court.

In *Bhulabai wd/o Barkaji Matre* v. *Shankar Barkaji Matre,* 1999 (3) Mh LJ 227 reminded the police officers that it is obligatory on the part of the investigating agency to conclude investigation within the prescribed period of 60/90 days, as contemplated in section 167(2) of the Code. The Hon'ble Court further directed the Magistrates to issue show cause notice to concerned police officer as to why he could not file the charge-sheet within the prescribed time. The Court further held that *"if the Magistrate finds that there is no justifiable reason for not filing the charge-sheet within prescribed time, then he should record so and then it will be the duty of the Public Prosecutor to submit his report to the Disciplinary authority of the investigation officer for appropriate action, against the investigation officer for such default in performing the duty."*

Police officer must remember that registration of FIR is mandatory in view of the recent judgment delivered by the Delhi High Court in *Laxminarayan Gupta* v. *Commissioner of Police,* 2007 (1) Crimes 608. The Hon'ble Court held that, *"provisions of section 154 of Cr.P.C. are mandatory and concerned officer is duty bound to register case on basis of an information disclosing cognizable offence."*

It is a common practice of police in India not to convey the action taken by them on the FIR lodged by the informant. However in *Bhagwant Singh* v. *Commissioner of Police,* (1985) 3 SCR: (1985) 87 Bom LR 421, the division Bench of the Apex Court has held that, *"action taken by the officer-in-charge of a police station on the FIR should be communicated to the informant."*

Where prosecution first recorded statement of prosecutrix under section 164, Cr.P.C. before Judicial Magistrate and only thereafter her further statement under section 161, Cr.P.C. was recorded, the Court held that procedure should have been otherwise and the Court drew the inference that right from the beginning prosecution was doubtful of trustworthiness of prosecutrix itself; *Krishna Kumar Malik* v. *State of Haryana*, (2011) 7 SCC 130.

In *Shailendra Kumar* v. *State of Bihar*, AIR 2002 SC 270: 2002 (1) SRJ 353, the Apex Court has held that *"the presence of Investigating Officer at the time of trial is must. It is his duty to keep the witnesses present. If there is failure on part of any witness to remain present, it is the duty of the Court to take appropriate action including issuance of bailable/non-bailable warrants as the case may be."*

In *State of Bihar* v. *J.A.C. Saldanna*, AIR 1980 SC 326: 1980 Cri LJ 98: (1980) 2 SCR 16, while pointing out the duty of police officers, the Apex Court directed that Police Officers should refrain from directly addressing communications to the Court when matters are required to be determined judicially.

It has been held by the Apex Court that section 161 of the Code casts a statutory duty upon the Police Officer investigating a case under Chapter XII to examine orally any person supposed to be acquainted with the facts of the case; *Ram Jethmalani* v. *Director, CBI*, 1987 Cri LJ 570 SC.

The Bombay High Court has held that suppression of vital piece of evidence casts a serious doubt about the genuineness and truthfulness of the dying declarations. It is not the duty of investigation officer to bolster the prosecution case by suppressing the evidence, but , he should present before the Court an unalloyed truth; *Prabhakar W. Salve* v. *State of Maharashtra*, 2006 All MR (Cri) 1274.

In this case the Apex Court held that the investigation should be judicious, fair, transparent and expeditious to ensure compliance to the basic rule of law. An investigation must be fair and effective and must proceed in proper direction in consonance with the ingredients of the offence and not in a haphazard manner; *Sidhartha Vashisht @ Manu Sharma* v. *State, (NCT of Delhi)*, (2010) 6 SCC 1: 2010 (2) Crimes 154 (SC).

Reminding Police Officers of their duty and responsibility during investigation, the High Court stated that Police Officers should understand their responsibility and not to approach the media to get cheap and objectionable publicity which makes the criminal justice system not transparent but patchy and hazy. Right to information is wrongly interpreted by the police as right to inform. High degree of secrecy is a must when the investigation is in process, *Deepti A. Devasthali* v. *State of Maharashtra, 2009* All MR (Cri) 3547 (Bom); Premature disclosure or leakage to media in a pending investigation will jeopardise and impede further investigation, and may allow real culprit to escape from the clutches of law. Hence, attempts to claim credit for imaginary investigation breakthroughs should be curbed; *Rajendran Chingaravelu* v. *R.K. Mishra*, (2010) 1 SCC 457.

Failure of Investigation Officer to perform his duty which may help or may result in helping the offender in avoiding the process of law against him in one way or the other, could be construed as gross criminal negligence. It is a serious offence and government should take appropriate action against the erring Police Officers and personnel. Mere disciplinary action in that regard would not be a sufficient answer; *Salma Babu Shaikh (Smt.)* v. *State of Maharashtra,* 2008 All MR (Cri) 2717 (Bom).

In this case, the Apex Court issued directions to State Government for fixing accountability on Investigating Officers in the cases of serious offences where accused is acquitted due to serious lapses done by the Investigating Officers in investigation. The Apex Court directed the State Government to identify all erring officials/officers responsible for failure of prosecution case because of culpable lapses and directed to take departmental action; *State of Gujarat* v. *Kishanbhai,* 2014 All MR (Cri) 759 (SC): 2014 (1) SCALE 177.

Police has the powers to conduct further investigation *de hors* any direction from the Court even after it had taken cognizance; *Hansabhai Valibhai Qureshi* v. *State of Gujarat,* (2004) 5 SCC 347: 2004 All MR (Cri) 1436 (SC).

CHAPTER X
RIGHTS OF VICTIMS

SYNOPSIS

Sections 357, 357A and 359 of Cr.P.C. deals with this aspect of law.

Apart from the above provisions, following rights have been recognised:—

(i) Right of Audience

In a criminal trial, the complainant has the following rights and options against the accused: (a) the right to be given notice on filing of police report, (b) the right to file a protest petition, which may be treated as a complaint by the Magistrate, and (c) the right to question the fairness of investigation and demand further investigation; *Kisan Lal* v. *Dharmendra Bafna*, (2009) 7 SCC 685.

In the under noted cases, the Apex Court held that informant is entitled to notice and an opportunity to be heard when a report made under section 173 (2), Cr.P.C. is under consideration by Court. The Court has held that Magistrate must issue notice to the informant at the time of considering the police report; *Gangadhar J. Mhatre* v. *State of Maharashtra*, (2004) 7 SCC 768; *Chittaranjan Mirdha* v. *Dulal Ghosh*, 2009 (3) Crimes 189 (SC); *NHRC* v. *State of Gujarat*, 2009 (2) Crimes 308 (SC).

Even where an order is passed by Magistrate under section 169 of Cr.P.C. discharging certain accused, the complainant should be given an opportunity of being heard before such order is passed; *Dina Chetan Shah* v. *Government of USSR through its Consulate General*, 2011 All MR (Cri) 2185 (Bom).

(ii) Right of Audience in Bail Matters

A lawyer engaged by first informant/complainant has no right of audience while opposing bail application. However, Counsel so engaged can brief the State Counsel and can also make a representation on behalf of complainant and can assist State Counsel while opposing bail application; *Dr. Sunil Puri* v. *State of Chhattisgarh*, 2006 (3) Crimes 733.

In this case, the Court held that though concept of *locus standi* of complainant was relaxed it would not mean an undisputed right of complainant to be heard at every stage including stage of arguments on bail. Submission sought to be addressed by complainant should be addressed through public prosecutor; *Ashok Jain* v. *State,* 2010 (1) Crimes 189 (Del).

However the Bombay High Court has taken a contrary view in this case. The Court held that when the complainant appears before Court in course of hearing of anticipatory bail, the Court is bound to hear him. Said right however could not be allowed to be exercised in manner which would delay disposal of application for bail; *Vinay Poddar* v. *State of Maharashtra,* 2009 (2) Crimes 305 (Bom) (SN).

In this case, the Hon'ble Apex Court has held that no vested right is granted to complainant or aggrieved party to directly conduct a prosecution. However, if Magistrate or Sessions Judge harbours opinion that prosecution is likely to fail, then the complainant or aggrieved party be given an informal hearing; *Sundeep K. Bafna* v. *State of Maharashtra,* 2014 All MR (Cri) 4113 (SC).

(iii) Right of Audience during Trials

The Apex Court held that even before the Sessions Court the role of a private person who is aggrieved by the offence is not altogether wiped out merely because the accused was charge-sheeted by the police. The Court permits written arguments to be filed by a private person before the Sessions Court and the Court is duty bound to consider the written arguments; *M/s. J.K. International* v. *State (Government of NCT of Delhi),* 2001 SCC (Cri) 547: AIR 2001 SC 1142.

This case known as '*Nirbhaya* case' relates to a ghastly incident of gang rape on 16th December, 2012 in a moving bus in the streets of Delhi. One of the arrested persons was juvenile. Petitioner approached the Juvenile Justice Board seeking impleadment in the proceedings before the Board. However, Board did not pass any written order in the matter. Thereafter petitioner filed a PIL in High Court of Delhi, but the High Court declined to answer the questions raised by the petitioner. Therefore petitioner filed special leave petition before Supreme Court. The Supreme Court held that in certain exceptional situations there is a recognition of a limited right in a victim or his family members to take part in the process, particularly, at the stage of the trial. The law, however, frowns upon and prohibits any abdication by the State of its role in the matter at each of the stages and, in fact, does not recognise the right of a third party/stranger to participate or even to come to the aid of the state at any of the stages; *Dr. Subramanian Swami* v. *Raju, through member, Juvenile Justice Board,* 2013 (4) Crimes 286 (SC).

(iv) Right to File Protest Petition

In this case, the Hon'ble Apex Court held that the Magistrate is not debarred from taking cognizance of a complaint merely on the ground that earlier he had declined to take cognizance of police report; *Gopal Vijay Verma* v. *Bhuneshwar Prasad Sinha,* (1982) (3) SCC 510.

A complainant can file protest petition. It has been held that the protest petition can always be treated as complaint and proceeded with in terms of Chapter XV of Cr.P.C. Therefore, in case there is no bar to entertain a second complaint on the same facts, in exceptional circumstances, the second protest petition can also similarly be entertained only under exceptional circumstances; *Shiv Shankar Singh* v. *State of Bihar,* 2012 (1) Crimes 16 (SC).

In this case, the Hon'ble Apex Court held that even the *de facto* complainant can raise objection to final report or file protest complaint after final report is submitted by police in Court; *Kishore Kumar Gyanchamlani* v. *G.D. Mehrotra,* 2001 (3) Crimes 205 (SC): (2001) 10 SCC 59: AIR 2002 SC 483.

Victim has right to file protest petition as victim is an aggrieved person not only in crime, but also in investigation, enquiry, trial, appeal, revision, review and also proceedings by which inherent powers of Court can be invoked. The legal heirs of deceased *de facto* complainant who are victims, can be allowed to file protest petition; *Debasish Bose* v. *State of West Bengal,* 2015 Cri LJ 2252 (Cal).

In this case, the Apex Court held that despite final report of police indicating that no case is made out against accused persons, Magistrate has the power to take cognizance while accepting the protest petition of complainant against the police report discharging accused persons. However, said protest petition must satisfy ingredients of complaint; *B. Chandrika* v. *Santosh,* 2013 All MR (Cri) 4418 (SC).

(v) Right to Documents

The Apex Court has held that while considering closure report submitted by police, Court must give notice to the complainant and furnish copies of statement of witnesses, other related documents and investigation report to the complainant; *Jakia Nasim Ahsan* v. *State of Gujarat,* (2011) 12 SCC 302.

(vi) Right of Intervener

Where application was filed by intervener at the stage when the Court was considering suspension of sentence pending appeal, the Apex Court held that High Court can in its inherent powers hear intervener and pass order on merits; *Kanaka Rekha Naik* v. *Manoj Kumar Pradhan,* 2011 ALL SCR 667.

(vii) Right of Appeal in Case of Acquittal

Section 378(4) of Cr.P.C. gives right of appeal to complainant in case of acquittal if such an order of acquittal is passed in any case instituted upon complaint and the High Court, on an application made to it by the complainant, can grant special leave to appeal.

(viii) Right to File Revision

The Apex Court has held that complainant has right to file revision against acquittal and the same is maintainable; *K. Pandurangan* v. *S.R.R. Velusamy,* AIR 2003 SC 3318: 2003 (4) Crimes 96 (SC): 2003 Cri LJ 4964 (SC).

(ix) Right of Victims of Acid Attack to Compensation

The Hon'ble Apex Court has taken judicial notice of rise in incidents of acid attack on girls and women. In a landmark judgement, Apex Court has given following directions to all States and Union Territories—(a) minimum compensation of Rs. 3,00,000 should made available to each victim. (b) victim compensation scheme of States and Union Territories should be accordingly amended and wide publicity be given. (c) free treatment should be made available by government and private hospitals (free treatment not only means provision of physical treatment to victim of acid attack but also availability of medicines, bed and food in the concerned hospital). (d) hospital should issue certificate that individual is acid attack victim. (e) District Legal Service Authority should function as Criminal Injuries Compensation Board and claims be decided by it. (f) bars to be imposed by States and Union Territories on the sale of acid across counter; *Laxmi* v. *Union of India,* AIR 2015 SC 3662: 2015 All MR (Cri) 2012 (SC).

In this case the Hon'ble Apex Court took judicial notice of plight of acid attack victims and emphasized the need to prevent such crimes and to pay enhanced compensation. In this case the Court directed the State to pay Rs. 10,00,000 to victim of acid attack and Rs. 3,00,000 to her younger sister who had also received acid injuries; *Parivartan Kendra* v. *Union of India,* 2016 All SCR (Cri) 157.

(x) Right of Victims of Atrocities to Compensation

The Union of India has amended The Scheduled Castes and The Scheduled Tribes (Prevention of Atrocities) Act, 1989 by The Scheduled Castes and The Scheduled Tribes (Prevention of Atrocities) Amendment Act, 2015 (1 of 2016). The Act received the assent of The President of India on 31st December, 2015 and it has been published in the Gazette of India, Ext., Pt. II, S. 1, dated 1st January, 2016. In the Amended Act new Chapter IV-A has been inserted which pertains to rights of victims and witnesses. New section 15A of the Amended Act provides that a victim or his dependent shall have the right to reasonable, accurate, and timely notice of any Court proceeding including any bail proceeding and the Special Public Prosecutor or the State Government shall informed the victim about any proceeding under the Act and shall be entitled to be heard at any proceeding under this Act in respect of bail, discharge, release, parole, conviction or sentence of an accused or any connected proceedings or arguments and file written submission on conviction, acquittal or sentencing. It has been further provided that the Special Court or the Exclusive Special Court shall provide to a victim, his dependent, informant or witnesses, the travelling and maintenance expenses during investigation, inquiry and trial.

The Central Government has amended the rules called The Scheduled Castes and The Scheduled Tribes (Prevention of Atrocities) Rules, 1995 *vide* G.S.R. 416(E) dated 23rd June, 2014 with effect from 23rd June, 2014. The Central Government has laid down the norms for relief amount (Schedule – Annexure I) to be given to the victims of atrocities and enhanced amount of relief to Rs. 90,000 upto Rs. 3,75,000 depending upon the nature and gravity of the offence. It has been specified in norms that 25% of the said amount shall be paid when the charge-sheet is sent to the Court and remaining 75% shall be paid when accused are convicted by the Court. The norms also provide pension to widow/dependent of deceased, full cost of the education and maintenance of the children of the victims, etc. for the murder, death, massacre, rape, mass rape and gang rape, permanent incapacitation and dacoity committed on members of.

(xi) Right of Victims of Gang Rape

News item was published in the Business and Financial News dated 23rd January, 2014 relating to the gang-rape of a 20 year old woman of Subalpur village, P.S. Labpur, Distt. Birbhum, State of West Bengal on the intervening night of 20th January, 2014/21st January, 2014 on the orders of community Panchayat as punishment for having relationship with a man from a different community, by order dated 24th January, 2014. The Hon'ble Apex Court took *suo motu* cognizance of the said news and directed that all hospitals, public or private, whether run by the Central Government, the State Government, local bodies or any other person, are statutorily obligated under section 357C of the Code of Criminal Procedure, 1973 to provide the first-aid or medical treatment, free of cost, to the victims of any offence covered under sections 326A, 376, 376A, 376B, 376C, 376D or section 376E of the IPC. The Court further directed that rehabilitation of victim must be given precedence as it is of paramount importance in each and every case; *In Re: Indian Women Says Gang-raped on orders of Village Court* published in Business and Financial News dated 23rd January, 2014 – *Suo Motu* Writ Petition (Criminal) No. 24 of 2014 reported in 2015 All SCR 3149.

CHAPTER XI
QUASHING OF F.I.R. AND PROCEEDINGS

Where the criminal proceedings are initiated with ulterior motive to harass, one can approach the High Court by filing writ petitions under Article 226 of the Constitution or under section 482 of Cr.P.C. instead of facing protracted trial. The lawyers can make use of the rulings in cases of *West Bengal* v. *Swapan Kumar Guha,* AIR 1982 SC 949: 1982 Cri LJ 819: (1982) 3 SCR 121 and *State of Haryana* v. *Ch. Bhajan Lal,* AIR 1992 SC 604.

The High Court may in exercise of powers under Article 226 of the Constitution and under section 482 of Cr.P.C. may interfere in proceedings relating to cognizable offences to prevent abuse of the process of any Court or otherwise to secure the ends of justice. The Apex Court in *State of Haryana* v. *Ch. Bhajan Lal,* AIR 1992 SC 604 while observing that this power should be exercised sparingly and that too in the rarest of rare cases, have given following categories of cases wherein such power could be exercised. (1) Where the allegations made in the first information report or the complaint, even if they are taken at their face value and accepted in their entirety do not *prima facie* constitute any offence or make out a case against the accused. (2) Where the allegations in the first information report and other materials, if any, accompanying the FIR do not disclose a cognizable offence, justifying an investigation by police officers under section 156(1) of the Code except under an order of a Magistrate within the purview of section 155(2) of the Code. (3) Where the uncontroverted allegations made in the FIR or complaint and the evidence collected in support of the same do not disclose the commission of any offence and make out a case against the accused. (4) Where, the allegations in the FIR do not constitute a cognizable offence but constitute only a non-cognizable offence, no investigation is permitted by a police officer without an order of a Magistrate under section 155(2) of the Code. (5) Where the allegations made in the F.I.R or complaint are so absurd and inherently improbable on the basis of which no prudent person can ever reach a just conclusion that there is sufficient ground for proceedings against the accused. (6) Where there is an express legal bar engrafted in any of the provisions of the Code or the concerned Act (under which a criminal proceeding is instituted) to the institution and continuance of the proceedings and/or where there is a specific provision in the Code or the concerned Act, providing efficacious redress for the grievance of the aggrieved party. (7) Where a criminal proceeding is manifestly attended with *mala fide* and/or where the proceeding is maliciously instituted with an ulterior motive for wreaking vengeance on the accused and with a view to spite him due to private and personal grudge.

In this case, the Apex Court issued the following guidelines for quashing a FIR or Complaint or criminal proceedings:

(a) The power of the High Court in quashing a criminal proceeding or FIR or Complaint in exercise of its inherent jurisdiction is distinct and different from the power given to a criminal court for compounding the offences under section 320 of the Code. Inherent power is of wide plenitude with no statutory limitation but it has to be exercised in accord with the guideline engrafted in such power *viz.*; (i) to secure the ends of justice or to prevent abuse of the process of any court. In what cases power to quash the criminal proceeding or complaint or FIR may be exercised where the offender and victim have settled their dispute would depend on the facts and circumstances of each case and no category can be prescribed. However, before exercise of such power, the High Court must have due regard to the nature and gravity of the crime. Heinous and serious offences of mental depravity or offences like murder, rape, dacoity, etc. cannot be fittingly quashed even though the victim or victim's family and the offender have settled the dispute. Such offences are not private in nature and have serious impact on society. Similarly, any compromise between the victim and offender in relation to the offences under special statutes like Prevention of Corruption Act or the offences committed by public servant while working in that capacity etc; cannot provide for any basis for quashing criminal proceedings involving such offences. But the criminal cases having overwhelmingly and pre-dominatingly civil flavour stand on different footing for the purposes of quashing, particularly the offences arising from commercial, financial , mercantile, civil, partnership or such like transactions or the offences arising out of matrimony relating to dowry etc. or the family disputes where the wrong is basically private or personal in nature and the parties have resolved their entire dispute. In this category of cases, High Court may quash criminal proceedings if in its view, because of the compromise between the offender and victim, the possibility of conviction is remote and bleak and continuation of criminal case would put accused to great oppression and prejudice and extreme injustice would be caused to him by not quashing the criminal case despite full and complete settlement and compromise with the victim. In other words, the High Court must consider whether it would be unfair or contrary to the interest of justice to continue with the criminal proceeding or continuation of the criminal proceeding would tantamount to abuse of process of law despite settlement and compromise between the victim and wrongdoer and whether to secure the ends of justice, it is appropriate that criminal case is put to an end and if the answer to the above question(s) is in affirmative, the High Court shall be well within its jurisdiction to quash the criminal proceedings; *Gian Singh* v. *State of Punjab*, 2013 ALL SCR 171.

In this case, the Apex Court summed up and laid down the following principles by which the High Court would be guided in giving adequate treatment to the settlement between the parties and exercising its power under section 482 of the Code:

(I) Power conferred under section 482 of the Code is to be distinguished from the power which lies in the Court to compound the offences under section 320 of the Code. The High Court has inherent power under section 482 of the Code to quash the criminal proceedings even in those cases which are not compoundable, where the parties have settled the matter between themselves. However, this power is to be exercised sparingly and with caution.

(II) When the parties have reached the settlement and on that basis petition for quashing the criminal proceedings is filed, the guiding factor in such cases would be to secure:

(i) ends of justice, or

(ii) to prevent abuse of the process of any court.

While exercising the power the High Court is to form an opinion on either of the aforesaid two objectives.

(III) Such a power is not to be exercised in those prosecutions which involved heinous and serious offences of mental depravity or offences like murder, rape, dacoity, etc. Such offences are not private in nature and have a serious impact on society. Similarly, for offences alleged to have been committed under special statute like the Prevention of Corruption Act or the offences committed by public servants while working in that capacity are not to be quashed merely on the basis of compromise between the victim and the offender.

(IV) On the other, those criminal cases having overwhelmingly and predominantly civil character, particularly those arising out of commercial transactions or arising out of matrimonial relationship or family disputes should be quashed when the parties resolved their entire disputes among themselves.

(V) While exercising its powers the High Court is to examine as to whether the possibility of conviction is remote and bleak and continuation of criminal cases would put the accused to great oppression and prejudice and extreme injustice would be caused to him by not quashing the criminal cases.

(VI) Offences under section 307, IPC would fall in the category of heinous and serious offences and therefore is to be generally treated as crime against the society and not against the individual alone. However, the High Court would not rest its decision merely because there is a mention of section 307, IPC in the FIR or the charge is framed under this provision. It would be open to the High Court to examine as to whether incorporation of section 307, IPC is there for the sake of it or the prosecution has collected sufficient evidence, which if proved, would lead to proving the charge under section 307, IPC. For this purpose, it would be open to the High Court to go by the nature of injury sustained, whether such injury is inflicted on the vital/delicate parts of the body, nature of weapons used, etc. Medical report in respect of injuries suffered by the victim can generally be the guiding factor. On the basis of this prima facie analysis, the High Court can examine as to whether there is a strong possibility of conviction or the chances of conviction are remote and bleak. In the former case it can refuse to accept the settlement and refuse to quash the criminal proceedings whereas in the later case it would be permissible for the High Court to accept the plea compounding the offence based on complete settlement between the parties. At this stage, the Court can also be swayed by the fact that the settlement between the parties is going to result in harmony between them which may improve their future relationship.

(VII) While deciding whether to exercise its power under section 482 of the Code or not, timings of settlement play a crucial role. Those cases where the settlement is arrived at immediately after the alleged commission of offence and matter is still under investigation, the High Court may be liberal in accepting the settlement to quash the criminal proceedings/ investigation. It is because of the reason that at this stage the investigation is still on and even the charge-sheet has not been filed. Likewise, those cases where the charge is framed but the evidence is yet to start or the evidence is still at infancy stage, the High Court can show benevolence in exercising its powers favourably, but after prima facie assessment of the circumstances/material mentioned above. On the other hand, where the prosecution evidence is almost complete or after the conclusion of the evidence the matter is at the stage of argument, normally the High Court should refrain from exercising its power under section 482 of the Code, as in such cases the trial Court would be in a position to decide the case finally on merits and to come to a conclusion as to whether the offence under section 307, IPC is committed or not. Similarly, in those cases where the conviction is already recorded by the trial Court and the matter is at the appellate stage before the High Court, mere compromise between the parties would not be a ground to accept the same resulting in acquittal of the offender who has already been convicted by the trial Court; *Narinder Singh* v. *State of Punjab,* 2014 All MR (Cri) 1886 (SC): (2014) 6 SCC 466.

Few cases are given below to illustrate the approach of the Courts as regards the quashing of F.I.R. and proceedings.

In *Madhavrao Jiwaji Rao Scindia* v. *Sambhajirao Chandrojirao Angre,* (1988) 2 SCR 930 the Apex Court has held that, "*When a prosecution at the initial stage is asked to be quashed, the test to be applied by Court is as to whether the uncontroverted allegations, as made, prima facie establish the offence. It is also for the Court to take into consideration any special features which appear in a particular case to consider whether it is expedient and in the interest of justice to permit a prosecution to continue. This is so on the basis that the Court cannot be utilised for any oblique purpose and where in the opinion of the Court chances of an ultimate conviction is bleak and, therefore, no useful purpose is likely to be served by allowing a criminal prosecution to continue, the Court may while taking into consideration the special facts of a case also quash the proceeding even though it may be at a preliminary stage. .... A case of breach of trust may be both a civil wrong and criminal offence. But there would be certain situations where it would predominantly be a civil wrong and may or may not amount to criminal offence....... Where facts constitute a civil wrong but the ingredients of criminal offence are wanting, the Court can quash the criminal proceedings."*

In *Shri Vasant Waman Pradhan* v. *Shri Dattatraya Vithal Salvi,* 2003 All MR (Cri.) 2523, the Bombay High Court while pointing out the duty of Court as regards the administration of criminal justice has held that, *"Cases/litigations which are not fit to be continued should be wiped out by taking courageous bold steps suo moto."*

In *State of Uttar Pradesh through C.B.I.* v. *R. K. Srivastava,* 1989 (3) Crimes 109, the Apex Court quashed the criminal proceedings on the ground that no document was referred to in the FIR as the outcome of forgery and the allegations made in the FIR taken at their face value and accepted in their entirety did not constitute an offence under sectiona 120B, 420, 471 of I.P.C.

This was a case *P.S. Rajya* v. *State of Bihar,* (1996) Supp 2 SCR 631 instituted under section 5(2) read with 5(1)(e) of Prevention of Corruption Act, 1947. In this case charge against the accused was not established in departmental proceedings and hence he was absolved. The Apex Court held that, *"when the charge which is identical could not be established in departmental proceedings, criminal proceedings can be quashed."*

In *Amarjeet Singh s/o Jeevan Singh* v. *State of Maharashtra,* 2006 All MR (Cri) 489, the Bombay Court quashed the prosecution on the ground that Kerosene was seized by an unauthorised officer who was not empowered to investigate the offence.

This was a case *Sardar Awartar Singh* v. *State of Uttar Pradesh,* 2006 (1) ABR (NOC) 147 (All): 2006 (1) ALJ 457 of assault and criminal intimidation where there was absence of proof of injury report and non-production of independent witnesses. The Lucknow Bench held that the complaint is *mala fide,* frivolous and vexatious and therefore quashed the criminal proceedings to prevent abuse of process of law and to secure ends of justice.

In this case *Darshan Singh* v. *State of Uttar Pradesh,* 2006 (1) ABR (NOC) 133 (All): 2006 (1) ALJ 374 main accused was acquitted and finding had been recorded that there was no conspiracy. The Court held that principal of *'stare decisis '* would be applicable and co-accused is entitled to same relief and chargesheet against him was quashed.

This was a case *Dhirendra Kumar Banerjee* v. *State of Bihar,* 2006 (1) ABR (NOC) 189 (Jhar): 2005 Cri LJ 4791 of cheating where the accused took the money. But the Court while observing that alleged act of taking money and other activities were done for benefit of co-operative society and not for personal benefit, quashed the order taking cognizance on the ground that there was not intent of cheating and allegations showed that the case was of civil nature.

The Bombay High Court in *Gambhir Rajaram Chaudhari* v. *Nirmala w/o Bhaskar Chaudhari,* 2005 (2) Mh LJ 36 has held that, *"High Court in exercise of its inherent powers can quashed criminal proceedings or FIR or complaint and section 320 of Cr.P.C. does not limit or affect the powers under section 482 of the Code."*

After coming into force of The Scheduled Castes and Scheduled Tribes (Prevention of Atrocities) Act, 1989, tendency to file complaints under the said Act has increased and FIR's are frequently registered without making any preliminary inquiry, thus jeopardising the liberty of a person. This Act is being used for settling personal and political scores. Therefore, few cases are given below which would help the aggrieved persons to avail appropriate remedy.

In *Manohar s/o Martandrao Kulkarni* v. *State of Maharashtra,* 2005 All MR (Cri) 2602, the Bombay High Court while quashing the proceedings has held that, *"there can be no registration of a crime under the Atrocities Act, or investigation as regards the said crime, if the caste of the complainant and/or the accused is not contained in the body of the FIR and there is no averment in the FIR that the accused does not belong to a Scheduled Caste or Scheduled Tribe...... All investigations and further Court proceedings on the basis of such investigations, cannot be maintained in law."*

[**Note**.—The view taken by the Bombay High Court does not seem to be a correct interpretation of the law in view of Judgement of the Apex Court rendered in *Ashabai M. Adhagale* v. *State of Maharashtra*, 2009 AIR Bom R 119 (SC): 2009 All MR (Cri) 1806 (SC). In this case, the Apex Court held that non-mentioning caste of accused in FIR is no ground to quash proceedings.]

In *Ashok Lakhaji Halmara* v. *State of Maharshtra,* 2005 All MR (Cri) 2489, the Bombay High Court quashed the proceedings on the ground that, every quarrel or altercation between the member of the Higher Caste and that of the Scheduled Castes and Scheduled Tribes would not ipso facto constitute acts of commission of offence which are capable of cognizance under the Scheduled Castes and Scheduled Tribes (Prevention of Atrocities) Act and Protection of Civil Rights Act as the case may be. The Court held that, *"if the imputations are grossly vague and perfunctory, it would be appropriate to quash the proceedings being abuse of process of law and Courts. ...... Even when the complaint may technically answer the ingredients of offence sought to be complained of, but the evidence be so perfunctory to raise prima facie case for trial, the proceedings deserved to be quashed."*

This was a case *Laxman Jayram Shant* v. *State of Maharashtra*, 1980 Bom CR 609 under the Protection of Civil Rights Act, 1955. While acquitting the accused the Court held that, *"abuses must, in some way or other be connected with preaching of untouchability."*

Note.—Lawyers are requested to read the following cases:

(1) *Satish Mehra* v. *Delhi Admn.,* 1996 SCC (Cri) 1104.

(2) *Superintendent & Remembrances of Legal Affairs, West Bengal* v. *Birendra Chandra Chakravarty,* AIR 1974 SC 290.

3) *M/s. Indian Oil Corporation* v. *M/s. NEPC India Ltd.,* 2006 (3) Crimes 182 (SC).

CHAPTER XII
REMANDS

The Magistrate has power to remand an accused person either to judicial custody (MCR) or Police Custody (PCR) under section 167(2) of Cr.P.C. for further investigation when there are reasonable grounds for believing that the accused is involved in the same and where it is necessary to do so in the interest of investigation. As the liberty of an individual is at stake, this stage is very important from the point of view of the accused. Experience has shown that, Magistrates authorise detention to police custody as a matter of routine, though the Apex Court in *Natabar Parida* v. *State of Orissa,* AIR 1975 SC 1465 and *State of Maharashtra* v. Tukaram Shiva Patil, 78 Bom LR has warned the Magistrates not to allow remand applications without being satisfied that there are really good grounds or reasonable grounds for the same.

In *Dr. Ajay Kisanlal Soni* v. *State of Maharashtra,* 1992 (1) Mh LR 226: 1992 Mh LJ 505: 1992 Bom Cri Cases 225, the Bombay High Court has observed that, *"Police Custody Remand is granted only for furthering the investigation in proper direction .... Police is bound to investigate the offence during the period of Police Custody Remand in preference to other problems of the Police Station ...... If the Police neglectes to perform these functions and come forth with a case that they were busy with law and order problems, such contention cannot be countenanced by the Courts .... Further Police Custody Remand cannot be granted."*

Power of remand is to be exercised when investigation is not complete. Once charge-sheet is filed and cognizance of the offence is taken, Court cannot exercise its power to remand an accused to custody for investigation under section 167(2), Cr.P.C. After cognizance of offence is taken, Court can remand accused to custody only in terms of section 309(2), Cr.P.C. In the present case, as the appellants were not in custody but released on bail, they could not be remanded unless bail was cancelled; *Mithabhai Pashabhai Patel* v. *State of Gujarat,* (2009) 6 SCC 332: 2009 (2) Crimes 475 (SC).

As to the police remand of accused arrested during further investigation, the Apex Court held that remand of such accused can be sought under section 167(2) and not under section 309(2) of Cr.P.C. Expression 'accused if in custody' in section 309(2) does not include the accused who is arrested on further investigation before supplementary charge-sheet is filed; *State through CBI* v. *Dawood Ibrahim Kaskar,* (2000) 10 SCC 438; *Dinesh Dalmiya* v. *CBI,* (2007) 8 SCC 770: 2007 All MR (Cri) 3290 (SC); *CBI* v. *Rathin Dandapat,* 2015 All MR (Cri) 3678 (SC): 2015 SAR (Cri) 1063 (SC).

In *T.N. Jayadeesh Devidas* v. *State of Kerala*, 1980 Cri LJ 906, the Kerala High Court while advising the deletion of section 27 of the The Evidence Act held the order of the Magistrate remanding accused to Police custody for securing recovery under section 27 of the Evidence Act to be violative of Article 20(3) of the Constitution.

In *Chadayam Makki* v. *State of Kerala*, 1980 Cri LJ 1195, the Kerala High Court has held that, "*application for Police Custody Remand of accused should be supported by the affidavit of investigation officer or Police Inspector or Police Sub- Inspector.*"

In this case [*CBI, Special Investigation Cell-I, New Delhi* v. *Anupam J. Kulkarni*, (1992) 3 SCR 158,] question arose as to whether a person arrested and produced before the nearest Magistrate as required under section 167(1) of Cr.P.C. could still be remanded to police custody after the expiry of the initial period of 15 days. The Apex Court held that, "*there cannot be any detention in the police custody after the expiry of first 15 days even in a case where some more offences either serious or otherwise committed by him in the same transaction come to light at a later stage. But this bar does not apply if the same arrested accused in involved in a different case arising out of a different transaction. Even if he is in judicial custody in connection with the investigation of the earlier case he can formally be arrested regarding his involvement in the different case and associate him with the investigation of that other case and the Magistrate can act as provided under section 167(2) and proviso and can remand him to such custody as mentioned therein during the first period of 15 days and thereafter in accordance with the proviso. ..... However after the expiry of the first period of 15 days the further remand during the period of investigation can only be in judicial custody.*"

In this case, the Apex Court held that change of custody to judicial to police or *vice versa* is permissible if it is within time limit of section 167(2), Cr.P.C.; *Kosanapu Ramreddy* v. *State of Andhra Pradesh*, AIR 1994 SC 1447: 1994 Cri LJ 2121.

Where police pray for extension of police custody remand it is obligatory on the part of police to give reasons and prayer has to be substantiated by the investigation officer not only by putting forth reasons but also by pointing out progress in investigation carried out when accused persons were in his custody; *Shivnath V. Lambe* v. *State of Maharashtra*, 2015 All MR (Cri) 2555.

Where the Investigation Officer sought police custody remand of the accused to know the whereabouts of the absconding accused, the Court held that mere apprehension that accused might have connection with other absconding accused and that he knows the hiding places of absconding accused, it not enough to grant police custody remand; *State* v. *Sundaramoorthy*, 2008 Cri LJ 898 (Mad): 2008 (3) ABR (NOC) 522.

In this case, the Apex Court has directed all the Magistrates to ascertain from physical appearance whether accused is an adult or a juvenile in conflict with law and further directed to follow the procedures laid down in sections 41B, 50A and 54 of Cr.P.C. before granting remands; *Jitendra Singh @ Babboo Singh* v. *State of Uttar Pradesh*, 2013 All MR (Cri) 2984 (SC).

However it has been held in *Velu Vishwanathan* v. *State,* 1971 Cri LJ 725 that, *"police can request the Magistrate to give custody to them for interrogation of the persons who surrendered before him."*

The Court declared the action of Magistrate as *ultra vires* of the Constitution where the custody of the accused person was given to Army under the order of remand; *Joyanta Boseboosa* v. *State of Assam,* 1992 Cri LJ 2147.

In *Gaibidingpoo Kabui* v. *Union Territory of Manipur,* AIR 1963 Manipur 12 and *R.K. Nabachandra Singh* v. *Manipur Administration,* AIR 1964 Manipur 39, the Courts have held that, *"If the police do not transmit to the Court a copy of the entries in the diary relating to the case, to satisfy the Magistrate that there are grounds for believing that the accusation or information is well founded, and that a remand is absolutely necessary for the purpose of investigation, the Magistrate has no jurisdiction to direct the detention of the arrested person."*

Judicial Custody

The Apex Court in *Nimeon Sangma* v. *Home Secretary, Govt. of Meghalaya,* (1979) 3 SCR 785 has condemned the practice of long pre-trial detention under guise of the judicial process and directed the State to release all persons who have been in custody for more than 6 months or against whom summons cases are pending.

It has been held by the Constitution Bench of the Apex Court in *Raj Narain* v. *Superintendent Central Jail, New Delhi,* (1971) 2 SCR 147 that, *"An order of remand without physical production of accused is not illegal but it is extremely unsatisfactory."*

In *Ramesh Kumar Ravi* alias *Ram Prasad* v. *State of Bihar,* 1987 Cri LJ 1489 (Pat), the Court has held that, *"remand orders can be passed despite the absence of written application or request."*

In *Gian Singh* v. *State (Delhi Admin.),* 1981 Cri LJ 100, the Court has held that, *"the accused can be questioned by the police even after his remand to judicial custody, subject to his right to silence, with the permission of the Magistrate in any place and manner which do not amount to custody in the police."*

In *Swami Hariharanand* v. *Jailer,* AIR 1954 All 601: 1954 Cri LJ 1317, the Court has held that, *"Magistrate directing the arrest cannot himself pass an order of remand under section 167 of Cr.P.C."*

Recently the Bombay High Court has held that, *"the accused booked under Maharashtra Control of Organised Crime Act, (30 of 1999) is not entitled to know the contents of remand application submitted by the police"*; *Mohd. Shakil* v *State of Maharashtra,* 2000 (3) Mh LJ 413.

CHAPTER XIII
CONFESSIONS
(Sections 24 to 27 of Evidence Act)

SYNOPSIS

Confession in ordinary parlance means admission or acknowledgement of guilt. However there is a distinction between "admission" and "confession". This distinction has been explained by the Apex Court in *CBI* v. *V.C. Shukla*, 1998 All MR (Cri) 629: (1998) 1 SCR 1153 wherein the Court observed: "...... *only voluntary and direct acknowledgement of guilt is a confession but when a confession falls short of actual admission of guilt it may nevertheless be used as evidence against the person who made it or his authorised agent as 'admission' under section 21."*

When a person confesses about the commission of crime, his statement becomes admissible in evidence and can be proved against him. Unless a person accused of committing crime shows that the confession was obtained by police by inducement, threat or promise, there is no inhibition in law to accept the same. But, it rarely happens that a person accused of commission of crime acknowledges his guilt on his own volition. Experience has shown that confessions are obtained by police by threat, harassment and torture. Unfortunately instead of discarding the confessional statement given to police, the Constitution Bench in *Prakash Kumar Bhutto* v. *State of Gujarat*, 2005 (1) Crimes 163 accepted confessional statement recorded under section 15 of TADA and Rules framed there under and held that, *"It would continue to remain admissible for the offences under any other law which were tried along with TADA offences under section 12 of the Act, notwithstanding that the accused was acquitted of offences under TADA in the same trial."* It is submitted with due respect that the approach of the Hon'ble Supreme Court of India is erroneous as it has not taken into consideration the ground realities and the environment prevalent in police stations and particularly the history of police torture and atrocities. The reason for opposing any move on the part of the State to make the confessions admissible in evidence can be understood from the following experiment conducted in a laboratory setting by Kassin and Kiechel in 1996. In this experiment certain college students were called and each male research participant interacted with a female student who was actually an experimental assistant. The two individuals were assigned a task in which the assistant read letters of the alphabet, which the participant then typed on a keyboard. They were warned *never* to press the ALT key because this would cause the program to crash and the data to be lost. No one actually did hit that key, but during the experiment, the computer suddenly ceased functioning. The experimenter rushed in, pretending to be upset, and accused the participant of having ruined everything by pressing the forbidden key. Each participant was asked, "Did you press the ALT key?" The innocent students would (1) *comply* by signing a false confession, (2) *internalize* the false confession by telling another student privately that he really did press the key, or (3) *confabulate* by letter, "recalling" false details of his supposed "crime". Two conditions were varied to determine their effects on false confessions. One, the accomplice either read the letters at a fast or a slow pace. Presumably, the participant would be less able to remember exactly what he did in the fast condition. Two, the accomplice either said that she has not seen what happened or that she had seen the student hit the key – thus providing false evidence against him. Altogether even though all were innocent of wrongdoing, 69 percent of the students signed the false confession, 28 percent internalized their guilt, and 9 percent confabulated and "remembered" false details about what happened. Thus, Kassin and Kiechel (1996) were able to obtain false confessions from college students in a laboratory setting. The celebrated writers (Kassin and Kiechel) observe *"if such confessions can be obtained in a laboratory experiment at a university, it seems very likely that they can take place in actual interrogations as well."* Kassin (1997) concludes that the criminal justice system does not provide adequate protection for the innocent person who becomes a suspect. He further argues that a confession obtained by means that involve manipulations such as providing the suspect with fake evidence should not be considered credible in a Court of Law. Thus, social psychology and forensic psychology may play an important role in its application to Law.

Few cases are given below on various types of confessions from the practical point of criminal trials:

(i) Extra-Judicial Confessions

The correct law as regards the extra-judicial confession has been propounded by the Apex Court in following two cases – In *Narayan Singh* v. *State of Madhya Pradesh,* (1985) Supp 2 SCR 319, the Apex Court has held that, *"It is not open to any Court to start with a presumption that extra-judicial confession in a weak type of evidence. It would depend on the nature of the circumstances, the time when the confession was made and the credibility of the witnesses who speak to such a confession."*

In *Thimma* v. *State of Mysore,* AIR 1971 SC 1871: (1971)1 SCR 215, the Division Bench of the Apex Court has held that, *"An extra-judicial confession made to one who is not a person in authority and which is free from any suspicion as to its voluntary character and has also a ring of truth in it, is admissible in evidence against the accused and deserves to be acted upon."*

In this case *Sahoo* v. *State of Uttar Pradesh,* (1965) 3 SCR 86, the facts were that the appellant developed illicit intimacy with his daughter-in-law named

Sunderpatti but there were incessant quarrels between them. On13th August 1963, she was found with serious injuries in the room where she was sleeping. She died on26th August 1963.. The appellant was put on trial for offence under section 302 of IPC and was convicted by Sessions Courts. High Court affirmed the conviction. The PW's 11, 13 and 15 deposed that they clearly heard the accused say when he opened the door of the house and came out at 6 o'clock in the morning of the fateful day that, *"he had finished Sunderpatti, his daughter-in-law, and thereby finished the daily quarrels."* This extra-judicial confession was held to be a relevant piece of evidence which corroborated the circumstantial evidence adduced in the case. While affirming the finding of both the Courts, the Apex Court held that (1) It is not a necessary ingredient of the term confession that it shall be communicated to another. (2) A confessional soliloquy is a direct piece of evidence. Generally such soliloquies are mutterings of a confused mind. Before such evidence can be accepted, it must the established by cogent evidence what were the exact words used by the accused. Even if so much was established, prudence and justice demand that such evidence cannot be made to sole ground of conviction. It may be used only as a corroborative piece of evidence.

In this case, the mother of accused, Smt. Dhillo Devi stated before the police that her son (the accused) had told her that he had killed Seema. Smt. Dhillo Devi appeared as a witness before the trial Court. However she was declared hostile by the prosecution as she resiled from her earlier statement to the police. During her cross-examination by the prosecution, she was confronted with her statement to the police to whom she had stated that her son (the accused) had told her that he had killed Seema. On being so confronted with her statement to the police she denied that she had made such statement. The Hon'ble Apex Court held that a statement to the police is ordinarily not admissible in evidence in view of section 162(1), Cr.P.C., but as mentioned in the proviso to section 162(1), Cr.P.C., it can be used to contradict the testimony of a witness. The Court opined that the statement of Smt. Dhillo Devi to the police can be taken into consideration in view of the proviso to section 162(1), Cr.P.C., and her subsequent denial is not believable as she wanted to save her son (the accused) from punishment. The Court further held that statement of the accused to his mother, the Apex Court held that it is an extra-judicial confession; *Bhagwan Dass* v. *State (NCT) of Delhi*, 2011 All MR (Cri) 2028.

In *State of Karnataka* v. *M.N. Ramdas*, AIR 2002 SC 3109, the Apex Court convicted the accused on the basis of extra-judicial confession made to a stranger at the earliest point of time.

In *Surendra Chauhan* v. *State of Madhya Pradesh*, (2000) 2 SCR 515, the Apex Court upheld the conviction based on the extra-judicial confession of accused made to mother of victim.

However, in *Makhan Singh* v. *State of Punjab*, AIR 1988 SC 1705, the Apex Court held the extra-judicial confession to be a weak piece of evidence as the same was made to police to avoid harassment.

Where it was alleged that extra-judicial confession was made by accused after consumption of liquor, it was held that the said extra-judicial confession is not voluntary and has to be excluded from consideration; *C.K. Reveendran* v. *State of Kerala,* 2000 Cri LJ 497 (SC).

This case of *Palvinder Kaur* v. *State of Punjab,* 1953 SCR 94 would make the concept of confession clear. Prosecution's case was that appellant administered potassium cyanide poison to her husband with the help of Mohinderpal on 6th February, 1950. The dead body was then put into a large trunk and kept in one of the rooms in the house in Ambala city. About ten days later, Mohinderpal during the absence of the appellant, removed the trunk from the house in a jeep and the trunk was then taken to Baldevnagar camp and was kept in a store room there. Three days later, on 19th February, 1950, Mohinderpal accompanied by Palvinder and a domestic servant, took the trunk a few miles on the road leading to Rajpura and threw the box in it. Appellant was tried for the offences under sections 302, 201 of I.P.C. She was convicted under section 302 by the Sessions Judge. On appeal, High Court acquitted her of the charge of murder but convicted under section 201 of I.P.C. Prosecution relied on an alleged confession of the appellant made to the Magistrate on 15th April, 1950. In appeal, the Apex Court held that, (1) Where the evidence showed that a person had died, that his body was found in a trunk and was discovered in a well and that the accused took part in disposal of the body but there was no evidence to show the cause of his death or the manner or circumstances in which it came about, then the accused could not be convicted for an offence under section 201. (2) A statement that contains self-exculpatory matter cannot amount to a confession, if the exculpatory matter is of some fact, which if true would negative the offence alleged to be confessed. A confession must either admit in terms the offence or at any rate substantially all the facts that constitute the offence. (3) It is well accepted rule regarding the use of confessions and admissions that these must either be accepted as a whole or rejected as a whole and that the Court is not competent to accept only the inculpatory part while rejecting the exculpatory part as inherently incredible. (4) When the statement made by the accused contained an admission that 'She had placed the dead body of her husband in a trunk and had carried it in jeep and thrown it into a well,' but with regard to the cause of the death the statement made by her was that, 'her husband had accidently taken a poisonous substance which was meant for washing photos erroneously thinking it to be a medicine'; the statement read as a whole was exculpatory in character and the whole statement was inadmissible in evidence.

In *B.A. Ramaiah* v. *State of Andhra Pradesh,* 1996 Cri LJ 4463 (SC), the Apex Court has held that, *"A statement contained in the F.I.R. furnished by one of the accused in the case cannot, in any manner, be used against another accused. Even as against the accused who made it, the statement cannot be used if it is inculpatory in nature nor can it be used for the purpose of corroboration or contradiction unless its maker offers himself as a witness in the trial. The very limited used of it is an admission under section 21 of the Evidence Act against its maker alone unless the admission does not amount to confession."*

In the instant case *Madhavgir s/o Gururantangir* v. *State of Maharashtra,* 2005 (1) Mh LJ 165 (DB) (Bom) the accused himself lodged F.I.R. in the police station which was in the nature of confession. The Bombay High Court has held that, *"the explanation for murder in a confession by the accused to the police in a F.I.R. may be relied on to prove motive or provocation with a view to extenuate the offence or sentence. In other words, there is no bar to a confession in first information being used in favour of the accused."*

In another case *Smt. Kusum Sagun Malmanke* v. *State of Maharashtra,* 2005 All MR (Cri) 2398 (DB) (Bom) the Bombay High Court has held that, *"Confessional statement and/or extra-judicial confession cannot be the basis of conviction unless it is corroborated by other piece of evidence."*

This was a case *Nishi Kant Jha* v. *State of Bihar,* (1969) 2 SCR 1033 where the appellant was charged for the murder of a fellow student in a railway compartment. The appellant was noticed washing blood – stained clothes, and bathing in a river. He was taken to the village Mukhia, where he made a statement and signed it. In this statement, he admitted his presence at the scene of murder but stated that crime was committed by someone else, that he was injured by the knife of assailant when he tried to prevent the crime, and that when the assailant jumped off the train he followed suit being apprehensive of arrest on the charge of murder. However in his statement under section 342, Cr.P.C. (old Code) the appellant denied all connections with the crime stating that he was injured at another place in a scuffle – blood – staining his clothes, books etc. He admitted being taken to the Mukhia's house, and stated that he had signed a blank paper there on being assaulted and threatened, but denied making the statement in writing ascribed to him. He was acquitted by the Sessions Court but in appeal the High Court convicted him for the charge of murder. Appellant filed special leave petition to the Supreme Court. In appeal, the Constitution Bench of the Supreme Court while upholding the conviction and sentence passed by the High Court, held that statement made to village Mukhia before accused was handed over to police is admissible in evidence. But in peculiar circumstances of the case, the exculpatory part of the statement made before the Mukhia being not only inherently improbable but also contradicted by the other evidence was rejected and the inculpatory part was accepted.

In this case *State of Kerala* v. *Ammini,* 1988 Cri LJ 107 (Ker) the accused made a statement to a doctor admitting his guilt. The Full Bench of the Kerala High Court held that, *"Statement made by the accused to the doctor of Government Hospital, though incriminating, is not a confession. It is not hit by section 26 of the Evidence Act and therefore it is admissible in evidence."* The view taken by the Kerala High Court in this case has been upheld by the Apex Court in *Ammini* v. *State of Kerala,* 1998 All MR (Cri) 287.

The following case is the *locus classicus* of the Judgement delivered on the point of admissibility of confession of accused against co-accused. In *Kashmira Singh* v. *State of Madhya Pradesh,* (1952) 1 SCR 526: AIR 1952 SC 159 – one accused namely Gurubachan Singh confessed his guilt and accordingly he was convicted and sentenced to death. He did not file appeal before the Supreme Court. However Kashmira Singh filed appeal to the Supreme Court. The appellant was convicted for the murder of one Ramesh (aged 5 years) and was sentenced to death by Additional Sessions Judge, Bhandara. The conviction was confirmed by the Division Bench of High Court, Nagpur. The prosecution story runs as thus – L.P. Tiwari was the food officer at Gondia at the relevant time. Appellant was an Asst. Food Procurement Inspector there. On 1st July, 1949, L.P. Tiwari found the appellant and Harbilas getting rice polished at a rice mill. The polishing of rice was prohibited by a State Law. Tiwari accordingly reported the matter to the Deputy Commissioner of Bhandara who suspended the appellant and later his services were terminated. This embittered the appellant and was heard to take revenge. There after the boy (Ramesh) was enticed to the house of the appellant's brother Gurudayal Singh and was done to death with the active assistance of Gurubachan Singh. The body was then tied up in a gunny bag and rolled up in a roll of bedding and allowed to lie in Gurudayal's house till about 7 p.m. At 7 p.m. the body wrapped as above was carried by Gurubachan on his head to a chowkidar's hut near the Sikh Gurudwara. The appellant accompanied him. Shortly before midnight the appellant and Gurubachan carried the body in a rikshaw and was thrown into the well. In this case, Gurubachan's confession played an important role in implication the appellant. The Apex Court acquitted the appellant of the charge of murder, conspiracy and kidnapping but convicted him for the offence punishable under section 201 of I.P.C and sentenced him to suffer rigiorous imprisonment for 7 years. The Apex Court as regards confession of co-accused and its use another accused has held that, *"The confession of an accused person against a co-accused is not evidence in the ordinary sense of the term. It does not come within the meaning of evidence cotained in section 3 of the Evidence Act in as much as it is not required to be given on oath, nor in the presence of the accused and cannot be tested by cross-examination. It is a much weaker type of evidence than the evidence of an approver which is not subject to any of these infirmities ...... Such a confession can only be used to lend assurance to other evidence against a co-accused. The proper way to approach a case of this kind is, first, to marshal the evidence against the accused excluding the confession altogether from consideration and see whether, if it is* believed, *a conviction could safely be based on it. If it is capable of belief independently of the confession, then it is not necessary to call the confession in aid. But cases may arise where the Judge is not prepared to act on the other evidence as its stands even though, if believed, it would be sufficient to sustain a conviction. In such an event the Judge may call in aid the confession and use it to lend assurance to the other evidence and thus fortify himself in believing what without the aid of the confession he would not be prepared to accept....... A conviction can be based on the uncorroborated testimony of an accomplice provided the judge has the rule of caution, which experience dictates, in mind ..... The rule of caution is that* save in exceptional circumstances *one accomplice cannot be used to corroborate another, nor can he be used to corroborate a person who though not an accomplice is no more reliable than one."*

The distinction between confession of accomplice under section 133 and confession under section 33, can be understood from the decision of the Constitution Bench of the Apex Court rendered in *Hari Charan Kurmi & Jogia Hajam* v. *State of Bihar,* AIR 1964 SC 1184: (1964) 6 SCR 623. In this case the appellants along with four others were tried and convicted for the offences of dacoity and murder and sentenced to undergo imprisonment for life. The conviction was confirmed by the High Court. In appeal the Supreme Court while *setting aside the conviction and sentence, held that, "Though the confession mentioned in section 30 of the Evidence Act is not evidence as defined by section 3 of the Act, it is an element which may be taken into consideration by the criminal Courts and in that sense, it may be described as evidence in a non-technical way. But in dealing with a case against an accused person, the Court cannot start with the confession of a co-accused. It must begin with other evidence adduced by the prosecution and after it has framed its opinion with regard to the quality and effect of the said evidence, then it is permissiable to turn to the confession in order to lend assurance to the conclusion of guilt which the judicial mind is about to reach on the said other evidence. .... .. The distinction between evidence of accomplice under section 133 and confession under section 33 of the Evidence Act is that the former is evidence under section 3 of the Evidence Act and Court may treat it as substantive evidence but the later is not evidence under section 3 of the Evidence Act and the Court should first start from other evidence and then find assurance in the confessional statement for conviction."*

The Hon'ble Apex Court has summarized and restated the principles regarding acceptability and evidentiary value of extra judicial confession: (i) It is a weak evidence by itself. (ii) It should be made voluntarily and should be truthful. (iii) It should inspire confidence. (iv) It attains greater credibility and evidentiary value if it is supported by a chain of cogent circumstances and is further corroborated by other prosecution evidence. (v) For an extra-judicial confession to be the basis of conviction, it should not suffer from any material discrepancies and inherent improbabilities. (vi) such statement essentially has to be proved like any other fact and in accordance with law; *Sahadevan* v. *State of Tamil Nadu,* 2012 ALL SCR 1956.

(ii) Other Cases

Armogam M. Kounder v. *State of Maharashtra,* 2015 All MR (Cri) 626: Extra-Judicial confession made before doctor in presence of Head Constable is hit by section 26 of Evidence Act and hence is not admissible.

Tejinder Singh @ Kaka v. *State of Punjab,* 2013 SAR (Cri) 708 (SC): In this case, extra-judicial confession was disclosed after 16 days. The Apex Court held that non-disclosure of extra-judicial confession either on same day or within reasonable time either to the police or to the family members of deceased does not inspire confidence to the accepted as testimony to sustain conviction and sentence.

Vijay Shankar v. *State of Haryana,* 2015 All MR (Cri) 4950 (SC): In this case prosecution claimed that extra-judicial confession of inflicting injuries to deceased was allegedly made by the appellant to witness who was only a member of Gram *Panchayat* and not a person of influence with police. The Apex Court held the said extra-judicial confession to be doubtful and refused to rely on same as it was unlikely that appellant approached him and made extra judicial confession and requested to save him.

State of Punjab v. *Jagga Singh,* 2015 All SCR 186: In this case, witness before whom extra-judicial confession was made, was not a person from whom accused could get any assistance by confessing his guilt. The Apex Court held that in absence of any corroboration, testimony of such person cannot be relied upon.

Pancho v. *State of Haryana,* 2012 All SCR 365: Extra-judicial confession of co-accused cannot be treated as substantive evidence against co-accused and the same cannot be used without corroboration from other evidence on record.

(2011) 10 SCC 165: Court cannot start with the confession of a co-accused. It must begin with other evidence. If Court has formed its opinion with regard to quality and effect of other evidence, then only it is permissible to turn to confession in order to receive assurance as to conclusion of guilt.

Mohd. Khalid v. *State of West Bengal,* (2002) 7 SCC 334: The prolonged custody immediately preceding the making of the confession is sufficient, unless it is properly explained, to stamp it as involuntary. It is necessary to prove the circumstances under which this unusual step was taken.

(iii) Confession to Police

Section 25 of the Evidence Act mandates that no confession made to a police officer, shall be proved as against a person accused of any offence while section 26 of the Evidence Act mandates that no confession made by any person whilst he is in the custody of a police officer, unless it be made in the immediate presence of a Magistrate, shall be proved as against such person.

The Supreme Court of United States of America has summarised the law regarding admissibility of confession in this case. The Court held that admissibility of a confession must be based on a reliable determination on the voluntariness issue which satisfies the constitutional rights of the defendant. A plea of guilty is more than a confession. The same standard must be applied to determining whether a guilty plea is voluntarily made. Ignorance, incomprehension, coercion, terror, inducements, subtle or blatant threats might be a perfect cover-up of unconstitutionality..... Several constitutional rights are involved in a waiver. *First* is the privilege against compulsory self-incrimination. *Second* is the right to trial by jury. *Third* is the right to confront one's accusers. Court cannot presume a waiver of these three important rights from a silent record; *Edward Boykin Jr* v. *State of Alabama,* (1969) 23 Law Ed. 2nd 274: AIR 1970 USSC 10 (12).

The Full Bench of the Bombay High Court has held that confession made to a police officer is inadmissible in evidence; *Rajeshwar H. Mohurle* v. *State of Maharashtra,* 2009 All MR (Cri) 1926.

In this case, the Apex Court held that if confession is made by a person while in the custody of the police, it shall be presumed to have been obtained under the circumstance mentioned in section 24 of The Evidence Act and, therefore, inadmissible, except so far as is provided by section 27 of the Evidence Act; *Commissioner of Police* v. *Narender Singh,* AIR 2006 SC 1800.

In this case, the Apex Court held that confession made by a person while in police custody, even to a third person other than a police officer, shall also become inadmissible; *Indra Dalal* v. *State of Haryana,* 2015 All SCR 2836.

(iv) Confession to Magistrate – (Section 164 of Cr.P.C.)

A person who is neither an accused nor sponsored by the investigating agency, has no *locus standi* to apply to the Magistrate to record his statement under section 164, Cr.P.C. However, evidence of such person can, at the instance of any of the parties, be taken during the trial; [*Jogendra Nahak* v. *State of Orissa*, AIR 1999 SC 2565: (2000) 1 SCC 272].

However, in this case, the Apex Court has held that a witness can appear before a Magistrate directly to get his statement recorded and Judicial Magistrate is duty bound to take his statement under section 164, Cr.P.C.; [*Mahabir Singh* v. *State of Haryana*, AIR 2001 SC 2503].

The Apex Court has enumerated following considerations and principles for recording confession under section 164, Cr.P.C.:

(i) The provisions of section 164, Cr.P.C. must be complied with not only in form, but in essence.

(ii) Before proceeding to record the confessional statement, a searching enquiry must be made from the accused as to the custody from which he was produced and the treatment he had been receiving in such custody in order to ensure that there is no scope for doubt of any sort of extraneous influence proceeding from a source interested in the prosecution.

(iii) A Magistrate should ask the accused as to why he wants to make a statement which surely shall go against his interest in the trial.

(iv) The maker should be granted sufficient time for reflection.

(v) He should be assured of protection from any sort of apprehended torture or pressure from the police in case he declines to make a confessional statement.

(vi) A judicial confession not given voluntarily is unreliable, more so, when such a confession is retracted, the conviction cannot be based on such retracted judicial confession.

(vii) Non-compliance of section 164, Cr.P.C. goes to the root of the Magistrate's jurisdiction to record the confession and renders the confession unworthy of credence.

(viii) During the time of reflection, the accused should be completely out of police influence. The judicial officer, who is entrusted with the duty of recording confession, must apply his judicial mind to ascertain and satisfy his conscience that the statement of the accused is not on account of any extraneous influence on him.

(ix) At the time of recording the statement of the accused, no police or police official shall be present in the open court.

(x) Confession of a co-accused is a weak type of evidence.

(xi) Usually the Court requires some corroboration from the confessional statement before convicting the accused person on such a statement; *Rabindra Kumar Pal @ Dara Singh* v. *Republic of India*, 2011 All MR (Cri) 673 (SC).

In this case, the Karnataka High Court has held that mere marking of document is not proof of its contents. Any document placed on record by parties if marked while evidence is recorded, that itself is not sufficient to accept such document as having evidentiary value. Order marking voluntary statements of accused and admitting them in evidence is not proper; *Muddoru R. Tipanna* v. *State of Karnataka*, 2015 Crl LJ 3354 (Kar).

Where the statement was recorded in derogation of section 164, Cr.P.C., the Apex Court held that such statement is not admissible under section 9 of the Evidence Act. However, memorandum of condition of house by Magistrate and his evidence thereon is admissible under section 9 of the Evidence Act; *Deep Chand* v. *State of Rajasthan*, AIR 1961 SC 1527: 1961 (2) Cri LJ 705 (SC).

In this case, statement of P.W. 1/injured was recorded by Magistrate as a dying declaration. The Apex Court held that on his survival, said statement is to be treated as a statement recorded under section 164, Cr.P.C. and can be used for corroboration or contradiction; *Sunil Kumar* v. *State of Madhya Pradesh*, (1997) 1 SCR 589.

When the Court is of the view that the witness has been won over by the defence, his statement under section 164 must be ignored. A statement under section 164 cannot be admitted as substantive evidence against an accused person but it can be used only for the purpose of corroborating or contradicting the maker of the said statement; *Mamand* v. *Emperor*, AIR 1946 PC 45.

The Apex Court has held that though the evidence of witness whose statement has been recorded under section 164, Cr.P.C. be viewed with some initial distrust, it is not invariably a rule of law; *Kanwar Pal Singh* v. *State of Haryana*, 1994 Cri LJ 1392 (SC).

Where a Magistrate has recorded a confession under section 164, Cr.P.C., he must substantially comply with its provisions as required under section 463, Cr.P.C. failing which the confession would be inadmissible; *Nazir Ahmad* v. *King Emperor*, AIR 1936 PC 253: 166 Indian Cases 793: (1936) 44 LW 213.

(v) Retracted Confession

In this topic we shall see the effect and evidentiary value of a retracted confession. The celebrated case on this point is *Ram Prakash* v. *State of Punjab*, (1959) SCR 1219. In this case the appellant was tried along with 'P' for the murder of Nirmala Devi, wife of Banwari Lal, a practising lawyer at Rupar. The appellant was sentenced to death while 'P' was sentenced to imprisonment for life. The appellant and 'P' appealed to the High Court but their conviction and sentence were affirmed by the High Court. The appellant obtained special leave to appeal to Supreme Court. The evidence upon which the prosecution relied consisted of the confession of 'P', the statement of the appellant which led to the recovery of the ornaments from the possession of the mistress of the appellant and recovery of a blood – stained dagger from him. The confession of 'P' was later retracted by him in the Court of Sessions. The three-Judge Bench of the Apex Court while maintaining the decision of the High Court dismissed the appeal of the appellant and held that *"a voluntary and true confession made by an accused though it was subsequently retracted by him can be taken into consideration against a co-accused by a virtue of section 30 of the Indian Evidence Act, but as a matter of prudence and practice the Court should not act upon it to sustain a conviction of the accused without full and strong corroboration in material particulars both as to the crime and as to his connection with that crime. .... The amount of credibility to be attached to a retracted confession would depend upon the circumstances of each particular case."*

The Apex Court has considered the effect of retracted confession and the manner of appreciation of the same in the following case. The facts of the case are as under: Accused *A* and *B* were charged and convicted of offences under sections 457, 380 and 461, IPC and their conviction was confirmed on appeal. The High Court in revision upheld *B's* conviction but acquitted A recording its findings which destroyed the prosecution case almost in its entirety. The conclusion of *B's* guilt rested solely on his retracted confession, not only uncorroborated in material particulars but devoid of truth in many substantial particulars. In using the confession for this purpose the High Court did not advert to substantial truth of the story as narrated by accused, but rested their view on a line of reasoning which was entirely at variance with the confession and in fact outside its scope. In such facts and circumstances, the Apex Court set aside the conviction; *Arjuna Lal Misra* v. *The State,* AIR 1953 SC 411.

Where the confession was not retracted at the earliest opportunity but after lapse of several months and when prosecution evidence was closed and during examination of accused under section 313, Cr.P.C., the circumstance reinforces the conclusion that the confession was voluntary; *Shankaria* v. *State of Rajasthan,* AIR 1978 SC 1248: 1978 Cri LJ 1251 SC: (1978) 3 SCR 736.

(vi) Disclosure Statement (Evidence Act, Section 27)

It is the common practice of police to extract disclosure statement from the accused persons who are in their custody. Though such statements are not voluntarily given by the accused person in custody, they are shown to be voluntary and truthful by the police. Such disclosure statements are often tendered in evidence and may form the basis for a judgement. Therefore, these statements are important from the point of defence.

In this case, after arrest, one of the accused persons made a statement to police that 'the spear with which I stabbed I hid in a particular place'. As a result of this disclosure statement, spears were recovered. As to the admissibility of the above statement, the Privy Council held that section 27, which is not artistically worded provides an exception to the prohibition imposed by the preceding section, and enables certain statements made by a person in police custody to be proved. The condition necessary to bring the section into operation is that the discovery of a fact in consequence of information received from a person accused of any offence in the custody of a police officer must be deposed to, and thereupon so much of the information as relates distinctly to the fact thereby discovered may be proved; *Pulukuri Kotayya* v. *King Emperor,* (1947) 74 IA 65.

As regards the admissibility of such disclosure statements, the Apex Court in *Bheru Singh* v. *State of Rajasthan,* (1994) 1 SCR 559, has held that *"a confession or an admission is evidence against the maker of it so long as its admissibility is not excluded by some provision of law .... Where the accused himself lodges the FIR, the fact of his giving the information to the police is, in view of section 27 of the Evidence Act, admissible against him as evidence of his conduct under section 8 of the Evidence Act and to the extent it is non-confessional in nature, it would also be relevant under section 21 of the Evidence Act; but the confessional part of the FIR cannot be used at all against the accused in view of the bar of section 25 of the Evidence Act."*

However, under section 27 of the Evidence Act, only so much of the statement of an accused is admissible in evidence as distinctly leads to the discovery of a fact. Therefore, once the fact has been discovered, section 27 cannot again be made use of to 're-discover' the discovered fact. It would be a total misuse even abuse of the provisions of section 27; *Sukhvinder Singh* v. *State of Punjab,* (1994) 3 SCR 1061.

As far as the law regarding the admissibility of such disclosure statements is concerned, the correct law seems to be the one rendered in *State of Himachal Pradesh* v. *Jeet Singh,* (1999) 1 SCR 1033. In this case the Division Bench of the Apex Court held that, *"it is a fallacious notion that when recovery of any incriminating article was made from a place which is open or accessible to others, it would vitiate the evidence under section 27 of the Evidence Act. Any object can be concealed in places which are open and accessible to others. For example, if the article is burried on the main road side or if it is concealed beneath dry leaves lying on public places or kept hidden in a public office, the article would remain out of the visibility of others in normal circumstances. ..... It is not whether the place is accessible to others are not but whether it was ordinarily visible to other. If it is not visible then it is immaterial that the concealed place is accessible to others. Discovery of fact is not the object recovered but the knowledge of the accused about it. It is now well settled that the discovery of the fact referred to in section 27 is not the object recovered but the fact embraces the place from which the object is recovered and the knowledge of the accused about it."*

In this case, the Apex Court held that the discoveries under section 27 of the Evidence Act are not of guns and daggers used in a crime. Guns and daggers have an ancient origin and one does not have to hunt for an accused to discover them. The discovery, mostly and really, is as regards the authorship of concealment. Conduct and concealment are incriminating circumstances and their discovery becomes relevant and admissible under section 27 of the Evidence Act; *State of Uttar Pradesh* v. *Jageshwar,* AIR 1983 SC 349: (1983) 2 SCC 305: (1983) 1 Crimes 978 (SC): 1983 Cri LJ 686 (SC).

In the case *State of Uttar Pradesh* v. *Deoman Upadhyaya,* AIR 1960 SC 1125: (1961) 1 SCR 14 the respondent-accused was tried for the murder of one Sukhdei on 19th June, 1958. The evidence against him was entirely circumstantial and one of the pieces of evidence was "confession" made by the respondent-accused leading to the discovery of the '*gandasa*' thrown into the tank. This *gandasa* was found by the chemical analyzer and serologist to be stained with human blood. The Sessions Judge convicted the respondent and sentenced him to death. On appeal, High Court held that section 27 of the Evidence Act offend Article 14 of the Constitution and ruled out the confession of the respondent to be inadmissible and acquitted him. On appeal to Supreme Court, the Constitution

Bench held that, (1) section 27 of the Evidence Act, and sub-section (2) of section 162 of Cr.P.C. did not offend Article 14 of the Constitution and were not void. (2) A person who approaches a police officer investigating an offence and offers to give information leading to the discovery of an incrimination fact must be deemed to have surrendered himself to the police and to be in custody within the meaning of section 27 of Evidence Act. (3) The expression "a person accused of any offence" in section 27 is merely descriptive of the persons against whom evidence is sought to be led in a criminal proceeding. It is not necessary that the person should have been accused of an offence at the time when he made the statement leading to the discovery of a fact. (4) The statement made by the respondent-accused that 'he will recover the *gandasa* which he has thrown in the tank' is admissible in evidence and may be used against him.

In *Bodh Raj* v. *State of Jammu and Kashmir,* AIR 2002 SC 3164, the Apex Court has held that, *"the information permitted to be admitted in evidence under section 27 of the Evidence Act is confined to that portion of the information which 'distinctly relates to the fact thereby discovered'. But the information to get admissibility need not be so truncated as to make it insensible or incomprehensible. The extent of information admitted should be consistent with understandability. Mere statement that the accused led the police and the witnesses to the place where he had concealed the articles is not indicative of the information given."*

This case *Krishan Mohar* v. *State of Goa,* AIR 1999 SC 3842 was under N.D.P.S. Act, 1985. '*Charas* was recovered from the accused – appellant in pursuance of disclosure statement made by the accused. Evidence however, showed that police were already informed about the place where *charas* was kept. In this case *charas* was found concealed in the stem of coconut tree which was standing on an open place accessible to all. The Apex Court while setting aside the conviction held that , *"it cannot be said that it was accused who had concealed the charas there and that it was found out on the basis of the disclosure statement made by the accused."*

In *Rammi* v. *State of Madhya Pradesh,* AIR 1999 SC 3544, the Apex Court has held that, *"though information furnished by the accused to police officer which led to the recovery of the weapons is admissible in evidence under section 27 of the Evidence Act, but admissibility alone would not render the evidence pertaining to the above information reliable. Court has to see whether it was voluntarily stated. ...... Evidence of investigation officer regarding recovery of weapons cannot be relied upon as there was material discrepancy in evidence of eye witnesses and that of investigation officer regarding the time when police took the accused in custody. And moreso when public prosecutor has avoided putting any question in that regard to those witnesses when opportunity for examination was provided to him."*

In this case *State of Haryana* v. *Ram Singh with Rai Saheb* v. *State of Haryana,* AIR 2002 SC 620, the accused made a disclosure statement to police officer which led to the discovery of some articles. The Apex Court while acquitting the accused by giving benefit of doubt held the evidence of interested witnesses to be unreliable in whose presence discovery was made on the ground that no independent witness was found out for the said purpose.

In this case *Bheru Shingh* v. *State of Rajasthan,* (1994) 1 SCR 559 the accused was charged for the offence of murder of his wife and five children. The accused himself lodged the F.I.R. disclosing motive of crime, manner in which he committed crime and produced weapon used in the crime. His confession under section 164 of Cr. P.C. was also recorded by the Magistrate. While considering the admissibility of F.I.R., the Apex Court held that, *"A confession or an admission is evidence against the maker of it so long as its admissibility is not excluded by some provision of law. ..... Where the accused himself lodges the F.I.R., the fact of his giving the information to the police is, in view of section 27 of the Evidence Act, admissible against him as evidence of his conduct under section 8 of the Evidence Act and to the extent it is non-cofessional in nature, it would also be relevant under section 21 of the Evidence Act; but the confessional part of the F.I.R. cannot be used at all against the accused in view of the bar of section 25 of the Evidence Act."*

In the instant case *Mohd. Inayatullah* v. *State of Maharashtra,* (1976) 1 SCR 715, the accused made a disclosure statement to the police saying *"I will tell the place of deposit of the three chemical drums which I took out from the Haji Bunder on 1st August." While dealing with the said disclosure statement, the Apex Court held that in the instant case only the first part of the statement namely "I will tell the place of deposit of three chemical drums" was admissible under section 27 of the Evidence Act. The rest of the statement was not a distinct and a proximate cause of the discovery and had to be ruled out altogether."* The Apex Court further observed that the drums were in a Musafirkhana which was a place accessible to all and sundry. The drums were not alleged to be lying concealed nor was the compound under the lock and key of the appellant and therefore the appellant was acquitted by giving the benefit of doubt.

In this case, the appellant was convicted for the murder of one *B.* Axe, shirt and *dhoti* stained with human blood were recovered at the instance of appellant pursuant to his disclosure statement. Statement of appellant was recorded by police sub-inspector under section 27 of the Evidence Act wherein he stated that ' the axe was one with which he had killed *B* and that the shirt and *dhoti* belonged to him.' However, no independent evidence was led by the prosecution to prove that the axe, shirt and *dhoti* belonged to the appellant. As regards the admissibility of the disclosure statement made by the appellant, the Apex Court held that the statements made by the appellant were inadmissible and remaining evidence was not sufficient to bring home the guilt of the appellant. The statements were incriminating ones made to a police officer and were hit by sections 25 and 26 of the Evidence Act. The Court further held that the statements were not admissible under section 27 of the Evidence Act as they did not lead to any discovery within the meaning of that section; *Prabhu* v. *State of Uttar Pradesh,* (1963) 2 SCR 881.

The Apex Court in *Suresh Budharmal Kalani* v. *State of Maharashtra,* 1988 Cri LJ 4592 has held that where a person making confession has been discharged, his confession cannot be used against other co-accused.

(vii) Notes

(i) Since, police Patil is a police officer, confession made to him by the accused is not admissible [1978 Cri LJ 891 (Bom)].

(**Note:** However, the observation "police Patil is a police officer" made in the above case has been overruled by the Full Bench of the Bombay High Court in *Rajeshwar H. Mohurle* v. *State of Maharashtra*, 2009 All MR (Cri) 1926).

(ii) The confession given by accused while he is in police custody, cannot be considered. [2005 Cri LJ 2346 (Karn)].

(iii) Confession was made by accused while he was in police custody. The statements given by three accused were in the form of history to doctor who examined injuries sustained by one accused. The Court held that since the statements are in the nature of confession, they transgress into forbidden field of Section 26 of the Evidence Act and therefore said statements are not admissible; *Prakash Parab* v. *State of Maharashtra*, 2006 (1) AIR Bom R 775 (DB) (Bom).

(iv) Four accused alleged to have conspired to commit crime. Confession was made by one of the accused, referring to what other accused have said and done in reference to common intention of conspiration. The Court held that the confession is usable under section 10 of the Evidence Act against those accused as well in the same manner in which it is usable against confessor himself; *State of Maharashtra* v. *Damu Gopinath Shinde*, AIR 2000 SC 1691: (2000) 3 SCR 880.

(v) A joint statement by two or more accused persons under section 27 of Evidence Act is not admissible; [*Govind Kishor Jadhav* v. *State of Maharashtra*, (1980) 82 Bom LR 173].

(vi) A confession of co-accused recorded under section 15 of TADA Act if found to be voluntary can be used as substantive evidence against the co-accused; *State of Tamil Nadu* v. *Nalini*, 1999 Cri LJ 3124 (SC): AIR 1999 SC 2640: 1999 AIR SCW 1899.

(vii) A confession under section 15 of TADA Act given by main accused cannot be examined with reference to confession by co-accused. Hence conviction of main accused cannot be refused on the basis of contradictions between the said two confessions; *Ravinder Singh* v. *State of Maharashtra*, AIR 2002 SC 2241.

(**Note:** *Kalpnath* v. *State*, AIR 1998 SC 201: 1997 AIR SCW 4166 has been held to be no longer a good law.).

(viii) An admission made by a person whether amounting to a confession or not cannot be split up and part of it used against him. It must be used either as a whole or not at all; *Hanumant Govind Nagundkar* v. *The State of Madhya Pradesh and Raojibhai* v. *The State of Madhya Pradesh*, AIR 1952 SC 343: 1953 Cri LJ 129: (1952) SCR 1091.

(ix) An admission made by Counsel on behalf of the accused is binding on the accused; *Raghunath* v. *State of Uttar Pradesh*, AIR 1973 SC 1100: 1973 Cri LJ 858.

(x) Before a confession is relied on, it must be clear and unequivocal, whether it is judicial or extra-judicial confession. Confession by a large number of persons more in general and vague terms is unreliable; *Kishan Lal* v. *State of Rajasthan,* 1999 Cri LJ 4076 (SC).

(xi) While in the confessional statement the accused stated that, *"he had stabbed the deceased in her belly"*, but the injuries found by the medical officer were on the chest of the deceased, it was held that the confessional statement is not true and therefore ruled out of consideration; *Union Territory of Mizoram* v. *Vanallawamma,* 1977 Cri LJ 1831.

(xii) Absence of signature or thumb mark of accused on the disclosure statement under section 27 of Evidence Act makes the statement unreliable; [AIR 1995 SC 2345: 1995 Cri LJ 3993].

(xiii) Words *"shall be signed by the person making the confession"* in section 164(4) of Cr.P.C. are mandatory in nature. Omission to get signature of person making confessional statement is fatal to prosecution; *Dhananjaya Reddy* v. *State of Karnataka,* AIR 2001 SC 1512.

(xiv) The rules or the guidelines framed by the Bombay High Court for recording confession by a Magistrate under section 164 of Cr.P.C. did not by themselves apply to recording of a confession under section 15 of the TADA; *S.N. Dubey* v. *N.B. Bhoir,* (2000) 1 SCR 200.

(xv) In this case some offences under TADA Act were incorporated initially but later on the same were dropped. In such facts and circumstances the Apex Court held that confessional statement made by accused under TADA Act, in different case, cannot be utilised by prosecution in the instant case as charges were framed only for the offences under IPC; *Sunderlal K. Bhatija* v. *State of Maharashtra,* AIR 2010 SC 1666.

(xvi) Though confessional statements of accused made to police officer or while in police custody is not admissible, it can be proved against him if same leads to discovery of new facts; *Madhu* v. *State of Kerala,* AIR 2012 SC 664: 2012 ALL SCR 528.

(xvii) Confession is a very weak type of evidence, particularly when alleged to have been made to the police, and it is not safe to convict on its basis unless there is adequate corroborative material; *Sri Indra Das* v. *State of Assam,* 2011 (2) Crimes 20 (SC).

(xviii) Extra-judicial confessional statement made orally before a person with whom the maker of the confession has no intimate relationship is not a very strong piece of evidence. It can only be used for corroboration. However, extra judicial confession of one accused cannot be fastened upon other accused; *Sunil Rai @ Paua* v. *Union Territory, Chandigarh,* 2011 (3) Crimes 111 (SC).

(xix) In a murder case, extra-judicial confession was made by accused to his wife. The Court held that in view of section 122 of the Evidence Act, such an extra-judicial confession cannot be taken into consideration; *Vilas R. Kurhade* v. *State of Maharashtra,* 2012 All MR (Cri) 547.

(xx) If extra-judicial confession is made during the presence of police, it would not be admissible in evidence; *Hari Tiriya* v. *State of Orissa,* 2011 (2) Crimes 315.

(xxi) Where exact words of the accused have not been uttered by any of the witnesses, extra-judicial confession is not reliable; *Roopsena Khatun* v. *State of West Bengal*, 2011 All SCR 2917.

(xxii) Confessional statement made by accused under section 32 of Prevention of Terrorism Act, 2002 cannot be used as a piece of evidence for any purpose against other co-accused; *Saquib Abdul Hameed Nachan* v. *State of Maharashtra*, (2010) 9 SCC 93.

CHAPTER XIV

BAIL

(Sections 436 to 439 Cr.P.C.)

SYNOPSIS

Section 436 of Cr.P.C. deals with bail in bailable offences. A person accused of committing a bailable offence can seek the same as a matter of right but it is not so in non-bailable offences.

Section 437 deals with the powers of the Court to grant bail in case of non-bailable offences. It is difficult to obtain bail when there are reasonable grounds for believing that accused has been guilty of an offence punishable with death or imprisonment for life and where a person has been previously convicted of an offence punishable with death, imprisonment for life or imprisonment for seven years or more. However person under the age of 16 years or a women or a sick or infirm person may be released on bail under the proviso to section 437 Cr.P.C.

Section 439 Cr.P.C. deals with special powers of High Court or Court of Session regarding bail. There are no limitations on the powers of High Court and Court of Session and these courts can grant bail even in cases where offence is punishable with death or imprisonment for life.

(i) Regular Bail In Non-Bailable Offences

In non-bailable offences number of factors are considered before granting bail such as seriousness of offence, evidence against the applicant and peculiar or special factors relating to him. Therefore, application for grant of bail must disclose such facts which would make the Court to lean in favour of granting bail.

In *2G Spectrum* case, the Apex Court laid down the law as regards grant of bail in case of non-bailable offences. The Court observed that "*bail is the rule and committal to jail an exception. Refusal is restriction on personal liberty guaranteed under Article 21 of the Constitution of India. ...... Seriousness of the charge is not the only factor to be considered. Apart from this, Court must also keep in mind punishment that could be imposed after trial and conviction..... Bail cannot be denied merely because of sentiments of community against the applicant..... Object of bail is neither punitive nor preventive. It is to secure appearance of accused at his trial by reasonable amount of bail"*; *Sanjay Chandra* v. *CBI,* AIR 2010 SC 830: 2011 All SCR 2930.

Though grant of bail is the rule and jail the exception, it is the discretion of the Court to grant or not to grant bail in non-bailable offences. However, it is expected that discretion should be exercised in judicious manner.

While exercising discretion Judges must be guided by well-settled principles of law as misuse of discretion may lead to injustice. The following observation will guide Judges in exercising discretion. The Court explained the discretion as: *"discretion is a science, not to act arbitrarily according to men's will and private affection: so the discretion which is exercised here, is to be governed by rules of law and equity, which are to oppose, but each, in its turn, to be subservient to the other. This discretion, in some cases follows the law implicitly, in others or allays the rigour of it, but in no case does it contradict or overturned the grounds or principles thereof, as has been sometimes ignorantly imputed to this Court. That is a discretionary power, which neither this nor any other Court, not even the highest, acting in a judicial capacity is by the constitution entrusted with"*; *Rookey's* case, 77 ER 209: (1597) 5 Co Rep 99 (King's Bench).

There is another passage which explains the discretion. Benjamin N. Cardozo in *'The Nature of The Judicial Process' says: *"The judge, even when he is free, is still not wholly free. He is not to innovate at pleasure. He is not a knight – errant roaming at will in pursuit of his own ideal of beauty or of goodness. He is to draw his inspiration from consecrated principles. He is not to yield to spasmodic sentiment, to vague and unregulated benevolence. He is to exercise a discretion informed by tradition, methodized by analogy, disciplined by system, and subordinated to "the primordial necessity of order in all the social life". Wide enough in all conscience is the field of discretion that remains."*

Section 439 and 389 are the provisions dealing with bail. While section 439 provides for bail at pre-conviction stage, section 389 provides for bail at post-conviction bail. A notice to the public prosecutor is sufficient in case of bail application filed under section 439 of Cr.P.C. But in case of bail application filed under section 389, Cr.P.C., it is *mandatory* that the appellate court gives an opportunity to the public prosecutor for showing cause in writing against such release; *Atul Tripathi* v. *State of Uttar Pradesh,* 2015 (2) Crimes 32 (SC).

There is no limit for filing bail applications. If application for bail is rejected at earlier stage, it does not bar fresh application on later occasion giving more details, further developments and different considerations; *Babu Singh* v. *State of Uttar Pradesh,* 1978 Cri LJ 651 (SC): (1978) 2 SCR 777.

Same view has been taken by the Apex Court in *Kalyan Chandra Sarkar* v. *Rajesh Ranjan @ Pappu Yadav,* 2005 (1) Crimes 202 and by the Bombay High Court in *Ganesh* v. *State of Maharashtra,* 2006 All MR (Cri) 450.

---

* 'The Nature of The Judicial Process' [The Storrs lectures delivered at Yale University by Benjamin N. Cardozo], page No. 141, Sixth Indian Reprint, 2005, published by Universal Law Publishing Co. Pvt. Ltd., Delhi.]

In this case, Apex Court held that though the principles of *res judicata* are not applicable to bail applications, repeated filing of the bail applications without there being any change of circumstances would lead to bad precedents; *State of Tamil Nadu* v. *S.A. Raja,* AIR 2005 SC 4462: 2005 (4) Crimes 186 (SC).

Where first bail application was rejected by Sessions Court as well as by High Court, second bail application can be made directly to High Court; *Twinkle Soni* v. *State of Jharkhand,* 2010 All MR (Cri) Journal 176 (Jha).

However in this case, the Court held that there is no requirement for accused to place his application for bail before the same judge who had rejected bail application of the co-accused as bail applications of two accused in the same case may not pertain to same subject-matter; *Firos Ali* v. *State of Kerala,* 2017 All MR (Cri) Journal 49 (Ker).

In this case, the Court held that if petitioner directly chooses to approach High Court, he cannot be thrown out merely on the ground that he has failed to approach to Sessions Court. Equally, it cannot also be said that he must make out an exceptional case before his petition for bail can be entertained; *Balan* v. *State of Kerala,* 2004 (1) Crimes 23 (Ker).

In this case, the Court held that even after rejection of bail by the High Court, the accused may again approach Sessions Court for bail on disclosing the facts of refusal by the High Court; *Chandramani* v. *State of Madhya Pradesh,* 1993 (2) Crimes 659 (Ori).

Where investigation is carried out by the National Investigation Agency (NIA) in a case registered under the provisions of MCOCA (1999) and UAPA (1967), application for bail filed before High Court under section 439 or under section 482 of CrPC is not maintainable. The application for bail will have to be made before Special Court under The National Investigation Agency Act, 2008 (34 of 2008). The Apex Court further ruled that appeal preferred under section 21(4) of NIA Act before single judge of the High Court is not maintainable. Appeal should be heard only by a Bench of two judges of High Court; *State of Andhra Pradesh* v. *Md. Hussain @ Saleem,* 2013 All SCR 3386.

In this case, the accused was denied bail on the ground that he committed offence under some other Act while on bail. The Apex Court struck down the words "or under any other Act" in section 21(5) of MCOCA (1999) as it puts excessive restriction on the right of person to seek bail; *State of Maharashtra* v. *Bharat Shantilal Shah,* 2009 All MR (Cri) 624 (SC).

(ii) Important Cases on Bail

1. The Bombay High Court in *State of Maharashtra* v. *Kaushar Yasin,* 1996 (2) Mh LJ 485, has held that before refusing bail, the Magistrate should see that there are reasonable grounds for believing that the accused is guilty of offence punishable with death or imprisonment for life. ..... Reasonable grounds mean that there should be rational or logical basis for inferring that the person is guilty of offence punishable with death of imprisonment for life.
2. *Lambert Kroger* v. *State,* 2000 (3) Crimes 521—While dealing with Court's power to grant bail under section 439 of Cr.P.C., the Delhi High Court

held that, *"In all non-bailable cases except cases relating to offences punishable with death or imprisonment for life, judicial discretion would always be exercised by Court in favour of granting bail unless exceptional circumstance were brought to the notice of Court which might defeat proper investigation and fair trial."*

3. *Devendra Singh Negi @ Debu* v. *State of Uttar Pradesh,* 1994 Cri LJ 1783 (All)—In this case the applicant accused surrendered before the Court and applied for bail under section 437 of Cr.P.C. Name of the applicant was not mentioned in F.I.R.. The applicant accused specifically mentioned that he is wanted in a crime. The Court held that practice of Magistrates in postponing surrender application is not proper.
4. *Khemlo Sakharam Sawant* v. *State,* 2002 (1) Bom CR 689 (Panaji Bench)—While allowing the bail to the applicant, the Court condemned the practice of Sessions Judge to adjourn the case for order after four days after hearing arguments and observed that," *Court should not get swayed by perception of morality but should confine its decision to the requirement of law...... In case of offences not punishable with death or imprisonment for life, grant of bail is rule and jail an exception."*
5. In *Hussaninara Khatoon* v. *Home Secretary, State of Bihar,* AIR 1979 SC 1040: 1979 Cri LJ 1036, the Apex Court has held that, "If the Court is satisfied on a consideration of the relevant factors that the accused has his ties in the community and there is no substantial risk of non-appearance, the accused may, as far as possible, be released on his personal bond."
6. In *Harsh Sawhney (Miss)* v. *Union Territory of Chandigarh,* AIR 1978 SC 1016: (1978) 3 SCR 129, the Apex Court has held that, *"Bail cannot be refused on the ground that the accused's presence for interrogation in connection with the investigation was necessary."*
7. In *State of Maharashtra* v. *N.P. Shah,* (1970) 1 SCWR 373, the Apex Court has held that, *"Bail cannot be refused on the ground that he will abscond or tamper with the evidence."*
8. In *Gurucharan Singh* v. *State (Delhi Admin.),* AIR 1978 SC 179: (1978) 2 SCR 358, the Apex Court has held that, *"unless exceptional circumstances are brought to the notice of the Court which may defeat proper investigation and a fair trial, the Court will not decline to grant bail to a person who is not accused of an offence punishable with death or imprisonment for life."*
9. *Brij Mohan* v. *State of Rajasthan,* 1989 (3) Crimes 213 and *Mohar Singh* v. *State of Rajasthan,* 1989 (3) Crimes 435—Accused may be released on bail when his name is not mentioned in F.I.R.
10. *Marigowda* v. *State of Karnataka,* 1998 Cri LJ 1864—When there is no overt act alleged against the petitioners by the complainant with respect to the attack on deceased, then such petitioners are entitled to bail.
11. *Ram Sanehi* v. *State of Uttar Pradesh,* 1999 Cri LJ 3708 (All)—When the role of accused is of mere exhortation, then bail may be granted to him.

12. *Prem Singh* v. *State of Rajasthan,* 1989 (2) Crimes 303 and *Babu Lal* v. *State,* 1989 (3) crimes 379—When there are "cross- cases" and both sides have received injuries and one party has been admitted to bail, the other party has to be released on bail.
13. *Amba Lal* v. *State of Rajasthan,* 1995 (3) Crimes 467—"Cross F.I.R." were registered against both parties. One person from each side died and it was difficult to decide as to which of the parties was aggressor. Right of private defence also claimed. The Court held that members of both the parties should be released on bail.
14. *Ram Charan* v. *State of Rajasthan,* 1989 (3) Crimes 631 (632)—When no fatal injury could be assigned to the accused and a cross case has also been registered with police, then accused may be released on bail on appropriate conditions even in a murder case.
15. *Badri* v. *State of Rajasthan,* 1992 (1) Crimes 1026—Where a "cross case" out of the same incident has been registered against complainant party and the police during investigation has found possession of disputed field with accused party, it is a proper case to grant bail to the accused.
16. *Naziri* v. *State of Uttar Pradesh,* 1993 (1) Crimes 358—When there is a "cross version" and both sides sustained injuries and when the injuries on the side of accused party are also on vital parts, then accused person may be released on bail.
17. *Ahmed Nadi* v. *State of Uttar Pradesh,* 1986 All Cri R 143—Non-compliance of sections 157 and 158 of Cr.P.C. entitles the accused to be released on bail.
18. *Binoy Jacob* v. *C.B.I.,* 1993 Cri LJ 1293 (Del)—Where the main accused is not arrested by the investigating agency, co-accused are entitled to bail.
19. *C.R. Patil* v. *State of Gujrat,* 2005 AII MR (Cri) 2537 (SC)—There was misappropriation of huge amount running into crores. Accused was granted temporary bail pending SLP against rejection of bail by High Court. Prayer was made for extension of bail to enable accused to make arrangements to repay amount. The Apex Court held that, *"In view of peculiar facts and circumstances of this case and in view of fact that temporary bail granted was not misused by applicants and their release on bail was in the interest of several investors/depositors of the Bank, they may be enlarged on bail."*
20. *Dr. Suresh G. Motwani* v. *State of Maharashtra,* 2003 All MR (Cri) 2212 (Bom)—The Court held that in case of economic offences the object of criminal prosecution is to protect the investors and help them in recovery of the money. Detention of offenders may not aid in the recovery and therefore bail may be granted.
21. *Sunil Hanumantrao Koppal* v. *State of Maharashtra,* 2006 (2) ABR (NOC) 207 (Bom)—F.I.R. was registered under sections 406, 408, 409, I.P.C. There were allegations of fraud and siphoning off amounts in crores. Accused was not the prime accused having no criminal antecedents. On mere

statement that accused might have been involved is not sufficient for further detention. The Court granted bail to the applicant/petitioner.

22. *Birajit Sinha* v. *State of Tripura,* 2005 (3) Crimes 15 (Gau)—Case was registered under sections 148, 149, 506, 511, 326, 302, I.P.C. and section 27 of Arms Act. Petitioner No. 1 a sitting M.L.A., No. 2 and 3 leaders of party and security guard were arrested. Deceased sustained bullet injuries due to indiscriminate firing resorted to by accused. However Ballistic report showed that deceased was not shot from revolver of petitioner No. 1 as claimed in F.I.R. but from firearm of petitioner No. 5. The Court held that it probablised story of defence and therefore granted bail.
23. *Pralhad Singh Bhati* v. *N.C.T., Delhi,* 2001 All MR (Cri) 739 (SC)—In this case anticipatory bail was granted in a case registered under sections 306, 498A of I.P.C. But later on offence was altered to section 302 of I.P.C. The Apex Court held that accused has to seek fresh bail.
24. *Subash N. Bhandare* v. *State of Maharashtra,* 2003 All MR (Cri) 1209—The Case was registered under sections 304B, 498A read with section 34 of I.P.C. Co-accused father-in-law and mother-in-law of deceased already released on bail. F.I.R. lodged after 6-7 days. Statements of neighbours were not recorded. Deceased had not written a single letter to her parents. Allegations in F.I.R. were general in character and therefore bail was granted.
25. *Aatif Nasir Mulla* v. *State of Maharashtra,* 2006 (2) AIR Bom R 229 (DB) Bom—It was a case under POTA. The Bombay High Court has held that confessional statement of co-accused cannot be taken into consideration while considering bail application of accused.
26. *Vasanthi* v. *State of Andhra Pradesh,* 2005 All MR (Cri) 2560 (SC)—In this the applicant/accused was booked under section 364A of I.P.C. and sections 18(1), 21(4) of A.P. Control of Organised Crime Act, 2001. It was alleged that applicant lent her car for being used in carrying the kidnapped boy. Car was seized from her residence. Her confessional statement was not recorded in accordance with the provisions of A.P. Act, 2001. She was in jail for fifteen months. The Apex Court granted bail to her holding that probability of conviction was not bright and possibility of her engaging in similar crimes on organised scale if released on bail was also very remote.
27. *Ranjitsingh Bramhajitsingh Sharma* v. *State of Maharashtra,* 2005 (2) Crimes 168 (SC): 2005 All MR (Cri) 1538 (SC)—The Apex Court held that, "if the Court, having regard to the materials brought on record, is satisfied that in all probability he may not be ultimately convicted, an order granting bail may be passed."
28. *Govindaprasad Amritlal Burman* v. *State of Maharashtra,* 2004 All MR (Cri) 635 (Bom)—Where quantity of *ganja* found to be with the applicant was less than the commercial quantity, the Court granted bail to the applicant.

29. *Sk. Chhotu Sk. Roshan* v. *State of Maharashtra,* 1995 (1) Mh LJ 228 (Bom)—In this case *ganja* was seized from the person of accused on the basis of prior information. But, search was conducted by a constable not validly authorised by Magistrate or any authorised officer. The Court granted bail to the accused holding that mandatory provisions of sections 41, 42 and 50 of the NDPS Act were not complied with.
30. *Wernli Monika Barbara* v. *State,* 2005 (3) Crimes 740 (Del)—The applicant was accompanying co-accused and was charged under section 29 of N.D.P.S. Act. The Delhi High Court held that if Court is satisfied that in all probability accused ultimately may not be convicted, bail could be granted.
31. *A.V. Dharamsingh.* v. *State of Karnataka,* 1993 Cri LJ 94 (Karn)—In this case accused was arrested for the offence punishable under section 20 of N.D.P.S. Act, 1985. The Hon'ble Court released the applicant/accused on Bail on the ground that offence under section 20 is punishable with imprisonment of less than five years and hence, section 37 is not attracted.
32. *Sanjay Narhar Malshe* v. *State of Maharashtra,* 2005 All MR (Cri) 1927 (DB) (Bom)—The Court has held that section 18 of the SC and ST (Prevention of Atrocities) Act, 1989 nowhere debars the Magistrate from exercising the powers under section 437 of Cr. P.C. and Judicial Magistrates have jurisdiction to grant bail; [The same view has been taken by the Courts in *Shanu* v. *State of Kerala,* 2001 (1) Crimes 292; *A. Mali* v. *State of Kerala,* 2000 Cri LJ 2721 and *Ram Bharoshi* v. *State of Uttar Pradesh,* 2004 (3) Crimes 651].
33. *State of Sikkim* v. *Utpal Dorjee Yongda,* 2005 (3) Crimes 476—Case was registered under sections 420, 468/471 read with 34 of I.P.C. and accused were remanded to four days police custody. On the same day both accused were granted bail on their application. The Court held that, *"though existence of remand order did not operate as a bar to hear bail application, taking up two applications at two different point of times on same day is undesirable. ...... Both matters (remand application and bail application) should be heard together and dispose them by common order to avoid passing contradictory orders."*
34. *Bishnu Mallick* v. *State of Orissa,* 1993 Cri LJ 3817—"Surrender Bail" – The Court held that since offence in question under section 436 of I.P.C. being exclusively triable by the Court of Sessions, Sessions Judge can accept surrender and consider bail application.
35. *Balkrshna Dhondu Raut* v. *Manik Motiram Jagtap,* 2005 All MR (Cri) 2193 (Bom)—"Surrender Bail" – The Bombay Court has held that the accused named in offences punishable with imprisonment for life can surrender before the Court of Sessions and avail of remedy of bail as permissible under provisions of the Code.
36. *Niranjan Singh* v. *Prabhakar,* AIR 1980 SC 785: 1980 Cri LJ 426—"Surrender Bail" – The Apex Court has held that, *"the accused can be in custody not*

merely when the police arrest him, produces him before a Magistrate and gets a remand to judicial or other custody but he can be stated to be in judicial custody where he surrenders before the Court and submits to its directions....... The Court is competent to accept surrender and decide the bail application."

Note: However the Apex Court in *Sunita Devi* v. *State of Bihar,* 2005 (1) Crimes 86 (SC): 2005 All MR (Cri) 511 (SC) has held that for making an application under section 439 of Cr.P.C., the fundamental requirement is that the accused should be in custody.

Sunita Devi's case has been overruled by *Siddharam Satlingappa Mhetre* v. *State of Maharashtra.,* 2010 All SCR 2725.

37. *Devendra Singh Negi* alias *Debu* v. *State of Uttar Pradesh,* 1994 Cri LJ 1783 (All)—"Surrender Bail" – Accused specifically mentioning that he is wanted in a crime. The Court held that practice of Magistrates in postponing surrender bail application is not proper.
38. *Supreme Court Legal Aid Committee representing under trial Prisoners* v. *Union of India,* (1994) Supp 4 SCR 386: 1994 AIR SCW 5115: (1995) 4 SCC 695: (1995) 1 Bom. Cri Cases 149 (SC)—Writ petition was filed on behalf of undertrial prisoners on the ground that the trial of the cases under N.D.P.S. Act has not yet commenced and delay in trial would affect their right of speedy trial. The Apex Court has directed that, *"Undertrials, whose trial would not be completed within the half period of the proposed punishment, should be released on bail in the amount of the maximum fine amount with two sureties."*
39. *Rejendra Singh* v. *State of Rajasthan,* 1988 (1) Cri Law Cases 713 (Raj)—Accused was arrested for the offence punishable under sections 304B, 498A of I.P.C. The Court released him on bail holding that allegations of demand of dowry and ill-treatment of deceased were made only after deceased committed suicide and not prior to it.
40. *Kamalabai (Smt.)* v. *State of Karnataka*—In this case accused was arrested for the offence committed by him under N.D.P.S. Act and *ganja* was seized from him. The Court while allowing the bail to the accused held that mere seizure memo is not sufficient for denying bail to accused persons in view of the fact that none of the accused was owner of or in exclusive possession of house from where *ganja* was seized.
41. *Lawarance D'Souza* v. *State of Maharashtra,* 1992 Cri LJ 399 (Bom)—Accused was arrested for the offence committed by him under N.D.P.S Act, 1985. The Bombay High Court held that question of non-compliance with provisions of sections 41 to 58 can be looked into even at the stage of bail.
42. *Om Prakash Malhotra* v. *State (Delhi Admin.),* 1990 (2) Cri Law Cases 505 (Del)—Accused was arrested for the offence punishable under sections 302, 498A read with 120B of I.P.C. Facts of the case were that deceased-wife died of burns after a gap of seven days and she made five statements before different officers and persons. In earlier statement deceased admitted that burning was of her own doing but according to

final statement she implicated her husband. The Court while granting bail to the petitioner held that the complicity of the petitioner is not made out *prima facie* and there is no prima facie evidence against him.

43. *K.K. Girdhar* v. *M.S. Kathuria,* 1989 Cri LJ 1094 (Del): 1988 (3) Crimes 61 (Del)—In this case application for bail was moved by accused before the Magistrate at a time when he was dealing with application for remand of accused moved on behalf of investigating agency. The Delhi high Court has held that the Magistrate was bound to deal with the application of remand and the bail application together at one and the same time and without further postponement of the hearing of either of them. Notice of bail application to the agency is not necessary.

44. *Bharat Abhiman Marathe* v. *State of Maharashtra,* 2007 All MR (Cri) 3510 (Bom)—The Hon'ble Court held that since offence under section 409 of IPC is punishable with imprisonment for life, Magistrate has no jurisdiction to grant bail. However accused can surrender before Sessions Court and avail of the remedy of bail.

(iii) Surrender Bail

In this case, the Gujarat High Court has laid down the procedure for dealing with the surrender of an accused and application for grant of bail before the Court of Sessions. The Court observed that the surrender of an accused before the Sessions Judge can be in two situations: (i) without the orders of the High Court; and (ii) under the orders of the High Court:

(I) In the first situation, where the accused surrenders before the Sessions Judge for an offence under the IPC or under any other enactment and files an application for bail under section 439 of the Code and the Judge does not have the record of the case before him and the same cannot be procured on that day and the Public Prosecutor also is not in a position to say anything in the matter, the only proper course to be adopted by the Sessions Judge would be to refuse to accept the surrender and ask the person to surrender himself before the Magistrate having jurisdiction in the matter.

(II) On the other hand, if there is sufficient material before the Sessions Judge on which the matter of surrender as also the bail application filed by the accused may be considered, he may take the person in custody and decide the bail application. In the event of the bail application being rejected, the only proper order that can be passed by the Sessions Judge is to direct him to be produced before the Judicial Magistrate having jurisdiction in the matter.

(III) As regards the second situation wherein the accused surrenders himself before the Sessions judge under the directions of the High Court, it pre-supposes that the High Court has considered the material and it was satisfied that there was a case pending investigation against that person under the IPC or any other Act. In that case, the surrender by the person before the Sessions Court cannot be said to be without any reason. In such a situation, if an accused surrenders himself before the Sessions

Judge, the Sessions Judge should not refuse to accept his surrender without recording any reason.

(IV) If the surrender is made by an accused under the orders of the High Court, but without prior notice to the public prosecutor, and the Sessions Judge does not have enough material before him to consider his bail application, the appropriate order that should be passed by the Sessions Judge is to accept his surrender and take the accused in custody and forward him to the Magistrate having jurisdiction in the matter for the purpose of passing appropriate orders as to his proper custody. The Sessions Judge cannot be equated with a Magistrate and, therefore, he cannot consider about his remand to the police custody. It is only the Magistrate who can pass order of remand to the police custody under section 167 of the Code.

(V) In case, the Sessions Judge has enough materials before him to consider the bail application of the person surrendered under the orders of the High Court, he is not precluded from deciding bail application of that person after taking the person in custody. However, in the event of rejecting the bail application, the appropriate order, that can be passed, is to forward the person to the Magistrate having jurisdiction, who in his turn shall pass appropriate order as to his custody.

(VI) The Sessions Judge before whom the accused surrenders, while hearing his bail application, has no power to remand the accused to the police custody in a case when the offence is under the IPC, except in cases where the Sessions Judge is empowered by law under any special Act or enactment.

(VII) The Court, be it the Court of the Magistrate or the Court of the Sessions Judge before whom an accused appears in order to circumvent the provision regarding remand to the police custody, the Courts must be very careful in accepting surrender as a *bona fide* surrender, and in the first instance, the Court should inform the police concerned with the investigation regarding the intention of such a person to surrender. If that is done, the difficulty of the police would certainly be met with; *Urveshbhai Baldevbhai Patel* v. *State of Gujarat,* Special Criminal Application No. 4608 of 2014, 4609 of 2014 and 3642 of 2013, decided on 1st December, 2014.

(iv) Interim Bail

In this case the Apex Court held that reputation of a person is his valuable asset, and is a facet of his right under Article 21 of the Constitution of India. Court has discretionary power to grant interim bail pending his regular bail application, which is inherent in its power to grant bail; *Sukhwant Singh* v. *State of Punjab,* (2009) 7 SCC 559.

In this case, the Apex Court held that in appropriate cases, interim bail should be granted pending disposal of final application, since arrest and detention of a person can cause irreparable loss to a person's reputation; *Lal Kamlendra Pratap Singh* v. *State of Uttar Pradesh,* 2010 All MR (Cri) 2030 (SC).

Where the applicant was on interim bail, his regular bail application could be considered without his surrendering to custody again; *Reena Dutta* v. *State of Orissa*, 2009 (1) Crimes 491 (Ori).

(v) Release on Bail Pending Appeal

The Hon'ble Apex Court has enumerated the circumstances in which bail can be granted to the appellants who have been in custody for long period on the ground of delayed proceedings in pending trials/appeals. The Apex Court issued following directions:

(a) bail application be disposed of normally within one week;

(b) trial be concluded in Magistrate's Court within 6 months and within 2 years in sessions cases;

(c) five year old cases be disposed off by the end of the year;

(d) if undertrial has completed period of custody in excess of the sentence likely to be awarded, he must be released on personal bond;

(e) High Court should dispose of bail applications before them within one month;

(f) High Court should take necessary measures in light of judgement of the Supreme Court in Captain *Harish Uppal's* case; *Hussain* v. *Union of India with Aasu* v. *State of Rajasthan*, Criminal Appeal No. 509 and 511 of 2017 arising out of Sp LP (Crl) No. 4437 of 2016 and 348 of 2017, decided by the Supreme Court.

1. *Gudikanti Narasimhulu* v. *Public Prosecutor, High Court of Andhra Pradesh*, (1978) 2 SCR 371.—The principal rule to guide release on bail pending hearing of appeal should be to secure the presence of the applicant during trial.

2. *State of Rajasthan* v. *Balchand @ Baliay*, (1978) 1 SCR 535.—Interim bail pending the hearing of an appeal – The Apex Court has held that, *"The basic rule is bail, not jail, except where there are circumstances of fleeing from justice or thwarting the course of justice or creating other troubles in the shape of repeating offence or intimidating witnesses and the like by the petitioner who seeks enlargement on bail from the Court. When considering question of bail, the gravity of the offence involved and the heinousness of the crime which are likely to induce the petitioner to avoid the course of justice must weigh with the Court."* The Court further observed that, *"while the system of pecuniary bail has a tradition behind it, it may well be that in most cases not monetary suretyship but under taking by relations of the petitioner or organisation to which he belongs may be better and more socially relevant."*

3. *Bhagwan Rama Shinde Gosai* v. *State of Gujrath*, 1999 All MR (Cri) 985 (SC).—The Apex Court released the applicant on bail on stringent conditions on the ground that High Court found not inclined to hear appeal expeditiously and expected that every effort must be made to hear appeal expeditiously.

4. *Viradasayya P. Hallur* v. *State of Karnataka*, 2003 All MR (Cri) Journal 128 (Karn) (FB).—The Karnataka High Court has held that, *"Unless accused has a right of appeal in law under the Code of Criminal Procedure or the Constitution of India, he is not entitled to suspension of sentence or bail...... Where the Court has no power*

to suspend sentence and grant bail under section 389(3) of Cr.P.C., it has no inherent power to grant bail in exercise of its powers under section 482 of Cr.P.C."

5. *Surinder Singh @ Shingara Singh* v. *State of Punjab,* 200 5(3) Crimes 268 (SC).—While upholding High Court's judgement in *Dharampal's* case [*Dharampal* v. *State of Harayana,* 2000 (1) CLR 74] the Apex Court has approved following guide lines regarding bail in pending appeals which are as follows—

> *"Life convicts, who have undergone at least five years of imprisonment of which at least three years should be after conviction, should be released on bail pending the hearing of their appeals should they make an application for this purpose. ..... That the period of five years would be reduced to four for females and minors, with at least two years imprisonment after conviction..... However, these directions shall not be applicable in cases where the grant of bail is forbidden by law."*

6. *Kashmira Singh* v. *The State of Punjab,* (1978) 1 SCR 385.—The Apex Court has held that, *"So long as this Court is not in a position to hear the appeal of an accused within a reasonable period of time, the Court should ordinarily, unless there are cogent grounds for acting otherwise, release the accused on bail in cases where special leave has been granted to the accused to appeal against his conviction and sentence."*

(vi) Compulsive Bail Under Section 167(2) of Cr.P.C.

Order for release on bail under proviso (a) to section 167(2) Cr.P.C. is not an order on merits but an order-on-default of prosecuting agency. Such an order could be nullified for special reasons after defect/default has been cured. Accused cannot claim any special right to remain on bail. If investigation reveals that accused has committed a serious offence and charge-sheet is filed, bail granted under proviso (a) to 167(2) could be cancelled on application by prosecuting agency. *Order granting bail can be set aside by Court superior to Court which granted bail and not by same Court; Abdul Basit @ Raju* v. *Md. Abdul Kadir Chaudhary,* 2014 (4) Crimes 561 (SC).

The computation of period of 60 or 90 days for filing charge-sheet is vital for the exercise of right of default bail or statutory bail. Where initial period of filing charge-sheet is 90 days and prosecution neither filed charge-sheet prior to date of expiry of 90 days nor filed an application for extension of time, accused is entitled to bail. Asking accused to file a rejoinder affidavit to application for extension of time filed subsequently is improper. Application for statutory bail has to be decided on the same date it is filed; *Union of India through C.B.I* v. *Nirala Yadav @ Raja Ram Yadav @ Deepak Yadav,* AIR 2014 SC 3036: 2014 All SCR 3451.

[**Note:** The Court followed *Uday M Acharya's* case, AIR 2001 SC 1910 whereas *Pragnya Singh Thakur* v. *State of Maharashtra,* AIR 2011 SC (Supp) 755: (2011) 10 SCC 445 has been held to be not a good law].

In this case, bail application was filed by the applicant accused before filing of charge-sheet, but same was not decided by Magistrate immediately. On the contrary, Magistrate allowed CBI to file charge-sheet. The High Court set aside the order of Special Judge and held that once accused files application under section 167(2) of Cr.P.C., same is to be decided by Magistrate immediately after its presentation. The Court further held that period of 90 or 60 days is to be counted from the first date of production of accused before Magistrate, whether he has jurisdiction or not; *Rajesh N. Bangawala* v. *State of Maharashtra,* 2015 All MR (Cri) 3449.

In this case, it was alleged that accused was involved in explosion involving an Israeli Embassy vehicle carrying wife of an Israeli diplomat at New Delhi. The Additional Sessions Judge held first custody of 90 days to be illegal and therefore accused acquired right for grant of statutory bail. However, Chief Metropolitan Magistrate (CMM) extended custody of accused for further 90 days retrospectively. The Apex Court held that the order of CMM is illegal and statutory right of bail cannot be defeated by such order; *Sayed Mohd. Ahmed Kazmi* v. *State,* GNCTD, 2013 All SCR 947.

In this case, charge-sheet was filed within 90 days of arrest. Subsequently, Supreme Court directed further investigation by CBI. Pursuant thereof CBI filed second FIR. While investigation under second FIR was pending, accused sought bail under section 167(2) of Cr.P.C. on the ground that CBI had failed to file charge-sheet pursuant to such second FIR, within stipulated period of 90 days. The Hon'ble Apex Court rejected the plea of default bail as the applicant was under arrest in connection with first FIR and not under second FIR; *Vipul Shital Prasad Agarwal* v. *State of Gujarat,* 2013 All MR (Cri) 1084 (SC).

In this case, applicant/accused sought statutory bail on the ground that sanction for his prosecution under section 197, Cr.P.C. has not been obtained by the prosecuting agency. The Court negatived the contention of the applicant/ accused and held that once charge-sheet is filed within stipulated time, question of grant of default bail does not arise; *Suresh Kumar Bhikamchand Jain* v. *State of Maharashtra,* 2013 All SCR 1526: 2013 (3) Crimes 260 (SC).

However, the Apex Court denied the benefit of statutory bail to the applicant/accused though there was non-compliance of section 167, Cr.P.C. The Court held that economic offences constitute a class apart and need to be visited with a different approach in the matter of bail. As there were sufficient materials against the accused, statutory bail was denied to the accused; *Y.S. Jagan Mohan Reddy* v. *C.B.I.,* 2013 SAR (Cri) 619 (SC).

1. *Aslam Babalal Desai* v. *State of Maharashtra,* (1992) Supp 1 SCR 545.—The Apex Court held that once an accused is released on bail under section 167 (2) of CrPC he cannot be taken back in custody merely on the filing of a charge-sheet but there must exist special reasons for so doing besides the fact that the charge-sheet reveals the commission of a non-bailable crime.
2. *Uday Mohanlal Acharya* v. *State of Maharashtra,* 2001 All MR (Cri) 713: AIR 2001 SC 1910.—In this case accused applied for bail and offered to furnish bail. But the Magistrate refused the same. Charge-sheet was filed when matter remained pending before High Court. The Apex Court held that," *Subsequent filing of charge-sheet would not frustrate the indefeasible right of accused to be released on bail.*"

3. *Sanjay Dutt* v. *C.B.I., Bombay,* (1994) Supp 3 SCR 263.—The Constitution Bench held that, *"the indefeasible right of the accused to be released on bail in accordance with section 20(4)(bb) of the TADA read with section 167(2) of Cr.P.C. in default of completion of the investigation and filing of the challan within the time allowed, is a right which ensures to and is enforceable by the accused only from the time of default in filing of the challan and it does not survive or remain enforceable on the challan being filed. If the accused applies for bail under this provision on expiry of the period of 180 days or the extended period, as the case may be, then he has to be released on bail forthwith."*
4. *Rehemankha Kalukha* v. *State of Maharashtra,* 2001 All MR (Cri) 2237 (FB) (Bom).—The Bombay Court has held that, *"The provision of section 167(2) of Cr.P.C. is mandatory and therefore accused is entitled to be released on bail after expiry of period if no charge-sheet is filed. ..... His right is not extinguished if charge-sheet is filed subsequently."*
5. *Santosh Singh S/o Govardhan Singh* v. *State of Maharashtra,* 1999 All MR (Cri) 1813 (Bom).—In this case the accused was arrested for the offences punishable under sections 363, 366 of I.P.C. But the charge-sheet was not filed within 60 days. The Bombay Court has held that, *"the applicant is entitled to be released on bail as the maximum punishment prescribed for offence under section 366 is ten years and case falls under section 167(2) (a) (ii) of Cr.P.C."*
6. *Pralhad Vitthal Giri* v. *State of Maharashtra,* 2002 All MR (Cri) 1502 (Bom).—The accused was arrested for the offence punishable under section 306 of I.P.C. But the charge-sheet was not filed within 60 days. While allowing the bail to the accused, the Court observed that, *"since the offence is punishable with imprisonment which may extent to ten years, it means that punishment can also be for less than 10 years and therefore detention period of 90 days cannot apply."*
7. *State of Maharashtra* v. *Bharati Chandmal Varma (Mrs.),* 2002 All MR (Cri) 1215 (SC).—The Apex Court has held that, *"period of 60 or 90 days is to be counted from the first day of remand when the accused is produced before Court."*

(vii) Pre-arrest bail (Anticipatory Bail)

(Section 438 Cr.P.C.)

A person accused of committing a non-bailable offence and who has reasons to believe that he may be arrested in such crime, can apply to the Court of Sessions or High Court for grant of pre-arrest bail. Unless there are special or extraordinary circumstances, one cannot directly approach the High Court. Ordinarily one has to approach the Court of Sessions in the first instance. However, there is no bar in filing second or successive application for anticipatory bail. In *Maya Rani Guin* v. *State of West Bengal,* 2003 Cri LJ 1: 2003All MR (Cri) Journal 117, the full Bench of the Calcutta High Court has held that, *"If accused makes an application for anticipatory bail to Sessions Judge and application is rejected, he can make subsequent application for bail to High Court if there is a change in fact situation or in law..... But second or successive application for anticipatory bail before the Court of Sessions is not entertainable.*" (This case has been followed by Rajasthan High Court in *Ganesh Raj* v. *State of Rajasthan*, 2005 (3) Crimes 205: 2005 Cri LJ 2086).

The State of Maharashtra has amended section 438 *vide* Maharashtra Act No. 24 of 1993 which has come into force on 28th July, 1993. The Amendment gives discretion to Court either to reject the application forthwith or issue an interim order for the grant of anticipatory bail. Further the presence of the applicant seeking anticipatory bail has been made obligatory at the time of final hearing of the application and passing of final order by the Court if such an application is filed by the public prosecutor and the Court considers such presence necessary in the interest of justice. The words "*either to reject the application forthwith or issue an interim order for the grant of anticipatory bail*" have created a lot of confusion. This has been clear by the Court which observed that the words "*either to reject the application forthwith or issue an interim order for the grant of anticipatory bail*" is to be read with its subject and the verb which precedes and also the proviso. ..... The verb *i.e.*, "court may" cannot be disjuncted from the phrase "either reject ...". The verb "may" gives discretion to the Court to pass the order either way; *Shrenik J. Jain* v. *State of Maharashtra*, 2014 (3) Bom CrC 52.

1. *Gurubaksh Singh Sibbia*, v. *State of Punjab* (1980) 3 SCR 383: AIR 1980 SC 1672: 1980 Cri LJ 1125.—The Constitution Bench of the Apex Court has held that, "*filing of F.I.R. is not a condition precedent to the exercise of power under section 438 of Cr.P.C. The imminence of a likely arrest on a reasonable belief can be shown the exist even if an F.I.R. is not yet filed...... The applicant must show that he has "reason to believe" that he may be arrested for a non-bailable offence. The use of the expression "reason to believe" shows that the belief that the applicant may be so arrested must be founded on reasonable ground. Mere 'fear' is not belief. ...... The grounds on which his belief is based must be capable of being examined by the Court objectively. ...... Section 438(1) cannot be invoked on the basis of vague and general allegations, as if to arm oneself in perpetuity against a possible arrest...... Anticipatory bail is a device to secure the individual's liberty; it is neither a passport to the commission of crime nor a shield against any and all kinds of accusations likely or unlikely. ...... The operation of an order passed under section 438(1) need not necessarily be limited in point of time. The Court may, if there are reasons for doing so, limit the operation of the order to a short period until after the filing of an F.I.R. in respect of the matter covered by the order. The applicant in such cases may be directed to obtain an order of bail under section 437 or 439 of Cr.P.C within a reasonably short period after the filing of the F.I.R. as aforesaid. But this need not be followed as an invariable rule. ...... The normal rule should be not to limit the operation of the order in relation to a period of time.*"

2. In *Re: Digendra Sarkar*, 1982 Cri LJ 2199.—The Court held that filing of F.I.R. is not a condition precedent to the application for Anticipatory Bail.

State of Maharashtra v. *Ishan V. Deshmukh*, 2011 All MR (Cri) 3687.—The Bombay High Court has held that anticipatory bail can be granted for a limited period till completion of investigation even if FIR is not registered.

3. *Shamin Ahmed* v. *State (F.B.)*, 2003 All MR (Cri) 2031 (SC).—The Apex Court has held that application for anticipatory bail is maintainable at post-

cognizance state of a case i.e. after filing of the charge-sheet or after issuance of a warrant of arrest in a complaint case.

4. *Meer Ahmed Ali Khan* v. *State of Maharashtra,* 2001 All MR (Cri) 1696 (Bom).—As regards the Jurisdiction of Court, the Bombay High Court has held that, *"Court within whose jurisdiction only arrest is apprehended but offence is not registered, has the jurisdiction to entertain application for anticipatory bail....... Such application can be entertained by a Court within whose territorial jurisdiction the applicant resides and therefore apprehends arrest."*

5. *Akhalaq Ahmed F. Patel* v. *State of Maharashtra,* 1998 All MR (Cri) 1070 (Bom).—The Bombay High Court granted bail to the accused/petitioner who was in government service as there was no likelihood of his absconding or tampering with the evidence and observed that, *"Anticipatory Bail can be granted even after summons or warrant is issued against the accused."*

6. *Kalyan* v. *State of Rajasthan,* 1982 Cri Law Cases 550 (Raj).—The High Court granted bail to the accused/petitioner who was a student of second year Arts and whose examination was likely to commence soon.

7. *Erachikkaiah* v. *State of Karnataka,* 1986 (1) Cri Law Cases 394.—The Court granted Anticipatory bail to the accused/petitioner as the case was based on mere suspicion.

8. *Bimal Kaur* v. *State of Punjab,* 1986 (1) Cri Law Cases 604 (P&H).—The Court granted bail to a female co-accused having minor children.

9. *Mithun* v. *State of Madhya Pradesh,* 1987 Cri LJ 1100.—The Court granted bail to an undertrial prisoner to ensure speedy trial.

10. *Shaik Khasim Bi (Smt.)* v. *State of Andhra Pradesh,* 1986 (2) Cri Law Cases 234.—The Court held that mere filing of the charge-sheet by the police and issuance of a warrant by the Magistrate do not put an end to the power to grant bail under section 438 of Cr. P.C.

11. *Jagannath* v. *State of Maharashtra,* 1981 Mh LJ 791: 1981 Cri LJ 1808 (Bom).—The Bombay High Court has held that merely because prosecution claims that accused is wanted in police custody for investigation is no ground to refuse bail.

12. *R.L. Jalappa* v. *Delhi Police Establishment,* 1988 (2) Cri Law Cases 363 (Karn).—Hon'ble Karnataka High Court held that, *"the fact that offence is a serious one is not by itself a good ground to refuse bail .... Although news reports are not admissible in evidence, they can form basis of reasonable belief in the mind of applicant."*

13. *Shaikh Muneer S/o Shaikh Gafoor* v. *State of Maharashtra,* 1992 (1) Mh LR 166 (Bom): 1992 Bombay Criminal Cases 160.—The Bombay High Court has held that, *"if the accused is already released on bail, it would not be necessary in all cases, for the Magistrate to take the accused again in custody......... The accused has already been granted anticipatory bail and he is released on bail after arrest. Therefore, the bail continues and it is not necessary for the learned Magistrate to take the accused in custody."*

14. *Laxmikant Shankarlal Sarda* v. *State of Maharashtra*, 2001 All MR (Cri) 2330 (Bom).—In this case offence was registered under sections 3 and 10AA of the Essential Commodities Act (1955) and clause 3 of Kerosene (Restriction on Use and Fixation of Ceiling Price) Order, 1993, and raid was conducted on prior information and it was not a case of chance recovery. Police sub-inspector who conducted raid was not an officer empowered to do so. Seizure *panchanama* did not show that raid was conducted under supervision of ACP. In such circumstances the Bombay High Court granted anticipatory bail.

Vilas P. Pawar v. *State of Maharashtra*, 2012 All MR (Cri) 3743 (SC): 2012 (8) SCALE 577.—No court shall entertain an application for anticipatory bail unless it, *prima facie*, finds that an offence under the SC & ST (Prevention of Atrocities) Act (1989) is not made out.

Tara Chand v. *State of Rajasthan*, 2007 Cri LJ 3047 (Raj).—Notwithstanding the provisions of section 18 of the SC & ST (Prevention of Atrocities) Act (1989), the Juvenile Board has jurisdiction to grant bail in the light of section 6(2) of Juvenile Justice (Care & Protection) Act, 2000. As section 12 of the Juvenile Justice (Care & Protection) Act, 2000 is a special provision meant exclusively for juveniles, exclusion of section 438 Cr.P.C. shall not apply to a case of juvenile who is governed by Juvenile Justice (Care & Protection) Act, 2000.

15. *Daulatrao Nanasaheb Pisal* v. *Bhuinj Police Station.*, 1998 All MR (Cri) 1181 (Bom).—In this case offence was registered under sections 354, 504, 506 read with sections 18, 3(i) and 3(ix) of the SC & ST (Prevention of Atrocities) Act (1989). The complainant – Woman belonged to 'Scheduled Caste' who married to 'Hindu-Maratha'. The Bombay High Court while granting anticipatory bail to the petitioner/applicant held that, "*After marriage, caste rigidity breaks down and would stand no impediment to her becoming member of the family to which the husband belongs and she gets herself transplanted. ..... In view of this legal position, once the marriage was celebrated between Mrs. Parate and her husband, she lost the benefit of belonging to Scheduled caste.*"

16. *Mukesh Kumar Saini* v. *State (Delhi Admin.)*, 2002 All MR (Cri) Journal 41 (Del).—In this case the allegations were that humiliating words were uttered while victim was being dragged inside before the arrival of the neighbours. The Court held that, "*humiliating words cannot be said to have been uttered within 'Public view'.... mention of SC/ST offence in F.I.R. is not by itself a ground to decline pre-arrest bail...... Judicial scrutiny of the documents is permissible.*"

17. *Ramchandra* v. *State of Maharashtra*, 1995 Mh LJ 669 (Bom).—The Bombay High Court has held that anticipatory bail can be granted in offences under the SC & ST (Prevention of Atrocities) Act (1989) if no offence is disclosed *prima facie* under the said Act.

18. *Chandra Poojari* v. *State of Karnataka*, 1998 Cri LJ 53.—The Karnataka High Court has held that anticipatory bail can be granted in offences under the SC & ST (Prevention of Atrocities) Act (1989) if any of the ingredients is lacking as it would not constitute the offence under the Act. (Similar view has been taken in *Haridas* v. *State of Maharashtra*, 1997 Cri LJ 122; *Ramesh Prasad Bhanja* v. *State of Orissa*, 1996 Cri LJ 2743; *Karan Singh* v. *State of Madhya Pradesh*, 1992 Cri LJ 3054).

19. *Mahender Rani Johar* v. *State of NCT of Delhi,* 2005 All MR (Cri) Journal 213.—The Court held that anticipatory bail can be granted where live link between conduct of petitioner and deceased is absent.

20. *M.P. Lohia* v. *State of West Bengal,* AIR 2005 SC 790.—In this case young wife committed suicide at her parents' home. Allegations of demand of dowry were made by her parents. Her in-laws were taking plea that she was suffering from mental illness and filing application for anticipatory bail. Both sides were making attempts to create documents to support their charges. The Apex Court granted anticipatory bail to the husband and in-laws of the deceased observing that, *"correctness or genuineness of said documents could be gone into during full-fledged trial and not at the stage of considering application for grant of anticipatory bail."*

21. *Shantilal Jethalal Vasa* v. *State of Maharashtra,* 1981 Bom CR 142.—In this case complaint case was filed in Court for cheating (Section 420, I.P.C.). Accused gave assurance for payment of cheque amount in two instalments. Rs. 5,00,000 were paid by draft. However the petitioner could not honour the said assurance due to financial stringency. Then complainant filed application in trial court for cancellation of bail on the ground that petitioner/accused played a fraud on the Court by giving a false assurance. The trial Court cancelled the bail. The accused moved the High Court for grant of anticipatory bail. While granting anticipatory bail to the petitioner the Court held that there was no justification for cancellation bail by Magistrate and that bail should be rule in such cases.

22. *Usman* v. *The Sub-Inspector of Police,* 2003 Cri LJ 3928 (Ker).—The Kerala High Court has given directions to all subordinate Courts that (a) Every application for bail/anticipatory bail must be disposed of by the subordinate Court including the Sessions Court within the outer limit of three working days of their filing without fail. (b) Copies of order in every bail application (whether regular or anticipatory) shall be furnished to the accused/counsel free of cost and acknowledgement obtained from the respective counsel/accused (one copy in each application irrespective of the number of petitioners) immediately after pronouncement of orders on the same day as mandated in section 363(1), Cr.P.C.

23. *R.L. Jalappa* v. *Delhi Police Establishment,* 1989 (3) Crimes 113.—In this case offence was registered under sections 302, 201 of I.P.C. The applicant/accused moved an application for grant of anticipatory bail. While allowing the application for bail, the Court held that (i) The fact that the offence is serious one is not by itself a good ground for refusal if otherwise entitled to .... discretion should be exercised judiciously having regard to the peculiar fact and circumstances of each case. (ii) Anticipatory bail cannot be refused merely because investigation is still incomplete....... Freedom of an individual and presumption of innocence still hold the field. (iii) The power to grant anticipatory bail should be exercised with due care and circumspection. However the grant of bail is the rule and refusal is the exception. (iv) If the proposed accusations appear to stem from some ulterior motive the object being to injure or humiliate the applicant by having him arrested, a direction for his release on bail in the event of his arrest would generally be made.

24. *Shamim Ahmed.* v. *State,* 2003 All MR (Cri) 2031 (SC) (FB).—The Apex Court held that application for anticipatory bail is maintainable at post-cognizance stage of a case *i.e.,* after filing of the charge-sheet or after the issuance of a process under section 204 of Cr.P.C. or after the issuance of a warrant of arrest in a complaint case.

25. *Bharat Choudhari* v. *State of Bihar,* 2003 All MR (Cri) 2379 (SC).—The Apex Court held that Courts can grant anticipatory bail even when cognizance is taken or charge-sheet is filed provided facts of the case require the Court to do so.

26. *Manoranjan Jana* v. *State of West Bengal,* 2006 All MR (Cri) Journal 17.—In this case, petitioner surrendered before Magistrate after anticipatory bail was granted and prayed for regular bail. The Court held that the petitioner can be stated to be in judicial custody when he surrendered and submitted to the jurisdiction of Court. He is entitled for regular bail.

Salauddin A. Shaikh v. *State of Maharashtra,* (1995) Supp 6 SCR 556.—The Apex Court held that *"ordinarily the regular Court which is to deal with that particular offence cannot be by-passed. Court granting anticipatory bail should not substitute itself for the original Court. ..... An order of anticipatory bail could even be obtained in cases of serious nature such as murder, it is essential that the duration of that order should be limited."*

While overruling *Salauddin A. Shaikh* v. *State of Maharashtra,* (1995) Supp 6 SCR 556: (1996) 1 SCC 667; *K.L. Verma* v. *State,* (1998) 9 SCC 348; *Adri D. Das* v. *State of West Bengal,* (2005) 4 SCC 303: 2005 All MR (Cri) 1097 (SC); *Sunita Devi* v. *State of Bihar,* (2005) 1 SCC 608: 2005 All MR (Cri) 511 (SC), a three-Judge Bench of the Apex Court held that the bail granted by the Court should ordinarily be continued till the trial of the case; *Siddharam-Satlingappa Mhetre* v. *State of Maharashtra,* 2010 All SCR 2725.

Abdul Razzak Abdul Sattar v. *State of Maharashtra,* 2011 All MR (Cri) 3660.—The Bombay High Court has held that presence of person apprehending arrest is not necessary in all cases at final hearing of anticipatory bail application. It is necessary only in such cases where an application has been filed by the public prosecutor for the presence of the petitioner and the Court considers the presence of such person necessary in the interest of justice.

Ashik R. Shah v. *State of Maharashtra,* 2010 All MR (Cri) 2524.—In this case, the Bombay High Court held that order directing applicant to remain present in the Court without granting any interim protection to him is not proper.

Maya Rani Guin v. *State of West Bengal,* 2003 Cri LJ 1 (Cal) (FB).—The full bench of the Calcutta High Court has held that a fresh application for anticipatory bail under section 438 of Cr.P.C. after rejection of the prayer for regular bail is not maintainable.

Jagmohan Bahal v. *State (NCT of Delhi),* 2015 ALL SCR 3478.—If a second application for pre-arrest bail is filed, the same should be heard and decided by the same judge who had rejected the first application unless such judge incapacitated due to transfer, superannuation, etc. If second application is placed before some other judge, it is his duty to place the matter before the first judge.

(a) Transit Bail

Pre-Arrest transit bail can be granted till filing of the petition before the concerned jurisdictional Court for a limited period. Court has jurisdiction to entertain application for pre-arrest transit bail of a petitioner who resides within the jurisdiction of the Court, though he apprehends arrest in connection with a case which has been started or registered outside the jurisdiction of this Court; *Pritam Singh* v. *State of Punjab*, 1980 Cri LJ 1174 (Delhi High Court).

The Bombay High Court had granted pre-arrest transit bail to Teesta Setalvad and her husband Javed Anand in a case where complaint was registered against them in Ahmedabad (Gujarat) and directed them to approach Gujarat High Court and seek anticipatory bail.

Other cases

(i) *Sudam Charan Dash* v. *State of Orissa*, SLP (Crl) No. 8291 of 2013, decided on 25th October, 2013 by Supreme Court.

(b) Ad-Interim Pre-Arrest Bail

The Court of Sessions or the High Court has the power to grant ad-interim pre-arrest bail.

(i) *Sukhwant Singh* v. *State of Punjab*, (2009) 7 SCC 559.

(ii) *Lal K. Pratap Singh* v. *State of Uttar Pradesh*, 2010 All MR (Cri) 2030 (SC).

(iii) *Mukesh Kishanpuria* v. *State of West Bengal*, 2011 All MR (Cri) 659 (SC).

(viii) Cancellation of Bail

1. *Bashir* v. *State of Haryana*, (1978) 1 SCR 585: AIR 1978 SC 55.—The Apex Court held that, "*the cancellation of a bail can only be on the grounds known to law and the receipt of the charge-sheet/challan in Court can by itself be no ground for cancellation of bail.*"

2. *Simranjit Singh Mann* v. *Union of India*, AIR 1993 SC 280.—The Apex Court held that, "Strangers or third party cannot move a petition for cancellation of bail."

3. *Puran* v. *Rambilas*, 2001 All MR (Cri) 1210.—This was a case of bride burning wherein father of deceased applied for cancellation of bail. The Apex Court held that the application is maintainable.

(ix) Bonds for Release, Discharge of Surety and Forfeiture of Bond

1. *Moti Ram* v. *State of Madhya Pradesh*, AIR 1978 SC 1594: 1978 Cri LJ 1703: 1979 Mh LJ 372.—The Apex Court held that, "*It is shocking to ask a poor mason to furnish surety for Rs. 10000. Asking accused to furnish excessive amount of surety virtually amounts to denial of bail.*"

2. *Keshab Narayan Banerjee* v. *State of Bihar*, AIR 1985 SC 1666: 1985 Cri LJ 1857: 1985 (2) Crimes 304.—The Apex Court held that, "*Asking accused to furnish security of Rs. 1,00,000 in cash of fixed deposit in nationalised bank with two sureties residing in the State for like amount, amounts to denial of bail.*"

3. *Mohd. Salam Mohd. Sakir Ansari* v. *L.S. Danekar*, 1999 (3) Mh LJ 864.—The Bombay High Court held that, "*Order of the Executive Magistrate calling upon*

accused to furnish two sureties, one from Hindu community and other from Muslim community is illegal and improper."

4. *Sandeep Jain* v. *State (NCT of Delhi)*, 2000 Cri LJ 807 (SC): 2000 SCC (Cri) 316.—The Apex Court held that, *"Conditions and amount of surety should not be excessive."*

5. *Ram Chandra Pd.* v. *State of Sikkim*, 1981 Cri LJ 1580.—The Court held that, *"Where a surety bond is taken by a Judicial Magistrate for appearance in that Court, the Additional Sessions Judge to whose Court the case of the accused was subsequently transferred for trial by an order of the Sessions Judge, cannot forfeit the bond and impose penalty."*

6. *State of Madhya Pradesh* v. *Savji*, 1987 Cri LJ 1353 (MP).—The Court held that, *"Order of the Court laying condition for release of accused that sureties must be such who do not possess less than particular hectors of land is violative of Article 21 of the Constitution of India."*

7. *State of Rajasthan* v. *Lal Singh*, 1987 Cri LJ 269 (Raj).—The Court held that, *"If there is any doubt regarding sufficiency of surety, the proper course is to accept surety as interim measure and release accused and then send it for verification."*

8. *Bekaru Singh* v. *State of Uttar Pradesh*, AIR 1963 SC 430: 1963 (1) Cri LJ 335.—The Apex Court held that, *"Surety bond cannot be forfeited without complying with section 444 (2) of the Code."*

9. *Gulam Mehdi* v. *State of Rajasthan*, AIR 1960 SC 1185: 1960 Cri LJ 1527.—The Apex Court held that, *"Before a surety becomes liable to pay the amount of the bond forfeited it is necessary to give notice to the surety why the amount should not be paid and if he fails to show sufficient cause, only then the Court can proceed to recover the money."*

10. *Tarani Yadav* v. *State*, 1962 (2) Cri LJ 627.—The Court held that, *"The Court is under a legal obligation to take all the evidence adduced by the person showing cause. Failure to do so, vitiates the proceedings."*

11. In *Re: K. Sivaswami Servai*, 1962 (2) Cri LJ 377: AIR 1962 Mad 340.—The Court held that, *"Under section 446(3) of Cr.P.C., the liability under the surety bond can be reduced in proper cases."*

CHAPTER XV
INVESTIGATION

SYNOPSIS

(i) Further Investigation/Re-investigation (ii) *De Novo* Investigation

Section 2(h) of the Code defines investigation as:

"investigation" includes all the proceedings under the Code for the collection of evidence conducted by a police officer or by any person (other than a Magistrate) who is authorised by a Magistrate in this behalf.

In other words *all proceedings permissible under Criminal Procedure Code for collection of evidence is investigation in terms of section 2(h); **Allan John Waters* v. *State of Maharashtra,* 2012 All MR (Cri) 1485.

Under the Code, investigation consists generally of the following steps—

(i) proceeding to the spot,

(ii) ascertainment of facts and circumstances of the case,

(iii) discovery and arrest of suspected offender,

(iv) collection of evidence relating to the commission of offence which may consist of (a) the examination of various persons (including accused) and the reduction of their statements into writing, if the officer thinks fit (b) the search of places and seizure of things considered necessary for the investigation and to be produced at the trial; and

(v) formation of the opinion as to whether on the material collected there is a case to place the accused before a Magistrate for trial and if so taking the necessary steps for the same by filing of a charge sheet under section 173. *H.N. Rishbud* v. *State of Delhi,* (1955) 1 SCR 1150. [The above steps involved in the course of investigation have been reiterated in; *State of Madhya Pradesh* v. *Mubarak Ali,* AIR 1959 SC 707: (1959) Supp 2 SCR 201].

The Full Bench of the Bombay High Court has held that 'inquiry' falls in the domain of the Court while 'investigation' and all its facets exclusively come under the domain of the investigation agency; *Sandip R. Shukla* v. *State of Maharashtra,* 2009 (1) Mh LJ 97 (FB).

In Sohrabuddin and Tulsiram Prajapati encounter case, the Apex Court has held that investigation in every criminal case is conducted on the basis of suspicion and reason to believe and to apply the standard of proof beyond doubt at a stage when a full-fledged investigation is yet to be launched is incorrect; *Narmada Bai* v. *State of Gujarat,* 2011 (2) Crimes 142 (SC).

In this case, the Apex Court held that local police can investigate a senior government official without prior approval of Central Government. But CBI cannot do it in view of section 6A of Delhi Special Police Establishment Act, 1946. However, section 6A of Delhi Special Police Establishment Act, 1946 cannot be interpreted to be putting a fetter on the power of a constitutional Court in a case of a continuing mandamus. Previous approval of central government is not required in court monitored investigation; *Manohar Lal Sharma* v. *The Principal Secretory*, 2014 (1) Crimes 16 (SC).

The core of sections 156, 157 and 159 of the Code is that if a police officer has reason to suspect the commission of a cognizable offence, he must either proceed with the investigation or cause an investigation to be proceeded with by his subordinate; that in a case where the police officer sees no sufficient ground for investigation, he can dispense with the investigation altogether; that the field of investigation of any cognizable offence is exclusively within the domain of the investigation agencies over which the Courts cannot have control and have no power to stifle or impinge upon the proceedings in the investigation so long as the investigation proceeds in compliance with the provisions relating to investigation and that it is only in a case wherein a police officer decides not to investigate an offence, the concerned Magistrate can intervene and either direct an investigation or in the alternative, if he thinks fit, he himself can, at once proceed or depute any Magistrate subordinate to him to proceed to hold an preliminary inquiry into or otherwise to dispose of the case in the manner provided in the Code. The expression 'reason to suspect the commission of an offence' used in section 154(1), Cr.P.C. would mean the sagacity of rationally inferring the commission of a cognizable offence based on the specific articulate facts mentioned in the FIR as well in the Annexures, if any, enclosed and any attending circumstances which may not amount to proof. In other words, the meaning of the expression 'reason to suspect' has to be governed and dictated by the facts and circumstances of each case and at that stage the question of adequate proof of facts alleged in the FIR does not arise. The commencement of investigation by a police officer is subject to two conditions, *firstly*, the police officer should have reason to suspect the commission of a cognizable offence as required by section 157(1) and *secondly*, the police officer should subjectively satisfy himself as to whether there is sufficient ground for entering on an investigation even before he starts an investigation into the facts and circumstances of the case as contemplated under clause (b) of the proviso to section 157(1) of the Code; *State of Haryana* v. *Ch. Bhajan Lal*, (1990) Supp 3 SCR 259.

As far as investigation by complainant is concerned, the Apex Court held that there is no legal bar to such course; *Rasiklal D. Thakkar* v. *State of Gujarat*, (2010) 1 SCC 1: 2010 All MR (Cri) 342 (SC).

Where high police officials are involved in the crime and investigation done by state police and eight action taken reports filed before Court are not satisfactory, the Court can entrust case for proper investigation to independent agency like CBI notwithstanding filing a charge-sheet; *Rubabbuddin Sheikh* v. *State of Gujarat*, 2010 All MR (Cri) 966 (SC): AIR 2010 SC 3175.

It has been held by the Apex Court that fair investigation and fair trial are concomitant to preservation of fundamental right of an accused under Article 21 of the Constitution of India; *Nirmal Singh Kahlon* v. *State of Punjab*, 2009 All SCR 1266.

However overzealous investigation officer may adopt unfair tactics during investigation. The effect of unfair methods of investigation has been stated by the Apex Court in one of the following cases. The Court held that "*there are no statutory guidelines in the matter of showing photographs to the witness during the stage of investigation. But nevertheless, the police is entitled to show photographs to confirm whether the investigation is going on in the right direction. ... If the suspect is available for identification or for video identification, the photograph shall never be shown to the witnesses in advance. In the instant case, the investigation officer procured the album containing the photographs with the names written underneath and showed this album to the eye witnesses and recorded their statements under section 161, Cr.P.C. The procedure adopted by the police is not justified under law as it will affect fair and proper investigation and may sometimes lead to a situation where wrong persons are identified as assailants*; *Dr. Gopalkrishnan* v. *Sadanand Naik*, 2004 (5) Mh LJ 83 (SC).

In this case, FIR alleged commission of offences under sections 419, 420, 467 and 468, IPC in course of proceedings of Civil Court. However the High Court quashed the FIR on the ground that section 195(1)(b)(ii) of the Code prohibited entertainment and investigation into the same by the police. Setting aside the order of the High Court, the Apex Court held that statutory power of the police to investigate under the Code is not in any way controlled or circumscribed by section 195 and procedure under section 340 should be followed; *State of Punjab* v. *Raj Singh* (1998) 1 SCR 223.

If the facts reported to the police disclose both cognizable and non-cognizable offences the police would be acting within the scope of its authority in investigating both the offences as the legal fiction enacted in sub-section (4) of section 155, Cr.P.C. provides that even non-cognizable case shall, in that situation, be treated as cognizable; *State of Orissa* v. *Sharat Chandra Sahu*, (1996) Supp 7 SCR 304.

(i) Further Investigation/Re-investigation

Section 173(8) of Cr.P.C. enables the police to carry further investigation. Even the Magistrate can order further investigation. Direction for further investigation is given when police does not act honestly and defective investigation comes into light during the course of trial.

In this case, Hon'ble Apex Court held that bringing out the truth of the case is *raison d'etre* for the investigating agency's existence. Re-investigation can be ordered even after submission of charge-sheet for securing a fair, honest and complete investigation; and, consolidating confidence of victim and public in general in the interest of administering mechanism; *Pooja Pal* v. *Union of India*, 2016 (1) Crimes 626 (SC).

In this case, the Apex Court has held that, "*though final report under section 173(2) of Cr.P.C. has been submitted by the investigating agency, Special Judge can order further investigation for the ends of justice. However, Special Judge cannot direct that further investigation shall be conducted by an officer of D.I.G. rank of CBI; Hemant Dhasmana* v. *Central Bureau of Investigation,* AIR 2001 SC 2721.

In this case, the Apex Court has held that re-investigation can be ordered by a Magistrate without affording opportunity of hearing to accused even after receipt of first report of police; *Sri Bhagwan Samardha Sreepada Vallabha Venkata Vishwandabha Maharaj* v. *State of Andhra Pradesh,* AIR 1999 SC 2332: 1999 Cri LJ 3661: 1995 (5) SCC 740.

In this case, the Hon'ble Apex Court held that once a Magistrate takes cognizance of an offence under section 190 of Cr.P.C., he cannot order of his own further investigation in the case under section 156(3) of Cr.P.C. But, if subsequently the Sessions Court passes an order discharging the accused persons, further investigation by the police on its own would be permissible, which may also result in submission of fresh charge-sheet; *Randhir Singh Rana* v. *State (Delhi Administration),* AIR 1997 SC 639: (1997) 1 SCC 361 and *Nupur Talwar* v. *C.B.I.,* AIR 2012 SC 1921.

In this case the Hon'ble Apex Court held that notwithstanding the practice of CBI in naming the second FIR as "Fresh FIR", investigation conducted by it is in the nature of further investigation under section 173(8) of Cr.P.C. Even where direction for further investigation has been given, it does not mean that earlier charge-sheet based on earlier investigation is rejected; *Vipul Shital Prasad Agarwal* v. *State of Gujarat,* 2013 All MR (Cri) 1084 (SC).

Where new facts are brought to the notice of the investigation officer by a witness of a case after filing of charge-sheet, the investigation officer should not wait for court's order, as statute itself gives him power of further investigation and he should submit the supplementary report; *Smt. Pratima Saha* v. *State of Tripura,* AIR 2014 Tripura 13

Where the police filed report stating that "crime not detected", it does not terminate investigation which is construed to be still in progress. Such an interim report does not fall within the scope of section 173(2) of Cr.P.C. Where the Magistrate ordered further investigation after acceptance of police report under section 173(2) to the effect that "crime not detected", the Full Bench of the Madras High Court held that there is no legal bar against such course of action. There is no requirement for police to firstly get the earlier report under section 173(2) set aside and then seek permission under section 173(8). Power of Magistrate under section 173(8) is independent judicial power but it is not a power to review, revise, vary or cancel earlier order under section 173(2) of Cr.P.C. The Court summarised the law as regards powers and conditions to order further investigation and stated that:

(i) An order of the Magistrate taking cognizance of offences on a police report is a judicial order.

(ii) An order of a Magistrate ordering further investigation on receiving a police report is a non-judicial order.

(iii) An order of a Magistrate accepting a negative police report after hearing the parties is a judicial order.

(iv) An order of a Magistrate recording the report of the police as "undetectable" is not a judicial order.

(v) The power of the Magistrate to permit the police to further investigate the case as provided under section 173(8) of the Code is an independent power and the exercise of the said power shall not amount to varying, modifying, or cancelling the earlier order of the Magistrate on the report of the police, notwithstanding the fact whether the said earlier order is a judicial order or a non-judicial order of the Magistrate.

(vi) For seeking permission for further investigation under section 173(8) of Cr.P.C. by the police, the earlier order, either judicial or non-judicial, passed by the Magistrate on the report of the police need not be challenged before the higher forum.

(vii) The power to grant permission for further investigation under section 173(8) of Cr.P.C. after cognizance has been taken on the police report can be exercised by the Magistrate only on a request made by investigating agency and not, at the instance of anyone other than the investigating agency or even *suo motu*.

(viii) The power to grant permission for further investigation under section 173(8) of Cr.P.C. can be exercised by the Magistrate before accepting the negative police report thereby acting on the protest petition by the victim or the *de facto* complainant.

(ix) Anyone who is aggrieved by any order made by the Magistrate on a police report as aforesaid in sub-paragraphs (i) to (iv) hereinabove may approach the higher forum for remedy, if any; *Chinnathambi @ Subramani* v. *State of Tamil Nadu*, 2017 All MR (Cri) Journal 212 (Mad) (FB).

(ii) *De Novo* Investigation

In this case, the Apex Court held that further investigation under section 173(8), Cr.P.C. can be done not only at the instance of the police, but even at the instance of the *de facto* complainant. However, subordinate Court is not competent to direct fresh, new, *de novo* investigation which is entirely different from further investigation; *Vinay Tyagi* v. *Irshad Ali*, 2016 (SC) and *Chandra Babu* v. *State*, 2015 Cri LJ 4538 (SC).

[**Note:** *Reeta Nag* v. *State of West Bengal*, (2009) 9 SCC 129: AIR 2010 SC (Cri) 401 has been held to be 'not a good law'].

In exceptional circumstances, the Court in order to prevent the miscarriage of criminal justice, if considers necessary, may direct for investigation *de novo* wherein the case presents exceptional circumstances; *Babubhai* v. *State of Gujarat*, (2010) 12 SCC 254.

CHAPTER XVI

CAUSE OF ACTION AND TERRITORIAL JURISDICTION

Every offence shall ordinarily be inquired into and tried by a Court within whose local jurisdiction it was committed. (Section 177, Cr.P.C.).

The use of the word "ordinarily" in section 177, Cr.P.C. indicates that the provision is a general one and must be read subject to special provisions contained in the Criminal Procedure Code. The exceptions implied by the word "ordinarily" need not be limited to those specially provided for by the law and exceptions may be provided by law on considerations of convenience or may be implied from other provisions of law permitting joint trial of offences by the same Court; *Purshottamdas Dalmia* v. *State of West Bengal,* AIR 1961 SC 1589: (1961) 2 Cri LJ 728: (1962) 2 SCR 101.

While in civil cases, normally the expression "cause of action" is used, in criminal cases as stated in section 177 of Cr.P.C., reference is to the local jurisdiction where the offence is committed. These variations in etymological expression do not really make the position different. The expression "cause of action" is therefore not a stranger to criminal cases. It is settled law that cause of action consists of bundle of facts, which give cause to enforce the legal injury for redress in a Court of law; *Y. Abraham Ajith* v. *Inspector of Police, Chennai,* 2004 All MR (Cri) 3400 SC.

If the investigation officer arrives at the conclusion that the crime was not committed within the territorial jurisdiction of the police station, then FIR can be forwarded to the police station having jurisdiction over the area in which the crime is committed; *Satvinder Kaur* v. *State (Govt. of NCT of Delhi),* (1999) 8 SCC 728.

The Apex Court has held that trial can take place where act has been done or where its consequence takes place; *State of Madhya Pradesh* v. *Suresh Kaushal,* 2001 All MR (Cri) 1974 (SC).

In this case wife filed FIR at Gaya under sections 498A, 406 read with 34 of IPC read with sections 3, 4 of Dowry Prohibition Act, 1961. Wife was tortured for dowry at Gaya. When she refused, her husband brought her from Ranchi to Gaya and left her at her parental house warning that till his demands are met she shall stay at Gaya and if she returns without meeting those demands she would be killed. The issue for consideration in appeal before Apex Court was whether criminal proceedings initiated by the appellant at Gaya against her husband and his relatives are maintainable or not for lack of jurisdiction. Answering the issue in affirmative, the Apex Court held that offence was continuing one and episode at Gaya was only a consequence of continuing offence of harassment and ill-treatment meted out to complainant; *Sunita Kumari Kashyap* v. *State of Bihar,* 2010 All MR (Cri) 1648 (SC).

In this case wife was subjected to torture at her matrimonial home at Sangamner and was forced to live at her parental house at Vaijapur. Wife suffered mental agony at parental house at Vaijapur on account of her estrangement. Therefore the High Court held that Courts at Sangamner as well as at Vaijapur have territorial jurisdiction to try the case; *Jairam M. Kahane* v. *State of Maharashtra,* 2006 All MR (Cri) 2466.

Where offence is committed by an Indian citizen outside India and if such a person is found anywhere in India, the offence can be inquired into and tried by any Court that may be approached by the victim as the legal fiction makes the place at which the offender may be found, to be a place of commission of offence; *Om Hemrajani* v. *State of Uttar Pradesh,* 2005 (2) Mh LJ 442 (SC).

Where allegations pertain to cheating and criminal breach of trust, absence of accused in India when offence was allegedly committed, their foreign nationality and residence outside India do not exempt them from being tried under Penal Code; *Lee Kun Hee* v. *State of Uttar Pradesh,* AIR 2012 SC 1007.

It was a case of dishonour of cheque under section 138 N.I. Act, 1881, where demand notice was issued from some other place where complainant does not ordinarily reside or carry on his business. The Court held that merely because a notice is issued from such a place, it would not give jurisdiction to the Court at the said place to entertain the complaint; *Hemlata R. Pendharkar* v. *Jaswantsingh R. Sonawane,* 2010 All MR (Cri) 3201.

Where doubt arises as to the jurisdiction of two or more courts who have taken cognizance of the same offence and where a question arises as to which of them ought to inquire into or try that offence, the question shall be decided by the High Court. (Section 186, Cr.P.C.).

In this case, explosives were supplied with forged documentation whereas it was allegedly supplied for terrorist activities at another place. The accused applied for discontinuation of similar proceedings at different Court. The Apex Court held that discontinuation of proceedings at other Courts cannot be ordered as nature and manner of offences are not identical. The Apex Court observed that section 186, Cr.P.C. is based on principle of convenience and expediency. To invoke the provisions of section 186, Cr.P.C., offences should be one and same in all cases. The Court further clarified that same offence means acts and omission constituting the offence should be one and same; *State of Rajasthan* v. *Bhagwan Das Agrawal,* 2014 ALL SCR 274.

In this case, offence was committed by a person in Pakistan. Thereafter, he migrated to India and acquired domicile. Question arose as to whether said person can be tried for that offence by a criminal Court in India. The Constitution Bench of Apex Court held that he cannot be tried for that offence by a criminal court in India as he was not a citizen of India at the time of the commission of the offence; *Central Bank of India* v. *Ram Narain*, (1955) SCR 697.

Where the Magistrate returned complaint holding that he has no pecuniary jurisdiction to try the case, the High Court set aside the order of Magistrate and held that no pecuniary jurisdiction is prescribed for the Magistrate Court; *The Catholic Syrian Bank* v. *A. Suguna Saraswathi*, 2007 (4) CRJ 216 (Mad).

CHAPTER XVII

CHARGESHEET

Chargesheet is the report which is submitted under section 170, Cr.P.C. by police indicating that it has found sufficient material in support of complaint, while final report is a report submitted under section 169, Cr.P.C. by police indicating that either it has not found sufficient materials in support of accusations made or the accusation as made is found false; *Atul Chandra Buragohain* v. *State of Assam,* 2007 (4) CRJ 141 (Gau).

Every investigation under Chapter XII of Cr.P.C. shall be completed without unnecessary delay [section 173(1)] and the investigation in relation to rape of a child may be completed within three months from the date on which the information was recorded by the officer-in-charge of the police station. [Section 173(1A)].

After completion of the investigation, while making report to the Magistrate under section 173, the requisite details have to be submitted by the officer-in-charge of the police station without any kind of interference or direction of a Magistrate and this will include a report regarding the fact whether any offence appears to have been committed and if so, by whom, as provided by clause (d) of sub-section 2(i) of section 173; *Union of India* v. *Prakash P. Hinduja,* AIR 2003 SC 2612: 2003 (3) Crimes 142 (SC): 2003(6) SCC 195.

A report under section 173 is an intimation to the Court about the completion of the investigation and mere fact that some document is not produced before the Court or the accused is not produced along with the charge-sheet or the copies submitted are not legible or any other reason like this, would be hardly a justification for refusing to accept the chargesheet; *Balaji V. Suwarnkar* v. *State of Maharashtra,* 1992 (1) Mh LJ 159: 1993 Bom Cr C 36.

In this case police filed closure report under section 169, Cr.P.C.. However Magistrate directed police to submit chargesheet under section 173(2) of Cr.P.C. While setting aside the order of the Magistrate, the Apex Court held that the order of the Magistrate is invalid as Magistrate straightway directed submission of chargesheet without conducting independent enquiry himself; *Wasanty Dubey* v. *State of Madhya Pradesh,* (2012) 2 SCC 731.

It has been held by the Apex Court that investigating agency is not precluded from further investigation in spite of forwarding report under section 173(2) on previous occasion; *Bank of Rajasthan* v. *Keshav Bangur,* AIR 2008 SC 202.

Investigation officer is entitled to file supplementary chargesheet. However obtaining further evidence after further investigation subsequent to first chargesheet is condition precedent for filing supplementary charge-sheet; *Yamuna Pathak* v. *State of Bihar,* 1994 Cri LJ (NOC) 112 (Pat).

Even the Orissa High Court has held that supplementary chargesheet cannot be submitted without making further investigation and without obtaining further evidence oral or documentary in respect of an offence; *Kunjalata Dei* v. *State of Orissa,* 1985 Cri LJ 1047.

If no offence is made out, investigation officer has jurisdiction to submit a final report under section 169, Cr.P.C.; *Moreshwar Savey* v. *State of Uttar Pradesh,* 2001 (2) B Cr C 116.

The Bombay Police Manual classifies the orders which may be requested by the investigation officer when he is of the opinion that no judicial proceeding need be initiated, as Summaries "A", "B", and "C". A request for "A" Summary is to be made when the police officer investigating the case is of the view that the offence is true but undetected and where there is no clue whatever about the culprits or property or where the accused is known but there is no evidence to justify his being sent up for trial. Request for "B" Summary is to be made when the complaint is maliciously false and for "C" Summary when the complaint is neither true nor false, that is, due to mistake of facts of being of a civil nature. Commissioner of Police or an officer duly nominated by him has no jurisdiction to grant summaries. Issuance of summaries A, B, C being a judicial function, same has to be performed exclusively by the Magistrate. However aggrieved party can challenge the order of Court by filing either a revision application under the Code or writ petition under Article 226 or 227 of the Constitution of India; *Shravan Baburao Dinkar* v. *N.B. Hirve,* 1997 (1) Mh LJ 412 (DB) (Bom).

In this case, the Apex Court held that investigation officer is required to produce all the relevant documents at the time of submitting the chargesheet as provided in section 173(5), Cr.P.C. At the same time, as there is no specific prohibition, it cannot be held that additional documents cannot be produced subsequently. If some mistake is committed in not producing the relevant documents at the time of submitting the report or the chargesheet, it is always open to the investigating officer to produce the same with the permission of the Court. The word "shall" used in sub-section (5) cannot be interpreted as mandatory; *C.B.I.* v. *R.S. Pai,* (2002) 5 SCC 82.

Other Cases

Ghanashyam Jena v. *State of Orissa,* 2003 Cri LJ 4794: It is always desirable that prior permission of the Magistrate is taken before a case is re-opened or re-investigated.

Mool Chand v. *State of Rajasthan,* 2009 Cri LJ 3158: The investigating agency is expected to inform the Court concerned for further investigation so as to express their regard and respect for it, before whom the challan has already been filed.

Mrs. Rameeja v. *State,* (2004) 4 Crimes 217 (Mad): Before conducting further investigation, the investigation officer must formally apply to the Magistrate/ Special Judge and get his permission.

Augustine v. *State of Kerala,* 1982 Cri LJ 1557 (FB): It is not incumbent upon the investigation officer to file chargesheet in both the cases *i.e.,* cross-cases.

Valummel Thommachan v. *State of Kerala,* 1994 Cri LJ 1738: Where during investigation, injuries were found on the person of the accused, and those injuries were received while exercising the right of private defence, filing of final report instead of chargesheet is proper.

Manilal Keshri v. *State of Bihar,* 2006 Cri LJ 3981 (Pata): Submission of chargesheet on the basis of stale material cannot be justified.

CHAPTER XVIII

COGNIZANCE AND BAR TO COGNIZANCE

SYNOPSIS

(i) Bar to cognizance (Section 195 Cr.P.C.)

(ii) Bar to taking cognizance of certain offences (Section 196 Cr.P.C.)

(iii) Prohibition to taking cognizance of offences [Section 197, Cr.P.C.]

(iv) Bar to take cognizance after lapse of the period of limitation

Section 190 of the Code deals with cognizance of offences by Magistrates. However the term 'cognizance' has not been defined in the Code of Criminal Procedure, 1973.

The Apex Court has held that the term "cognizance" though not statutorily defined, yet judicial pronouncements give it a definite meaning and connotation. Cognizance broadly means taking judicial notice by competent Court of a cause or matter presented before it so as to decide whether there is basis for initiating proceedings for judicial determination; *Subramanyam Swamy* v. *Manmohan Singh,* (2012) 3 SCC 64.

The word "cognizance" has no esoteric or mystic significance in criminal law or procedure. It merely means – become aware of and when used with reference to a Court or Judge, to take notice of judicially; *Ajit Kumar Palit* v. *State of West Bengal,* (1963) SUPP 1 SCR 953.

The expression "Cognizance" has not been defined in the Code. But the word (cognizance) is of definite import. It has no esoteric or mystic significance in criminal law. It merely means "become aware of" and when used with reference to a Court or a Judge, it connotes to take notice of judicially. It indicates the point when a Court or a Magistrate takes judicial notice of an offence with a view to initiating proceedings in respect of such offence said to have been committed by someone. ..... "Taking cognizance" does not involve any formal action of any kind. It occurs as soon as a Magistrate applies his mind to the suspected commission of an offence. Cognizance is taken prior to commencement of criminal proceedings. Taking of cognizance is thus, a sine qua non or condition precedent for holding a valid trial. Cognizance is taken of an offence and not of an offender. Whether or not a Magistrate has taken cognizance of an offence depends on the facts and circumstances of each case and no rule of universal application can be laid down as to when a Magistrate can be said to have taken cognizance; *S.K. Sinha* v. *Videocon International Ltd.,* (2008) 2 SCC 492: 2008 All SCR 517.

[**Note:**—*This case has been followed by the Apex Court in; Dr. Mrs. Nupur Talwar* v. *C.B.I., Delhi,* 2012 All MR (Cri) 729 (SC)].

The word "may" in section 190 Cr.P.C. cannot be construed as "must" and therefore Magistrate is not bound to take cognizance of each and every case. ..... When a Magistrate applies his mind not for the purpose of proceeding under the various sections of Chapter XVI of the Code but for taking action of some other kind, e.g., ordering investigation under section 156(3) or issuing a search warrant for the purpose of investigation, he cannot be said to have taken cognizance of any offence; *Gopal Das Sindhi* v. *State of Assam,* AIR 1961 SC 986.

In this case the Court held that when Magistrate applies mind to decide the course of action to be followed that does not mean that he has taken cognizance. Cognizance can be said to be taken only when Magistrate proceeds to record verification statement of the complainant. ..... If the complainant is not examined, no cognizance is said to be taken at all; *Manish M. Mate* v. *State of Maharashtra,* 2008 (1) Mh LJ 130.

Stage of issuing directions to carry out investigation under section 156(3) is a pre-cognizance stage. It can be said that the Court has taken cognizance of the complaint only when process is issued against the accused; *Syed M.K.M.A. Qayyum* v. *Mohd. Abdul Q.M.A. Mobood,* 2012 All MR (Cri) 1091.

Before it can be said that a Magistrate has taken cognizance of an offence under section 190(1)(a) of Cr.P.C, he must not only have applied his mind to the contents of the petition but have done so for the purpose of proceeding under section 200 and the subsequent provisions of the Code. Where he applied his mind only for ordering investigation or issuing a warrant for purpose of investigation he cannot be said to have taken cognizance of the offence; *R.R. Chari* v. *State of U.P.,* (1951) SCR 312.

In this case, the Apex Court held that cognizance of offence on complaint is taken for the purpose of issuing process to accused. However, Magistrate should not act as post office in taking cognizance of each and every complaint filed before him and issue process as a matter of course. Though no formal order or a speaking order is required to be passed at the stage of sections 190/204 Cr.P.C., there must be sufficient indication on application of mind by Magistrate to facts constituting commission of offence and statements recorded u/s 200 Cr.P.C. so as to proceed against offender; *Mehmood Ul Rehman* v. *Khazir Mohammad Tunda,* 2015 All SCR 2242.

In this case, the Apex Court held that cognizance of offence relates to application of judicial mind by Magistrate in connection with the commission of offence. When complainant is examined, Magistrate cannot be said to have *ipso facto* taken cognizance; *S.R. Sukumar* v. *S. Sunaad Raghuram,* 2015 All MR (Cri) 2898 (SC).

This case relates to corruption in allocation of additional spectrum in conspiracy with the public servant. The Appellants – Directors of the company were summoned by the trial Court though they were not named in the chargesheet. The appellants challenged the order of summoning. The Hon'ble Apex Court set aside the order of summoning and held that application of mind by Magistrate and his satisfaction that allegation, if proved, would constitute an offence, is sine qua non for taking cognizance. Cognizance of offence and prosecution of an offender are two different things. The Court further held that Appellants/Directors cannot be implicated as accused persons in chargesheet and they cannot be summoned treating them as "*alter ego*" of their respective Companies. Though criminal intent of persons controlling affairs of company can be imputed to Company, principle of *alter-ego* cannot be applied *vice-versa* where Company is accused; *Sunil Bharti Mittal* v. *C.B.I.*, 2015 All MR (Cri) 812 (SC).

Other Cases

State of Maharashtra v. *Sharadchandra V. Dongre*, AIR 1995 SC 231: 1994 AIR SCW 4301: 1995 (1) SCC 42: 1995 (1) Mh LJ 432: Magistrate alone has jurisdiction to decide if materials placed by prosecution u/s 173(2) of Cr.P.C. is sufficient to take cognizance of offence or not. Such power cannot be controlled by the investigating agency. While condoning delay in launching prosecution, notice to accused and recording of reasons is necessary.

Trisuns Chemical India Ltd. v. *Rajesh Agrawal*, AIR 1999 SC 3499: 1999 Cr LJ 4325: 1999 AIR SCW 3492: 1999 (8) SCC 686: It is an erroneous view that the Magistrate taking cognizance of an offence u/s 190 of Cr.P.C. must necessarily have territorial jurisdiction to try case as well.

Kishore Kumar v. *G.D. Mahrotra*, 2002 AIR SCW 12: 2001 (4) Supreme 584: 2001 (3) Crimes 205: AIR 2002 SC 483: Power of Magistrate to take cognizance in cases instituted otherwise than on police report is not lost merely because Magistrate has accepted final form submitted by police investigating the incident in question on the basis of F.I.R."

M/s Swill Ltd. v. *State of Delhi*, AIR 2001 SC 2747: 2001 Cr LJ 4173: 2001 AIR SCW 3017: 2001 (6) SCC 970: The Court can summon the person not joined as accused in chargesheet at the stage of taking cognizance u/s 190 of Cr.P.C. At this stage, Magistrate can ascertain from statement of witnesses examined by investigating officer as to who the offenders really are.

Bharat Damodhar Kale v. *State of A.P.*, 2003 All MR (Cri) 2681 (SC): 2003 Cr LJ 4543: AIR 2003 SC 4560: 2003 AIR SCW 5333: Limitation period prescribed in chapter 36 of the Code (Sections 469, 471) is only for the filing of the complaint or initiation of prosecution and not for taking cognizance. Maxim *'actus curiae neminem gravabit'* which means an act of the Court shall prejudice no man also supports the view that limitation is not prescribed for taking cognizance.

Bhiku Yeshwant Dhangat v. *Baban Maroti Barate*, 2001 Cr LJ 295: 2000 (4) Mh LJ 861: Taking cognizance of the complaint without there being any disclosure as to the witnesses whom the complainant would be examining, is improper. However it is sufficient if the complainant incorporates the names of the witnesses in the complaint itself instead of giving a separate list.

A.R. Antulay v. *Ramdas S. Nayak*, AIR 1984 SC 718: 1984 Cr LJ 647: 1984 (2) SCC 500: (1984) 2 SCR 914: It is well recognised principle of criminal jurisprudence that anyone can set or put the criminal law into motion except where the statute indicates to the contrary. *Locus standi* of the complainant is a concept foreign to criminal jurisprudence. A private complaint filed in the respect of the offences committed by public servants as enumerated in Section 6(1)

& (b) of the Criminal Law (Amendment) Act, 1952 can be entertained by the special Judge and taken cognizance of. The same is perfectly legal.

Vidyadharan v. *State of Kerala,* AIR 2004 SC 536: 2004 Cr LJ 605: 2003 AIR SCW 6511: 2003 (9) SCALE 581: Cognizance of offence under the SC & ST (Prevention of Atrocities) Act, 1989 cannot be taken directly by Special Court/ Sessions Courts without case being committed to it by Magistrate.

Nandkishore Choube v. *State of Maharashtra,* 2000 (2) Mh LJ 770: Magistrate cannot take cognizance of the offence under the SC & ST (Prevention of Atrocities) Act, 1989. Private complaint presented before Magistrate must be returned to complainant to present it before Special Court.

Ashok Gyanchand Vohra v. *State of Maharashtra,* 2006 Cr LJ 1270: 2006 (1) AIR Bom R 855: Special Court constituted to try the offences under MCOCA (30 of 1991)has power to order investigation u/s 156(3) of Cr.P.C. on receipt of private complaint. Sanction u/s 23(2) of MCOCA is not sine-qua-non for taking cognizance of private complaint.

Gangula Ashok v. *State of A.P.,* AIR 2000 SC 740: 2000 Cr LJ 819: 2000 AIR SCW 279: 2000 (2) SCC 504: A complaint or a chargesheet cannot straightway be laid before the Special Court under the SC & ST (Prevention of Atrocities) Act, 1989. Special Court can take cognizance only if the case has been committed to it by a Magistrate as provided in the Code.

Kishor Kumar v. *G.D. Mehrotra,* AIR 2002 SC 483: 2002 AIR SCW 12: 2001 (4) Supreme 584: 2001 (3) Crimes 205: In a complaint case power of Magistrate to take cognizance is not lost merely because Magistrate has accepted final form submitted by Police investigating the incident in question on the basis of FIR.

Aggarwal, A.C., Sub-Divisional Magistrate, Delhi v. *Mst. Ram Kali,* 1967 (2) SCA 621: AIR 1968 SC 1: 1968 Cr LJ 82: (1968) 1 SCR 205: The words "may take cognizance" in the context of section 190(1)(b) of Cr.P.C. means "must take cognizance". Magistrate has no discretion in the matter, otherwise that section will be violative of Article 14 of The Constitution of India.

Ram Lal Narang v. *State (Delhi Administration),* AIR 1979 SC 1791: 1979 Cr LJ 1346: (1979) 2 SCR 923: Further investigation by police is not barred even if cognizance of offence is taken by a Magistrate.

Gopal Das Sindhi v. *State of Assam,* AIR 1961 SC 986: 1961 (2) Cr LJ 39: 1961 (1) SCJ 573: (1961) 1 SCR 573: When a Magistrate applies his mind not for the purpose of proceeding under the various sections of Chapter XVI of Cr.P.C. but for taking action of some kind, e.g., ordering investigation under section 156(3) or issuing a search warrant for the purpose of investigation, he cannot be said to have taken cognizance of any offence.

Narayandas Bhagwandas v. *State of West Bengal,* 1959 Cr LJ 1368: AIR 1959 SC 1118: (1960) 1 SCR 93: It is only when a Magistrate applies his mind for the purpose of proceeding under section 200 of Cr.P.C. and subsequent sections of Chapter XVI or under Section 204 of Chapter XVII of the Code that it can be positively stated that he had applied his mind and therefore had taken cognizance.

H.N. Rishbud & Inder Singh v. *The State of Delhi,* (1955) 1 SCR 1150: AIR 1955 SC 196: 1955 Cr LJ 526: If cognizance is in fact taken on a police report in breach of a mandatory provision relating to investigation, the results which follow cannot be set aside unless the illegality in the investigation can be shown to have brought about a miscarriage of justice.

(i) Bar to cognizance (Section 195 Cr.P.C.)

The Bar contained in section 195(1)(b)(ii) of the Code is not applicable to a case where forgery of the document was committed before the document was produced in a Court. Section 340(1) of the Code has an interlink with section 195(1)(b). So no complaint can be made by a Court regarding any offence falling within the ambit of section 195(1)(b) of the Code without first adopting procedural requirements of section 340(1); *Sachida Nand Singh* v. *State of Bihar,* (1998) 1 SCR 492.

The Constitution Bench of the Apex Court has held that the expression when such offence is alleged to have been committed in respect of a document produced or given in evidence in a proceeding in a Court occurring in clause (b)(ii) should normally mean commission of such an offence after the document has actually been produced or given in evidence in the Court. Section 195(1) mandates a complaint in writing of the Court for taking cognizance of the offences enumerated in clauses (b)(i) and (b)(ii) thereof; *Iqbal Singh Marwah* v. *Meenakshi Marwah,* 2005 (2) Crimes 11 (SC).

In this case question arose as to whether section 195 and 340 of the Code affect the power of the police to investigate into a cognizable offence. Answering the question in negative the Court held that from a plain reading of section 195 Cr.P.C. it is manifest that it comes into operation at the stage when the Court intends to take cognizance of an offence u/s 190(1) Cr.P.C., and it has nothing to do with the statutory power of the police to investigate into an FIR, in accordance with Chapter XII of the Code even if the offence is alleged to have been committed in, or in relation to, any proceedings in Court. In other words, the statutory power of the police to investigate under the Code is not in any way controlled or circumscribed by section 195 Cr.P.C. It is of course true that upon the chargesheet (challan), if any, filed on completion of the investigation into such an offence the Court would not be competent to take cognizance thereof in view of the embargo of section 195(1)(b) Cr.P.C., but nothing therein deters the Court from filing a complaint for the offence on the basis of the FIR (filed by the aggrieved private party) and the materials collected during investigation, provided it forms the requisite opinion and follows the procedure laid down in section 340 Cr.P.C.; *State of Punjab* v. *Raj Singh,* (1998) 2 SCC 391.

(ii) Bar to taking cognizance of certain offences (Section 196 Cr.P.C.)

There is bar to taking cognizance by court of any offence punishable under Chapter VI or under section 153A, section 295A or sub-section (1) of section 505 of IPC or a criminal conspiracy to commit such offence, or any such abetment, as is described in section 108 A of IPC, without the previous sanction of the Central Government or of the State Government.

Further, Court cannot take cognizance of any offence punishable under section 153B or sub-section (2) or sub-section (3) of section 505 of IPC, or a criminal conspiracy to commit such offence, without the previous sanction of the Central Government or of the State Government or of the District Magistrate.

Specific provisions have been made in Statues like The Unlawful Activities (Prevention) Act, 1967 where Court cannot take cognizance of any offence specified therein without the previous sanction of the Central Government or the State Government.

It has been held by the Apex Court that when the power is conferred on a particular authority, that authority alone must exercise power to accord sanction for prosecution; *State* v. *Gordhandas Bhanji,* AIR 1952 SC 16: 1952 SCR 135.

Where cognizance of offence u/s 466 r/w section 120B, IPC was taken without the sanction of the Government, the Apex Court held that cognizance taken is without jurisdiction; *S.L. Goswami* v. *High Court of M.P. at Jabalpur,* (1979) 2 SCR 385.

(iii) Prohibition to taking cognizance of offences [Section 197, Cr.P.C.]

The words *"any offence alleged to have been committed by him while acting or purporating to act in the discharge of his official duty"* in section 197(1) are capable of a narrow as well as wide interpretation. If these words are construed too narrowly, the section will be rendered altogether sterile, for it is no part of an official duty to commit an offence. The Court further held that the question of sanction under section 197 can be raised and considered at any stage of proceedings; *B. Saha* v. *M.S. Kochar,* (1980) 1 SCR 111.

In 2G Spectrum Case the Apex Court delivered landmark judgement. The Court refused to hold that question of granting sanction for prosecution arises only at the stage of cognizance and not before that. The Court held that grant or refusal of sanction for prosecution is not a quasi-judicial function and person for whose prosecution sanction is sought is not required to be heard by competent authority. The Court further granted 3 months time for sanctioning authority to decide the question of sanction and held that if decision is not taken within time limits, sanction should be deemed to have been granted; *Dr. Subramanian Swamy* v. *Dr. Manmohan Singh,* 2012 All SCR 273.

While dealing with a case under Prevention of Corruption Act, 1988, the Apex Court held that even if a public servant ceased to be so he is liable to be prosecuted under the Act. However, Court can take cognizance of offence even without sanction if he ceased to be a public servant; *Kalicharan Mahapatra* v. *State of Orissa,* (1998) 3 SCR 961.

In this case also, the Apex Court held that protection u/s 197 is not available if offender ceased to be a public servant on the day of taking of cognizance; *Raghunath A. Govilkar* v. *State of Maharashra,* 2008 (1) BCrC 565 (SC).

Where sanction was refused by government when public servant was in service, the Court held that he cannot be prosecuted later after his retirement; *Chittaranjan Das* v. *State of Orissa,* 2011 All SCR 1639.

In this case, the Apex Court held that sanction to prosecute is not necessary if accused public servant is holding different office than the one held at the time of cognizance; *Abhay Singh Chautala* v. *C.B.I.,* 2011 All SCR 1848.

In this case the Apex Court held that the protection by way of sanction under section 197 is not applicable to the officers of Government companies or the public undertakings even when such public undertaking are "State" within the meaning of Article 12 of the Constitution of India on account of deep and pervasive control of the Government. *Mohd. Hadi Raja* v. *State of Bihar,* (1998) 3 SCR 22.

Where investigation officer went to the house of complainant and threatened her husband to make a tutored statement and tried to obtain his signature on a blank paper, the Court held that for such excess or misuse of authority, no protection can be claimed by the public servant concerned; *Choudhury Parveen Sultana* v. *State of West Bengal,* 2009 All MR (Cri) 504 (SC).

While denying protection u/s 161 of Bombay Police Act and section 197(2) of Cr.P.C., the Court held that act of giving third degree treatment to person in police custody is not an act done in discharge or purported discharge of duty; *Kashinath L. Marwalikar* v. *State of Maharashtra,* 2002 All MR (Cri) 1791.

Where a public servant allegedly committed offence punishable under sections 409, 420, 467, 471, IPC, the Court held that section 197 is not attracted as these offences can by no stretch of imagination by their very nature be regarded as having been committed by a public servant while acting or purporting to act in discharge of official duty; *Bholu Ram* v. *State of Punjab,* 2008 All MR (Cri) 3557 (SC): 2008 (4) Crimes 260 (SC).

In this case, complaint u/s 409, 420, IPC was dismissed by the trial Court holding that sanction to prosecution has not been obtained. While restoring the complaint, the Apex Court held that it is not the official duty of the public servant to fabricate false record and misappropriate public funds in furtherance or in discharge of his official duties. Discharge of official duty is not integrally connected nor is it inseparably interlinked with the crime committed in the course of same transaction; *Sambhoo Nath Misra* v. *State of U.P.,* (1997) 2 SCR 1139.

Where police officer made statement of a witness the part of record though said witness never gave any statement, the Court held that sanction to prosecute is not necessary as preparation of false record of investigation cannot be a part of his official duty; *Nandkumar S. Kale* v. *Bhaurao C. Tidke,* 2007 (5) AIR Bom R 547.

In this case, the Apex Court held that, it is for the accused to produce relevant material to show whether necessary ingredients to attract section 197 are present or not as the matter relates to the jurisdiction of the Court to take cognizance and accused is not required to wait till the stage under section 246(4), Cr.P.C. is reached; *Suresh Kumar Bhikamchand Jain* v. *Pandey Ajay Bhushan,* 1998 Cr LJ 1242 (SC): 1998 (2) BCrC 285 (SC).

(iv) Bar to take cognizance after lapse of the period of limitation

Sections 468 to 473 of the Code deal with this aspect of procedure.

Where complaint was filed after 8 years, the Court held the same to be barred by limitation. The Court held that cognizance of an offence u/s 403, 406 I.PC. for criminal breach of trust cannot be taken as the offence is not continuing offence; *Sesa Goa Ltd.* v. *State of Maharasthra,* 2009 (4) AIR Bom R 18.

The Apex Court has held that section 473 Cr.P.C. provides that any Court may take cognizance of an offence after the expiry of the period of limitation, if it is satisfied that the delay has been properly explained or it is necessary to do so in the interest of justice; *Srinivasa Gopal* v. *Union Territory of Arunachal Pradesh,* (1988) SUPP 1 SCR 477.

CHAPTER XIX

CHARGE, DISCHARGE AND FRAMING OF CHARGE

It is observed that serious attention is not paid by the advocates to this stage, though this is very important from the point of defence. Instead of facing the protracted trial, the accused can be given relief under these provisions if his lawyer is vigilant and diligent. Therefore certain cases are given under this chapter which would help the trial Court advocates in giving relief to their clients.

The provisions regarding charge, discharge and framing of charge are given below:—

(i) **Chapter XVIII of Cr. P.C.** – Trial before a Court of Session – Section 226 – Opening case for prosecution

Section 227 – Discharge

Section 228 – Framing of charge

(ii) **Chapter XIX of Cr.P.C.** – Trial of warrant cases by Magistrate – (A) Cases instituted on a police report—

Section 239 – When accused shall be discharged

Section 240 – Framing of charge

(iii) Chapter XIX of Cr.P.C. – Cases instituted otherwise than on police report – (Complaint Cases)

Section 245 – When accused shall be discharged

Section 249 – Absence of Complainant

(iv) Chapter XX of Cr.P.C. – Trial of summons cases by Magistrate – Section 256 – Non-appearance or death of Complainant

Section 258 – Power to stop proceeding in certain cases

The correct interpretation of Section 227 of Cr.P.C. has been done by the Apex Court in *Union of India* v. *Prafulla Kumar Samal,* (1979) 2 SCR 229. The Apex Court held that, *"the considerations governing the interpretation of section 227 of Cr.P.C. apply mutatis mutandis to the proceedings under the Prevention of Corruption Act, after the chargesheet is submitted before the Special Judge. At the stage of section 227, the Judge has merely to sift the evidence in order to find out whether or not, there is sufficient ground for proceeding against the accused. ..... The sufficiency of ground would take within its fold, the nature of the evidence recorded by the police, or the documents produced before the Court, which ex-facie disclose that there are suspicious circumstances against the accused so as to frame a charge against him."*

In *Dilawar* v. *State of Maharashtra,* AIR 2002 SC 564, the Apex Court has propounded the law as regards discharge under section 227 of Cr.P.C. as under *"In exercising power under section 227 of Cr.P.C., the Court has power to sift and weigh the evidence for the limited purpose of finding out whether or not a prima facie case against the accused has been made out. ..... If two views are equally possible and the judge is satisfied that the evidence produced before him while giving rise to some suspicion but not grave suspicion against the accused, he will be fully justified to discharge the accused. ...... In exercising jurisdiction under section 227 of Cr.P.C., the judge cannot act merely as a post office or mouthpiece of the prosecution but has to consider the broad probabilities of the case, the total effect of evidence and documents produced before Court but should not have made roving enquiry into the pros and cons of the matter and weighed the evidence as if he was conducting trial."*

Relying on the law laid down in *R.S. Naik* v. *A.R. Antulay,* AIR 1986 SC 2045, the Bombay High Court has observed in *Ramdas Kachru Wadkar* v. *State of Maharashtra,* 2006 (1) AIR Bom R 623, that, *"Guiding principle for discharging accused should be whether material on record is sufficient for proceeding against him. ...... Appreciation of evidence on record at this stage is unnecessary and statements made should be accepted as they are."*

Where the accused was neither named in F.I.R. nor named by witnesses nor any property was recovered from his possession, he was discharged by the Court holding that it is a case of no evidence. Plea of the prosecution that his name was taken by co-accused was negatived by the Court holding that this fact cannot be legally proved in view of sections 25 & 26 of the Evidence Act. *Anant Kumar* v. *State of M.P.,* 1993, Cr LJ 1499 (MP).

The Bombay High Court in *Shri Vasant Waman Pradhan* v. *Dattatraya Vitthal Salvi,* 2003 All MR (Cri) 2523, has directed the Magistrates to wipe out cases/ litigations which are not fit to be continued by taking courageous bold steps *suo motu.* The Court further observed that the Magistrates and Judges should not feel any hesitation in adjudication whenever called on by the litigants, being specially moved by the applications at various stages.

In *Nandkishor R. Lohiya* v. *State of Maharashtra,* 2000 (4) Mh LJ 616, the Bombay High Court has held that, *"the accused can claim discharge when there is no ground to sustain charge. But he must exhaust this remedy of discharge before the stage of framing charge and not thereafter. .... After framing charge under section 228 and after recording plea of accused, procedure in Section 229 to 235 is to be followed. ..... There is no procedure for dropping charge under section 216 of Cr.P.C."*

This is a case known as "Bombay Blast Case" *State of Maharashtra* v. *Som Nath Thapa,* (1996) SUPP 1 SCR 189: where the charges were framed against the appellant for the alleged offence of criminal conspiracy. Appellant Abu Asim Azmi was charged with booking air tickets for accused to facilitate their weapon training in Pakistan out of his own funds thus, abetting terrorist act whereas appellant Amjad Aziz Meharbaksh was charged to have asked accused to remove jeep with arms and ammunations in his compound. The appellants challenged the order of TADA Court framing charge against them. While allowing the appeals of Abu Asim Azmi & Amjad Aziz Meharbaksh, the Apex Court has held that, *"If on the basis of materials on record, a Court could come to the conclusion that commission of the offence is a probable consequence, case for framing of charge exists. To put it differently, if the Court were to think that the accused might have committed the offence it can frame the charge, though for conviction the conclusion is required to be that the accused has committed the offence. It is apparent that at the stage of framing of charge, probative value of the materials on record cannnot be gone into; the materials brought on record by the prosecution has to be accepted as true at that stage."*

In *State of Maharashtra* v. *Salman Salim Khan*, 2004 All MR (Cri) 600 (SC), the Apex Court while deprecating the practice of intervention by the superior Courts at this stage, has held that, *"Alteration of charge or framing of a proper charge should best be left to be decided by trial Court at an appropriate stage of the trial."*

In *Prabhakar s/o Krushnaji Deshmukh* v. *Subhash Jasraj Karnawat*, 2004 All MR (Cri) 710, while dealing with the power of Magistrate under section 240 & 245 of Cr.P.C., the Court held that, *"Magistrate has power not to frame charge and discharge the accused for reasons to be recorded. The yardsticks, however, in the cases which are instituted on police report and which are instituted otherwise than on police report are different. Before discharging the accused in a police case the Magistrate has to come to the conclusion on the basis of material and documents that the charge against the accused is groundless. Thus, if there is prima facie case, the charge will have to be framed and the person must be tried. .... In the cases which are instituted otherwise than on police report, the Magistrate is expected to examine the evidence adduced by the complainant. The evidence should be such which, if unrebutted, would result in conviction. In other words, it is not sufficient at this stage in such cases that there is a prima facie case against the accused."*

In *Dinesh Ramsanehi Yadav* v. *State of Maharashtra*, 1998 All MR (Cri) 1330, the Bombay High Court set aside the order of the Special Judge of framing charge under section 3(1)(iv)(v) of SC & ST (Prevention of Atrocities) Act, (1989). The facts of the case were that the complainant belonging to SC & ST community alleged that the accused encroached on land belonging to them. Title of land was claimed by both the parties. The Special Judge framed charge of encroachment without identifying such land. The Bombay High Court held that, "The Special Court committed serious error in not examining title-deeds adduced before framing charge."

In *Kaimala Bhargavi Amma* v. *Kundumadathi R. Nair*, AIR 1979 (NOC) 177 (Ker), the Full Bench of the Kerala High Court while pointing out the duty of Magistrate in committal of a case exclusively triable by the Court of Sessions held that, *"Magistrate can dismiss the complaint not making out any case prima facie. ...... The Magistrate cannot hold preliminary enquiry preparatory to committal."*

In *Luis* v. *Mahadeo*, 1984 Cr LJ 513 (Goa), The Court held that, *"Section 245 of Cr.P.C. unmistakably and undoubtedly shows that even before recording the evidence referred to in Section 244 of Cr. P.C., the Magistrate can discharge the accused for reasons to be recorded."*

The Apex Court while dealing with the scope of section 249 of Cr.P.C. in *Ratilal Bhanji Mithani* v. *State*, AIR 1979 SC 94, has held that, *"If in any particular case, complainant fails to produce his witness for which he has assumed responsibility and the case is dragged due to such successive lapses on the part of the complainant, there is nothing inherently unreasonable for the Magistrates to come to the conclusion that the charge is groundless so as to discharge the accused. ...... To hold the contrary would be to grant a premium to complainant to prolong the matter to cause the harassment to the accused."*

In *A.H. Pathan* v. *Amin Textiles,* 1995 Cr LJ 1843, the Gujarat High Court has held that, *"non-appearance of the complainant is a valid ground for discharging the accused."* The same view has been taken by the Courts in *Nabaghan* v. *Brundaban,* 1987 Cr LJ 381 (Orissa); *State of M.P.* v. *Punamchand,* 1987 Cr LJ 1232 (MP).

In *Associated Cement Co. Ltd.* v. *Keshavanand,* AIR 1998 SC 596, the Apex Court while dealing with the scope of Section 256 of Cr.P.C. held that, *"...... If the situation does not justify the case being adjourned to another date, the Court is free to dismiss the complaint and acquit the accused. But if the presence of the complainant on that day was quite unnecessary then resorting to the step of axing down the complaint may not be a proper exercise of the power envisaged in the Section. ..... The discretion must, therefore, be exercised judicially and fairly without impairing the cause of administration of criminal justice."*

While dealing with the ambit of section 167(5) of Cr.P.C., the Apex Court in *Nirmal Kanti Roy* v. *State of West Bengal,* 1998 All MR (Cri) 1295, has held that, *"time schedule provided under section 167 (5) of Cr.P.C. is not rigid.......... It is not mandatory to discharge accused on expiry of such time schedule."*

In *Dinesh Dutt Joshi* v. *State of Rajasthan,* 2001 All MR (Cri) 2401, the Apex Court has held that, *"while exercising inherent powers under section 482 of Cr.P.C. for setting aside discharge order passed by the trial Court, person likely to be affected by proposed order must be served with a show-cause notice against proposed order."*

Where accused – husband was charged only under section 304B of I.P.C., his conviction under section 300 read with 109 of I.P.C. was set aside by the Apex Court holding that abetment is a substantive offence and failure to frame charge under section 109 of I.P.C. caused prejudiced to the accused; *Sohan Lal alias Sohan Singh* v. *State of Punjab,* AIR 2003 SC 4466.

Where the charged was altered but it was not read and explained to accused, the Apex Court held that requirement of section 216(2) is not fulfilled; *Sabbi Mallesu* v. *State of A.P.,* AIR 2006 SC 2747: 2006 (3) Crimes 146 (SC).

In this case, the Court deprecated the practice of directly framing charges against accused without hearing accused. The Court held that framing of charge without hearing accused is not permissible. Compliance of provisions of sections 226, 227 Cr.P.C. is not an empty formality. The Court directed that the judgment of this case be circulated to all Sessions Judges; *Ambadas Kashirao Kharad* v. *State of Maharashtra,* 2007 (5) ABR (NOC) 701 (Bom): 2007 All MR (Cri) 1916: 2007 (1) Bom CR (Cri) 881.

Even the Karnataka High Court has held that hearing parties before charge is mandatory. *State of Karnataka* v. *Abdul Rahim,* 2006 AIR Bom R (NOC) 846 (Kant).

In this case, question arose as to whether charge can be framed even though in earlier proceedings under section 482 Cr.P.C. High Court quashed the chargesheet in respect of one of the offence charged. The Apex Court held that trial Court can still frame the charge quashed, on the basis of materials available under section 216 Cr.P.C. as the order passed by the High Court under section 482 Cr.P.C. cannot be termed as final decision. The trial Court can add or alter charges according to evidence available on record; *Umesh Kumar* v. *State of A.P.*, (2013) 10 SCC 591: 2013 AIR SCW 6062: 2014 All SCR 661.

In this case, the Apex Court held that trial Court is empowered to add/alter charges at any stage before conclusion of trial. Such power can also be exercised by appellate court in exercise of its powers under sections 385(2), 386 Cr.P.C.; *Bhimanna* v. *State of Karnataka*, (2012) 9 SCC 650: AIR 2012 SC 3026: 2013 AIR SCW 498: 2014 All SCR 594.

In this case, the Apex Court directed all trial courts in India to ordinarily add section 302 IPC to a charge of section 304B, IPC so that death sentence can be imposed in heinous and barbaric crimes against women; *Rajbir @ Raju* v. *State of Haryana*, AIR 2011 SC 568: 2011 All SCR 48.

In this case, trial Court by framing additional charge under section 302 without adverting to evidence adduced in case and simply on the basis of Apex Court's direction has acted mechanically. The Apex Court remitted the matter back to trial Court for a fresh order. The Court held that directions of Apex Court in *Rajbir @ Raju* v. *State of Haryana*, reported in AIR 2011 SC 568: 2011 All SCR 48 regarding compulsory addition of charge under section 302 IPC in dowry death cases is not to be followed mechanically; *Jaswinder Saini* v. *State (Govt. of NCT of Delhi)*, 2013 All MR (Cri) 3006 (SC): AIR 2014 SC 841.

In this case, the Apex Court held that where evidence shows that the offence falls under section 302 IPC, trial Court should frame the charge under section 302 even if the police has not expressed any opinion in that regard in the report under section 173(2) Cr.P.C. Section 304B IPC can be put as an alternative charge if the trial Court feels so; *Vijay Pal Singh* v. *State of Uttarakhand*, 2015 (1) Crime 167 (SC).

In this case, while diluting the charge from section 302 IPC to section 304 IPC, the learned Judge merely stated that on consideration of case-diary no sufficient material was found frame charge under section 302 IPC. However such a statement was clearly against the evidence on record. The learned Judge did not give reasons as to why case-diary material was found insufficient. The Apex Court held that dilution of charge is serious matter and is untenable. The Apex Court raised doubt about *bonafide* of judge and held that in view of failure of judge to pass correct legal order despite possessing requisite experience and in view of his service record which was not good, selection grade was denied to the judge; *R.S. Mishra* v. *State of Orissa*, 2012 All SCR 882.

In this case, the Apex Court held that prosecution is bound to recall witnesses, examine them with regard to altered charge and allow accused to cross examine witnesses where original charge under section 306 IPC is altered to one under section 302 IPC. Even new trial can also be insisted in such cases where charge is altogether different and distinct; *R. Rachaiah* v. *Home Secretary, Bangalore*, 2016 All SCR (Cri) 916.

In this case, the Apex Court held that accused summoned under section 319 Cr.P.C. as additional accused is not entitled to relief of discharge under section 227 Cr.P.C. since it would be contrary to the scheme and intent of the Code of Criminal Procedure; *Jogendra Yadav* v. *State of Bihar*, 2015 All MR (Cri) 3707 (SC): 2015 SAR (Cri) 1027.

Add – *State of Haryana* v. *Bhajan Lal*, (1992) SUPP 1 SCC 335; *State of M.P.* v. *S.B. Johari*, (2008) 2 SCC 57; *Gunwantlal* v. *State of M.P.*, (1972) 2 SCC 194; *Sajjan* v. *C.B.I.*, 2011 All SCR 24.

Other Cases:

Sh. Satish Mehra v. *State (Delhi Administration)*, (1996) SUPP 4 SCR 197: The Apex Court held that section 228 of Cr.P.C. contemplates the stage after the case survives the stage envisaged in section 227. When the Court is of opinion that there is ground to presume that the accused has committed an offence the procedure laid down therein has to be adopted. When those two sections are put in juxtaposition with each other the test to be adopted discernible. It is axiomatic that the standard of proof normally adhered to at the final stage is not to be applied at the stage where the scope of consideration is where there is sufficient ground for proceeding.

State of M.P. v. *Sheetla Sahai*, 2009 (8) SCC 617: 2010 All SCR 980: The Apex Court held that at the time of framing charges, Court cannot confine to material supporting the prosecution and ignore the material favouring accused. .... Charges can be framed where two views are possible. But where only one view is possible, accused should not be put to trial considering his right to fair inquiry and trial under Article 21 of the Constitution of India.

P. Vijayan v. *State of Kerala*, AIR 2010 SC 663: The Apex Court held that Court is empowered to discharge accused if two views are possible and one of them gives rise to suspicion only, as distinguished from grave suspicion. Whether trial will end in conviction or acquittal is not relevant at this stage. ..... Words "not sufficient ground for proceeding against the accused" clearly show that Judge is not a mere post office to frame the charge at the behest of prosecution. But has to exercise his judicial mind to facts of case in order to determine whether a case for trial has been made out by prosecution.

Govind S. Ubhe v. *State of Maharashtra*, 2009 All MR (Cri) 1903: Where application for discharge is made, the Court can consider basic infirmities and broad probabilities but Court cannot make roving enquiry into pros and cons and weigh evidence as if it is conducting a trial.

Shilchandra R. Ingle v. *State of Maharashtra*, 2009 (4) BCrC 341: The Court held that normally framing of additional charge would be permissible if such request is made by prosecutor. Exercise of such power that too without affording an opportunity of hearing to accused is illegal.

Rukmini Narvekar v. *Vijaya Satardekar*, 2008 (14) SCC 1: AIR 2009 SC 1013: 2009 Cr LJ 822 (SC): The Apex Court held that defence is entitled to place materials before Court at the time of framing of charge only in some of the rare and exceptional cases and the material so placed should convincingly establish that the whole prosecution version is totally absurd, preposterous and concocted.

State of Maharashtra v. *Priya Sharan Maharaj,* (1997) 2 SCR 933: At the time of framing of charge, Court can sift evidence on record only for the limited purpose of finding out whether a *prima facie* case is made out against the accused.

State of Bihar v. *Ramesh Singh,* (1978) 1 SCR 257: In this case, the Apex Court has given tests for discharging an accused. The Court held that reading the two provisions together in juxtaposition at the initial stage of the trial, the truth, veracity and effect of the evidence which the prosecutor proposes to adduce are not to be meticulously judged. Nor is any weight to be attached to the probable defence of the accused. .... The standard of test and judgement which is to be finally applied before recording a finding regarding the guilt or otherwise of accused, is not exactly to be applied at the stage of deciding the matter under sections 227 and 228.

State of West Bengal v. *Mohd. Khalid,* 1995 (1) SCC 684: At the stage of framing of charge, what the Court has to see is whether the materials brought on record would reasonably connect the accused with the crime. No more is required to be inquired into.

Niranjan Singh Karam Singh Panjabi v. *Jitendra Bhimraj Bijja,* AIR 1990 SC 1962: 1990 Cr LJ 1869 (SC): While considering the application for discharge, the Court is not expected to accept all that the prosecution states as gospel truth even if it is opposed to common sense or the broad probabilities of the case.

Dina Chetan Shah v. *Govt. of USSR Through its Consulate General,* 2011 All MR (Cri) 2185: When an order is passed by Magistrate under section 169 discharging certain accused, the complainant should be given an opportunity of being heard before such order is passed.

Pravin M. Naik v. *State of Maharashtra,* 2012 All MR (Cri) 1189: Police cannot omit those persons named in FIR as they have no right to discharge the accused.

Baliram M. Jogdand v. *State of Maharashtra,* 2012 All MR (Cri) 1080: Where application for discharge for some of the offences alleged was filed and the Court pass the order stating that the said application will be decided at final stage of hearing, the Court held that impugned order is totally unknown to criminal law. ..... Application cannot be kept in abeyance till final hearing of case.

Subramanium Sethuraman v. *State of Maharashtra,* 2005 (1) Mh LJ 626 (SC): Once the plea of the accused in summons case is recorded the procedure contemplated under chapter XX has to be followed and the trial has to be taken to its logical conclusion. Chapter XX of the Code does not contemplate a stage of discharge like section 239 which provides for a discharge in a warrant case.

CHAPTER XX

PROCEDURE IN SEARCHES AND SEIZURES

General provisions relating to search are contained in sections 99 to 103 and 165, 166 of the Code of Criminal Procedure 1973.

While conducting search due process of law must be followed by police. Lord Denning has explained the due process of law as: the measures authorised by the law so as to keep the streams of justice pure: to see that trials and inquiries are fairly conducted; that arrests and searches are properly made; that lawful remedies are readily available; and that unnecessary delay is eliminated.

The improper conduct of search and seizures and sealings of incriminating articles affect the credibility of prosecution case. Some cases are given below to show the judicial approach regarding search, seizures and sealings of articles conducted without following the due process of law:

State of Punjab v. *Baldev Singh,* (1999) 3 SCR 977: The Constitution Bench of the Apex Court held that an illicit article seized from the person of an accused, during search conducted in violation of the safeguards provided in section 50 of NDPS Act, cannot by itself be used as admissible evidence of proof of unlawful possession of the contraband on the accused. Any other material/article recovered during that search may, however, be relied upon by the prosecution in other /independent proceedings against an accused notwithstanding the recovery of that material during an illegal search and its admissibility would depend upon the relevancy of that material and the facts and circumstances of that case.

In *Ronny @ Ronald James Alwaris* v. *State of Maharashtra,* AIR 1998 SC 1251: 1998 Cr LJ 168: 1998 (2) Mh LR 769 (SC), the Apex Court held that sections 100(4) & section 166(3)(4) of Cr.P.C. require the officer making the search under Chapter VII of Cr.P.C. to call two or more respectable inhabitants of the locality in which the place to be searched is situated. The Court further held that list of things should be prepared on the spot.

In *Radha Krishan* v. *State of U.P.,* AIR 1963 SC 822, the Apex Court held that mere non-compliance of the provisions of sections 100 and 165 of the Cr.P.C. is an irregularity and all that is required by the Court is to examine carefully the evidence regarding search and seizure to find out if such irregularity has caused any prejudice to the accused.

In *Malak Khan* v. *King Emperor,* AIR 1946 PC 16, the court held that section 165 Cr.P.C. was engrafted to make a search without warrant because lack of time in procuring the search warrant would render the search infructuous.

In *State of Rajasthan* v. *Rehman,* AIR 1960 SC 210: 1960 Cr LJ 286, the Apex Court held that the requirements of sub-section (1) are mandatory and non-compliance of the same would render the search illegal.

In *Hira Lal* v. *Emperor,* AIR 1935 Nag 237, the Court held that an oral order will not suffice for conducting a search by a subordinate Police Officer in terms of sub-section 3 of section 165 CrPC.

State of Haryana v. *Rajmal,* 2011 All SCR 2978: The Apex Court held that illegal search does not vitiate seizure of article.

In this case, the Apex Court held that recoveries made pursuant to disclosure statement under section 27 Evidence Act must be found to have been made as consequence to statement made by accused in custody. If nexus in between them is not established, the said statement would be inadmissible in evidence; *Sanjay Dutt* v. *State of Maharashtra,* AIR 2013 SC 2687: 2013 Cr LJ 3538: 2013 All MR (Cri) 1498 (SC).

State of Haryana v. *Ram Singh,* AIR 2002 SC 620: 2001 (4) All MR (Cri) 544 (SC): Where all disclosures, discoveries and even arrests have been made in the presence of the same three totally interested witnesses and no independent witness was found out for the said purpose, it creates doubt, benefit of which must go to the accused.

Pancho v. *State of Haryana,* AIR 2012 SC 523: In this case, articles of tractor discovered were easily available in market and there was nothing special about them. Belated discovery of these articles raised a question about their intrinsic evidentiary value and therefore discovery evidence was rejected.

Bharama P. Kudhachkar v. *State of Karnataka,* AIR 2012 SC 570: In this case, mangalsutra, ring and chain were seized pursuant to disclosure statement made by accused. During trial said articles were produced in Court for identification. However no attempt was made by police to get these articles identified at the earliest point of time. The Apex Court held that identification of articles and involvement of accused persons is doubtful as the ornaments like mangalsutra, ring and chain as easily available to all.

Kishore K. Patil v. *State of Maharashtra,* 2011 All MR (Cri) 3796: The Court held that discovery of weapons cannot be proved by relying on solitary statement of investigation officer. The Court further held that I.O. ought to have deposed as to how accused came to disclose about concealment of weapons used and as to how weapon came to be discovered at the instance of accused. In such facts and circumstances the Court discarded the discovery evidence.

Mustkeen @ Sirajudeen v. *State of Rajasthan,* 2011 All SCR 2662: The Apex Court held that disclosure alone does not connect accused with the crime. Close link between discovery of material objects and their use in the commission of offence must be proved by prosecution. If recovery memo is prepared at police station itself, it would lose its sanctity.

Murlidhar I. Suryawanshi & Anr v. *State of Maharashtra,* 2011 All MR (Cri) 2159: Where currency notes were recovered pursuant to disclosure statement but the number and denominations were not noted, the Court discarded the recovery evidence holding that money cannot be identified unless the numbers and denominations of the currency notes are previously noted down and subsequently proved to be the same.

State of Maharashtra v. *Manisha M. Sohoni,* 2006 All MR (Cri) NOC 221 (Bom): Where grinding stone was recovered from the house of accused prior to his arrest, the Court held that recovery cannot be taken to be the one u/s 27 of the Evidence Act.

Rajkumar B. Dube v. *State of Maharashtra,* 2006 All MR (Cri) 2765: Where knife was recovered at the instance of accused after one month from the date of incident and investigators did not obtain finger prints from the knife, the Court held that no credence can be placed on recovery evidence.

State of Maharashtra v. *Tanaji S. Gawai,* 2006 All MR (Cri) 1080: This was a case of robbery where articles were recovered from accused after three days. The Court while disbelieving the recovery evidence held that testimony of investigation officer is not reliable and credible as robber would not keep articles in his pant for three days after the incident, just waiting for the police to nab him with the incriminating articles.

Shiri @ Shrikant R. Gaonkar v. *State of Goa,* 2006 All MR (Cri) NOC 207: Where pen and cap was recovered pursuant to disclosure statement but no identification parade was conducted to get the articles identified, the Court held that identification of said articles for first time before Court after a gap of more than 2½ years cannot be accepted.

Pramil @ Premanand Rao v. *State of Goa,* 2006 All MR (Cri) 3413: The Court held that identification of a common article of day to day use cannot be accepted as a circumstance against accused in serious crimes like murder.

Asaram R. Jadhav v. *State of Maharashtra,* 2004 All MR (Cri) 1201: Where stolen articles were recovered after a long gap, the Court held that it is necessary for prosecution to examine person to whom stolen articles were sold.

Ahmad @ Ahmad Chakri v. *State of Maharashtra,* 1994 Cr LJ 274 (Bom): In this case accused was in police custody but discoveries were made after five days. In such facts and circumstances, the Court held that discovery evidence gets weakened because of unexplained delay.

Rammi @ Rameshwar v. *State of M.P.,* 2000 All MR (Cri) 275 (SC): In this case arms were recovered at the instance of accused but there was discrepancy in evidence of eye witness and investigation officer about time of taking accused in custody. During trial public prosecutor avoided putting any question to investigation officer in re-examination regarding the said discrepancy. In such facts and circumstances the Court discarded recovery evidence.

Mujeeb v. *State of Kerala,* 2000 All MR (Cri) 573 (SC): Where investigation officer recorded disclosure statement of accused which led to discovery of articles but the investigation officer did not record actual words in verbatim, the Court held that it cannot be treated as a statement of accused leading to discovery.

John Crasto v. *State of Goa,* 2005 (2) BCrC 236: In this case shoes and clothes were recovered from one house but there was no whisper as to who was in possession of the searched house. Accused admitted that articles seized belong to him. The Court held that in absence of proof as to exclusive possession of the seized articles at the time of commission of crime, recovery cannot be said to be proved only on admission of accused before police.

Niranjan Panja v. *State of West Bengal,* 2010 All MR (Cri) 2283 (SC): The Apex Court held that discovery evidence cannot be relied upon in absence of weapon being produced before Court during trial.

Bhanudas B. Salve v. *State of Maharashra,* 2005 (3) BCrC 263: In this case, prosecution did not examine panch witnesses to prove arrest as well as seizure panchanamas of clothes and knife. Further articles were lying in police station for a period of 22 days in unsealed condition. In such facts and circumstances the Court held that recovery evidence is not reliable.

Mani v. *State of Tamil Nadu,* AIR 2008 SC 1021: Where certain articles were recovered pursuant to disclosure statement given by accused from open ground after more than 10 days of incident and about 300 feet away from dead body, the Apex Court held recovery evidence to be unbelievable.

Dashrath M. Borate v. *State of Maharashtra,* 1996 (2) BCrC 22: The Court held that prosecution must establish that right from the time the articles seized till sending the same to the Chemical Analyser, those were kept throughout in sealed condition.

Sahib Singh v. *State of Punjab,* (1996) SUPP 6 SCR 245: In this case, revolver and six live cartridges were recovered during search. However no independent person witnessed the search. The seized articles were not packeted and sealed. There was no evidence to indicate with whom revolver was after seizure till it was sent to arms expert. In such facts and circumstances, the Court disbelieved the recovery evidence and benefit of doubt was given to accused.

Kailash R. Ambekar v. *State of Maharashtra,* 2004 (3) BCrC 719: The Court held that possibility of tampering with attached articles cannot be ruled out where attached articles were not properly sealed.

Lakshmi Jani v. *State,* 1986 Cr LJ 513: The Court held that police officer should take immediate steps to seal articles and evidence should be produced that the seals were not tampered with till the articles were sent to chemical analyser.

Dasu v. *State of Maharasthra,* 1985 Cr LJ 1933 (Bom): In this case, it was mentioned in forwarding letter issued by investigation officer to chemical analyser that all the articles were wrapped in brown papers and were duly sealed. But there was no evidence as to when they were wrapped and sealed. The Court held that non-sealing of articles immediately after seizure is bound to affect the probative value of the findings of the chemical analyser.

Lalchand C. Yadav v. *State of Maharashtra,* 2000 All MR (Cri) 1485: In this case, person who carried the knife to chemical analyst was not examined. Sealing of knife was found doubtful. Even police officer gave evasive answer to question whether panch was a habitual witness. In such facts and circumstances, the Court held that it is unsafe to rely on recovery evidence.

Mahendra M. Thakur v. *State of Mahrashtra,* 2011 All MR (Cri) 3849: The Court held that if blood stained clothes are not wrapped and sealed immediately after the seizure in presence of panchas, it is bound to affect the probative value of the findings of the chemical analyser.

Pawan Kumar v. *State (Delhi Administration),* 1989 Cr LJ 127 (Delhi): Where no effort was made by police to join any independent witness at the time of search though several persons were present, the Court held that this circumstance creates doubt about arrest of accused and recovery of knife.

Smt. Prem Lata v. *State of Himachal Pradesh,* 1987 Cr LJ 1539: In this case, the investigation officer admitted in cross-examination about presence of number of persons at the time of search. However no independent witness was called to act as panch. The Court held that non-compliance of section 100 (4), Cr.P.C. would give rise to doubt about the accuracy of the prosecution case and the benefit of doubt goes to accused.

Resham Singh v. *State,* 1981 Cr LJ 1691 (P&H): Where investigation officer did not offer his personal search before effecting the search of the appellant, the Court held the alleged recovery to be useless.

In *Mohamud Shadab* v. *State of Maharashtra,* 2012 All MR (Cri) 2255, it was claimed by prosecution that articles were recovered from accused at his instance. However said articles were missing from police station. The Court held that mere seizure or a recovery of articles is of no help to prosecution in absence of identification of articles in Court during trial.

In *State of Rajasthan* v. *Teg Bahadur,* 2005 All MR (Cri) 2045 (SC), it was claimed by prosecution that articles worn by deceased woman were recovered from accused. The Apex Court held that this circumstance is not material unless family member of deceased identified them as belonging to deceased which she was wearing at the time of occurrence.

In *Vijay @ Gaddu B. Mahakalkar* v. *State of Maharashtra,* 2015 All MR (Cri) 180, blood of victim was detected on clothes of accused as per CA report. However, clothes of accused persons were seized almost after 7 days of their arrest. Even seized clothes were not sealed. The Court held that CA report is not admissible in evidence and cannot be used against accused.

CHAPTER XXI
JOINT TRIALS

Sections 177 to 189 and 210 and 218 to 224 of the Code deal with this aspect of procedure.

Under section 210 Cr.P.C. Magistrate may try two cases arising out of a police report and a private complaint together. Where having taken cognizance of an offence in respect of an accused in a complaint case, in a separate police investigation such a person is again made an accused, then the Magistrate may inquire into or try together the complaint case and the case arising out of the police report as if both cases were instituted on a police report. However on facts, the Court directed that both the cases be tried separately; *Pal @ Palla* v. *State of U.P.*, 2010 (4) Crimes 184 SC.

Joint trial is an exception to the normal rule provided in the Code which enjoins that each accused should be tried separately when the offence committed by him is distinct and separate; *V.M. Kundan* v. *Municipal Corporation*, (1973) 2 SCC 207: 1973 SCC (Cri) 783.

Proviso to section 218 applies only in such a case where the distinct offences for which the accused is charged are being tried before the same Magistrate. However section 220 applies where anyone series of acts are so connected together as to form the same transaction and where more than one offences committed; *State of Punjab* v. *Rajesh Syal*, 2003 All MR (Cri) 342 (SC).

In this case, the Apex Court held that section 233 of Cr.P.C. embodies the general mandatory rule providing for a separate charge for every distinct offence and for separate trial for every such charge. The broad object underlying the general rule seems to be to give to the accused a notice of the precise accusation and to save him from being embarrassed in his defence by the confusion which is likely to result from lumping together in a single charge distinct offences and from combining several charges at one trial. There are, however exceptions to this general rule and they are found in sections 234, 235, 236 and 239 Cr.P.C. These exceptions embrace cases in which one trial for more than one offence is not considered likely to embarrass or prejudice the accused in his defence. The matter of joinder of charges is, however, in the general discretion of the Court and the principle consideration controlling the judicial exercise of this discrition should be to avoid embarrassment to the defence by joinder of charges; *Chandra Bhal* v. *State of U.P.*, (1971) 3 SCC 983.

In this case, the High Court held that evidence should be recorded in cross-cases, except to the extent that witnesses of prosecution which were/are common can be examined in one case and their evidence be read as evidence in other case. However, cases should be disposed of simultaneously. While pronouncing two separate judgments care should be taken that judgement in one's case was/ is not based upon evidence recorded in other case; *Randhir Singh* v. *Hari Chand* 2014 Crimes 665 (Delhi) (DB).

In 2G Scam Case, CBI filed first chargesheet under the provisions of Prevention of Corruption Act, 1988 not impleading the present petitioners. CBI again filed second chargesheet against present petitioners charging them under the provisions of IPC. Petitioners filed application and prayed for joint trial. However, special judge rejected the prayer of petitioners holding that provisions of sections 220 and 223 CrPC are enabling provisions and it is not obligatory on the Court to hold joint trial. The petitioner challenged the said order in Apex Court. The Apex Court held that order of the Special Judge is not illegal and accused cannot insist that he be tried as co-accused with other accused, that too in a different case. Trial in main chargesheet was in advance stage and holding joint trial might lead to miscarriage of justice; *Essar Teleholdings Ltd.* v. *C.B.I.*, 2015 (4) Crimes 95 (SC).

In this case, the High Court justified the conduction of joint trial in a case where accused in both the cases are common and two incidents occurred in course of same transaction. The Court further observed that intention of the accused in both the cases is common and prosecution is likely to lead common evidence in both the cases and therefore no prejudice would be caused to any parties; *Raghunath S. Karke* v. *State of Maharashtra,* 2000 All MR (Cri) 15.

In this case, the Privy council held that in a case of criminal conspiracy, it is not necessary for the validity of a trial to ultimately prove that the conspiracy alleged actually existed. The validity of joint trial upon charges for offences alleged to be part of the conspiracy is determined by the initial accusation levelled by the prosecution against the whole body of the accused persons; *Babu Lal* v. *Emperor,* AIR 1938 PC 130.

In this case complaint alleging commission of offence against accused persons under sections 304-B/34/406, IPC was filed in Court at place 'B'. Accused took the plea that since incident constituting offence punishable under section 304-B IPC had taken place at place "J" in another State, the Court at place "B" lacks territorial jurisdiction. However the Court negatived the plea raised by accused and held that jurisdiction of Court at place "B" cannot be ousted for offence under section 304-B, IPC as the events in FIR as well as in complaint culminating in death of deceased showed that there was continuity of action and incident constituting offence under section 304-B can be held to be a part of same transaction; *Mohan Baitha* v. *State of Bihar,* AIR 2001 SC 1490.

It is not permissible for the Court under section 223 to club and consolidate the case on a police challan and the case on a complaint where the prosecution version in the police challan case and the complaint case are materially different, contradictory and mutually exclusive; *Harinder Singh* v. *State of Punjab,* AIR 1985 SC 404: 1986 Cr LJ 831 (SC).

The cross-cases should be simultaneously decided by the same judgement, but each case must be decided on the basis of the evidence on record of the case and not on the evidence of the cross-case; *Hakim Singh* v. *State of M.P.*, 1994 Cr LJ 2463 (DB) (MP).

The objection to joint trial must be raised at the earliest opportunity; *Mangaldas Raghavji Ruparel* v. *State of Maharashra,* AIR 1966 SC 128: 1966 Cr LJ 106.

The Apex Court has held that prohibition of a second trial is only with respect to the very same person who had been earlier convicted or acquitted and would not bring within its ambit the case of a co-accused. Burden of proving *'autrefois acquit'* or *'autrefois convict'* is on the accused; *Gulshan Rai Nagpal* v. *State of Sikkim,* 2011 (3) Crimes 770 (Sik) (DB) (SN).

In this case, the Apex Court held that the crucial requirement to attract Article 20 (2) is that the two offences should be identical. It is, therefore, necessary to analyse and compare the ingredients of the two offences and not the allegations made in the two complaints, to see whether their identity is established; *State of Bombay* v. *S.L. Apte,* (1961) 3 SCR 107.

In this case it has been held that case diary of a counter case cannot be referred to as evidence in another case; *Sashi Behera* v. *State of Orissa,* 1986 Cr LJ 1145.

CHAPTER XXII

PROCEDURE OF TRIAL IN CERTAIN CONTINGENCIES

SYNOPSIS

Sections 70, 82, 83 and 299 of the Code deal with procedure for recording evidence in absence of accused.

The Court has held that before recording of evidence in absence of accused, Court is required to take steps contemplated under section 70, 82 and 83 of Cr.P.C.; *Anil K. Lodha* v. *State of Maharashtra,* 2010 All MR (Cri) 808.

Both conditions in first part of section 299 must be read conjunctively and not disjunctively. Court must be satisfied about both the conditions. For invoking section 299, the Magistrate is required to hold that the accused was absconding on that date. Non-observance of principles of natural justice is itself a prejudice to any man. An order passed in violation of fundamental right or in breach of natural justice, would be a nullity; *Jayendra V. Thakur* v. *State of Maharashtra,* 2009 (3) Crimes 76 (SC).

Section 33 of the Evidence Act and section 299 of Cr.P.C. provide pre-conditions, which must be established if the statement recorded in the absence of accused is to be used in evidence against him. Statement of witnesses recorded under section 299 of Cr.P.C. before the arrest of accused, can be utilised in evidence in trial after the arrest of such accused, only if the persons making statement are dead or would not be available or any condition enumerated in the second part of section 299 is established; *Nirmal Singh* v. *State of Haryana,* AIR 2000 SC 1416: 2000 (2) Crimes 101 (SC).

(i) Duty of Court when acccused is absconding

With a view to achieving uniformity in the trial of absconding accused, it is directed that the Courts need not pass orders in respect of the accused shown as absconding in red ink in column No. 2 of the chargesheet filed by the police, since they are not before the Court. However, if such accused are traced during the pendency of the trial of the accused who is/are sent up to the Court, the former should not be tried with the latter, if the prosecution evidence has already commenced. In such cases and in cases where the absconding accused is/are apprehended after the disposal of the trial, separate proceeding should be entertained on a supplementary chargesheet, submitted by the police as per Rule 218(3) of the Bombay Police Manual, 1959 (Volume III). [Paragraph 2(2) of Chapter VI of Criminal Manual issued by The High Court of Judicature (Appellate Site) Bombay].

(ii) Procedure of Trial of newly added persons

When Court proceeds under section 319 against any person not initially being an accused, it must commence *de novo* proceedings *qua* such person from the stage of section 244, and after witnesses are reheard, allow such accused person to cross-examine them before framing of charge. Newly joined accused person has a right of cross-examination of witnesses before framing of charge against him; *Harinarayan G. Bajaj* v. *State of Maharashra,* (2010) 11 SCC 520: 2010 All MR (Cri) 1001 (SC).

In this case, the Apex Court held that newly added accused could be tried after conclusion of trial of other accused. Expression "could be tried together" does not prevent prosecution of newly added accused after trial of others. Holding that newly added accused ought to be tried with other accused would result in delaying trial of other accused and offending their right of speedy trial; *Babubhai B. Bokhiria* v. *State of Gujarat,* AIR 2013 SC 3648.

Whole case against all accused should be tried and disposed of not only expeditiously but also simultaneously. Cognizance against newly added accused should be taken in the same case and in the same manner as against the original accused; *Bholu Ram* v. *State of Punjab,* AIR 2008 SC (Supp) 550: JT 2008 (9) SC 504: 2008 (4) Crimes 260 (SC).

The controversy as regards the scope and extent of the powers of the courts under the criminal justice system to arraign any person as an accused during the course of inquiry or trial as contemplated under section 319 of the Code of criminal procedure, 1973 has been resolved by the Constitution Bench of the Apex Court. The Hon'ble Supreme Court of India held that:

(i) After committal, cognizance of an offence can be taken against a person not named as an accused but against whom materials are available from the papers filed by the police after completion of investigation. Such cognizance can be taken under section 193 Cr.P.C. and the Sessions Judge need not wait till 'evidence' under section 319 Cr.P.C. becomes available for summoning an additional accused.

(ii) Summoning of addition accused is not permissible at the stage of committal.

(iii) Once examination-in-chief is conducted, it becomes part of record. It is evidence as per law on the basis of which court can add a person as an accused who may be corrected with the offence. There is no logic behind waiting till cross-examination is over.

(iv) Power under section 319 Cr.P.C. can be invoked at the stage of trial in complaint case when evidence of complainant as well as his witness is being recorded.

(v) Section 319 Cr.P.C. can be invoked by court against person already discharged by it only after inquiry under section 300(5) and 398 Cr.P.C.

(vi) The degree of satisfaction that will be required for summoning a person under section 319 Cr.P.C. would be the same as for framing a charge; *Hardeep Singh* v. *State of Punjab,* 2014 All MR (Cri) 801 (SC).

In this case, the Apex Court held that the degree of satisfaction to exercise power under section 319 Cr.P.C. to summon persons not arraigned as accused is more than the degree warranted at the time of framing of charges against others in respect of whom chargesheet was filed. The *prima facie* opinion to be formed requires stronger evidence than mere probability of his complicity. The power under section 319 Cr.P.C. should be exercised sparingly and only in those cases where the circumstances of the case so warrants; *Brijendra Singh* v. *State of Rajasthan,* Criminal Appeal No. 763 of 2017, Decided on 27th April 2017 by the Apex Court.

In this case, the Constitution Bench of the Apex Court held that a Court of Sessions can with the aid of section 193 Cr.P.C. proceed to array any other person and summon him for being tried even if the provisions of section 319 Cr.P.C. could not be pressed in service at the stage of committal; *Dharam Pal* v. *State of Haryana,* AIR 2013 SC 3018: 2013 All MR (Cri) 3266 (SC).

CHAPTER XXIII
PROCEDURE FOR GRANTING PARDON

The provisions regarding tender of pardon to accomplice are contained in sections 306, 307 and 308 of Cr.P.C.

The Chief Judicial Magistrate or Metropolitan Magistrate or Magistrate of the First Class may tender a pardon to any person supposed to have been directly or indirectly concerned in or privy to an offence, on condition of his making a full and true disclosure of the whole of the circumstances within his knowledge relating to the offence and to every other person concerned, whether as principal or abettor, in the commission thereof.

Section 306 Cr.P.C. applies to any offence triable exclusively by the Court of Session or by the Court of a Special Judge appointed under the Criminal Law Amendment Act, 1952 (46 of 1952) and any offence punishable with imprisonment which may extent to seven years or with a more severe sentence.

It is mandatory for Magistrate who tenders a pardon to record reasons for so doing and whether the tender was or was not accepted by the person to whom it was made. The Magistrate is duty bound to furnish a copy of such record free of cost to the accused if application is made by him.

A person accepting a tender of pardon shall be examined as a witness in the Court of the Magistrate taking cognizance of the offence and in the subsequent trial, if any, and he shall be detained in custody until the termination of the trial, if he is already on bail.

The Apex Court has observed that the object and purpose of enacting the provision is obviously intended to provide a safeguard to the accused inasmuch as the approver has to make a statement disclosing his evidence at the preliminary stage before the committal order is made and accused not only becomes aware of the evidence against him, but he is also afforded an opportunity to meet with the evidence of the approver before the committing court itself at the very threshold so that he may take steps to show that the approver's evidence at the trial was untrustworthy, in case there are any contradictions or improvements made by him during his evidence at the trial; *Suresh Chandra Bahri* v. *State of Bihar,* AIR 1994 SC 2020: (1994) Supp 1 SCR 483: (1995) Supp 1 SCC 80.

In this case, the Apex Court held that the purpose of granting pardon is not to judge extent of culpability of person pardoned but to prevent failure of justice by not allowing offender to escape from lack of evidence. Special Judge can grant pardon even at the stage of investigation i.e. prior to filing of the chargesheet. The power under section 5(2) of the Prevention of Corruption Act (1988) to grant pardon is an unfettered power subject to stipulation made in the section itself; *Bangaru Laxman* v. *State (Through CBI)*, AIR 2012 SC 873: 2012 All MR (Cri) 337 (SC): (2012) 1 SCC 500.

Tender of pardon can be granted to any person supposed to have been directly or indirectly concerned in, or privy to, any such offence. This tender of pardon can be tendered at any time after commitment of a case but before the judgement is pronounced.

This is a case of murder of one Tapan Chakraborti (a local leader of CPI(M)). Trial commenced on 11th March 2003 and accused No. 12 moved an application to before the trial court to become an approver on 16th June 2014. The evidence of accused No. 12 who as examined as P.W. 6 was considered by the Hon'ble High Court. In appeal before Supreme Court, the appellants contended that evidence of approver ought to have been discarded as there was delay in tendering pardon to him. The Hon'ble Apex Court negatived the contention of the appellants and held that tender of pardon was given before the judgement is pronounced; *Mrinaldas* v. *State of Tripura*, 2011 All MR (Cri) 3256 (SC).

As a matter of practice and procedure, approver has to be examined as a witness first in the Court of Magistrate and then in the trial Court. Where tender of pardon is given to accused, he ceases to be an accused and becomes a witness for prosecution. It is obligatory on the part of approver to comply with the conditions on which pardon is granted and he has to make a true and full disclosure of the circumstances within his knowledge, relating to the offence and to every other person concerned, whether as principal or abettor, in the commission thereof. It is also obligatory on the part of approver to implicate himself in the said offence. However evidence of approver cannot be rejected on the ground that he has not inculpated himself and was not privy to the crime. The Court held that extent of culpability of accomplice is not material; *State of Rajasthan* v. *Balveer @ Balli*, 2013 All SCR 3721.

In this case question arose as to whether the pardon provision contained in sections 306 and 307 of the Code apply or not to the proceedings before the Special Court constituted under Special Court (Trial of Offences Relating to Transactions In Securities) Act (27 of 1992). The Apex Court held that the Special Court established under the Act is a Court of exclusive jurisdiction. Sections 6 and 7 confer on that Court wide powers. It is a Court of original criminal jurisdiction and has all the powers of such a Court under the Code including those of sections 306 to 308 of Cr.P.C.; *Harshad S. Mehta* v. *State of Maharashtra*, AIR 2001 SC 3774: 2001 Cr LJ 4259: 2002 (1) Mh LJ 63 (SC).

The Bombay High Court has held that granting pardon is not the discretion of the police authorities. It is a judicial function; *Udaysingh Jagtap* v. *State of Maharashtra*, 2001 (2) Mh. LJ 231.

Ordinarily, it is for the prosecution to ask that a particular accused out of several may be tendered pardon. But when the accused applies directly, the Special Judge must first refer the request to the prosecution. It is only when the prosecution joins in the request that the Special Judge should exercise his powers; *Lt. Commander Pascal Fernandes* v. *State of Maharashtra*, (1968) 1 SCR 695.

However co-accused have no right to audience when the Magistrate is considering the request of an accused for tendering pardon under section 306 of Cr.P.C.; *CBI* v. *N.K. Amin* 2010 (6) CRJ 622 (Guj).

In this case, the Apex Court held that it is a mandate of the provisions of the Cr.P.C. to the prosecution to examine the approver to whom pardon had been granted as a witness both in the committing court as well as in the trial Court; *State (Delhi Administration)* v. *Jagjit Singh,* (1988) Supp 3 SCR 1093: AIR 1989 SC 598.

However it has been held that the provisions of section 306 (4) (a) of Cr.P.C. are not mandatory. Where the approver is not examined before the Magistrate, the trial is not vitiated. The Court further held that at the time of investigation or inquiry for the offence triable by Sessions Court accused persons have no right to cross-examine the approver; *State of Himachal Pradesh* v. *Surinder Mohan,* (2000) 1 SCR 659: 2000 Cr LJ 1429 (SC).

In this case, the Apex Court held that while investigation is going on, Magistrate as well as Special Judge has concurrent jurisdiction in granting pardon. But where Magistrate exercised his jurisdiction under section 306 CrPC even after appointment of a Special Judge, same is only a curable irregularity and does not vitiate the proceedings, provided the order is passed in good faith; *P.C. Mishra* v. *State Through CBI,* AIR 2014 SC 1921: 2014 All SCR 1545.

In this case, the Apex Court held that section 307 Cr.P.C. authorised even a Court conducting trial to tender pardon against whom there is some material indicating his participation in crime after following appropriate procedure of law; 2015 SAR (Criminal) 787.

In this case, the Apex Court held that approver's evidence should be tested by the touchstone of independent credible evidence. Ordinarily, an approver's statement has to be corroborated in material particulars bridging closely the distance between the crime and the criminal; *Ravinder Singh* v. *State of Haryana,* (1975) 3 SCR 453.

In this case, the Apex Court held that a statement of approver in regard to the manner in which crime has been committed *vis-a-vis* the role played by the accused, on the one hand, and that of the approver, on the other, must be tested on the touchstone of the prudence doctrine; *Santosh K.S. Bariyar* v. *State of Maharashtra,* 2009 All SCR 1421: (2009) 6 SCC 498: AIR 2010 SC (Supp) 612: 2010 AIR SCW 1130.

In this case, the Bombay High Court held that recommendation and opinion of the investigation officer rather than that of the public prosecutor must be considered while granting pardon where accused himself requests for the grant of pardon under section 307 of Cr.P.C.; *Tukaram R. Waze* v. *State of Maharashtra,* 1993 (2) Mh LJ 1693.

Trial of person not complying with conditions of pardon (Section 308 CrPC)

(1) Where, in regard to a person who has accepted a tender of pardon made under section 306 or section 307, the Public Prosecutor certifies that in his opinion such person has, either by wilfully concealing anything essential or

by giving false evidence, not complied with the condition on which the tender was made, such person may be tried for the offence in respect of which the pardon was so tendered or for any other offence of which he appears to have been guilty in connection with the same matter, and also for the offence of giving false evidence:

Provided that such person shall not be tried jointly with any of the other accused:

Provided further that such person shall not be tried for the offence of giving false evidence except with the sanction of the High Court, and nothing contained in section 195 or section 340 shall apply to that offence.

(2) Any statement made by such person accepting the tender of pardon and recorded by a Magistrate under section 164 or by a Court under sub-section (4) of section 306 may be given in evidence against him at such trial.

(3) At such trial, the accused shall be entitled to plead that he has complied with the condition upon which such tender was made, in which case it shall be for the prosecution to prove that the condition has not been complied with.

(4) At such trial, the Court shall—

(a) if it is a Court of Session, before the charge is read out and explained to the accused;

(b) if it is the Court of a Magistrate before the evidence of the witnesses for the prosecution is taken, ask the accused whether he pleads that he has complied with the conditions on which the tender of pardon was made.

(5) If the accused does so plead, the Court shall record the plea and proceed with the trial and it shall, before passing judgment in the case, find whether or not the accused has complied with the conditions of the pardon, and, if it finds that he has so complied, it shall, notwithstanding anything contained in this Code, pass judgment of acquittal.

CHAPTER XXIV

DEPOSITIONS AND REMAKS RESPECTING DEMEANOUR OF WITNESSES

The Bombay High Court has laid down certain rules for recording evidence and depositions in Criminal Manual. Rules/Paragraph 14 to 28 of Chapter VI of the Criminal Manual issued by The High Court of Judicature (Appellate Site) Bombay deal with this aspect of procedure. Important rules are given below—

Paragraph 17(2) The particulars of the village, caste or sub-caste of the person concerned should not be mentioned unless such reference is necessary for the purposes of administering the oath, or for determining the law by which the person concerned is governed or for determining any of the issues or points involved in the proceeding.

Paragraph 18(1) Subject to the statutory alternatives in the matter of recording evidence as contained in sections 275 and 276 of Cr.P.C., as far as possible, the Sessions Judges and Judicial Magistrates should record memorandum of evidence in English in all cases and proceedings.

Paragraph 18(3) While the Sessions Judges and Magistrates may only make a memorandum of the substance of the deposition of each witness, they should take care to see that all answers given by him are recorded in the regional language, provided of course that they are relevant and admissible in evidence. They should compare the memorandum of substance of the deposition made by them with the deposition recorded in the regional language when it is read out in open Court and see that none of the statements contained in the memorandum are omitted from the record of the deposition made in the regional language.

Paragraph 19 The deposition in the regional language and the memorandum of the substance thereof taken down by the Sessions Judge or Magistrate, should bear the same exhibit number. There should not be a separate series of exhibits for depositions; all the exhibits; including depositions should be made in one series.

Paragraph 20 The Presiding Officer should make a note about the demeanour of a witness in the deposition recorded by him when such demeanour is noteworthy and is likely to affect his estimate of the value of the evidence given by the witness.

Even Section 280 of the Code provides that when a Presiding Judge or Magistrate has recorded the evidence of a witness, he shall also record such remark (if any) as he thinks material respecting the demeanour of such witness whilst under examination. However experience in Court room shows that it rarely happens that a Judge or Magistrate records demeanour of a witness. If a Judge or a Magistrate does not make a note of demeanour of a witness even on oral request of the advocate, written application should be filed for the same.

The Apex Court has held that the omission to record remarks respecting the demeanour of the witness as provided in section 363 of the Criminal Procedure Code (1898) by the trial Judge either during or at the close of the examination of the witness does not mean that the recording of the remarks about the demeanour by him later in the judgement is not to be taken into consideration. The remarks made in the judgement will be given due weight by the Appellate Court in the appraisal of the witness; *Ganeshbhai Shankarbhai* v. *State of Gujarat,* AIR 1972 SC 1618.

While recording deposition of witnesses, the Apex Court directed that the trial Court should indicate the rank of the accused, besides using the name, while recording evidence in cases involving multiplicity of accused. The Apex Court directed all the High Courts to issue circulars to the trial Courts to implement this practical suggestion; *Mohd. Rafiz H. Thakor* v. *State of Gujarat,* (1996) Supp 9 SCR 504.

It is emphasised for the guidance of all the trial Judges/Magistrates, that whenever there is an occasion to decide whether oath should be given to a child witness before recording his/her evidence, it is desirable that they should not only put certain questions to such child witnesses to ascertain whether they understood the sanctity of oath or not, but also incorporate, at the top of deposition the questions put by the Court and the answers given by the child witnesses; *Sadashiv T. Dipke* v. *State of Maharashtra,* 2000 (1) Mh LJ 339 (DB) (Bom).

As regards the recording of evidence of a deaf and dumb person, the Apex Court has held that a deaf and dumb person is a competent witness. If in the opinion of the Court, oath can be administered to him/her, it should be so done. Such a witness, if able to read and write, it is desirable to record his statement giving him questions in writing and seeking answers in writing. If a deaf and dumb witness is not able to read and write, his statement can be recorded in sign language with the aid of interpreter, if found necessary. In case interpreter is provided, he should be a person of same surrounding but should not have any interest in the case and he should be administered oath; *State of Rajasthan* v. *Darshan Singh @ Darshan Lal,* 2012 (2) Crimes 318 (SC).

CHAPTER XXV

FIR: IT'S SIGNIFICANCE AND EVIDENTIARY VALUE

SYNOPSIS

Procedure for recording information in cognizable cases is laid down in section 154 of Cr.P.C.

It has been held that the word "shall" appearing in section 154 is mandatory. The section places an absolute duty on the part of the officer-in-charge of a police station to record information and place substance thereof in the prescribed book, where the information supplied or brought to his notice shows commission of a cognizable offence; *Sandeep R. Shukla* v. *State of Maharastra,* 2008 All MR (Cri) 3486 (FB): 2009 (1) Mh LJ 97 (FB).

In this case, the Bombay High Court directed Commissioner of Police to enquire and take appropriate action against police officer concerned who did not register FIR within 48 hours of receipt of information disclosing commission of cognizable offence; *Girdhari R. Bhagwani* v. *State of Maharashtra,* 2013 All MR (Cri) 1266.

In this case, the Bombay High Court held that falsity of allegation is no ground to decline registration of FIR in respect of offence under section 354 IPC and preliminary inquiry is not permissible. The Court directed police to register FIR; *Priya G. Gaokar* v. *State of Maharashtra,* 2014 All MR (Cri) 4200.

In this case, the Bombay High Court held that no previous sanction under section 197 Cr.P.C. is required for the purpose of registration of offence against a public servant; *Bhagwan Y. Kulkarni* v. *State of Maharashtra,* 2006 (2) Mh LJ (Cri) 975.

Even the Apex Court has held that provision of section 154 of Cr.P.C. is mandatory and concerned officer is duty bound to register FIR immediately on the basis of information disclosing a cognizable offence. However, the police officer can conduct a preliminary inquiry only to ascertain whether cognizable offence is disclosed or not in exceptional cases where the information received does not disclose a cognizable offence. But the same should not exceed 7 days in any case. [examples where preliminary inquiry is permissible are: matrimonial disputes/family disputes, commercial offences, medical negligence cases, corruption cases, and cases where there is abnormal delay/laches in initiating criminal prosecution, for example, over three months delay in reporting the matter without satisfactorily explaining the reasons for delay. Entries of all information received in a police station must be mandatorily reflected/noted in general diary/station diary/daily diary; *Lalita Kumari* v. *Government of Uttar Pradesh,* 2013 (4) Crimes 243 (SC): 2013 All MR (Cri) 4444 (SC): AIR 2014 SC 187: 2014 All SCR 1893 (Constitution Bench).

In this case, Inspector of Police attached to Lokayukta registered FIR *suo motu* in P.S. of Lokayukta on the basis of news report published against the appellant showing commission of cognizable offences by applicant/accused. The Apex Court held that no illegality has been committed by Inspector of Police attach to Lokayukta. The Court further held that registration of FIR under section 9 of Lokayukta Act is not necessary; *Yunus Zia* v. *State of Karnataka,* AIR 2015 SC 2376.

In this case, Apex Court held that prior registration of FIR is essential to start investigation by police whereas CBI, in terms of its manual may conduct a limited pre-investigation inquiry which may lead to registration of an FIR and thereafter regular investigation may begin. The Apex Court further held that for initiation of investigation, suspect does not have right of prior hearing; *Samaj Parivartan Samudaya* v. *State of Karnataka,* AIR 2012 SC 2326: 2012 All SCR 1570.

In this case the Apex Court held that information given on telephone to police is not for the purpose of lodging FIR, but rather to request police to reach the place of occurrence, whereas information given in person is for lodging FIR. Furthermore, merely because information given on phone is prior in time would not mean that the same would be treated as FIR; *Manu Sharma* v. *State (NCT of Delhi),* (2010) 6 SCC 1.

However the Apex Court has held in this case that section 154 Cr.P.C. does not require that the report must be given by a person who has personal knowledge of the incident reported; *Hally* v. *State of M.P.,* AIR 1974 SC 1936.

There can be no second FIR in respect of the same offence/event. If the subsequent information is consequence of the first event, the same can be incorporated in the first FIR; *Chirra Shivraj* v. *State of A.P.,* 2011 (1) Crimes 92 (SC).

In this case, the Apex Court held that the lodgement of two FIR's is not permissible in respect of one and the same incident. The concept of sameness has been given a restricted meaning. It does not encompass filing of a counter FIR relating to the same or connected cognizable offence. What is prohibited is any further complaint by the same complainant and others against the same accused subsequent to the registration of the case under the Code, for an investigation in that regard would have already commenced and allowing registration of further complaint would amount to an improvement of the facts mentioned in the original complaint. However the prohibition does not cover the allegations made by the accused in the first FIR alleging a different version of the same incident. Thus, a rival version in respect of the same incident do take different shapes and in the event, lodgement of two FIR's is permissible; *Upkar Singh* v. *Ved Prakash*, AIR 2004 SC 4320: (2004) 13 SCC 292: 2004 All MR (Cri) 3118 (SC).

In this case, the Apex Court held that prohibition on filing second FIR does not encompass filing of counter FIR. Prohibition applies only to filing of second FIR by same complainant against same accused against whom investigation has already started. The Apex Court refused to quash the FIR where FIR had different spectrum and where FIR filed against each other alleged offence of fabrication of documents; *Surender Kaushik* v. *State of U.P.*, AIR 2013 SC 3614.

However, in this case, the Apex Court has held that the law does not prohibit registration and investigation of two FIR's in respect of same incident having different versions of events; *Shiv Shankar Singh* v. *State of Bihar*, (2012) 1 SCC 130: 2012 (1) Crimes 16 (SC): 2012 All MR (Cri) 354 (SC).

In this case, material on record showing killing of Soharabuddin and Kaisarbi and Tulsiram Prajapati to be part and continuance of the same series of acts. The Apex Court held that it is not permissible to allow registration of second FIR as second FIR and fresh chargesheet violates Article 21 of the Constitution of India. However, second chargesheet can be treated as supplementary chargesheet in first FIR; *Amitbhai Anilchandra Shah* v. *CBI*, 2013 (2) Crimes 171 (SC).

An FIR is not the encyclopaedia of all the facts relating to crime. The only requirement is that at the time of lodging FIR, the informant should state all those facts which normally strike to mind and help in assessing the gravity of the crime or identity of the culprit briefly; *Jarnail Singh* v. *State of Punjab*, 2009 (4) Crimes 30 (SC).

In this case the Apex Court has held that FIR should at least mention the broad story of the prosecution. Non-mentioning of material and vital facts may affect credibility of FIR; *Arulvelu* v. *State*, (2009) 10 SCC 206.

In this case, the Apex Court directed the Union of India and all States to upload FIR's on websites within 24 hours from registration of FIR. This time limit has been extended to 72 hours for the states of difficult terrains. However the Court has made one exception/relaxation as regards the FIR in cases of terror, insurgency and sexual offences where there is no need to upload FIR's on websites; *Youth Bar Association of India* v. *Union of India*, 2006 All MR (Cri) 4957 (SC): AIR 2016 SC 4136: (2016) 9 SCC 473.

(i) Ante-timed/ante-dated or fabricated FIR

In this case the Apex Court has given the circumstances to judge as to whether an FIR is ante-timed or fabricated. The Court held that with a view to determine whether the FIR was lodged at the time it is alleged to have been recorded, the Courts generally look for certain external checks. One of the checks is the receipt of the copy of the FIR, called a special report in a murder case, by the local Magistrate. If this report is received by the Magistrate late it can give rise to an inference that the FIR was not lodged at the time it is alleged to have been recorded unless, of course, the prosecution can offer a satisfactory explanation for the delay in despatching or receipt of the copy of the FIR by the local Magistrate. The second external check equally important is the sending of the copy of the FIR along with the dead body and its reference in the inquest report, prepared under section 174 Cr.P.C. is aimed at serving a statutory function, to lend credence to the prosecution case, the details of the FIR and the gist of the statements recorded during inquest proceedings get reflected in the report. The absence of those details is indicative of the fact that the prosecution story was still in an embryo state and had not been given any shape and that the FIR came to be recorded later on after due deliberations and consultations and was then ante-timed to give it the colour of a promptly lodged FIR; *Meharaj Singh, Etc.* v. *State of U.P.*, (1994) 5 SCC 188: II (1994) CCR 516 (SC).

Readers are adviced to read following cases for other list of checks; *Girish Yadav* v. *State of M.P.*, AIR 1996 SC 552: 1996 Cr LJ 2159 (SC): II (1996) CCR 21 (SC) and *Jagdish Murav* v. *State of U.P.*, 2006 (8) SCALE 433.

In this case statement of the informant contained only the short name of the accused. However, the formal FIR made on the basis of the statement contains surname with full name of the accused persons. The Court held that FIR was not at all prepared at the time alleged by the prosecution. It was indeed on the basis of the investigation. FIR was not the basis of the investigation as it should be but was the outcome of investigation. Such FIR cannot be relied on; *Ravindra @ Ravi Bansi Gohar* v. *State of Maharashtra*, 1999 (1) BCrC 1 (SC).

In this case the time of occurrence and report was not mentioned in the FIR and the columns meant to mention these particulars were quite blank. The Court held that FIR is not reliable; *Ram Naresh Singh* v. *State of Bihar*, 1988 (2) Cr LC 98 (Pat).

In this case it was held that the FIR is ante-timed as if the station house diary which contains the contents of the FIR does not mention that Ishrat had visited the police station and lodged the complaint and I.O. left the police station for hospital accompanied by the complainant; *Mohanlal Gangaram Grehani* v. *State of Maharashtra*, AIR 1982 SC 839: 1982 (9) SCC 334.

In this case court held that an FIR cannot be lodged in a murder case after the inquest has been held..... where enmity between two groups is admitted, it requires serious consideration as to whether the FIR was ante-timed or not; *Ramesh B. Devaskar* v. *State of Maharashtra*, 2008 All MR (Cri) 293 SC.

Where prosecution has suppressed the genesis of the case, adverse inference can be drawn that the FIR is a fabricated document. Once FIR is held to be fabricated or brought into existence long after the occurrence, the entire prosecution case would collapse; *Marudanal Augusti* v. *State of Kerla*, 1980 (4) SCC 425: 1980 SCC (Cri) 985.

Before an inference is drawn that FIR is ante-dated, some circumstances have to be shown either from the cross-examination of the relevant witness or from material appearing on record that would probabilise such an inference; *Siddhappa Andappa Andolgi* v. *State of Maharashtra*, 2008 All MR (Cri) 2625.

However it has been held by the Apex Court that exhaustive report is not necessarily ante-timed particularly where maker was not cross-examined on this aspects. It cannot be presumed that the FIR is ante-timed; *State of U.P.* v. *Anil Singh*, AIR 1988 SC 1998: (1988) 3 Crimes 367 (SC): 1989 Cr LJ 88 (SC).

(ii) Effect of Delay in Lodging FIR

Delay in lodging FIR, more often than not, results in embellishment and exaggeration, which is a creature of an afterthought. A delayed report not only gets bereft of the advantage of spontaneity, the danger of the introduction of coloured version, exaggerated account of the incident or a concocted story as a result of deliberations and consultations, also creeps in, casting a serious doubt on its veracity. Therefore, it is essential that the delay in lodging the report should be satisfactorily explained; *State of A.P.* v. *M. Madhusudhan Rao,* 2009 All MR (Cri) 547 (SC): (2009) ACR 118.

In this case the Apex Court held that in absence of any explanation, the delay may give presumption that allegations/accusations were false and had been given after thought or had given a coloured version of events. Deliberate delay in lodging the complaint is always fatal; *Bhagaloo Lodh* v. *State of U.P.,* AIR 2011 SC 2292: 2011 AIR SCW 3710: 2011 All MR (Cri) 2373 (SC).

In this case, the Apex Court held that when an FIR has been lodged belatedly, an inference can rightly follow that the prosecution story may not be true but equally on the other side, if it is found that there is no delay in the recording of the FIR, it does not mean that the prosecution story stands immeasurably strengthened; *Kilakkatha Parambath Sasi* v. *State of Kerala,* AIR 2011 SC 1064: 2011 AIR SCW 3618.

Delay in lodging FIR has great importance when incident takes place out of enmity. Discrepancy as regards timing of lodging FIR is fatal to prosecution case; *Om Prakash* v. *State of U.P.,* (2008) 17 SCC 249: 2009 AIR SCW 1: 2009 (1) Crimes 183 (SC).

In this case the Apex Court held that if FIR is belatedly filed with a view to enmesh the other party in long and arduous criminal proceedings, the Court may take a view that it amounts to an abuse of the process of law and delay in lodging of FIR in such cases is fatal to prosecution; *Bhajan Singh @ Harbhajan Singh* v. *State of Haryana,* AIR 2011 SC 2552: 2011 All SCR 1626.

Where investigation had commenced much prior to lodging of FIR, FIR is hit by section 162 Cr.P.C. There was delay in lodging FIR as well as reaching the same to Magistrate but there was no explanation for delay. The Court held that there was every scope for investigating agency to introduce a coloured version on account of commencement of investigation much earlier to lodging of FIR; *Lingala Lasmaiah* v. State of A.P., 2009 (3) Crimes 129 (AP).

Where accused persons belonged to two rival political parties and where there was delay in lodging FIR, the Court held that possibility of implication as afterthought out of political bitterness is not ruled out; *Rajeevan* v. *State of Kerala,* 2003 All MR (Cri) 820 (SC).

In this case, police went to the place of incident after incident took place. Person who was on the spot and had seen occurrence was not questioned by investigation officer. The investigation officer, however, completed inquest, prepared site plan, got post-mortem of dead persons conducted but FIR was recorded late at night on the next day. The Apex Court held that such delay casts a serious doubt about whole prosecution case especially when no explanation is offered for the delay; *Kailas Gour* v. *State of Assam*, AIR 2012 SC 786: 2012 All SCR 93.

In this case enmity between the informant and accused is established. Incident is alleged to have taken place at 1.00 am but FIR shows that it was recorded at 6.15 am. The informant has deposed that information was recorded by the police at 8.00 am. Thus there was serious contradiction between the informant and the investigation officer about the timing of FIR. In such facts and circumstances, the Court held that such FIR is not reliable as the delay could have been utilised by the informant to implicate the accused in the offence; *Bharat Y. Hegade* v. *State of Maharashtra*, 1995 (1) BCrC 82 (Bom).

In this case there was delay in recording FIR. Explanation for this delay was that it was the practice of his police station not to record such information until a message was received from the hospital with regard to the condition of the injured person. The Apex Court held the prosecution story to be suspicious and further held that the explanation given by the police was mere moonshine for his failure to do what was his statutory duty; *G.B. Patel* v. *State of Maharashtra*, AIR 1979 SC 135: 1979 Cr LJ 51 (SC): 1978 (4) SCC 371: (1979) 2 SCR 94.

(iii) Delay in sending copy of FIR to Magistrates

Delay in conveying the FIR itself does not make the investigation tainted. However it needs to be noted that where an explanation is offered by the prosecution for the delay, that has to be tested. The unexplained delay by itself may not be fatal, but is a certainly relevant aspect which can be taken note of while considering the role of the accused persons for the offence; *State of Kerala* v. *Anilachandran @ Madhu*, (2009) 2 Crimes 225 (SC).

There was delay in transmitting FIR and FIR reached the Magistrate belatedly. The Court held that such delay is fatal to prosecution particularly when there is doubt on whereabouts of complainant and also with respect to genesis of complaint; *Chikkarangaiah* v. *State of Karnataka*, 2009 All MR (Cri) 3060 (SC).

Where defence did not put any question to investigation officer with regard to delay of five days in sending special report to Magistrate, the Apex Court held that no explanation was required to be furnished by investigation officer; *Brahm Swaroop* v. *State of U.P.*, 2010 All MR (Cri) 3975 (SC): (2010) 4 Crimes 267 (SC).

In this case, the Apex Court held that no judicial notice can be taken as to whether FIR was sent to the concerned Magistrate. It has to be proved like any other fact; *Bir Singh* v. *State of U.P.*, AIR 1978 SC 59: 1978 Cr LJ 177.

(iv) Use of FIR during trial

An FIR is not substantive piece of evidence and can only be used to corroborate the statement of the maker under section 157 of the Evidence Act or to contradict it under section 145 of that Act. It cannot be used as evidence against maker at the trial if he himself becomes an accused nor to corroborate or contradict other witness; *Nisar Ali* v. *State of U.P.*, AIR 1957 SC 366: 1957 Cr LJ 550 (SC).

An FIR is a previous statement which can, strictly speaking, be only used to corroborate or contradict the maker of it. But, omissions of important facts affecting the probabilities of the case, are relevant under section 11 of the Evidence Act in judging the veracity of the prosecution case; *R.K. Pandey* v. *State of M.P.*, AIR 1975 SC 1026: 1975 Cr LJ 870 (SC): (1975) 3 SCC 815.

An FIR cannot be used as a substantive evidence or corroborating statement of third party; *State of M.P.* v. *Surbhan*, (1996) SUPP 1 SCR 333.

It has been held by the Apex Court that where first informant turned hostile, FIR cannot be used to corroborate the informant or to discredit other prosecution witnesses before whom deceased made dying declaration. The Court further held that statements recorded under section 164 Cr.P.C. cannot be used as substantive evidence; *George* v. *State of Kerala*, (1998) 2 SCR 303.

If the complaint made by informant to the police is not the first one, it is not the FIR. So, it is hit by sections 161 and 162, Cr.P.C. and the Judge should not rely upon it except to the extent permitted by the proviso to section 162 i.e. to contradict the informant with reference to any particular statement therein; *State of Bombay* v. *Rucy Mistry*, AIR 1960 SC 391: 1960 Cr LJ 532 (SC).

If the FIR given by accused contains any admission as defined in section 17 of the Evidence Act, there is no bar in using of such an admission against the maker thereof as permitted under section 21 of the Act provided such admission is not inculpatory in character; *Faddi* v. *State of M.P.*, (1964) 6 SCR 312.

When the statement in the FIR given by an accused contains incriminating material and it is difficult to sift the exculpatory portion therefrom, the whole of it must be excluded from evidence; *Agnoo Nagesia* v. *State of Bihar*, (1966) 1 SCR 134.

It has been held by the Apex Court that FIR can be used by the defence to impeach the credit of the maker under section 155(3) of the Evidence Act; *Shanker* v. *State of U.P.*, AIR 1975 SC 757: 1975 Cr LJ 634 (SC).

In this case, the Apex Court held that where FIR was not proved through its maker when he gave evidence in the trial Court, the High Court was wrong in holding that FIR is admissible under section 157 of the Evidence Act; *Damodarprasad Chandrikaprasad* v. *State of Maharashtra*, (1972) 2 SCR 622: AIR 1972 SC 622: 1972 Cr LJ 451(SC).

The Prosecution did not examine the informant who lodged the report at police station but actual lodging of FIR was proved by prosecution through the head constable. The Court held that evidence of head constable is not at all sufficient to prove the contents of the FIR; *Raju Sawla Shinde* v. *State of Maharashtra*, 1998 (2) BCrC 165.

Where contents of FIR were never put to the victim, the Apex Court held that the same cannot be used against victim; *Utpal Das* v. *State of West Bengal*, AIR 2010 SC 1894: 2010 All SCR 1269: 2010 (6) SCC 493.

Where the informer had died a natural death long after the occurrence but prior to the initiation of the commitment proceedings, the Court held that FIR cannot be used either for corroboration or for contradiction of the maker who is dead. .... As the statement in FIR did not relate to the cause of the informer's death, the FIR was not admissible under section 32 (1) of the Evidence Act; *State of Orissa* v. *Chakradhar Behera,* AIR 1964 Orissa 262: 1964 (2) Cr LJ 696.

In this case PSI again recorded dying declaration and treated it as FIR though the dying declaration was immediately recorded by the Magistrate. The Court held that the course adopted by PSI is not proper and first dying declaration recorded by the Magistrate should have been treated as FIR for registration of crime; *Hanumant K. Karale* v. *State of Maharashtra,* 2005 (3) BCrC 252 (DB) (Bom).

(v) Other Cases

Ramesh Kumari v. *State,* 2006 (1) Crimes 229 (SC): Where report discloses commission of a cognizable offence, recording of FIR is mandatory.

Kari Choudhary v. *Mst. Sita Devi,* 2002 (1) SCC 714: 2002 All MR (Cri) 426 SC: There cannot be two FIR's against the same accused in respect of the same case. But when there are rival versions in respect of the same episode, they would normally take the shape of two different FIR's and investigation can be carried out under both of them by the same investigating agency.

Mahesh S. Puthran v. *Commissioner of Police, Thane,* 2012 All MR (Cri) 1715: Registration of FIR by Police Officer in relation to offence under Maharashtra Regional and Town Planning Act (1966) cannot be countenanced as the Act is a special enactment and provides mechanism for initiating prosecution.

Husna v. *State of Punjab,* III (1996) CCR 209 (SC): Appellants were not named in the FIR but were named in the supplementary statement recorded during investigation. The Court held that the statement which was recorded during the investigation was hit by section 162 Cr.P.C. and the trial Court could not have relied upon the same as part of the FIR.

Lala Ram. v. *State,* 1989 Cr LJ 572 (Del): Neither names of accused nor names of witnesses, nor any other details of occurrence were mentioned in daily diary. There was non-compliance with section 154 of Cr.P.C. and rule 24.1 of the Punjab Police Rules (1934). Thus at the time of making entry in daily diary, full facts in regard to the occurrence were not known.

Kotak Mahindra Bank Ltd. v. *Nobiletto Finlease & Investment Ltd.,* 2005 (3) BCrC 60: The Court held that before recording FIR, entry regarding filing of complaint, preliminary steps taken pursuant to complaint, particulars about calling of any person for inquiry such as purpose, time duration of his attending police station should find place in station diary.

Gowrishankara Swamigalu v. *State of Karnataka,* (2008) 14 SCC 411: 2008 All SCR 1354: 2009 (2) SCC (Cri) 813: Although statements under section 161 Cr.P.C. were not part of the FIR, defence is entitled to show improvements *vis-a-vis* the allegations in the FIR. Where there was delay in filing FIR and contents of FIR clearly demonstrated that same has been drafted by a person well versed in legal language, the Apex Court held the acquittal to be proper.

State of A.P. v. *V.V. Panduranga Rao,* 2009 (2) Crimes 425 SC: If the police goes to the place of occurrence on the basis of a telephonic information, then any statement made by any person about the offence shall be a statement under section 162, but not FIR. When the information is only one which required the police to move to the place of occurrence and as a matter of fact the detailed statement was recorded after going to the place of occurrence, the said statement is to be treated as FIR.

Shivaji C. Khillare v. *State of Maharashtra*, 2006 (1) BCrC 522: Where report in question was recorded after recording of inquest panchanama *i.e.*, after commencement of investigation, it cannot be treated as FIR and can be used for contradicting the informant and not for the purpose of corroboration.

Sri Sambhu Das @ Bijoy Das v. *State of Assam*, 2010 All SCR 2484: Information regarding cognizable offence furnished to police will be regarded as FIR and all enquiries held by the police subsequent thereto would be treated as investigation, even though the formal registration of the FIR takes place only later.

State of Maharashtra v. *Bittu @ Gurmitsingh*, 2006 All MR (Cri) 1058: Information was recorded in station diary and investigation in the matter started on the basis of that information. The Court held that the station diary entry can be treated as FIR, though names of all the assailants were not mentioned in the said information.

Kishore G. Thawani v. *State of Maharashtra*, 2000 All MR (Cri) 20: In this case, FIR was on plain paper and not in prescribed form. No time or crime number was mentioned. Further there was no acknowledgement of any officer endorsed on it to show that the said document was treated as FIR. Such discrepancies remained unexplained. The Court held that such document cannot be treated as FIR.

Dilip D. Chandiwade v. *State of Maharashtra*, 1995 (2) BCrC 218: When there was conflict between the recitals as contained in the complaint/FIR with these as found in the statement of the complainant, the Court held that it was bounden duty of the prosecution to have got that conflict clarified in the trial Court and advantage goes to the appellant.

C. Magesh v. *State of Karnataka*, 2010 All SCR 1933: Lodger coming with typed complaint which was registered and FIR was lodged. Origin of typed complaint was not known and no secondary evidence was led to ascertain veracity of FIR. The Court held that it would not be correct to wholly place reliance on the FIR.

Hallu v. *State of M.P.*, AIR 1974 SC 1936: 1974 Mh LJ 694 (SC): Absence of names of accused in report/FIR though person making report had learnt of their names, is a serious infirmity in the report.

Bandlamuddi Atchuta Ramaiah v. *State of A.P.*, 1997 (2) BCrC 131 (SC): The Apex Court held that FIR containing statement of one accused cannot be used against another accused. Inculpatory statement cannot be used against accused who made it nor can be used for corroboration or contradiction unless its maker offers himself as a witness in the trial. The very limited use of it is an admission under section 21 of the Evidence Act against its maker alone unless it does not amount to confession.

Somappa v. *State of Mysore*, AIR 1979 SC 1831: 1979 Cr LJ 1358 (SC): Where, on receipt of information about occurrence, investigation officer reached the spot, recorded the statement of the witness, and took other investigation steps, it was held that statement of the witness under section 161, Cr.P.C. cannot be treated as FIR.

Ashok T. Bhutia v. *State of Sikkim*, 2011 All MR (Cri) 2003 (SC): In this case, complaint was lodged against public servant alleged to be having disproportionate assets and FIR was registered without any preliminary enquiry. The Court held that registration of FIR without any preliminary enquiry is illegal and such an irregularity is not curable.

Boddella Babul Reddy v. *Public Prosecutor*, 2010 (3) SCC 648: Complaint was recorded at behest of P.W. 1 at the hospital after MLA and legal advisors of the Party has visited injured. And it was proved that FIR itself was given with consultation of legal advisors and under the guidance of MLA who was inimical towards appellants on account of political rivalry. The Apex Court held the prosecution version to be suspicious.

Channappa A. Siddareddy v. *State*, 1980 Cr LJ 1022: Since FIR is a public document, any person is entitled to obtain the copy of the same.

Sevi v. *State of Tamil Nadu*, AIR 1981 SC 1230: 1981 Cr LJ 736 (SC): Where original FIR were suppressed, the Apex Court held that the entire prosecution case becomes suspect.

State of Himachal Pradesh v. *Rakesh Kumar*, 2009 (6) SCC 308: The Apex Court held that the foremost priority of a person is to shift an injured victim in any accident to the hospital and Courts cannot insist that FIR should be recorded first.

Balaka Singh v. *State of Punjab*, AIR 1975 SC 1962: In this case FIR was written after inquest report was prepared by ASI. The Apex Court held that FIR lost its authenticity.

Smt. Ramani Bala Devi v. *Kanai Lal Malakar*, AIR 1965 Tripura 17: Where an occurrence forms the subject of two cross-cases, the FIR in one case is admissible in the counter-case in which the informants themselves stand their trial, though in every case the entire statement may not be admissible. In view of the occurrence being the subject of two cross-cases, it is admissible in evidence.

Vishal Agrawal v. *Chhattisgarh State Electiricity Board*, 2014 (1) Crimes 181 (SC): FIR can be filed for the theft of electricity with the police notwithstanding provisions of section 151 of the Electricity Act, 2003. Procedure contained in the Code of Criminal Procedure, 1973 is applicable to offences triable under the Act.

M. Saravana @ K.D. Saravana v. *State of Karnataka*, 2012 All MR (Cri) 2737 (SC): 2012 AIR SCW 4292: 2012 Cr LJ 3877: 2012 (4) Mh LJ (Cri) 598 (SC): (2012) 7 SCC 636: FIR can be lodged by any person even by telephonic information and informant need not be an eye witness to the incident.

Dr. Subraminian Swamy v. *Raju Through Member, Juvenile Justice Board*, 2014 (2) Crimes 307 (SC): In view of Rule 11(11) of Juvenile Justice Rules, 2007, the police are not required to file an FIR or a chargesheet while dealing with cases of juvenile in conflict with law. Instead they must only record the information of the offence in the general daily diary, followed by a report containing the social background of the juvenile, circumstances of the apprehension and the alleged offence. An FIR is necessary only if the juvenile has allegedly committed a serious offence like rape or murder or has allegedly committed the offence with an adult.

Sandeep I Sagar v. *State of Maharashtra,* 2013 All MR (Cri) 1781: Registration of FIR is not necessary in offence of drunk and driving since offence under section 185 of Motor Vehicles Act, 1988.

State v. *N.S. Gnaneswaran,* AIR 2013 SC 3673: (2013) 3 SCC 594: 2013 AIR SCW 3806: 2013 Cr LJ 3619: 2014 All SCR 201: The provision contained in section 154(2) Cr.P.C. as regards supply of copy of FIR to the informant, is merely directory and not mandatory.

CHAPTER XXVI

TRIALS BEFORE COURT OF SESSIONS AND SPECIAL COURTS

SYNOPSIS

(1) Preparation and Conduct of the Trial

Conducting a criminal trial on behalf of the accused is not an easy task. The defence lawyer has to perform various jobs to defend his client. It is advisable to visit the spot of incident which may afford certain clues for cross examination. Second thing is that we get a clear picture regarding the alleged incident. Another thing which a lawyer has to do is that he has to collect evidence to rebut the charge against his client. Dedication and hardwork have no alternative. Students may go through a story of a lady advocate given in 'RAGE OF ANGELS'. The Story runs as *'A lady named Connie Garrett met with an accident in which she looses her arms and become amputee. Her suit for damages is dismissed in trial Court and her appeal also gets dismissed in appellate Court, thus practically loosing any hope of getting damages in Court of law. Her Advocate named Jennifer Parker collects evidence and finds that Nationwide Motors Corporation has had fifteen accidents in a last five years, and some of their trucks have been recalled. Further she discovers that a deficiency in the braking system that causes the rear end of the truck to swing around when the brakes are hit hard. With this evidence, she won the suit and six million dollars were awarded as the amount of damages to the plaintiff. It is said that it was the largest personal injury award in the history of the State of New York.'*

P. Ramanatha Aiyer (Author of ' Cross Examination - Principles & Precedents') has advised students and trial Court advocates to *'Watch the witness when he is on the direct examination and his impression upon the jury, but make no note except that which is indispensable train your memory so that you can direct your attention to what is going on in the Court room, and keep yourself free to think and plan.' Further the author has advised students and trial Court advocates not to make ill-timed and useless objection during direct examination of the witness. The author says that, 'let trivial an unimportant breaches of the rules of evidence pass unnoticed and never, never make an objection without good grounds for believing that it will be sustained unless it relates, of course, to some fundamental legal proposition in your case in which you must have a ruling to preserve some basic right upon appeal.'* For every time you are overruled, the jury think that you do not know your business or that you are merely there to obstruct, and every answer given after an unsuccessful objection is doubly emphasized. No knowledge of the rules of evidence is too much; you must know and feel the rules, feel them in your knee-joints. But you are not there to display that knowledge. Never for an instant forget your jury and remember that they do not like objections to the evidence, believing in their lay fashion that these are mere excuses for attempting to conceal truth.

Provisions relating to order of production and examination of witnesses, examination-in-chief, cross-examination and re-examination in the Evidence Act are reproduced below:—

Section 137 - Examination-in-chief.—The examination of a party by the party who calls him shall be called his examination-in-chief.

Cross-examination.—The examination of a witness by the adverse party shall be called his cross-examination.

Re-examination.—The examination of a witness, subsequent to the cross-examination by the party who called him, shall be called his re-examination.

Section 138 - Order of examinations.—Witnesses shall be first examined-in-chief, then (if the adverse party so desires) cross-examined, then (if the party calling him so desires) re-examined.

The examination and cross-examination must relate to relevant fact, but the cross-examination need not be confined to the facts to which the witness testified on his examination-in-chief.

Direction for re-examination.—The re-examination shall be directed to the explanation of matters referred to in cross-examination; and, if new matter is, by permission of the Court, introduced in re-examination, the adverse party may further cross-examine upon that matter.

Order of Examination of Witnesses (Section 135 Evidence Act)

Section 135 of the Evidence Act regulates the order of production and examination of witnesses and it is regulated by the law and practice for the time being relating to criminal procedure and, in the absence of any such law, by the discretion of the Court.

The prosecution is the best judge of the order in which witnesses will be examined in Court. But expert witnesses need to be examined after the examination of other material witnesses.

Section 135-**Order of production and Examination of Witnesses** - The order in which witnesses are produced and examined shall be regulated by the law and practice for the time being relating to civil and criminal procedure respectively, and, in the absence of any such law, by the discretion of the Court.

Under section 135 of the Evidence Act, Court has discretion to decide order of examination of witnesses; *Jarat Kumari Dassi* v. *Bissessur Dutt,* ILR 39 Cal 245.

However the above old view has been impliedly overruled by the Apex Court in this case where the Court held that it is the sole and absolute discretion of the Public Prosecutor to whom he should examine and the sequence and manner of examination of its witnesses. Nobody, nor even the Court can interfere with such an exercise of power by him; *Dr. Rajesh Talwar* v. *C.B.I.,* 2013 (82) ACC 303.

Read: *Abuthagir* v. *State,* 2009 Cr LJ 3987 (SC).

Ram Singh v. *State of M.P.,* 1989 Cr LJ (NOC) 206 (MP).

Sometimes prosecution adopts unfair practice of examining an approver as a witness at the end. The Apex Court has deprecated such practice and held that an approver should ordinarily be examined as a first witness at a trial and not at the end when he has had occasion to know the other evidence led by the prosecution; *Rampal* v. *State of Maharashtra,* (1994) 2 SCR 179.

Judge to Decide as to Admissibility of Evidence – (Section 136 of Evidence Act)

If defence objects to introduction of any piece of evidence during trial, the Court is bound to decide it's admissibility.

Where the defence has taken objection to exhibit the FIR on the ground that the same is not the report first in point of time, the trial Court should put exhibit mark on FIR only after examination of investigation officer; *Mulu Laxman* v. *State of Gujarat,* AIR 1965 Guj 319 (DB).

The Hon'ble Apex Court has recast the practice regarding such objections taken during the course of trial and held that whenever an objection is raised during evidence, the trial Court can make a note of such objection and marked the objected document tentatively as an exhibit in the case (or record the objected part of the oral evidence) subject to such objections to be decided at the last stage in the final judgement. If objection relates to deficiency of stamp duty of a document, the Court has to decide the objection before proceeding further; *Bipin S. Panchal* v. *State of Gujarat,* AIR 2001 SC 1158: (2001) 3 SCC 1.

Principles of Examination of Witnesses

In this case, the Gujarat High Court held that witness could be examined to establish a fact in issue or a relevant fact. Examination-in-chief and cross-examination must relate to relevant facts. As long as cross-examination is related to relevant facts, it could not be confined to any limits. Once a question which is not relevant is put, matter is within discretion of Court to decide whether witness has to be compelled to answer such question or whether warning should ensure that witness is not obliged to answer the same. Where there is a dispute with regard to relevancy and admissibility of a question, Court's endeavour should be to elicit answer of witness after noting objection and final decision to reject a particular piece of evidence as irrelevant or inadmissible, can be taken at the end of the trial; *Prashant M. Pandya* v. *State of Gujarat,* 2016 (3) Crimes 90 (Guj).

When State is interested in the outcome of a criminal case, witnesses are tutored and forced to depose as per their theory and they are kept confined under the police protection. It often happens that examined witnesses and prospective witnesses are allowed to consult each other. This causes prejudice to defence of accused persons. Celebrated authors Wigmore, Best and Roscoe Pound have suggested that in order to prevent communication between witnesses who have been examined and those awaiting examination, Court can order that the former must remain in Court until the latter are examined. Wigmore calls this as process of sequestration. But there is no such provision in the Code of Criminal Procedure, 1973. It is expected that academicians, jurists and Law Commission of India should propose to incorporate such provision in the Code of Criminal Procedure, 1973. Incorporation of such provision is necessary for fair trial. Even the Hon'ble Apex Court has held that fair trial obviously would mean a trial before an impartial Judge, a fair prosecutor and atmosphere of judicial calm. Fair trial means a trial in which bias or prejudice for or against the accused, the witness, or the cause which is being tried is eliminated; *Zahira H.H. Sheikh* v. *State of Gujarat,* Appeal (Crl) 446-449 of 2004, Decided on 12th April 2004 by the Supreme Court of India.

Under section 352 Cr.P.C. (Old Code), Court has power to order any particular person, witness, or Police Officer to go out of the Court room, if their presence is objected to by the accused; See: *Nathusingh* v. *Emperor,* AIR 1925 Nag 296: 88 IC 362: 26 Cr LJ 1130.

In this case also, the Court held that no witness who is to give evidence should be present in the Court room when the deposition of another witness is being recorded; *Subh Karam Singh* v. *Kedar Nath,* AIR 1941 All 314: ILR (1941) All 612.

The rule as to the exclusion of witnesses from Court until they have been examined is not without exceptions. It does not extent to the parties themselves in civil cases, so long as they conduct themselves properly; *In Re: Vemureddy Babureddy,* AIR 1921 Mad 424: ILR 44 Mad 916.

According to Roscoe Pound, rule as to the exclusion of witnesses from Court until they have been examined also applies to criminal cases.

Examination-in-chief

While deprecating habit of granting adjournments frequently and deferring the same for a long time, the Apex Court directed all the Courts to see that cross-examination is completed on the same day after the examination-in-chief is over. However, if examination continues till late hours, cross-examination can be adjourned to next date; *Vinoth Kumar* v. *State of Punjab,* 2015 All SCR 900: 2015 (1) Mh LJ (Crl) 288 (SC).

However, the Court should not examine witnesses when his counsel has sought adjournment on valid and genuine reasons; *Bashira* v. *State of U.P.,* AIR 1968 SC 1313.

In this case, the Apex Court held that if accused protracts the trial, he can be remanded to custody and his bail cancelled; *State of U.P.* v. *Shambhu Nath Singh,* JT 2001 (4) SC 319.

In this case, the hon'ble Apex Court condemned practice of tendering a witness for cross-examination only and held that section 138 of the Evidence Act envisages that a witness would first be examined-in-chief and then subjected to cross-examination and for seeking any clarification. There is no meaning in tendering a witness for cross-examination only. Tendering of a witness for cross-examination, as a matter of fact, amounts to giving up of the witness by the prosecution as it does not choose to examine him in chief. Non-examination of a witness seriously affects the credibility of the prosecution case and it also detracts materially from its reliability; *Sukhwant Singh* v. *State of Punjab,* AIR 1995 SC 1601: (1995) 2 SCR 1190: (1995) 3 SCC 367.

The defence counsel must object to the presence of Investigating Officer-cum-witness or other material witnesses when other witnesses are being examined. If such witnesses are present, the Court may order them to retire; *Nathu Singh* v. *The Crown,* AIR 1925 Nag 296; *A.P. Sarma* v. *G.C. Veerayya,* AIR 1961 AP 420; *Kasi Iyer* v. *State,* AIR 1966 Ker 316: 1966 Cr LJ 1445.

In this case, the High Court held that defence can examine a prosecution witness as defence witness who was given up by it. However police statement recorded under section 162 Cr.P.C. cannot be made available to defence to cross-examine such witness; (1977) 18 Guj LR 896 (DB): 1977 Cri LR (Mah) 281.

Provisions relating to leading questions are reproduced below:

Evidence Act, Section 141.—Leading questions.—Any question suggesting the answer which the person putting it wishes or expects to receive is called a leading question.

Evidence Act, Section 142.—When they must not be asked.—Leading question must not, if objected to by the adverse party, be asked in an examination-in-chief, or in a re-examination, except with the permission of the Court.

The Court shall permit leading questions as to matters which are introductory or undisputed, or which have, in its opinion, been already sufficiently proved.

Evidence Act, Section 143.—When they may be asked.—Leading questions may be asked in cross-examination.

What amounts to leading question, is a question of fact which has to be decided taking into consideration the facts and circumstances of each case.

While explaining the concept of leading question and duty of the public prosecutor, the Hon'ble Apex Court has held that leading question to be one which indicates to the witnesses the real or supposed fact which the prosecutor expects and desires to have confirmed by the answer. Leading question may be used to prepare him to give the answers to the questions about to be put to him for the purpose of identification or to lead him to the main evidence or fact in dispute. The attention of the witness cannot be directed in chief examination to the subject of the enquiry/trial. The Court may permit leading question to draw the attention of the witness which cannot otherwise be called to the matter under enquiry, trial or investigation. The discretion of the Court must only be controlled towards that end but a question which suggest to the witness, the answer to prosecutor expects must not be allowed unless the witness, with the permission of the Court, is declared hostile and cross-examination is directed thereafter in that behalf. Therefore, as soon as the witness has been conducted to the material portion of his examination, it is generally the duty of the prosecutor to ask the witness to state the facts or to give him own account of the matter making him to speak as to what he had seen. The prosecutor will not be allowed to frame his questions in such a manner that the witness by answering merely "yes" or "no" will give the evidence which the prosecutor wishes to elicit. The witness must account for what he himself had seen. Sections 145 and 154 of the Evidence Act are intended to provide for cases to contradict the previous statement of the witnesses called by the prosecution. Sections 143 and 154 provides the right to cross-examination of the witnesses by the adverse party even by leading questions to contradict answers given by the witnesses of to test the veracity or to drag the truth of the statements made by him. Therein the adverse party is entitled to put leading questions but section 142 does not give such power to the prosecutor to put leading questions on the material part of the evidence which the witness intends to speak against the accused and the prosecutor shall not be allowed to frame questions in such a manner to which the witness by answer merely "yes" or "no" but he shall be directed to give evidence which he witnessed. The question shall not be put to enable the witness to give evidence which the prosecutor wishes to elicite from the witness not the prosecutor shall put into witness's mouth the words which he hoped that the witness will utter nor in any other way suggest to him the answer which it is desired that the witness would give. The counsel must leave the witness to tell unvarnished tale of his own account; *Varkey Joseph* v. *State of Kerala,* (1993) 3 SCR 390.

Provisions relating to refreshing memory by a witness are reproduced below—

Evidence Act, Section 159.—Refreshing memory.—A witness may, while under examination, refresh his memory by referring to any writing made by himself at the time of the transaction concerning which he is questioned, or so soon afterwards that the Court considers it likely that the transaction was at that time fresh in his memory.

The witness may also refer to any such writing made by any other person, and read by the witness within the time aforesaid, if when he read it he knew it to be correct.

When witness may use copy of document to refresh memory.—Whenever a witness may refresh his memory by reference to any document, he may, with the permission of the Court, refer to a copy of such document:

Provided the Court be satisfied that there is sufficient reason for the non-production of the original.

An expert may refresh his memory by reference to professional treatises.

Evidence Act, Section 160.—Testimony to facts stated in document mentioned in section 159.—A witness may also testify to facts mentioned in any such document as is mentioned in section 159, although he has no specific recollection of the facts themselves, if he is sure that the facts were correctly recorded in the document.

Evidence Act, Section 161.—Right of adverse party as to writing used to refresh memory.—Any writing referred to under the provisions of the two last preceding section must be produced and shown to the adverse party if he requires it; such party may, if he pleases, cross-examine the witness thereupon.

Cross-examination of own witness by prosecution.—The word 'hostile' has not been defined either in the Evidence Act or in the Code of Criminal

Procedure. But it has assumed meaning by virtue of various decisions of Court. A hostile witness is the one who from the manner in which he gives evidence shows that he is not desirous of telling the truth to the Court. However Court should not readily conclude that the witness was suppressing the truth. Hostility of a witness should be judged from the answers given by him and attitude and demeanour shown by him at the time of his examination in chief.

Court can permit prosecution to cross-examine its own witness if he shows hostile attitude during examination-in-chief. The Gujarat High Court has held that it is not correct to say that the prosecution cannot be allowed to contradict the evidence given by its witness under the proviso to section 162(1), Cr.P.C., without declaring him hostile and save in his cross-examination. However party should give sufficient reasons to satisfy the Court that it is proper in the circumstances to exercise its discretion and permit the person who calls a witness to put questions to him in the nature of cross-examination. The word "cross-examination" found at the end of the proviso to section 162(1) Cr.P.C., refers to the cross-examination of a witness by the accused and not to the questions put under section 154 of the Evidence Act. It is therefore clear that the answers to questions put to a witness after permission is obtained by the party who calls him, are answers given in the examination-in-chief, although they are in the nature of cross-examination; *State of Gujarat* v. *Mohan Hira,* AIR 1960 Guj 9.

In this case, the Apex Court held that the Court can permit a person, who calls a witness, to put questions to him which might be put in the cross-examination, at any stage of the examination of the witness, provided it takes care to give an opportunity to the accused to cross-examine him on the answers elicited which do not find place in the examination-in-chief; *Dahyabhai Chhaganbhai Thakker* v. *State of Gujarat,* AIR 1964 SC 1563: (1964) 7 SCR 361: (1964) 2 Cr LJ 472 (SC).

During the examination-in-chief of a witness, it often happens that public prosecutor seeks permission to declare the witness as hostile and Courts also grant permission to cross examine such witness in terms of Section 154 of the Evidence Act and as a matter of routine and mechanically too. But the Apex Court in *Gura Singh* v. *State of Rajasthan,* AIR 2001 SC 330, has held that, *"permission to cross examine hostile witness in terms of Section 154 of the Evidence Act cannot and should not be granted at mere asking of party calling the witness."* Same view has been taken by the Madras High Court in; *S. Murugesan* v. *S. Pethaperumal,* AIR 1999 Mad 76.

In this case, after declaring the witnesses hostile, the public prosecutor drew the attention of the Court to their previous statements recorded by the investigation officer under section 161 of Cr.P.C. and marked them as exhibits without specifically drawing the attention of witnesses to the particular parts of their previous statement. The Gauhati High Court held that the public prosecutor has not followed the procedure required in terms of section 145 of the Evidence Act and cannot be considered as proved contradictions; *Jiban Das* v. *State of Tripura,* 2012 Cr LJ 3237 (Gau).

In this case, P.W. 39 was examined in Court and he mentioned about a document executed in 1993 styling the same as a sale deed executed. After referring to the same in the chief-examination, the same witness further stated that he received the consideration thereof in 1983. The said last part of the chief-examination is obviously not in consonance with the prosecution case. But the public prosecutor did not choose to seek permission of the trial Court to put questions to the witness which might be put in cross-examination by the adverse party. Hence, the examination proceeded to the cross-examination by the adverse party. It was in the cross-examination that the witness gave further details of how he received the consideration. At the said stage (after cross-examination was over) public prosecutor requested for permission to treat the said witness as hostile. The trial Judge declined permission to the public prosecutor to cross-examine the witness. The CBI took up the matter before the High Court. Even the High Court declined to interfere in the order of the trial Court. Hence appeal was filed by special leave. The Hon'ble Apex Court declined to interfere on the ground that the public prosecutor did not seek permission to cross question the said witness at the stage of chief-examination when the witness has resiled from his expected stand even in chief-examination; *State of Bihar* v. *Lalu Prasad @ Lalu Prasad Yadav,* AIR 2002 SC 2432.

In this case, prosecution witness was declared hostile and was permitted to be cross-examined by public prosecutor. The said witness in his cross- examination contradicted himself in relation to the statements/admissions made by him in examination-in-chief. In such circumstances the Bombay High Court held that petitioner-accused is entitled to cross- examine the witness to the extent of contradictions; *Pradhan Murlidhar Potdar* v. *State of Maharshtra,* 2005 (2) Mh LJ 226 (Bom).

Cross-Examination

(A) Principles of cross-examination

The cross-examination is a double-edged weapon and therefore it should be used very judiciously. Injudicious use of this weapon results in disaster. This has been aptly illustrated by Stephen Tumim in his book titled **'Great Legal Disasters'**. In this case a lady was accused of having picked someone's pocket. The counsel of the accused who was holding his first brief cross-examined the policeman as under—

GILBERT:—You say you found the purse in her pocket, my man?

CONSTABLE:—Yes, sir.

GILBERT:—Did you find anything else ?

CONSTABLE:—Yes, sir.

GILBERT:—What ?

CONSTABLE:—Two other purses, a watch with the bow broken, three handkerchiefs, two silver pencil-cases, and a hymn-book.

The above example shows the importance of the art of cross-examination. Views of eminent jurists have been given below-

The objects of cross-examination are to impeach the accuracy, credibility, and general value of the evidence given in-chief; to shift the facts already stated by the witness, to detect and expose discrepancies, or to elicit suppressed facts which will support the case of the cross-examining party. Therefore keeping in view the above objects of cross-examination, advocates should use this weapon judiciously and to advance the cause of your client. Eminent personalities have evolved different rules of cross-examination which are given below.

Eminent Jurist Dr. Paul Brown has given following golden rules for the cross-examination of the witnesses—

(a) Except in indifferent matters, never take your eye from that of the witness. This is a channel of communication from mind to mind the loss of which nothing can compensate:- 'Truth, falsehood, hatred, anger, scorn, despair, And all the passions, - all the soul is there.'

(b) Be not regardless, either, of the voice of the witness. Next to the eye this is perhaps the best interpreter of his mind. The very design to screen conscience from crime - the mental reservation of the witness - is often manifested in the tone or accent or emphasis of the voice.

(c) Be mild with the mild; shrewd with the crafty; confiding with the honest; merciful to the young, the frail, or the fearful; rough to the ruffian, and thunderbolt to the liar. But in all this, never be unmindful of your own dignity. Bring to bear all the powers of your mind, not that you may shine, but that virtue may triumph, and your cause may prosper.

(d) In a criminal, especially, in a capital case, so long as your cause stands well, ask but few questions; and be certain never to ask any the answer to which, if against you, may destroy your client, unless you know the witness perfectly well, and know that his answer will be favourable equally well; or unless you be prepared with testimony to destroy him, if he play traitor to the truth and your expectations.

(e) An equivocal question is almost as much to be avoided and condemned as an equivocal answer; and it always leads to or excuses an equivocal answer. Singleness of purpose, clearly expressed, is the best trait in the examination of the witnesses, whether they be honest or the reverse. Falsehood is not detected by cunning, but by the light of truth; or if by cunning, it is the cunning of the witness, and not of the counsel.

(f) If the witness determine to be witty or refractory with you, you had better settle that account with him at first or its items will increase with the examination. Let him have an opportunity of satisfying himself either that he has mistaken your power or his own. But, in any result, be careful that you do not lose your temper. *Anger is always either the precursor or evidence of assured defeat in every intellectual conflict.*

(g) Let a skilful chess player, in every move, fix your mind upon the combinations and relations of the game; partial and temporary success may otherwise end in total and remediless defeat.

(h) Never undervalue your adversary, but stand steadily upon your guard: a random blow may be just as fatal as though it were directed by the most consummate skill; the negligence of one often cures, and sometimes renders effective the blunders of another.

(i) Be respectful to the Court and Jury, kind to your colleague,civil to your antagonist; but never sacrifice the slightest principle of duty to an overweening deference towards either.

Judge Parry has given following rules for cross examination—

(a) Never ask a question without having a good reason to assign for asking it.

(b) Never hazard a critical question without having good ground to believe that the answer will be in your favour.

Judge Donovan has evolved following principles for cross-examination -

(a) Know what you need and stop when you get it;

(b) Risk no case on the hazard of an answer that may destroy it;

(c) Hold your temper while you lead the witness, if convenient, to lose his;

(d) Ask as if wanting one answer when you desire the opposite, if the witness is against you, and reverse the tactics if he is more tractable;

(e) Treat a witness like a young runaway colt, and see that he does not get too much the start of his master; and if his does, let go to the reins at the first safe turns in the testimony; but if you see any object to break his running, call the turn quickly.

(f) Use as much brevity as is compatible with clearness and stop when you get through.

Remember the advice given by Hon'ble N.D. Norris who said, "*Never cross-examine at large. Cases are lost rather by too much than by too little cross examination.*"

Mr. Johnson has given following cardinal rules for cross-examination — The *First* is the examining counsel must have a *continuity* and *concentration* of thought. By concentration means that which eliminates and excludes every other thought excepting the subject in hand, and the witness he is dealing with. By continuity it means that it is not to be in broken patches, the his concentration is not to be fixed here this moment and somewhere else the next, but there should be a continuity throughout the whole of his cross-examination. And that leads to the *second rule,* which is: never let the witness get away with you. Then the, *third* cardinal rule is that don't begin to cross examine upon any point unless you have a good ground for gaining that point, and stop absolutely short when you gain it. The *fourth rule* is important as regards policy and that is: always? attack your witness in the weakest point at the opening unless it is some complicated matter involving long accounts or something of that kind. Always attack your witness where he is least prepared or protected. As regards the subject, the point is that: Counsel should always keep to the level of witness. Mr. Johnson further says that, "In cross-examination it is important to eliminate any concern about your own case, because the moment you are thinking about what your case is or will be, or what effect the evidence will have on your case, your mind is distracted from a subject which requires singleness of eye and purpose, and singleness of mental action........ Then it is very important that we should determine a line of attack on each point."

Norton has said that, "*Cross-examination, though a very powerful, is also a very dangerous engine. It is a double - edged weapon, and as often wounds him who wields it, as him at whom it is aimed. To wield it to advantage requires grate practice and natural tact.*"

An observed fact and evidence can be tested by asking following questions in cross-examination—

(a) What are the circumstances at the time of observation;

(b) Whether the observation was causal or deliberate;

(c) Whether the observer is the observing type and what was his state of mind at that time;

(d) Whether the observer was fully aware of the danger of unconscious elaboration and distortion, both at the time of incident and afterwards;

(e) The length of time which had elapsed between the observation and its being recorded;

(f) Amount of confirmation forthcoming from other observers;

(g) Whether the witnesses are telling what they honestly believe to be the whole truth;

(h) Whether the witnesses have any motive to falsely depose against the complainant.

The party who has a right to take part in any enquiry or trial, can cross-examine the witness or witnesses. A party can ask questions on every issue to establish his case. There is no rule of procedure which deprives a party of his right to cross-examine a witness in respect of the whole case. It should be remembered that while cross-examining a witness, advocates should maintain decorum and decency. When a witness is cross-examined, he may be asked any question which tend to test his veracity, to discover who he is and what is his position in life, or to shake his credit, by injuring his character, although the answer to such questions might tend directly or indirectly to criminate him or might expose or tend directly or indirectly to expose him to a penalty or forfeiture. [**Section 146, Evidence Act**]. However, proviso has been added by the Criminal Law (Amendment) Act, 2013 (13 of 2013) with effect from3rd February 2013. Due to addition of this proviso, now it is not permissible to adduce evidence or to put questions in the cross-examination of the victim as to the general immoral character, or previous sexual experience, of such victim with any person for proving such consent or the quality of consent.

Provisions relating to impeaching credit of the witness and manner of proving former statements of witness are reproduced below—

Evidence Act, Section 155.—Impeaching credit of witness.—The credit of a witness may be impeached in the following ways by the adverse party, or, with the consent of the Court, by the party who calls him:—

(1) by the evidence of persons who testify that they, from their knowledge of the witness, believe him to be unworthy of credit;

(2) by proof that the witness has been bribed, or has accepted the offer of a bribe, or has received any other corrupt inducement to give his evidence;

(3) by proof of former statements inconsistent with any part of his evidence which is liable to be contradicted;

(4) when a man is prosecuted for rape or an attempt to ravish, it may be shown that the prosecutrix was of generally immoral character. [This sub-clause has been omitted by Indian Evidence (Amendment) Act, 2002 (4 of 2003), section 3 (w.e.f. 1-1-2003)]

Explanation.—A witness declaring another witness to be unworthy of credit may not, upon his examination-in-chief, give reasons for his belief, but he may be asked his reasons in cross-examination, and the answers which he gives cannot be contradicted, though, if they are false, he may afterwards be charged with giving false evidence.

Evidence Act, Section 156.—Questions tending to corroborate evidence of relevant fact, admissible.—When a witness whom it is intended to corroborate gives evidence of any relevant fact, he may be questioned as to any other circumstances which he observed at or near to the time of place at which such relevant fact occurred, if the Court is of opinion that such circumstances, if proved, would corroborate the testimony of the witness as to the relevant fact which he testifies.

Evidence Act, Section 157.—Former statements of witness may be proved to corroborate later testimony as to same fact.—In order to corroborate the testimony of a witness, any former statement made by such witness relating to the same fact, at or about the time when the fact took place, or before any authority legally competent to investigate the fact, may be proved;

(B) Cases on Cross-Examination

In *Deb Narayan Halder* v. *Smt. Anushree Halder,* AIR 2003 SC 3174, proceeding for maintenance was filed by wife. Though there was nothing in pleadings or in evidence examined by wife that husband had affair with any other lady, questions were asked to the witnesses in cross-examination. It was held by the Apex Court that putting questions in that regard to the witness produced by husband is not permissible.

In *Onkar Bhikaram* v. *Balmukund Javerchand,* AIR 1957 MB 135, the Court has held that *"Under section 138 of the Evidence Act, cross examination need not be confined to the facts to which the witness testifies in his examination-in-chief; he can be cross- examine as to the whole of the case."* It has been held in *State* v. *Md. Misir Ali,* AIR 1963 Assam 151, that *"Mere suggestions during cross-examination, not supported by specific statements by the accused and defence evidence, have no evidentiary value in a criminal trial."*

In *State of Himachal Pradesh* v. *Thakurdas,* 1983 Cr LJ 1694, the Court has held that *"When a party has declined to avail himself of the opportunity to put his essential and material case in cross-examination, it must follow that he believed that the testimony given could not be disputed....... This is not merely a technical rule of evidence. It is a rule of essential justice."*

In *Yusuf Ali* v. *State of Maharashtra,* AIR 1968 SC 147, it has been held by the Apex Court that, *"When the accused did not suggest to prosecution witnesses in a cross examination indicating his defence, the defence version may be rejected as an after thought."*

It has been held by the Apex Court in *State of U.P.* v. *Nahar Singh,* AIR 1998 SC 1328: 1998 Cr LJ 2006, that *"Where the first informant was not cross-examined on his explanation about delay in lodging the F.I.R., his evidence remained unchallenged and must be believed."*

However, it has been held by the Apex Court in *Juwar Singh* v. *State of M.P.,* AIR 1981 SC 373, that *"Failure to cross-examine a witness would not mean that the testimony of the witness is true and acceptable, and it may be discarded if his testimony is on the face of it unacceptable."*

In *Mohan Rai* v. *State of Bihar,* AIR 1968 SC 1281 two complaints one by A and the other by M in respect of the same incident having divergent versions were lodged. Both the complaints were investigated simultaneously by police. Statement of A was recorded as First Information in one case and statement of M as First Information in the other. B was questioned during investigation and prosecution was launched against B & M. As regards the use of statement, the Apex Court held that *"no portion of B's statement could be used to contradict statement of M in his complaint, either under section 157 or under section 145 of the Evidence Act............ Since B was not examined as a witness in the case, his previous statement could not be used either to contradict his evidence or corroborate it even if it is to be held that it is a statement coming under section 154 of Cr.PC."*

It has been held by the Gujarat High Court in *Lal Pratap Singh* v. *State of Gujarat,* 1963 (1) Cr LJ 355, that cross-complaint by accused to police can be used to corroborate or contradict the accused, if the accused gives evidence in Court.

While cross-examining a witness the defence counsel should take precaution not to put improper suggestion as it may sometimes be used against the defence. The case on this point is the decision of the Division Bench of the Bombay High Court reported in *Rajesh Namdeo Mhatre* v. *State of Maharashtra,* 2002 (4) Mh LJ 266: 2003 (1) All MR (Cri) 298. In this case the Court has held that *"suggestions made to prosecution witnesses in their cross-examination are not evidence but they may be called in aid only to lend assurance to prosecution case particularly when other evidence establishes the guilt of the accused."*

In *State of Karnataka* v. *Annegowda,* 2006 All MR (Cri) 3230 (SC): AIR 2006 SC 2641: 2006 Cr LJ 3630: 2006 AIR SCW 3562, the Apex Court held that common trial and clubbing of cases registered against accused is not permitted by section 242 of the Code. However, proviso to section 242 of the Code permits the cross-examination of any witness to be deferred until any other witness or witnesses have been examined or recall any witness for further cross-examination.

In this case question arose as to whether defence is entitled to cross-examine approver whose pardon was withdrawn. The Apex Court held that on forfeiture of such pardon, he is relegated to the position of an accused. However, he cannot be compelled to be a witness. His evidence is rendered useless for the purpose of trial of co-accused. Thus, no occasion arises for defence to cross-examine him; *State of Maharashtra* v. *Abu Salem Abdul Kayyum Ansari,* (2010) 10 SCC 179: 2011 All MR (Cri) 280 (SC).

Cross-Examiantion as to Previous Statement

In this case, the Apex Court held that a previous statement made by a person and recorded on tape, can be used not only to corroborate the evidence given by the witness in Court but also to contradict the evidence given before the Court, as well as to test the veracity of the witness and also to impeach his partiality; *N. Sri Rama Reddy* v. *V.V. Giri,* AIR 1971 SC 1162: (1971) 1 SCR 399.

In this case, statement of complainant was recorded on CD during an interview. Accused sought permission to contradict the evidence given by complainant by confronting him with his statement recorded on CD. However, trial Court refused permission. The High Court held that trial court's order is improper. It further held that the CD to be used for the purpose of confronting the witness must fulfil the necessary requirements of being primary evidence; *Dilip Takhtani* v. *State of M.P.,* 2011 Cr LJ 2025 (MP).

In the offence of kidnapping, during the cross-examination of victim, permission was sought by defence to put forward CD containing interview of victim on local T.V. channel and for watching the same on CD player. Trial Court granted permission to the accused. This order of the trial Court was challenge before High Court which held that grant of permission for the same by the trial Court is illegal; *State of Gujarat* v. *Shailendra K. Pande,* 2008 Cr LJ 953 (Guj).

In this case, the High Court held that CD itself is a primary and direct evidence admissible as to what has been said and picked up by the recorder. A previous statement made by a witness and recorded on CD can be used not only to corroborate the evidence given by the witness in the Court, but also to contradict the evidence given before the Court as well as to test the veracity of the witness and also to impeach his impartiality. Apart from this, the evidence is admissible in respect to three other matters *i.e.* under section 146 (1) of the Evidence Act, which provides questions lawful in cross-examination; *Ghanshyambhai M. Patel* v. *State of Gujarat,* 2014 SCC Online Guj 7196.

In this case, son of deceased deposed that he saw his mother being killed by the accused. He was sought to be contradicted by his earlier statement in which he said that his father had killed his mother. The Court disallowed the same as the earlier statement of son of deceased was not in writing; *Majid* v. *State of Haryana,* AIR 2002 SC 382.

In this case, the Court held that section 162 Cr.P.C. does not prohibit the use of statement recorded by police in connection with another case. Where the Court permitted the defence counsel to use the statement recorded by police in connection with another case for cross-examining the prosecution witness concern, the Court held that such order of the trial court is not illegal as sections 145,

146 and 155(3) of the Evidence Act are complementary to each other; *Surendran* v. *State*, 1994 Cr LJ 464.

As to the use of written report filed by witness to the police, the Court held that those parts of the report on which the defence relied were not duly proved as required under the proviso to section 162(1), Cr.P.C.: they, therefore, could not be used by the defence in contradicting the witness. Section 145 of the Evidence Act requires that the witness must be confronted with those parts of the earlier statement on which the defence relies for the purpose of contradicting him. The report as such being a statement made to a police officer cannot be used by the defence by reason of prohibition contained in section 162(1) Cr.P.C. However, the defence can rely only on those parts of the report with which the witness was confronted by virtue of proviso to section 162(1), Cr.P.C. and no part of that report can be used by the defence for the purpose of contradiction without complying with the provisions of section 145 of the Evidence Act; *Pangi Jogi Naik* v. *State of Orissa*, AIR 1965 Ori 205.

In a case where the police refuses to submit chargesheet against the accused persons after investigation, and the accused are summoned to a trial on a private earn plaint, the provision of section 162, Cr.P.C. still applies and the accused can get copies of the statements previously made by the prosecution witness for the purpose of contradicting the prosecution witnesses in the manner provided under section 145 of the Evidence Act; *Hari Mahadeo Gore* v. *Emperor*, AIR 1927 Nag 24.

In this case, the Apex Court held that the testimony of the witness would not be allowed to be used for corroborating the testimony of other prosecution witnesses where the trial Court did not permit the defence counsel to cross-examine a prosecution witness with reference to an important point in his earlier statement to police; *Badri* v. *State of Rajasthan*, AIR 1976 SC 560: (1976) 1 SCC 442.

Cross-ExaminAtion of co-accused's Witness

There is no provision either in the Evidence Act or the Code of Criminal Procedure to allow one accused to cross-examine the witness of another co-accused. Moreover, cross-examination is the right of adverse party only and co-accused cannot be said to be an adverse party in relation to another accused. But one accused can be allowed to cross-examine the witness of another co-accused on the principle of equity, fair trial and to avoid failure of justice. Where a witness of co-accused gives evidence against accused tending to injure or affect the defence of the accused, he has right to cross-examine the witness of another co-accused; *Chaman Lal* v. *Emperor*, AIR 1940 Lah 210: ILR 1940 Lah 521: 1941 Cr LJ 639.

Cross-ExaminAtion of Court Witness

In this case, the Court held that accused in entitled to cross-examine the Court witness; *Sadanand* v. *Emperor*, AIR 1931 Bom 413.

In this case, Apex Court held that where the Court summons a witness as a Court witness, the complainant is entitled to cross-examine the witness; *Jagat Rai* v. *State of Maharashtra*, AIR 1968 SC 178.

In this case, the Court held that if the witness called by the Court gives evidence against the complainant, he would have right to cross-examine such a witness; *Pradeep Kumar Agarwal* v. *State*, 1995 Cr LJ 76.

In this case, the Apex Court held that if a witness called by court gives evidence against the complainant, he should be allowed to cross-examine; *Iddar* v. *Aabida*, AIR 2007 SC 3029: 2007 Cr LJ 4313: 2007 All MR (Cri) 2073 (SC).

In this case, the Court held that witnesses examined by the Court in the interests of justice cannot be said to be witnesses called for prosecution. Section 145 of the Evidence Act is controlled by section 162 Cr.P.C. and the prohibition contained in section 162 Cr.P.C. cannot be permitted by law. Consequently, statement of the court witnesses recorded by the police cannot be used by the prosecution under section 162 Cr.P.C. to contradict them, even though they were cited as prosecution witnesses; See: *Bhupal Chandra* v. *Emperor*, 44 Cal WN 451; *Sheo Shankar* v. *State*, AIR 1953 All 652; *In Re Koti Reddy*, AIR 1960 AP 76.

In this case, trial Court asked certain questions to a witness under section 165 of the Evidence Act. The High Court held that adverse party against whom the witness has given evidence pursuant to the Court question, is entitled to cross-examine on matter referred to in the answer given in reply to any such question; *Popatlal J. Shah* v. *State of Maharashtra*, 2007 All MR (Cri) 950: 2007 (4) AIR Bom R 67.

Cross-examination of Defence Witness

In this case, an interesting question arose as to whether a witness who was examined in chief, cross-examined and discharged as prosecution witness, can reappear as defence witness under section 233 of Cr.P.C. The Hon'ble Apex Court answered the question in negative; *Yakub Ismail Bhai Patel* v. *State of Gujarat*, AIR 2004 SC 4209: (2004) 12 SCC 229. However, the defence is entitled to examine a witness skipped by the prosecution who is cited as a witness and whose statement is filed on record. If the accused examines a prosecution witness as a defence witness, prosecution cannot make use of his police statement for contradicting him during his cross-examination. It has been held by the Hon'ble Apex Court that under section 162 of Cr. P.C. only witnesses on behalf of the prosecution could be contradicted by reference to the statements made to the police, and not court witnesses or defence witnesses; *Mrs. Shakila Khader* v. *Nausher Gama*, AIR 1975 SC 1324.

Re-cross Examination

In *Muniappan* v. *State of Madras*, AIR 1961 SC 175, the Apex Court has held that, *"The accused in entitled in law to put further question to a prosecution witness by way of cross-examination in respect of what he had stated in reply to questions put to him in cross-examination by? the other accused. Each accused is entitled in law to test the evidence given against him by a prosecution witness, by cross-examination. And such cross-examination need not be limited only to what has been stated by him in examination-in-chief. Though Section 137 & Section 138 do not in words speak of a further round of cross-examination, there is neither in these section nor anywhere else in the Evidence Act and thing to bar the accused from exercising his right of cross-examination afresh if and when the prosecution witness makes a further statement of facts prejudicial to him."*

In this case prosecution witness was declared hostile and was permitted to be cross-examined by public prosecutor. However witness in cross-examination contradicted himself in relation to the statements/admission made by him in the examination-in-chief. The Court held that petitioner/accused is entitled to cross-examine the witness to the extent of contradictions; *Pradhan M. Potdar* v. *State of Maharashtra,* 2005 (2) Mh LJ 226.

In this case witness turned hostile in examination-in-chief and he was cross-examined by defence. Thereafter prosecution sought permission to cross-examine the witness. However the Court refused the permission. The Apex Court held that refusal cannot be said to be a wrong exercise of discretion; *State of Bihar* v. *Lalu Prasad Yadav,* AIR 2002 SC 2432: 2002 Cr LJ 3236 (SC).

In this case, accused sought permission for recalling of witness for re-cross-examination as some vital questions remained to be put to a witness inadvertently during his earlier cross-examination in respect of certain documents. The Court granted permission to accused observing that if such questions were not permitted to be put to complainant, accused would be unable to put forth his defence and principles of natural justice would also be violated. However, the court directed that such re-cross-examination should be restricted to the extent documents produced by complainant and not beyond that; *Vikas S. Waghmare* v. *Moreshwar B. Kadam,* AIR 2011 (NOC) 357 (Bom).

Re-examination

In this case, the Apex Court held that re-examination cannot be allowed for introducing new matters except with the leave of the Court. The Court further held that while conducting re-examination of a witness, it is not permissible to put two or three questions into one question; *Chanan Singh* v. *State of Haryana,* AIR 1971 SC 1554: 1971 SCC (Cri) 714: (1971) 3 SCC 466.

The scope of re-examination of a witness under section 138 of the Evidence Act, has been considered by the Apex Court in this case wherein the Apex Court has held that questions cannot be confined to ambiguities alone which arose in cross-examination. Questions can be put to obtain explanation required for any matter referred to in cross-examination; *Rammi @ Rameshwar* v. *State of M.P.,* AIR 1999 SC 3544: 1999 Cr LJ 4561.

While considering the scope of re-examination, the Apex Court held that doubts created in cross-examination can only be clarified and nothing can be supplemented to examination-in-chief by way of re-examination; *Pannayar* v. *State of Tamil Nadu,* (2009) 9 SCC 152: 2009 (4) BCrC 753 (SC): AIR 2010 SC 85.

Recently The Bombay High Court has held that re-examination of a witness to explain or clarify ambiguities brought down in cross-examination is a legal right of defence. [2006 AIR Bom R (DOC) 44 (Bom)].

Cross-examination after Re-examination

In this case, question arose as to whether a witness who was examined in chief, cross-examined and discharged as prosecution witness, could be allowed to resile from their testimony by filing affidavit saying that what they deposed was false and was done at the instance of the police. The Hon'ble Apex Court answered the question in negative and deprecated such practice; *State of M.P.* v. *Badri Yadav,* AIR 2006 SC 1769: (2006) 9 SCC 549.

However if the witness who deposed one way earlier comes before the appellate Court with a prayer that he is prepared to give evidence which is materially different from what he has given earlier at the trial with the reasons for the earlier lapse, the Court can consider the genuineness of the prayer in the context as to whether the party concerned had a fair opportunity to speak the truth earlier and in an appropriate case accept it. But such power should be exercised in exceptional cases or extra-ordinary situation: *Anil Sharma* v. *State of Jharkhand,* AIR 2004 SC 2294.

Cross-examination of Witnesses before Framing of Charge

In this case, the Apex Court held that accused has right to cross examine the witnesses under section 244 Cr.P.C. and also when a new accused is added under section 319 Cr.P.C.. The Court further held that the right of an accused to cross-examine witnesses produced by the prosecution before framing of charge against him is a valuable right. It was only through cross-examination that the accused could show to the Court that there was no need for a trial against him and that the denial of an opportunity to the accused to show to the Magistrate that the allegations made against him were groundless and that there was no reason for framing a charge against him; *Harinarayan G Bajaj* v. *State of Maharashtra,* (2010) 11 SCC 520.

Re-calling of a Witness

Provisions relating to re-calling of witness are reproduced here:—

Cr.P.C. Section 311 - Power to summon material witness, or examine person present.—Any Court may, at any stage of any inquiry, trial or other proceeding under this Code, summon any person as a witness, or examine any person in attendance, though not summoned as a witness, or recall and re-examine any person already examined; and the Court shall summon and examine or recall and re-examine any such person if his evidence appears to it to be essential to the just decision of the case.

Cr.P.C. Section 391 - Appellate Court may take further evidence or direct it to be taken.—(1) In dealing with any appeal under this Chapter, the Appellate Court, if it thinks additional evidence to be necessary, shall record its reasons and may either take such evidence itself, or direct it to be taken by a Magistrate, or when the Appellate Court is a High Court, by a Court of Sessions or a Magistrate. (2) When the additional evidence is taken by the Court of Sessions or the Magistrate, it or he shall certify such evidence to the Appellate Court, and such Court shall thereupon proceed to dispose of the appeal. (3) The accused or his pleader shall have the right to be present when the additional evidence is taken. (4) The taking of evidence under this section shall be subject to the provisions of Chapter XXIII, as if it were an inquiry.

Courts have ample power to recall a witness for re-examination. Section 165 of Evidence Act and section 311 of Cr.P.C. are complementary to each other and they confer jurisdiction on the judge to act in aid of justice. It is well accepted and settled principle that a court must discharge its statutory functions whether discretionary or obligatory according to law in dispensing justice because it is the duty of Court not only to do justice but also to ensure that justice is being done; *Mohanlal Shamji Soni* v. *Union of India,* 1991 Supp (1) SCC 271.

In this case, the Apex Court held that recall of witness under section 311 of Cr.P.C. is not a matter of course and discretion given to the Court has to be exercised judiciously. Mere observation that recall was necessary for ensuring fair trial is not enough unless there are tangible reasons to show how the fair trial suffered without recall. Recall of witness cannot be allowed at the fag end of the trial. Mere change of counsel cannot be ground to recall the witness of cross-examination. Where accused jumped bail and was arrested with great difficulty witnesses cannot be recalled for cross-examination on the demand of accused; *AG* v. *Shiv Kumar Yadav,* AIR 2015 SC 3501: (2015) 9 SCALE 649: 2015 All SCR 3113.

In this case the Apex Court held that it is open to the defence to request the Court for re-calling the witness for the purpose of further cross-examination to impeach his veracity on the strength of the alleged former statement which came on record subsequently; *State of Rajasthan* v. *Tejaram,* AIR 1999 SC 1776: (1999) 2 SCR 29.

While setting aside the order of the trial Court rejecting the application filed by the accused for recalling the witness for cross-examination, the Bombay High Court allowed the application of the accused for recalling the witness for cross-examination as his counsel was not present during the chief examination of witness; *Rameshwar Bhagwat Dhawad* v. *State of Maharashtra,* 2004 All MR (Cri) 3226.

The Court has power to summon a material witness or examine any person present under section 311 of the Code. Witness already examined-in-chief can be recalled for re-examination even after cross-examination is over. But that can be done in the interest of justice and keeping in view the legal precedents; *G.G.A. Naidu* v. *State of Maharashtra,* 2002 All MR (Cri) 1465.

Where the charge was amended and it was a material change, the Court held that it was just and expedient to recall the prosecution witness on the request of the revisionist for further cross-examination so that veracity of the statements of the witnesses already examined may be tested in regard to the amended charge; *Dharam Pal Singh* v. *State of U.P.,* 2010 (1) Crimes 975 (All).

Where prosecution filed application under section 311 of the Code for recalling witness, the Court held that prosecution cannot be allowed to fill-up the lacunae in examination-in-chief; *B.D. Goel* v. *Ibrahim Haji,* 2001 Cr LJ 450 (Bom).

In this case application under section 311 of the Code was filed for permission to cross-examine prosecution witness. However permission was denied by the trial Court on the ground of non-disclosure in application as to what questions petitioners intended to put to P.W.1. The Court set aside the order of trial Court and held that if some new evidence beneficial to defence has come to light and cross-examination of prosecution witness is found necessary, then the Court cannot deny permission for the same; *Rajesh* v. *State*, 2006 (2) Crimes 449 (Kant).

In this case, witness was once recalled and cross-examined. It has been held by the Hon'ble Apex Court that this does not prevent the Court from further recalling him if his evidence appears to the Court to be essential to the just decision of the case; *Manna Sk.* v. *State of West Bengal*, AIR 2014 SC 2950: 2014 All MR (Cri) 4463 (SC).

In this case, instead of senior counsel, junior counsel conducted cross-examination of complainant though not prepared thoroughly. As such, no effective cross-examination was done. Considering gravity of the offence, the hon'ble High Court granted opportunity to accused to cross-examine complainant by recalling him and matter was remanded back for considering it afresh; *Prashant W. Zore* v. *State of Maharashtra*, 2015 All MR (Cri) 4687.

However, once the accused has been examined under section 313 Cr.P.C., powers under section 311 of the Code cannot be exercised as it would amount to filling up a lacuna existing in the case of the prosecution; *Mir Mohd. Omar* v. *State of West Bengal*, AIR 1989 SC 1785.

In this case, the Apex Court held that if the new counsel thought to have the material witnesses further examined, the Court could adopt latitude and a liberal view in the interest of justice, particularly when the Court has unbridled powers in the matter as enshrined in section 311 Cr.P.C. Grant of fairest opportunity to the accused to prove his innocence is the object of every fair trial; *Hoffman Andreas* v. *Inspector of Customs, Amritsar*, (2000) 10 SCC 430.

The Apex Court has held that under section 391 of the Code, appellate Court is entitled to take further evidence. A witness may be recalled not only for further cross-examination but for recording additional evidence, if necessary. When some statement is made which is not within legal framework, section 391 comes to help for bringing it on record. The Court further held that where approver made diametrically opposite statements incriminating himself and other accused in the case, prayer for further cross-examination of the approver ought not to have been denied on ground of further likely delay in the trial; *Sudevanand* v. *State Through C.B.I.*, 2012 (1) Crimes 137 (SC): 2012 All SCR 518.

Exclusion of Evidence to Contradict Answers to Questions Testing Veracity (Section 153 Evidence Act)

In this case, the Apex Court while considering the scope of Section 153 of the Evidence Act has held that the rule limiting the right to call evidence to contradict a witness on collateral issues excludes all evidence of facts which are incapable of affording any reasonable presumption or inference as to the principal matter in dispute. But when the issue is whether prosecution witness was present at the scene of occurrence evidence can be offered to show that at the very time he was at the different place. Evidence of that type is not aimed at shaking the credit of the witness by injuring his character. It affects only the veracity of the testimony irrespective of his character. (On facts, the eye witness recorded as being present in the inquest report is of no consequence); *Vijayan @ Vijay Kumar* v. *State*, (1999) 2 SCR 89.

Refreshing Memory (Section 159 Evidence Act)

It often happens during the course of examination-in-chief that witness deposes that he does not remember whether his statement was recorded by the police or not and his whole statement is shown to him to refresh his memory However, the Kerala High Court has held that a witness cannot be allowed to refresh his memory with his prior statement recorded under section 161 of Cr.P.C; *Simon* v. *State of Kerala,* 1996 Cr LJ 3368.

The Bombay High Court has condemned the practice of witnesses refreshing their memory outside the Court. The Court held that there would indeed be nothing wrong in the witness refreshing his memory, but that ought to be done before the Court and not outside the Court. In order to test the veracity of a witness, he would be required to recollect the incident out of his own memory and should he falter on some material aspect, he could be allowed to refresh his memory with reference to the contemporaneous records of the incident created by the police. It is not permissible for a witness to stealthily refresh his memory before entering the Court and deposing about entire evidence giving minute details as if he was reeling them out from his memory; *Shri. Sharad s/o Namdeorao Shirbhate* v. *State of Maharashtra,* 2007 All MR (Cri) 352.

In this case, witness did not depose about particular incident by recollecting evidence of that incident but he deposed about the incident as his police statement was read out to him short time before he deposed. The Bombay High Court held that evidence of such witness becomes inadmissible; *Rustam U. Jadhav* v. *State of Maharashtra,* 2016 All MR (Cri) 248.

In this case, the Bombay High Court has held that allowing a witness to read his supplementary statement recorded by police in the course of investigation, for refresing his memory, is in express violation of the provisions of section 162 Cr.P.C.. Apart from this, there was no question of refreshing memory, as memory can be refreshed only in the circumstances mentioned in section 159 of the Evidence Act, and there was no evidence that the conditions requisite for permitting the complainant to refer to his supplementary statement recorded by the police had been fulfilled. This is apart from the express bar created by section 162 of the Code, which would override the provisions of section 159 of the Evidence Act; *Shridhar Chavan* v. *State of Maharashtra,* 2016 All MR (Cri) 88.

However, the Gujarat High Court has held that reading over of the police statement to the witness before he enters the witness box does not amount to contravention of the prohibition contained in section 162(1) Cr.P.C.. But the fact of reading over of the statement may affect the probative value of the evidence of said witness; *Natthu Manchhu* v. *State of Gujarat,* 1978 Cr LJ 448 (Guj).

Record of Evidence (section 275, 276, 278 Cr.P.C.)

Section 278 of Cr.P.C. provides that as soon as evidence of each witness is completed as per the procedure under sections 275 or 276 of Cr.P.C., the deposition is required to be read over to him in the presence of the accused. It has been held by the Hon'ble Bombay High Court that reading over of recorded evidence of each witness to him in the presence of the accused is *mandatory; Vilas N. Sandal* v. *State of Maharashtra,* 2007 All MR (Cri) 2573: 2007 (4) AIR Bom R 42.

Transfer of Depositions from One Case to Another (Cr.P.C Section 299)

In this case, the Apex Court held that for invoking the provisions of section 299 of the Code, the principle of natural justice is inbuilt in the right of an accused. Non-observance of principles of natural justice is itself a prejudice to any man. An order passed in violation of fundamental right or in breach of natural justice would be nullity. Both the conditions contained in the first part of section 299 of the Code must be read conjunctively and not disjunctively. Satisfaction of one of the requirements should not be sufficient. It is obligatory on the part of the court to arrive at a finding on the basis of the materials brought on record by bringing a cogent evidence that the jurisdictional facts existed so as to enable the Court concerned to pass an appropriate order on the application filed by the Special Public Prosecutor. For invoking section 299 Cr.P.C., the Magistrate is required to hold that the accused was absconding on that date. However, once a person is arrested and/or is otherwise capable of being brought to Court, the proclamation issued under section 82 of Cr.P.C. ceases to have any effect. The Court further held that the provisions of section 299 of the Code must receive strict interpretation and scrupulous compliance thereof is imperative in character; *Jayendra Vishnu Thakur* v. *State of Maharashtra*, 2009 (3) Crimes 76 (SC).

In this case, appellant being absconder was tried subsequently in a separate trial. His conviction at appellate stage was based mostly on depositions made by witnesses in previous trial against other accused though depositions were not transferred validly as per section 299 Cr.P.C. The hon'ble Apex Court held that remitted the matter back for deciding the same in accordance with law as the appellate Court committed serious error in not taking note of the fact that application for transfer of deposition was rejected during trial by the trial court; *Vijay R. Chorasiya* v. *State of Gujarat*, 2014 All SCR 3253.

Use of Statement Made to Police

In this case, the Court held that the statements are required to be recorded to put a check upon witnesses to a new story at a trial and/or putting a check upon prosecution to rope/plant altogether new witnesses at a trial and for the purposes of the defence knowing the case required to be met at a trial; *Wasudeo C. Yadav* v. *State of Maharashtra*, 2010 All MR (Cri) 673 (Bom).

In this case, the Apex Court held that it is not mandatory for police to record every statement of every witness *i.e.* law contemplates situation where there might be witness who depose in Court but whose previous statements have not been recorded. Statement made by a witness under section 161 Cr.P.C. and signed by him, is hit by bar under section 162 Cr.P.C. However, evidence deposed in Court by said witness is admissible; *Manu Sharma* v. *State (NCT of Delhi)*, (2010) 6 SCC 1.

In this case, some of the witnesses had stated in their evidence that they had heard the name of the accused being called but neither this fact nor the name of the accused was mentioned in the FIR. However the High Court took into consideration the contents of the statements recorded under section 161 of Cr.P.C. of the various witnesses, during the course of investigation, for the purpose of finding corroboration of their statements in Court that the name of the accused was disclosed to the police. The Hon'ble Apex Court held that the High Court committed serious error in taking into consideration the contents of the statements recorded under section 161 Cr.P.C. for finding corroboration of their statements in Court; *Rameshwar Singh* v. *State of J&K,* (1972) 1 SCR 627.

The Apex Court has held that under section 162 Cr.P.C only witnesses on behalf of the prosecution could be contradicted by reference to their statements made to the police, and not Court witnesses or defence witnesses; *Mrs. Shakila Khader,* v. *Nausher Gama,* AIR 1975 SC 1324.

In this case, P.W.1 was not confronted with his statement recorded by the police under section 161 Cr.P.C. to prove the contradiction nor his statement marked for the purpose of contradiction was read out to the investigation officer. However the court used police statements of witnesses to contradict them under proviso to section 162 Cr.P.C. As regards the procedure adopted by the trial Court, the hon'ble Apex Court held that Court cannot *suo motu* make use of statements to police not proved and ask question with reference to them which are inconsistent with the testimony of the witness in Court. Words *"if duly proved" in section 162 Cr.P.C. clearly show that the record of the statement of witnesses cannot be admitted in evidence straightway nor can be looked into but they must be duly proved for the purpose of contradiction by eliciting admission from the witness during cross-examination and also during the cross-examination of the investigation officer; V.K. Mishra* v. *State of Uttarakhand,* 2015 SAR (Criminal) 1008 (SC): 2015 All MR (Cri) 3298 (SC).

The Apex Court has expressed its displeasure regarding the fact that our law does not admit of cross-examination of defence witness in respect of his previous statement made to police; *Laxman Kalu Nikalje* v. *State of Maharashtra,* AIR 1968 SC 1390: 1968 Cr LJ 1647 (SC).

In this case, a witness denied in court that his statement was recorded by police. As to the mode and manner of proving a statement of witness, the High Court directed to follow following procedure: when a witness is to be confronted with any statement or part thereof made before the police, the same has to be put to that witness while deposing in the Court and if the same is denied, it has to be proved to have been so stated by that witness, by confirmation through the investigation officer, who recorded the same. When any part of the statement so used in the cross-examination requires explanation, then such explanation has to be brought on record by re-examination; *Wasudeo M. Khadatkar* v. *State of Maharashtra,* 2011 All MR (Cri) 2591 (Bom).

Use of Previous Statements

In this case Sessions Court allowed defence request for recalling prosecution witness for confronting his statement subsequently recorded before Juvenile Court. The Apex Court held that procedure adopted by the Sessions Judge was not in accordance with the law and Court reminded that a witness could be confronted only with his previous statement and not subsequent statement made by him, even if it is inconsistent with the earlier; *Mishrilal* v. *State of M.P.,* 2005 (3) BCrC 476 (SC).

It has been held by the Bombay High Court that non-cognizable report lodged with police under section 155 Cr.P.C. would be a previous statement for the purposes of section 145 of the Evidence Act. Mere fact that under section 155 Cr.P.C. only gist was recorded and not entire version was not sufficient to hold that same was not a previous statement; *Mr. Gopal B. Prabhu Konkar* v. *Mr. Babuso K. Naik,* 2009 (2) Crimes 601 (Bom).

In this case, the High Court held that where previous statements have been denied by maker thereof, such statements even if proved by recording officer, cannot be used as substantive piece of evidence; *State of Maharashtra* v. *Goraksha A. Adsul,* 2005 All MR (Cri) 2969 (Bom).

Procedure in Impeaching Credit of Witness *[section 155 of the Evidence Act]*

The credit of a witness may be impeached by proof of former statements inconsistent with any part of his evidence which is liable to be contradicted. [Section 145 r/w section 155(3) of Evidence Act].

In this case, the Apex Court explained the principle contained in section 155(3) of the Evidence Act in relation to section 145 of the Evidence Act and held that the credit of a witness can be impeached by proof of any statement which is inconsistent with any part of his evidence in Court. This principle is delineated in Section 155(3) of the Evidence Act and it must be borne in mind when reading Section 145 which consists of two limbs. It is provided in the first limb of section 145 that a witness may be cross-examined as to the previous statement made by him without such writing being shown to him. But the second limb provides that, *"if it is intended to contradict him by the writing his attention must, before the writing can be proved, be called to those parts of it which are to be used for the purpose of contradicting him. There is thus a distinction between the two vivid limbs, though subtle it may be. The first limb does not envisage impeaching the credit of a witness, but it merely enables the opposite party to cross-examine the witness with reference to the previous statements made by him. He may at that stage succeed in eliciting materials to his benefit through such cross-examination even without resorting to the procedure laid down in the second limb. But if the witness disowns having made any statement which is inconsistent with his present stand his testimony in Court on that score would not be vitiated until the cross-examiner proceeds to comply with the procedure prescribed in the second limb of section 145; Binay Kumar Singh* v. *State of Bihar,* IV (1996) CCR 253.

Use of former Statement *[section 157 of the Evidence Act]*

Former statements of witnesses may be proved to corroborate later testimony as to same fact. Word "Statement" in section 157 only means "something that is stated" and the element of communication to another person is not necessary before "something that is stated" becomes a statement under section 157; *Bhogilal Chunilal Pandya* v. *State of Bombay,* AIR 1959 SC 356: 1959 Cr LJ 389: 1959 SCJ 240: (1959) SUPP I SCR 310.

This was a case of shoot out in neighbouring house where inmates of neighbouring house reached the spot and stated that victims mentioned names of accused as assailants. As to admissibility of such evidence, the Apex Court held that such evidence may not be substantive evidence but has utility at the trial as it would fall under section 157. What is important is that interval between the incident and the utterance of the statement should not be such as to afford occasion for reflection or even contemplation; *Nathuni Yadav* v. *State of Bihar*, AIR 1997 SC 1808: 1997 AIR SCW 1158: 1997 (1) JT 406: 1997 (1) Supreme 490: 1997 (1) SCALE 56: (1998) 9 SCC 238.

However it has been held by the Apex Court that where statement of witness in Court was not believed, his former statement cannot be used as independent evidence in support of other evidence; *Moti Singh* v. *State of U.P.*, AIR 1964 SC 900: 1964 (1) Cr LJ 727: 1963 (2) SCJ 714: (1964) 1 SCR 688.

Explaining the meaning of words "at or about the time" in section 157, the Apex Court held that there can be no hard and fast rule about "at or about" condition in section 157. The main test is whether the statement was made as early as can reasonably be expected in the circumstances of the case and before there was opportunity for tutoring or concoction; *Rameshwar* v. *State of Rajasthan*, AIR 1952 SC 54: (1952) SCR 377: 1952 Cr LJ 547: 1952 SCJ 46.

In this case, the Apex Court held that it is not necessary under section 157 of the Evidence Act that the witness to be corroborated must also say in his testimony in Court that he had made the former statement to the witness who was corroborating him. What section 157 required was that the witness to be corroborated must give evidence in Court of some fact and if that was done his testimony in Court relating to that fact could be corroborated by any former statement made by him relating to the same fact; *Ramratan* v. *The State of Rajasthan*, (1962) 3 SCR 590.

In this case complainant narrated to her colleagues that transpired earlier. The Hon'ble Apex Court held that this is not *res gestae* and hence is inadmissible under section 6 of the Evidence Act. But the same when corroborated by those witnesses, is clearly admissible under section 157 of the Evidence Act; *Chander Kala* v. *Ramkishan*, AIR 1985 SC 1268.

In this case, prosecutrix narrated the incident to so many independent witnesses without any discrepancy soon after the incident. The order of the trial Court admitting the narration under section 157 of the Evidence Act as corroborative of prosecutrix's testimony was upheld as correct by the hon'ble Apex Court; ....AIR 2000 SC 2231.

Use of Statement in Panchanama

Statement in Panchanama can be used in evidence only for contradicting witness under section 145 of the Evidence Act whose statement is contained in panchanama. But his attention must, before writing can be so used, be called to parts sought to be used for contradicting him; *Kanu Ambu Vish* v. *State of Maharashtra*, AIR 1971 SC 2256: 1971 Cr LJ 1547: (1971) 1 SCC 503.

Use of Statement of Witnesses During Test Identification Parade

...............In the case of a test identification parade arranged by the police and held in the presence of panch witnesses, the statements involved in the process of identification would be the statements made by the identifying witnesses to the panch witnesses and would be outside the purview of section 162 Cr.P.C., provided the process of identification is carried out under the exclusive direction and supervision of the panch witnesses and the police had completely obliterated themselves from the parade. Where the test identification parade is carried out by the police in their presence, no distinction can be made between the statements made to the police officers and the statements made to the panch witnesses called by the police officers when conducting the test identification parade; *Ramkishan Mithanlal Sharma* v. *State of Bombay*, AIR 1955 SC 104.

Use of Statements in Pre-trap and Post-trap Panchanamas in Anti-corruption Cases

As regards the use of statements in pre-trap and post-trap panchanamas in anti-corruption cases, the Full Bench of the Bombay High Court in *Vishnu Krishna Belurkar* v. *The State of Maharashtra*, 1974 Bom LR 627 has held that *"the previous statements of panchas which are to be found in pre-trap and post-trap panchanamas in anti-corruption cases do not fall within the phrase"* statement made to the police officer *"as contemplated in section 162, Criminal Procedure Code 1898, and the contents of such panchanamas do not fall within the ban of that section. Such previous statements can legitimately be used for purposes of corroboration under section 157 of the Indian Evidence Act, 1872. However, if a panchanama incorporates a statement which amounts to a statement intended as a narration to a police officer during his investigation then it would fall under section 162, Criminal Procedure Code and will have to be excluded. That, however, is a duty which the Court must perform every time a panchanama is tendered in evidence."*

In this case *Maha Singh* v. *State (Delhi Administration)*, (1976) 3 SCR 119: AIR 1976 SC 449: 1976 Cr LJ 346 the Inspector of the Anti-Corruption Department on a complaint made to him recorded the same, arranged for the raid by noting each step taken, thereafter in a regular manner the steps taken by him in order to detect the accused while taking the bribe comes within the term "investigation" under section 4(1) of the Cr.P.C. 1898. The fact that he had also later on forwarded the complaint for formal registration of the case at the police station having the jurisdiction did not do away with the character of the "investigation" already commenced, by the Inspector on recording the complainant's statement disclosing a cognizable offence........ Therefore any statement made by the accused in answer to questions put by the Inspector is inadmissible under section 162, Cr.P.C. and neither the prosecution nor the accused can take advantage of these answers.

Use of Inquest Report, Seizure List and Site Plans

The basic purpose of holding an inquest is to report regarding the apparent cause of death, namely whether it is suicidal, homicidal, accidental or by some machinery, etc. For the purpose of holding the inquest it is neither necessary nor obligatory on the part of investigation officer to investigate into or ascertain who were the persons responsible for the death; *Amar Singh* v. *Balwindar Singh*, 2003 Cr LJ 1282 (SC): 2003 (2) Bom Cr C 187 (SC): (2003) 2 SCC 518.

In this case, the Hon'ble Apex Court held that contents of inquest report cannot be treated as evidence but it can be looked into to test veracity of the witness who attested the same as a panch witness; *Kuldip Singh* v. *State of Punjab*, AIR 1992 SC 1944: 1992 Cr LJ 3592 (SC).

Documents like the inquest report, seizure lists or the site plans consist of two parts, one of which is admissible and the other is inadmissible. That part of such documents which is based on the actual observation of the witness at the spot being direct evidence in the case, is clearly admissible under section 60 of the Evidence Act, whereas the other part which is based on information given to the investigation officer; or on the statement recorded by him is inadmissible under section 162 Cr. P.C., except for the limited purpose mentioned in that section; *Rameshwar Dayal* v. *State of U.P.*, (1978) 3 SCR 59.

Inquest report cannot be used to contradict the prosecution witness to whom the deceased made dying declaration. Statements are admissible only to the extent of what the investigation officer saw and found. The rest would be hit by section 162 of Cr.P.C.; *George* v. *State of Kerala*, (1998) 2 SCR 303.

In this case, the Apex Court held that inquest report cannot be treated as substantive evidence but may be utilised for contradicting the witness of the inquest. Provisions of sections 174 and 175 Cr.P.C. afford a complete Code in itself for the purpose of inquiries in cases of accidental or suspicious deaths; *Sambhu Das @ Bijoy Das* v. *State of Assam*, 2010 All SCR 2484.

Use of Statement of Accused Made to Witnesses

In this case, it was alleged that accused made certain statements before one of the witnesses(P.W.1). This witness *i.e.* P.W.1 narrated the statement made by accused, Sandeep which consisted of mixture of admission as well as confession. As regards the admissibility of the statement, the Apex Court held that since the last part of the statement would fall under the category of confession, it would be hit by section 25 of the Evidence Act, whereas the former statements which do not implicate the accused to the offence, would be protected by section 8 of the Evidence Act and consequently the said part of the statement was fully admissible; *Sandeep* v. *State of U.P.*, 2012 (2) Crimes 254 (SC).

use of Statement made by A Witness During Media Interview

In this case, the Hon'ble Apex Court held that expression "previous statement" in section 145 of the Evidence Act would not include interview on television given by a witness, after filing of the chargesheet. Section 146 of the Evidence Act does not contemplate such a situation. The aforesaid expression must, therefore, be confined to statement made by a witness before the police during investigation and not thereafter; *State of NTC of Delhi* v. *Mukesh*, 2015 All SCR 3474.

Use of Statement of Accused Made During Media Interview

In this case, police in an overzealous manner arranged media interview of accused namely Afzal. During the said interview accused made certain statements to press and T.V. reporters in the presence of police. As to use and admissibility of the statements made by said accused during media interview, the Apex Court held that the same should not be relied upon irrespective of the fact whether the statement was made to a police officer within the meaning of section 162, Cr.P.C. or not; *State (N.C.T. of Delhi)* v. *Navjot Sandhu*, 2005 All MR (Cri) 2805 (SC).

Use of Statement of Co-accused

In this case, prosecution failed to substantiate the allegation of conspiracy against the appellant. The Court observed that he could not be under any circumstance called a co-conspirator so as to attract the provisions of section 10 of the Evidence Act. Therefore, statement of co-accused in police custody cannot be used to implicate the appellant in the conspiracy to murder; *S. Arul Raja* v. *State of Tamil Nadu,* 2010 All SCR 2252: 2010 (10) SRJ 78 (SC).

Use of Statement of Co-conspirator

In this case, the appellants were prosecuted on charges under section 120 B r/w section 165A of the IPC, for having conspired to commit the offence of bribing a public servant in connection with the discharge of his public duties. The case against them was that on August 24, 1953, when the Inspector of Police who was in charge of the investigation of a case in which the second appellant was involved, was on his way to the police station, the appellants accosted him on the road and the second appellant asked him to hush up the case for valuable consideration. Some days later, on August 31 the first appellant offered to the Inspector at the police station a packet containing Rs. 500 in currency notes and told him that the second appellant had sent the money through him in pursuance of the talk that they had with him on August 24, as a consideration for hushing up the case. As to the use and admissibility of the statement of co-conspirator, the Apex Court held that the incident of August 24 was evidence that the intention to commit the offence had been entertained by both the appellants on or before that date showing a clear indication of the existence of the conspiracy, and that the statement made by the first appellant on August 31 was admissible not only to prove that the second appellant had constituted the first appellant his agent in the perpetration of the crime but also to prove the existence of the conspiracy. The payment of the bribe and the statement of August 31 accompanying it, were part of the same transaction, having been made in the course of the conspiracy and the statement in question was therefore admissible under section 10 of the Evidence Act; *Badri Rai* v. *State of Bihar,* (1959) SCR 1141.

In this case, after the examination-in-chief of PW64 (the second respondent herein) was over, the petitioner herein filed a petition under section 319 of Cr.P.C. seeking to summon the second respondent/PW 64 as an additional accused so as to be tried together with the rest of the accused, who are already facing trial. That petition was dismissed by the trial Court. The said order was challenged before the Apex Court. The facts showed that PW 64 was examined by the police on 11th September 2008 and his statement under section 161 was recorded. Subsequently, on 26/09/2008, his statement was recorded under section 164 Cr.P.C. by the Metropolitan Magistrate, George Town, Chennai. The second respondent was examined as PW64 in the trial of the above mentioned case. The substance of the statements of PW64 is that initially he was involved in conspiracy of murder but later on he withdrew and did not take part in the commission of murder. But he stated that the second accused and the third accused were in contact with each other. The Apex Court held that both the evidence and the statement under section 164 Cr.P.C. of PW 64 prima facie indicate a conspiracy to kill Vijayan to which conspiracy PW 64 was a party at least at the initial stage. According to PW 64, he developed cold feet after the initial stage and withdrew from the conspiracy and did not participate in the actual killing of Vijayan. The Apex Court held that offence of conspiracy is disclosed against PW 64 and it also formed part of same transaction, warranting joint trial. The Apex Court further held that, the statement of PW 64 being an incriminatory statement, is hit by proviso to section 132 of the Evidence Act and cannot be used against him and he cannot be summoned as additional accused. However the Apex Court directed the trial Court to grant him pardon and record his evidence afresh; *R. Dineshkumar @ Deena* v. *State,* 2015 All SCR 1241.

Use of Statement Made by Accused in Another Case

In this case (Bombay Blast Case), prosecution tried to make use of the confessional statements made by accused persons in another case. As to the relevancy and use of confessional statements made by accused persons in another case, the Hon'ble Apex Court held that confessional statements made by accused persons in another case would only constitute *"a statement as to the existence of such fact"* and that would not be a direct/primary evidence. The same would clearly fall within the mischief of "hearsay rule". In order to be relevant under section 11 of the Evidence Act, such statement ought to be a statement about the existence of a fact and not a statement as to its existence. Further no reliance could be place under section 32 of the Evidence Act since authors of confessional statements are very much available and their presence can be procured for deposition; *State of Maharashtra* v. *Kamal Ahemad Mohd. Vakil Ansari,* AIR 2013 SC 1441: 2013 AIR SCW 1652: 2013 Cr LJ 2069 (SC): 2013 All MR (Cri) 2590 (SC).

Use of Statement of Witness in Subsequent Proceeding

In this case, the Apex Court has held that the statement of the injured under section 161 Cr.P.C. is not admissible under section 33 of the Evidence Act; *Sukhar* v. *State of U.P.,* 2000 Cr LJ 29 (SC).

Use of Statements Recorded in Mutation Proceedings

In *Mahila Bajrangi* v. *Badribai,* 2003 AIR SCW 129 the Apex Court held that the statements recorded in mutation proceedings are not admissible in absence of independent corroboration since mutation proceedings before Tahsildar under Madhya Pradesh Land Revenue Code are not judicial proceedings.

Use of Statement in Cross-cases

In this case, the Court held that cross-complaint by accused to police can be used to corroborate or contradict the accused, if the accused gives evidence in Court; *Lal Pratap Singh* v. *State of Gujarat,* 1963 (1) Cr LJ 355.

Statement made by a witness under section 161 Cr.P.C. during investigation of a cross-case is not admissible in evidence in other case; *Gajendra Singh* v. *State of U.P.,* AIR 1975 SC 1703.

Where previous statement of a witness recorded during the course of investigation of another case is intended to be used, restrictions imposed under section 162 Cr.P.C. and section 145 of the Evidence Act would apply; *State of Kerala* v. *Babu,* AIR 1999 SC 2161: (1999) 4 SCC 621.

Use of Statement Made in Enquiry under section 202 Cr.P.C.

In this case, the Apex Court held that the statement of solitary witness recorded during the course of inquiry under section 202 Cr.P.C. cannot be proved under section 157 of the Evidence Act to corroborate evidence of other witnesses. A plain reading of the section would show that previous statement of a particular witness can be used to corroborate only his own evidence during trial and not evidence of other witnesses; *Sashi Jena* v. *Khadal Swain,* AIR 2004 SC 1492: (2004) 4 SCC 236: 2004 Cr LJ 1394: 2004 (2) BCrC 326 (SC).

Use of Statement Recorded under section 164 Cr.P.C.

It has been held by the High Court that statement under section 164 CrPC can be recorded not only at the instance of police, but also at the instance of accused or aggrieved person or on request of witness himself; *Bhima Mallik* v. *State of Orissa,* 1994 Cr LJ (NOC) 390 (Ori).

In this case, the High Court held that statement of victim-girl in a rape case recorded under section 164 Cr.P.C. can be admitted into evidence and be marked as exhibit without Magistrate who recorded it being examined in Court; *Sk. Khelafat Mojhi* v. *State of West Bengal,* 2010 (4) Crimes 666 (Cal).

In this case, Privy Council held that the statement made under section 164 CrPC is not admissible in evidence and may be used to corroborate or contradict a statement made in Court in the manner provided by sections 145 and 157 of the Evidence Act; *Bhuboni Sahu* v. *The King,* AIR 1949 PC 257.

In this case, the Hon'ble Apex Court has stated the procedure and pre-requisites of recording statement under section 164 Cr.P.C. The Court held that before recording the confession, the Magistrate is required to satisfy himself that accused was making a voluntary statement and that the accused was cautioned about the use of such confession at the trial. This satisfaction of the Magistrate and caution given to the accused must be recorded before recording of confession by putting questions to the accused. The Court held that a mere endorsement in accordance with sub-section (4) of section 164 Cr.P.C. after recording it would not fulfil the requirements of the former sub-section; *Tulsi Singh* v. *State of Punjab,* III (1996) CCR 106 (SC).

The statement recorded under section 164 Cr.P.C. is not substantive evidence and it can be used only to corroborate the witness under section 157 of the Evidence Act or contradict the witness under section 145 of the Evidence Act; *Ram Kishan Singh* v. *Harmit Kaur,* AIR 1972 SC 468.

In this case, the Court held that statement of accused recorded under section 164 Cr.P.C. cannot be used as substantive evidence. It can be used to contradict or corroborate a witness who has made the statement. Maker of such statement may be cross-examined by using statement made by him under section 164 Cr.P.C. to demonstrate that evidence of witness is false. Credibility of prosecution witness can be impeached with the aid of statement under section 164 Cr.P.C; *Mohan Singh* v. *State of West Bengal,* 2015 (3) Crimes 81 (Cal).

A Magistrate can record the statement of a person as provided in section 164 of the Code and such a statement would either the elevated to the status of section 32 if the maker of the statement subsequently dies or it would remain within the realm of what it was originally. A statement recorded by a Magistrate under section 164 of the Code becomes usable to corroborate the witness as provided in section 157 of the Evidence Act or to contradict him as provided in section 155 thereof; *Ramprasad* v. *State of Maharashtra,* (1999) 5 SCC 30: (1999) 3 SCR 519.

In this case, dying declaration was recorded under the impression that there was no chance of survival of victim. However, declarant survives. The Apex Court held that such statement is in essence a statement under section 164 CrPC and it can be used under section 157 of the Evidence Act for the purpose of corroboration and under section 155 of the Evidence Act for the purpose of contradiction; *State of U.P.* v. *Veer Singh,* 2004 All MR (Cri) 3190.

In this case, statement of victim was recorded as dying declaration. However, declarant survived. The Bombay High Court held that it is to be treated as a statement under section 164 Cr,P.C. and not a previous statement under section 161 Cr.P.C. It can be used for corroboration or contradiction; *Ramesh G. Kamble* v. *State of Maharashtra,* 2011 All MR (Cri) 3536: 2011 (6) Mh LJ 927: 2011 (6) AIR Bom R 412 (FB).

In this case, statement of child witness was recorded under section 164 of the Code not only by investigation officer but also by the Judicial Magistrate. During trial child witness turned hostile. But, the public prosecutor did not put the statement to him after he was declared hostile and he was allowed to be cross-examined. As to the use and admissibility of the statement of child witness, the Apex Court held that as the statement under section 164 of the Code was not put to the witness by the public prosecutor, same cannot be relied upon and is liable to be rejected; *Ashok Gavade* v. *State of Goa,* 1995 (1) BCrC 41 (Bom).

In this case, statement of witness was recorded under section 164 Cr.P.C. before Magistrate. As to the use of statement recorded under section 164 Cr.P.C. in different contingencies, the Apex Court held that if the witness sticks to the statement given by him under section 164 Cr.P.C, no problem arises. If the witness resiles from the statement under section 164 Cr.P.C. in committal Court, he can be cross-examined on his earlier statement. But if he sticks to the statement given by him under section 164 Cr.P.C before committal enquiry and resiles from it in the Sessions Court, the procedure prescribed under section 288 Cr.P.C. will have to be observed. Equally, a statement recorded under section 288 Cr.P.C. of one witness can be taken to corroborate the statement of another witness under section 288 Cr.P.C; *Dhanabal* v. *State of Tamil Nadu,* AIR 1980 SC 628.

In this case, prosecution witness deposed in statement under section 164 Cr.P.C. that initially he was involved in conspiracy of murder but later on he withdrew and did not take part in commission of murder. However offence of conspiracy disclosed against said prosecution witness and it also form part of same transaction, warranting joint trial. But, being an incriminatory statement, it is hit by proviso to section 132 of Evidence Act which grant immunity to such a witness; *R. Dineshkumar @ Deena* v. *State,* 2015 (2) Crimes 50 (SC): 2015 All SCR 1241.

Use of Statement Recorded as Dying Declaration

In this case, statement of injured was recorded as dying declaration. However injured survives. As to use and admissibility of the said statement, the Apex Court held that statement cannot be treated as dying declaration but has to be treated as of a superior quality/high degree than that of a statement recorded under section 161, Cr.P.C. It can be used as provided under section 157 of the Evidence Act; *Ranjit Singh* v. *State of M.P.*, AIR 2011 SC 255.

Use of Statement of Victim to Doctor

Statement made by victim to doctor examining her and other witnesses after the incident cannot be simply discarded as hearsay evidence. Section 6 of the Evidence Act permits proof of collateral statements which was so connected with the fact in issue to be a part of the same transaction. In order to constitute same transaction the series of acts should be connected together and in this respect the proximity of timeassume significance. Section 8, illustration (J) of the Evidence Act makes it abundantly clear that the facts, shortly after the alleged rape, are relevant; *Lalmand N. Chaudhary* v. *State,* 2010 All MR (Cri) 102 (Bom).

The history of assault narrated by the victim and noted by the doctor in medical examination report is not a substantive piece of evidence, but said statement could be used to contradict the testimony of the person who gave the narrative; *Sujit G. Sohatre* v. *State of Maharashtra,* 1997 Cr LJ 454 (Bom).

Use of Post Mortem Report

In this case, the Apex Court held that post mortem report by itself is not a substantive evidence but it is the doctor's statement in court which has the credibility of a substantive evidence. Post-mortem report in normal circumstances is used only for refreshing the memory of the doctor or to contradict whatever he might say for the witness-box; *Munshi Prasad* v. *State of Bihar,* 2002 SCC (Cri) 175.

Use of Confessional Statements

In the case of conspiracy one of the accused persons made a confessional statements after common intention of parties was no longer in existence. Further, statements made in confession related to past acts done by accused. As to use and admissibility of the said confessional statement, the Apex Court held that section 10 of the Evidence Act cannot be invoked as against other accused/ appellants; *Sidharth* v. *State of Bihar,* 2006 All MR (Cri) 888 (SC).

Where co-accused was not being tried along with the other accused, the confession of co-accused cannot be used against other accused persons; *Yakub P. Nadar* v. *State of Maharashtra,* 2006 All MR (Cri) 1983.

In this case, the Hon'ble Delhi High Court held that confession of a co-accused cannot be treated as substantive evidence and can be pressed into service only when Court is inclined to accept other evidence and feels necessity of seeking for assurance in support of its conclusion deducible from the said evidence. In criminal trial, there is no scope for applying principle of moral conviction or grave suspicion. In criminal cases where oral evidence adduced against an accused person is fully unsatisfactory and prosecution seeks to rely on confession of a co-accused, presumption of innocence which is the basis of criminal jurisprudence assist the accused and compels the court to render verdict that charge is not proved against him; *Jaffar @ Raju* v. *State,* 2013 (4) Crimes 356 (Del).

Where consent statement was signed by appellant and it was not by way of confession, said statement is admissible and bar under section 25 of the Evidence Act would not be applicable; *Jarnail Singh* v. *State of Punjab,* 2011 All SCR 541.

Use of Documents on Record

Where defence thinks that evidence on record might aid defence, the Court held that it was for defence and not for prosecution to make use of such evidence. It was for appellant to prove evidence favourable to him, by exhibiting relevant documents and calling necessary witnesses; *Santosh Kumar Singh* v. *State,* (2010) 9 SCC 747.

Use of Case - Diary

The Bombay High Court has issued directions to Director of Prosecution to issue appropriate orders calling upon prosecutors to ensure that case-diary is produced in trial Court before the trial begins; *Akram Khan Sirajulhaq* v. *State of Maharashtra,* 2010 All MR (Cri) 2154.

In this case, the Court directed Secretary of Home Department to issue appropriate instructions to all concerned to comply with the mandate of changed legal position which has come into force with effect from 31/12/2009. The Court has drawn the attention to the mandatory requirement specified in section 172 (1-B) which stipulates that the diary referred to in section 172(1) shall be in volume and duly paginated; *Mrs. Atluri P.V. Rao* v. *Police Inspector Pawar,* 2011 All MR (Cri) 1759.

Section 172 requires a police officer to enter his proceedings in a diary day by day. It also empowers a criminal Court to look into diaries, not as evidence, but to aid it in enquiry or trial. Object of requiring a diary to be maintained day by day is obviously to avoid concoction of evidence, or changing chronology to suit investigation. Every authority whose actions have a potential of jeopardising liberty of a citizen must ensure a transparency in its actions by scrupulously following requirement to keep a record of such activities; *State* v. *Anil Jacob,* 2009 All MR (Cri) 427 (Bom).

As regards the use of case diary during inquiry or trial, the Apex Court held that section 162 of the Code bars the use of any statement made before a police officer in the course of an investigation under chapter XII, whether recorded in a police diary or otherwise. If such statement is sought to be used in any proceeding other than an inquiry or trial or even at an inquiry or trial but in respect of an offence other than that which was under investigation at the time when such statement was made, the bar of section 162 would not be attracted. Section 162 has been enacted for benefit of the accused and to protect him against overzealous police officers and untruthful witnesses. However, it has no application in a civil proceeding or in a proceeding under Article 32 of 226 of the Constitution. The Apex Court further held that criminal Court can use such diary, not as evidence in the case, but to aid it in such inquiry or trial. If, however, the case diary is used by the police officer who has made it to refresh his memory or if the criminal court uses it for the purpose of contradicting such police officer in the inquiry or trial, the provisions of section 161 Cr.P.C. or section 145 of the Evidence Act, as the case may be, would apply and the accused would be entitled to see the particular entry in the case diary; *Khatri* v. *State of Bihar*, (1981) 3 SCR 145. The law laid down in this case has been followed in *Shamshul Kanwar* v. *State of U.P.*, (1995) 3 SCR 1197.

In *Malkiat Singh* v. *State of Punjab*, (1991) 2 SCR 256, the Apex Court has held that, *"If the police officer who made the entries in the case diary uses it to refresh his memory or if the Court uses it for the purpose of contradicting such witness, by operation of Section 161 of Cr.P.C. and Section 145 of the Evidence Act, the accused can use it for the purpose of contradicting the witness i.e. investigation officer or to explain it in re-examination by the prosecution, with permission of the Court."*

However in *Mahabir* v. *State of Haryana*, AIR 2001 SC 2503, the Apex Court has held that, *"If the Court uses the entries in a case diary for contradicting a police officer, it should be done only in the manner provided in Section 145 of the Evidence Act,.... The interdict contained in Section 162 of Cr.P.C. debars the Court from using the power under section 172 of Cr.P.C. for explaining a contradiction."*

It has been held by the Apex Court in *State of Kerala* v. *Babu*, (1999) 2 SCR 978, that, *"Court can summon the case diary of a different case not pertaining to the one in hand...... Power to summon the case diary of another case emanates not from Section 172 of Cr.P.C. but from Section 91(1) of the Evidence Act.*

Use of Daily Diary

As regards the production of daily diary in Court, the Apex Court in *Kalpanath Rai* v. *State (through C.B.I.)*, AIR 1998 SC 201, has held that, *"it cannot be produced as a matter of course in every case....... Of course it is open to the defence to move the Court for getting down such diaries if the defence wants to make use of it."*

The Bombay High Court has held that the station diary is a public record and even a certified copy of the same can be obtained. There is no prohibition under law that accused cannot call for the station diary or cannot see the same. [*Sureshbabu D. Talbhandare* v. *State of Maharashtra*, 2011 All MR (Cri) 1515].

Record of the Judge

If a judge does not record the evidence of the witness properly and it does not depict true state of affairs that has taken place during the trial of a case, it is the duty of a lawyer to point out the same at the earliest opportunity to the judge concerned. If some thing wrong has been recorded or improperly recorded by a judge in deposition or in any inquiry, objection should be taken immediately when the matter is still fresh in the mind of the judge.

During the course of hearing of special leave to appeal, the Counsel for respondent intervened and protested that he never made any such concession and invited the Judges to peruse the written submissions made by him in the High Court. As to propriety of submissions made by the counsel for respondent, the hon'ble Apex Court held that the Court cannot launch into an inquiry as to what transpired in the High Court. The Supreme Court is bound to accept the statement of the Judges recorded in the their judgement, as to what transpired in Court. Statement of the Judges recorded in their judgements cannot be allowed to be contradicted by statements at the Bar or by affidavit and other evidence. If the judges say in their judgement that something was done, said or admitted before them, that has to be the last word on the subject. If a party thinks that the happenings in Court have been wrongly recorded in a judgement, it is incumbent upon the party, while the matter is still fresh in the minds of the judges, to call attention of the very judges who have made the record to the fact that the statement made with regard to his conduct was a statement that had been made in error. That is the only way to have the record corrected. If no such step is taken, the matter must necessarily end there. Of course a party may resile and an Appellate Court may permit him in rare and appropriate cases to resile from a concession on the ground that the concession was made on a wrong appreciation of the law and had led to gross injustice; but, he may not call in question the very fact of making the concession as recorded in the judgement; *State of Maharashtra* v. *Ramdas S. Nayak,* AIR 1982 SC 1249: (1983) 1 SCR 8.

The Division Bench of the Bombay High Court has followed the above case and held that the Judge's record is conclusive and neither lawyer nor litigant may claim to contradict it except before the judge himself, but nowhere else. *Olaf Wumling* v. *State of Goa,* 2000 (4) Mh LJ 72.

Consequences of not Putting Questions to Witnesses During Cross-examination

In this case, the Apex Court held that if the question is not put to the witness in cross-examination who could furnish explanation on a particular issue, the correctness or legality of the said fact/issue could not be raised; *Atluri Brahamanandan* v. *Anne Sai Bapuji,* AIR 2011 SC 545.

Contradictions and Omissions

Provisions relating to procedure of bringing contradictions and omissions on record during the cross-examination of a witness are reproduced below:—

Evidence Act, Section 145.—Cross-examination as to previous statements in writing.—A witness may be cross-examined as to previous statements made by him in writing or reduced into writing, and relevant to matters in question, without such writing being shown to him, or being proved; but, if it is intended to contradict him by the writing, his attention must, before the writing can be proved, be called to those parts of it which are to be used for the purpose of contradicting him.

Cr.P.C. Section 162.—Statement to police not to be signed: Use of statements in evidence.—(1) No statement made by any person to a police officer in the course of an investigation under this Chapter, shall, if reduced to writing, be signed by he person making it; nor shall any such statement or any record thereof, whether in a police diary or otherwise, or any part of such statement or record, be used for any purpose, save as hereinafter provided, at any inquiry or trial in respect of any offence under investigation at the time when such statement was made.:

Provided that when any witness is called for the prosecution in such inquiry or trial whose statement has been reduced into writing as aforesaid, any part of his statement, if duly proved, may be used by the accused, and with the permission of the Court, by the prosecution, to contradict such witness in the manner provided by section 145 of the Indian Evidence Act, 1872 (1 of 1872); and when any part of such statement is so used, any part thereof may also be used in the re-examination of such witness, but for the purpose only of explaining any matter referred to in his cross-examination.

(2) Nothing in this section shall be deemed to apply to any statement falling within the provisions of clause (1) of section 32 of the Indian Evidence Act, 1872 (1 of 1872), or to affect the provisions of section 27 of that Act.

Explanation.—An omission to state a fact or circumstance in the statement referred to in sub-section (1) may amount to contradiction if the same appears to be significant and otherwise relevant having regard to the context in which such omission occurs and whether any omission amounts to a contradiction in the particular context shall be a question of fact.

Omissions

Section 11 of the Evidence Act states that facts not otherwise relevant are relevant if they are inconsistent with any fact in issue or relevant fact and if by themselves or in connection with other facts they make the existence or non-existence of any fact in issue or relevant fact highly probable or improbable.

As a matter of practice and procedure, question relating to each omission ought to be separately asked and answer to said question have to be recorded separately and each omission ought to be proved through investigation officer separately; *Anil Daggi s/o Tukaram Mandhare* v. *State of Maharashtrra*, 2009 (4) B Cr C 27 (Bom) (DB).

The principle embodied in section 11 of the Evidence Act has been stated by Prof. Wigmore in simple and lucid manner. He pointed out that *'a failure to assert a fact, when it would have been natural to assert it, amounts in effect to an assertion of the non-existence of the fact.'* Therefore, omissions of important facts affecting the probabilities of the case are held to be relevant under section 11 of the Evidence Act in judging the veracity of the prosecution case; *Ram Kumar Pande* v. *State of M.P.*, AIR 1975 SC 1026: (1975) 3 SCR 519.

In this case, the Hon'ble Apex Court held that omission to mention name of accused in FIR before the investigation officer soon after the incident or at the time of inquest, is relevant under section 11 of the Evidence Act in judging the veracity of prosecution case; *Siddanki Ram Reddy* v. *State of A.P.*, (2010) 7 SCC 697: 2011 All SCR 49.

In this case, the Hon'ble Apex Court held that omission of material facts pertaining to the crime is relevant in judging veracity of prosecution case though it does not constitute substantive evidence; *State of Maharashtra* v. *Ahmed Sheikh Babajan*, (2009) 14 SCC 267.

In this case, the Apex Court held that omission to state fact if significant, may amount to contradiction. Omission of witness as to who caused which injury to whom was not contradictory when witness states the incident and the manner in which it occurred; *Jaswant Singh* v. *State of Haryana*, (2000) 4 SCC 848: JT 2000 (4) SC 114.

This judgement has become *locus classic* of the judgement rendered on the point as to when an omission in earlier statement can be relied upon to contradict subsequent statement in Court. The Hon'ble Apex Court has evolved a test for ascertaining under what circumstances an alleged omission can be relied upon to contradict the positive evidence in Court. The Hon'ble Apex Court held that: (1) A statement in writing made by a witness before a police officer in the course of investigation can be used only to contradict his statement in the witness box and for no other purpose; (2) statements not reduced to writing by the police officer cannot be used for contradiction; though a particular statement is not expressly recorded, a statement that can be deemed to be part of that expressly recorded can be used for contradiction, not because it is an omission strictly so-called but because it is deemed to form part of the recorded statement; (4) such a fiction is permissible by construction only in the following three cases:

(i) when a recital is necessarily implied from the recital or recitals found in the statement. (illustration: in the recorded statement before the police the witness states that he saw A stabbing B at a particular point of time, but in the witness-box he says that he saw A & C stabbing B at the same point of time; In the statement before the police the word "only" can be implied, *i.e.*, the witness saw A only stabbing B;)

(ii) a negative aspect of a positive recital in a statement; (illustration: in the recorded statement before the police the witness says that a dark man stabbed B, but in the witness-box he says that a fair man stabbed B; the earlier statement must be deemed to contain the recital not only that the culprit was a dark complexioned man but also that he was not of a fair complexion); and

(iii) when the statement before the police and that before the Court cannot stand together, (illustration: the witness says in the recorded statement before the police that A after stabbing B ran away by a northern lane, but in the Court he says that immediately after stabbing he ran away towards the southern lane; as he could not have run away immediately after the stabbing, *i.e.*, at the same point of time, towards the northern lane as well as towards the southern land, if one statement is true, the other must necessarily be false.)

The Court further held that the aforesaid examples are not intended to be exhaustive but only illustrative. The same instance may fall under one or more heads. It is for the trial Judge to decide in each case, after comparing the part or parts of the statement recorded by the police with that made in the witness-box, to give a ruling, having regard to the aforesaid principles, whether the recital intended to be used for contradiction satisfies the requirement of law; *Tahsildar Singh* v. *State of U.P.*, AIR 1959 SC 1012: (1959) SUPP 2 SCR 875.

Whether an omission to mention fact in statement made to police amounts to contradiction, the Court held that it is a question of fact to be decided considering significance and relevance of omission in context of such omission occurred; *Satya Pal* v. *State of Haryana,* AIR 2013 SC 2015.

In this case Hon'ble Apex Court held that if there are omissions in previous statement which do not amount to contradictions but throw some doubt on the veracity of what was omitted, the uncertainty or doubt may be capable of removal by questions in re-examination. Neither proof nor use of such omissions, which do not amount to contradictions is barred by section 145 of the Evidence Act. It is not possible to lay down a general rule as to what effect a particular omission for previous statement should have on the probative value of what was so omitted by a witness. The effect will depend upon the totality of proved facts and circumstances in which the omission might have taken place. It will often be determined by the importance of what was omitted. The Law of Evidence contains nothing more than section 3 and section 114 of the Evidence Act to indicate and illustrate the standards and methods employed in assessing the evidence; *Laxman* v. *State of Maharashtra,* AIR 1974 SC 308: 1974 Cr LJ 369: (1974) 2 SCR 505: 1974 Mh LJ 229.

In this case, a copy of statement of a witness furnished to accused contained material omission as regards the actual role played by the accused whereas no such omission was found in the original statement of the said witness recorded by the investigation officer. The Apex Court held that the defence was legitimately entitled to bring material omission on record and rely upon same; *Golla J. Reddy* v. *State of A.P.,* (1996) SUPP 1 SCR 772: AIR 1996 3244: 1996 Cr LJ 2470 (SC).

In this case, the Bombay High Court held that material omissions in evidence of witnesses if brought on record and proved through investigation officer, then they are ready to be in evidence and they do carry substantial evidentiary value. For appreciating these omissions, Court has to consider other prevailing circumstances and other corroborative evidence. Such omissions cannot be given weightage in isolation; *Manohar B. Dubale* v. *State of Maharashtra,* 2014 All MR (Cri) 3793.

Contradictions

Bringing out contradictions and omissions in former statement of a witness, is very important to demolish the case of the prosecution. For this purpose, the contradictions and omissions brought on record have to be proved through the investigation officer. Unless the contradictions and omissions brought on record are proved through the investigation officer, the Court is not bound to consider the same.

The procedure for bringing out contradictions and omissions and proving the same has been explained in various judgements. Few such judgements are given below—

In this case, the Hon'ble High Court has held that if it is intended by an accused to contradict the evidence given by a prosecution witness at the trial, with a statement made by him before the police during the investigation, the correct thing to do is to draw the attention of the witness to that part of the contradictory statement which he made before the police, and question him whether he did in fact make the statement. If the witness admits having made the particular statement to the police, that admission will go into evidence and will be recorded as part of the evidence of the witness and can be relied on by the accused as establishing the contradiction. If, on the other hand, the witness denies having made such a statement before the police, the particular portion of the statement recorded under section 162, Cr.P.C. should be provisionally marked for identification, and when investigation officer comes into the witness box, he should be questioned as to whether that particular statement has been made to him during investigation. The answer of investigation officer would prove the statement, which is then exhibited and accused may rely on it as contradiction; *State of Assam* v. *Md. Misir Ali,* AIR 1963 Assam 151.

The Division Bench of the Gauhati High Court has given the procedure for contradicting a witness with his previous statement as under - (a) If a witness admits having made particular statement to police, the admission will go into the evidence and will be recorded as part of the evidence and can be relied on by the accused as establishing the contradiction. (b) If, on the other hand, the witness denies to have made such statement before the police, the particular portion of the statement recorded, should be previously marked for identification as B-1 to B-1, B-2 to B-2 (or any identification mark), etc. and when the investigation officer comes into the witness box, he should be questions as to whether these particular statement had been made during the course of investigation by the particular witness. The answer of the investigation officer would prove the statement B-1 to B-1, B-2 to B-2 which are then exhibited as Ex. D-1, Ex. D-2, etc. (Exhibition marks); *Gandkanta Das* v. *State Assam,* 1990 Cr LJ 219.

In this case, the Hon'ble Apex Court while pointing out the duty of the trial court as to regards the recording of contradiction, has held that while recording the deposition of a witness, it becomes the duty of the trial Court to ensure that the part of the police statement with which it is intended to contradict the witness is brought to the notice of the witness in his cross-examination. The attention of the witness should be drawn to that part and this must reflect in his cross-examination by reproducing it. If the witness admits the part intended to contradict him, it stands proved and there is no need to further proof of contradiction and it will be read while appreciating the evidence. If he denies, his attention must be drawn to that statement and must be mentioned in the deposition. Thereafter attention of the investigation officer should be drawn to the passage marked for the purpose of contradition; *V.K. Mishra* v. *State of Uttarakhand,* 2015 All MR (Cri) 3298 (SC): 2015 SAR (Criminal) 1008 (SC).

In this case, the Apex Court distinguished the case of *Tara Singh* v. *State of Punjab,* AIR 1951 SC 441: 1951 SCJ 518: (1951) SCR 729 and explained the law of contradiction as: (a) section 145 of the Evidence Act applies when same person makes two contradictory statements either in different proceedings or in two different stages of a proceeding. (b) section 145 of the Evidence Act applies only if a witness denies that he made the former statement. (c) When the witness admits the former statement, all that is necessary is to look to the former statement on which no further proof is necessary because of the admission that it was made; *Bhaskar Singh* v. *State of Punjab,* (1952) SCR 812.

In this case, the defence counsel merely asked the witness as to whether he stated before the Magistrate that accused Surendra has assaulted Kameshwar to which he had replied: "he does not recall" as to what he stated before Magistrate. The Apex Court held that it cannot be called as contradiction as the provisions of section 145 of the Evidence Act have not been complied with; *Rajendra Singh* v. *State of Bihar,* AIR 2000 SC 1779: 2000 (3) Crimes 21 (SC): 2000 Cr LJ 2199 (SC).

During trial witness stated that he had gone to the spot on hearing the sound of a gunshot and tried to snatch away the gun from the accused. But in his police statement he did not state anything regarding snatching of the gun. The Apex Court held that this omission amounts to contradiction creating serious doubt about the truthfulness of the witness; *State of Rajasthan* v. *Rajendra Singh,* (2009) 11 SCC 106.

In this case, witnesses omitted the fact of oral dying declaration made by victim to them in statement recorded under section 161 Cr.P.C. The Apex Court held that significant omission so made in statement of witnesses recorded under section 161, Cr.P.C. amounts to contradiction; *Subhash* v. *State of Haryana,* AIR 2011 SC 349.

In this case, the Apex Court while refusing to consider the omissions as "contradictions" as the investigation officer was not asked whether he had put questions to the eye witness, has held that reading section 161 (2) of Cr.P.C. with the explanation to Section 162, and omission in order to be significant must depend upon, whether the specific question, the answer to which is omitted, was asked of the witness; *Jaswant Singh* v. *State of Haryana,* AIR 2000 SC 1833.

In this case, the Apex Court has held that resort to section 145 of the Evidence Act, is necessary only if a witness denies that he made the former statement; *Bhagwan Singh* v. *State of Punjab,* AIR 1952 SC 214: (1952) SCR 812.

In this case PW 1, PW 5 and PW 10 did not make any allegation as regards the alleged exhortation on part of all accused. However it appears that PW 3, PW 4 and PW 8 stated before the police that there had been such exhortations by the respondents therein. The Apex Court held that such omission on the part of PW 3, PW4 and PW 8, in the facts and circumstances of the case, being very material, would amount to contradiction; *Gopal* v. *Subhash,* AIR 2004 SC 4900.

In this case, during cross-examination of witness as to previous statement made before police almost all contradictions or omissions were brought on record, which were portions from the statement made before police that were not deposed before the Court. The Hon'ble Bombay High Court held that these were not the contradictions as contemplated under section 145 of the Evidence Act; *Sheshrao Nanu Dhawale* v. *State of Maharashtra,* 2009 (3) AIR Bom R 705: 2009 Cr LJ (NOC) 869 (Bom).

Other Important Cases on the Principle of Contradiction

Dhanabal v. *State of T.N.,* AIR 1980 SC 628 & *State of Rajsthan* v. *Kartar Singh,* AIR 1970 SC 1305: (1971) 1 SCR 56: A witness can be contradicted under section 145 of the Evidence Act only when he denies his statement and not when he admits it.

Mohanlal Gangaram Gehani v. *State of Maharashtra,* AIR 1982 SC 839: 1982 Cr LJ 630: 1982 Mah LR 117: Section 145 of the Evidence Act, applies only to cases where the same person makes two contradictory statements either in different proceedings or in two different stages of a proceeding....... Where the statement made by a person or witness is contradicted not by his own statement but by the statement of another prosecution witness, the question of the application of Section 145 does not arise.

State of Kerala v. *Babu,* AIR 1999 SC 2161: The statement recorded by police officer under section 161 of Cr.P.C. even though is a previous statement under section 145 of the Evidence Act, can be used for the purpose of establishing a contradiction or impeaching the credit of the witness but only in the manner provided for in Section 162 of Cr.P.C....... Accused has a right to make use of the previous statement of a witness including the statements recorded by the investigation agency under section 162 of Cr.P.C. during the course of an investigation for the purpose of establishing a contradiction in the evidence of a witness or discredit the witness.

State of Maharashtra v. *Kalu Shivram,* AIR 1980 SC 879: 1980 Cr LJ 564: Statement by prosecution witness before police can only be used to contradict such witness as provided in Section 145 of the Evidence Act...... It cannot be used as substantive evidence in favour of or against the accused.

Chinnammal v. *State of Tamil Nadu,* (1997) 1 SCC 145: 1997 SCC (Cri) 51: Previous statement of witness cannot be used as substantive evidence...... It can only be used by the defence to contradict or discredit any witness.

Prakash Chand v. *State (Delhi Admn.),* AIR 1979 SC 400: It is permissible to use the statements made under section 162 (1) of Cr. P.C. to the police, when the prosecution witness turns hostile, for the purpose of contradicting the witness with reference to the statements.

Faddi v. *State of M.P.,* AIR 1964 SC 1850: (1964) 6 SCR 312: In this case, the person lodging the F.I.R. subsequently was arraigned as an accused and was tried. The F.I.R. contained admission of facts by accused. As regards that admissibility of F.I.R. and its use against the accused, the Apex Court held that the F.I.R. being neither a confession nor a statement made to a police officer during the course of investigation, its admissibility is not barred either by Section 25 of Evidence Act or by Section 162 of Cr.P.C........ The report was an admission by the accused of certain facts which had a bearing on the question to be determined by the Court viz., how and by whom the murder was committed, or whether the accused's statement in Court denying the correctness of certain statements of the prosecution witnesses was correct or not...... Admissions are admissible in evidence under section 21 of the Evidence Act and admission of an accused can be proved against him.

Sukar v. *State of U.P.,* AIR 1999 SC 3883: A statement of injured recorded under section 161 of Cr.P.C. cannot be held admissible in evidence under section 33 of the Evidence Act.

Mohan Rai v. *State of Bihar,* AIR 1968 SC 1281: In this case, two complaints were lodged, one by 'A' and the other by 'M' in respect of same incident and divergent versions were given. Both the complaints were investigated simultaneously. Statement of 'A' was recorded as first information in one case and statement of 'M' as first information in the other. 'B' was questioned during investigation and prosecution was initiated against 'B' and 'M'. As regards the use of statement, the Apex held that no portion of 'B's statement could be used to contradict statement of 'M' in his complaint either under section 157 or Section 145 of the Evidence Act. As 'B' was not examined as a witness in a case, his previous statement could not be used either to contradict his evidence or corroborate it, even if it is to be held that it is a statement coming under section 154 of Cr.P.C.

Mahabir Singh v. *State of Haryana,* AIR 2001 SC 2503: Where the statement was made by a solitary eye-witness soon after the occurrence of crime to his father, the Apex Court held that it did not cross boundaries envisaged by words *"at or about the time when the fact took place"* in section 157 of the Evidence Act and testimony of father can be used for corroboration of evidence of eye-witness, his son.

Mathu Naikar v. *State of Tamil Nadu,* AIR 1978 SC 1647: (1978) 4 SCC 385: In this case, the Hon'ble Apex Court held that the practice of permitting the public prosecutor to explain omission or contradiction in deposition of a witness with reference to his statement recorded under section 161 of the Code is not permissible under law.

Effect of Omissions and Contradictions

Material discrepancies are those which are not normal, and not expected of a normal person. While normal discrepancies do not corrode the credibility of a party's case, material discrepancies do so; *State of Rajasthan* v. *Kalki,* (1981) 2 SCC 752.

However, it has been held by the Bombay High Court that minor discrepancies assume significance not in the evidence of independent witnesses but only in the evidence of interested witnesses; *State of Maharashtra* v. *Vazir Hakki,* 2005 Cr LJ 2719: 2005 (2) BCrC 195.

The omissions which amount to contradictions in material particulars, *i.e.,* materially affect the trial or core of the prosecution's case, render the testimony of the witness liable to be discredited and it is unsafe to rely upon such evidence; *A. Shankar* v. *State of Karnataka,* 2011 All MR (Cri) 2357 (SC). Same view has been taken by the Apex Court in *State of M.P.* v. *Dal Singh,* 2013 All SCR 2161.

It has been held by the Apex Court that only such omissions which amount to contradiction in material particular can be used to discredit the testimony of the witness unreliable. When the version given by the witness in the Court is different in material particulars from that disclosed in his earlier statement, the case of the prosecution becomes doubtful and not otherwise. Minor contradictions are bound to appear in the statements of truthful witnesses as memory sometimes plays false and the sense of observation differ from person to person; *Narayan C. Chaudhary* v. *State of Maharashtra,* (2000) 8 SCC 457.

While considering the effect of contradictions on the case of prosecution, the Hon'ble Apex Court observed that it is a settled proposition of law that there is possibility of some variations in the exhibits, medical and ocular evidence and it cannot be ruled out. But it is not that every minor variation or inconsistency would tilt the balance of justice in favour of the accused. Where contradictions and variations are of a serious nature, which apparently or impliedly are destructive of the substantive case sought to be proved by the prosecution, they may provide an advantage to the accused; 2015 SAR (Criminal) 455.

In this case, the Apex Court held that duly proved contradictions make motive also doubtful; *State of M.P.* v. *Surpa,* AIR 2001 SC 2408.

In a case of murder based on the evidence of last seen theory, vacillations in deposition of prosecution witnesses cannot be brushed aside as "minor discrepancy" especially when it is to form the basis for life sentences to three persons. The Hon'ble Apex Court held that said witness cannot be said to be trustworthy; *Sunil Rai @ Pauna* v. *Union Territory Chandigarh,* AIR 2011 SC 2545.

(2) Examination of Certain Categories of Witnesses

In the Court rooms the defence lawyers are confronted with different types of witnesses. Unless the defence lawyer knows his social background and antecedents, it will be difficult for him to cross-examine such witness. Further it is submitted that most of the people suffer from one or the other personality disorder. This leads to faulty perceptions about facts and things. In Psychiatry the characteristics of different types of personalities are given and the same are reproduced below which would help the defence lawyers during cross-examination—

(a) Paranoid Personality Disorder - Persons with paranoid personality disorder are characterized by longstanding suspiciousness and mistrust of people in general. They refuse responsibility for their own feelings and assign responsibility to others. They are often hostile, irritable, and angry. The bigot, the injustice collector, the pathologically jealous spouse, and the litigious crank often have paranoid personality disorder.

    In some persons the paranoid personality disorder is lifelong. In others it is a harbinger of schizophrenia. In still others, as they mature or as stress diminishes, paranoid traits give way to reaction formation, appropriate concern with morality, and altruistic concerns. In general, however, patients with paranoid personality disorder have lifelong problems working and living with others. Occupational and marital problems are common.

(b) Schizoid Personality Disorder - Schizoid personality disorder is diagnosed in patients who display a lifelong pattern of social withdrawal. Their discomfort with human interaction, their introversion, and their bland, constricted affect are noteworthy. Persons with schizoid personality disorder are often seen by others as eccentric, isolated, or lonely. Persons with the disorder tend to gravitate toward solitary jobs and involve almost no contact with others. Many prefer night work to day work, so that they do not have to deal with many people.

(c) Schizotypal Personality Disorder - Persons with Schizotypal personality disorder are strikingly odd or strange, even to laypersons. Magical thinking, peculiar ideas, ideas of reference, illusions, and derealisation are part of the schizotypal person's everyday world. In schizotypal personality disorder, thinking and communicating are disturbed. Like schizophrenic patients, persons with Schizotypal personality disorder may not know their own feelings; yet they are exquisitely sensitive to detecting the feelings of others, especially negative affect like anger. They may be superstitions or claim clairvoyance. Their inner world may be filled with vivid imaginary relationships and childlike fears and fantasies. They?may believe that they have special power and thought and insight. Although frank thought disorder is absent, their speech may often require interpretation. They may admit that they have perceptual illusions or macropsia or that people appear to them as wooden and alike. The speech of person with Schizotypal personality disorder may by odd or peculiar and have meaning only to them. They show poor interpersonal relationship and may act inappropriately. As a result, they are isolated and have few, if any, friends.

(d) Antisocial Personality Disorder - Antisocial personality disorder is characterized by continual antisocial or criminal acts, but it is not synonymous with criminality. Instead, it is an inability to conform to social norms that involves many aspects of the patient's adolescent and adult development. Antisocial personality disorder patients are highly represented by so-called con men. They are highly manipulative and are frequently able to convince others to participate in schemes that involve easy ways to make money or achieve fame or notoriety, which may eventually lead the unwary to financial ruin, social embarrassment, or both. Antisocial personality disorder patients do not tell the truth and cannot be trusted to carry out any? task or follow any conventional standard of morality. Promiscuity, spouse abuse, child abuse, and drunk driving are common events in the patients' lives. A notable finding is a lack of remorse for those actions; that is, the patients appear to lack a conscience. Depressive disorders, alcohol use disorders and other substance abuse are common.

(e) Borderline Personality Disorder - Borderline personality disorder patients stand on the border between neurosis and psychosis and are characterized by extraordinarily unstable affect, mood, behaviour, object relations, and self-image. These patients almost always appear to be in a state of crisis. Mood swings are common. The patients can be argumentative at one moment and depressed at the next and then complain of having no feelings at another time. The behaviour of borderline personality disorder patients is highly unpredictable. The painful nature of their lives is reflected in repetitive self-destructive acts. Such patients may slash their wrists and perform other self-mutilations to elicit help from others, to express anger, or to numb themselves to overwhelming affect.

(f) Histrionic Personality Disorder - Histrionic personality disorder is characterised by colourful, dramatic, extroverted behaviour in excitable, emotional persons. Accompanying their flamboyant presentations, however, is often an inability to maintain deep, long - lasting attachments. Gestures and dramatic punctuations in their conversations are common. They may make frequent slips of the tongue, and their language is colourful. The patients are sensation seekers and may get into trouble with the law, abuse substances, and act promiscuously.

(g) Narcissistic Personality Disorder - Persons with narcissistic personality disorder are characterized by a heightened sense of self-importance and grandiose feelings that they are unique in some way. They handle criticism poorly and may become enraged that anyone would dare to criticize them, or they may appear to be completely indifferent to criticism.

(h) Avoidant Personality Disorder - Persons with avoidant personality disorder show an extreme sensitivity to rejection, which may lead to a socially withdrawn life. They are not asocial and show a great desire for companionship but are shy; they need unusually strong guarantees of uncritical acceptance. Such persons are commonly referred to as having an inferiority complex. The main trait of their personality is timidity.

(i) Dependent Personality Disorder - Persons with dependent personality disorder subordinate their own needs to those of other, get others to assume responsibility for major areas in their lives, lack self-confidence, and may experience intense discomfort when alone for more than a brief period. This disorder is more common in women than in men. Persons with the disorder are unable to make decisions without an excessive amount of advice and reassurance from others. Pessimism, self-doubt, passivity, and fears of expressing sexual and aggressive feeling characterized the behaviour of the persons of this group.

(j) Obsessive-Compulsive Personality Disorder - Obsessive - compulsive personality disorder is characterized by emotional constriction, orderliness, perseverance, stubbornness, and indecisiveness. The essential features of the disorder is a pervasive pattern of perfectionism and inflexibility. Patients often have backgrounds characterized by harsh discipline. Their mood is usually serious. They may do well in positions demanding methodical, deductive, or detailed work, but they are vulnerable to unexpected changes, and their personal lives may remain barren.

(k) Passive-Aggressive Personality Disorder - The person with passive-aggressive personality disorder is characterized by covert obstructionism, procrastination, stubbornness, and inefficiency. Such behaviour is a manifestation of underlying aggression, which is expressed passively. Such persons find excuses for delays, and find fault with those on whom they depend.

(l) Depressive Personality Disorder - Persons with depressive personality disorder are characterized by lifelong traits that fall along the depressive spectrum. They are pessimistic, anhedonic, duty-bound, self-doubting, and chronically unhappy.

(m) Sadomasochistic Personality Disorder - These persons are characterised by elements of sadism or masochism or a combination of both. These persons experience sexual pleasure while inflicting pain on others.

(n) Sadistic Personality Disorder - Persons with sadistic personality disorder show a pervasive pattern of cruel, demeaning, and aggressive behaviour, beginning in early adulthood, that is directed toward others. Persons with the disorder like to humiliate or demean people in front of others. In general persons with sadistic personality disorder are fascinated by violence, weapons, injury, or torture.

The students and young lawyers are advised to read '**Body Language**' by Allan Pease and '**The Power of Your Subconscious Mind**' by Joseph Murphy which will enable you to read the minds of witnesses in the dock.

Child Witness

Child may testify and is a competent witness. As per section 118 of the Evidence Act, all persons shall be competent to testify unless the Court considers that they are prevented from understanding the questions put to them, or from giving rational answers to those questions, by tender years, extreme old age, disease, whether of body or mind, or any other cause of the same kind.

The maturation of sense organs is a very important factor in perception. Due to immaturity and tender age he is prone to tutoring and prompting. Therefore this class of witness is regarded as most dangerous. Even the Courts have insisted on adequate corroboration to the evidence of child, before accepting the same.

Evidence of Child should not be accepted without adequate corroboration; *Bhagwan Singh* v. *State of M.P.*, 2003 All MR (Cri) 564.

Where the Court was dealing with the evidence of a child of five years. The Apex Court held that a witness who, by reason of his immature understanding was not administered oath and who was privileged, by reason of his years, not to make his answer in an intelligible and coherent manner is unsafe to be trusted wholesale; *Suresh* v. *State of U.P.*, (1981) 3 SCR 259.

In this case, the Apex Court held that it is safe and prudent to look for corroboration for the evidence of a child witness from the other evidence on record; *K. Venkateshwarlu* v. *State of A.P.*, 2012 All SCR 2328.

In this case, son of deceased aged 7 years on the date of incident deposed that his mother was killed by her in laws. However said fact was not disclosed by him to police on the date of incident, but said to have been told to her maternal aunt. Child was staying with mother's parents after incident and was examined in Court after lapse of 7 years. The Apex Court held that it is unsafe to convict accused only on the evidence of child as possibility of parents of mother tutoring him could not be ruled out; *Hamza* v. *Muhammadkutty @ Mani*, 2014 All MR (Cri) 1108 (SC).

Chance Witness

A person who comes for a particular purpose to the place of occurrence cannot be described as a chance witness. Unless a person gives a satisfactory explanation to account for his presence at a particular place by chance, he cannot be characterized as 'chance witness'.

In this case, the Apex Court held that the evidence of a chance witness requires a very cautious and close scrutiny. A chance witness must adequately explain his presence at the place of occurrence. Conduct of the chance witness, subsequent to the incident may also be taken into consideration particularly as to whether he has informed anyone else in the village about the incident; *Jarnail Singh* v. *State of Punjab,* 2009 (4) Crimes 30 (SC).

In this case, the Apex Court held that the evidence of chance witness is not necessarily incredible or unbelievable but it only requires caution and close scrutiny before acceptance; *Satbir* v. *Surat Singh,* (1997) 2 SCR 1.

However, it has been held that if a chance witness happens to be a relative or a friend of the victim or inimically deposed towards the accused, his evidence is viewed with suspicion and requires caution and close scrutiny; *Bahal Singh* v. *State of Haryana,* AIR 1976 SC 2032: 1976 Cr LJ 1568.

Hostile Witness

A hostile witness is one, who from the manner in which he gives evidence, shows that he is not desirous to tell the truth to the Court, and who has deposed contrary to the case of the party who produces him. But, the mere fact that the evidence of a witness tends to be favourable to the accused would not be a valid ground to declare such a witness as hostile. As regards the appreciation of evidence of a hostile witness, the correct law is the one which has been rendered in *Gurpreet Singh* v. *State of Haryana,* AIR 2002 SC 3217. In this case, the Apex Court held that, "*It is now well settled that in the event of a portion of evidence not being consistent with the statement given under section 161 of Cr.P.C. and the witness stands declared hostile, that does not, however, mean and imply total rejection of the evidence....... The portion which stands in favour of the prosecution or the accused may be accepted but the same shall be subjected to close scrutiny.*"

In *Dhananjay* v. *State of West Bengal,* (1994) 1 SCR 37, the Apex Court has held that, "*that part of the testimony of ? a hostile witness which receives corroboration from other evidence on record could be accepted.*"

In *George* v. *State of Kerala,* (1998) 2 SCR 303, the Apex Court has held that, "*F.I.R. cannot be used to corroborate the informant or to discredit other prosecution withess before whom deceased made dying declaration when the first informant turned hostile.*"

Accomplice as a Witness

Relevant provisions relating to accomplice witness are given below:

Indian Evidence Act, 1872, section 133 - An accomplice shall be a competent witness against an accused person; and a conviction is not illegal merely because it proceeds upon the uncorroborated testimony of an accomplice.

Indian Evidence Act, 1872, section 114 - The Court may presume the existence of any fact which it thinks likely to have happened, regard being had to the common course of natural events, human conduct and public and private business, in their relation to the facts of the particular case. **Illustration (b)** - That an accomplice is unworthy of credit, unless he is corroborated in material particulars.

According to Wharton's Law Lexicon, 'accomplice' is a person concerned with another or others in the commission of a crime whereas according the Webster's dictionary 'accomplice' means an associate in wrong or crime, whether as a principal or accessory.

Section 133 of the Evidence Act is a rule of law and it states that an accomplice shall be a competent witness against an accused person whereas illustration (b) to section 114 of the Evidence Act is a rule of practice and caution. However illustration does not control main section and drawing of presumption is not mandatory. It is well settled law that court cannot accept evidence of accomplice unless it is corroborated in material particular.

An accomplice shall be a competent witness against an accused person; and a conviction is not illegal merely because it proceeds upon the uncorroborated testimony of an accomplice. [Evidence Act, Section 133]

The principle laid down in this case is known as "Baskerville Rule" and has been followed by the Indian Courts. In this case, Lord Reading said: there is no doubt that the uncorroborated evidence of an accomplice is admissible in law. But it has long being rule of practice at common law for the Judge to warn the jury of the danger of convicting a prisoner on the uncorroborated testimony of an accomplice or accomplices, and, in the discretion of the Judge to advise them not to convict upon such evidence; but the judge should point out to the jury that it is within their legal province to convict upon such unconfirmed evidence. This rule of practice has become virtually equivalent to a rule of law, and since the Court of Criminal Appeal came into operation this Court has held that, in the absence of such a warning by the Judge, the conviction must be quashed. If after the proper caution by the Judge the jury nevertheless convict the prisoner, this Court will not quash the conviction merely upon the ground that the accomplice's testimony was uncorroborated; *Kings* v. *Baskerville,* (1916) 2 KB 658: (1916) 2 JOB. 658.

In this case, the Apex Court held that an accomplice, by long legal tradition, is a notoriously infamous witness, one who being *partipes-criminis,* purchase his immunity by accepting to accuse others. Section 114, illustration (b) of the Evidence Act envisages the presumptive uncredit worthiness of an accomplice. But then, section 133 provides that a conviction is not illegal merely because it rests upon an accomplice's uncorroborated testimony; *Balwant Kaur* v. *Union Territory of Chandigarh,* (1988) 1 SCR 745.

In this case, three appellants were convicted under section 120B IPC and section 167(81) of the Sea Customs Act for having entered into a criminal conspiracy among themselves and with a Chinese citizen in Hong Kong to smuggle gold into India with the help of Ethyl Wong, an Airlines Stewardess. She gave evidence at the trial as a witness for the prosecution. Her testimony was clearly that of an accomplice. Although she could have been prosecuted, she was not arraigned and it is her testimony which has been the subject of a major part of the arguments before the Apex Court. As to the competency of her to give evidence and the evidence of accomplice, the hon'ble Apex Court held that under section 118 of the Evidence Act, all persons are competent to testify unless the Court considers that they are prevented from understanding the question put to them for reasons indicated in that section. Under section 132 of the Evidence Act, a witness is not excused from answering any relevant question upon the ground that the answer will incriminate him or expose him to a penalty of forfeiture of any kind and when compelled to answer such question is protected against arrest or prosecution by the safe guard in the proviso to section 132 as well as in Article 20(3). The evidence of Ethyl Wong could not therefore be ruled out as that of an incompetent witness. Since Ethyl Wong was a self-confessed criminal, in conspiracy with others who were being tried, her evidence was accomplice evidence. Section 133 of the Evidence Act makes the accomplice a competent witness against an accused person. For this reason also her testimony was that of a competent witness. The competency of an accomplice is not destroyed because he/she could have been tried jointly with the accused but was not and was instead made to give evidence in the case. Section 5 of the Indian Oaths Act and section 342 of the Code of Criminal Procedure, 1898 do not stand in the way of such a procedure. If any accomplice is not prosecuted but is tendered as a witness, the bar of the Indian Oaths Act ceases because the person is not an accused person in a criminal proceeding. The interrelation of section 342(4) of the Code and section 5 of the India Oaths Act, both of which prohibited the giving of oath or affirmation to an accused on trial is fully evidenced by the simultaneous amendment of the Code in 1955 by which the right to give evidence on oath is conferred on the accused and provisions in *pari materia* are made in section 5 of the Oaths Act. The only prohibition against the use of accomplice testimony exists in the rule of caution about the corroboration and the interdiction of influence in any form by section 343 of the Code. If any influence by way of promise of pardon has to be made, the provisions of sections 337 and 338 or of the Criminal Law Amendment Act, 1955 have to be observed. That, however, applies to special kinds of cases of which the present was not one. The expression 'criminal proceeding' in the exclusionary clause of section 5 of the Indian Oaths Act cannot be used to widen the meaning of the word 'accused'. The same expression is used in the proviso to section 132 of the Indian Evidence Act and there it means a criminal trial and not investigation. The same meaning must be given to the exclusionary clause of section 5 of the Oaths Act to make it conform to the provisions in *pari materia* to be found in section 342, 342A of the Code and section 132 of the Evidence Act. The expression is also not rendered superfluous because, given this meaning, it limits the operation of the exclusionary clause to criminal prosecutions as opposed to investigation and civil proceedings; *Laxmipat Choraria* v. *State of Maharashtra*, AIR 1968 SC 938: (1968) 2 SCR 624.

In this case, the Hon'ble Apex Court held that though an accomplice is a competent witness and though a conviction may lawfully rest upon his uncorroborated testimony, yet the court is entitled to presume and may be justified in presuming in the generality of cases that no reliance can be placed on the evidence of an accomplice unless the evidence is corroborated in material particulars, by which is meant that there has to be some independent evidence tending to incriminate the particular accused in the commission of the crime. The Court further held that there is no antithesis between section 133 and Illustration (b) to section 114 of the Evidence Act; *Dagdu* v. *State of Maharashtra*, (1977) 3 SCR 372.

In this case, the Apex Court held that there is no prohibition to act upon the deposition of accomplice not put on trial, without corroboration. An accomplice who has not been put on trial is a competent witness as he deposes in the Court after taking oath; *Prithipal Singh* v. *State of Punjab*, 2011 All MR (Cri) 3931 (SC).

As regards the use of evidence of an accomplice who has not been put to trial, the hon'ble Apex Court held that the does not prohibit taking into consideration even the evidence provided by an accomplice, who has not been put to trial. It is a well settled legal proposition that the evidence provided by a person who has not been put to trial, and who could not have been tried jointly with the accused can be considered, if the Court finds his evidence reliable, and conviction can also safely be based upon it. However, such evidence is required to be considered with care and caution. An accomplice who has not been put to trial is a competent witness as he deposes in Court after taking an oath, there is no prohibition under any law to act upon his deposition without corroboration; *R. Shaji* v. *State of Kerala*, 2013 (1) Crimes 217 (SC).

In this case, the hon'ble Apex Court held that the presumption under section 114 (b) of the Evidence Act is in the nature of a precautionary provision in corroborating the rule of prudence which is ingrained in the appreciation of accomplice's evidence. Therefore, the Court should be guarded before accepting the accomplice's evidence and look for corroborating evidence; *M.O. Shamsudhin* v. *State of Kerala*, (1995) 3 SCR 900.

Accomplice means a partner in crime. As regards the appreciation of evidence of an accomplice, the Constitution Bench of the Apex Court held that if any of the witnesses are accomplices, their evidence is admissible in law. Evidence of partisan or interested witnesses must be tested in the same way as any other interested evidence is tested, and in a proper case, the Court may look for independent corroboration before convicting the accused person; *The State of Bihar* v. *Basawan Singh*, (1959) SCR 195.

Approver as a Witness

An approver, who is admittedly guilty of the crime is an accomplice who has betrayed his associates and has apparently sought pardon for saving his skin, thereby getting immunity from prosecution. Therefore he is not termed as a witness of character.

As a matter of procedure, approver has to be examined as witness in committing court and in trial court also; *State (Delhi Admn.)* v. *Jagjit Singh*, AIR 1989 SC 598. However, the trial does not get vitiated due to non-examination of the approver in the committing Court as section 306(4)(a) CrPC is not manadatory; *State of Himachal Pradesh* v. *Surinder Mohan,* (2000) 1 SCR 659.

Ordinarily an approver's statement has to be corroborated in material particulars. Certain clinching features of involvement disclosed directly to an accused by an approver must be tested *qua* each accused from independent credible evidence and on being satisfied, the evidence of an approver can be accepted. What is the extent of corroboration that is required under the acceptance of the evidence of the approver would depend upon the facts and circumstances of the case. The corroboration required, however, must be in material particulars connecting each of the accused with the offence. In other words, the evidence of the approver implicating several accused persons in commission of the offence could not only be corroborated generally but also qua each accused. But that does not mean that there should be independent corroboration of every particular circumstance from an independent source. All that is required is that there must be some additional evidence rendering it probable that the story of accomplice is true. Corroboration also could be both by direct or circumstantial evidence; *A. Deivendran* v. *State of Tamil Nadu,* AIR 1998 SC 2821: 1998 AIR SCW 285.

As regards the appreciation of evidence of an approver, the Apex Court held that law is settled that an approver is a competent witness against the accused persons. But the Court, to satisfy its conscience, insists as caution and prudence to seek, as a rule, corroboration to the evidence of the approver, *particips criminis* from independent evidence ocular or circumstantial, of general particulars regarding the story spoken of by the approver of the commission of the crime and the part played by the accused therein to find whether it is true and worthy of acceptance. The reliability of the evidence of an approver should be considered from totality of the fact and circumstances; *Sevaka Perumal* v. *State of Tamil Nadu,* (1991) 2 SCR 711: AIR 1991 SC 1463: 1991 AIR SCW 1368.

In this case, the Hon'ble Apex Court held that though the conviction can be based on uncorroborated testimony of an accomplice, but as a rule of prudence, it is unsafe to place reliance on the uncorroborated testimony of an approver as required by illustration (b) to Section 114 of the Evidence Act; *S.C. Bahri* v. *State of Bihar,* AIR 1994 SC 2020: 1994 Cr LJ 3271: (1994) SUPP 1 SCR 483.

Accused as a Witness

The testimony of the accused as a witness if found cogent, credible and trustworthy can be accepted. It cannot be totally wiped out because of the only circumstance that they were accused in counter-case; *Raj Kishore Jha* v. *State of Bihar,* AIR 2003 SC 4664.

Defence Witnesses

It has been held by catina of judgements that defence witnesses are entitled to equal treatment as that of prosecution witnesses and their testimony can be accepted if found reliable and trustworthy.

In this case, the Apex Court held that defence witnesses are entitled to equal treatment with those of the prosecution. Courts ought to overcome their traditional instinctive disbelief in defence witnesses; *Dudh Nath Pandey* v. *State of U.P.*, AIR 1981 SC 911: (1981) 2 SCC 166.

Where the special judge refused to summon six defence witnesses, the Apex Court has held that, *"the trial was vitiated by his failure in summoning the defence witnesses and denying the fullest opportunity to defend himself;" Habeeb Mohammad* v. *State of Hyderabad,* AIR 1954 SC 51: (1954) SCR 475.

However it has been held by the Apex Court in *Arivazhagan* v. *State,* (2000) 2 SCR 155, that, *"if the Court feels that the list of defence witnesses is intended only to delay the proceedings, the Court is well within its powers to disallow even the whole of it....... It is the duty of Court to short list such proceedings."*

Expert Witness

When the Court has to form an opinion upon a point of foreign law, or of science or art, or as to identity of handwriting or finger impressions, the opinions upon that point of persons specially skilled in such foreign law, science or art, or in questions as to identity of handwriting or finger impressions are relevant facts. Such persons are called experts. [***Evidence Act, Section 45***].

In order to bring the evidence of a witness as that of an expert, it has to be shown that he has made a special study of the subject or acquired a special experience therein. Credibility of the expert's evidence depends on the reasons stated in support of his conclusions and the data and materials furnished which form the basis of his conclusions. Report submitted by an expert does not go in evidence automatically. He is to be examined in Court and has to face cross-examination; *State of Himachal Pradesh* v. *Jai Lal,* 1999 All MR (Cri) 1790.

In this case, Apex Court held that expert does not act as a judge or jury. His function is advisory in character. Credibility of expert evidence depends on the reasons stated in support of his conclusions and the data and material furnished which form the basis of his conclusions; *Ramesh Chandra Agrawal* v. *Regency Hospital Ltd.,* AIR 2010 SC 806: 2010 All SCR 165.

Recently, the Madras High Court has held that there is no expert available in India to offer any opinion regarding age of ink used for writing disputed document so as to satisfy requirements of section 45 of the Evidence Act. Therefore Court refused to send disputed handwriting for opinion to expert; *K. Vairavan* v. *Selvaraj,* 2013 (3) Crimes 177 (Mad).

Police Witness

Police witnesses are considered to be dangerous persons as they are professional witnesses. **Harris** has said that while cross-examining such witnesses 'try him with something, just a little out of the common line, by way of experiment. To be effective with policeman your questions must be rapidly put. Although he has a trained mind for the witness-box, it is trained in a very narrow grove; it moves as he himself moves, slowly and ponderously along its particular beat; it travels slowly because of its discipline, and is by no means able to keep pace with yours, or ought not to be. You should not permit him to trace the connection between one question and another when you desire that he should not do so. While this mental exertion is going on, interrept him suddenly with a question you have good reason for putting, and in all probability you will get something near the answer you require. It is dangerous to put "fishing" question to this class of witness. Your are almost sure to catch the wrong answer. Your safer course will be to cross-examine for contradictions and improbabilities, not forgetting where necessary to give the witness the opportunity of denying anything upon which you intend to contradict him. Cross-examine for prejudices, and as to opportunities, remembering always that there is often as much in the manner as in the matter of cross-examination, and much more at times in silence than in both.' **P. Ramanatha Aiyer** has said that, "*A police officer is a very difficult witness to cross-examine. In order that a police officer should be cross-examine effectively, the defence counsel should prepare himself with all details and the steps taken in investigation by the said officer. The Police officer generally idenfies himself with the case as if it is his personal one. Therefore, it is risky to question him in a haphazard manner unless you know that he can be caught in the net......... A rapid and minute examination on details upon which he may be unprepared will be the safest plan to be adopted especially upon matters bordering on, or connected with, those portions of his evidence, in which one's instructions or one's instinct, lead one to believe that there have been delinquencies on his part. A fear of underhand or illegal doings being disclosed or brought to light may tend to put him in a flutter: and to this, a real or assumed air of having some dangerous knowledge, or information, will be of assistance, if coupled with fineness. Should such a witness evidence an attempt to escape a point that is pressed in a manner that shows his desire to conceal his attempt to do so, he should be brought up sharply and the point should pressed home.*" **Morrison on Advocacy** says that, "*with this class of witnesses, as with every other, the chief rules to remember are not to cross-examine too far on any point and, if possible, never to cross-examine minutely upon any point upon which any other witnesses have been cross-examined.*"

Stock Witness

In this case this witness was examined by police in some other case also and he was said to be a police tout. The Apex Court held that evidence of stock witness cannot be relied upon for recording conviction; *Baldev Singh* v. *State of Punjab*, (2009) 6 SCC 564.

Interested Witness

Term 'interested' postulates that witness must have some direct interest in having accused somehow or the other convicted for some other reason; *Takdir S. Sheikh* v. *State of Gujarat*, 2012 All MR (Cri) 688 (SC).

In this case, the Apex Court held that merely because eye witnesses are family members, their evidence cannot *per se* be discarded. When there is allegation of interestedness, the same has to be established by the defence. Mere statement that being relatives of deceased they are likely to falsely implicate accused, cannot be a ground to discard evidence, which is otherwise cogent and reliable; *Bhupendra Singh* v. *State of U.P.*, (2009) 12 SCC 447.

In this case, where the incident took place between the two rival political factions, the Apex Court held that eye witnesses belonging to victim party can be stamped as interested witnesses. Evidence of such witnesses has to be examined with great care and caution to obviate possibility of false implication or over-implication; *Pandurang C. Mhatre* v. *State of Maharashtra,* (2009) 10 SCC 773: 2009 All SCR 2348.

In a case of murder enmity between accused family and deceased family was admitted. All the prosecution witnesses belonged to deceased family and were inimical to the accused person. The prosecution witnesses denied injuries on accused. However medical evidence established several injuries on the person of accused. The Apex Court held that non-explanation of injuries sustained by accused or denial of such injuries by witnesses makes their evidence unreliable; *Ganesh Datt* v. *State of Uttarakhand,* 2014 All SCR 2278: 2014 (3) Crimes 47 (SC).

Partisan Witnesses

(3) Special Types of Evidence

Handwriting

When the Court has to form an opinion as to the person by whom any document was written or signed, the opinion of any person acquainted with the handwriting of the person by whom it is supposed to be written or signed that it was or was not written or signed by that person, is a relevant fact. [***Evidence Act, Section 47***]

The science of handwriting is not an exact science unlike the science of fingerprints; *Vandavasi Karthikeya* v. *S. Kamalamma,* AIR 1994 AP 102.

The Expert evidence as to handwriting is opinion evidence and it cannot take the place of substantive evidence; *Ram Chandra* v. *State of U.P.,* AIR 1957 SC 381.

The Court cannot afford to overlook the fact that the science of identification of handwriting is an imperfect and frail one as compared to the science of identification of finger-prints and therefore looked for corroboration. The Court should be extremely slow in venturing and opinion on the basis of mere comparison, more so, when the quality of evidence in respect of specimen/ admitted writings is not of high standard. Before a Court can act on the opinion evidence of a handwriting expert two things must be proved beyond any manner of doubt, namely, (i) the genuineness of the specimen/admitted handwriting of the concerned accused and (ii) the handwriting expert is a competent, reliable and dependable witness whose evidence inspires confidence; *State of Maharashtra* v. *Sukhdeo Singh,* (1992) 3 SCR 480.

In this case, the Apex Court held that the writing may be proved to be in the handwriting of a particular individual by the evidence of a person familiar with the handwriting of that individual or by the testimony of an expert competent to make the comparison of handwritings on a scientific basis. A third method of comparison is comparison by the Court with the writing made in the presence of the Court or admitted or proved to be the writing of the person; *Fakhriddin* v. *State of M.P.,* AIR 1967 SC 1326.

In this case, it is alleged that General Manager and Trustee of Canbank Mutual Fund (CMF) have made false endorsement on a letter relating to disbursement of brokerage. Witness claimed to be conversant with the handwriting of accused.

However, material on which he is making such claim, not produced. The Apex Court held the evidence of said witness to be unreliable as the facts and circumstances showed that said witness was not part of chain of correspondence to speak its author; *R. Raghuvir Acharya* v. *C.B.I.*, 2013 All SCR 3354: 2013 (3) Bom CR (Cri) 289 (SC).

In this case, when prosecution witness testified that the letter was written by accused, was suggested that the same was forged and fabricated, the Apex Court held that it became incumbent upon prosecution to prove handwriting and signature of accused thereon by sending it to handwriting expert; *Pawan Kumar* v. *State of Haryana*, 2004 (1) BCrC 479 (SC).

Finger Prints and Foot Prints

In this case, the Apex Court held that evidence of finger print expert falls under the category of expert evidence under section 45 of the evidence Act. However evidence of finger print expert is not substantive evidence but can only be used for corroboration; *Musheer Khan @ Badshah Khan* v. *State of M.P.*, 2010 All MR (Cri) 933 SC.

However, the science of identification of footprints is not a fully developed science and therefore no reliance can be placed on the report of foot print experts; *Mohd. Aman* v. *State of Rajasthan*, AIR 1997 SC 2960: 1997 Cr LJ 3567.

In this case, the Apex Court held that the circumstances of matching of shoeprints found at the spot with that of the accused is considered insufficient to establish the offence against accused; *State of Haryana* v. *Ved Prakash*, AIR 1994 SC 468.

In this case, vehicle was recovered on the basis of statements of a witness who could see only one digit from number plate of vehicle. There was no evidence that marks of motor cycle tyre were lifted from the place of offence and compared with marks of vehicle recovered. Further, marks of tyre received by FSL were also not sealed. The Apex Court held that it would be unsafe to rely on above evidence in order to establish presence of vehicle at the place of offence; *Varun Chaudhary* v. *State of Rajasthan*, 2012 All SCR 821.

Electronic & Digital Evidence

The Central Government has amended Indian Evidence Act, 1872 and introduced sections 65-A, 65-B and 67-A by Act No. 21 of 2000, section 92 and Sch. II with effect from17th October 2000. The newly inserted provisions are special provisions as to evidence and admissibility relating to electronic records.

Relevant provisions pertaining to electronic and digital evidence are reproduced below:

Evidence Act Section 45-A.—When in a proceeding, the court has to form an opinion on any matter relating to any information transmitted or stored in any computer resource or any other electronic or digital form, the opinion of the Examiner of Electronic Evidence referred to in section 79-A of the Information Technology Act, 2000 (21 of 2000), is a relevant fact.

Explanation.—For the purposes of this section, an Examiner of Electronic Evidence shall be an expert.

Information Technology Act, 2000, Section 79-A.—The central government may for the purpose of providing expert opinion on electronic form evidence before any Court or other authority specify, by notification in the Official Gazette, any Department, Body or agency of the Central Government or a State Government as an Examiner of Electronic Evidence.

Explanation.—For the purposes of this section, "electronic form evidence" means any information of probative value that is either stored or transmitted in electronic form and includes computer evidence, digital audio, digital video, cell phones, digital fax machines.

Evidence Act section 65A & 65B. In this case, the Court held that evidence of video and photo identification must satisfy the tests laid down in Turnbull; *R.* v. *Turnbull,* 1977 QB 224 (CA).

The Supreme Court of Canada held that identification of accused through video tape is permissible provided the video is clear and is of quality and depends on the time for which the accused is shown; but the weight to be given to the tape is for the Judge to decide; *R.* v. *Nikolovsk,* (1996) 141 DLR (4d) 647.

Where the authenticity of the video and audio recording has not been certified by the Foresic Laboratory, the same is not admissible; *Mahendra Singh* v. *Gulab,* AIR 2005 SC 2515.

A three-Judge Bench of The Supreme Court overruled the decision in the case of *State (NCT of Delhi)* v. *Navjog Sandhu @ Afsan Guru,* AIR 2005 SC 3820: (2005) 11 SCC 600: 2005 AIR SCW 4148 and held that proof of electronic record is a special provision introduced under the Evidence Act. The very caption of section 65-A of the Evidence Act read with section 59 and 65-B is sufficient to hold that the special provisions on evidence relating to electronic record shall be governed by the procedure prescribed under section 65-B of the Evidence Act. That is a complete Code in itself. Being a special law, the general law on secodary evidence under sections 63 and 65 has to yield. An electronic record by way of secondary evidence therefore, shall not be admitted in evidence unless the requirements under section 65-B are satisfied. Thus, in the case of CD, VCD, chip, etc., the same shall be accompanied by the certificate in terms of section 65-B obtained at the time of taking the document, without which, the secondary evidence pertaining to that electronic record, is inadmissible; *Anwar P.V.* v. *P.K. Basheer,* AIR 2015 SC 180.

In this case, the Apex Court held that sub-section (1) of the section 65-B of the Evidence Act makes admissible as a document, paper print out of electronic records stored in optical or magnetic media produced by a computer, subject to the fulfilment of the conditions specified in sub-section (2) of section 65-B of the Evidence Act. Secondary evidence of contents of documents can also be led under section 65 of the Evidence Act; *Tomaso Bruno* v. *State of U.P.,* (2015) 7 SCC 178.

In this case, the Bombay High Court held that certificate under section 65-B of the Evidence Act must be signed by person occupying a responsible official position in relation to operation of relevant device or the management of relevant activities so that electronic record produced could be taken as admissible evidence; *M/s Shradha Shipping Co. Pvt. Ltd.* v. *M/s Adhithri Trading Co.*, 2015 (4) Crimes 319 (Bom).

In this case, the Bombay High Court held that it is mandatory for prosecuting agency to produce certificate in terms of section 65-B of the Evidence Act obtained at a time of collecting call details record of mobile phone. In absence of its compliance, secondary evidence pertaining to that electronic record is inadmissible; *Faim @ Lala Ibrahim Khan* v. *State of Maharashtra*, 2016 All MR (Cri) 4225.

In this case, question arose as to whether call details record (CDR) can be admitted in evidence without requisite certificate on call details record as per the provisions of law contained in section 65-B of the Evidence Act. The Hon'ble Bombay High Court held that call details record is inadmissible in law where requisite certificate as per law has not been filed; *Balasaheb G. Todkari* v. *State of Maharashtra*, 2015 All MR (Cri) 3464.

Where Magistrate passed the order directing exhibit of electronic record without considering objection of petitioner as to non-compliance of mandatory conditions laid down under section 65-B(2) & (4) of Evidence Act. The High Court held that order of the Magistrate is illegal. The Court further held that order of exhibit shall be subject to objections of petitioner and it shall be decided by trial Court at the time of final hearing; *Aum International Inc.* v. *Indian Hotels Co. Ltd.*, 2017 All MR (Cri) 1071 (Bom).

See: (i) *Sanjay Singh R. Chavhan* v. *Dattatraya G. Fhalke*, 2015 SC; (ii) *Amar Singh* v. *Union of India*, (2011) 7 SCC 69; (iii) *Ratan Tata* v. *Union of India*, (WP (C) 398 of 2010; (iv) *Lorraine* v. *Markel American Insurance Co.*, 2007 USA; (v) *Kubor* v. *Dickson*, SC of Nigera.

Voice Identification Evidence

This is a case where an FIR was registered on a complaint made by Rajiv Bhadauria of Jindal Steel Company Pvt. Ltd. alleging that the appellants demanded a sum of money to refrain from telecasting programmes on a television channel pertaining to the alleged involvement of a corporate entity in a wrongful activity pertaining to the allocation of coal blocks. The appellants were arrested in connection with the said crime. An application was moved by the investigating officer when the appellants were in police custody, requesting the Court to seek the consent of the appellants for obtaining their voice samples at the Central Forensic Laboratory, CBI for the purpose of comparing it with a recording which had been made in the course of a sting operation. The appellants consented for the same. But the appellants raised a grievance that they were being made to read out inculpatory material drawn from an audio recording of the alleged sting operation. Thereafter the matter reached the Apex Court. The Apex Court held that the underlying process for drawing the voice samples should be fair and reasonable, having due regard to the mandate of Article 21. On the other hand, it is not open to the accused to dictate the course of investigation. The text which the appellants would be called upon to read out for the purpose of drawing their voice samples will not have sentences from the inculpatory text. Similarly, permitting the text to contain words drawn from the disputed conversation would meet the legitimate concern of the investigating authorities for making a fair comparison; *Sudhir Chaudhary,* v. *State (NCT of Delhi),* Criminal Appeal Nos. 700-701 of 2016, decided on 29th July 2016.

In this case, the Apex Court held that the evidence of voice identification is at best suspect, if not, wholly unreliable. Accurate voice identification is much more difficult than visual identification. It is prone to such extensive and sophisticated tampering, doctoring and editing that the reality can be completely replaced by fiction. Therefore, the Courts have to be extremely cautious in basing a conviction purely on the evidence of voice identification; *Nilesh Dinkar Paradkar* v. *State of Maharashtra,* 2011 All SCR 796.

Tape Recorder

A previous statement made by a person and recorded on tape, can be used not only to corroborate the evidence given by the witness in Court but also to contradict the evidence given before the Court as well as to test the veracity of the witness and also to impeach his impartiality. However the Apex Court in *Ram Singh* v. *Col. Ram Singh,* (1985) SUPP 2 SCR 399, has held that following conditions must be fulfilled before accepting the same - (i) The voice of the speaker must be identified by the maker of the record or by others who recognise his voice. Where the voice is denied by the maker it will require very strict proof to determine whether or not it was really the voice of speaker. (ii) The voice of the speaker should be audible and not distorted by other sounds or disturbances. (iii) The accuracy of the tape recorded statements has to be proved by the maker of the record by satisfactory evidence. (iv) Every possibility of tampering with or erasure of a part of the tape recorded statement must be ruled out. (v) The statement must be relevant according to the rules of evidence. (vi) The recorded cassette must be carefully sealed and kept in safe custody. The Court further held that, *"Court must be satisfied beyond reasonable doubt that the record has not been tampered with."* Other celebrated cases on the point are; *Sri. Ram Reddy* v. *V.V. Giri,* AIR 1971 SC 1162: (1971) 1 SCR 399, and *Yusuffalli Esmail Nagree* v. *State of Maharashtra,* AIR 1968 SC 147: (1967) 3 SCR 720.

Dog Tracking

It has been held that dog tracking evidence is a weak piece of evidence. The Apex Court has held that Iddentification of accused by dogs of police squad is not sufficient to connect him with the crime; *Surinder Pal Jain* v. *State (Delhi Admn.),* 1993 Cr LJ 1871.

Serologist

Where in a case of burning, the serologist failed to give opinion in respect of origin, sex, and age of the deceased from bones recovered from spot, the Apex Court declined to consider his report and set aside the conviction; *Bhupendra Singh* v. *State of U.P.,* AIR 1991 SC 1083.

Typewriter

The Constitution Bench of the Apex Court in *State (through C.B.I., New Delhi)* v. *S.J. Choudhary,* (1996) 2 SCR 556: I (1996) CCR 156, has held that, *"the opinion of a typewriter expert comes within the ambit of section 45 of the Evidence Act and is admissible."*

[**Note** - This Constitution Bench has overruled the observations made in *Hanumant* v. *State of Maharashtra,* AIR 1952 SC 343: (1952) SCR 1091 pertaining to typewriter expert and evidence on the basis of concession.].

Dying Declarations

A statement made by a person as to the cause of his death, or as to any of the circumstances of the transaction which resulted in his death, in cases in which the cause of that person's death comes into question is relevant under section 32 of the Evidence Act. Dying declarations form a special class of evidence and the Courts have given sanctity to such statements if they are found trustworthy.

Section 60 of the Evidence Act lays down that the oral evidence must be direct. Dying declaration is an exception to the general rule that heresay evidence is not admissible. This exception has been devised out of necessity as there would be no evidence to such incidents. It is accepted on the principle that a person who is about to die would not make a false statement. It is said that a person who is on the verge of death, when there is no hope of survival and when every motive has gone, no person would lie.

There is no particular form or procedure for recording dying declaration. It should be recorded, as far as practicable, in the language of the declarant. There is no requirement of law it should be recorded in the question and answer form. As a matter of general rule and caution, mental and physical state of the declarant should be certified through doctor. Though dying declaration recorded by police is viewed with suspicion, it can be recorded by police in case of emergency and where there is no time to call magistrate or doctor. Examination of scribe who recorded dying declaration is obligatory. Where no reason's were given for non-examination of scribe, dying declaration was discarded.

The general principle on which this species of evidence is admitted is, that they are declarations made in extremity, when the party is at the point of death, and when every hope of this world is gone; when every motive to falsehood is silenced, and the mind is induced by the most powerful considerations to speak the truth; a situation so solemn, and so awful, is considered by the law as creating an obligation equal to that which is created by a positive oath administered in a Court of Justice.* *Rex* v. *Woodcock,* (1789) 168 Eng. Rep. 352 (KB).

Where the dying declaration was recorded by constable on the dictations of police sub-inspector, the hon'ble Apex Court held that it is not safe to rely upon said dying declaration as the narration was not in the actual words of deceased; *Muralidhar @ Gidda* v. *State of Karnataka,* 2014 All SCR 1571.

By merely exhibiting dying declaration, its contents is not proved unless such witness or magistrate vouchsafes before the trial Court; *Jivan T. Dhavali* v. *State of Maharashtra,* 2008 All MR (Cri) 2018 (Bom).

A statement of declarant recorded as dying declaration by nods, gestures or signs is admissible; *Meesala Ramakishan* v. *State of A.P.,* (1994) 4 SCC 182: 1994 SCC (Cri) 838.

In this case, the Apex Court held that absence of medical certificate does not render a dying declaration to be unacceptable. What is essentially required is that the person who records it must be satisfied that the injured person was in a fit state of mind. The medical certificate is only a rule of caution; *Koli Chunilal Savji* v. *State of Gujarat,* AIR 1999 SC 3696: 1999 Cr LJ 4582: (1999) 9 SCC 562.

In this case, appellants were convicted by Additional Sessions Judge, Chandrapur for the offence punishable under section 302 and 201 of IPC. One of the items in evidence was writing on the wall with the help of *lipstick.* And the same was found to be in handwriting of the deceased. Deceased wrote on the wall with the help of lipstick that she wanted to commit suicide. It was contended on behalf of the defence/appellants that the trial Court committed a grave error by ignoring the said dying declaration. In appeal, the hon'ble Bombay High Court held that writing by lipstick on the wall cannot be treated as dying declaration to hold that deceased committed suicide; *Gowardhan B. Ashtekar* v. *State of Maharashtra,* 2015 All MR (Cri) 1441.

Dying declaration can be oral or recorded. Oral dying declaration has to be conveyed to the Court at the trial in precisely the same words used by the maker of the statement: *Kamal R. Jadhav* v. *State of Maharahshtra,* 2006 All MR (Cri) NOC 220. But, ordinarily it is not safe to rely on oral dying declaration; *Bhagwan Das* v. *State of Rajasthan,* AIR 1957 SC 589. And it is an extremely weak type of evidence; *Puran Chand* v. *State of Haryana,* 2010 All MR (Cri) 2625 (SC).

In this case, doctor recorded statement of the deceased on admission in hospital but said statement was neither read over to her nor her signature or thumb impression was obtained. It was also not attested by any other person. The Court held that it would not be safe to convict the accused solely on the basis of dying declaration; *Jai Karan* v. *State (NCT of Delhi),* 2000 All MR (Cri) 682 (SC). Though there was no mention in the dying declaration that it was read over and explained to the deceased, the trial Court and the High Court concluded that it has to be presumed that it was read over and explained to the deceased. The Apex Court held that view of the trial Court and the High Court is unacceptable; *Shaikh Bakshu* v. *State of Maharashtra,* 2007 All SCR 2407: (2008) 1 SCC (Cri) 679. The requirement of an endorsement that the contents of the dying declaration were read over to and admitted by its declarant is not an empty formality. In absence of such endorsement, dying declaration is rendered unsafe to rely upon; *Datta T. Malwad* v. *State of Maharashtra,* 2014 All MR (Cri) 3967. Where the dying declaration was not read over to the declarant and there was no evidence that deceased admitted the contents of the dying declaration to have been correctly recorded, the Court did not place any reliance on the said dying declaration; *Raju K. Adangale* v. *State of Maharashtra,* 2014 All MR (Cri) 4085.

In *Patel Hiralal Joitaram* v. *State of Gujrat,* 2002 All MR (Cri) 460 SC, the Apex Court while dealing with the admissibility of a dying declaration held that *"admissibility is the first step and once it is admitted, the Court has to consider how far it is reliable........ Once the test of reliability is found positive, the Court has to consider the utility of that statement in the particular case."*

In this case, accused was charged with the offence of murder. The body of deceased was recovered from a trunk in railway compartment. It was claimed by prosecution that deceased made a statement to his wife that he received a letter asking him to go to the house of the accused for receiving money due to him and that he was so doing. The prosecution introduced this statement as a piece of evidence. As regards that admissibility of this statement, Privy Council held that the statement is admissible in evidence and it was rightly admitted under section 32 (1) of the Evidence Act. For admissibility under the section, the statement may be made before the cause of death has arisen, or before the deceased has any reason to anticipate being killed. The statement made by deceased to his wife can certainly be held to be a circumstance of the transaction which resulted in his death; *Pakala Narayan Swamy* v. *Emperor*, (1939) LR 66 IA 66.

In *Uka Ram* v. *State of Rajsthan*, AIR 2001 SC 1814, the Apex Court explained the circumstances under which conviction for murder can be based solely on dying declaration. The Court held that, *"The admissibility of the dying declaration rests upon the principle that a sense of impending death produses in a man's mind the same filling as that of a conscientious and virtuous man under oath - "Nemo moriturus praesumuntur mentire". Such statements are admitted, upon consideration that their declarations made in extremity, when the maker is at the point of death and when every hope of this world is gone, when every motive to falsehood is silenced and the mind induced by the most powerful consideration to speak the truth. The Principle on which the dying declaration are admitted in evidence, is based upon the legal maxim" Nemo moriturus praesumuntur mentire "i.e., a man will not meet his maker with a lie in his mouth. It has always to be kept in mind that though a dying declaration is entitled to great weight, yet it is worthwhile to note that as the maker of the statement is not subjected to cross-examination, it is essential for the Court to insist that dying declaration should be of such nature as to inspire full confidence of Court in its correctness. The Court is obliged to rule out the possibility of the statement being the result of either tutoring, prompting or vindictive or product of imagination. Before relying upon a dying declaration, the Court should be satisfied that the deceased was in a fit state of mind to make the statement. Once the Court is satisfied that the dying declaration was true, voluntary and not influence by any extraneous consideration, it can base it conviction with any further corroboration as rule requiring corroboration is not a rule of law but only a rule of prudence."*

The Constitution Bench of the Apex Court consisting of five Judges in *Laxman* v. *State of Maharashtra*, AIR 2002 SC 2973: 2002 (6) SCC 710: 2002 All MR (Cri) 2259, has held that, *"Normally the Court in order to satisfy whether the deceased was in a fit mental condition to make the dying declaration look upto the medical opinion. But where the eye - witnesses state that the deceased was in a fit and conscious state to make the declaration, the medical opinion will not prevail, not can it be said that since there is no certification of the doctor as to the fitness of the mind of the declarant, the dying declaration is not acceptable......... There is no requirement of law that a dying declaration must necessarily be made to a Magistrate....... What is essentially required is that the person who records a dying declaration must be satisfied that the deceased was in a fit state of mind......... A certification by the doctor is essentially a rule of caution and therefore the voluntary and truthful nature of the declaration can be established otherwise."*

In this case, the hon'ble Apex Court, has summarized the principles governing dying declarations which are as under:—

(i) There is neither rule of law nor of prudence that dying declaration cannot be acted upon without corroboration.

(ii) If the Court is satisfied that the dying declaration is true and voluntary, it can base conviction on it, without corroboration.

(iii) The Court has to scrutinize the dying declaration and must ensure that the declaration is not the result of tutoring, prompting or imagination. The Court has to further scrutinize as to whether the deceased had an opportunity to observe and indentify the assailants and whether he/she was in a fit state to made the declaration.

(iv) Where dying declaration is suspicious, it should not be acted upon without corroborative evidence.

(v) Where the deceased was unconscious and could never make any dying declaration the evidence with regard to it is to be rejected.

(vi) A dying declaration which suffers from infirmity cannot form the basis of conviction.

(vii) Merely because a dying declaration does contain the details as to be occurrence, it is not to be rejected.

(viii) Equally, merely because it is a brief statement, it is not to be discarded. On the contrary, the shortness of the statement itself guarantees truth.

(ix) Normally the Court in order to satisfy whether deceased was in a fit mental condition to make the dying declaration look up to the medical opinion. But where the eye-witness said that the deceased was in a fit and conscious state to make the dying declaration, the medical opinion cannot prevail.

(x) Where the prosecution version differs from the version as given in the dying declaration, the said declaration cannot be acted upon.

(xi) Where there are more than one statement in the nature of dying declaration, one first in point of time must be preferred. Of course, if the plurality of dying declaration could be held to be trustworthy and reliable, it has to be accepted; *P.V. Radhakrishna* v. *State of Karnataka,* 2003 All MR (Cri) 1792. Another Bench of the Hon'ble Apex Court has also reiterated the above principles governing dying declarations; *Atbir* v. *Government (NCT of Delhi),* 2010 All MR (Cri) 3998 (SC): (2010) 9 SCC 1.

This was a case *Moti Singh* v. *State of U.P.,* (1964) 1 SCR 688 of murder where some persons including the appellants were convicted by the Sessions Judge. High Court acquitted other five but appellants were convicted for murder. The facts of the case are that one 'G' was injured during the occurrence and had been taken to the hospital where his dying declaration was recorded. He left the hospital and died twenty days later. Before any post-mortem examination could be held, his body was cremated. In appeal to Supreme Court the appellants contended that the dying declaration was inadmissible and they were entitled to an acquittal. The Apex Court held that, *"The dying declaration was inadmissible in evidence as there was no evidence on record as to what caused the death of 'G'. The mere fact that 'G' had received two gun shot injury during the occurrence which in the opinion of the doctor were dangerous to life was not sufficient for holding that 'G' must have died on account of these injuries....... When it was not established that 'G' had died as a result of the injuries received at the incident, his statement did not relate to the cause of his death or to the circumstances of the transaction which resulted in his death and did not fall within the ambit of Section 32(1) of the Evidence Act."*

In this case *Sukhar* v. *State of U.P.*, AIR 1999 SC 3883 statement was given by injured to investigation officer and F.I.R. also was lodged by him. As regards the admissibility of the statement, the Apex Court held that, *"F.I.R. is not admissible as dying declaration under section 32 of the Evidence Act."*

In this case *Kajal Sen* v. *State of Assam*, AIR 2002 SC 617 no bed-head ticket was taken out in which statement and condition of patient was recorded. Further the person recording the dying declaration also admitted that deceased was surrounded by many attendants who were talking with deceased. In particular facts and circumstances of the case, the Apex Court held the dying declaration to be doubtful and therefore ruled out of consideration.

This was a case *Kans Raj* v. *State of Punjab*, (2000) 3 SCR 662 of dowry death. The Apex Court held that, *"if dying declaration is in writing, then the scribe must be produced in the Court. If the statement is verbal then the person who had heard the deceased making statement must be examined."* The Apex Court while convicting the accused, explained the meaning of expression "soon before" as:

> *"...... However such death should "soon before" be preceded by cruelty or harassment by the husband/relatives in connection with dowry demand. Proximate or live links must be shown to exist between the course of conduct relating to such cruelty/harassment and consequential death........ Mere lapse of time by itself does not provide the accused a defence that the cruelty/ harassment was not soon before."*

In this case *Pawan Kumar* v. *State of Haryana*, AIR 2001 SC 1324 accused was tried for the offence punishable under section 306, 498 A of I.P.C. Death was caused due to burn injuries. However dying declaration put up story that kerosene in stove got finished and while filling kerosene clothes of deceased caught fire. The Apex Court while dismissing the appeal held that, *"Story in dying declaration is falsified by the fact that absence of kerosene would put off the ignition of stove........ Story of accidental death is unbelievable."*

In *Smt. Laxmi* v. *Om Prakash*, AIR 2001 SC 2283, the Apex Court held that, *"One of the important tests of the reliability of the dying declaration is a finding arrived at by the Court as to satisfaction that the deceased was in a fit state of mind and capable of making a statement at the point of time when the dying declaration purports to have been made and/or recorded. If the Court finds that the capacity of the maker of the statement to narrate the facts was impaired or the Court entertains graved doubts whether the deceased was in a fit physical and mental state to make the statement, the Court may in the absence of corroborative evidence lending assurance to the containtents of the declaration, refuse to act on it........ It is not the number of dying declaration which will weigh with the Court. A singular dying declaration not suffering from any infirmity and found worthy of being relied on may form the basis of conviction. On the other hand if every individual dying declaration consisting in a plurality is found to be infirm, the Court would not be persuaded to act thereon merely because the dying declarations are more than one and apparently consistent."*

Where the dying declarations were inconsistent with each other, conviction based on one of the dying declarations implicating accused, was set aside; *Smt. Kamla* v. *State of Punjab*, 1993 Cr LJ 68 (SC).

In this case *Chacko* v. *State of Kerala*, AIR 2003 SC 265 deceased aged about 70 years of age had suffered 80 % burn injuries. Dying declaration was made 8 to 9 hours of incident giving material details of motive and manner of incident. Though doctor was present while recording dying declaration, certificate of doctor was absent. Inquest report though prepared after dying declaration, deceased did not give the name of accused. The Apex Court held the dying declaration to be doubtful and therefore set aside the conviction.

In this case *Gananath Pattanaik* v. *State of Orissa*, (2002) 1 SCR 845 wife of appellant committed suicide by hanging herself in the house. The Appellant was tried and convicted by the trial Court for the offence punishable under section 304B & 498A. And his conviction was upheld by High Court. In appeal, the Apex Court while acquitting the appellant by giving benefit of doubt held that, *"The statement of the deceased made to her family members, which had been taken on record with the aid of section 32 of the Evidence Act, 1872 for the offence under section 304B IPC is not admissible in evidence for the offence punishable under section 498A IPC. It has to be termed as being only a hearsay evidence. Section 32 of the Evidence Act is an exception to the hearsay rule and deals with the statement or declarations by a person, since dead, relating to the cause of his/her death or the circumstances leading to such death. If a statement which otherwise is covered by the hearsay rule does not fall within the exceptions of section 32 of the Evidence Act, the same cannot be relied upon for finding the guilt of the accused........ There is no evidence on record to hold that the deceased had conceived the apprehension of the appellant having illicit relations with his sister-in-law, which led the deceased to end her life."*

Where the death caused was not due to injuries inflicted but was on account complications leading to renal failure as a result of disturbance in electrolytic balance, the statement if any made by the injured relating to the cause of his injury could not be termed as dying declaration; *Hathabhai Jethabhai* v. *State of Gujarat*, 1994 CCR 711 (DB) (Guj).

In this case *Sudhakar* v. *State of Maharashtra*, 2000 (2) All MR (Cri) 1389 it was alleged that a twenty year old teacher was raped by Head-master and co-teacher. F.I.R. was lodged by prosecutrix 11 days after incident and she was attending school from next day. The prosecutrix committed suicide after 5½ months. The Apex Court while acquitting the appellant held that, *"Statement to police made after 11 days of incident cannot be treated as dying declaration......... There is no legal evidence on record that the prosecutrix at or about the time of making the statement had a disclosed her mind for committing suicide allegedly on account of humiliation to which she was subjected to on account of rape committed on her person. The prosecution evidence does not even disclose the cause of death of the deceased."*

However it has been held by the Apex Court that when a person who has made a statement, even if it be in expectation of death but is not dead, it is not a dying declaration and is not admissible under section 32 of the Evidence Act. Such statements are admissible under section 157 of the Evidence Act as former statements made by them to corroborate their testimony in the Court; *Maqsoodan* v. *State of U.P.*, (1983) 2 SCR 45: AIR 1983 SC 216.

In this case, statement of declarant was recorded as dying declaration. But the declarant survived. As to the use and evidentiary value of such statement, the Full Bench of the Bombay High Court held that dying declaration, in eventuality of declarant surviving it, is to be treated as a statement under section 164 Cr.P.C. and not a previous statement under section 161 Cr.P.C. It can be used for corroboration or contradiction unlike statement under section 161 Cr.P.C. which can be used only for contradiction; *Ramesh G. Kambale* v. *State of Maharashtra*, 2011 All MR (Cri) 3536 (Bom) (FB).

In this case, question arose as to whether statement made by deceased to Magistrate under section 164 of Cr.P.C. can be elevated to the status of Section 32 of the Evidence Act if maker dies subsequently. The Apex Court while giving affirmative answer to the point involved held that a statement made to a Magistrate is not affected by the prohibition as he can record the statement of a person as provided in Section 164 of the Code. Such a statement would either be elevated to the status of Section 32 of the Evidence Act if the maker subsequently dies or it would remain within the realm of what it was originally. This statement becomes usable to corroborate the witness as provided in Section 157 of the Evidence Act or to contradict him as provided in Section 155 thereof; *Ram Prasad* v. *State of Maharashtra*, (1999) 3 SCR 519.

In this case, the statement of a deceased was recorded by a police officer as a complaint and not as a dying declaration. The Court held that said statement can in fact be treated as a dying declaration if the other requirements in this regard are satisfied; *Paras Yadav* v. *State of Bihar*, (1999) 2 SCC 126.

Where there are plural/multiple dying declarations, the Court has to scrutinise the evidence cautiously and must find out whether there is consistency particularly in material particulars. In case there are *inter se* discrepancies in the depositions of the witnesses given in support of one of the dying declarations, it would not be safe to rely upon the same; *Bhadragiri Venkata Ravi* v. *Public Prosecutor, High Court of A.P., Hyderabad*, 2013 SAR (Criminal) 753 (SC). The Hon'ble Apex Court did not place reliance on the dying declarations as prosecution failed to explain as to why second dying declaration was taken two days after the first dying declaration was recorded; *Suryakant D. Bitale* v. *Dilip B. Kale*, 2014 All SCR 2578.

In this case, deceased lived for about seven weeks after recording of dying declaration. She sustained only 40 to 45 % burn injury which was not fatal. She died not because of burns but due to improper management of wounds. The Hon'ble Apex Court did not place any reliance on the said dying declaration on the ground that deceased did not apprehend her death on the date of recording of dying declaration. The dying declaration does not show either the cause of death or the circumstances which resulted in the death of declarant; *Banarasi Dass* v. *State of Haryana,* 2015 All SCR 308.

It is not an invariable rule of law that every dying declaration should be accepted as true and correct. There are exceptions to this rule. Experience has shown that the dying man very often takes that last opportunity to implicate his enemies and wreak sweet vengeance on them. Therefore Court has to be circumspect and cautious before accepting dying declaration; *Samson Hyam Kemkar* v. *State of Maharashtra,* (1974) 3 SCC 494: *Hazara Singh* v. *State of U.P.,* (1969) 2 SCC 22.

Other Cases on Dying Declaration

(a) Dying declaration was discarded as there was no endorsement of attestation by the Executive Magistrate to identify that is was a thumb impression of victim; *State of Maharashtra* v. *Rambhau Dahibhajan,* 2005 All MR (Cri) 849 (DB) (Bom).

(b) Even though deceased suffered 90% burns on her hands, thumb impression was put and therefore dying declaration was discarded; *State of Punjab* v. *Gian Kaur,* 1998 CCR 38 (SC).

(c) Dying declaration recorded by Head Constable was held to be not reliable as police had abundant time to summon Executive Magistrate who was residing a few yards away from police station; *Meera* v. *State of Rajasthan,* AIR 2004 SC 1879.

(d) In cases where there are multiple dying declarations and acceptance of one dying declaration falsifies the other, the dying declarations have to be necessarily rejected; *Suresh Arjun Dodorkar (Sonar)* v. *State of Maharashtra,* 2005 All MR (Cri) 1599 (DB) (Bom).

(e) Dying declaration was discarded as there was endorsements in medical record at one place as 'accidental burns' and another place it was recorded as 'self-inflicted'; *Sheikh Mehbood @ Hetak* v. *State of Maharashtra,* AIR 2005 SC 1805.

(f) In this case, medical evidence showed that brain functions of the injured were impaired due to brain injury. The Apex Court held that, *"Even if the injured were able to speak out something after sustaining injuries, such dying declaration cannot be relied upon."*; *State of Rajasthan* v. *Teja Ram,* (1999) 1 SCR 29.

(g) In this case deceased made a statement that people close to co-accused killed him. However there was no evidence to indicate that deceased new accused earlier. In such circumstances, the Apex Court held that, *"Such statement, even if accepted, cannot be said to be the clinching material to hold that it refers to the accused"*; *Vijayan* v. *State of Kerala,* (1999) 1 SCR 659.

(h) In this case, Apex Court held that the statement of a deceased recorded by a police officer as a complaint and not as a dying declaration can in fact be treated as a dying declaration if the other requirement in this regard are satisfied; *Paras Yadav* v. *State of Bihar,* (1999) 2 SCC 126.

(i) Where the dying declarations are contradictory and self destructive and the acceptance of one necessarily falsifies other, no reliance can be placed on either of the dying declarations; *Smt. Radhabai F. Pawar* v. *State of Maharashtra*, 2014 All MR (Cri) 4364.

(j) In this case, statement of deceased was recorded under section 161 Cr.P.C. by the investigation officer when he was taken in injured condition at police station immediately after the occurrence. Said statement narrated the details of prosecution case which ultimately resulted in death of deceased. The court held that conviction relying on said dying declaration is proper; *Rafique @ Rauf* v. *State of U.P.*, 2013 All SCR 2500.

(k) Where witnesses did not disclose the fact of making oral dying declaration by the deceased to then for two days and there was no independent corroboration to the same, it was held that such oral dying declaration is not reliable; *Ramsai* v. *State of M.P.*, 1994 Cr LJ 138 (SC).

(l) In this case, two deaths took place in the course of same transaction. The Apex Court held that in such a case, dying declaration of one person would also be relevant for the cause of death of another; *Tejram Patil* v. *State of Maharashtra*, 2015 All SCR 1301.

CHAPTER XXVII
APPRECIATION OF EVIDENCE

SYNOPSIS

(A) Proof Beyond Reasonable Doubt

Advocates who conduct criminal trials must be conversant with the rules of appreciation of evidence. Before dealing with appreciation of evidence, let us know the difference between the appreciation of evidence in criminal and civil cases. In civil cases, plaintiff has to prove his case on the principle of preponderance of probabilities. This principle has been explained by the Apex Court in *Narayan Ganesh Dastane* v. *Sucheta Narayan Dastane*, (1975) 3 SCR 967: AIR 1975 SC 1534, wherein the Apex Court held that, "*The normal rule which governs civil proceedings is that a fact is said to be established if it is proved by preponderance of probabilities. Under section 3 of the Evidence Act a fact is said to be proved when the Court either believes it to exist or it considers its existence so probable that a prudent man ought, in the circumstances, to act upon the supposition that it exists. The belief regarding the existence of a fact may thus be founded on a balance of probabilities. The first step in this process is to fix the probabilities, the second to weigh them, though the two may often intermingle. The impossible is weeded out in the first stage, the improbable at the second. Within the wide range of probabilities the Court has often a difficult choice to make but it is this choice which ultimately determines where the preponderance of probabilities lies. .... Proof beyond reasonable ground is proof by a higher standards which generally governs criminal trial or trials involving enquiries into issues of quasi-criminal nature. A criminal trial involves the liberty of the subject which may not be taken away on a mere preponderance of probabilities. If the probabilities are so nicely balanced that a reasonable, not a vascillating, mind cannot find where the preponderance lies, a doubt arises regarding the existence of the fact to be proved and the benefit of such reasonable doubt goes to the accused.*"

In *State of Uttar Pradesh* v. *Krishna Gopal*, AIR 1988 SC 2154, the Apex Court has explained the proof beyond reasonable doubt as: "......... *Though this standard is a higher standard, there is, however, no absolute standard. What degree of probability amounts to "proof" is an exercise particular to each case. Doubts would be called reasonable if they are free from a zest of abstract speculation. Law cannot afford any favourite other than truth. To constitute reasonable doubt, it must be free from an over emotional response. Doubts must be actual and substantial doubts as to the guilt of the accused person arising from the evidence, or from the lack of it, as opposed to mere vague apprehensions. A reasonable doubt is not imaginary, trivial or a merely possible doubt; but a fair doubt based upon reason and common sense."*

Explaining the principle of reasonable doubt, the Apex Court in *Vijayee Singh* v. *State of Uttar Pradesh,* AIR 1990 SC 1459: (1990) 2 SCR 573 has observed that *"...... But where the accused introduces material to displace the presumption which may affect the prosecution case or create a reasonable doubt about the existence of one or other ingredients of the offence, it would amount to failure of prosecution to prove a case beyond reasonable doubt. .... But a reasonable though incompletely proved plea which casts a genuine doubt on the prosecution version indirectly succeeds. However it must be the doubt of the prudent man who is assumed to possess the capacity to seperate the chaff from the grain."*

(B) General Rules of Appreciation of Evidence

The Apex Court in *State of Uttar Pradesh* v. *M.K. Anthony,* AIR 1985 SC 48, has propounded the principle of appreciation of evidence in a criminal trials as under: *"While appreciating the evidence of a witness, the approach must be whether evidence of the witness read as a whole appears to have a ring of truth. Once that impression is found it is undoubtedly necessary for the Court to scrutinize the evidence more particuraly keeping in view the deficiencies , drawbacks and infirmities pointed out in the evidence as a whole and evaluate them to find out whether it is against the general tenor of the evidence and whether the earlier evaluation of the evidence is shaken as to render it unworthy of belief. Minor discrepancies on trivial matters not touching the core of the case and hyper-technical approach in persuasion of the evidence should be avoided."*

While pointing out the duty of Court in appreciation of evidence, the Apex Court in *Chet Ram* v. *State,* 1971 Cr LJ 1246, has explained the principle of separating the chaff from grain as under: *"Courts, in search of truth, have to beware of being misled by half-truths or individually defective pieces of evidence. Firstly, undeniable facts and circumstances should be examined. Secondly, the pattern of case thus revealed in the context of a whole sequence of proved facts must be scrutinized to determine whether a natural, or probable and therefore a credible course of events is disclosed. Thirdly, the minutiae of evidence including established discrepancies should be put in the crucible of the whole context of an alleged crime or occurrence and tested particularly with reference to the proved circumstances which generally provide a more reliable indication of truth than the faulty human testimony, so that the process of separating the grain from the chaff may take place. Fourthly, in arriving at an assessment of credibility of individual witnesses, regard must be had to the possible motives of either deliberate medacity of subconscious mind. Lastly, the demeanour and bearing of a witness in Court should be carefully noticed and appellate Court should remember that a trial Court has had in this respect, an advantage which it does not possess."*

In *K.N. Virji* v. *State of Gujrath,* AIR 1970 SC 245, the Apex Court has held that, *"...... It is true that oftentimes the Courts have to separate the truth from falsehood. But where the two are so intermingled as to make it impossible to separate them, the evidence has to be rejected in its entirety."*

In *Garib Singh* v. *State of Punjab,* AIR 1973 SC 460: 1972 Cr LJ 1286, the Apex Court has held that, *"Appraisement involves weighing of one set of facts or inferences from them against the opposite ones fairly and reasonably."*

In *Milkiyat Singh* v. *State of Rajasthan,* AIR 1981 SC 1579, the Apex Court has held that, *"It is true that if a part of the story is found doubtful, it would not necessarily falsify the whole account, but in that case the rest of the story told by the alleged eye-witnesses must be examined carefully before it is relied on."*

The Apex Court in *Laxman Prasad* v. *State of Bihar,* AIR 1981 SC 1388, had held that, *"...... Mere congruity or consistency in evidence are not the sole test of truth. Sometimes even falsehood is given an adroit appearance of truth so that truth disappears and falsehood comes to the surface."*

(C) Doctrine of Benefit of Doubt

The Constitution Bench of the Apex Court in *M.G. Agarwal* v. *State of Maharashtra,* AIR 1963 SC 200: (1963) 2 SCR 405, has explained this doctrine in cases based on circumstantial evidence as under: *"It is well-settled rule in criminal jurisprudence that circumstantial evidence can be reasonably made the basis of an accused person's conviction if it is of such a character that it is wholly inconsistent with the innocence of the accused and is consistent with the innocence of the accused and is consistent only with his guilt. If the circumstances proved in the case are consistent either with the innocence of the accused or with his guilt, then the accused is entitled to the benefit of doubt. ...... But in applying the principle, it is necessary to distinguish between facts which may be called primary or basic on the one hand and inference of facts to be drawn from them on the other. In regard to the proof of basic or primary facts, the Court has to judge the evidence in the ordinary way, and in the appreciation of evidence in respect of proof of these basic or primary facts there is no scope for the application of the doctrine of benefit of doubt. The Court considers the evidence and decides whether that evidence proves a particular fact or not. When it is held that a certain fact is proved, the question arises whether that fact leads to the inference of guilt of the accused person or not and dealing with this aspect of the problem, the doctrine of benefit of doubt would apply and an inference of guilt can be drawn only if the proved fact is wholly inconsistent with the innocence of the accused and is consistent with his guilt."*

As regards the appreciation of evidence in cases based on circumstantial evidence, the Apex Court in *Kishore Chand* v. *State of Himachal Pradesh,* AIR 1990 SC 2140: (1990) Supp 1 SCR 105, has held that, *"....... imaginary possibilities have no role to play. What is to be considered are ordinary human probabilities. It is not necessary that circumstances by itself be conclusive but cumulatively must form unbroken chain of events leading to the proof of the guilt of the accused. If any of the said circumstances are consistent with the innocence of the accused or the chain of the continuity of the circumstances is broken, the accused is entitled to benefit of doubt."*

The Apex Court in *Machhi Singh* v. *State of Punjab,* (1983) 3 SCR 413: AIR 1983 SC 379, explained the doctrine of benefit of doubt as: *"When a piece of evidence introduced and relied upon by the prosecution itself creates a doubt (a reasonable doubt) as regards the complicity of the accused, even if there are no infirmities in other evidence, the doctrine of benefit of doubt must be invoked by the Court in favour of the accused."*

The Constitution Bench of the Apex Court in *Hari Charan Kurmi & Jogia Hajam* v. *State of Bihar*, (1964) 6 SCR 623: AIR 1964 SC 1184, has held that, *"In criminal trials, there is no scope for applying the principle of moral conviction or grave suspicion. In criminal cases where the other evidence adduced against an accused person is wholly unsatisfactory and the prosecution seeks to rely on confession of a co-accused person, the presumption of innocence which is the basis of criminal jurisprudence assists the accused person and compels the Court to render the verdict that the charge is not proved against him, and so, he is entitled to the benefit of doubt."* (*Page No. 635, 636*)

(D) Burden of Proof

The burden to prove a criminal case always lies on prosecution and it never shifts. Even where accused brings his case within the general exceptions provided under Chapter IV of the Code, initial burden of proof still lies on the prosecution. It is only when the prosecution discharges its initial burden, the onus of proof shifts on the accused and thereafter the question of considering the defence of the accused arises.

This was a case [*Abdul Rashid Ibrahim Mansuri* v. *State of Gujarat*, (2000) 1 SCR 542] under NDPS Act, 1985 wherein prior information regarding possession of *charas* by the accused was not reduced to writing and the said information was not communicated to superior officer. As regards burden of proof on accused, the Apex Court held that, *"Burden of proof would be discharged if it appears from prosecution case that accused could not have had knowledge or required intention, even though accused has not adduced evidence of his own; in the instant case non-recording of information at first instance was a circumstance in favour of accused leading to discharge of burden of proof and he was not liable to be convicted."*

The Apex Court in *State of Maharashtra* v. *W.R. Kaidalwar*, (1981) 3 SCR 675, has explained the meaning of expression "burden of proof" in a case under Prevention of Corruption Act, 1947 as: *"The expression 'burden of proof' has to distinct meanings: (i) the legal burden, that is, the burden of establishing the guilt and (ii) the evidential burden, that is, the burden of leading evidence. Notwithstanding the general rule that the burden of proof lies exclusively upon the prosecution, in the case of certain offences, the burden of proving a particular fact in issue may be laid by law upon the accused. This burden is not so onerous as that which lies on the prosecution and is discharged by proof of a balance of probabilities. .... The extent and nature of burden of proof resting upon the public servant cannot be higher than establishing his case by a preponderance of probability. ...... The phrase 'burden of proof' in Section 106 of the Evidence Act is clearly used in the secondary sense, namely the duty of introducing evidence."*

(E) Standard of Proof

The Apex Court in *State of Maharashtra* v. *Chandraprakash*, AIR 1990 SC 658, has explained "standard of proof" required to convict a person accused of committing rape as under: *"What is necessary is that the Court must be alive and conscious of the fact that it is dealing with the evidence of a person who is interested in the outcome of the charge levelled by her. .... If for some reason the Court is hesitant to place implicit reliance on the testimony of prosecutrix, it may look for evidence which may lend assurance to her testimony short of corroboration required in the case of an accomplice. ..... If the totality of circumstances disclose that the pro secutrix does not have a strong motive to falsely involve accused, Court should accept her evidence..... The degree of proof required must not be higher than is expected of an injured witness."*

As regards the standard of proof in rape cases, the Apex Court in *Shankarlal Gyarasilal Dixit* v. *State of Maharashtra,* (1981) 2 SCR 384, has held that, *"..... 'Shadow of doubt' even in cases which depend on direct evidence is shadow of 'reasonable' doubt. In its practical application the test which requires the exclusion of other alternative hypotheses is far more rigorous than the test of proof beyond reasonable doubt."*

In *M. Narsinga Rao* v. *State of Andhra Pradesh,* AIR 2001 SC 318 the Apex Court while explaining the concept of standard of proof required to convict a person, held that *"the word 'proof' needs to be understood in the sense in which it is define in the Evidence Act because proof depends upon the admissibility of evidence. A fact is said to be proved when, after considering the matters before it, the Court either believes it to exist, or consider its existence so probable that prudent man ought, under the circumstances of the particular case, to act upon the supposition that it exists. This is the definition given for the word 'proved' in the Evidence Act. What is required is production of such materials on which the Court can reasonably act to reach the supposition that a fact exists. Proof of the fact depends upon the degree of probability of its having existed. The standard required for reaching the supposition is that of a prudent man acting in any important matter concerning him."* The Apex Court further cited Fletcher Moulton L.J. [in *Hawkins* v. *Powells Tillery Steam Coal Company Ltd.,* (1911) 1 KB 988] who observed that *"proof does not mean proof to rigid mathematical demostration, because that is impossible; it must mean such evidence as would induced a reasonable man to come to a particular conclusion."*

However the Apex Court in *Ashish Batham* v. *State of Madhya Pradesh,* AIR 2002 SC 3206 has held that *"suspicion however strong is not the substitute for legal proof. Graver the charge greater has to be the standard of proof. Courts must keep in mind that there lies long mental distance between 'may be true' and 'must be true'."*

As regards the standard of proof required to convict a person in a case based on circumstantial evidence, the Apex Court in *Akhilesh* v. *State of Bihar,* (1995) 3 SCR 864 has explained the concept and held that *"the standard of proof required to convict a person on circumstantial evidence is now well-settled. According to the standard enunciated by this Court the circumstances relied upon by the prosecution in support of the case must not only be fully established but the chain of evidence furnished by those circumstances must be so complete as not to leave any reasonable ground for a conclusion consistent with the innocence of the accused. The circumstances from which the conclusions of the guilt of the accused is to be inferred, should be of conclusive nature and consistent only with the hypothesis of the guilt of the accused and the same should not be capable of being explained by any other hypothesis, except the guilt of the accused. ...."*

(F) Elements of Crime

There are certain principles (elements of crime) in criminal law which are relevant in judging the culpability of a person. These are given below:

Actus reus

Actus reus i.e., guilty act is the physical element of committing a crime. It is the actual conduct which caused the crime. It can be in the form of an act, an omission or a state of affairs. Exceptionally, on omission or failure to act can result in criminal liability.

Mens rea

Mens rea means guilty mind. It is the mental element of committing a crime and establishes the element of intent. *Mens rea* is what goes on inside the accused's mind. Both *actus reus* and *mens rea* must coincide to constitute a crime.

Intent or Intention

This is the explicit and conscious desire to commit a dangerous or illegal act.

Knowledge

This term applies if a person is aware that his or her actions will have certain results, but does not seem to care.

Recklessness

It is the decision to commit a certain action despite knowing about associated risks.

Negligence

This is the mildest form of criminal culpability. A person commits negligence when she fails to meet a reasonable standard of behaviour for her circumstances.

Motive

It is the reason the accused commits the criminal act or *actus reus*. Motive can generate intent, support a defence, and be used to determine sentencing. Motive alone does not constitute *mens rea* and does not act as a substitute for criminal intent.

Vicarious liability

It is the transfer of criminal liability from one criminal to another based on a special relationship. Under this theory, accused need not commit the criminal act supported by criminal intent.

Strict liability

It is an exception to the requirement of a criminal intent element. (Example – cases of vehicular accidents, tax violations, etc.).

Causation

Another principle is the principle of causation. "Causation" is that "but for" the defendant's conduct, the victim would not have been harmed. If more than one cause form harm exists, the rule states that to be responsible, one's action must have more than a slight or trifling link to be harm. Another rule of causation is that one must *"take his victim as he finds him"*. For instance, if *P* gives his friend *Q* a playful slap on the head, but *Q* suffers from a rare cranial condition and dies, then *P* can be guilty of manslaughter regardless of how unlucky he is to have bickered with *Q*. This is known as the *"thin skull rule"*.

There are various steps to determine causation. When there are multiple causes that lead to a particular consequence, the issue of intervention becomes relevant. Between the defendant's act and the victim's harm, the chain of causation must be unbroken. It could be broken by *novus actus interveniens* i.e., break in the chain of causation of a third party, the victim's own conduct or another unpredictable event.

It has been held in this case that victim's mere self-neglect is no break in the chain whereas the victim's gross self-neglect is a break in the chain of causation; *R.* v. *Dear,* (1996) CLR 595.

In this case, the defendant held a girl in front of him as a shield and shot at armed police men, to resist lawful arrest. The police instinctively fired back and killed the girl. The Court held that defendant's act caused the death of girl and had not broken the chain of causation; *R.* v. *Pagett,* (1983) 76 Cr App R 279.

Retired Supreme Court Justice Mr. Markandeya Katju criticised the judgment of the Apex Court in the cases of *State* v. *Govind Swami,* 2017 by writing various blogs. He criticised the Apex Court for failing to take notice of the doctrine of *novus actus interveniens*. However he was held guilty for committing contempt of Court.

Doctrine of Transferred Malice

Transferred intent (transferred malice in English Law) is a legal doctrine that holds that, when the intention to harm one individual inadvertently causes a second person to be hurt instead, the perpetrator is still held responsible.

This principle can be better understood from an English Case. This incident occurred on 2nd October, 2007. There was cross-fire between two gunmen in which a lady was killed by the bullet of defendant No. 1. At the time of incident she was talking to her sister on mobile phone and she was hit by a single shot to the head and was killed. In this case fact showed that defendant one and defendant two were voluntarily engaged in fighting each other, each intending to kill or cause grievous bodily harm to the other and each foreseeing that the other has the reciprocal intention. The Supreme Court of United Kingdom held defendant one to be guilty of committing murder of deceased on the doctrine of joint enterprise and transferred malice; *Regina* v. *Armel Gnango,* (2011) UKSC 59: (2012) 2 WLR 17: (2012) 1 Cr App R 18.

The above principle is embodied in section 301 of I.P.C. The Indian case on the principle embodied in section 301 of I.P.C. is given below.

In this case, the accused aimed at complainant 'S' but shot fired by him accidently hit 'J' and caused her death. The Apex Court held that accused would be liable to be convicted under section 304, Part II of the I.P.C. with the aid of section 301 of I.P.C. The Apex Court further held that if accused had injured the complainant 'S', he would have been liable to be convicted under section 304 Part II, IPC. In spite of complainant 'S' having escaped unhurt and yet 'J' having been injured though not aimed at, on the *doctrine of transferred malice* as contained in section 301, I.P.C. the liability of the accused remains the same; *Kashi Ram* v. *State of Madhya Pradesh,* AIR 2001 SC 2902.

(G) Appreciation of Evidence in Certain Categories of Cases

In this chapter important cases are given to let the readers know the judicial reasoning and approach in appreciating evidence.

Criminal Conspiracy (Section 120 A, 120 B IPC)

Criminal conspiracy as defined in section 120 A of the I.P.C. is an agreement by two or more persons to do or cause to be done an illegal act or an act which is not illegal by illegal means. The agreement is the gist of the offence. In order to constitute a single general conspiracy there mu1st be a common design and a common intention to all to work in furtherance of the common design. A general conspiracy must be distinguished from a number of separate conspiracies having a similar purpose. Where different groups of persons cooperate towards their separate ends without any privity with each other, each combination constitutes a separate conspiracy. The common intention of the conspirators is then to work for the furtherance of the common design of his group only; *Mohd. Hussain Umar Kochra* v. *K.S. Dalipsinghji,* (1970) 1 SCR 130.

In this case, the Court held that the offence of criminal conspiracy requires detailed and specific proof against each of the accused that he individually participated in a particular design to do a particular criminal act; *Emperor* v. *Aftab Mohamed Khan,* AIR 1940 All 291: 1941 Cr LJ 647.

In this case, the Court held that the agreement can be inferred from collateral acts, but these acts must show a common plan so as to exclude a reasonable possibility of the acts of the conspirators having been done separately and connected only by coincidence; *Benoyendra Chandra Pandey* v. *Emperor,* AIR 1936 Cal 73: 1937 Cr LJ 394.

In this case the Court held that the doing of an overt act, independent of the agreement, is a step further in prosecution of the object of the conspiracy and stamps it as criminal within the meaning of the section. The overt act must be something distinct from that tending to prove merely the agreement; *Bachcha Babu* v. *Emperor,* AIR 1935 All 162.

In this case, the Court held that there should be *prima facie* evidence that a person was a party to the conspiracy before his acts can be used against his co-conspirators. It is obligatory on the prosecution to establish such link as would join up the several activities of the accused person to be in furtherance of the common intention, *i.e.,* conspiracy. Existence of conspiracy cannot be assumed from a set of unconnected facts or from a set of conduct exhibited by different accused persons at different places and times without a reasonable justification for drawing the link; *Jagannath Misra* v. *State of Orissa,* (1974) 40 Cut LT 1253.

In this case, the Hon'ble Apex Court has stated the principles of law relating to conspiracy as: the essence of conspiracy is that there should be an agreement between persons to do one or other of the acts described in the section. The said agreement may be proved by direct evidence or may be inferred from acts and conduct of the parties. There is no difference between the mode of proof of the offence of conspiracy and that of any other offence. It can be established by direct evidence or by circumstantial evidence. But section 10 of the Evidence Act introduces the doctrine of agency and if the conditions laid down therein are satisfied, the acts done by one are admissible against the co-conspirator. The Court has further analysed the law contained in section 10 in relation to conspiracy and held that: (i) there shall be a prima facie evidence affording a reasonable ground for a Court to believe that two or more persons are members of a conspiracy; (ii) if the said condition is fulfilled, anything said , done or written by any one of them in reference to their common intention will be evidence against the other; (iii) anything said , done or written by him should have been said, done or written by him after the intention was formed by any one of them; (iv) it would also be relevant for the said purpose against another who entered the conspiracy whether it was said, done or written before he entered the conspiracy or after he left it; and (v) it can only be used against a co-conspirator and not in his favour; *Sardar Sardul Singh Caveeshar* v. *State of Maharashtra,* (1964) 2 SCR 378.

Explaining the law of criminal conspiracy, the Apex Court held that a criminal conspiracy is partnership in crime, and there is in each conspiracy a joint or mutual agency for the prosecution of a common plan. Thus, if two or more persons enter into a conspiracy any act done by any of them pursuant to the agreement is, in contemplation of law, the act of each of them and they are jointly responsible therefore. This means that everything said, written or done by any of the conspirators in execution or furtherance of the common purpose is deemed to have been said, done or written by each of them. And this joint responsibility extends not only to what is done by any of the conspirators pursuant to the original agreement but also to collateral acts incidental to and growing out of the original purpose. A conspirator is not responsible however, for acts done by a co-conspirator after termination of the conspiracy. The joinder of a conspiracy by a new member does not create a new conspiracy nor does it change the status of the other conspirators and the mere fact that conspirators individually or in groups perform different tasks to a common end does not split up a conspiracy into several different conspiracies. .... A man may join a conspiracy by word or by deed. However, criminal responsibility for a conspiracy requires more than a merely passive attitude towards an existing conspiracy. One who commits an over tact with knowledge of the conspiracy is guilty. And one who tacitly consents to the object of a conspiracy and goes along with other conspirators, actually standing by while the others put the conspiracy into effect, is guilty though he intends to take no active part in the crime; *State through C.B.I.* v. *Nalini,* (1999) 3 SCR 1.

It has been held by the Apex Court that conspiracy to commit a crime itself is punishable as a substantive offence and every individual offence committed pursuant to the conspiracy is separate and distinct offence to which individual offenders are liable to punishment, independent of the conspiracy; *Ajay Agarwal* v. *Union of India,* (1993) 3 SCR 543.

In order to prove a criminal conspiracy which is punishable under section 120B of the IPC, there must be direct or circumstantial evidence to show that there was an agreement between two or more persons to commit an offence. This clearly envisages that there must be a meeting of the minds resulting in an ultimate decision taken by the conspirators regarding the commission of an offence. A conspiracy can be inferred even from the circumstances giving rise to a conclusive or irresistible inference of an agreement between two or more persons to commit an offence; *V.C. Shukla* v. *State (Delhi Administration)*, (1980) 3 SCR 500.

In this case, several accused persons were charged for hatching a conspiracy to commit defalcation of properties and they were tried for the offence punishable under sections 120B, 109, 408, 467 and 471 of the IPC. Explaining the law regarding conspiracy, the Apex Court held that unless the prosecution proved that there was a close cohesion and collusion between all the accused which formed the subject matter of a conspiracy, it would be difficult to prove the charges against the appellant. The charge of conspiracy having failed, the most material and integral part of the prosecution story against the appellant disappeared. In a criminal case of such serious nature *mens rea* cannot be excluded. Once the charge of conspiracy has failed the onus lay on the prosecution to prove affirmatively that the appellant was directly and personally connected with acts or omissions pertaining to the items purchased; *Jethsur Surangbhai* v. *State of Gujarat*, (1984) 1 SCR 797.

In this case, one Lalit Suneja was shot dead by two unknown persons near to his house. The respondent and other accused persons were tried for the offence punishable under sections 302/34 and 120B of the IPC. The respondent and one Om Prakash Shrivastava @ Babloo were convicted but accused Manjeet Singh was acquitted. The High Court set aside the conviction of the respondents. The State has challenged the judgement of acquittal passed by the High Court of Delhi. In appeal, the Hon'ble Apex Court upheld the judgement of High Court and held that for proving criminal conspiracy, meeting of mind is essential. Mere knowledge or discussion regarding the plan would not be sufficient. Though prosecution proved that all the accused were present in Delhi on the day of occurrence, it failed to prove any prior meeting of mind of the accused or any action, individually or in concert against any of the accused; *State (Govt. of NCT of Delhi)* v. *Nitin Gunwant Shah*, 2015 (4) Crimes 51 (SC).

In this case, the High Court has culled out the principles as to how criminal conspiracy should be proved. These principles are: (i) Circumstances when taken together on face value should indicate meeting of minds between conspirators. (ii) It has to be shown that all means adopted and illegal acts done were in furtherance of object of conspiracy hatched. (iii) A systemic role played by each accused should be highlighted. (iv) Each circumstance should be proved beyond reasonable doubt. (v) Conspiracy has to be proved by leading substantive evidence; *Jaffar @ Raju* v. *State*, 2013 (4) Crimes 356 (Del).

Other Cases

Topandas v. *State of Bombay*, (1955) 2 SCR 881: One person alone cannot be held guilty if other alleged co-conspirators are acquitted of the charge.

Indresh Kumar v. *Ramphal,* (2010) 2 SCC 241: When charge of criminal conspiracy fails but individual act of accused is established, accused would be guilty and can be convicted.

Kehar Singh v. *State (Delhi Administration),* (1988) 3 SCC 609: 1988 (2) Crimes 981 (SC): Mere knowledge, or even discussion, of the plan is not, per say enough to constitute conspiracy.

R. Venkatkrishnan v. *C.B.I.,* (2009) 11 SCC 737: Criminal conspiracy is an offence which is independent of other offences. In the absence of agreement, mere thought to commit a crime does not constitute offence.

(i) Murder

Culpable homicide is the genus and murder its specie. All murders are culpable homicide but not *vice versa*. Generally, culpable homicide sans special characteristics of murder are culpable homicide not amounting to murder; *Budhi Lal* v. *State of Uttarakhand,* 2008 (4) Crimes 68 (SC): 2008 (12) SCALE 848: 2008 (10) JT 572: 2008 (7) Supreme 4. There are three degrees of culpable homicide *i.e.,* lowest degree (Section 304-II), middle degree (Section 304-I) and highest degree or murder (Section 302). It is the degree of probability of death which determines whether a culpable homicide is of the gravest, medium or the lowest degree; *Shri Harendra Nath Borah* v. *State of Assam,* 2007 (1) Crimes 303 (SC).

In another case, the Apex Court held that it is the degree of probability of death resulting from the intended bodily injury whether a culpable homicide is of the gravest, medium or the lowest degree; *Sellappan* v. *State of Tamil Nadu,* 2007 (1) Crimes 289 (SC).

Murder is an aggravated form of culpable homicide. Even without bringing into the radius of the exceptions enumerated in section 300 of IPC, an offence may still be culpable homicide if it does not possess the attributes of murder; *Willie (William) Slaney* v. *State of Madhya Pradesh,* AIR 1956 SC 116: 1956 Cr LJ 291 (SC).

In has been held by the Court that injury to a vital part of the body is not necessarily an ingredient to determine whether the case falls under section 300 or not. If the bodily injury intended to be inflicted is sufficient in the ordinary course of nature to cause death, the offence falls under section 300, IPC; *Babu Lal Behari Lal* v. *Emperor,* AIR 1946 Nag 120: 47 Cr LJ 441.

To constitute a criminal offence, intention, motive, preparation and act is necessary. In criminal cases, all the ingredients of the offence in question have to be established by the prosecution in order to secure the conviction of the accused. Therefore defence must try to bring such evidence on record which would disprove one or the other ingredient of the offence. Before dealing with the cases on murder, let us see the difference between above terms. This has been explained by the Apex Court in *Jai Prakash* v. *State (Delhi Administration),* (1991) 1 SCR 202. The Court held: *'Intention' is different from 'motive' or ignorance or 'negligence'. It is the 'knowledge' or 'intention' with which the act is done that makes difference, in arriving at a conclusion whether the offence is culpable homicide or murder. .... The 'intention' and 'knowledge' of the accused are subjective and invisible states of mind and their existence has to be gathered from the circumstances, such as the weapon used, the ferocity of attack, multiplicity of injuries and all other surrounding circumstances. ...... It is accepted that the knowledge of the consequences which may result in doing an act is not the same thing as the intention that such consequences should ensue. Firstly, when an act is done by a person, it is presumed that he must have been aware that certain specified harmful consequences would or could follow. But the knowledge is bare awareness and not the same thing as 'intention' that such consequences should ensue. As compared to 'knowledge', 'intention' requires something more than the mere foresight of the consequences, namely the purposely doing of a thing to achieve a particular end. .... 'Knowledge' as contrasted with 'intention' signify a state of mental realisation with the bare state of conscious awareness of certain facts in which human mind remains supine or inactive. On the other hand, 'intention' is a conscious state in which mental faculties are aroused into activity and summoned into action for the purpose of achieving a conceived end.*

Motive is relevant factor in criminal cases as has been observed by the Apex Court in *State of Uttar Pradesh* v. *Babu Ram*, AIR 2000 SC 1735. In this case the Court observed that, *"Motive is relevant factor in all criminal cases whether based on testimony of eye witness or circumstantial evidence. .... It cannot be laid down that motive may not be very much material in cases depending on direct evidence whereas motive is material only when the case depends upon the circumstantial evidence. There is no legal warrant for making such a hiatus a criminal cases as for the motive for committing the crime."*

It is often argued in Courts that failure to prove motive must entail acquittal of accused. However, in *Nathuni Yadav* v. *State of Bihar*, (1978) 9 SCC 238, the Apex Court has held that, *"Motive for doing a criminal act is generally a difficult area for prosecution. One cannot normally see into the mind of another. Motive is the emotion which impels a man to do a particular act. Such impelling cause need not necessarily be proportionally grave to do grave crimes. Many a murders have been committed without any known or prominent motive. It is quite possible that the aforesaid impelling factor would remain undiscoverable."*

The Apex Court in *Shivaji Sahebrao Bobade* v. *State of Maharashtra*, (1974) 1 SCR 489, has held that, *"Proof of motive satisfies the judicial mind about the likelihood of the authorship but its absence only demands deeper forensic search and cannot undo the effect of evidence otherwise sufficient. Motives of men are often subjective, submerged and unamenable to easy proof that Courts have to go without clear evidence thereon if other clinching evidence exists."*

It has been held by the Apex Court in *Dhananjay Shankar Shetty* v. *State of Maharashtra*, AIR 2002 SC 2787, that *"Failure to allege and prove the motive of accused in committing crime assumes significance when there are other circumstances creating doubt about the prosecution case."*

In *Sakharam* v. *State of Madhya Pradesh*, (1992) 1 SCR 638, the Apex Court has held that, *"Absence of motive is a plus point for the accused in a case where the evidence against him is only circumstantial."*

Cases on Clause "firstly" of Section 300, IPC

In this case, appellant was put on trial under section 302 and 304 Part I of I.P.C. for the alleged murder of his wife's paramour. He was tried by the

Sessions Judge, Greater Bombay, with the aid of Special Jury. The Jury brought in a verdict of "not guilty" by 8:1 under both the sections; but the Sessions Judge did not agree with the verdict of the Jury and hence he submitted the case under section 307 of the Code (old) to the Bombay High Court after recording the grounds for his opinion. The said reference was heard by Division Bench of Bombay High Court which held the accused guilty of the offence of murder under section 302 of I.P.C. and sentenced him to undergo rigorous imprisonment for life.

Prosecution story is that on April 27, 1959, Sylvia confessed to Nanavati of her illicit intimacy with Ahuja. Enraged at the conduct of Ahuja, accused went to the flat of Ahuja, entered his bed-room and shot him dead. Accused himself surrendered before police.

The defence story is that wife of accused confessed him of her illicit intimacy with Ahuja. Sylvia did not tell accused if Ahuja would marry her and take charge of their children and therefore he decided to go and settle the matter with him. Accused went to the flat of Ahuja and asked him whether he would marry Sylvia and look after the children. The deceased retorted, *"Am I to marry every woman I sleep with?"* The accused became enraged, put the envelope containing the revolver on a cabinet nearby, and threatened to thrash the deceased. A struggle ensued between the two and during the struggle two shots went off accidently and hit Ahuja resulting in his death.

The Apex Court while upholding the conviction under section 302, I.P.C. held that it was the case of intentional shooting to wreak vengeance. The Court took into consideration post-incident conduct of the accused for judging his defence story of sudden and grave provocation. As regards the defence taken by the accused and his attempt to bring his case within the exception embodied in section 80, I.P.C. the Court held that, *"No abstract standard of reasonableness can be laid down for the application of doctrine of grave and sudden provocation. What a reasonable man will do in certain circumstances depends upon the customs, manners, way of life, traditional values, etc.; in short, the cultural, social and emotional background of the society to which an accused belongs; K.M. Nanavati* v. *State of Maharashtra,* (1961) 1 SCR 567.

Advocates should not get swayed by the defences taken by famous advocates and should not imitate others. If we go through the facts of the above case, it reveals that spot room did not show any indication of struggle or fight. Spectacle of the deceased was not broken but it was intact lying by side. Towel wrapped around waist of deceased was intact. There was no bruise on the body of deceased. There was no blood on clothes. Also there were no injuries on the body of accused. In such circumstances, the defence taken does not seem to be proper. These observations are not made to criticise the great lawyers who have conducted trial but these are only given with a view that defence taken in one case may not be appropriate in another case.

In this case it was alleged that appellants set fire to the room in which deceased was sleeping. They locked the door of the room from outside where servant of the deceased was sleeping. When villagers were coming towards the room which was set on fire, they were prevented from rendering any help to the victim. The Apex Court held that the case falls under clause "firstly" of section 300, IPC as there was a clear intention to kill the victim; *Rawalpenta Venkalu* v. *State of Hyderabad,* AIR 1956 SC 171.

Where accused hit the deceased with the blade of the sword-stick which was two feet in length, on the chest with such force as to impair the liver and aorta, the Apex Court held that case falls under clause "firstly" of section 300, IPC and it is a case of murder; *Rau Bhagwanta Hargude* v. *State of Maharashtra,* 1979 Cr LJ 1022.

Cases on Clause "secondly" of Section 300, IPC

In this case, accused gave three blows on the body of deceased by knife. However depth of injury on chest which was grave and fatal was not more than cavity deep. Taking into consideration the depth of the injury, the Apex Court held that accused has not given knife blows with full force. It also indicates lack of intention to kill. Though accused had ample opportunity to inflict more injuries, he fled from the seen without inflicting more injuries. The Apex Court held that the case falls under clause "secondly" of section 300 of IPC and convicted the accused under section 304, Part I of IPC; *Mangesh* v. *State of Maharashtra,* AIR 2011 SC 637.

In this case deceased was assaulted by kitchen knife when a quarrel took place in sudden altercation. Facts showed that appellants had not come to assault deceased. During the said quarrel deceased entered into house and bolted from inside. At this time accused broke open door and went inside, picked up weapon and assaulted deceased. Only two knife blow injuries were inflicted one of which proved fatal as the same was on vital part. The High Court held that had appellant desired to kill deceased, they could have repeated knife stabs. This shows that there was no intention to murder the deceased. Therefore the offence falls under section 304, Part I of IPC; *Surinder Singh* v. *State,* 2010 (1) Crimes 734 (Del).

Cases on Clause "Thirdly" of Section 300, IPC

The facts of the case are: the accused thrust a spear into the abdomen of the deceased which caused death. In the opinion of the doctor the injury was sufficient to cause death in the ordinary course of nature. The Sessions Judge convicted the accused under section 302 of I.P.C. The High Court upheld the conviction. In appeal, it was argued that the third clause of section 300 of I.P.C. did not apply as it was not proved that the accused intended to inflict a bodily injury that was sufficient to cause death in the ordinary course of nature. The Apex Court while pointing out the duty of the prosecution to bring a case under clause thirdly of section 300 of I.P.C., has held that: (i) It must establish, quite objectively, that a bodily injury is present. (ii) The nature of the injury must be proved; these are purely objective investigations. (iii) It must be proved that there was an intention to inflict that particular injury, that is to say, that it was not accidental or intentional, or that some other kind of injury was intended. (iv) It must be proved that the injury of the type just described made up of the three elements set out above was sufficient to cause death in the ordinary course of nature. This part of the enquiry is purely objective and inferential and has nothing to do with the intention of the offender.

The third clause of section 300, I.P.C. consists of two parts. Under the first part it must be proved that there was an intention to inflict the injury that is found to be present and under the second part it must be proved that the injury was sufficient in the ordinary course of nature to cause death. The words *"and the bodily injury intended to be inflicted"* are merely descriptive. All this means is, that it is not enough to prove that the injury found to be present is sufficient to cause death in the ordinary course of nature; it must in addition be shown that the injury found to be present was the injury intended to be inflicted. Whether it was sufficient to cause death in the ordinary course of nature is a matter of inference or deduction from the proved facts about the nature of the injury and has nothing to do with the question of intention. .... It is true that in a given case the enquiry may be linked up with the seriousness of the injury. For example, if it can be proved, or if the totality of the circumstances justify an inference, that the prisoner only intended a superficial scratch and that by accident his victim stumbled and fell on the sword or spear that was used, then of course the offence is not murder; *Virsa Singh* v. *State of Punjab,* 1958 SCR 1495.

In order that a case falls under section 300, clause "thirdly", prosecution must prove (i) that the bodily injury is present, (ii) that the injury is sufficient in the ordinary course of nature to cause death, and (iii) that the accused intended to inflict that particular injury that is to say it was not accidental or unintentional or that some other kind of injury was intended; *State of Haryana* v. *Pala,* 1996 Cr LJ 1872 (SC) and *Jai Prakash* v. *State (Delhi Administration),* (1991) 1 JT (SC) 288: (1991) 1 SCR 202.

Cases on Clause "Forthly" of Section 300, IPC

The Apex Court has held that where the intention was not to kill or cause such bodily injury as was sufficient in the ordinary course of nature to cause death but the accused had knowledge that his act was so imminently dangerous that it must in all probability cause death or such bodily injury as was likely to cause death, the case would fall under section 300, clause "fourthly"; *Mohinder Pal* v. *State of Punjab,* AIR 1979 SC 577: 1979 Cr LJ 584 (SC).

Both clause (c) of section 299 and clause (4) of section 300 required knowledge of probability of the act causing death. Clause (4) of section 300 of IPC would be applicable where knowledge of the offender as to the probability of death of a person being caused from his imminently dangerous act approximated to a practical certainty. Such knowledge on the part of the offender must be of the highest degree of probability, the act having been committed by the offender without any excuse for incurring the risk of causing death or such injury as aforesaid. But sometimes the facts are so intertwined and the second and the third stages so telescoped into each other that it may not be convenient to give a separate treatment to the matters involved in the section and third stages; *Rajinder* v. *State of Haryana,* 2006 (2) Crimes 303 (SC).

Cases on Exception I to Section 300, IPC

Provocation is an external stimulus which can result into loss of self control. Such provocation and the resulting reaction need not be measured from the surrounding circumstances. However the provocation must be such as will upset not merely a hasty, hot tempered and hypersensitive person but also a person with calm nature and ordinary sense. Protection extended by *Exception I* is to the normal person acting normally in the given situation; *Arun Raj* v. *Union of India,* (2010) 6 SCC 457: 2010 All SCR 1507.

In this case, incident took place at spur of moment when accused visited house of deceased, a maid servant for asking her to rejoin duty. Accused had gone unarmed. Accused had no premeditation to kill deceased or cause any bodily injury to her. The Apex Court convicted the appellant for the offence punishable under section 304, Part II of the IPC holding that possibility of accused losing self-control on some provocative utterances of deceased cannot be ruled out; *Yomeshbhai P. Bhatt* v. *State of Gujarat,* AIR 2011 SC 2328.

In this case, alleged incident happened all of sudden on drain. Evidence showed that some altercation took place between the deceased and the accused. The accused hit deceased by *Gandasi* but he used its blunt side. The weapons used in the alleged incident were implements of common use which are normally carried by villagers. Doctor deposed that accused had used *Gandasi* from its blunt side. In such facts and circumstances, the Hon'ble Apex Court held that prior intention to commit murder cannot be inferred and therefore held the accused liable for offence under section 304, Part I read with section 34, IPC; *Gurdial Singh* v. *State of Punjab,* AIR 2011 SC 840.

In this case, alleged incident occurred on petty dispute regarding grazing of goats by accused. Accused used to carry bamboo stick with him and same was not brought specially to assault deceased. There was no previous enmity between accused and deceased. The Hon'ble High Court held that in absence of premeditation, it can be said that accused had no intention to kill. The Court convicted the accused for the offence punishable under section 304, Part I, IPC; *Kanuram Birua* v. *State of Goa,* 2011 All MR (Cri) 3852.

In this case, there was no evidence of animosity, premeditation or intention to kill. Accused came to the spot on hearing shout of his father with weapon which is used regularly by communities. The Apex Court held that Act of the accused was the result of grave and sudden provocation where father of both deceased and accused was being abused and ill-treated by accused in a drunken state and therefore offence false within the ambit of exception I to section 300, IPC and was convicted for the offence punishable under section 304, Part I, IPC. The Court further observed that premeditation and intention to kill are two vital circumstances amongst others to be considered by Court before holding accused guilty of offence under section 302 or 304, IPC. The Apex Court observed that grave and sudden provocation would normally mean that a person in a circumstance could lose self-control but only temporarily and that too in proximity to time of provocation; *Bodhi Singh* v. *State of Himachal Pradesh,* 2014 All SCR 3828.

Cases on Exception II to Section 300, IPC

In this case, deceased first pulled collar of appellant's shirt and tried to press his neck. Appellant tried to overpower him by inflicting knife blow. However appellant exceeding his right of private defence in doing so. In such facts and circumstances the Apex Court held that the case of appellant falls under section 304, Part I; *Raman* v. *State of Kerala,* 2008 All SCR 2732.

Cases on Exception IV to Section 300, IPC

It was a case of sudden fight between two parties. The Apex Court held that in such a case whole blame cannot be placed on one side as sudden fight implies mutual provocation and blows on each side. In such cases, apportionment of share of blame which attaches to fight is difficult. Where accused claims the benefit of *Exception IV,* he has to further prove that he has not taken undue advantage. The Apex Court altered the conviction to one under section 304, Part I; *Shambhoo Singh* v. *State of Rajasthan,* AIR 2008 SC 3200.

In this case, accused launched attack on deceased after 15 minutes of quarrel as deceased denied food to the appellant. The appellant was denied food as he was jobless. The Court held that the case is covered by *Exception IV* to section 300 as the hunger and humiliation provoked the attack and convicted the appellant under section 304, Part I of IPC; *Ashok R. Sutar* v. *State of Maharashtra,* 2012 All MR (Cri) 506 (Bom) (DB).

The facts of the case are: the appellant first threw water pot made of brass under the influence of liquor and thereafter threw a burning kerosene lamp upon deceased. At the time of incident deceased was wearing nylon sari which immediately caught fire and she was engulfed by flames and succumbed to the injuries. The appellant was convicted by the trial Court for the offence punishable under section 302, IPC. The Judgment of the trial Court was affirmed by the High Court. The Hon'ble Apex Court altered the conviction to one under section 304, Part I holding that the case clearly falls under *Exception IV* of section 300. The Apex Court observed that there was no intention on the part of the accused to cause death or such bodily injury as would have resulted in the death of his wife. There was no premeditation and the incident occurred in a sudden quarrel; *Sayaji Hanmat Bankar* v. *State of Maharashtra,* 2011 (3) Crimes 129 (SC).

In this case, deceased was called by his wife to settle the score where sudden fight arose out of trivial issue amongst neighbourers. There were two accused on one side and deceased on the other side. During scuffle, deceased overpowered one accused. This provoked the other accused to take wooden log from vicinity and hit the deceased. Single blow was given by the accused on head of deceased due to which he died. The Apex Court held that single blow given by accused shows that he did not behave in cruel or unusual manner and the said blow was unintentional as the scuffling parties were in motion. The Court held that all the four ingredients of *Exception IV* to section 300, IPC are made out and therefore this is case of culpable homicide not amounting to murder. The Court awarded 10 years imprisonment to the accused; *Chenda @ Chanda Ram* v. *State of Chhattisgarh,* 2013 All SCR 3372.

Cases on Exception V to Section 300, IPC

In this case, deceased Nathi after leaving her matrimonial home, while she was residing at her maternal home, developed love and intense relationship with the accused. Since the deceased and the accused were of the same *gotra,* their relationship was not accepted by the villagers. Even during the course of trial PW-3 admitted that Nathi and accused were in love and that Nathi and the accused eloped and lived together for about 10-15 days. A *panchayat* was convened after Nathi returned home. PW-3 further deposed that Nathi having left her previous husband, wanted to marry the accused; but to *gotra* of both being one, the marriage could not be held. As their desire of marriage was not accepted by the villagers, accused and the deceased were dejected.

The accused-appellant has taken the defence plea of suicide pact. The appellant explained the circumstances in which he caused the death of the deceased. He stated that he and deceased were in love and they solemnised their marriage. He stated that the villagers had objections for the relationship and therefore both tried to commit suicide. He further stated that acting on the consent of Nathi, he inflicted sword injuries on Nathi and she died. However, before the appellant could kill himself, there was intervention and therefore he could not kill himself. Evidence on record showed that at the time of incident, accused and deceased were in a closed room and accused had not come armed. The sword was taken from inside the room. The witness who saw the incident from peep hole of the door, did not state that the deceased was quarrelling or shouting for help. The appellant contended that his act of causing death of Nathi falls under *Exception V* of section 300, IPC.

The Hon'ble Apex Court held that the death of deceased was not premeditated and the act of the accused causing death of Nathi appears to be in furtherance of the understanding between them to commit suicide and the consent of the deceased and the act of the accused falls under *Exception V* of section 300, IPC. The Court accepted the defence version and held the appellant guilty under section 304, Part I, IPC. However conviction of the appellant under section 309, IPC was maintained; *Narendra* v. *State of Rajastan*, 2014 All MR (Cri) 3760 (SC).

Duty of Court while Appreciating Evidence

In this case, the Court had stated the proper mode of approaching cases under sections 299, 300, IPC. The Court held that "*the proper way to approach facts and apply law in cases were one man has by his act caused the death of another is to deal with the case in the four staged given below:*

Stage 1 – It should be first established to the satisfaction of the Court that the accused person has done an act by doing which he has caused the death of another. This is the starting point.

Stage 2 – Next it should be considered whether the act on the part of the accused amounts to culpable homicide.

Stage 3 – It is only after considering the two stages that section 300 comes into operation. Therefore the next thing to do is to ascertain whether the ingredients of section 300 have been satisfied.

Stage 4 – Lastly it must be considered on the facts of the particular case whether the culpable homicide is brought from the higher plane of murder to which it has been raised, to the lower plane of culpable homicide not amounting to murder by reason of the case falling within any of the exceptions of section 300.

If culpable homicide is not murder, the only matter to be considered at the fourth stage is whether the accused has established (if such is his case) the right of private defence as a complete defence under section 96.

If culpable homicide is murder and it is not established that the case comes under any of the exceptions to section 300 then it remains a case of murder.

Questions of knowledge, intention and the like such as these which arise in such cases are always essentially questions of facts falling to be decided solely on the particular facts and circumstances of each individual case." [* *Nga Chit Tin* v. *The King,* AIR 1939 Rangoon 225].

Others Cases

Dwarka Prasad v. *State of Uttar Pradesh,* (1993) 2 SCR 70: It was the case of murder wherein the motive for the occurrence was that about 10 or 12 days before the date of occurrence, the appellant abused the P.W. 2 and the deceased. They gave two/three slaps to the appellant. While allowing the appeal of the appellant in part, the Apex Court held that the motive disclosed on behalf of the prosecution for the occurrence is not acceptable. Even if it is assumed that because of some altercation 10/12 days before the date of occurrence, the appellant had decided to cause the murder of the deceased, then more injuries would have been caused on the person of the victim by the appellant.

State of Madhya Pradesh v. *Surbhan,* (1996) Supp 1 SCR 333: In this case while the deceased was returning after taking water from the tank, the respondent-accused came from behind and gave a blow with *'Falia'* and went away. P.W. 2, Ratan Singh, son of the deceased who is an eye witness to the occurrence narrated to other persons/witnesses that the accused came from behind and attacked the deceased. The deceased was taken to hospital and declared dead. The Trial Court convicted the respondent/accused for the offence of murder under section 302, I.P.C. and sentenced him to undergo life imprisonment. On appeal High Court acquitted the respondent. The State appealed to Supreme Court. In appeal, while dismissing the appeal, the Apex Court held that, "...... *A reading of the medical evidence clearly indicates that there are three separate injuries inflicted upon the deceased, by three separate blows but PW2 does not speak of the accused having inflicted those three injuries. ..... The single blow cannot cause three incised injuries of different dimensions at three different places."*

Theory of "Last Seen"

In murder trials based on circumstantial evidence, circumstance of accused being last seen together with the deceased is often introduced by the prosecution. In such circumstances theory of last seen comes into picture. Therefore few cases are given on this point.

The principle which underlies section 106 of the Evidence Act is applied in the context of the last seen theory when certain facts are especially within the knowledge of a person; *State of Rajastha* v. *Kashi Ram,* (2006) 12 SCC 254: AIR 2007 SC 144: 2007 All MR (Cri) 525 SC.

This theory comes into play where the time gap between the point of time when the accused and the deceased is found dead is so small that possibility of any person other than the accused being the author of crime becomes impossible. Even in such a case Courts should look for some corroboration; *Yuvraj Ambar Mohite* v. *State of Maharashtra*, 2007 (1) CRJ 442 (SC).

Even in this case, the Apex Court held that the last seen theory comes into play where the time gap between the point of time when the accused and deceased were last seen alive and when the deceased is found dead is so small that possibility of any person other than the accused being the author of crime becomes impossible; *Bodh Raj* v. *State of Jammu & Kashmir*, AIR 2002 SC 3164: 2002 Cr LJ 4664: 2002 AIR SCW 3655: 2002 (8) SCC 45.

In this case, accused was charged for committing murder. It was alleged that appellant was last seen with the deceased. Defence of the accused was that son-in-law of deceased took away deceased to his place on pretext of illness of his wife i.e. daughter of deceased. Son-in-law though present in Court was not examined. The prosecution did not produce any witness connected with deceased to suggest that deceased was not seen after he was alleged to be last seen with the appellant. The Apex Court did not consider the evidence as to last seen against the accused and acquitted him; *Makhan Singh* v. *State of Punjab*, AIR 1988 SC 1705: 1988 Supp SCC 526: 1988 SCC (Cri) 917: (1988) 3 JT 1262.

In this case, accused was charged for the offence of murder. Prosecution alleged that the accused and deceased were last seen together before murder. However weapon of offence was recovered from another accused who had grudge against the deceased and who has been discharged. The Apex Court did not consider the evidence as to last seen and acquitted the appellant; *Kansa Behera* v. *State of Orissa*, AIR 1987 SC 1507: 1987 Cr LJ 1852: 1987 (3) SCC 480: 1987 SCC (Cri) 601.

In this case, it was alleged that Dr. M.S. Dahiya (accused) committed murder of wife Namita, a British national of Indian origin at Hotel Arenberg, Brussels, Belgium. It is the prosecution case that accused dismembered and extensively mutilated the body and disposed of the body parts at different places in the city of Brussels. The investigation was conducted in three countries-Belgium, London and concluded in India. The prosecution relied on last seen theory. The Accused did not dispute the fact that deceased was with him in room throughout night. But he consistently took a stand that deceased had left him voluntarily early in the morning. As to last seen evidence introduced by the prosecution, the Apex Court held that last seen evidence would not necessarily mean that the respondent/accused had killed his wife. In view of previous attitude of deceased, it is quite possible that she had walked out on her own. The Court further held that merely because the respondent accused objected to the behaviour of deceased towards her male friends at the birthday party of her sister prior to marriage would not constitute sufficient motive to kill her. Order of Delhi High Court acquitting the accused is upheld; *State Through C.B.I.* v. *Mahendra Singh Dahiya*, 2011 All MR (Cri) 1295 (SC).

Where deceased was seen following accused one day earlier whereas body of deceased was recovered on next day, the Apex Court held that this circumstance cannot be relied on to invoke last seen together theory; *Roopsena Khatum* v. *State of West Bengal*, 2011 All SCR 2917.

In this case, it was alleged that witnesses saw accused and her juvenile son near dead body at a distance of about 30-40 meters from the house which was an open space accessible to anyone. This circumstance was relied on by the prosecution as the evidence of last seen together. The Court discarded the last seen together evidence as prosecution failed to establish that the accused was last seen in the company of the deceased; *Smt. Angela Diniz* v. *State,* 2012 All MR (Cri) (Bom) 423.

In this case, the Apex Court held that theory of last seen is not independently sufficient to lead to a finding of guilt of accused where there are contradictions between the evidence of witnesses; *Sahadevan* v. *State of Tamil Nadu,* 2012 All SCR 1956.

In this case, the Apex Court held that prosecution must essentially establish the time when the accused and deceased were last seen together as well as the time of the death of the deceased; *Sk. Yusuf* v. *State of West Bengal,* (2011) 11 SCC 754: 2011 All MR (Cri) 2365 (SC).

In this case, prosecution claim that deceased was strangulated before her death and her body was burnt by accused. Prosecution claim that accused was last seen in the company of deceased. On facts, the Court held that burden under section 106 of the Evidence Act would not shift on accused to explain the alleged occurrence on the basis of last seen theory as prosecution failed to discharge initial burden of showing presence of accused at his residence shortly prior to occurrence of the incident; *Mohd. Sadiq Mohd. Rafiq* v. *State of Maharashtra,* 2014 All MR (Cri) 1974.

In this case, prosecution claimed that accused accompanied by deceased had gone in car borrowed by accused. One witness to whom accused visited deposed that accused and deceased left his farm together but accused returned alone with soiled cloths. It was claimed that motive for the crime was that accused wanted to take away car. The Apex Court held that though evidence creates suspicion, it is not sufficient to incriminate accused as there is no evidence as to how and where deceased was done to death; *Rishi Pal* v. *State of Uttarakhand,* AIR 2013 SC 3641.

In this case, prosecution claim that accused was last seen in the company of deceased and he murdered deceased. It was further claimed by prosecution that motive for the crime was alleged intimacy of accused with the wife of younger brother of deceased. However this fact was not proved by the prosecution. The Apex Court acquitted the accused by giving benefit of doubt to him holding that circumstance of last seen does not by itself and necessarily lead to inference that it was accused who committed crime; *Kanhaiya Lal* v. *State of Rajasthan,* 2014 All SCR 1542.

In this case, mutilated body was found in a train. Prosecution claim that accused was last seen in the company of deceased in train. The Court acquitted the accused on the ground that it was not just appellants who were last seen together with deceased and prosecution failed to prove that there were no other persons in the train. The Court observed that if theory of last seen together is to be accepted then there should be no other persons in the company of accused and victim when they are seen together for last time; *Mohan Singh* v. *State of West Bengal,* 2015 (3) Crimes 81 (Cal).

In this case, prosecution alleged that accused murdered his wife with grinding stone. Police did not notice weapon of crime *viz.* grinding stone in house though spot *panchanama* was effected on the date of incident. Therefore Court disbelieved discovery of said stone at the instance of accused. There was no evidence to show that accused was last seen in the company of deceased. The Court held that merely because dead body was found in house belonging to both accused and deceased, would not attract section 106 of Evidence Act particularly when there is no evidence about the presence of accused in house; *Rekha S. Chavan* v. *State of Maharashta,* 2014 All MR (Cri) 3279.

Murder by Poisoning

The law regarding the mode and manner of proof in cases of murder by administration of poison has been laid down by the Apex Court in *Ramgopal* v. *State of Maharashtra,* AIR 1972 SC 656. The Apex Court laid down the following tests—(a) Whether there is a clear motive for an accused to administer poison to the deceased. (b) Whether the deceased died of poison which is said to have been administered. (c) Whether the accused had poison in his possession and (d) Whether the accused had an opportunity to administer it to the deceased. [This case has been followed by the Apex Court in *Sharad Birdhi Chand Sarda* v. *State of Maharashtra,* (1985) 1 SCR 88: AIR 1984 SC 1622].

This is an interesting case of murder by poisoning based on circumstantial evidence. The judgment was delivered by a majority of 2 : 1. A.K. Sarkar, Justice delivered a dissenting judgment thereby acquitting the accused. This minority judgment is also well-reasoned and appeals to common sense and logic. The facts of the case were that the appellant was travelling with one Laxmibai Karve and it was alleged that the appellant administered some unrecognised poison or drug to her in the course of a railway journey between Puna and Bombay with the intention of causing her death and which did cause her death. Appellant was the family doctor of said Laxmibai. In the autopsy no ante-mortem injury was found on her person. No poison was detected either in post-mortem report or in chemical analyser's report. Even cause of death was not established. (Medical opinion did not state anything about poison). While dismissing the appeal of the appellant the Apex Court laid down the law as regards murder by poisoning based on circumstantial evidence as: At the trial of a person for murder by alleged poisoning, the fact of death by poisoning is provable by circumstantial evidence, notwithstanding that the autopsy as well as the chemical analysis fail to disclose any poison; though the cause of death may not appear to be established by direct evidence, the medical evidence of experts and the circumstances of the case may be sufficient to infer that the death must be the result of the administration to the victim of some unrecognised poison or drug with acts as a poison, and a conviction can be rested on circumstantial evidence provided that it is so decisive that the Court can unhesitatingly hold that the death was not a natural one. ...... If the deceased died in circumstances which *prima facie* admit of either disease or homicide by poisoning one must look at the conduct of the appellant both before and after the death of the deceased; *Anant Chintaman Lagu* v. *State of Bombay*, (1960) 2 SCR 460.

Charles G. Sobhraj, a French national facing criminal trials in seven countries is recently languishing in Nepal's prison as he was found guilty for murder and was awarded a twenty year jail term. He was tried in India for the murder of one A.A. Jacobs, an Israeli national by administration of zinc phosphide. It was alleged that the accused gave a pill to deceased who swallowed it with water. The glass of water was ordered by accused which was brought by waiter. According to the prosecution this glass contained a poisonous substance which ultimately resulted in the death of A.A. Jacobs. Chemical examiner reported that the viscera contained decomposition products of zinc phosphide poison and parts thereof also contained chlorpromazine in traces. Dismissing the appeal of the state, the Apex Court held that apart from its inability to accept the evidence of Somaru (PW 2) regarding identification of Sobhraj as the foreigner who came to Natraj Hotel, the High Court further found that his statement that on 5th January, 1976 at or about 4.30 p.m. he brought a glass of water as ordered by Sobhraj and that Jacobs swallowed a pill offered by Sobhraj with the water from that glass (which according to the prosecution contained a poisonous substance and ultimately resulted in the death of Jacobs) was wholly unacceptable. The grounds canvassed by the High Court for such conclusion were that Somaru did not disclose such an important fact to the police till 28th May, 1976, even though since the offence was committed, he had met them on a number of occasions; that it was unlikely that Sobhraj would have asked him to fetch a glass of water to give a pill to the deceased for PW 1 had stated that a glass is normally kept in the rooms in the Hotel and there is also running water in the tap in the bathroom; and that if Sobhraj wanted to give a poisonous pill to the deceased he could have done it secretly, when he had such an opportunity instead of doing it in the presence of a waiter of the Hotel; *State of Uttar Pradesh* v. *Charles Gurmukh Sobhraj*, IV (1996) CCR 90 (SC).

Other Cases on Murder by Poisoning

Jaipal v. *State of Haryana*, AIR 2002 SC 3447: In this case it was alleged that death was caused due to tablet of aluminium phosphide (celphos) administered by accused. Doctors did not positively approving that suggestion. Medical evidence was that congestion of organs as found could be due to other reasons. There was omission on part of the police to protect the place where sample of vomits could be found. There was no motive on part of accused to commit the crime. In such facts and circumstances of the case, the Apex Court set aside the conviction the accused.

Culpable Homicide not Amounting to Murder

To explain this concept few cases are given below:

In this case [*Sardar Khan* v. *State of Assam*, 1983 Cr LJ (NOC) 120 (Gauhati)] accused was tried for the offence punishable under section 304, Part I of I.P.C. It was alleged that deceased died due to subdural haemorrhage which was caused due to fall on ground as a result of fist blow given by accused. The Court while holding the accused guilty for the offence punishable under section 323, I.P.C.

but not under section 304 Part I of I.P.C. observed that, "...... *That the haemorrhage had not occurred as a result of the fist blow on the abdomen but it was due to impact of the fall on the ground caused by the fist blow on the abdomen of the deceased. Since only one fist blow was given, it cannot be said that the accused can be attributed with the knowledge that it was likely to cause an injury which would cause death."*

This was a case [*Shankar* v. *State of Maharashtra,* 1995 (1) Mh LJ 416 (DB) (Bom)] wherein accused was charged for the death of the deceased by a stab injury over abdomen which internally punctured the right artery at ileum. The Bombay High Court while altering the conviction of accused from murder to one under section 304, Part II, held that, *"In absence of intention of puncturing the artery, case fell under section 299, I.P.C. and not under section 300, I.P.C."*

In this case, accused was driving BMW Car in high speed and in rash and negligent manner. At the time of incident the accused was in an inebriated State after consuming alcohol. He gave a violent dash to a group of persons standing on the road resulting in death of six persons and injury to one person. The impact was so great and severe that they flew in the air and fell on the bonnet and wind screen of the car. Some of them rolled down and came beneath the car. Though injured persons were shouting and crying for help, the accused drove away the car at high speed. The trial Court convicted the accused for the offence punishable under section 304, Part II of IPC. However the Delhi High Court altered the order of the trial Court and convicted the accused for the offence punishable under section 304A of the IPC. On appeal by the State, the Hon'ble Supreme Court framed solitary question as to whether respondent accused deserves to be held guilty of commission of offence under section 304, Part II of the IPC or the conviction and sentence awarded to him by the High Court of Delhi, under section 304A of the IPC should be held to be good and legally tenable. The Hon'ble Apex Court held that the High Court of Delhi has committed an error in converting the conviction of accused to section 304A of the IPC from that of section 304, Part II of IPC. The Hon'ble Apex Court held that accused had the knowledge that his action was likely to cause death of so many human beings, lying on the road unattended. The Court further observed that had the accused extended a helping hand to the victims of the accident, caused by him by making arrangements to give immediate medical attention, perhaps lives of some of the victims could have been saved. Ever after committing the accident, he only thought of his safety, did not care for the victims and escaped from the site showing lease concern to the human beings lying on the road with serious injuries. Conduct of the accused is highly reprehensible and cannot be countenanced by any Court of law; *State* v. *Sanjeev Nanda,* 2012 All MR (Cri) 3005 (SC).

In case of drunken driving there is presumption that the accused has the knowledge that his act is likely to cause death. The Apex Court held that a presumption is that a person knows natural and likely consequences, even if unforeseen, do not render the act involuntary. Act of negligent, rash or dangerous driving, is not devoid of element of voluntariness. Sections 279, 304A and 336 to 338 are premised entirely on negligent *i.e.,* non-voluntary act or omissions. Charges under sections 304-I, 304-II and 338 are not mutually destructive and can coexist. The Apex Court held that offence under section 304-II, IPC is proved against the appellant; *Alister A. Pareira* v. *State of Maharashtra,* (2012) 2 SCC 648: 2012 All SCR 654.

Other Cases

1. *Kallikatt Kunhu* v. *State of Kerala,* (2000) 1 SCR 1162: This was a case of murder wherein it was alleged that the accused stabbed the deceased with dagger. However no blood stains were found on dagger. The Apex Court held that, *"If the dagger was used to inflict injuries upon the deceased, the same could not have been found enclosed in a sheath near the basement of the* chappa *(shed). It should have been found unsheathed and ought to have had some blood stains. ..... If, as alleged, the incident had taken place in the shed, it is not probable that the* dhoti *and bottle could have been found in the pathway."*

2. *Akhilesh Hazam* v. *State of Bihar,* (1995) 3 SCR 864: This was a case of murder based on circumstantial evidence wherein the accused was charged for murdering his mother, sister, wife and daughter. Accused made a disclosure statement which led to the discovery of iron angle. However there was absence of report of serologist as to the presence of human blood on iron angle. The Apex Court acquitted the accused by giving benefit of doubt. The Court took the conduct of the accused of not absconding into consideration and also the failure of the prosecution to prove motive.

3. *State of Rajasthan* v. *Maniram,* AIR 2001 SC 2430: This was a case of murder wherein the version of eye witnesses about number and nature of injuries received by deceased was not supported by medical evidence. Conduct of one of the eye witnesses in not making any attempt to save deceased who was his grandmother and with whom he was living, is not natural. His explanation that he was frightened due to sudden attack is also not normal and natural as he was healthier than the accused. Therefore order of acquittal was upheld.

4. *Awadhesh* v. *State of Madhya Pradesh,* 1988 Cr LJ 1154 (SC): This was a case of murder wherein the doctor opined that person who caused injuries to deceased was at higher level that the deceased. Evidence of doctor was not consistent with the testimony of the eye witnesses. Medical expert's opinion was corroborated by other circumstances indicating that eye witnesses had not seen the actual occurrence. Hence the Apex Court set aside the conviction.

5. *Prafulla Bora* v. *State of Assam,* 1988 Cr LJ 428 (Gauhati): This was a case of murder where a lady about 80 years of age was the eye witness. Evidence disclosed that her vision was weak and she was also hard of hearing. Occurrence took place after the dark. The Court did not place reliance on her evidence.

6. *Hardeep* v. *State of Haryana,* AIR 2002 SC 3018: In this case father and son were charged for the offence of murder. Quarrel took place few days before the incident between deceased and accused over repayment of loan of Rs. 250. Festival of Holi was being celebrated. Prosecution alleged that father caught hold of deceased from behind and his son stabbed him right on the chest. All three eye witnesses were closely related to the deceased. The Apex Court while acquitting the accused held that, *"It does not appeal to the reason that for this kind*

of a dispute the father will allow his son to commit murder at the young age when he has only passed out high school and get his son condemned for whole life."

7. *Chandu Bhai* v. *State of Gujarat,* AIR 1982 SC 1022: This was a case of murder wherein the eye witness stated in statement made to police that the appellant was armed with a *'stick'* during the incident. But during the trial, all the three eye witnesses stated that he was armed with a *'dharia'*. The Apex Court rejected the ocular evidence and appellant was acquitted by giving benefit of doubt.

8. *Valson* v. *State of Kerala,* AIR 2002 SC 2339: This was a case of murder wherein it was alleged that accused inflicted knife blow on his brother, the deceased. The Court altered the conviction to one under section 304, Part I holding that sites at which the fatal blow fell was not chosen or intended by the accused.

Honour Killing

Murders committed for the alleged honour of family are known as 'honour killing' and number of such incidents are increasing. The Hon'ble Apex Court has taken judicial notice of the increase in number of such incidents and warned that all persons who are planning to perpetrate honour killing should know that the gallows await them. The Court further held that honour killing comes within the category of rarest of rare cases and deserves death punishment; *Bhagwan Dass* v. *State (NCT) of Delhi,* AIR 2011 SC 1863.

This is a case of honour killing. In this case, deceased Nitish Katara was in love with accused Vikas's sister Bharti. Deceased was abducted and brutally murdered on the night of 16th February, 2002 to 17th February, 2002. The Apex Court upheld the conviction of accused Vikas, his cousin Vishal Yadav and Sukhdeo awarded by the High Court. The Apex Court awarded life sentence of 25 years to them without remission. While confirming the order of the High Court, the Apex Court held that crime was committed in a planned and cold-blooded manner with the motive that has emanated due to feeling of some kind uncalled for and unwarranted superiority based on caste feeling that has blinded the thought of "choice available" to a sister – a representative of women as a class. In review petition filed by the convicts, the Apex Court modified the order with singular modification in the sentence and held that the sentence under section 201/34, IPC shall run concurrently; *Vikas Yadav* v. *State of Uttar Pradesh,* 2016 SC.

In *suo motu* writ petition filed by a woman who alleged that she was gang rapped on orders of village court the Hon'ble Apex Court, directed concerned authority to register FIR and take action against the culprits. [*In Re* v. *Indian Woman Says Gang-Raped on Orders of Village Court* published in Business and Financial News Dated 23rd January, 2014, *Suo Motu* W.P. (Cri) No. 24 of 2014].

In this case, petitioner filed writ petition before the Supreme Court alleging that her brothers are harassing her husband and husband's relatives as she has performed inter-caste marriage. The Apex Court observed that such Acts of violence or threats or harassment are wholly illegal and those who commit them must be severely punished. This is a free and democratic country, and once a person becomes a major he or she can marry whosoever he/she likes. The Court further observed that there is nothing honourable in such killings, and in fact they are nothing but barbaric and shameful acts of murder committed by brutal, feudal minded persons who deserve harsh punishment. The Court issued directions to register FIR against the culprit; *Lata Singh* v. *State of Uttar Pradesh*, WP (Crl) 208 of 2004, decided on 7th July. 2006.

In this case, accused was charged with the murder of his niece for marrying a man belonging to Scheduled Caste community. However the deceased was killed after six years of her marriage. Only evidence against the accused was recovery of ornaments from his pocket which allegedly belonged to deceased. Said ornaments were however recovered after a period of about three weeks in a personal search. The Hon'ble Apex Court set aside the conviction of accused for murder on the reasoning that a person who has allegedly killed his niece for honour of family would not act so low as to steal jewellery; *Dandu Jaggaraju* v. *State of Andhra Pradesh*, 2012 All SCR 138.

Murders in Fake Encounter

Police and para-military forces are killing persons in encounters with alleged extremists and maoists. Many such incidents are reported in the press and electronic media. The Hon'ble Apex Court has held that fake encounters are nothing but cold blooded, brutal murders by persons who are supposed to uphold law and further held that where a fake encounter is proved against policemen in a trial, they must be given death sentence, treating it as a rarest of rare case; *Prakash Kadam* v. *Ramprasad V. Gupta*, 2011 All SCR 1402: 2011 (2) Crimes 279 (SC).

Though the criminal appeal filed before the Hon'ble Apex Court pertains to discharge application, the facts of this case are interesting and unique. This is a case of one naxalite being killed in alleged police encounter in 1970. However, reports appear in various newspaper in Kerala in the year 1998 that the killing of Varghese (naxalite) in the year 1970 was a fake encounter and that senior police officers are involved in the said fake encounter. Pursuant to the said news reports, several writ petitions were filed by various individuals and organization before the High Court of Kerala with a prayer that the investigation may be transfer to CBI. In the said writ petition, one constable filed counter affidavit, making a confessional statement that he shot the said naxalite on the instruction of his superior officers. High Court of Kerala passed an order directing the CBI to register an FIR. Accordingly, the CBI registered FIR against the appellant and other two persons for the offence under section 302, IPC read with section 34, IPC. After investigation, the CBI filed the chargesheet before the Special Judge (CBI). The appellant filed a petition for discharge, but the learned trial judge dismissed the said petition. The appellant filed criminal revision before the High Court but the same was also dismissed. Thereafter appellants filed Criminal Appeal before Hon'ble Apex Court against the said order. The Apex Court dismissed the appeal filed by the appellant and directed the trial judge to dispose of the case expeditiously. Result of the case is awaited; *P. Vijayan* v. *State of Kerala*, (2010) 2 SCC 398: 2010 All MR (Cri) 588 (SC).

The conduct of police administration in Mumbai and the State of Maharashtra shows the activism to target and brand Muslim community as anti-nationals. The proceeding relate to the aftermath of the demolition of Babri Masjid in December 1992. During the period (December 1992 and January 1993), the city of Mumbai had witnessed incidents of riot on a large scale with complete breakdown of law and order. The incident in question occurred on 9th January, 1993 near Suleman Usman Bakery in which firing was resorted to by the Special Operation Squad led by R.D. Tyagi (Additional Commissioner of Police, Mumbai) in which 9 persons had died. Two revision petitions were filed before Sessions Court, one against the order of framing of charge and second, against the order rejecting applications for discharge from sessions case. However FIR was registered against the persons present inside the premises of Suleman Bakery and Chunnabatti Masjid alleging that they had become violent and aggressive and that their Act of aggression had led to the police firing.

The Government of Maharashtra set-up a commission under the Chairmanship of Justice Shrikrishna for enquiry. The Shrikrishna Commission filed report on 16th February, 1998. However, the findings and recommendations of the Commission were not accepted by Government of Maharashtra. This led to filing of number of writ petitions before High Court as well as before the Supreme Court. As a result of constant monitoring by the Supreme Court, the State of Maharashtra filed affidavit on 23rd March, 2001 stating that it had passed resolution to initiate further investigation to implement recommendations of the Commission. The Government also constituted Special Task Force (STF) for carrying out further investigation. STF found that the firing dated 9th January, 1993 was totally unjustified and police personnel had in fact committed murder of nine persons. On the basis of said enquiry, STF registered fresh FIR against the delinquent police personnel and filed chargesheet in 2001.

The Hon'ble Bombay High Court held that first FIR filed against persons is bogus and therefore discharge those accused. However as regards the fresh FIR/second FIR in respect of the same incident, the Court held that the only course open to STF was to forward further report under section 173(2), Cr.P.C. with alteration in offences and indicating the accused in second FIR which would have resulted in withdrawal of prosecution against applicants-accused in first FIR. (The result of the trial is awaited); *Ashfaque Ahmed* v. *State of Maharashtra*, 2013 All MR (Cri) 563.

Attempt to Commit Murder (I.P.C. Section 307)

The cases under this section often involve the question whether there was an attempt to commit crime or intent to commit crime. The law and the difference between the two has been stated by the Apex Court in *Sagayam* v. *State*, (2000) 3 SCR 565. This was a case where the appellant in order to spread fear in the minds of the people and for extorting money and valuables, stored lethal weapons in his house. When PW 2 (ASI) went to his house for search, appellant unsuccessfully tried to assault him. While allowing the appeal the Apex Court held that, *"In the instant case, the evidence of PW 2 only establish that there was a threat to assault him but the overt acts attributed to the appellant could not amount to attempt to murder, at best it can be one of attempt to assault but there is not even an injury upon the victim. It is possible that accused confronted PW 2 but that by itself could not result in coming to the conclusion that it was an attempt to murder him. .... To justify conviction under section 307, I.P.C., it is not essential that bodily injury capable of causing death should have been inflicted. An attempt in order to be criminal need not be the penultimate act fore-boding death. It is sufficient in law if there is present an intent coupled with some overt act in execution thereof, such act being proximate to the crime intended and if the attempt has gone so far that it would have been complete but for the extraneous intervention which frustrated its consummation. .... There are different stages in a crime. First, intention to commit it; second, preparation to commit it; third, an attempt to commit it. If at the third stage, the attempt falls, the crime is not complete but law punishes for attempting the same. .... An attempt to commit crime must be distinguished from an intent to commit it or preparation of its commission."*

In another case [*State of Maharashtra* v. *Mohd. Yakub S/o Abdul Hamid,* (1980) 2 SCR 1158] the Apex Court has explained the meaning of "attempt" and the distinction between "preparation" and "attempt" as: *"The expression" attempt "within the meaning of the penal provisions is wide enough to take in its fold any one or series of acts committed beyond the stage of preparation. .... What constitutes an "attempt" is a mixed question of law and fact, depending largely on the circumstances of the particular case. "Attempt" defines a precise and exact definition. Broadly speaking, all crimes which consist of the commission of affirmative acts are preceded by some covert or overt conduct which may be divided into three stages: the first stage exists when the culprit first entertains the idea or intention to commit an offence; in the second stage he makes preparations to commit it; and the third stage is reached when the culprit takes deliberate overt steps to commit the offence. Such overt act or step, in order to be criminal, need not be the penultimate act towards the commission of the offence. It is sufficient if such act or acts were deliberately done and manifest a clear intention to commit the offence aimed, being reasonably proximate to the consummation of the offence. ...... There is a distinction between "preparation" and "attempt". Attempt begins where preparation ends. In sum, a person commits the offence of 'attempt to commit a particular offence' when (i) he intends to commit that particular offence and (ii) he, having made preparations and with the intention to commit the offence, does an act towards its commission; such an act need not be the penultimate act towards the commission of that offence, but must be an act during the course of committing that offence."*

This was a case, where it was alleged that both the accused attempted to commit murder of the complainant. However injuries sustained by the complainant were simple in nature and he was discharged from hospital within three days of his admission. Further, evidence showed that both the accused gave a single blow to the complainant even though there was no protest on part of the complainant. The Bombay High Court held that offence under section 307, I.P.C. is not made out and therefore altered the conviction to one under section 324, I.P.C.; *Ashok Chaudhari* v. *State of Maharashtra,* 2001 (2) Mh LJ 31.

In this case, accused though armed with *ballam* used only the blunt side of it. The Apex Court while justifying the acquittal held that no offence is made out under section 307 of I.P.C. as there was no intention to commit murder; *Hari Singh* v. *Sukhbir*, 1988 (3) Crimes 541.

In this case, accused was convicted under section 307, IPC. It was alleged by prosecution that the accused-appellant hurled abuses on complainant and thereafter threw a burning chimney at him thereby attempting to commit murder. The Bombay High Court held that accused is not guilty for the offence punishable under section 307, IPC as there was no intention to attempt to commit murder; *Anant N. Mankar* v. *State of Maharashtra*, 2011 (2) Crimes 5C (Bom).

In this case, it was alleged that appellants armed with *bhala* and other weapons assaulted victim on a dispute over passage. While setting aside conviction, the Patna High Court held that both injured had sustained simple injury and witnesses did not explain counter version which could not be denied in the facts of the case when specific evidence was lead by defence. Denial of counter version raised a reasonable doubt if correct version of incident suppressed; *Narendra Kumar* v. *State of Bihar*, 2012 (1) Crimes 511 (Pat).

In this case, accused was convicted for the offence punishable under section 307 of IPC. It was alleged that accused husband set his wife on fire. However evidence on record showed that accused immediately tried to extinguish fire. In such facts and circumstances, the Court altered the conviction from section 307 to one under section 326 of IPC holding that accused only wanted to cause hurt to his wife and requisite *mens rea* is absent; *Jairam J. Salve* v. *State of Maharashtra*, 2012 All MR (Cri) 1704.

In this case, prosecution claim that accused persons assaulted their senior officer with *lathi* for recording absence from work place and they intended to commit murder. Senior Officer received 18 injuries but they were not on vital parts of the body. The Apex Court set aside the conviction under section 307, IPC and altered the same to one under section 325, IPC holding that there was no intention to commit murder. The Court further held that whether there is an attempt to murder or whether there is an attempt to cause hurt is a question to fact and it can be determined on considering the nature of injuries, nature of weapons, parts of body were injury is cause, severity of blows, motive, etc.; *Fireman Ghulam Mustafa* v. *State of Uttaranchal*, 2015 All MR (Cri) 3698 (SC).

Abetment of Suicide – (Section 306, I.P.C.)

Before any person is convicted for the offence punishable under section 306, IPC, it is incumbent upon the prosecution to prove that the accused has abetted the commission of such suicide. In other words, the prosecution is required to prove that the act of the accused falls under any of the clauses of section 107 of the IPC.

Section 107 of I.P.C. does not itself create a substantive offence. Abetment is a separate and distinct offence provided the thing abetted is an offence. Abetment does not involve the actual commission of the crime abetted; it is a crime apart. Even after the introduction of section 498A of the IPC and section 113A of the Indian Evidence Act, the proof must be beyond any shadow of reasonable doubt. There is a higher standard of proof in criminal cases than in civil cases, but there is no absolute standard in either of the cases. The standard adopted must be the standard adopted by a prudent man; *Gurubachan Singh* v. *Satpal Singh,* (1989) Supp 1 SCR 292.

In this case, the Apex Court devised a "4-C Test" which has to be followed by Courts while appreciating evidence on record. The Court held that contiguity, continuity, culpability and complicity of the indictable Acts or omissions are the concomitant indices of abatement. The Court held that for drawing presumption under section 113A of the Evidence Act, offence should be proved beyond reasonable doubt. The Court further held that intention and involvement of the accused to aid or instigate the commission of suicide is imperative to constitute abatement. Remoteness of the culpable Acts or omissions rooted in the intention of the accused to actualise the suicide would fall short as well of the offence of abatement essential to attract the punitive mandate of section 306, IPC; *Gurcharan Singh* v. *State of Punjab,* 2017 All SCR (Cri) 42.

In this case, deceased committed suicide by consuming poison. Trial Court convicted the accused under section 304B of IPC. In appeal, High Court held that deceased committed suicide not due to dowry harassment but due to harassment by the husband unrelated to dowry and therefore converted the conviction into section 306, IPC. The Apex Court upheld the order of High Court and held that the cruelty or harassment sans any dowry demands which drives the wife to commit suicide, attracts the offence under section 306 and not section 304B even though the specific charge had not been framed; *Narwindar Singh* v. *State of Punjab,* Criminal Appeal No. 590 of 2005, decided on 5th January, 2011.

In this case, the Apex Court held that a person abets the doing of a thing when (i) he instigates any person to do that thing, or (ii) engages with one or more other person or persons in any conspiracy for the doing of that thing, or (iii) intentionally aids, by act or illegal omission, the doing of that thing; *Faguna Kanta* v. *State of Assam,* AIR 1959 SC 673. The division bench of the Allahabad High Court in *State of Uttar Pradesh* v. *Sarju Prasad,* 1996 Cr LJ 3833, has held that, "*A person will be said to aid the commission of offence of abetment either prior to or at the time of the commission of an Act, if he does something in order to facilitate the commission of that Act.*"

However the Madras High Court in *Anandha Thandavam* v. *Udaya Sundaram,* 1989 (3) Crimes 209, has held that, "*An unintentional aiding is not an abetment within the meaning of section 107, I.P.C. ...... Intentional aiding and active complicity is the gist of the offence of abetment.*"

The Apex Court in *Satvir Singh* v. *State of Punjab,* 2002 All MR (Cri) 194, has held that, "*Condition precedent to attract section 116 read with section 306, I.P.C. is that suicide should necessarily have been committed. .... Law does not penalise an abetment to the offence of mere attempt to commit suicide.*"

The facts of this case are that: appellant is the brother of Neelam Sengar, wife of the deceased Chander Bhushan *alias* Babloo. It was alleged that the marriage between the sister of the appellant and the deceased took place in 1993. Further it was alleged that immediately after marriage she was subjected to continuous ill-treatment by the deceased and the family members forcing her to live separately along with her husband and children for about a year. Thereafter, she went to her parents house. About two months prior to the incident, the appellant advised the deceased to take his sister back to her matrimonial house and treat her properly. On 25th July, 1998 the appellant visited the place of the parents of the deceased where it is alleged that the appellant threatened the parents of the deceased that if they do not mend their behaviour towards his sister, he would be compelled to resort to filing a complaint under section 498A of the I.P.C. Thereafter the deceased returned alone and told his brothers and other acquaintances that the appellant had threatened and abused him by using filthy words. On the next date *i.e.,* 27th July, 1998, the deceased was found hanging with a rope by neck on the raft of his house and he was found dead. The deceased also left a suicide note on a stray piece of wrapping paper which reads as Gosalpur Sengar has threatened to report under dowry demand and threatened to involve family members due to this I am writing in my full senses that Sanjay Sangar is responsible for my death. .... The appellant filed a petition under section 482 of the Cr.P.C. for quashing the charge before the High Court but his appeal was dismissed. In appeal, the Apex Court quashed the chargesheet framed against the appellant and held that, *"The words 'to go and die' uttered by the accused to the deceased by itself would not constitute ingredient of 'instigation'. Presence of* mens rea *is necessary concomitant of instigation. Fact that deceased committed suicide after two days of quarrel during which said words were uttered by accused would show that suicide was not direct result of quarrel. Suicide note left by the deceased showed that he was in great stress and depression"; Sanju* alias *Sanjay Singh Sengar* v. *State of Madhya Pradesh,* AIR 2002 SC 1998.

Other Cases on Abetment to Suicide

Najjam Faroqui v. *State,* 1992 Cr LJ 2574 (Cal) (DB) – Where no injury was found on the front of trunk of the deceased, the theory of suicide by kerosene burning injuries was rejected.

Cyriac s/o Devassai v. *Sub-Inspector of Police, Kaduthuruthy,* 2006 All MR (Cri) Journal 27 (Kerala) – In this case deceased owed rupees 200 to accused. Accused merely told him in public that, *"why are you remaining as a burden on earth, why can't you go and die?"* and deceased committed suicide. The Court held that, *"The act of accused though insulting and abusive would not by itself constitute abetment of suicide. .... It is not what deceased 'felt' but what accused 'intended' by his act is more important. .... In order to prove that the accused abetted commission of a suicide of a person, prosecution has to establish that: (i) The accused kept on irritating or annoying the deceased by words, deed or wilful omission or conduct which may even be a wilful silence until the deceased reacted; or, that the accused strongly advised or persuaded the deceased to do something; or pushed or forced the deceased by deed, words, or wilful omission or conduct which may even be a wilful silence to make the deceased to move forward more quickly in a forward direction. (ii) That the accused had the intention to provoke, incite, urge or encourage the deceased to commit suicide, while acting in manner stated above."*

Joseph Kurien v. *State of Kerala,* (1994) Supp 4 SCR 122 – The Apex Court held that, *"when direct involvement is not established, accused cannot without a formal charge be held guilty of abetment. .... The roles of the perpetrator and abettor of the crime are different."*

State of Himachal Pradesh v. *Nikku Ram,* (1995) Supp 3 SCR 177 – This was a case under sections 306, 107, 498A, I.P.C. wherein the Court held that, *"since evidence of demands amounting to cruelty of married person having been disbelieved by Court, offence of abetment of suicide is not made out. ..... Presumption under section 113A of the Evidence Act as to the abetment of suicide cannot be drawn."*

State of Punjab v. *Iqbal Singh,* (1991) 2 SCR 790. In this case the Apex Court held that, *"Section 113A or 113B of the Evidence Act cannot be invoked as the prosecution had not brought the exact date of marriage on record.*

A.K. Chaudhary v. *State of Gujarat,* 2006 Cr LJ 726: 2006 (2) ABR (NOC) 361 (Guj) – In this case there was official relationship between accused and deceased. The deceased who committed suicide was suspended by accused officer accordingly to employment regulation. In such circumstances it was held that no offence is made out under section 306 of IPC as the action of suicide in such case can be said to fall under exceptions provided under section 80 of IPC.

Swamy Prahladdas v. *State of Madhya Pradesh,* 1995 SCC (Cri) 943: 1995 Supp (3) SCC 438 – In this case it was alleged that deceased committed suicide due to utterances of words 'go and die' by the accused. The Apex Court held that *"utterances of words to 'go and die' does not reflect requisite* mens rea *on assumption that words would be carried out. ...... Deceased had plenty of time to weigh pros and cons of act by which he ultimately ended his life. ...... Suicide is not the direct result of words uttered.*

Sonti Rama Krishna v. *Sonti Shanti Sree,* 2009 (1) Crimes 83 (SC): Words uttered in a fit of anger or emotion without any intention cannot be termed as instigation.

Ganpat D. Garje v. *State of Maharashtra,* 2012 All MR (Cri) 1255: In this case, frequent quarrels used to take place between accused and the victim. The said quarrels were on account of victim's desire to stay separately from joint family of the accused. The Court set aside the conviction holding that even if victim had committed suicide on being fed up by frequent quarrels with accused within a span of about six months before the incident, accused cannot be said to have abetted the commission of suicide of deceased.

Nachhattar Singh v. *State of Punjab,* 2011 All SCR 2957: In this case, prosecution alleged that deceased committed suicide as accused were expecting her to work and look after aged in-laws. The prosecution further alleged that the act of the accused constitutes cruelty. The Apex Court held that the act of the accused does not constitute cruelty within the meaning of section 498A and it cannot be said that the in-laws abetted the commission of suicide of their daughter-in-law.

Punishment of abetment if the Act abetted is committed in consequence, and where no express provision is made for its punishment (Section 109, IPC).

Where a person aids and abets the perpetrator of a crime at the very time the crime is committed, he is a principal of the second degree and section 109 applies. But mere failure to prevent the commission of an offence is not by itself an abetment of that offence. Mere help in preparation for commission of an offence which is not ultimately committed, is not covered under section 109 of the IPC. For constituting offence of abetment, intentional and active participation by the abettor is necessary. .... Section 114 of IPC applies where a criminal first abets an offence to be committed by another person and is subsequently present at its commission. Section 114 is not applicable in every case in which the abettor is present at commission of offence abetted; *Kulwant Singh @ Kulbansh Singh* v. *State of Bihar,* (2007) 15 SCC 670: 2007 (5) CRJ 318 (SC).

In this case, the Apex Court held that where a person is charged with having committed an offence and another is charged with having abetted him in the commission thereof, and the prosecution fails to substantiate the commission of the principal offence, there can be no conviction for abetment; *Gallu Sah* v. *State of Bihar,* (1959) SCR 861.

Cases of Dowry Deaths and Bride Burning (Section 304B, IPC)

The increasing malady of the bride burning is a matter of serious concern not only for the Courts but also for the civilised society. This concern is reflected in one of the judgments rendered by the Apex Court where the Apex Court said that social reformist and legal jurists may evolve a machinery for debarring such a boy from remarriage irrespective of the member of family who committed the crime and in violation penalise the whole family including those who participate in it. That is, social ostracisation is needed to curtail increasing malady of bride burning; *Ashok Kumar* v. *State of Rajasthan,* (1990) Supp 1 SCR 401.

Section 304B, IPC creates a new offence and it is not merely a rule of evidence. Their trial and punishment for the offence of dowry death provided in section 304B with the minimum sentence of seven years imprisonment for an act done by them prior to creation of the new offence of dowry death would clearly deny to them the protection afforded by clause (1) of Article 20 of the Constitution. Thus there is protection under Article 20(1) of the Constitution against conviction for a new offence created subsequent to the commission of offence; *Soni D. Babubhai* v. *State of Gujarat,* (1991) 3 SCR 812.

In this case, the Hon'ble Apex Court has stated that the following necessary ingredients must be proved by the prosecution in cases of dowry deaths: (i) That the death of a woman is caused by any burns or bodily injury or occurs otherwise than under normal circumstances; (ii) That the death of a woman occurred within seven years of her marriage; (iii) It must be shown that she was subjected to cruelty or harassment by her husband or any relative of the husband for or in connection with the demand of dowry. The Apex Court further held that, "the presumption under section 113B of the Evidence Act would follow only when the above three essentials of section 304B, I.P.C. are satisfactorily proved. However this is a rebuttable presumption; *Arun Garg* v. *State of Punjab,* 2005 All MR (Cri) 2551.

To attract section 304B, IPC, the death should be dowry death, *i.e.,* in connection with the demand of dowry as defined in section 2 of the Dowry Prohibition Act, 1961. 'Dowry means any money or property or valuable security demanded by any of the persons mentioned in section 2 of the Dowry Prohibition Act, 1961, at or before or at any time after the marriage. Such demand if reasonably connected to the death of a married woman, would necessarily make it 'Dowry Death'. The Court held that provisions of section 304B, IPC, must be given a fair, pragmatic and common sense interpretation so as to fulfil the object sought to be achieved by the Parliament; *Rajinder Singh* v. *State of Punjab,* 2015 (2) Crimes 90 (SC): 2015 All SCR 1226.

A demand for money on account of some financial stringency or for meeting some urgent domestic expenses or for purchasing manure cannot be term as a demand for dowry as the said word is normally understood; *Appasaheb* v. *State of Maharashtra,* AIR 2007 SC 763: (2007) 1 SCC 721: 2007 All MR (Cri) 859 (SC). This judgement was reconsidered by the Court and it held that the judgment does not lay down a law of universal application. If a demand for property or valuable security, directly or indirectly, has nexus with the marriage, such demand would constitute demand for dowry. The cause of raising of such demand remains immaterial; *Bachni Devi* v. *State of Maharashtra,* AIR 2011 SC 1098: (2011) 4 SCC 427. Even a three-Judges bench held that *Appasaheb's* case is not a good law; *Rajinder Singh* v. *State of Punjab,* 2015 (2) Crimes 90 (SC): 2015 All SCR 1226.

Parliament has shifted the burden of proof in contradistinction to the *onus* of proof on to the husband and his relatives in the cases where it has been shown that a dowry death has occurred. The inroad into or dilution of the presumption of innocence of an accused has, even *de hors* statutory sanction, been recognised by Courts in those cases where death occurs in a home where only the other spouse is present; as also where an individual is last seen with the deceased. The deeming provision in section 304B is, therefore, neither a novelty in nor an anathema to our criminal law jurisprudence; *Mir Mohammad Umar* v. *State of Tamil Nadu,* (2009) 14 SCC 415: 2009 All MR (Cri) 2118 (SC).

While interpreting the word "it" in relation to word "shown" in section 304B, IPC, the Court held that Parliament has employed the amorphous pronoun/noun "it" (which we think should be construed as an allusion to the prosecution), followed by the word "shown", and it has to be read up to mean "prove" and the word "deemed" has to be read down to mean "presumed"; *Mithu* v. *State of Punjab,* AIR 1983 SC 473.

Presumption as to Dowry Death (Section 113B, Evidence Act)

Section 113B has been inserted in the Evidence Act by Act 43 of 1986 with effect from 1st May, 1986. This newly inserted provision raises a mandatory presumption as regards the death of such a person as the dowry death when it is shown that soon before her death such women was subjected to cruelty or harassment for, or in connection with, any demand for dowry.

In this case, the Apex Court held that provisions of Penal Code and Act of 1861 not only discourage demand for dowry but also penalize any such Act. Sections 304B of IPC and section 113B of the Evidence Act do supplement each other to effectuate legislative mandate of statutory presumption of guilt, the contingencies warranted being present; *M. Narayan* v. *State of Karnataka,* 2015 All SCR 2215.

For raising presumption under section 113B of the Evidence Act, prosecution has to prove that the death of women occurred in unnatural condition and it took place within seven years of marriage and that cruelty or harassment was for or in connection with demand of dowry; *Hem Chand* v. *State of Haryana*, (1994) Supp 4 SCR 295. Prosecution further has to rule out the possibility of a natural or accidental death so as to bring it within the purview of *"death occurring otherwise than in normal circumstances; Bakshish Ram* v. *State of Punjab*, 2013 SAR (Criminal) 545 (SC): 2013 All SCR 2480. *Presumption of dowry death would be attracted only in a case of suicidal or homicidal death and not in a case of accidental death; Sultan Singh* v. *State of Haryana*, 2014 All MR (Cri) 4468 (SC). *Where injuries on the person of the deceased were not sufficient to cause death, section 304B is not attracted;* AIR 1996 SC 67. *Where there was no evidence showing any persistent dowry demand, once stray instance of demand of dowry is not enough to attract section 304B; Baljinder Kaur* v. *State of Punjab*, 2014 (4) Crimes 293 (SC): 2015 All SCR 244. *Once the basic ingredients of the offence under section 304B, IPC, are established or shown or proved by the prosecution, even by preponderance of possibility, the initial presumption of innocence is replaced by an assumption of guilt of the accused. Thereupon, the burden of proof is transferred upon the accused and it requires him to produce evidence dislodging his guilt beyond reasonable doubt: Sher Singh © Partapa* v. *State of Haryana*, 2015 All MR (Cri) 2817 (SC). *However, presumption that the death has been caused by husband or relatives of deceased, who caused cruelty or harassment, can be rebutted even without direct evidence; Vijay Pal Singh* v. *State of Uttarakhand*, 2015 All MR (Cri) 2841 (SC).

The Apex Court has culled out the principles laid down in various decisions of the Supreme Court as regards the presumption of dowry death: (a) To attract the provision of section 304B, IPC, the main ingredient of the offence to be established is that soon before the death of the deceased she was subjected to cruelty and harassment in connection with the demand of dowry. (b) the death of the deceased women was caused by any burn or bodily injury or some other circumstance which was not normal. (c) such death occurs within seven years from the date of her marriage. (d) that the victim was subjected to cruelty or harassment by her husband or any relative of her husband. (e) such cruelty or harassment should be for or in connection with demand of dowry. (f) it should be established that such cruelty and harassment was made soon before her death. (g) the expression (soon before) is a relative term and it would depend upon circumstances of each case and no straightjacket formula can be laid down as to what would constitute a period of soon before the occurrence. (h) it would be hazardous to indicate any fixed period and that brings in importance of a proximity test both for the proof of an offence of dowry death as well as for raising a presumption under section 113B of the Evidence Act. (i) the expression "soon before" would normally imply that the interval should not be much between the concerned cruelty or harassment and the death in question. There must be existence of a proximate or live link between the effect of cruelty based on dowry demand and the concerned death. In other words , it should not be remote in point of time and thereby make it a stale one. (j) however , the expression "soon before" should not be given a narrow meaning which would otherwise defeat the very purpose of the provisions of the Act and should not lead to absurd results. (k) section 304B is an exception to the cardinal principles of criminal jurisprudence that a suspect in the Indian Law is entitled to the protection of Article 20 of the Constitution, as well as, a presumption of innocence in his favour. The concept of deeming fiction is hardly applicable to criminal jurisprudence but in contradiction to this aspect of criminal law, the legislature applied the concept of deeming fiction to the provisions of section 304B. (l) such deeming fiction resulting in a presumption is, however, a rebuttable presumption and the husband and his relatives, can, by leading their defence prove that the ingredients of section 304B were not satisfied. (m) the specific significance to be attached is to the time of the alleged cruelty and harassment to which the victim was subjected to, the time of her death and whether the alleged demand of dowry was in connection with the marriage. Once the said ingredients were satisfied it will be called dowry death and by deemed fiction of law the husband or the relatives will be deemed to have committed that offence; *Kashmir Kaur* v. *State of Punjab,* 2013 All MR (Cri) 1090 (SC).

In this case, the Apex Court held that drawing of presumption as to abetment is not mandatory in each and every case. Presumption has to be drawn having regard to "all other circumstances" of the case. Cause and effect relationship between cruelty and suicide has to be established before drawing presumption; *Ramesh Kumar* v. *State of Chhattisgarh,* AIR 2001 SC 3837.

In this case, the Apex Court held that even if a single ingredient of section 304B, IPC is not made out, presumption under section 113B of the Evidence Act will not be available to prosecution and the burden would not shift on defence. Mere fact that deceased happened to be a young woman would not lead to inference that she had died an unnatural death. Where demand of money was made prior to one year of the incident, it fails the proximity test.; *Gurdeep Singh* v. *State of Punjab,* 2012 All MR (Cri) 693 (SC).

Though death of deceased was unnatural and it took place within 7 years of marriage, the Apex Court refused to draw presumption under section 113B of the Evidence Act as the demand for dowry soon before death was not proved; *Shindo @ Sawinder Kaur* v. *State of Punjab,* 2011 All SCR 1008.

In this case, the Apex Court held that mere evidence of cruelty and harassment is not sufficient to bring in application of section 304B but it needs to be established that soon before death, deceased was subjected to cruelty or harassment by her husband or in connection with demand for dowry; *Narayanamurthy* v. *State of Karnataka,* (2008) 16 SCC 512: AIR 2008 SC 2377: 2008 AIR SCW 3931.

In this case, the appellant-accused and her son were charged with offences under section 302 read with section 34, IPC or alternatively under section 306 read with section 34, IPC for causing the death of, or abetment to cause suicide by the daughter-in-law/wife of the accused. According to the prosecution, it was a case of dowry death. The dead body was found in a completely burnt condition in the matrimonial house of the deceased. The trial Court convicted both the accused under section 302 read with section 34, IPC and sentenced them to undergo rigorous imprisonment for life. On appeal, the High Court acquitted both the mother and son for the offences under section 302 read with section 34, IPC but convicted the mother under section 201, IPC and sentenced her to undergo rigorous imprisonment for 5 years. The State preferred and appeal against the acquittal whereas the convicted accused preferred an appeal against her conviction and sentence. On behalf of the appellant/accused it was contended that the deceased either committed suicide or died due to fire accident; that the husband of the deceased was not present at the time of occurrence; and that the mother-in-law was entitled to acquittal under section 201 of IPC. Allowing the appeal of the State and dismissing the appeal filed by the accused, the Apex Court held that the conduct of the appellant-accused as evidenced by Ex. P-1 to P-4 the pre-marital demand for dowry and non-compliance thereof is a relevant fact to establish motive as rightly found by the Court below. The fact that daughter-in-law met with homicidal death within three months from the date of marriage is also a relevant fact to conclude that the death was due to the failure to comply with the demand for dowry. At the earliest the appellant-accused came forward with the plea that the deceased committed suicide at 8.00 or 8.30 a.m. after taking meal, which is found to be false, is also a relevant fact in completing the chain of circumstances. The fact that more than one participated in the commission of the crime and the fact that there is no other person inimical to the deceased to commit the crime and the fact that it is not impossible for the accused-husband to immediately leave after committing the crime, would clearly connect him to be a *participis criminis* in committing homicide of his wife. Without his cooperation and participation in committing the crime, on the facts and circumstances, it is impossible for his mother alone to commit the crime. Except denial he offered no explanation in his statement under section 313, Cr.P.C. The false theory of suicide is also a circumstance to be taken into account. The remorseless conduct of the appellant is a relevant fact. Also the conduct of the accused-husband is inculpatory. The normal human conduct would be that on hearing the news of the death of his wife he was expected to immediately reach home; to make enquiry for the cause of death, and to take further actions, which are absent in this case. The Court further observed that as per the evidence of DW-4, the deceased was happy in the marital home. It would, therefore, conclusively exclude the theory of suicide. Thus, she must have been done to death by none other than the inmates of the matrimonial home; *Sarojini* v. *State of Madhya Pradesh,* (1992) Supp 2 SCR 25: (1993) Supp 4 SCC 632.

In this case, the Apex Court held that in dowry deaths prosecution must prove that the death of married woman was within seven years of marriage and a little prior to death, her husband or relative on the point of demand of dowry subjected her to cruelty or harass her. The prosecution has to rule out the possibility of a natural or accidental death so as to bring it within the purview of *"death occurring otherwise than in normal circumstances"*. Initial burden of proof lies on prosecution. This burden will not shift on accused merely on the basis of prosecution's allegation that the death had occurred within seven year of marriage. Recovery of belongings of the deceased like earrings, bangles, hair clip etc. from the well upon the discloser statement is not material as no family member of the deceased identified or claimed that the same belonged to the deceased and/or she was wearing the same at the time of occurrence. Such articles are of common use and can be found in any house; *State of Rajasthan* v. *Teg Bahadur,* 2005 All MR (Cri) 2045.

In this case, wife of appellant committed suicide by hanging herself in the house. An F.I.R. was lodged with the police by the father of the deceased alleging murder of his daughter by the appellant and his family members. The prosecution established that the deceased committed suicide due to ill-treatment, harassment and cruelty by the appellant and his family members for a bringing insufficient dowry. The appellant was convicted under sections 304B and 498A, I.P.C. for the offence of dowry death and cruelty. Trial Court convinced the appellant for cruelty under section 498A of I.P.C. and sentenced him to three years rigorous imprisonment which was upheld by High Court. Allowing the appeal by giving him the benefit of doubt, the Apex Court held that the concept of cruelty and its effect varies from individual to individual and also depending upon the social and economic status to which such persons belongs. Cruelty for the purposes of constituting the offence under section 498A. I.P.C. need not be physical. Even mental torture or abnormal behaviour may amount to cruelty and harassment in a given case. The statement of the deceased made to her family members which had been taken on record with the aid of section 32 of the Evidence Act for the offence under section 304B, I.P.C. is not admissible in evidence for the offence punishable under section 498A, I.P.C. It has to be termed as being only a hearsay evidence. If a statement which otherwise is covered by the hearsay rule does not fall within the exceptions of section 32 of the Evidence Act, the same cannot be relied upon for finding the guilt of the deceased. .... There is no evidence on record to hold that the deceased had conceived the apprehension of the appellant having illicit relations with his sister-in-law which led the deceased to end her life; *Gananath Pattanaik* v. *State of Orissa,* (2002) 1 SCR 845.

In this case, the appellant Reema was admitted on having consumed poisonous substance. Appellant stated before the investigation officer that she was married to Anupam the respondent No. 1 on 25th January, 1998 and after the marriage, she was harassed by her husband-respondent No. 1, mother-in-law, father-in-law and brother-in-law (respondent Nos. 2, 3 and 4) respectively for not bringing sufficient and more dowry. It was also disclosed that it was the second marriage of both the appellant and respondent No. 1. On the date of incident, all the four accused persons forced her to take something to put an end to her life and forcibly put some acidic substance in her mouth. After completion of the investigation chargesheet was filed and charges were frame under sections 307 and 498A of I.P.C. The Trial Court acquitted the accused persons. The Punjab and Haryana High Court declined leave to appeal to the State. In appeal, the Apex Court held that dowry may not be legally recognizable but in view of purpose of sections 498A, 304B, I.P.C. and section 113B of the Evidence Act, *ostensible husband* would also be liable for dowry death...... The absence of a definition of 'husband' to specifically include such persons who contract marriages ostensibly and co-habitate with such woman, in the purported exercise of his role and status as 'husband' is no ground to exclude them from the purview of section 304B or 498A, I.P.C. viewed in the context of the very object and aim of the legislations introducing those provisions; *Reema Aggarwal* v. *Anupam*, 2004 All MR (Cri) 1124.

Other Cases on Dowry Death and Presumptions

Kans Raj v. *State of Punjab*, 2000 Cr LJ 2993: 2000 AIR SCW 2093: 2000 (5) SCC 207: AIR 2000 SC 2324: The Apex Court held that no presumption under section 113B of the Evidence Act would be drawn against the accused if it is shown that after the alleged demand, cruelty or harassment, the dispute stood resolved and there was no evidence of cruelty and harassment thereafter.

Harjit Singh v. *State of Punjab*, 2006 All MR (Cri) 250: The Apex Court acquitted the appellant on the ground that prosecution failed to prove that deceased was subjected to cruelty with the meaning of section 498A, I.P.C.

Suvarnasingh T. Dhanjal v. *State of Maharashtra*, 2006 All MR (Cri) 58: The Bombay High Court refused to draw presumption against the accused under section 113A or 113B of the Evidence Act as the cruelty and harassment was not in connection with the demand of dowry.

P. Mani v. *State of Tamil Nadu*, AIR 2006 SC 1319: The Apex Court held that presumption of abetment under section 113A of the Evidence Act in offence against married woman is not available when charge is under section 302 of I.P.C.

Akula Ravinder v. *State of Andhra Pradesh*, AIR 1991 SC 1142: The Apex Court while acquitting the accused held that, *"Though the prosecution proved that the death occurred within seven years of the marriage and that before her death they have harassed her for demand of dowry, the prosecution failed to establish that death was otherwise than in normal condition."*

Keshab Chandra Panda v. *State of Orissa*, 1995 Cri LJ 174: The Orissa High Court has held that, *"The expression 'soon before her death' in both sections 304B, I.P.C. and 113B Evidence Act is incorporated with the idea of 'proximity test' which would normally imply that the interval should not be much between the concerned cruelty or harassment and the death in question. There must be existence of a proximate and live link between the effect of cruelty based on dowry demand and the concerned death........ If the alleged incident of cruelty is remote in time and has become stale enough, not to disturb mental equilibrium of the woman concerned, it would be of no consequence."*

Hem Chand v. *State of Haryana*, (1994) Supp 4 SCR 295: The Apex Court held that *"for drawing presumption under section 113B of the Evidence Act, the prosecution is required to show and prove that soon before her unnatural death, which took place within 7 years of marriage, the deceased had been subjected, by such person, to cruelty or harassment for or in connection with demand of dowry."*

Kamesh alias *Kamlesh Panjiyar* v. *State of Bihar*, (2005) 1 Crimes 277 SC: The Apex Court held that *"presumption under section 113B of the Evidence Act is a presumption of law and on proof of essentials, it becomes obligatory on Court to raise a presumption that accused caused death. .... However, prosecution has to rule out possibility of a natural, or accidental death so as to bring it within purview of death occurring otherwise than in normal circumstances."*

John V. Khandagale v. *State of Maharashtra*, 2011 All MR (Cri) 1142 (Bom): Merely because a woman dies unnatural death within 7 years of marriage, it cannot be said to be a dowry death unless the death can be related to demand of dowry.

Shamnsaheb M. Multani v. *State of Karnataka*, AIR 2001 SC 921: (2001) 2 SCC 577: If any accused wants to escape from the said presumption, the burden is on him to disprove it. If he fails to rebut the presumption, the Court is bound to act on it.

Rape

To convict a person for the offence of rape, the prosecution must prove that sexual intercourse with a woman falls under any of the circumstances mentioned in section 375 of I.P.C. The Apex Court in its various judgements has held that no corroboration is required to the testimony of the prosecutrix in convicting accused person and accused persons can be convicted on the sole testimony of the prosecutrix if it is trustworthy and inspires confidence in the mind of the Court.

The Bombay High Court has stated the law regarding credibility of the testimony of the prosecutrix in *Sitaram* v. *State of Maharashtra*, 1974 Cri LJ 82 as:

(a) Circumstances showing on the part of prosecutrix an animus against the accused;

(b) Circumstances tending to show consent *e.g.*, absence of material showing an attempt at resistance and absence of any marks of struggle;

(c) Attempts at improvement or exaggeration in the version as attempted by the prosecution;

(d) Elements of artificiality or unnaturalness in the story as attempted by the prosecutrix;

(e) Conduct of the part of the prosecutrix, inconsistency with the credibility of the version, *e.g.*, omission to make a disclosure at the earliest opportunity; and

(f) Absence of signs of rape in the findings of the medical examination or of chemical analysis.

In *State of Rajasthan* v. *N.K.-The Accused*, (2000) 2 SCR 818, the accused/respondent was charged under section 376, I.P.C. for the offence of committing rape on a minor girl. The trial Court convicted the accused for the offence under section 376 of I.P.C. but the High Court acquitted him holding that the prosecutrix was not proved beyond reasonable doubt to be below sixteen years of age and that absence of injuries on the person of the prosecutrix infers the possibility of the prosecutrix being the consenting party to the act. The State preferred appeal to the Supreme Court. Allowing the appeal of the State, the Apex Court held that, "*A prosecutrix complaining of having been a victim of the offence of rape is not an accomplice after the crime. There is no rule of law that her testimony cannot be acted without corroboration in material particulars. Her testimony has to be appreciated on the principle of probabilities just as the testimony of any other witness; a high degree of probability having been shown to exist in view of the subject matter being a criminal charge. However, if the Court of facts may find it difficult to accept the version of the prosecutrix on its face value it may search for evidence direct or circumstantial which would lend assurance to her testimony. Assurance, short of corroboration as understood in the context of an accomplice would do. ..... Absence of injuries on the person of the prosecutrix is not necessarily an evidence of falsity of the allegation or an evidence of consent on the part of the prosecutrix. It will all depend on the facts and circumstances of each case. ...... The injuries suffered by the prosecutrix were abrasions or bruises which would heal up in ordinary course of nature within two to three days of the incident. The absence of visible marks of injuries on the person of the prosecutrix on the date of her medical examination would not necessarily mean that she had not suffered any injuries or that she had offered no resistance at the time of the commission of the crime...... Consent is immaterial in certain circumstances covered by clauses thirdly to sixthly, the last one being when the woman is under 16 years of age. Certainly consent is no defence if the victim has been proved to be under sixteen years of age. .... If she be of sixteen years of age or above, her consent cannot be presumed. An inference as to consent can be drawn only if it is based on evidence or probabilities of the case."*

In this case, the Apex Court held that an act of helplessness in the face of inevitable compulsions is not consent in law. Actual use of force is not always necessary. A threat of use of force is sufficient to negative the alleged consent. If prosecution establishes that there was no consent on the part of prosecutrix, issue of majority became irrelevant; *Satpal Singh* v. *State of Haryana,* (2010) 8 SCC 714.

In this case, semen stains were found on vaginal swab and salwar and it was contended by prosecution that it is the evidence of rape. However the Apex Court held that merely because vaginal swab and salwar had semen stains thereon, would at the best, be evidence of sexual intercourse but not of rape. It is true that in a case of rape the evidence of prosecutrix must be given predominant consideration, but to hold that this evidence has to be accepted even if the story is improbable and belies logic, would be doing violence to the very principles which govern the appreciation of evidence in a criminal matter; *Tameezuddin @ Tammu* v. *State of NCT of Delhi,* 2010 (1) CRJ 110 (SC).

In this case, the Apex Court held that an argument that a prosecutrix must be believed irrespective of improbabilities in her case, can never be accepted. Test always is as to whether given story prima facie inspire confidence; *Dinesh Jaiswal* v. *State of Madhya Pradesh,* 2010 All SCR 790.

In this case [*Uday* v. *State of Karnataka,* AIR 2003 SC 1639: 2003 SCC (Cri) 775] in this case it was alleged that accused expressed love and promised to marry prosecutrix and committed sexual intercourse with her due to which she became pregnant. However prosecutrix were aware of the fact that they belonged to different castes and proposal of their marriage will be opposed by their family members. Yet prosecutrix started cohabiting with accused consciously. Defence of the prosecutrix was that she gave consent to sexual intercourse under misconception of fact. In such facts and circumstances of the case, the Apex Court while acquitting the accused held that, *"consent given by prosecutrix to sexual intercourse cannot be said to be given under misconception of fact i.e., promise to marry, but because she also desired for it. .... False promise is not a fact."* Same view has been taken in *Krishna Pada Mahato* v. *State of West Bengal*, 2005 (3) Crimes 644 (Cal).

In this case, victim, an Australian national, major in age alleged rape and wrongful confinement by the accused. There were two versions of incident, one given by the victim and other given by the accused. The defence of the accused is that victim consented to sexual intercourse with him. It had come on record that victim had five boy friends since the age of 15 years and was habituated to sex. The Court acquitted the accused on the ground that conduct of victim in remaining silent is unnatural and that victim implicated him to claim insurance; *Obi Okoroafor* v. *State of Goa*, 2015 All MR (Cri) 662.

In this case, prosecution alleged that while prosecutrix, a 13 year old girl, was sleeping in between her mother and brother, accused took her to adjoining room on point of knife and committed rape on her. During trial witness stated that both of them remained there for couple of hours and only when mother and sister of prosecutrix opened the door, they were found hiding behind bags. The Apex Court acquitted the accused on the ground that prosecution failed to prove the age of the prosecutrix and the narration of events leads to inference that prosecutrix was a consenting party; *State of Madhya Pradesh* v. *Munna @ Shambhoo Nath*, 2015 All SCR 3184.

In this case, it was alleged that teacher committed rape on a student. After the commencement of trial, matter for adjourned for several times and accused tried to prolong the matter. The trial Court adjourned proceedings for a long period giving defence an opportunity to win prosecutrix and her mother. No attempt was made by any accused persons to rebut the presumption arising under section 114A of the Evidence Act. While upholding the conviction of the accused, the Apex Court held that provision of section 114A of the Evidence Act is attracted; *Mohan Lal* v. *State of Punjab*, 2013 All MR (Cri) 1860 SC.

In this case, prosecutrix who is aged about 19 years of age had willingly gone with accused to get married. Physical relationship between parties had clearly developed with the consent of prosecutrix. There was no evidence to prove conclusively that appellant had never intended to marry prosecutrix. The Apex Court held that presumption under section 114A of the Evidence Act, that prosecutrix did not in fact, give such consent, is not attracted. The Court further held that mere failure to keep his promise to marry prosecutrix due to reasons not clear from evidence, does not amount to misconception of fact; *Deepak Gulati* v. *State of Haryana*, AIR 2013 SC 2071: 2013 All SCR 2170: 2013 SAR (Cri) 747 SC.

Other Cases on Rape, Abduction, Murder, etc.

State of Rajasthan v. *Kishanlal*, AIR 2002 SC 2250: The Apex Court acquitted the accused on the ground that the prosecutrix did not raise alarm and that version of the prosecutrix regarding threat given by the accused with knife was belied by non recovery of knife from accused.

Joseph v. *State of Kerela,* (2000) 3 SCR 729: The Apex Court acquitted the accused by giving benefit of doubt on the ground that no injuries were found on the body of the victim and that no blood stains or semen were found on the *dhoti* of the accused.

Jawharlal Das v. *State of Orissa,* (1991) 2 SCR 298: The Apex Court acquitted the accused on the ground that the prosecution failed to establish that the accused had an intercourse on the day of occurrence.

Tukaram v. *State of Maharashtra,* AIR 1979 SC 185: The Apex Court held that the fear which clause thirdly of section 375, I.P.C. speaks is negatived when the girl is taken by the accused right from amongst her near and dear ones.

Paramjit Singh v. *State of Himachal Pradesh,* 1987 Cri LJ 1266: Where according to Radiologist the age of the victim is 16 or 17 years, margin of error in test is 1½ to 2 years, the benefit of margin of error has to be given to the accused if the age of the victim has been found to be above 18 years.

Koli Jaga Rana v. *State of Gujarat,* 1992 Cri LJ 2080: The Division Bench of the Gujarat High Court has held that, *"The burden lies on the prosecution to prove each ingredient of the offence. ...... The accused is not required to explain as to why victim and other witnesses have falsely implicated him."*

Ravindra D. Patil v. *State of Maharashtra,* 1989 Cri LJ 394 (Bom): Where penetration was not proved, accused was acquitted of the charge under section 376 of I.P.C. even though hymen of the prosecutrix was found torn and blood stains were also found on her underwear.

Palli Venkateswarlu v. *State,* 2002 All MR (Cri) 842 (Panji Bench): In this case the accused was charged for committing the offence under sections 363, 376 of I.P.C. It was alleged that the accused committed forcible intercourse with her. However facts revealed that prosecutrix aged about 17 years was in love with accused and abandoned her parent's house and went with accused on her own. The Court acquitted the accused holding that no case is made out under sections 376, 363, I.P.C.

Bhagwan Charan Mate v. *State of Maharashtra,* 2006 (1) AIR Bom R 145: 2006 ALL MR (Cri) 1366: In this case it was alleged that the accused forcibly dragged and raped the prosecutrix. However, neither there were any injuries on private parts nor any marks of assault on the body of the prosecutrix. Further there was no evidence to suggest that the prosecutrix cried for held. In such circumstances the Bombay High Court set aside the conviction of the accused.

Ronal K. Ramakant v. *State of Haryana,* AIR 2001 SC 2488: In this case it was alleged that the accused committed rape and murder of the victim. However accused's version was that they were in love and some assailants assaulted victim and she died on spot. The facts revealed that victim was in totally naked condition and underclothes of victim and accused were found in same room. In such circumstances, the Apex Court held that it is an intercourse by a consent and set aside the conviction.

Anwar Khan v. *State of Maharashtra,* 2010 AllMR (Cri) 2124 (Bom): The Court held that where prosecutrix is of the age of maturity, it cannot be believed that she does not have the knowledge of the consequences of the sex. Where facts showed that the consent is not given by the prosecutrix because of criminal force, assertion of mistaken belief cannot be accepted.

Vijayan v. *State of Kerala,* (2008) 14 SCC 763: Where prosecutrix waited for seven months for filing FIR, the Court held that in absence of any other supporting evidence it would be unsafe to convict appellant wholly on the basis of testimony of the prosecutrix.

Vishwanathan v. *State of Tamil Nadu,* 2008 (4) CRJ 777 (SC): In cases of gang rape, identification parade and proof of potency are necessary.

(H) Abduction, Kidnapping etc. – (I.P.C. 363, 366)

Section 366 is an aggravated form of section 363. In order to bring home the charge against the accused the prosecution must established that: (a) The accused induced the complainant to go from any place; (b) Such inducement was by deceitful means; (c) Such abduction took place with intent that the complainant may be seduced to illicit intercourse; (d) The accused knew it to be likely that the complainant may be seduced to illicit intercourse as a result of her abduction.

In this case, the Apex Court held that mere abduction and finding that a woman was abducted is not enough. Prosecution must prove that abduction is for the purposes mentioned in section 366 of the IPC; *Gabbu* v. *State of Madhya Pradesh,* 2006 (2) B Cr C 668 (SC).

In trials for the offence of abduction or kidnapping, question often arises whether the act of the accused falls within the purview of *"taking out of lawful guardianship"* or not. This has been explained by the Apex Court in *S. Varadarajan* v. *State of Madras,* (1965) 1 SCR 243. The Apex Court held that *"Where a minor girl, alleged to be taken away by the accused person, had left her father's protection knowing and having capacity to know the full import of what she was doing and voluntarily joined the accused, it could not be said that the accused had taken her away from the keeping of her lawful guardian within the meaning of section 361 of I.P.C. ...... Something more had to be done in a case of that kind, such as an inducement held out by the accused person or an active participation by him in the formation of the intention, either immediately prior to the minor leaving her father's protection or at some earlier stage. If the evidence failed to establish one of these things, the accused would not be guilty of the offence merely because after she had actually left her guardian's house or a house where her guardian had kept her she joined the accused, and the accused and the accused helped her in her design not to return to her guardian's house by taking her along with him from place to place. No doubt, the part played by the accused could be regarded as facilitating the fulfilment of the intention of the girl. That part, in our opinion, falls short of an inducement to the minor to slip out of the keeping of her lawful guardian and is, therefore, not tantamount to 'taking'."*

In this case [*Jinish Lal Shah* v. *State of Bihar,* AIR 2003 SC 2081] the accused was charged for kidnapping and raping a girl. However sequence of events showed that prosecutrix accompanied accused willingly. Even the father of prosecutrix stated in F.I.R. that she went away by taking clothes and gold chain and some cash. The Apex Court acquitted the accused holding that circumstances show that there was no threat or inducement to her.

In a case of abduction and murder when it is proved that accused abducted deceased the deceased alone knew what happened to him until he was with him. If he was found murdered within a short time after the abduction, the permitted reasoning process would enable the Court to draw the presumption that the accused have murdered him. Such inference can be disrupted if the accused would tell the Court what else happened to deceased at least until he was in their custody; *State of West Bengal* v. *Mir Mohammad Omar,* (2000) 8 SCC 382.

It was a case of abduction and murder. During trial prosecution examined eye witness to prove the death of deceased and took burden of proving as to how death was caused on its own shoulders. But prosecution miserably failed to prove the same. While setting aside the conviction for murder and maintaining the conviction for abduction, the Apex Court held that merely because deceased was abducted and accused failed to offer explanation as to what transpired after abduction, Court would not be justified in drawing inference of murder at the hands of abductor especially when prosecution did not allege that what happened after abduction is within the knowledge of abductor only; *Murlidhar* v. *State of Rajasthan,* 2005 (2) B Cr C 174 (SC).

Where victim did not offer any resistance or raised any protest while she was being taken away, the Court held that it could not be presumed that she was being taken by the accused against her will and for the purpose of seducing her to illicit intercourse against her will; *Rattan Suka Lilke* v. *State of Maharashtra,* 2012 All MR (Cri) 923 (Bom).

Other Cases on Abduction and Kidnapping

Chhote Lal v. *State of Haryana,* AIR 1979 SC 1494: 1979 Cri LJ 1126: The Apex Court held that mere finding that accused abducted the woman, the charge under section 366 cannot be held to have been proved. It is further necessary to find out that they abducted the woman for any of the purposes mentioned in section 366 of I.P.C.

Shyam v. *State of Maharashtra,* AIR 1995 SC 2169: 1995 Cri LJ 3974: 1995 SCC (Cri) 851: Where the prosecutrix a fully grown up woman moved on the carrier of the bicycle of the accused, did not jump down from the bicycle, nor raised any alarm, there was no question of taking her out of the lawful guardianship of her mother, she was a willing party. The Apex Court acquitted the accused of the charge of abduction under section 366 of I.P.C.

State of Karnataka v. *Sureshbabu Puk Raj Porral,* 1994 Cri LJ 1216 (SC): Where the age of the victim was doubtful, and the victim herself deposed that she went with the accused voluntarily, the offence of taking the victim from the lawful guardianship did not arise. The Apex Court acquitted the accused.

State of West Bengal v. *Mir Mohd. Omer,* AIR 2000 SC 2988: The Apex Court held that, *"Unless abductors explain otherwise to court as to what else they did with victim, Court can draw presumption under section 106 of the Evidence Act that all abductors are responsible for murder."*

State of Maharashtra v. *Surendrakumar M. Mahesh,* 1998 All MR (Cri) 1142: 1998 (2) B Cr C 381: Where there was love affair of a girl below 18 years and where she voluntarily went away with the accused and joined his company, the Court held that accused is entitled to acquittal.

Naresh Sonkusare v. *State of Maharashtra,* 2006 All MR (Cri) 2099: In this case, victim admitted love affair with the accused and that she eloped with him. Medical evidence showed the age of victim as 17, plus minus one year. There were various contradictions in victim's police statement. There was difference in duration of alleged kidnapping. In such facts and circumstances, the High Court set aside the conviction.

(I) The Protection of Children from Sexual Offences Act, 2012

This Act has been enacted to protect children from offences of sexual assault, sexual harassment and pornography and provides for establishment of Special Courts for trial of such offences.

A Special Court may take cognizance of any offence, without the accused being committed to it for trial, upon receiving a complaint of facts which constitute such offence, or upon a police report of such facts. It also provides that questions to be put to a child while recording the examination-in-chief, cross-examination or re-examination of the child has to communicated to the special Court which shall in turn put the same to the child. (Section 33)

The evidence of the child has to be recorded within a period of 30 days of the special Court taking cognizance of the offence and trial has to be completed within a period one year from the date of taking cognizance of the offence. (Section 35)

The Special Court shall ensure that the child is not exposed in any way to the accused at the time of recording of the evidence and Court may record the statement of the child through video-conferencing or by utilising single visibility mirror or curtains or any other devise. (Section 36)

The Special Court has to try cases *in camera* and in the presence of the parents of the child or any other person in whom the child has trust or confidence. (Section 37)

In this case, it was stated by the prosecution that accused called prosecutrix girl aged about 8 years in his room, closed the door from inside and he molested her. The accused was convicted by the Special Court for the offence punishable under section 10 of the POCSO Act and under section 506 of the I.P.C. The Hon'ble High Court set aside the conviction and sentence imposed on the appellant on the ground that evidence of victim's mother is hearsay in nature, there is no medical evidence as to the examination of either victim or accused and there is no other corroborative evidence; *John & Vivek R. Jadhav* v. *State of Maharashtra,* 2015 All MR (Cri) 4053.

In this case, DNA report proved that appellant is father of child born to prosecutrix. However, prosecution neither proved birth date of victim nor proved that she was a child. Even report was not lodged promptly. In view of the facts and circumstances of the case and evidence on record, the Bombay High Court acquitted the accused; *Ravi Anandrao Gurpude* v. *State of Maharashtra,* 2017 All MR (Cri) 1509.

(J) Robbery and Dacoity – (Sections 390 to 399 I.P.C.)

(a) Robbery

Robbery is a aggravated form of theft or extortion. *Before theft can amount to robbery, *firstly,* the offender must have voluntarily caused or attempted to cause to any person death or hurt or wrongful restraint or fear of instant death or of instant hurt or of instant wrongful restraint, *secondly* this must be in order to the committing of theft, or in committing the theft, or in carrying away or attempting to carry away property obtained by the theft, *thirdly* the offender must voluntarily cause or attempt to cause to any person hurt etc., for the end, that is in order to committing theft or for carrying away or attempting to carry away property obtained by the theft. It is not sufficient that in the transaction of committing theft, hurt etc. had been caused. If hurt etc., is caused at the time of commission of theft, but for an object other than the one referred in section 390, theft would not amount to robbery. [**State of Maharashtra* v. *Vinayak Tukaram Utekar,* 1997 Cri LJ 3988 (Bom) (DB)].

In this case, the Apex Court held that robbery is only an aggravated form of offence of theft or extortion. Aggravation is in the use of violence to cause death, hurt or restraint. Violence must be in the course of theft and not subsequently. It is not necessary that violence actually should be committed. Even an attempt to commit it is enough; *Venu @ Venugopal* v. *State of Karnataka,* AIR 2008 SC 1199.

In *Harish Chandra* v. *State of Andhra Pradesh,* AIR 1976 SC 1458: 1976 Cri LJ 1168, the Apex Court held that, *"Theft is robbery under section 390, I.P.C. if, in order to the committing to the theft, or in committing the theft, or in carrying away or attempting to carry away property obtained by the theft, the offender for that end voluntarily causes or attempts to cause to any person death or hurt, or wrongful restraint or fear of instant death or of instant hurt or of instant wrongful restraint."*

(b) Dacoity

It has been held by the Division Bench of the Allahabad High Court in *Sirajuddin* v. *State of Uttar Pradesh,* AIR 1951 All 834: 1952 Cri LJ 1514, that, *"Dacoity is committed where a robbery is committed by five or more persons and also where five or more persons had attempted to commit a robbery. The offence of dacoity is committed even if the dacoits have failed to remove the booty."*

However it has been held by the Apex Court in *Sakhi* v. *State of Uttar Pradesh,* AIR 1973 SC 760: 1973 Cri LJ 599, that, *"Actual participation by every one of the five or more persons in commission of the robbery whether as major actors or aiders is necessary."*

It has been observed that Courts generally draw presumption under section 114(a) of the Evidence Act if articles are recovered from the accused person. But it has been held by the Apex Court in *Man Singh* v. *State of Madhya Pradesh,* 1993 Cri LJ 3669, that *"Merely because certain stolen articles were recovered from the accused, they cannot be held to be dacoits unless there is recent possession."*

This was a case [*Rampal Pithwas Rahidass* v. *State of Maharashtra,* (1994) 2 SCR 179] where it was alleged that nine assailants assaulted two watchmen on construction site near Chandrapur-Ballarshah Highway and then they waylay six other persons passing on the Highway and violently assaulted them and escaped from the spot after committing dacoity and consequently five victims of the assault died as a result of the injuries. Injured witness 'D' gave a statement which formed the basis for the F.I.R. No arrest was made for about four days leading to tension at the town Chandrapur and there were demonstrations in the town against the police inaction. One 'R' who later on turned an approver was arrested four days after the event in connection with an allegation regarding an innocuous incident involving touching of a bicycle under circumstances and for reasons not satisfactorily explained by the prosecution. It was alleged that during interrogation, 'R' disclosed his involvement in the sensational dacoity four days earlier and consequently to the information disclosed by 'R', all other accused and one more person 'M' were arrested. 'M', however, died in police custody within three days of his arrest. Thereafter, accused R made a voluntary statement under section 164 of the Cr.P.C. before the Judicial Magistrate giving details of the crime. This led to some recoveries and arrest of two more persons. On grant of pardon 'R' turned an approver. The Additional Sessions Judge, Chandrapur convicted all the eight accused under sections 302/149, I.P.C. as well as sections 307 and 395, I.P.C. and sentenced them to death. In appeal and confirmation proceeding in the High Court, three accused were acquitted and the conviction under section 302, I.P.C. and consequent death sentences were maintained in respect of five accused. All the five convicted accused and the State (against the acquittal of three accused persons) appealed to the Supreme Court. Allowing the appeals of the accused and dismissing that of the State, the Apex Court held that, *"The circumstances surrounding the initial arrest of the approver 'R' were curious and the prosecution concocted a false story about the arrest of 'R' who was planted as an accused in order to silence the large discontent against the police due to its inability to apprehend the culprits. The recovery of a bag at the instance of 'R' was also not free from doubt due to conflict in versions regarding its contents. The version in 'R's confessional statement under section 164 of Cr.P.C. dated 21st July, 1984 was departed from in his application dated 17th January, 1987 seeking bail where he disclaimed any knowledge about the incident and disclosed police pressure on him become an eye witness. 'R', the approver was throughout under pressure to become an approver due to the fact that the police was under constant attack from the media and the public and even his first confessional statement was not a voluntary one having come a couple of days after the death of another accused in police custody. The examination of 'R' as an approver at the fag end of the trial and not as the first prosecution witness enabled him to know the other evidence led in the case so that he could depose accordingly in support of the prosecution. .... Identification of all the appellants in the absence of any earlier test identification parade when the assailants were alleged to be wearing masks and were unknown to the victims or the injured witnesses, is of no significance. The conduct of the approver in going away without a penny and the co-accused permitting him to do so defies logic and common sense. .... The corroborating pieces of evidence of identification by the three injured witnesses in the absence of any earlier test identification parade or the recoveries made at different dates and different places at the instance of different accused in the presence of the same panch witness are not trustworthy or reliable. ....*

Investigating agencies must act fairly and honestly and not resort to fabricating false evidence or creating false clues only with a view to secure conviction because such acts shake the confidence of the common man not only in the investigation agency but also in the system of dispensation of criminal justice. Let no guilty man go unpunished but let the end not justify the means! Proper results must be obtained by proper means – otherwise it would be an invitation to anarchy."

In this case, accused was prosecuted for the offence punishable under sections 395, 396, 397 of the I.P.C. Stolen articles such as cash and vehicles were recovered from the possession of accused pursuant to his disclosure statement and this was the only evidence against him. Prosecution contended that presumption under section 114, *Illustration* (a) of the Evidence Act be raised against the accused. While setting aside the conviction, the Apex Court held that presumption as to his culpability is not to be raised. Availability of such presumption also depends on the nature of property recovered. If property recovered can change hands readily, presumption would not be available. In this case accused was not identified by witnesses to have participated in the crime ; recovery of stole articles on disclosure statement was not proximate in time to the date of incident and articles recovered were either cash or small things or vehicles which can change hands readily. Therefore the Apex Court refused to draw presumption under section 114, *Illustration* (a) of the Evidence Act against the accused; *State of Rajasthan* v. *Talevar,* AIR 2011 SC 2271.

Other Cases on Robbery and Dacoity

1. *Chandran* v. *State of Kerala,* AIR 1990 SC 2148: This was a case of robbery with murder based on circumstantial evidence. The Apex Court acquitted the accused on the ground that statement leading to the recovery of some articles was not made by the accused during first examination but was made at a subsequent stage of the examination.

2. *K. Venkateshwara Rao* v. *State,* (2002) 6 SCC 247: In this case accused was tried for the offence punishable under section 412 and 396 of I.P.C. It was alleged that certain documents alleged to be the property involved in the dacoity was seized from the accused consequent to a statement made by him to police. The Apex Court acquitted the accused holding that conviction under section 412, I.P.C. is not sustainable when charge of dacoity is not proved against him. The Apex Court further observed that recovery of documents from the accused having no direct bearing on the recovery itself is not admissible in evidence and cannot bind the accused.

3. *Shambhu Dayal* v. *Subhash Chandra,* AIR 1998 SC 1732: In this case accused was tried for the offence of dacoity with murder. The Investigation Officer did not record the statement of eye witnesses at the earliest opportunity and there was infirmity in evidence regarding identification of other dacoits. There was discovery of clothes and golden ring at the instance of alleged dacoit. The Apex Court while acquitting the accused held that, *"discovery of clothes and golden ring at the instance of alleged dacoit is doubtful as it was not probable that while committing dacoity they would have taken away clothes also and buried them in the courtyard."*

(K) Cases of Group Rivalaries and Communal Frenzy

In cases of riots the appreciation of evidence is a very difficult process. Therefore the Madras High Court in *Re: Arulanandu*, AIR 1952 Mad: 1952 Cri LJ 583, has given five fundamental principles for appreciation of evidence in such cases. These are: "*(a) The Court must see that all the ingredients required for unlawful assembly and rioting are strictly proved before convicting a particular accused. (b) Spectators, way farers, etc., should not be, by reason of their mere presence at the scene of rioting and with the rioters, held to be members of unlawful assembly or rioters. But if they are proved to have marched with the rioters for a long distance, it shall be for them to prove their innocence under section 106 of the Evidence Act. (c) An ordinary rule of caution and prudence will require that an accused identified only by one witness and not proved to have done any over Act etc., should be acquitted by giving him the benefit of doubt. (d) Where there are acute factions, one based on agrarian disputes and troubles, another on political wrangling and rivalry, and a third on caste division or the division of the haves and the have-nots, the greatest care must be exercised before believing the evidence of a particular witness belonging to one of these factions against an accused of the opposite views. This principle becomes of special importance when there are no overt Acts, etc., proved, and when there are only one or two witnesses speaking to the presence of the accused among the rioters, and they belong to the classes or factions opposed to the accused. (e) Mere followers in rioting deserve a much more lenient sentence than leaders who misled them into such violent acts, by emotional appeals, slogans and cries.*"

The facts of the case* were that: The agitation that started in February 1985 against Government policy of reservation in the state of Gujarat turned into communal riots of shocking magnitude between Hindus and Muslims in March 1985, and resulted in mass exodus of Dabgars, a Hindu community, from their houses in the affected locality. When calm was partially restored, some of them returned. Maniben, one of the deceased, however continued to live in her house with other members of her family. On 9th June, 1985, members of minority community converged from two sides and set the house of Maniben on fire and then chaining it from outside resulting in death of the lady, her two daughters, four grand children and son of a neighbour. Next house set ablaze was of Navin and then many others. Charge was framed against 63 persons under TADA Act and various offence including section 302 of I.P.C. 56 were acquitted by the Trial Judge. Those convicted filed appeal. At the same time a reference was made for confirmation of death sentence. The Apex Court allowed the appeals and acquitted the accused and reference was discharged. As regards the assessment of evidence in crime emanating from communal frenzy, the Apex Court in **Dilawar* v. *State of Gujarat*, (1990) Supp 2 SCR 108, has held that, "*Sentiments or emotions, however strong, are neither relevant nor have any place in a Court of law. Acquittal or conviction depends on proof or otherwise of the criminological chain which invariably comprises of why, where, when, how and who. Each knot of the claim has to be proved beyond shadow of doubt to bring home the guilt. Any crack or loosening in it weakens the prosecution. Heinousness of crime or cruelty in its execution however abhorring and hateful cannot reflect in deciding the guilt. .... To bring home the guilt the prosecution was required to prove the presence of witnesses, possibility of seeing* *the incident by them and identification of the appellant. But that is not the prosecution case. In fact prosecution is silent on this aspect. There is no whisper of the place from where the incident was seen by the witnesses. Was it front of house of Ambalal or inside or roof? This was very relevant as every witness admitted that from interior of Ambalal's house, the front of neither Maniben's nor Navin's house could be seen. Evidence thus regarding possibility of seeing the appellants from house of Ambalal is very shaky............. Identification of accused from out of the mob even if they were known from before becomes highly doubtful."*

This was a case [*Budhwa* alias *Ramcharan* v. *State of Madhya Pradesh*, (1990) Supp 2 101: AIR 1990 SC 4] where the appellants were convicted for offences under sections 147, 149 and 302, I.P.C. for murdering a villager. The prosecution case was that motivated by group rivalry the accused persons numbering over 15 attacked the deceased with *tabbals* and *lathis* while he accompanied by his mother and sister. As a result of injuries sustained the deceased died on the spot. When sister of deceased tried to intervene, she too was assaulted. She lodged the F.I.R. the same day against the appellants and others. The Trial Court and the High Court convicted the appellants. In appeal Supreme Court set aside the conviction and sentence of some of the appellants and dismissed the appeals of some of the appellants. The Apex Court held that, *"It is an accepted proposition that in the case of group rivalries and enmities, there is a general tendency to involve as many persons of the opposite factions as possible by merely naming them as having participated in the assault. The Court, therefore, has in all such cases to sift the evidence with utmost care and caution and convict only those persons against whom the prosecution witnesses can be safely relied upon without raising any element of doubt. .... In a melee, as in the instant case, where several people are giving blows at one and the same time it will be impossible to particularize the blows. If any witness attempts to do it, his veracity is doubtful. But, it is simpler to make an omnibus statement that all the accused assaulted with their weapons because that obviates close cross examination. Therefore the nature of injury sustained by the victim assumed importance. .... When the several blows with* lathis *and* tabbals *could produced only seven injuries on the person of the deceased the necessary inference would be that not more than seven persons might have participated in delivering the blows. Therefore, the presence of more than seven persons is doubtful. .... The manner in which the incident happened also makes it clear that the assailants acted in prosecution of the common object to cause the death of the victim."*

This was a case of group rivalry [*Bharwad J. Nagjibhai* v. *State of Gujarat*, (1995) Supp 3 SCR 23] where 40-50 member of Bharwad community armed with sticks, *dhavias* and *farsis* attacked three members of the Patel community killing one and injuring two. Case was registered against 15 persons. The Trial Court acquitted all the 15 persons. However High Court admitted appeals of the state against only seven accused persons and discharged the rest. High Court convicted all the seven persons under sections 148 and 326, I.P.C. read with section 149, I.P.C. and some under sections 324 and 326, I.P.C. simpliciter and rest under sections 149, I.P.C. In appeal while dismissing both the appeals of the appellants, held that, *"The nature, number and location of injuries are some of the indicia to ascertain the common object and for that matter the offence committed. Considering the nature of the injuries inflicted on the three persons, this Court agrees with the reasoning of the High Court that it could not be conclusively inferred that the common object of the assembly was to commit the murder. If really a mob of 50-60 persons wanted to commit murder, nothing prevented them from inflicting severe injuries on the persons of the two victims, more so, when some of them were armed with sharp cutting and dangerous weapon. The fact that accused / appellant 1 - 7 used blunt edges on the weapons and not their sharp edges goes a long way to show that they did not share a common intention to kill when they assaulted him. .... Section 149 of I.P.C. applies to offences not only actually committed in pursuance of common object , but also offences that members of the unlawful assembly knew was likely to be committed."*

In this case, accused persons were prosecuted for the offence punishable under sections 304, 323, 147 of the I.P.C. Defence of the accused-respondents is a cross version of the incident in which family members of both the sides gathered at the spot and started hurling brickbats on each other and consequently both sides suffered injuries. While confirming the acquittal, the Apex Court held that no authenticity can be attached to the version given by the informant in FIR as the presence of informant witness at the spot at the time of incident is doubtful. The Court further held that defence version that complainant were in fact aggressors cannot be discarded only on the basis of lesser number of injuries having been suffered by them; *State of Uttar Pradesh* v. *Munni Ram,* 2011 All MR (Cri) 1323(SC).

In such cases question of common object (section 149, I.P.C.) or common intention (section 34, I.P.C.) often arises. This has been explained by the Apex Court in *Jaswant Singh* v. *State of Haryana,* (2000) 2 SCR 903. The Apex Court held that, *"With regard to section 34, I.P.C., promotion and facilitation of crime is required in addition to common intention whereas regarding section 149, I.P.C., mere presence in the unlawful assembly is sufficient. .... The similarity of section 34 and section 149, I.P.C. lies in the requirement of a common object or intention or a pre-arranged plan in furtherance of which the act is done. The difference lies in the degree of actual participation required in the criminal enterprise. The emphasis is on physical presence and promotion of crime."*

Other Cases on Group Rivalaries and Communal Frenzy

1. *Bhima* v. *State of Maharashtra,* AIR 2002 SC 3086: This was a case of assault by mob where large number of persons armed with sticks attacked the victims and also pelted stones. While acquitting the accused of the charge under section 302 read with section 149, the Apex Court held that, *"It was not established as to who specifically attacked whom. It was not clear whether intention was to cause the death of deceased. .... It is more possible that intention was to give hard beating to the deceased who was said to be bully in village. In circumstances it can be inferred that common object was commit offences under sections 323, 325 read with sections 147/149 and not under section 302 read with section 149."*

2. *Kashi Ram* v. *State of Madhya Pradesh,* AIR 2001 SC 2902: The Apex Court held that, *"Accused acting in exercise of right of private defence cannot be said to form unlawful assembly. Therefore they cannot be convicted under section 148 or with the aid of 149 of I.P.C."*

3. *Hari Ram* v. *State of Haryana*, 1993 Cri LJ 3540 (SC): The Apex Court held that, *"For determination of aggressor in a bilateral clash, number of injuries found on side of complainant or accused cannot be a basis to determine aggressor. ....* Onus *is on prosecution to prove its case."*

4. *Babu* v. *State of Maharahstra*, 1995 (1) Mh LJ 843 (Bom): The Bombay Court has held that, *"Mere presence at the place of incident would not make a person member of unlawful assembly. .... In riot cases, conviction on the basis of testimony of single eye witness is not proper. Court should insist on plurality of eye witnesses."*

5. *Sone Lal* v. *State of Uttar Pradesh*, (1981) 3 SCR 352: This was a case of clash between two parties having enmity with each other. The appellants claimed right of private defence. The Apex Court held that, *"The appellants who were aggressors even if they received injuries from the victims cannot have any right of private defence."*

6. *Bhudeo Mandal* v. *State of Bihar*, (1981) 3 SCR 291: The incident in question took place as a result of irrigation dispute and the appellants were merely acting under a *bona fide* claim or belief that they had the right to irrigate the land. Further there was no overt act attributed to any of the appellants in regard to the deceased. The Apex Court held that, *"Mere fact that the appellants were armed with* lathis *by itself would not prove that they shared the common object with which the deceased was inspired."*

Sedition and Waging War against State

Every ruling party in the Centre or in the State has misused the provision of section 124A of the I.P.C. to silence the opponents who criticise the policies and programmes of the Government. The persons who were booked under the said provision include Arundhati Roy, Dr. Binayak Sen, Arun Jaitley, Aseem Trivedi (Cartoonist), Kanhaiya Kumar (JNU Student Leader), etc. Even Amnesty International India based in Bengaluru was booked under the provisions of sedition for alleged "anti-India slogans" at one of their events. The case of Punjab's IPS Officer – turned – pro Khalistan politician Simranjit Singh Mann is more interesting. He was booked under the sedition charges in more than 50 cases but has never been convicted in any case.

In this case, it was alleged that one Clarence Brandenburg, a leader in the Ku Klux Klan, gave a speech at a Klan ralley in the summer of 1964. Because of this speech – which included remarks accusing the United States Government of suppressing the "caucasian race". He was convicted of advocating violence under the Ohio Criminal Syndicalism Statute. This statue made it illegal to advocate crime, sabotage, violence, or unlawful methods of terrorism as a means of accomplishing industrial or political reform. The Supreme Court of the United States held that The Ohio law violated Brandenburg's right to free speech. The Court found that the Ohio Criminal Syndicalism Statute ignored whether or not the advocacy it criminalized actually led to imminent lawless action. The failure to make this distinction rendered the law overly broad and in violation of the Constitution. The Court further held that mere advocacy or teaching the duty, necessity, or propriety of violence as a means of accomplishing political or industrial reform, or publishing or circulating or displaying any book or paper containing such advocacy, or justifying the commission of violent acts with intent to exemplify, spread or advocate the propriety of the doctrines of criminal syndicalism, or to voluntarily assemble with a group formed to teach or advocate the doctrines of criminal syndicalism is not per se illegal. It will become illegal only if it incites to imminent law less action; *Clarence Brandenburg* v. *State of Ohio,* 395 U.S. 444 (1969).

The Supreme Court of India has relied on the above case in *Arup Bhuyan* v. *State of Assam,* AIR 2011 SC 957.

In a landmark judgment, the Constitution Bench has held that section 124A of the I.P.C. must be so construed as to limit its application to acts involving intention or tendency to create disorder, or disturbance of law and order; or incitement violence. The Court further held that a citizen has a right to say or write whatever he likes about the government, or its measures, by way of criticism or comment, so long as he does not incite people to violence against the government established by law or with the intention of creating public disorder; *Kedar Nath Singh* v. *State of Bihar,* AIR 1962 SC 955: (1962) Supp 2 SCR 769.

Cases under Tada

After peoples struggles the TADA Act has been repealed and consequently the designated Courts were also abolished. The Apex Court in *Bhaskar @ Prabhakar* v. *State,* AIR 1999 SC 3539 has held that after abolition of designated Court, offences not falling under TADA Act can be tried by regular Courts from stage at which designated Court ceases to function. ...... *De novo* trial cannot be held.

In this case [*Nazir Khan* v. *State of Delhi,* 2003 All MR (Cri) 2651 (SC)]. The accused persons took British and American nationals to the hideouts and were kept as hostages. The police rescued the hostages and arrested the accused persons who were members of Harkat-Ul-Mujahiddin (in short 'HUM') and they were put on trial. The TADA Court, New Delhi convicted some of the accused persons whereas two accused were acquitted. However before completion of trial, Umar Sheikh, the mastermind and the kingpin of the whole case was allowed to leave the country along with other militants in exchange of passengers who had been made hostages in Indian Air Lines hijacked flight AI-814. In appeal, while maintaining the conviction, the Apex Court held that, *"It is the fundamental right of every citizen to have his own political theories and ideas and to propagate them and work for their establishment so long as he does not seek to do so by force and violence or contravene any provision of law. Thus where the pledge of a society amounted only to an undertaking to propagate the political faith that capitalism and private ownership are dangerous to the advancement of society and work to bring about the end of capitalism and private ownership and the establishment of a socialist State for which others are already working under the lead of the working classes, it was held that it was opened to the members of the Society to achieve these objects by all peaceful means, ceaselessly fighting public opinion that might be against them and opposing those who desired the continuance of the existing order of society and the present Government; that it would also be legitimate to presume that they desired a change in the existing Government so that they could carry out their programme and policy. ..... The mere use of the words 'fight' and 'war' in their pledge did not necessarily mean that the society planned to achieve its objects by force and violence."*

In *Jamil Ahmed* v. *State of Rajasthan,* 2003 AIR SCW 6078: 2003 (9) SCC 673, the Apex Court held that, *"confessional statement of accused recorded under section 15 of the TADA Act, 1987 is a substantive piece of evidence even against co-accused provided concerned accused are tried together. However Court should look for general corroboration in such case. ....Acceptable confession of a co-accused can be used as corroborative confession of another accused in same trial..... Section 15 of the TADA Act by the use of* non obstante *clause has made confession recorded under section 15 admissible notwithstanding anything contained in the Evidence Act or Criminal Procedure Code. Section 15 excludes the application of section 36 of the Evidence Act."*

In *State of Punjab* v. *Jagga Singh,* AIR 1998 SC 3113, the accused was tried under TADA for the unlawful possession of arms. It was alleged that accused was found in possession of unlawful arms *i.e.,* a gun and cartridges. However, neither there was any evidence regarding the sending of arms and cartridges to CFSL for examination nor was there any report of CFSL that the said gun was in working condition and the cartridges were live. Further, entry in Malkhan register did not mention that said gun was sent to CFSL and there was no description of cartridges. In such facts and circumstances of the case the Apex Court set aside the conviction.

In *Sanjay Dutt* v. *C.B.I. Bombay,* (1994) Supp 3 SCR 263, the Constitution Bench has held that, *"Mere conscious possession of a forbidden substance is sufficient to constitute an offence and the offence created by section 5 in a statute like TADA is not extraordinarily or conceptually impermissible...... The net ingredient is that possession of such arms etc. should be unauthorised. The unauthorised possession in the context means without the authority of law."*

In *Ayyub* v. *State of Uttar Pradesh,* AIR 2002 SC 1192, the Apex Court acquitted the accused on the ground that confession made by the appellants did not indicate that same was voluntary in nature and that police officer who recorded the same did not certify that he believed the confession to be voluntarily made.

This is known as *Bombay Blast* case. The incident took place on 12th March, 1993 in which 257 persons lost their lives and 713 were injured. In addition thereto, there had been lost of property worth several crores.

This case is one of the cases in *Mumbai Blast* cases and it is numbered as *Bombay Blast* case No. 1/93. The respondent accused was charged for general conspiracy and for persuading his brother-in-law (A-39) to undergo weapons' training in Pakistan and keeping in his possession four hand grenades brought to him by A-39 and for handing over the same to A-93, showing that the same had been smuggled into India for committing terrorist activities. The designated Court acquitted the respondent-(A-72) of all the charges. State filed appeal before the Apex Court challenging the order of acquittal passed by the Special Judge of the designated Court under the TADA Act. The Hon'ble Supreme Court acquitted respondent/A-72 namely Ayub Ibrahim Patel on the ground that prosecution failed to establish that Ayub of Oshiwara could be Ayub (A-72) and that both are one and the same person; *State of Maharashtra* v. *Fazal Rehman Abdul*, 2013 (2) Crimes 255(SC).

In this case, accused were charged with criminal conspiracy to commit murders and cause injuries to RSS and Hindu leaders at Headquarter's building of RSS at Chennai by procuring explosives and other material for preparing suit case bombs on 8th August, 1993. The Designated Court convicted some accused whereas some accused were acquitted. Confessional statement of the accused stated that only gelatine sticks and detonators were bought by accused. Bombs exploded were found to have been made of RDX and PETN but no trace of gelatine was found. Prosecution failed to prove the source of RDX and what happened to the gelatine. The Hon'ble Apex Court acquitted the appellants and held that conclusion of trial Court "other materials" as mentioned in confession would bring in its sweep RDX and PETN was wholly without any basis and suspicion however strong cannot take the place of proof; *Abubucker Siddique* v. *State represented by Dy. S.P., CBI/SCB/Chennai, Tamil Nadu*, 2011 All MR (Cri) 302(SC).

(L) Prevention of Terrorism Act, 2002

The story of the prosecution is that on 24th September, 2002 at about 4.30 p.m., two persons armed with AK-56 rifles, hand grenades etc., entered the precincts of Swaminarayan Akshardham Temple situated at Gandhinagar, Gujarat from gate No. 3. They fired indiscriminately towards the children, games and rides and started throwing hand grenades. While continuing the attack, they reached gate No. 2 of the temple and fired at the worshippers, devotees, volunteers and visitors and then proceeded towards the main building. Since the main door of the temple was locked they moved towards the Sachchidananad Exhibition Hall, killing and injuring women, children and others. Thereafter, immediately CRPF personnel, Deputy Inspector General (DIG), Gujarat State and other Senior Police Officers along with SRP commandos rushed to the place of offence to return the fire. A fierce gun battle ensued between police and alleged terrorists (fidayeens) and there was also a bomb blast. Even National Security Guard (NSG) commandos was summoned from New Delhi they arrived at about 12.00 at midnight. They began the counter attack against the fidayeens. Exchange of firing continued and lasted for nearly five hours which went on into the wee hours of 25-9-2002. Eventually both of them were killed in early morning hours . It is further the case of prosecution that a large quantity of fire arms and explosive substances were carried by the two fidayeens. Some of the explosives were seized along with other articles from the premises. The attack resulted in the killing of 33 persons, including NSG commandos, personnel from the State Commandos Force and three other persons from the SRP group. Nearly 86 persons, including 22 police officers and jawans were grievously injured.

FIR was registered under various sections of I.P.C. and POTA Act. The ATS was shooting in the dark for about year without any result and was unable to trace the real culprits. The case was transferred to Crime Branch Ahmedabad on the morning of 28th March, 2003. Mr. D.G. Vanzara suddenly gave a lead and some persons were arrested. Police recorded confessional statement of accused. After completion of investigation, chargesheet was filed and the case was tried by the Special POTA Court. The appellants were convicted by the Special Court and it was confirmed by the High Court of Gujarat. In appeal, the Hon'ble Apex Court acquitted all the appellants, of all the charges framed against them. The main evidence against the appellants consisted of (a) the confession of accused persons recorded after 11 months of terrorists attack, (b) evidence of accomplice and (c) recovery of Urdu letters from dead bodies of the terrorists. The first piece of evidence was discarded on the ground that neither police officer nor Magistrate followed the statutory mandate under sections 32 and 52 of the POTA Act and the reflection time or cooling off time was only 15 minutes. As regards the evidence of accomplice, the Court rejected the same on the ground that evidence of accomplice does not satisfy the twin test (self implication and proof of guilt of accused beyond reasonable doubt) and is not reliable. As regards the recovery of Urdu letters from the dead bodies of terrorists, the Hon'ble Apex Court observed that the said letters were clean and spot less though the clothes worn by deceased person's were stained with blood and mud and all cloths bore multiple tears and holes due to perforation by bullets. In such a case, the fact that the letters remained clean, without any tear, soiling or stains of blood and soil is highly unnatural and improbable. The Court held that letters cannot be admitted as evidence as possibility of replacement of originals cannot be ruled out.

The Hon'ble Apex Court expressed anguish about the incompetence with which the investigating agencies conducted the investigation of the case of such grievous nature, involving the integrity and security of the nation. Instead of booking the real culprits responsible for taking so many precious lives, the police caught innocent people and got imposed the grievous charges against them which resulted in their conviction and subsequent sentencing. (Even after the above observations of the Hon'ble Apex Court, neither State Government nor the Central Government initiated any inquiry against the investigation officers nor have taken any action against them. This is nothing but the compromise with the integrity and security of the nation); *Adambhai Sulemanbhai Ajmeri* v. *State of Gujarat*, 2014 (3) Crimes 79 (SC): 2014 All MR (Cri) 2627 (SC).

(M) Cases under The Maharashtra Control of Organised Crime Act, 1999

This case relates to seven serial bomb blasts in seven different first class compartments of local trains of Mumbai Sub-urban Railways on 11th July, 2006. These blasts resulted in the death of 187 persons. The accused respondents had filed an application for examining witnesses in defence which are mentioned at serial no. 63 (Additional Chief Secretary, Home Department), 64 (Commissioner of Police), 65 (Deputy Commissioner of Police) and 66 (Deputy Commissioner of Police). But, the trial Court declined the prayer of the accused/respondent. The accused/respondent preferred appeal before the High Court. The appeal was allowed by the Bombay High Court. Aggrieved by the said order State of Maharashtra filed special leave petition before the Apex Court. The question which arose before the Hon'ble Apex Court is whether the confessional statements recorded before the witnesses at Sr. No. 64 to 66, by the persons who were accused in Special Case No. 4 of 2009 but who are not accused in Special Case No. 21/2006, would be admissible in special case No. 21/2006. The Hon'ble Apex Court held that confessional statement of the accused recorded two years after the occurrence in Special Case No. 4 of 2009 is not admissible in Special Case No. 21/2006 as the same is not part of 'facts in issue', *i.e.*, bomb blasts in 2006. The Court further held that section 18 of the MCOCA Act, 1999 is an exception to sections 25 and 26 of The Evidence Act only in a trial against an accused (or against a co-accused, abettor or conspirator) who has made the confession. Said exemption has not been extended to other trials in which the person who has made the confession is not an accused; *State of Maharashtra* v. *Kamal Ahmed Mohammed Vakil Ansari*, 2013 (2) Crimes 94 (SC): 2013 All MR (Cri) 2590 (SC): 2013 SAR (Criminal) 684: AIR 2013 (SC)1441.

In this case, the appellant was convicted by the Special Court under MCOCA. The accused challenged his conviction. The Apex Court observed that there was evidence showing that main accused was responsible for procuring pistol and handing over the same to co-accused which was used in the shoot-out. The said fact was established and proved by confessional statement of the co-accused. The Apex Court held that confessional statement of the co-accused could be the basis of conviction under the provisions of MCOCA as confessional statement of co-accused is admissible as piece of substantive evidence; *Mohd. Farook Abdul Gafur* v. *State of Maharashtra*, 2010 All SCR 1532.

In this case, accused was booked under the provisions of MCOCA. The Bombay High Court interpreted the expression "by use of violence" as: violence implies use of greater degree of force as defined in sections 349 and 350 of IPC. Offences like cheating or criminal breach of trust which have an element of passivity, but not feeling of being rendered helpless, cannot come within the sweep of activities covered in the expression "by use of violence". Unless involvement in offence of organised crime is proved, further inferences are not permissible. The Court further held that unless the crime was aimed at pecuniary or other like advantage, it would be of no avail for proving offence or organised crime; *Madan R. Gangwani* v. *State of Maharashtra*, 2009 All MR (Cri) 1447.

(N) Cases under NDPS Act 1985

As there was divergence of opinion between different Benches of the Apex Court with regard to the ambit and scope of section 50 of the Act, the batch of cases were placed before a three-Judge Bench. The three-Judge Bench was of the opinion that the judgment of a three-Judge Bench in *Saiyad Mohd. Saiyad Umar Saiyad's* case required reconsideration and therefore this batch of cases was required to be considered by a still larger Bench. Answering the reference referred by the three-Judge Bench, the Constitution Bench of the Apex Court in *The State of Punjab* v. *Baldev Singh*, (1999) 3 SCR 977, held that, *"It is an obligation of the empowered officer and his duty before conducting the search of the person of a suspect, on the basis of prior information, to inform the suspect that he has the right to require his search being conducted in the presence of a Gazetted Officer or a Magistrate and that the failure to so inform the suspect of his right, would render the search illegal because the suspect would not be able to avail of the protection which is inbuilt in section 50 of the Act. Similarly, if the concerned persons requires, on being so informed by the empowered officer or otherwise, that his search be conducted in the presence of a Gazetted Officer or a Magistrate, the empowered officer is obliged to do so and failure on his part to do so would also render the search illegal and the conviction and sentence of the accused bad. .... The provisions of the section 50 of the Act implicitly make it imperative and obligatory and cast a duty on the investigation officer to insure that search of the concerned person (suspect) is conducted in the manner prescribed by section 50, by intimating to the concerned person about the existence of his right, that if he so requires, he shall be searched before a Gazetted Officer or a Magistrate and in case he so opts, failure to conduct his search before a Gazetted Officer or a Magistrate, would cause prejudice to an accused and render the recovery of the illicit article suspect and vitiated the conviction and sentence of an accused, where the conviction has been recorded only on the basis of the possession of the illicit article, recovered during a search conducted in violation of the provisions of section 50 of the Act. The omission may not vitiate the trial as such, but because of the inherent prejudice, which would be caused to an accused by the omission to be informed of the existence of his right , it would render his conviction and sentenced unsustainable. The protection provided in the section to an accused to be intimated that he has the right to have his personal search conducted before a Gazetted Officer or a Magistrate, if he so requires, is sacrosanct and indefeasible — it cannot be disregarded by the prosecution except at its own peril........ An illicit article seized from the person of an accused, during search conduction in violation of the safeguards provided in Section 50 of the Act, cannot by itself be used as admissible evidence of proof of unlawful possession of the contraband on the accused."* However it is curious that the Constitution Bench did not express any opinion as to whether the provision of Section 50 of the Act are mandatory or not.

The question which was left unanswered by the above Bench has been finally answered by the Constitution Bench of the Apex Court in *Vijaysinh C. Jadeja* v. *State of Gujarat,* (2011) 1 SCC 609: 2010 All MR (Cri) 4023 (SC). In this case, the Court held that section 50 of the Act is a mandatory requirement and must be strictly construed.

In this case, the Apex Court held that procedure under section 50 of the Act is to be mandatorily followed. Merely informing accused of his option to be searched before Gazetted Officer or before Magistrate is not sufficient. Accused must be actually produced before Gazetted Officer or Magistrate; *Narcotics Central Bureau* v. *Sukhdev Raj Sodhi,* 2011 All MR (Cri) 2356 (SC).

This was a case where the Appellant who was driving an auto-rickshaw was intercepted by a posse of police personal while it was proceeding to Shahpur (Gujarat). Four gunny bags were found stacked in the vehicle which contained *'Charas'* (Cannabis hemp). Appellant was arrested and prosecuted for offences under section 20(b)(ii) of the NDPS Act besides section 66(1)(b) of the Bombay Prohibition Act. The trial Court acquitted the appellant but he was convicted by the Gujarat High Court. In appeal, while allowing the appeal and setting aside the conviction and sentence, the Apex Court held that, the non-recording of information had deprived the appellant as well as the Court of the material to ascertain the precise information received by PW-2 before proceeding to stop the vehicle. It could be counted as a circumstance in favour of the accused. .....

There was non-compliance with section 42 of the Act. It was imperative that the officer should take down in writing the information received from any person that any narcotic drug was kept or concealed in any building, conveyance or enclosed place and he shall forthwith send a copy thereof to his immediate official superior...... If the circumstances appearing in prosecution case were such as to give reasonable assurance to the Court that appellant could not have had the knowledge or the required intention, the burden cast on the accused under section 35 of the Act would stand discharged even if he had not adduced any other evidence of his own when called upon to enter on his defence; *Abdul Rashid Ibrahim Mansuri* v. *State of Gujarat,* (2000) 1 SCR 542.

This was a case where there was recovery of contraband from loud-speakers possessed by accused while she was going abroad. Plea of the accused was that her husband's friend gave her music system to be given to her husband who was running shop of electronic goods in abroad. Evidence on record showed that no steps were taken by prosecution to search said friend to go to root of matter. In such circumstances, the Court accepted the plea of the accused and set aside the conviction. Further the Court held that prosecution failed to establish beyond doubt that accused had knowledge of possession of contraband; *Mrs. Giva Fatimat Oluwaseyi* v. *Harbans Singh,* 2006 (1) AIR Bom R 329.

In this case, the Apex Court held that pre-search requirement of recording information received and sending it to superior officer demands exact and definite compliance as opposed to substantial compliance. Compliance with the provisions of section 57 does not dispense compliance with requirements of sections 42 and 50. Protections provided under sections 42, 50 and 57 are distinct and they are neither inter-linked nor inter-dependent. Compliance with one does not dispense compliance with other; *Kishan Chand* v. *State of Haryana,* AIR 2013 SC 357.

In this case, co-accused has signed on communication for himself and the respondent-accused. However accused has not signed on communication at all and did not give his independent consent. The Apex Court set aside the conviction and held that accused must be individually informed that he has a right to be searched before a nearest Gazetted Officer or before a nearest Magistrate. Joint communication of right may not be clear or unequivocal. It may create confusion and may result in diluting the right. It would frustrate very purpose of section 50; *State of Rajasthan* v. *Parmanand,* 2014 All MR (Cri) 1475 (SC).

Other Cases under NDPS Act

1. *Jayantilal Modi* v. *State of Maharashtra,* 2001 (2) Mh LJ 615 (Bom) (FB): The Bombay High Court has held that compliance with section 42 of the Act is necessary even with respect to commission of offence in public place of the like mentioned in the explanation to section 43 of the Act.

2. *Ahmed Kola* v. *V.M. Dosi,* 2001 (2) Mh LJ 515 (Bom): The Bombay High Court has held that search of body cavity or inside of abdomen of a person amounts to personal search and attracts provision of section 50 of the Act.

3. *Megha Singh* v. *State of Punjab,* AIR 2003 SC 3184: The Apex Court held that, *"The expression 'possession' is a polymorphous term which assumes different colours in different contexts. Possession in a given case need not be physical possession but can be constructive. ...... The word 'conscious' means awareness about a particular fact. It is a state of mind which is deliberated or intended. .... Provisions of section 50 of the Act do not extent to search of vehicle or a container or a bag or premises."*

4. *Mohd. Shaikh* v. *State of Maharashtra,* 2004 All MR (Cri) 53 (Bom): The Bombay High Court has held that, *"Leader of raiding party should not be the officer-in-charge of the police station in which such seized samples are kept of safe custody. Interestedness in success of the raid would pollute the safeness of the custody of the samples."*

5. *Mohd. Mansoori* v. *State of Maharashtra,* 2003 All MR (Cri) 506 (Bom): The Bombay High Court has held that, *"Prosecution is obliged to bring such evidence on record to convince a Court that such witness can be called as an expert in real sense."*

6. *State of Punjab* v. *Balbir Singh,* (1994) 2 SCR 208: The Apex Court has held that, *"If a police officer without any prior information makes a search or arrests a person in the normal course of investigation into an offence or suspected offence as provided under the provisions of the Cr.P.C. and when such search is completed, at that stage section 50 of the NDPS Act would not be attracted and the question of complying with the requirements thereunder would not arise. If during such search or arrest there is a chance recovery of any narcotic drug or psychotropic substance then the police officer, who is not empowered, should inform the empowered officer who should thereafter proceed in accordance with the provision of the NDPS Act."*

7. *Kishor Gopaldas Thawani* v. *State of Maharashtra,* 2000 (1) Mh LJ 813 (Bom) (DB): The Bombay High Court has held that, *"If the officer concerned has not given intimation in writing to his seniors about raid conducted by him, the effect of raid, the property seized and registration of offence within 48 hours as required by section 57 of the NDPS Act, accused is entitled to acquittal."*

8. *G. Srinivas Goud* v. *State of Andhra Pradesh,* 2005 AIR SCW 4905: The Apex Court held that, *"when search was conducted by Gazetted Officer, requirement of sending copy to superior officer is not mandatory."*

9. *Paramjit Singh* v. *Union of India,* 2000 Cri LJ 100 (Raj): The Rajasthan High Court has held that where in a case under NDPS Act, the accused was arrested much before the recording of his statement, there were chances of the statement being recorded under duress and as such the statement cannot be relied upon.

10. *Hasan I. Inamdar* v. *State of Maharashtra,* 2003 All MR (Cri) 1889: Illegal search cannot entitle the prosecution to raise presumption under section 54 of the Act.

11. *State of Karnataka* v. *Dondusa N. Baddi,* 2010 (6) CRJ 163 SC: (2010) 12 SCC 495: 2010 All SCR 2431: Where neither the information was taken down in writing nor was conveyed to immediate police officer, it was held that oral evidence of police officer is not acceptable. The Court further held that the

dispatch of a wireless message to officer does not amount to compliance with section 42(2) of the Act.

12. *Karnail Singh* v. *State of Haryana,* 2010 All SCR 968: (2009) 8 SCC 539: The Constitution Bench held that mandatory enforcement of section 42 has been restricted only to provision of sending a copy of the information written down by empowered officer to the immediate superior official and not to any other condition of the section.

13. *Kuldeep Singh* v. *State of Punjab,* 2011 All MR (Cri) 1013 (SC): In this case four bags of poppy husk were recovered. However no samples were taken at the place of occurrence. On the contrary four bags were taken to police station, their contents were mixed and after taking samples, said bags were resealed. The Apex Court held that failure to take samples at initial stage of seizure was an incurable defect and therefore entire trial stood vitiated.

14. *State of Rajasthan* v. *Tara Singh,* 2011 All SCR 1380: The Apex Court held that the question as to how and where the samples had been stored or as to when they had dispatched or received in the laboratory is a matter of great importance on account of the huge penalty involved in these matters.

(O) Cases under Prevention of Corruption Act, 1988

The brief facts of the case [*State of Maharashtra* v. *Wasudeo Ramchandra Kaidalwar,* (1981) 3 SCR 675] are that the respondent/accused was a Range Forest Officer on a monthly salary of Rs. 515. In a search conducted by an officer of the Anti-Corruption Bureau Rs. 26,000 in cash, Savings bank accounts in the names of himself, his wife and children, national savings certificates, postal saving certificates, gold and silver ornaments, sale deeds of certain properties in the name of his wife, sister-in-law and brother-in-law aggregating in all to over Rs. 79,000 were discovered from his house. On the allegation that he was found in possession of assets disproportionate to his known sources of income he was charged with offence punishable under section 5(2) read with section 5(1)(e) of the Prevention of Corruption Act, 1947. The defence of the respondent/accused was that he led a frugal life and that secondly much of the property found in his house belonged to his father-in-law Hanumanthu who was *pairokar* of Raja Dharmarao, *Zamindar* of Aheri Estate. He added that two sisters of his father-in-law were the kept mistresses of the *Zamindar* and enjoyed special favours from the late *Zamindar* who bestowed on them large amounts of cash, ornaments etc. They used to visit the house of his father-in-law once or twice a month, and used to keep all their cash, gold and silver ornaments. Hanumanthu owned a grocery shop. He and his father had a liquor shop besides forest contracts. Hanumanthu used to deal in money lending business. The *Zamindar* gave large amounts of cash and presents most of which were passed on his father-in-law. At the time of his death, his father-in-law entrusted his minor daughter and son to his care and instructed that his property should be divided among his three children equally and that therefore he was holding the property merely as a custodian and was not the owner thereof. Respondent/accused examined 12 witnesses in support of his defence including Dr. Chandrashekhar Merakar and Adv. V.N. Swamy of Chandrapur. The Special Judge, Chandrapur rejected the plea of the respondent and convicted and sentenced him under section 5(2) read with section 5(1)(e) of the Act. On appeal, a single Judge of the High Court acquitted him. The State preferred appeal to the Supreme Court. The Apex Court while dismissing the appeal and acquitting the accused held that, *"The expression 'burden of proof' has two distinct meanings: (i) the legal burden, that is, the burden of establishing the guilt and (ii) the evidential burden, that is, the burden of leading evidence. Notwithstanding the general rule that the burden of proof lies exclusively upon the prosecution, in the case of certain offences, the burden of proving a particular fact in issued may be laid by law upon the accused. This burden is not so onerous as that which lies on the prosecution and is discharged by proof of a balance of probabilities. To substantiate the charge of criminal misconduct under section 5(2) read with 5(1)(e) the prosecution must prove (a) that the accused was a public servant; (b) the nature and extent of the pecuniary resources or property in his possession; (c) his known sources of income,* i.e., *known to the prosecution; (d) that such sources or property were disproportionate to his known sources of income. Once these are established, the offence of criminal misconduct under section 5(1)(e) would be complete. The burden then shifts to the accused to substantially account for possession by him of assets disproportionate to his income. The extent and nature of burden of proof resting upon the public servant cannot be higher than establishing his case by a preponderance of probability. .... The phrase 'burden of proof' in section 106 of the Evidence Act is clearly used in the secondary sense, namely the duty of introducing evidence. The nature and extent of the burden cast on the accused is well settled. The Accused is not bound to prove his innocence beyond all reasonable doubt. All that he need do is to bring out a preponderance of probability. .... The evidence led in the case was sufficient to create a doubt whether the respondent was in possession of assets disproportionate to his known source of income. On the other hand there is preponderance of probability that the property in his possession belonged not to him, but to his father-in-law."*

In *Subhash Parbat Sonvane* v. *State of Gujarat,* 2002 (5) SCC 86: AIR 2003 SC 2169, the accused was tried for the offence punishable under section 13(1)(d(i) of the Prevention of Corruption Act, 1988. It was alleged that the accused obtained pecuniary advantage. However the facts and evidence revealed that complainant followed accused towards toilet and gave him something from his pocket which accused put in his pocket. While setting aside the conviction, the Apex Court held that, *"from the Evidence it cannot be inferred that accused had demanded any amount from the complainant or that he had obtained the same. Mere acceptance of money is not sufficient for convicting accused under section 13(1)(d)(i). There must be evidence on record that accused obtained any amount by corrupt or illegal means. .... The expression 'obtains pecuniary advantage' contemplates an element of effort or initiative on the part of the receiver of the advantage."*

In this case [*State of Bihar* v. *Basawan Singh,* (1959) SCR 195] question arose as to whether testimony of raiding party requires independent corroboration. The Constitution Bench of the Apex Court held that, *"The corroboration need not be by direct evidence that the accused committed the crime. It is sufficient even though it is merely by circumstantial evidence of his connection with the crime. .... If any of the witnesses are accomplices, their evidence is admissible in law. Evidence of partisan or interested witnesses must be tested in the same way as any other interested evidence is tested, and in a proper case, the Court may look for independent corroboration before convicting the accused person."*

In *2-G Spectrum* case, the petitioner filed petition for impleading Prime Minister as one of the accused persons on the ground that prices were fixed at 2001 level without resorting to auction method. The Apex Court held that a wrong judgment or an inaccurate or incorrect approach or poor management by itself, even after due deliberations between Ministers or even with Prime Minister, by itself cannot be said to be a product of criminal conspiracy and therefore refused to implead and issue process against the *Prime Minister; Subramanian Swamy* v. *A. Raja,* 2012 All SCR 2488.

Other Cases on Prevention of Corruption Act, 1988

State of Kerala v. *V. Padmnabhan,* (1999) 3 SCR 864: As regards whether sanction is required to prosecute a public servant, the Apex Court held that, *"Immunity on the ground of want of prior sanction cannot be claimed for offence under section 5(2) of the Act. Sections 406, 409, I.P.C. are cognate offences and it is no part of the duty of the public servant to enter into a criminal conspiracy for committing criminal breach of trust. .... Prior sanction under section 197 of Cr.P.C. is not required in case of offence under both sections."*

Prakash Singh Badal v. *State of Punjab,* AIR 2007 SC 1274: The Apex Court held that *"Where a criminal act is performed under the colour of authority but which in reality is for the public servant's own pleasure or benefit, then such acts shall not be protected under the doctrine of State Immunity and no sanction is required for prosecuting a public servant."*

Mahmood Khan Mahboob Khan Pathan v. *State of Maharashtra* AIR 1998 SC 2360: The Apex Court held that, *"unless money paid is proved to be for personal satisfaction or pleasure of recipient, Court cannot raise presumption under section 4(1) of the Prevention of Corruption Act, 1947."*

K.R. Purushothaman v. *State of Kerala,* AIR 2006 SC 35: In this case accused was tried for the offence punishable under section 13(1)(c) of Prevention of Corruption Act, 1988. However property in question was neither entrusted to accused nor was under his control. Further it was not proved that accused did obtain for himself or for any other person, any valuable thing or pecuniary advantage. In such circumstances accused was acquitted of the charge.

Kanwarjit Singh Kakkar v. *State of Punjab,* 2011 All SCR 1156: In this case, Government doctor was prosecuted for doing private practice and charging profession fee. It was alleged that he did not seek permission for private practice. The Apex Court quashed the FIR holding that such an act would be against service rules but is not an offence under Prevention of Corruption Act, 1988. Indulgence in private practice and charging profession fee would also not amount to 'trade' under section 168 of the I.P.C.

(P) Cases under the Scheduled Castes and Scheduled Tribes (Prevention of Atrocities) Act, 1989

The Central Government has made amendments in the Act by The Scheduled Castes and The Scheduled Tribes (Prevention of Atrocities) Amendment Act,

2015 (1 of 2016) and it has came into force from 1st January, 2016. Important amendments carried out in the Act pertaining to trial of cases under the Act are reproduced below:

(a) Trial of Offences

(i) Establishment of Special Court and Exclusive Special Court – (Section 14) – For the purpose of providing for speedy trial, an Exclusive Special Court to be established for one or more districts. Such Courts shall have power to directly take cognizance of offences under the Act.

(ii) The trial under the Act shall be completed within a period of two months from the filing of the charge sheet, as far as possible.

(iii) The trial under the Act in the Special Court or Exclusive Special Court or the Exclusive Special Court shall be continued from day-to-day until all the witnesses in the attendance have been examined.

(iv) No adjournment shall be granted. If special Court finds the adjournment necessary, it shall be adjourned till the following day.

(b) Appeals (Section 14A)

(i) An appeal shall lie from any judgement, sentence or order, of a Special Court or an Exclusive Special Court to the High Court both on facts and on law.

(ii) An appeal shall lie to the High Court against an order of the Special Court or the Exclusive Special Court granting or refusing bail.

(iii) Every appeal under this section shall be preferred within a period of 90 days from the date of the judgement, sentence or order appealed from.

(iv) High Court may entertain an appeal after the expiry of 90 days if it is satisfied that the appellant had sufficient cause for not preferring the appeal within the period of 90 days.

(v) No appeal shall be entertained after the expiry of the period of 180 days.

(vi) Every appeal shall be disposed off within a period of three months from the date of admission of the appeal.

(c) Special Public Prosecutor and Exclusive Special Prosecutor

(i) For every Special Court, the State Government shall, specify a Public Prosecutor or appoint an advocate who has been in practice as an advocate for not less than 7 years, as a Special Public Prosecutor for the purpose of conducting cases in the Court.

(ii) For every Exclusive Special Court, the State Government shall specify an Exclusive Special Public Prosecutor or appoint an advocate who has been in practice as an advocate for not less than 7 years, as an Exclusive Special Public Prosecutor for the purpose of conducting cases in the Court.

(d) Punishment for Neglect of Duties – (Section 4)

A Public servant who wilfully neglects his duties required to be performed by him under the Act and the rules shall be punishable with imprisonment for a term which shall not be less than six months but which may extend to one years.

(e) Presumption as to Offences – (Section 8)

In a prosecution for an offence under this Chapter, if it is proved that – (a) the accused rendered any financial assistance to a person accused of, or reasonably suspected of, committing, an offence under this Chapter, the Special Court shall presume, unless the contrary is proved, that such person had abetted the offence; (b) a group of persons committing an offence under this Chapter and if it is proved that the offence committed was a sequel to any existing dispute regarding land or any other matter, it shall be presumed that the offence was committed in furtherance of the common intention or in prosecution of the common object. (c) the accused was having personal knowledge of the victim or his family, the Court shall presume that the accused was aware of the caste or tribal identity of the victim, unless the contrary is proved.

In *State of Maharashtra* v. *Dnyaneshwar S/o Pandurang Bhokare,* 2006 All MR (Cri) 404 (Bom) (DB) prosecution alleged that the accused belonging to Hindu upper caste dragged the prosecutrix and pressed her lips to prevent her from shouting and committed rape on her. The accused was tried for the offence punishable under section 376, IPC read with sections 3(1)(xi), 3(1)(xii) and 3(2)(v) of the Act and was acquitted by the Special Judge, Amravati. Being aggrieved by the judgement, the State has preferred appeal before the High Court. Dismissing the appeal of the State, the Division Bench of the Bombay High Court held that, *"the charge in respect of offences punishable under the various clauses of section 3 of the Act was indeed uncalled for. Merely because the victim belongs to Scheduled Caste or the accused is upper caste Hindu, it does not follow that the offence punishable under section 3 of the Act would be made out. It is not the allegation of the prosecution that the accused committed the offences because the victim belong to the Scheduled Caste. It was simply a case of two young persons committing an indiscretion."*

In this case, the Court held that there must be intentional insult or intimidation with intent to humiliate a member of SC/ST by a non SC/ST. Merely calling a person by caste would not attract the provisions of the Act. There must be specific accusation alleged against each of the accused. Section 34 of the IPC cannot be pressed into service. Omnibus statement that all the accused persons uttered allegedly humiliating words may not be enough; *Mukesh Kumar Saini* v. *State (Delhi Administration),* 2001 Cri LJ 4587 (Del).

Other Cases on the Scheduled Castes and Scheduled Tribes (Prevention of Atrocities) Act, 1989

Gajana S/o Baliram Mehetre v. *State of Maharashtra,* 2006 All MR (Cri) 423 (Bom): The Bombay High Court has held that, *"what is necessary under section 3(1) (xi) of the Act is the assault or use of force with the intention to dishonour or outrage the modesty of woman. .... Verbal threats have no use of force or assault. Therefore when the section speaks of assault or use of force it will have to be interpreted as mere factual assault or factual use of force so seen."*

V.P. Shetty v. *Senior Inspector of Police,* 2005 All MR (Cri) 2384 (Bom) (DB): Where it was alleged that the accused insulted and humiliated the complainant in closed cabin of the accused in absence of any stranger, it was held that the accusation by the accused to the complainant does not fall in expression *"within the public view"* and therefore proceeding were quashed.

Ashok L. Halmare v. *State of Maharashtra,* 2005 All MR (Cri.) 2489 (Bom): The Bombay High Court quashed the proceeding on the ground that every quarrel or altercation between member of SC/ST and non SCST would not *ipso facto* constitute offence under the Act.

Manohar Martandrao Kulkarni v. *State of Maharashtra.* 2005 All MR (Cri) 2602 (Bom): The Bombay High Court held that where the FIR does not contain an averment that the accused does not belong to a Scheduled Caste or Scheduled Tribe, neither offence can be registered nor can there be any investigation as regards said crimes. [**Note**: The view taken by the Bombay High Court does not seem to be a correct interpretation of the law in view of Judgement of the Apex Court rendered in *Ashabai M. Adhagale* v. *State of Maharashtra,* 2009 AIR Bom R 119 (SC): 2009 All MR (Cri) 1806 (SC). In this case, the Apex Court held that non-mentioning caste of accused in FIR is no ground to quash proceedings.].

State of Andhra Pradesh v. *Viswanabula Chetti Babu,* 2011 All MR (Cri) 660 (SC): Offence under the Act must the investigated only by a specified Deputy Superintendent of Police and not by officer of the rank of Assistant Sub-Inspector of Police.

P.P. High Court of Andhra Pradesh v. *Kusuma Mallaiah,* 2005 Cri LJ 1162 (AP): Where Investigation Officer was not legally appointed by State Government, trial was vitiated as rule 7 has not been complied with.

State of Madhya Pradesh v. *Chunnilal @ Chunni Singh,* 2010 All SCR 693: Proceedings under section 3 of the Act without authorisation for investigation by competent authority was illegal but proceedings under IPC can continued in appropriate Court.

(Q) Cases under Exceptions/Special Pleas – (Chapter IV – Sections 76 to 106 I.P.C.)

Section 96, IPC – Nothing is an offence which is done in the exercise of the right of private defence.

Section 97, IPC – Every person has a right, subject to the restrictions contained in section 99,to defend- First.- His own body, and the body of any other person, against any offence affecting the human body; Secondly.- The property whether movable or immovable, of himself or of any other person, against any act which is an offence falling under the definition of theft, robbery, mischief or criminal trespass, or which is an attempt to commit theft, robbery, mischief or criminal trespass.

(R) Right of Private Defence of Body and Property

In this case, the appellant was the party man of *C* and *P*, the two accused. *B* and *H* were real brothers and the deceased was the wife of *H* and *J* was the nephew of *B* and *H*. *P* was the cousin of *H*. *B* was to celebrate Lohri festival in connection with the birth of his grand-child. *B* went to *J* to request him to join the celebration of Lohri festival at his house. The next day *J* came to the house of *B* and remained there till the evening on the occasion of the birth of his grand-child. In the evening *H*, his wife and *B* came out of the house along with *J* to see the latter off. They were standing in front of the gate of his (*H's*) house. At that time electric light which was fitted at his house, was illuminating in which a human being could be identified. *J* was going to connect his tractor with his trolley. Meanwhile, *P* accused armed with his D.B.B.L. gun, *W* appellant armed with a single barrelled gun and C accused armed with '*gandasa*' came to the house of *H* and *B* and *C* said that they were going to teach *H* and others a lesson for parking the tractor trolley in the lane. *P* opened the attack by firing from his D.B.B.L. gun towards H. However, the fire missed the target as he (*H*) had knelt down to save himself and the fire passed over his head. Thereafter appellant fired from his single barrelled gun and the shot hit the deceased near her pelvic. On receipt of the injury, she fell down on the ground. Thereafter *C* dealt a blow on the head of *B* from its sharp side. Meanwhile *P* dealt blow with his butt and his gun on the left hand of *J* and another blow from the said butt on his right ear. Then *C* dealt a blow on the head of *B* from its reverse side. Thereupon *H*, *B* and *J* raised and alarm and on this, the accused decamped with their weapons. Before that, *B* and *H* also caused injuries on person of appellant in their self-defence. The deceased '*B*' was placed in a car and she died on the way to the hospital and a First Information Report was lodged, and a post-mortem was held. On the basis of the evidence adduced on behalf of the prosecution, the Sessions Judge convicted the appellant for the offence punishable under section 304, Part I, I.P.C. and section 27 of the Arms Act. In appeal to the Supreme, it was contended on behalf of the appellant that he had a right of private defence of body. Allowing the appeal, the Apex Court held that, "*It is obvious that if an accused with an intention to kill his victim fires a shot at him which misses the target and hits any other innocent person fatally he would remain guilty of an offence of murder but if the accused had no such intention and was protected by right of private defence under the situation and circumstances in which it could extend to even causing death of assailant as laid down by section 100 and if in exercise of that right of private defence the blow fatally falls on an innocent person the action would still remain protected under section 100 of the I.P.C.. ..... For applicability of Section 301, the act must amount to culpable homicide in the first place. If the act is not culpable at all, then even if it results into homicide of an innocent person, in view of section 100 of I.P.C. as in the present case, section 301 will have no operation. ...... While judging the nature of apprehension which an accused can reasonably entertain in such circumstances requiring him to act on the spur of moment when he finds himself assaulted, by number of persons, it is difficult to judge the action of the accused from the cool atmosphere of the Court room. Such situations have to be judged in the light of what happens on the spur of the moment on spot and keeping in view the normal course of human conduct as to how a person would react under such circumstances in a sudden manner with an instinct of self-preservation. Such situations have to be judged from the subjective point of view of the accused concerned who is confronted with such a situation on the spot and cannot be subjected to any microscopic and pedantic scrutiny.*

..... *Under the circumstances of the case the appellant had the right of private defence which would extend to even causing death"*; *Wassan Singh* v. *The State of Punjab*, (1995) Supp 5 SCR 703: (1996) 1 CCR 107(SC).

The Apex Court in *Yogendra Morarji* v. *The State of Gujarat*, AIR 1980 SC 660, has stated the principles governing the burden of proof where the accused sets up a plea of private defence, which are as follows: Section 105, Evidence Act enacts an exception to the general rule whereby in a criminal trial the burden of proving everything necessary to establish the charge against the accused beyond reasonable doubt, rests on the prosecution. According to the section, the burden of proving the existence of circumstances bringing the case within any of the General *Exceptions* in the Penal Code; or within any special exceptions or proviso contained in any other part of the Code or in other Law, shall be on the accused person, and the Court shall presume the absence of such circumstances. But, the section does not neutralise or shift the general burden that lies on the prosecution to prove beyond reasonable doubt all the ingredients of the offence with which the accused stand charged. Therefore, where the charge about the accused is one of culpable homicide, the prosecution must prove beyond all manner of reasonable doubt that the accused caused the death with the requisite knowledge or intention described in section 299 of I.P.C. It is only after the prosecution so discharges its initial traditional burden establishing the complicity of the accused, that the question whether or not the accused had acted in the exercise of his right of private defence, arises. Under section 105 of the Evidence Act read with the definition of 'Shall presume' in section 5 of the Evidence Act, the Court shall regard the absence of circumstances on the basis of which the benefit of an Exception (such as the one on which right of private defence is claimed), as proved unless, after considering the matter before it, it believes that the said circumstances existed or their existence was so probable that a prudent man ought, under the circumstances of the particular case, to act upon the supposition that they did exists. The accused has to rebut the presumption envisaged in the last limb of section 105, by bringing on record evidential material before the Court sufficient for a prudent man to believe that the existence of such circumstances is probable. In other words, even under section 105, the standard of proof required to establish those circumstances is that of a prudent man as laid down in section 3 of the Evidence Act. But within that standard there are degrees of probability, and that is why under section 105, the nature of burden on an accused person claiming the benefit of an *Exception*, is not as onerous as the general burden of proving the charge beyond reasonable doubt cast on the prosecution. The accused may discharge his burden by establishing a mere balance of probabilities in his favour with regard to the said circumstances. "..... *The material before the Court to establish such a preponderance of probability in favour of the defence plea may consist of oral or documentary evidence, admissions appearing in evidence led by the prosecution or elicited from prosecution witnesses in cross-examination, presumptions, and the statement of the accused recorded under section 313 of the Cr.P.C. ..... Notwithstanding the failure of the accused to establish positively the existence of circumstances which would bring his case within an Exceptions, the circumstances proved by him may raise a reasonable doubt with regard to one or more of the necessary ingredients of the offence itself with which the accused stands charged."* The Apex Court further stated the general principles embodied in the Penal Code, Governing the exercise of the right of private defence, as follows: *"The Code excepts from the operation of its penal clauses large classes of act done in good faith for the purpose of repelling unlawful aggression but this right has been regulated and circumscribed by several principles and limitation. The most salient of them concerned the defence of body are as under:* Firstly, *there is no right of private defence against an act which is not in itself an offence under the Code;* Secondly, *the right commences as soon as – and not before – a reasonable apprehension of danger to the body arises from an attempt or threat to commit some offence although the offence may not have been committed and it is conterminous with the duration of such apprehension (section 102). That is to say, right avails only against a danger imminent, present and real;* Thirdly, *it is a defensive and not a punitive or retributive right. Consequently, in no case the right extends to the inflicting of more harm than it is necessary to inflict for the purpose of the defence, (section 99). In other words, the injury which is inflicted by the person exercising the right should be commensurate with the injury with which he is threatened. At the same time, it is difficult to expect from a person exercising this right in good faith, to weigh 'with golden scales' what maximum amount of force is necessary to keep within the right. Every reasonable allowance should be made for the* bona fide *defender 'if he with the instinct of self-preservation strong upon him, pursues his defence a little further than may be strictly necessary in the circumstances to avert the attack.' It would be wholly unrealistic to expect of a person under assault, to modulate his defence step by step according to the attack;* Fourthly, *the right extends to the killing on the actual or potential assailant when there is a reasonable and imminent apprehension of the atrocious crimes enumerated in the six clauses of section 100. The combined effect of the first two clauses is that taking the life of the assailant would be justified on the plea of private defence if the assault causes reasonable apprehension of death or grievous hurt to the person exercising the right. In other words, a person who is in imminent and reasonable danger of losing his life or limb may, in the exercise of right of self-defence, inflict any harm, even extending to death, on his assailant either when the assault is attempted or directly threatened. The principle is also subject to the preceding rule that the harm or death inflicted to avert the danger is not substantially disproportionate to an incommensurate with the quality and character of the perilous act or threat intended to be repelled;* Fifthly, *there must be no safe or reasonable mode of escape by retreat, for the person confronted with an impending peril to life or of grave bodily harm, except by inflicting death on the assailant;* Sixthly, *the right being, in essence, a defensive right, does not accrue and avail where there is 'time to have recourse to the protection of the public authorities'."*

The facts of the case are: the relations between one *G* and his wife were strained and she went to live with her father *B* and her brother *V*, the appellant. *G*, with three others, went to the quarter of *B* and he went inside and came out dragging his reluctant wife behind him. She caught hold of the door and *G* started pulling her. At this the appellant shouted to his father that *G* was adamant and thereupon *B* replied that he should be beaten. The Appellant took out a knife from his pocket and stabbed *G* once. The knife penetrated the heart of *G* and he died. *B* and the appellant were tried for the murder of *G*. *B* was acquitted whereas the appellant was convicted for the offence punishable under section 304, Part II of the IPC. While acquitting the appellant the Apex Court held that the appellant had the right of private defence of the body of his sister which extended to the causing of death of *G*. The extended right under section 100 of the IPC arose when there was the offence of assault of one of the types mentioned in the six clauses of that section. It was not necessary that the intention with which the assault was committed must always be an offence itself. The word 'abduction' used in the fifth clause of section 100 meant nothing more than what was defined as 'abduction' in section 362, and it was not necessary, to get the protection of this clause, that the abduction must be of a type punishable under the Penal Code. Further, the appellant had not inflicted more harm than was necessary and was not guilty of an offence; *Vishwanath* v. *State of Uttar Pradesh*, (1960) 1 SCR 646.

In this case, it was submitted by accused that when accused *M* (acquitted co-accused) was trying to drive out the goat which had entered the field of deceased, he was beaten by the deceased and two *lathi* blows were inflicted on him, and when respondent/accused came to his rescue he was also given two *lathi* blows whereupon in right of private defence he gave two blows to deceased, which resulted in his death. The Apex Court upheld the acquittal holding that accused acted in right of private defence; *Satya Narain Yadav* v. *Gajanand*, (2008) 16 SCC 609.

As regards the right of private defence where accused did not establish the same, the Apex Court in *Seriyal Udayar* v. *State of Tamil Nadu*, AIR 1987 SC 1289, has held that, *"Even if on the basis of material as it stands, the right of private defence of the accused/appellant is not established, still the material produced in cross examination and circumstances do indicate that the incident might have happened in a manner in which it was suggested by the accused, then it cannot be said that the prosecution has established the offence against the appellant accused beyond reasonable doubt and therefore he cannot be convicted."*

In *Laxman Sahu* v. *State of Orissa*, AIR 1988 SC 83, the Apex Court has held *"that the right of private defence of body is available to one who is suddenly confronted with immediate necessity of averting an impending danger not of his creation. The necessity must be present, real or apparent."*

In *Jassa Singh* v. *State of Haryana*, AIR 2002 SC 520, the Apex Court has held that, *"Right of private defence of property which may extend to causing death is not available in case of trespass in respect of open land."*

However, the Apex Court has recently in *Kishan Chand* v. *State of Uttar Pradesh*, 2007 All SCR 2739 has held that, *"there is no law that right of self-defence cannot be exercised in relation to a dispute over an open space."* In view of this latest pronouncement of the Apex Court, view taken in *Jassa Singh's* (*supra*) case does not seem to be a good law.

After scrutiny of various judgment, the Apex Court has culled out following principles:

(i) Self-preservation is the basic human instinct and is duly recognised by the criminal jurisprudence of all civilised countries. All free, democratic and civilized countries recognize the right of private defence within certain reasonable limits.

(ii) The right of private defence is available only to one who is suddenly confronted with the necessity of averting an impending danger and not of self-creation.

(iii) A mere reasonable apprehension is enough to put the right of self-defence into operation. In order words, it is not necessary that there should be an actual commission of the offence in order to give rise to the right of private defence. It is enough if the accused apprehended that such an offence is contemplated and it is likely to be committed if the right of private defence is not exercised.

(iv) The right of private defence commences as soon as a reasonable apprehension arises and it is co-terminus with the duration of such apprehension.

(v) It is unrealistic to expect a person under assault to modulate his defence step by step with any arithmetical exactitude.

(vi) In private defence the forced used by the accused ought not to be wholly disproportionate or much greater than necessary for protection of the person or property.

(vii) It is well settled that even if the accused does not plead self-defence, it is open to consider such a plea if the same arises from the material on record.

(viii) The accused need not prove the existence of the right of private defence beyond reasonable doubt.

(ix) The Indian Penal Code confers the right of private defence only when that unlawful or wrongful act is an offence.

(x) A person who is in imminent and reasonable danger of losing his life or limb may in exercise of self defence inflict any harm even extending death on his assailant either when the assault is attempted or directly threatened; *Darshan Singh* v. *State of Punjab*, 2010 (1) Crimes 78 SC: 2010 All MR (Cri) 622 (SC).

Other Cases on Private Defence of Body and Property

Buta Singh v. *State of Punjab*, AIR 1991 SC 1316:

In this case it was alleged that prosecution party went to the disputed land to have it tilled and launched attack on camp of accused. Accused and his wife fought to repel attack. Both sides suffered injuries. One of the persons belonging to prosecution party died. In such circumstances it was held that, "*Accused had the right of private defence and he did not exceed the same. .... He could not have weighed in golden scales in the heat of the moment the number of injuries required to disarm his assailants who were arm with lethal weapons.*"

Dwarka Prasad v. *State of Uttar Pradesh*, (1993) 2 SCR 70: It was a case of free-fight. As regards the question as to whether right of private defence is available or not in case of free-fight the Apex Court held that, *"If prosecution establishes free-fight, then no right of private defence is available to either party."*

Abdul Kadir v. *State of Assam,* AIR 1986 SC 305: In this case land was in the possession of accused persons and paddy crop had been grown by them and the same was ready to harvesting. The deceased and their people armed with sharp cutting instruments trespassed in to the property of the accused and were about to harvest the paddy. Theft and mischief were either being committed or threatened to be committed. In this incident accused persons received grievous injuries. The Apex Court held that, *"The accused persons were entitled to the right of private defence of body and property."*

State of Uttar Pradesh v. *Niyamat,* AIR 1987 SC 1652: The Apex Court held that, *"Where certain villagers tried, during night to rescue a person who was illegally arrested by police and was being carried away and launched attack on police resulting in death of one who was accompanying police, only after one of the constables fired three shots one after another, the villagers could be said to have acted in exercise of right of private defence as the act of firing shots caused reasonable apprehension of grievous injury or death in their minds."*

Chanan Singh v. *State of Punjab,* AIR 1979 SC 114: The Apex Court held that, *"If there is existence of probability of accused having acted in self-defence, he is entitled to benefit of doubt."*

Subramani v. *State of Tamil Nadu,* AIR 2002 SC 2980: The Apex Court held that, *"Persons exercising right of private defence do not intend to commit criminal act. Their object is to protect person or property. Therefore they cannot be convicted with the aid of section 34, I.P.C."*

Kashinath Ramchandra Patil v. *State of Maharashtra,* 2001 (1) Mh LJ 87 (Bom) (DB): The Court has held that, *"Section 34, I.P.C has no application where more than one person act in discharge of right of private defence of person or property. .... In such cases prosecution must establish who amongst them exceeded right of private defence. ..... Where prosecution and defence come with untrue facts, both versions have to be rejected and benefit of doubt has to be given to accused."*

Deo Narain v. *State of Uttar Pradesh,* AIR 1973 SC 473: (1973) 3 SCR 57: Where in the course of a melee a blow with *lathi* was aimed at a vulnerable part of the body of the accused who in order to defend himself caused a blow with considerable force with a spear on the chest of the deceased though he himself received a superficial *lathi* blow on his head, it was held that the accused acted in self-defence.

Jai Bhagwan v. *State of Haryana,* AIR 1999 SC 1083: Where evidence showed that accused who was one of the co-owners and possessor of land where occurrence took place, caused grievous hurt by dangerous weapon, it was held that the accused is entitled to protection of right of private defence of property under section 104, I.P.C.

Triloki Nath v. *State of Uttar Pradesh,* AIR 2006 SC 321 and *Bishna* alias *Bhiswadeb Mahato* v. *State of West Bengal,* AIR 2006 SC 302: The Apex Court has held that accused aggressors are not entitled to claim right of private defence.

Ravishwar Manjhi v. *State of Jharkhand*, (2008) 16 SCC 561: In such cases where both the versions are probable, *causa causans* of the incident is required to be considered. As plea of private defence raised by the appellant is probable, benefit is extended to the appellants.

State of Bihar v. *Nathu Pandey*, AIR 1970 SC 27: Persons who act in the exercise of right of private defence, do not form an unlawful assembly.

Defence of Insanity

Section 84, IPC: Nothing is an offence which is done by a person who, at the time of doing it, by reason of unsoundness of mind, is incapable of knowing the nature of the Act, or that he is doing what is either wrong or contrary to law.

A test applied to determine whether a person accused of crime was sane at the time of its commission and, therefore, criminally responsible for the wrongdoing. The rule laid down in *M'Naghten's* case has been accepted to be a test for criminal insanity. Under this rule, a criminal defendant is not guilty by reason of insanity if, at the time of the alleged criminal act, the defendant was so deranged that he/she did not know the nature or quality of her actions or, if she knew the nature and quality of her actions, she was deranged that she did not know that what she was doing was wrong. This rule is named for Daniel M'Naghten, who, in 1843, tried to kill England's Prime Minister Sir Robert Peel. M'Naghten thought Robert Peel wanted to kill him, so he tried to shoot Peel but instead shot and killed Peel's Secretary Edward Drummond. Medical experts testified that he was psychotic, and was not found guilty by reason of insanity; *Queen* v. *Daniel M'Naghten*, (1843) 8 Eng. Rep. 718: (1843) 10 CL.

Section 84 IPC embodies the fundamental maxim of criminal law, *i.e.*, *"actus non reum facit nisi mens sit rea"* which means that an act does not constitute guilt unless done with a guilty intention. In order to constitute an offence *actus reus* and *mens rea* must coincide. However no culpability can be fastened on insane person as they are incapable of forming any reasonable decision; *Bapu* v. *State of Rajasthan*, (2007) 8 SCC 66.

This was a case [*Bhikari* v. *State of Uttar Pradesh*, (1965) 3 SCR 194: AIR 1966 SC 1: 1966 Cri LJ 63] where the appellant who killed a child in a cruel manner and injured others was tried and convicted under section 302, I.P.C. and his appeal before the High Court also failed. In his statement at the trial he did not specifically plead insanity but in both the Court the plea that being insane he could not be credited with the intention requisite for the offence alleged was raised on his behalf. In appeal, the Supreme Court dismissed the appeal of the applicant and held that, *"the burden of proving the intention of the accused person, where intention is an ingredient of the offence is on the prosecution and this burden never shifts. But intention can sometimes be only proved from circumstances and therefore it is sufficient for the prosecution to prove the acts of the accused and the circumstances in which they were committed. If from these and inference of the requisite intention can be reasonably drawn, the prosecution must be deemed to have discharged its burden. .... Section 84 of the I.P.C. can no doubt be invoked by a person for nullifying the evidence adduced by the prosecution by establishing that he was at the relevant time incapable of knowing the nature of the act or that he was doing was wrong or contrary to law. The prosecution need not give evidence about the capacity of the accused the know the nature of the act or that it was wrong or contrary to law because these are matters of presumption. Everyone is presumed to know the natural consequences of his act. Similarly everyone is presumed to know the law. It is for this reason that section 105 of the Evidence Act places upon the accused person the burden of proving the exception on which he relies. ...... The second part of section 105 of the Evidence Act lays down that the Court shall presume the absence of circumstances on the basis of which the case could be said to come under a General Exception. But this presumption is rebuttable and the accused can rebut it either by leading evidence or by relying upon the prosecution evidence itself. If upon the evidence adduced in the case whether by the prosecution or by the accused a reasonable doubt is created in the mind of the Court as regards one or more of the ingredients of the offence including* mens rea *of the accused, he would be entitled to be acquitted. This is very different from saying that the prosecution must also establish the sanity of the accused at the time of the commission of the offence despite what has been expressly provided for in section 105 of the Evidence Act."*

In a case of murder, accused pleaded that he was under the influence of alcohol and therefore knowledge and intention to commit the offence is lacking and the same cannot be attributed to him. While dismissing his appeal, the Apex Court held that insanity, whether produced by drunkenness or otherwise is a defence to the crime charged. The evidence of drunkenness which renders the accused incapable of forming the specific intent essential to constitute the crime should be taken into consideration with the other facts proved in order to determine whether or not he had this intent. The evidence of drunkenness falling short of a proved incapacity in the accused to form the intent necessary to constitute the crime, and merely establishing that his mind was affected by drink so that he more readily gave way to some violent passion, does not rebut the presumption that a man intends the natural consequences of his acts; *Basdev* v. *State of Pepsu,* (1956) SCR 363.

In *Dahyabhai Chhaganbhai Thakker* v. *State of Gujarat,* (1964) 7 SCR 361, the three-Judge Bench of the Apex Court held that, *"Even if the accused is not able to establish conclusively that he was insane at the time he committed the offence, the evidence placed before the Court by the accused or by the prosecution may raise a reasonable doubt in the mind of the Court as regards one or more of the ingredients of the offence, including* mens rea *of the accused and in that case the Court would be entitled to acquit the accused on the ground that the general burden of proof resting on the prosecution was not discharged."*

In this case, it was pleaded that accused cannot be convicted on the ground of his insanity. The defence stated that he was being treated for a long time for insomnia. However, the defence did not examined the doctor who was treating the accused. The plea of insanity was neither substantiated nor probabilised by the accused. The Apex Court negatived the plea of insanity and held that insanity is a medical condition that cannot for long be concealed from friends and relatives of person concerned. Non-production of anyone who noticed any irrational or eccentric behaviour on part of appellant, is a serious lapse on the part of defence. The Court further observed that conduct of appellant not fleeing from scene of occurrence would not in itself show that person concerned was insane at the time of commission of offence; *Elavarasan* v. *State*, (2011) 7 SCC 110.

In this case, the appellant was put on trial for commission of offence under section 302 of IPC read with section 27 of the Arms Act. It was alleged by prosecution that the appellant all of a sudden came with a country-made pistol, and fired at point blank range at the deceased. During the course of trial, the appellant raised a plea of insanity but the same was negatived by both the trial court and the High Court. Both the Courts sentenced him to undergo imprisonment for life. While upholding the sentence imposed on the appellant , the Supreme Court held that an accused who seeks exoneration from liability of an act under section 84 of the IPC is to prove legal insanity and not medical insanity. Every person who is suffering from mental disease is not ipso facto exempted from criminal liability. The mere fact that the accused is conceited, odd, irascible and his brain is not quite all right , or that the physical and mental ailments from which he suffered had rendered his intellect weak and affected his emotions or indulges in certain unusual acts, or had fits of insanity at short intervals or that he was subject to epileptic fits and there was abnormal behaviour of the behaviour is queer are not sufficient to attract the application of section 84 of the IPC. .... Even if the accused establishes unsoundness of mind , section 84 will not be attracted in case it is found that the accused knew what he was doing was wrong or that it was contrary to law...... The entire conduct of the accused, from the time of the commission of the offence upto the time the sessions proceedings commenced is relevant for the purpose of ascertaining as to whether plea raised was genuine bona fide or an afterthought; *Surendra Mishra* v. *Jharkhand*, (2011) 11 SCC 495: 2011 (1) Crimes 192 (SC).

Other Cases on Plea of Insanity

Ratanlal v. *State of Madhya Pradesh*, (1971) 3 SCR 251: AIR 1971 SC 778: 1971 Cri LJ 654: The Apex Court held that, *"The crucial point of time at which unsoundness of mind should be established is the time when the crime was committed."*

Amrit Bhusan Gupta v. *Union of India*, AIR 1977 SC 608: The Apex Court held that, *"Only legal insanity is recognised of section 84 of I.P.C. A person suffers from legal insanity where his cognitive faculty of mind is destroyed as a result of unsoundness of mind to such an extent as to render him incapable of knowing the nature of the act or that what he was doing was contrary to law."*

Jailal v. *Delhi Administration*, AIR 1969 SC 15: 1968 Cri LJ 259: The Apex Court held that, *"The mental faculty of the accused must be so destroyed so as to recognise the character of the act."*

S. Murthy v. *State*, (1988) 1 Crimes 326 (Mad): The Court has held that, *"the disorder or disturbance must be of a such degree which would obliterate perceptual or volitional capacity of the accused."*

Sanna Eranna v. *State of Karnataka*, 1983 Cri LJ 619 (Kant): This was a case of murder. The accused raised the plea of insanity and proved that he had the previous history of lunacy. In such circumstance the Karnataka High Court held that, *"Burden shifts on prosecution to establish negatively that accused was not of unsound mind when he committed the offence."*

Plea of Alibi

According the Webster's Dictionary *"alibi "* means elsewhere. It is a form for defence by which the accused, in order to establish his innocence, undertakes to show that he was elsewhere when the crime was committed.

An *alibi* is not an exception (special or general) envisaged in the IPC or any other law. It is only a rule of evidence recognised in section 11, *Illustration* (a) of the Evidence Act that facts which are inconsistent with the fact in issue are relevant. The burden on prosecution would not be lessened by the mere fact that the accused has adopted the defence of *alibi*. The plea of the accused in such cases need be considered only when the initial burden has been discharged by the prosecution satisfactorily. But once the prosecution succeeds in discharging the burden it is incumbent on the accused, who adopts the plea of *alibi*, to prove it with absolute certainty so as to exclude the possibility of his presence at the place of occurrence. Strict proof is required for establishing the plea of *alibi*; *Binay Kumar Singh* v. *State of Bihar*, (1997) 1 SCC 283.

In this case, the Apex Court held that when an alibi is set-up, the burden is on the accused to lend credence to the defence put up by him or her. However, the approach of the Court should not be such as to pick holes in the case of the accused person. The defence evidence has to be tested like any other testimony, always keeping in mind that a person is presumed innocent until, he or she is found guilty; *Jumni* v. *State of Haryana*, 2014 (3) Crimes 14 (SC).

In this case, plea of *alibi** taken by the accused has failed. The defence witnesses examined by them have been disbelieved. It was contended on behalf of the prosecution that adverse inference should be drawn against the accused due to his failure to prove plea of alibi. The Apex Court rejected the submission and held that when the prosecution is not able to prove its case beyond reasonable doubt, it cannot take advantage of the fact that the accused have not been able to probablise their defence; *Sunil Kundu* v. *State of Jharkhand*, 2013 All SCR 1804.

This was a case [*Nesar Ahmed* v. *State of Bihar*, AIR 2001 SC 2416] of murder where the appellants along with two others (father and sister-in-law of appellant No. 1) were tried for offences under sections 302/34, I.P.C. and section 201, I.P.C. The trial Court acquitted all the four accused for the offence under section 201, I.P.C. but convicted them for offences under sections 302/34, I.P.C. and sentenced them to undergo life imprisonment. On appeal, the High Court acquitted the father and sister-in-law of accused No. 1 by giving them benefit of doubt but maintained conviction and sentence of both the appellants- husband and mother-in-law of deceased Aheleya Khantoon. There was no eye witness in this case and the entire case was based on circumstantial evidence. Prosecution case was that accused who were husband and in-laws of the deceased were seen leaving house at 10.00 a.m. whereas deceased died at 11.00 a.m. in that house according to prosecution witnesses. There was no evidence to show that the accused were in the house at the crucial time. As regards the plea of alibi set up by the accused, the Apex Court held that, *"previous quarrels between parties or refusal of her husband to refund loan taken from his father-in-law cannot be said to be clinching circumstances as to negate reasonable hypothesis inconsistent with innocence of accused. Link to complete chain of circumstantial evidence is doubtful in absence of proof of presence of accused at crucial time at the place of occurrence. .... Plea of alibi as set up by accused looks probable and therefore conviction of the accused is set aside by giving them the benefit of doubt."*

In *Nallamsetty Yanadaiah* v. *State of Andhra Pradesh,* 1993 Cri LJ 408, the Apex Court accepted the plea of alibi set-up by the accused on the ground that the name of the appellant was not mentioned by the eye witnesses in F.I.R or during inquest.

Defence of Intoxication (Drunkness)

Section 85, I.P.C.: Nothing is an offence which is done by a person who, at the time of doing it, is, by reason of intoxication, incapable of moving the nature of the act, or that he is doing what is either wrong, or contrary to law; provided that the thing which intoxicated him was administered to him without his knowledge or against his will

When defence of intoxication is raised, a phrase 'Dutch Courage' is often use. Dutch Courage is an English colloquialism tended to mean using spirits, not just beer, to stiffen resolve. According to British English, Dutch courage means the confidence that some people get from drinking alcohol before they do something that needs courage. According to researchers, 'Dutch Courage' has two possible origins. The first derives from the disparaging idea that Johnny Foreigner, whether sailing up the Medway or facing down the locals in the East Indies, needed a few drinks before a fight. The second theory relates more directly to the use of a specific drink-gin-to bolster one's courage.

The decision of the House of Lords in *Majewski's* case is a *locus classicus* of the judgment rendered on the defence of intoxication and it is known as "Majewski Rule". In this case, the court held that voluntary intoxication is no defence to crimes requiring only basic intent, the *mens rea* requirement for these being satisfied by the reckless behaviour of intoxicating oneself; *Director of Public Prosecution* v. *Majewski,* (1976) UKHL 2: AC 443: 2WLR 623: 2 All ER 142.

Defence of Mistake of Fact

Section 79, IPC.: Nothing is an offence which is done by any person who is justified by law, or who by reason of a mistake of fact and not by reason of a mistake of law in good faith, believes himself to be justified by law, in doing it.

Mistake of fact arises when a criminal defendant misunderstood some fact that negates an element of the crime i.e., *mens rea.* For raising this plea, mistake of fact must be *bona fide,* honest and reasonable. It is not available in respect of absolute liability offences. For example, defence of reasonable mistake of fact in manslaughter cases is not available in Australia.

In this case, on the date of incident when the deceased was returning from the house of PW 2 after reciting Bhagbat, where some other villagers including the respondent/accused were also present, and reached near the house of the respondent, he was assaulted by the respondent accused. The respondent/accused raised a plea of mistake of fact stating that during the day time his bell-metal utensils had been stolen and he was keeping a watch for the thief, he saw a person coming inside his premises and thinking him to be a thief he dealt a *lathi* blow but subsequently discovered that it was the deceased. On the basis of the evidence on record, the trial Court convicted and sentenced the respondent under section 304, Part II of IPC. However, in appeal, the High Court accepted the defence plea and held that respondent had not committed any offence and was protected under section 79 of the IPC and acquitted him. Allowing the appeal of the state, the Apex Court held that under section 79 of IPC although an act may not be justified by law, yet if it is done under a mistake of fact, in the belief of good faith that it is justified by law, it will not be an offence. The question of good faith must be considered with reference to the position of the accused and the circumstances under which he acted. In view of section 52 of the IPC "good faith" requires not logical infallibility but due care and attention. The question of good faith is always a question of fact to be determined in accordance with the proved facts and circumstances of each case. It may be laid down a general rule that an alleged offender is deemed to have acted under that state of things which he in good faith and on reasonable grounds believed to exist when he did the act alleged to be an offence. Section 79 is attracted where the circumstances showed that the accused acted under a *bona fide* belief that he was legally justified in doing the act owing to ignorance of the existence of relevant facts, or mistake as to them; *State of Orissa* v. *Bhagaban Barik*, (1987) 2 SCR 785.

CHAPTER XXVIII

RELEVANCY OF CERTAIN FACTS AND CIRCUMSTANCES

SYNOPSIS

Section 5 to section 55 of the Evidence Act deals with the relevancy of facts and during trial the relevant facts may be used for or against the accused. Few examples of relevancy of facts and circumstances during trial are given below:

1. Statement in F.I.R.

The Apex Court in *State of Rajasthan* v. *Nana,* 2007 All MR (Cri) 2938 (SC), has held that statement made in F.I.R. is a factor which is relevant so far as the statement of the maker of the F.I.R. is concerned. However, it does not have any effect on the credibility of evidence of other witnesses.

In this case, the Apex Court held that F.I.R. itself is not proof of a crime but it is a relevant piece of evidence which can be used for corroborating prosecution case. It should contain basic case, not all facts and circumstances on which prosecution relies; *Jitendra Kumar* v. *State of Haryana,* (2012) 6 SCC 204.

2. Delay in Lodging F.I.R.

It is not the every delay in lodging F.I.R. which is fatal to prosecution but if the delay is not satisfactorily explained, adverse inference may be drawn against the prosecution.

The Apex Court in *Ramdas* v. *State of Maharashtra*, 2007 All SCR 248, has held that lodging of report belatedly is a relevant fact of which Court must take notice. Delay will have to be considered in the light of other facts and circumstances.

Where the delay in lodging F.I.R. was inordinate and remained unexplained and also the statement in F.I.R. and his evidence were inconsistent, the conviction was set aside; *Bishnu Deo* v. *State of Orissa,* 1982 Cri LJ 493.

In *Peddireddy* v. *State of Andhra Pradesh,* AIR 1991 SC 1356, the Apex Court acquitted the accused on the ground that the eye witnesses did not report the occurrence to any of the villagers after witnessing the same and there was delay of 15 hours in lodging F.I.R.

However, it has been held by the Apex Court in *State of Rajasthan* v. *Maharaj Singh,* 2005 All MR (Cri) 2309 (SC), that, *"Delay in lodging F.I.R. would become material if there is any doubt regarding the prosecution case."*

3. Delay in Sending Copy of F.I.R to Magistrate

The Apex Court in *Bijoy Singh* v. *State of Bihar,* AIR 2002 SC 1949, has held that, *"If delay in sending copy of F.I.R. to Magistrate as required by section 157 of Cr.P.C. by itself, does not render the whole case of the prosecution to be doubtful. Where prosecution failed to explain the delay, the Court is required to minutely examine the prosecution version for ensuring itself as to whether any innocent person has been implicated in the crime or not. ..... However chances of roping accused person wrongly in the case allegedly on account of enmity between the parties cannot be ruled out."*

In *Anil Rai* v. *State of Bihar,* 2001 All MR (Cri)1930 (SC), the Apex Court has held that, *"only extraordinary and unexplained delay in sending copy of F.I.R. to Magistrate as mandated by section 157 of Cr.P.C. vitiates F.I.R."*

However, it has been held by the Apex Court in *Munshi Prasad* v. *State of Bihar,* AIR 2001 SC 3031, that, *"If delay in sending copy of F.I.R. to Magistrate is explained, such delay cannot demolish prosecution case if prosecution evidence on record is trustworthy."*

But it should be remembered that before calling upon the Court to draw adverse inference against the prosecution for delay in despatch of F.I.R. to the Court, there should be cross-examination by the defence on these matters; vide: *State of Uttar Pradesh* v. *Anil Singh,* AIR 1988 SC 1998: 1989 Cri LJ 88.

4. Omission of Name of Accused in F.I.R.

Where the F.I.R. did not show the name of one of the accused even though prosecution witnesses claimed to have known and seen the accused running away from the place of occurrence, it was held that they must not have seen the accused at the place of occurrence; *Mahesh Chander* v. *State (Delhi Admin.),* AIR 1991 SC 1108.

5. Omission of Material Facts in F.I.R.

It has been held by the Apex Court in *Ram Kumar Pande* v. *State of Madhya Pradesh,* AIR 1975 SC 1026: (1975) 3 SCR 519, that, *"omissions of important facts affecting the probabilities of the case are relevant under section 11 of the Evidence Act in judging the veracity of the prosecution case ."*

Where the report is lodged by a person claiming to be an eye witness to the occurrence, it is expected that he would not omit to state a striking feature about the incident. If such infirmity is found in the F.I.R. then the version of such eye witness who lodged the report is liable to be rejected; *State of Orissa* v. *Dilip Kumar,* 1987 Cri LJ 1242.

6. Absence of Names of Witnesses in F.I.R.

Where the names of witnesses who witnessed the incident were not mentioned in F.I.R. but at later stage attempt was made by the prosecution to rope in innocent persons, it was held that the evidence of so called eye witnesses is not reliable; *Yamanappa* v. *State of Karnataka,* 1981 Cri LJ 164 (SC).

7. Relevancy of Motive

The High Court has held that motive is a relevant factor when prosecution relies upon circumstantial evidence. However, mere proof of motive is not sufficient to connect a person to a crime though it may be one of the links in the chain of circumstances; *Sivan* v. *State of Kerala,* 2007 (4) CRJ 381.

8. Relevancy of Questions put in Cross-examination

In *Jesu Asir Singh* v. *State,* AIR 2007 SC 3015, the Apex Court held that questions put in cross-examination, though not always determinative in finding accused guilty, they are certainly relevant.

9. Conduct of Witnesses

Where prosecution witnesses claimed that they have seen the accused running away from the place of occurrence but they did not chase and attempt to apprehend the accused or at the worst did not raise a hue and cry, the Apex Court held that it created a hallow of suspicion in the veracity of the prosecution case; *Mahesh Chander* v. *State (Delhi Admin.),* AIR 1991 SC 1108.

In this case, victim survived for five days but no complaint was made by witnesses when she was alive. The Court held that no reliance can be placed on the oral testimony of such witnesses; *Krishna S. Shinde* v. *State of Maharashtra,* 2012 All MR (Cri) 1605.

10. Relevancy of Facts Forming Part of same Fransaction (*Res Gestae*) (Evidence Act, Section 6)

The rule embodied in section 6 of the Evidence Act is known as *res gestae.* This has been explained by the Apex Court in *Gentela Vijayavardhan Rao* v. *State of Andhra Pradesh,* (1996) Supp 5 SCR 273. The Court held that the principle of law embodied in section 6 of the Evidence Act is usually known as the rule of *res gestae* recognised in English Law. The essence of the doctrine is that a fact which, though not in issue, is so connected with the fact in issue *"as to form part of the same transaction"* becomes relevant by itself. This rule is, roughly speaking, an exception to the general rule that hearsay evidence is not admissible. The rationale in making certain statement or fact admissible under section 6 of the Evidence Act is on account of the spontaneity and immediacy of such statement or fact in relation to the fact in issue. But it is necessary that such fact or statement must be part of the same transaction. Such statement must have been made contemporaneous with the acts, which constitute the offence or at least immediately thereafter. But if there was an interval, however slight it may be, which was sufficient enough for fabrication then the statement is not part of *res gestae.*

To form particular statement as part of the same transaction, utterances must be simultaneous with the incident or substantial contemporaneous that is made either during or immediately before or after its occurrence. Statement of witnesses about what the deceased had told them against the accused about the treatment meted out to her has no connection with any circumstance or transaction which resulted in her death. Hence, provision of section 6 is not attracted; *Bhairon Singh* v. *State of Madhya Pradesh,* 2010 All SCR 213: 2010 (1) CRJ 627(SC).

Where the prosecution witness reached the scene of murder subsequent to the incident and was told about it by a bystander, the evidence of the witness is inadmissible as *res gestae* as the witness has not herself seen the incident; *Chotke* v. *State,* AIR 1958 Cal 482: 1958 Cr LJ 1170. However, where the statement is of a witness who came to the scene of the occurrence after it was over and did not see the accused attack the deceased but learnt it from the eye witnesses, it could be used for the purpose of corroboration under section 157 of the Evidence Act; *Mukhtiar Singh* v. *State of Punjab,* AIR 2009 SC 1854: (2009) 11 SCC 257.

In this case, a husband, his father and mother were prosecuted for the murder of his wife. Deceased cried out for help as soon as she was pushed into the room. Her children who were playing outside in the verandah exclaimed at the same time that there mother was being killed. The Court held that the exclamations of children are relevant as *res gestae* and can be admitted in evidence through the evidence of persons who heard them; *Sawaldas* v. *State of Bihar,* AIR 1974 SC 778: 1974 Cri LJ 664 (SC).

Another illustrated case on the principle of *res gestae* is *Rashtriya Mill Mazdoor Sangh through its President* v. *State of Maharashtra,* AIR 1996 SC 2797. In this case, it was alleged that accused set up hut on fire. Magistrate recorded statements of victims under expectation of death. The Apex Court held that *"in view of appreciable interval between acts of incendiarism and Magistrate recording statement, the statements are not admissible as forming part of* res gestae."

In this case, the Apex Court held that for the applicability of provision of section 6 of the Evidence Act which is an exception to hearsay rule, there must be no interval between alleged criminal act and recording or making of statement in question. Words sought to be proved by hearsay, if not absolutely contemporary with action or event, at least should be so clearly associated with it that they are part of such action or event; *Dhal Singh Dewangan* v. *State of Chhattisgarh,* 2016 All SCR (Cri) 1481.

11. Relevancy of Facts which are the Occasion, Cause or Effect of Facts in Issue (Evidence Act Section 7)

In this case, certain articles were recovered from the possession of the accused. It was claimed by the prosecution that said articles belong to deceased. On the basis of said recovery, it was claimed by the prosecution that accused committed murder of deceased. The High Court held that though recovery of articles from the possession of accused is a relevant fact under section 7 of the Evidence Act, unless it is conclusively established that the articles were with the accused at the time of the offence, possession of said articles by the accused would not be enough to establish nexus with the murder; *Annasuyamma* v. *State of Karnataka,* 2002 Cri LJ 4401 (Kant); *Ramdas* v. *State of Maharashtra,* AIR 2007 SC 155; *Bishna* v. *West Bengal,* AIR 2006 SC 302; *R.M. Malkani* v. *Maharashtra,* AIR 1973 SC 157.

12. Relevancy of Motive, Preparation and Previous and Sub-sequent Conduct (Evidence Act, Section 8)

(A) Motive

Absence of motive in case which depends on circumstantial evidence is relevant and favourable to defence; *Pannayar* v. *State of Tamil Nadu,* (2009) 9 SCC 152. Proof of motive only adds to weight and value of evidence adduced by the prosecution. Absence of proof of motive only demands careful assessment of evidence; *Vijay Shankar* v. *State of Haryana,* 2015 Cri LJ 4774 (SC).

Where accused was charged with murdering a person whom he suspected of having stolen his money, it was held that it is not sufficient motive to commit murder; *Sunil Rai @ Pauna* v. *Union Territory of Chandigarh,* AIR 2011 SC 2545: (2011) 12 SCC 258. Where deceased was on inimical terms with both the accused, fact that either may have his own motive for killing deceased, was not relevant in determining common intention as required under section 34 of IPC; AIR 2000 SC 2063.

Evidence of father and sister of the deceased is relevant under section 8 of the Evidence Act and it would raise presumption under section 113B of the Evidence Act in respect of offence under section 498A of IPC; *State of Uttar Pradesh* v. *Ramesh Prasad Misra,* (1996) Supp 4 SCR 631.

(B) Preparation

The distinction between attempt and preparation has been explained by the Apex Court in this case. The Court held that: a culprit first intends to commit the offence, then makes preparation for committing it and thereafter attempts to commit the offence. Attempt to commit an offence can be said to begin when the preparations are complete and the culprit commences to do something with the intention of committing the offence and which is a step towards the commission of the offence. Preparation to commit an offence is punishable only when the preparation is to commit offences under section 124A and section 399 of the IPC. The dividing line between a mere preparation and an attempt is sometimes thin and has to be decided on the facts of each case. There is a greater degree of determination in attempt as compared with preparation; *Ramkripal S. Charmakar* v. *State of Madhya Pradesh,* 2007 (3) Crimes 115 (SC): 2007 Cri LJ 2302 (SC): 2007 AIR SCW 2198.

(C) Previous or Subsequent Conduct

(i) Previous or Subsequent Conduct of Accused

Any behaviour or conduct of accused would be relevant if it had nexus with the offence alleged to have been committed by him; *Vivek Kalra* v. *State of Rajasthan,* 2013 All SCR 1231.

Conduct of each of the members of unlawful assembly, before and at the time of attack and thereafter, motive for crime, are some of the relevant considerations in determining common object of unlawful assembly; *Sikandar Singh* v. *State of Bihar,* AIR 2010 SC 3580.

Background of incident, motive, nature of assembly, nature of arms carried by members, their common object and behaviour of members soon before, at and after actual occurrence are relevant factors to draw inference of common object under section 149 of the IPC; *Munivel* v. *State of Tamil Nadu,* 2006 (2) Crimes 111 (SC).

In this case, the Court held that common intention to commit a criminal act has relevance only to offence and not to right of private defence. The Court further held that persons exercising right of private defence cannot be convicted with the help of section 34, IPC; *Subramani* v. *State of Tamil Nadu,* 2002 All MR (Cri) 2250 (SC).

In this case, the Apex Court held that the act of absconding is no doubt a relevant piece of evidence which should be considered along with other evidence, but its value would always depend on the circumstances of each case; *Matru @ Girish Chandra* v. *State of Uttar Pradesh,* AIR 1971 SC 1050.

Circumstance of abscondence is a relevant fact. But where accused were arrested from their houses on the third day of the incident and accused did not abscond, the Court refused to draw adverse inference of guilt against the accused; *Durga Burman (Roy)* v. *State of Sikkim,* 2014 (4) Crimes 192 (SC).

In this case, accused did not attend funeral, did not call upon the family of deceased to condole the death and was absconding for nearly 33 days. The Honourable Apex Court held that these circumstances by themselves will not implicate accused. However, cumulative effect of these circumstances along with the motive can be taken into consideration; *Kantilal Soni* v. *State of Gujarat,* 2003 All MR (Cri) 1774 (SC).

In number of decisions, Courts have taken note of pre and post incident conduct of the accused and failure to explain the same by the accused has led the Court to draw adverse inferences against him. For example, the abscondence of accused immediately after the incident has been held to be relevant circumstance in judging the involvement of the accused in crime.

In *Thimma* v. *State of Mysore*, (1971) 1 SCR 215: AIR 1971 SC 1871, the Apex Court has held that, *"Evidence of abscondence is relevant as evidence of conduct under section 8 of the Evidence Act but the guilty mind of the accused is not the only conclusion that could be drawn by the Court, because, even innocent persons may, when suspected of grave crimes, be tempted to evade arrest. Such is the instinct of self-preservation in an average human being."*

It has been held by the Allahabad High Court in *Devendra Singh Negi* alias *Debu* v. *State of Uttar Pradesh*, 1994 Cri LJ 1983 that, *"every person who is not immediately available cannot be characterised as an absconder. The Court has to record its satisfaction that the accused has absconded or is concealing in order to avoid execution of warrant. The provisions of section 82, Cr.P.C. are mandatory and have to be strictly construed."*

In *Anant Chintaman Lagu* v. *The State of Bombay*, (1960) 2 SCR 460, the accused/appellant was tried for the murder of one Laxmibai Karve by administration of some poison. The case entirely rested on circumstantial evidence. The Apex Court took the following pre and post incident conduct of the accused into consideration for convicting the accused: (i) The accused falsely stated to casualty Medical Officer that the lady had suddenly become unconscious. (ii) He told the wrong name of deceased to hospital authorities. (iii) Instead of giving address of the deceased, he gave his own address to hospital authorities. (iv) He wrote false letter to hospital authorities that the brother of deceased was coming from Calcutta to take charge of the dead body when in fact Laxmibai (deceased) had no brother. (v) He had withdrawn large amount from accounts of deceased by forging her signature and misappropriated the same. (vi) He removed jewellery from the person of deceased. (vii) He did not disclose the entire case history of Laxmibai and the treatment given to her to the hospital authorities. (viii) Though G.T. Hospital is situated at a distance of five or six furlongs from Victoria Terminus Station, he admitted deceased to distant hospital. (ix) He left the hospital after her death and did not take charge of her body. (x) He wrote false letters to the relatives of deceased that she is alive.

In *Jessica Lal Murder* case, the Apex Court held that a criminal trial is not an enquiry into the conduct of an accused for any purpose other than to determine whether he is guilty of the offence charged. In this connection, that piece of conduct can be held to be incriminatory which has no reasonable explanation except on the hypothesis that he is guilty. Conduct which destroys the presumption of innocence can alone be considered as material; *Sidhartha Vashisht @ Manu Sharma* v. *State (NCT of Delhi)*, 2010 (2) Crimes 154 (SC).

Recently, the Apex Court has held that conduct of accused subsequent to commission of crime may be relevant if there is sufficient evidence to show that he fabricated some evidence to screen/absolve himself from offence; *Prithipal Singh* v. *State of Punjab*, (2012) 1 SCC 10.

13. Relevancy of Facts Necessary to Explain or Introduce Relevant Facts (Evidence Act, Section 9)

(A) Test Identification Parade

In this case, the Court laid down important guidelines for judges in trials that involve identification evidence as there was widespread concern over the problems posed by cases of mistaken identification. These are: (a) It is imperative for the judge to warn the jury of the special need for caution before convicting the accused. (b) Judge should instruct jury as to the reason for the need of such warning. (c) Judge should direct the jury to examine closely the circumstances in which the identification of each witness can be made. These circumstances are – For how long was the accused under observation by the witness? At what distance was the witness from the accused? What length of time elapsed between the original observation and the subsequent identification to the police?

These directions were called "Turnbull Direction". The Court held that a Turnbull direction need not be provided unless the prosecution case depends wholly or substantially on visual identification; *Regina* v. *Turnbull,* (1977) QB 224 (CA).

Test identification parade is a part of investigation and is governed by section 162 of Cr.P.C.; *Heera* v. *State of Rajasthan,* AIR 2007 SC 2425.

The purpose of holding test identification parade is to form opinion about its evidentiary value for the purpose of corroborating or contradicting the statement of the identifying witnesses in Court; *Rameshwar Singh* v. *State of Jammu and Kashmir,* (1971) SCC (Cri) 638: AIR 1972 SC 102: 1972 Cri LJ 15 (SC): (1972) 1 SCR 627.

In this case, the Apex Court held that test identification parade is inherently weak in character and meant for helping investigating agency with an assurance that their investigation was proceeding on right lines. It can be used for corroboration, and what weight is to be attached thereto is a matter for Court; *Musheer Khan* v. *State of Madhya Pradesh,* (2010) 2 SCC 748.

In this case, the Honourable Apex Court analysed the law regarding test identification parade and stated the principles as under: (a) If an accused is well-known to the prosecution witnesses from before, no test identification parade is called for and it would be meaningless and sheer waste of public time to hold the same. (b) Where prosecution claims that accused is known to prosecution witnesses from before, but the said fact is denied by accused and files petition for holding test identification parade, Court may accede to the prayer. (c) Evidence of identification of an accused in Court by a witness is substantive evidence whereas that of identification in test identification parade is, though a primary evidence but is not substantive one. The evidence can be used only to corroborate identification of accused by a witness in Court. (d) Test identification parades are held during the course of investigation ordinarily at the instance of investigating agencies and should be held with reasonable despatch for the purpose of enabling the witnesses to identify either the properties which are subject matter of alleged offence or the accused persons involved in the offence so as to provide it with materials to assure itself if the investigation is proceeding on right lines and the persons whom it suspects to have committed the offence were the real culprits. (e) failure to hold test identification parade does not make the evidence of identification in Court inadmissible, rather the same is very much admissible in law, but ordinarily identification of an accused by a witness for the first time in Court should not form the basis of conviction. (f) Ordinarily, if an accused is not named in the first information report, his identification by witnesses in Court, should not be relied upon; *Dana Yadav @ Dahu* v. *State of Bihar*, AIR 2002 SC 3325: 2002 AIR SCW 3867.

Identification evidence is relevant under section 9 of the Evidence Act. Generally, identification parade is held where the accused is unknown or stranger. Identification evidence is often tendered in evidence by the prosecution and if the same remains unchallenged, it can be called into aid in judging the presence of accused at the spot of incident and the authorship of a crime. Therefore, defence counsel must know the procedure for holding identification parades. This would help them in cross-examination during trials.

The Bombay High Court in *Sayed Mohammed Owais* v. *State of Maharashtra*, 2002 All MR (Cri) 2472, has laid down following procedure for holding identification parade:

(i An Executive Magistrate/Honorary Magistrate, if called upon for the purpose of holding an identification parade, should remember that he is the person who conducts the parade; he will be in full and sole charge of the entire proceedings.

(ii) The Executive Magistrate/Honorary Magistrate should first acquaint himself, very briefly, with the facts of the case and find out who is to be put in the parade for identification and who are the witnesses to be called up for identification.

(iii) Two independent respectable persons (not being persons connected with the police) should be first called up. The Police themselves will have normally arranged to call up such persons; but the Executive Magistrate/Honorary Magistrate will question them and satisfy himself that they are independent and fairly intelligent persons. In order that they may follow the proceedings intelligently, the Executive Magistrate/Honorary Magistrate should acquaint them, briefly, with the facts of the case and as to who is sought to be identified and who are to come for identification.

(iv) The parade should then be arranged in a room or a place which is such that the identifying witnesses, as well as the persons connected with the Police, should not be able to look into it.

(v) If there is only one accused person to be identified, there should be at least half a dozen persons placed in the parade. If two accused persons are to be identified, then there should be about 10 or 12 persons in the parade. Not more than two accused should be placed in any single identification parade. Normally, the Police themselves will have called up the persons to be put in the parade; but the Executive Magistrate/Honorary Magistrate should see that they are persons of more or less the same physical appearance, and approximately of the same age, as the person to be identified. It is desirable that innocent persons to be mix should be different for each parade.

(vi) No person, other than the persons in the parade, and the two respectable persons, should be allowed to be remain in the room where the identification proceedings are being held. In particular, all police officers and constables should be asked to withdraw themselves completely from the room. There is no objection to any of them remaining outside the room or otherwise at hand, ready to be called up in case the accused creates trouble, or in case of emergency. They should, however, not be visible from the room or the place where the parade is being held.

(vii) After the parade is arranged, one of the two respectable persons should be sent up to bring the accused from the lockup. Care should be taken to see that when the accused is being brought from the lockup, the identifying witnesses do not have an opportunity of seeing him. They should be kept in quite a different room, out of sight of the lockup.

(viii) At this stage, the Executive Magistrate/Honorary Magistrate should commence to write the memorandum. It should include:—(a) the place at which and the date on which, parade is being held and the time at which it was commenced; (b) the names, ages, occupation and the full addresses of the two respectable persons; (c) the name and the approximate ages of the persons standing in the parade, mentioning clearly, one below the other, in numerical order their positions in the parade (which positions they should not be allowed afterwards to alter); (d) the fact that no persons, other than those, in the parade and the two respectable persons, were allowed to remain in the room and that all police officers and constables were asked to withdraw; and (e) that respectable persons so and so fetched the accused from the lockup, and that the identifying witnesses were in a different room so that they could not see him being brought from the lockup to the identification room.

(ix) When the accused is brought, the Executive Magistrate/Honorary Magistrate should ask him to take whatever place he likes in the parade. The place which he selects should be noted in the memorandum. For example, he may select to stand between numbers 3 and 4 in the parade; and it should then be noted that he took his position between Nos. 3 and 4 in the parade. The original numbering of the persons in the parade should not be altered simply because the accused has now joined in.

(x) The accused should then be asked if he wants to make any alteration in his dress. He may change his cap or coat, or he may decide to put on (or remove) a cap or a coat. He should be allowed to do this, and that fact should be noted in the memorandum. If he does not wish to change his dress, then that fact too should be noted in the memorandum.

(xi) One of the respectable persons should be asked to fetch the first identifying witness from the room in which he may be sitting. When the witness arrives, the Executive Magistrate/Honorary Magistrate should question him and ascertain from him whether he had an opportunity to see the culprit at any time subsequent to the offence or after the arrest. He may either record the statement separately or make a reference to the statement in the memorandum. The witness should then be asked to view the parade carefully and see whether he would be able to identify the person, who , for instance; stabbed him or whom he saw firing a shot from a revolver or whom he saw inside the flat in which a burglary may have taken place, or, as the case may be. The identifying witness will then go up and look closely at the parade. If he identifies any person, he should be asked to go forward and touch that person, and not merely to point him out from a distance. This is necessary in order that there may be no doubt afterwards as to whom exactly he had identified. The fact that identifying witness identified the accused, should be noted in the memorandum (along with the name of the accused) and, of course also if he failed to identify him or identified a wrong person. It should further be noted whether the witness identified the accused straightway or after some hesitation or after first pointing out a wrong person and then correcting himself and pointing out the accused. When this is over, the identifying witness should be asked to go away into a different room and not to contact the remaining identifying witnesses. He may even be asked to go away.

(xii) After he leaves the room the accused should be asked once again, whether he desires to change his place in the parade. If he changes his place, it should be noted in memorandum, and also if he declines to do so, he should be asked again, if he wants to change his dress; and if he does so, or if he declines to do so, that fact should also be noted in the memorandum.

(xiii) Then one of the respectable persons should be asked to fetch the second identifying witness. In regard to the identification by him also, the same procedure should be gone through as in the case of the first identifying witness, the memorandum being also written up side by side.

(xiv) This procedure should be followed for each subsequent identifying witness.

(xv) After all the identifying witnesses have thus been exhausted one after the other, the memorandum should be wound up by stating the time at which it was concluded. Then the memorandum should be read over and explained to the respectable persons in language which they understand. If the respectable persons know English well, then they should be asked in addition, to read over the memorandum for themselves.

(xvi) After the memorandum is completed, the Executive Magistrate/Honorary Magistrate should make the following endorsement as the end:

"Identification parade was conducted by me personally with the help of two respectable witnesses, namely Shri. .... and Shri. ...., whose signatures have been obtained in token of what transpired in their presence, and shall sign below this endorsement and put the date below his signature."

There shall be another endorsement to the following effect: "We read above memorandum (or it was explained to us) and it depicts the correct state of affairs as stated in the memorandum, and he shall obtain the signature of the two respectable persons with whose help he held the identification parade."

(xvii) The Executive Magistrate/Honorary Magistrate himself should also sign every sheet of the memorandum.

(xviii) All corrections and interlineations in the memorandum should be initialled by the Executive Magistrate/Honorary Magistrate.

(xix) The Memorandum should then be handed over to the police officer concerned.

(xx) Care should be taken to see that at no stage of the proceedings, police officer or any police constable comes into the room in which the parade is being held. The police should not be allowed to interfere with the proceedings, which are entirely to be conducted by the Executive Magistrate/Honorary Magistrate. It will be advisable to note in the memorandum itself that no police officer or constable was present at any time during the entire proceedings of the identification parade.

(xxi) The most important part of the memorandum will be the statements made by the identifying witnesses. These should be very carefully recorded along with the questions asked to the identifying witnesses. (This recording need not be in the question and answer form). For example, an identifying witness may be asked if he is able to identify any one in parade as the person who fired shot, and the identifying witness may point out the accused and may add that it was not the accused who actually fired, but that the accused was standing by the side of the man who had fired the shot. In that case, whatever the identifying witness states, should be carefully noted, as far as possible in his words (translated in to English).

(xxii) If more than one accused are placed in parade, then in the memorandum they should not be referred to as "Accused No. 1", "Accused No. 2" etc. But they should be referred by their full names.

(xxiii) The memorandum should be written in the language of the Court.

Apart from the above procedure, Advocates are advised to go through the guidelines issued by the High Court of Judicature (Appellate side) Bombay in Criminal Manual's Chapter I.

Where accused is arrested after a long gap, overzealous police officer may try to implicate innocent person by claiming that witnesses have identified the accused in test identification parade. In fact, the honourable Apex Court has taken judicial notice of such things and admitted that the one area of criminal evidence susceptible to miscarriage of criminal justice is the error in the identification of criminal; *Harinath* v. *State of Uttar Pradesh,* (1988) SCC (Cri) 14.

Where accused refused to take part in test identification parade, the Court held that this refusal to participate in test identification parade would go against him; *Shyam Babu* v. *State of Haryana,* (2008) 15 SCC 418.

Similarly, where no explanation was given by the accused in their statements recorded under section 313, CrPC for declining to appear in test identification parade, this circumstance was held against the accused persons and their conviction was upheld; *Pargan Singh* v. *State of Punjab,* 2014 All MR (Cri) 3775 (SC).

In this case, question arose as to whether adverse inference can be drawn against the accused persons for refusing to join test identification parade. Honourable Justice H.S. Bedi held that refusal of accused persons to join test identification parade was immaterial as they had been shown to eye witnesses in advance. However, Justice Gyan Sudha Misra disagreed with Justice H.S. Bedi and she held that adverse inference can surely be drawn against the accused persons at least in order to corroborate the prosecution case. (As there was disagreement between the members of the Bench, the matter has been referred to larger Bench for consideration); *Prem Singh* v. *State of Haryana,* (2011) 9 SCC 689.

Other cases

1. *Rakesh H. Kahar* v. *State of Maharashtra,* 2006 All MR (Cri) 3062: It is obligatory on the part of Special Executive Officer to ask the witness as to whether he had opportunity to see the suspect or his photograph prior to test identification parade.

2. *Ramcharan Bhudiram Gupta* v. *State of Maharashtra,* 1996 (1) Mh LR 702: 1996 (1) Bom CR 190: 1996 (1) B Cr C 285: Dummies to the mixed with suspects must bear similar physical appearance.

3. *Manohar Shankar Jadhav* v. *State of Maharashtra,* 1996 (2) Mh LR 511: Arrangements for test identification parade should be made by an independent authority like Executive Magistrate. Though test identification parade was conducted by the Magistrate, but it was arranged by the investigation officer, the Court held that such identification parade cannot be relied upon.

4. *Vilas V. Patil* v. *State of Maharashtra,* 1996 Cri LJ 1854 (Bom): Where there was non-compliance with instructions contained in Paras 16(3)(i) to (xxii) of Chapter I of Criminal Manual, the Court held that identification evidence cannot be relied upon.

5. *Ravindra @ Ravi Bansi Gohar* v. *State of Maharashtra,* 1998 SCC (Cri) 1527: Where the photographs of the accused were shown to the witnesses who were to identify them in the test identification parade, the Court held that showing photographs to the witnesses prior to the identification parade, vitiates the process.

6. *Kartar Singh* v. *State of Punjab,* 1994 SCC (Cri) 899: Identification on the basis of a photograph could not be held to have the same value as the evidence of a test identification parade.

7. *Budhesan* v. *State of Uttar Pradesh,* AIR 1970 SC 1321: 1970 Cri LJ 1149 (SC): (1970) 2 SCC 128: The Apex Court held that the evidence, in order to carry conviction, should ordinarily clarify as to how and under what circumstances the complainant or the witness came to pick out the particular accused person and the details of the part which he allegedly played in the crime in question with reasonable particularity.

8. *Siddanki Ram Reddy* v. *State of Andhra Pradesh,* (2010) 7 SCC 697: 2011 All SCR 49: Where there is attack in crowded place by a mob and when eye witnesses have little time to see accused, substantive evidence should be sufficiently

corroborated by a test identification parade held soon after occurrence and any delay in holding test identification parade may be fatal to prosecution.

9. *Ravindra Kumar Pal @ Dara Singh* v. *Republic of India,* 2011 All MR (Cri) 673 (SC): Photo identification and test identification parade are not substantive evidence.

10. *Prem Singh* v. *State of Haryana,* (2011) 9 SCC 689: In this case, accused refused to participate in test identification parade. Honourable Justice H.S. Bedi held that refusal of accused to join test identification parade was immaterial as they had been shown to eye witnesses in advance, whereas Justice G.S. Mishra held that adverse inference can surely be drawn against accused at least in order to corroborate prosecution case. (Due to disagreement between judges, the matter has been referred to larger Bench).

14. Relevancy of Things Said or Done by Conspirator in Reference to Common Design (Evidence Act, Section 10)

It is settled law that act or action of one of the accused cannot be used as evidence against the other, but section 10 of the Evidence Act carves out an exception to this general law in case of conspiracy. The first part of the section is attracted only when the Court is satisfied that there is a reasonable ground to believe that two or more persons have conspired together to commit an offence, that is to say, there should be a prima facie evidence that a person was a party to the conspiracy before his acts can be used against the conspirators; *Bhagwan Swarup* v. *State,* AIR 1965 SC 682: 1965 (1) Cri LJ 608 SC.

While interpreting the provision of section 10, the Apex Court held that: the words of section 10 are not capable of being widely construed so as to include a statement made by one conspirator in the absence of the other with reference to past acts done in the actual course of carrying out the conspiracy, after it has been completed. The words "common intention," signify a common intention existing at the time when the thing was said, done or written by one of them. Things said, done or written while the conspiracy was on foot are relevant as evidence of the common intention, once reasonable ground has been shown to believe in its existence. But it should be a very different matter to hold that any narrative or statement or confession made to a third party after the common intention or conspiracy was no longer operating and had ceased to exist is admissible against the other party. There is no common intention of the conspirators to which the statement can have reference; *Mirza Akbar* v. *King Emperor,* AIR 1940 PC 176.

In this case, under section 10 of the Evidence Act, the evidence of acts, statements or writings of a co-conspirator, either under trial or not on trial but outside the period of conspiracy, would not be admissible against the other conspirators in proof of the specific issue of the existence of the conspiracy; *Sardar Singh Caveeshar* v. *The State of Bombay,* (1958) SCR 161.

In this case, the Honourable Apex Court held that any statement of the accused after arrest whether confessional or not, cannot fall within the ambit of section 10 of the Evidence Act; *State of Gujarat* v. *Mohammad Atik,* 1998 Cri LJ 2251 (SC).

15. When Facts not Otherwise Relevant became Relevant (Evidence Act, Section 11)

Omissions of important facts affecting the probabilities of the case are relevant under section 11 of the Evidence Act in judging the veracity of prosecution case; *Ram Kumar Pande* v. *State of Madhya Pradesh,* AIR 1975 SC 1026: 1975 Cri LJ 870: (1975) 3 SCR 519.

Omission to State the motive for the crime in the first information report is an omission of an important fact. But when the FIR was filed by a villager, no much importance can be attached to the motive of the accused; *State of Uttar Pradesh* v. *Krishna Master,* AIR 2010 SC 3071: (2010) 12 SCC 324: 2010 Cri LJ 3889.

16. Relevancy of Facts Showing Existence of State of Mind, or of Body or Bodily Feeling (Evidence Act, Section 14)

In this case, the honourable Bombay High Court has held that existence of state of mind is relevant and admissible under section 14 of the Evidence Act. However, a distinction is to be made in the proof of actual act and the proof of his state of mind. The Court further held that no previous instance can be taken assistance of in examining as to whether the actual act of the accused is proved or not; *Arif Yusuf Sab Deshmukh* v. *State of Maharashtra,* 1997 (1) B Cr C 342: 1997(2) Mh LJ 568.

17. Facts Bearing on Question Whether Act was Accidental or Intentional (Evidence Act Section 15)

Under section 14 of the Evidence Act, facts showing existence of State of mind, or of body or bodily feeling which are in issue are relevant whereas the facts forming part of a series of similar occurrences are relevant under section 15 of the Evidence Act. Ernest Cockle has said that both under sections 14 and 15, the similar acts are not admissible to prove the *actus reus* but only to prove the *mens rea* (that is, similar acts cannot be adduced to show that, for instance, 'A' gave a counterfeit coin to 'B' but only to show that he did it with the knowledge that it was counterfeit).

Signature crimes or *modus operandi* or system crimes fall under this section. These are the cases of serial killers. Signature crime evidence has been held to be admissible when defendant raised defence of misidentification in rape prosecution; *Makin* v. *Attorney-General for New South Wales,* (1894) AC 57.

On the principle of section 15 of the Evidence Act (which says that 'When there is a question whether an act was accidental or intentional, or done with a particular knowledge or intention, the fact that such act formed part of a series of similar occurrences, in each of which the person doing the act was concerned, is relevant.), following is an interesting case which would make the concept underlying the section, clear: This is known as the "Brides in the Bath Tub case". The story of this case runs as: One George Joseph Smith was charged with the murder of a woman whom he has married, though his wife was living. She was found dead in her bath, death being due to drowning. The question that arose was whether the death was accidental or whether the prisoner was responsible. Evidence that the prisoner had married two other women, that those two also died in their baths, and that he had been the sole beneficiary under the wills executed by the unfortunate women was sought to be given by the prosecution and was objected to by the defence. The Presiding Judge admitted the evidence under the rule in English law corresponding to this section while warning the jury not to use the evidence to infer that the prisoner is a person likely to have committed murder. It was to be used only for deciding whether the death was accidental or intentional; *R.* v. *George Joseph Smith,* (1915) 11 Cr App R 2-9.

18. Absence of Name of Assailant in Medico-legal Papers

In *Rehmat* v. *State of Haryana,* (1996) 4 CCR 75 (SC): 1996 (3) Crimes 238 (SC), where the name of the assailant was not stated by the injured/complainant to the doctor who examined him and gave treatment, the Apex Court drew the adverse inference that the accused was not the assailant and he was later on implicated in the crime. (Same view has been expressed by the Apex Court in *Rajeevan* v. *State of Kerala,* AIR 2003 SC 1813.)

19. Absence of Blood Stains on Weapons and Articles

In *Kallikatt Kunhu* v. *State of Kerala,* (2000) 1 SCR 1162, it was alleged that the appellant stabbed the deceased by a dagger which was found enclosed in a sheath near the basement of the *chappa* (Shed). However, no blood stains were found on the dagger. The Apex Court held this circumstance to be against the prosecution and conviction of the accused was set aside.

Where blood stained clothes and knife were recovered pursuant to the disclosure statement given by the accused but the said recovery was after the second remand of the appellant, the Apex Court disbelieved the said recovery; *Ashish Batham* v. *State of Madhya Pradesh,* AIR 2002 SC 3206.

Where the accused was tried for the offence of murder and blood stains were found on his *dhoti*, the Apex Court held that, *"this circumstance by itself is not sufficient to prove the offence. .... Accused being an agriculturist there is nothing unusual in finding blood stains on his dhoti;"* [*Pohalaya* v. *State of Maharashtra,* AIR 1979 SC 1949.]

Where no blood was found at the place of occurrence and where witnesses were allegedly lying at the time of occurrence, the Apex Court held this circumstance against the prosecution; [*State of Uttar Pradesh* v. *Motiram,* AIR 1990 SC 1709.]

20. Delay in Recording Statement of Eye Witness or Material Witnesses

Where there was delay of nine days in recording statement of injured witness and the explanation given for delay was not sufficient, it was held that involvement of some accused is doubtful; [*Bijoy Singh* v. *State of Bihar,* AIR 2002 SC 1949.]

In *Balkrushna* v. *State of Orissa,* AIR 1971 SC 804: 1971 Cri LJ 670, the Apex Court held that, *"unjustified and unexplained delay in recording statement of material eye witnesses is fatal to prosecution"*.

21. Failure to State Identity in F.I.R.

It has been held by the Apex Court in *Hari Nath* v. *State of Uttar Pradesh,* 1988 Cri LJ 422 (SC): AIR 1988 SC 345, that, failure to state identity of accused in F.I.R. raises reasonable doubt about the complicity of accused in crime.

22. Non-Holding of Test Identification Parade

In *Kanan* v. *State of Kerala,* 1979 Cri LJ 919: 1979 SCC (Cri) 621: (1979) 3 SCC 319, the Apex Court has held that, *"It is well-settled that where a witness identifies an accused who is not known to him in the Court for the first time, his evidence is absolutely valueless unless there has been a previous test identification parade to test his powers of observation. The idea of holding test identification parade under Section 9 of the Evidence Act is to test the veracity of the witness on the question of his capability to identify an unknown person whom the witness may have seen only once. If no test identification parade is held then it will be wholly unsafe to rely on his testimony regarding the identification of an accused for the first time in Court."*

In *State of Maharashtra* v. *Sukhdeo Singh,* (1992) 3 SCR 480 (*Indira Gandhi Assassination* case), the Apex Court has held that, *"In the absence of test identification parade it would be extremely risky to place implicit reliance on the identification made for the first time in Court after a long lapse of time and that too of persons who had changed their appearance."*

23. Non-Examination of Material Witnesses

It has been held by the Kerala High Court in *Raghava Karup* v. *The State of Kerala,* AIR 1965 Ker 44 (DB), that, *"if a material witness is kept back from the Court, it would certainly give rise to adverse inference under section 114(g) of the Evidence Act against the prosecution case and casts serious reflection on the fairness of the trial...... However the test to determine whether he is a material witness or not is whether his evidence is essential to the unfolding of the narrative on which the prosecution is based."*

24. Non-Examination of Informant

It has been held by the Apex Court in *Krishna Mochi* v. *State of Bihar,* AIR 2002 SC 1965, that, *"if the prosecution does not examine the informant, First Information Report is not admissible in evidence but it would not be also a ground of acquittal."*

25. Non-Explanation of Injuries on the Person of Accused by the Prosecution

In *Rajendra Singh* v. *State of Bihar,* (2000) 2 SCR 1073, the Apex Court has held that, *"though prosecution is not obliged to explain each and every injury on the accused, failure to explain grievous injury creates suspicion on the ground that true version is concealed by the prosecution."*

The same view has been taken by the Apex Court in *Dhananjay* v. *State of Maharashtra,* AIR 2002 SC 2787.

26. Non-Filing of Injury Report of Injured

In *Shankar Mahto* v. *State of Bihar,* (2002) 6 SCC 431, the Apex Court has held that, *"If the prosecution does not file injury report in respect of the injuries suffered by the eye witnesses in the incident, it could be a ground for raising doubt on the point of their receiving injuries, but not to discard their entire evidence."*

27. Relevancy of Deposition of Witnesses in Absence of Accused

As regards the admissibility of deposition of witnesses in absence of accused, the Apex Court in *Nirmal Singh* v. *State of Haryana,* (2000) 2 SCR 807, has held that *'Section 299 of Cr.P.C. consists of two parts. The first part speaks of the circumstances under which witnesses produced by the prosecution could be examined in the absence of the accused and the second part speaks of the circumstances, when such deposition can be given in evidence against the accused in any inquiry or trial for the offence with which he is charged. This procedure contemplated under section 299 of the Code is thus an exception to the principle embodied in section 33 of the Evidence Act in as much as under section 33 the evidence of a witness, which a party has no right or opportunity to cross examine is not legally admissible. Being an exception, it is necessary, therefore that all the conditions prescribed, must be strictly complied with. In other words, before recording the statement of the witnesses, produced by the prosecution the court must be satisfied that accused has absconded or that there is no immediate prospect of arresting him, as provided under first part of section 299(1) of the Cr.P.C. ...... On perusal of section 299 of Cr.P.C. as well as section 33 of the Evidence Act, it is evident that the pre-conditions in both the sections must be established by the prosecution and it is only then, the statements of witnesses recorded under section 299 of Cr.P.C. before the arrest of the accused can be utilised in evidence in trial after the arrest of such accused only if the persons are dead or would not be available or any other condition enumerated in the second part of section 299(1) of the Cr.P.C. is established.'*

28. Relevancy of Certain Evidence for Proving, in Subsequent Proceeding, the Truth of Facts therein Stated (Evidence Act, Section 33)

In this case, the first informant deposed before Magistrate when accused was being tried for offence under section 304A of IPC. Subsequently, charge was converted into section 304 Part II of IPC and case was committed to the Court of Sessions. The question arose before the High Court as to whether deposition of first informant is relevant in subsequent proceeding before the Court of Session. The honourable High Court held that ingredients of offence being different in both the proceedings, section 33 of the Evidence Act would not be invocable. The Court further observed that the important requirement for accepting the evidence from the earlier judicial proceeding in the later part of the proceedings or in subsequent judicial proceeding is that the question in issue must substantially be same in the first as in the second proceeding; *Salman Salim Khan* v. *State of Maharashtra*, 2016 ALL MR (Cri) 1.

29. Relevancy of Civil Court Decision in Criminal Proceedings (Evidence Act, Section 40 to 43)

In *K.G. Premshankar* v. *Inspector of Police*, 2003 (1) Mh LJ 1 (SC), the Apex Court held that *"if the criminal case and civil proceedings are for the same cause, judgment of Civil Court would be relevant if conditions of any of the sections 40 to 43 of the Evidence Act are satisfied."*

In *Syed Askari Hadi Ali Augustine Imam* v. *State (Delhi Administration)*, AIR 2009 SC 3232, the Apex Court held that to attract section 41, judgment has to be pronounced. Mere pendency of the two proceedings, whether civil or criminal, by itself would not attract the provisions of section 41. Judgment rendered by probate Court is judgment *in rem* and is binding on all Courts and authorities. Judgment *in rem* indisputably is conclusive in a criminal as well as in civil proceeding.

However, it should be remembered that finding of Civil Court cannot be mechanically followed in criminal proceedings as has been held by the Bombay High Court in *Sulabha Pradip Vasa* v. *Pradip P. Vasa*, 2000 (2) Mh LJ 262.

30. Relevancy of Character (Evidence Act, Sections 53, 53A, 54, 55)

In this case, the Apex Court held that the evidence of general reputation and general disposition is relevant under section 53 and explanation to section 55 of the Evidence Act in a criminal proceeding. But in any case, the character evidence is a very weak evidence and it cannot outweigh the positive evidence in regard to the guilt of a person. However, it may be useful in doubtful cases to tilt the balance in favour of the accused or it may also afford a background for appreciating his reactions in a given situation; *Sardar Sardul Singh Caveeshar* v. *State of Maharashtra*, (1964) 2 SCR 378.

In the trial of abetment to suicide of first wife, second wife deposed that accused-husband had tendency of ill-treating. However, defence did not lead any evidence as to good character of the accused. The Court held that there is no occasion for the prosecution to tender any evidence on tendency of ill-treating wives. Therefore, evidence of second wife is not relevant and cannot be considered; *Sambhaji S. Rupnavar* v. *State of Maharashtra*, 2013 All MR (Cri) 507.

In a case under TADA Act, 1985, there was no evidence to show that the appellant had ever acted in any manner indicating that he was indulging in terrorist or disruptive activity. He is also not a previous convict. The prosecution case vested entirely on the presumption under section 5 of the Act. The appellant adduced positive evidence to show that his antecedents are good enough and he bears a good moral character. The honourable Apex Court held that positive evidence led by the appellant regarding his good moral character is relevant and admissible in evidence and his evidence probabilises the plea of defence and is enough to rebut the presumption under section 5 of the Act; *Mohan Singh* v. *State of Haryana*, 1995(2) SCR 610.

31. Relevancy of Abscondance

In this case, the Apex Court held that the act of absconding is no doubt a relevant piece of evidence which should be considered along with other evidence, but its value would always depend on the circumstances of each case; *Matru @ Girish Chandra* v. *State of Uttar Pradesh*, AIR 1971 SC 1050: (1971) 3 SCR 914: 1971 Cri LJ 913 (SC).

32. Relevancy of Common Intention

In this case, the Apex Court held that common intention to commit a criminal act has relevance only to offence and not to right of private defence. The Court further held that persons exercising right of private defence cannot be convicted with the help of section 34, IPC; *Subramani* v. *State of Tamil Nadu*, AIR 2002 SC 2980: 2002 AIR SCW 3488: 2002 All MR (Cri) 2250 (SC).

CHAPTER XXIX

TRIALS BEFORE MOFUSSIL COURT (MAGISTRATE'S COURT)

SYNOPSIS

(A) Certain Trials of Warrant Cases Instituted on Police Report (Warrant Trials)

(i) Arms Act, 1959

This was a case [*Sahib Singh* v. *State of Punjab*, (1996) Supp 6 SCR 245] under TADA and Arms Act where the appellant was convicted and sentenced under section 25 of the Arms Act, 1959 and section 5 of the TADA Act, 1987. According to the prosecution, the appellant was apprehended on suspicion and on search by police officers a revolver with six live cartridges were recovered from the bag the appellant was holding in his right hand. Allowing the appeal, the Apex Court held that, "*Before conducting a search the concerned police officer is required to call upon some independent and respectable people of the locality to witness the search. In a given case it may so happen that no such person is available or, even if available, is not willing to be a party to such search. It may also be that after joining the search, such persons later on turn hostile. In any of these eventualities the evidence of the police officers who conducted the search cannot be disbelieved solely on the ground that no independent and respectable witness was examined to prove the search but if it is found – as in the present case – that no attempt was even made by he concerned police officer to join with him some persons of the locality who were admittedly available to witness the recovery, it would affect the weight of evidence of the police officer, though not its admissibility. The arms and ammunitions allegedly recovered from the appellant and seized were not packeted and sealed. There was no evidence to indicate with whom the revolver was after its seizure till it was sent to the Arms Expert for testing. This missing link also weakens the prosecution case. For all these infirmities the appellant is entitled to benefit of reasonable doubt."*

In this case, appellant-accused allegedly injured four persons by a single gunshot, resulting in death of one of them. It is the prosecution version that appellant-accused had used 315 bore rifle, owned by his father. Appellant was charged and tried for the offence punishable under section 27 of using the said firearm. However the High Court convicted the appellant under section 25 of the Act. In appeal, the Apex Court held that appellant could not have been convicted and punished by the High Court for committing offence under section 25. The High Court clearly erred while convicting appellant under section 25 without caring to go through the provisions of the Act; *Mahendra Pratap Singh* v. *State of Uttar Pradesh,* (2009) 11 SCC 334.

In this case, Apex Court held that for inviting conviction under section 27, it has to be proved that firearm was used in contravention of section 5 or 7 of the Act. In the instant case, since it was a licenced gun, there was no question of section 7 coming within mischief of section 5(1). Therefore appellant is liable to be acquitted under section section 27 of the Act; *Deomuni Sharma* v. *State of Jharkhand,* (2009) 10 SCC 80.

Other Cases on Arms Act, 1959

1. *Kamal Singh Mata Singh* v. *State of Maharashtra,* 2005 (1) Mh LJ 218: The Bombay High Court quashed and set aside the conviction as there was no sanction from District Magistrate. The Bombay High Court ruled that, *"For prosecution of accused for offence under section 3 of the Arms Act, previous sanction of District Magistrate is necessary."*

2. *Nanhey* v. *State of Uttar Pradesh,* 1978 Cri LJ 1001 (All): It has been held by the Allahabad that, *"Where the District Magistrate gave the sanction without considering the evidence, such a sanction is no sanction in the eyes of law and the prosecution based upon such sanction is not in accordance with law and therefore accused is entitled to acquittal."*

3. *Amarjit Singh* v. *State of Punjab,* (1995) 3 SCC 217: The Apex Court has held that, *"Non-sealing of the revolver at the spot is a serious infirmity because the possibility of tampering with the weapon cannot be ruled out."*

4. *Gyasudding Khan* v. *State of Bihar,* AIR 2004 SC 210: The Apex Court set aside the conviction on the ground that there was no evidence on record to show that stengun and SLR used, answers the description of "Prohibited Arms" within the meaning of section 2(1)(i) of the Arms Act and that there was no discussion regarding this aspect by the trial Court.

5. *Subhash Ramkumar Bind* alia *Vakil* v. *State of Maharashtra,* 2003 All MR (Cri) 188 (SC): The Apex Court held that, *"Arm can be prohibited only by notification and*

not by administrative instruction. This requirement is sacrosanct and since the issue shall have to be dealt with utmost care and caution, without the issuance of a notification question of a conviction under section 27(3) of the Arms Act would not arise."

6. *Jagjit Singh* v. *State of Punjab,* (1994) 4 SCC 726: In this case the accused was charged under section 3(1) of the TADA Act 1987. As regards the proof for offence under section 3(1) of the Act, the Apex Court held that, *"Mere finding of articles described as pistol and cartridges is not sufficient .... Prosecution must prove that the article in question was in working order and not a toy gun or the like and the cartridges were in fact live cartridges. This can be proved by evidence of ballistic expert or even by a police personnel who has tested the same."*

7. *Basant Raj* v. *State of Rajasthan,* 1994 Cri LJ 2137: Where the accused merely carried revolver in pocket of his pant but did not use it, it was held that accused cannot be convicted under section 27 of the Arms Act.

8. *Salim Akhtar* alias *Mota* v. *State of Uttar Pradesh,* 2003 All MR (Cri) 1167 (SC): The Apex Court held that where the pistol was recovered from the appellant was not sealed on the spot and neither its number nor make noted in recovery memo, it raises considerable doubt about factum of recovery.

(ii) Explosive Substances Act, 1908

In this case, the Apex Court held that where the Central Government has delegated its powers to grant consent to District Magistrate, the State Government cannot further delegate it to Additional District Magistrate. Moreover, power which has been delegated to District Magistrate cannot be exercised by Additional District Magistrate simply because he is invested with all powers of District Magistrate. The Apex Court further held that explosive substances as defined in section 5 of the TADA Act, 1987 cannot be given the same meaning as under the Explosive Substances Act (6 of 1908). It must be complete article or device capable of exploding. Empty cells or parts for making bomb are not covered under the meaning of "Explosive Substances". However gelatine sticks are explosive substances; *State of Madhya Pradesh* v. *Bhupendra Singh,* AIR 2000 SC 679.

In this case, accused was prosecuted for possessing explosives. It was alleged by the prosecution that the accused illegally possessed explosives and had sustained injuries on account of blast of explosive substance. The Court acquitted him by giving benefit of doubt as there was no proof that accused was in possession or actual control of explosives. The Court held that merely because accused had sustained injuries on account of blast of explosive substance, it cannot be concluded that he was in actual possession of said explosive substance; *Sikandar Axamani* v. *State of Goa,* 2014 All MR (Cri) 1728.

(iii) Cases of Hurt, Grievous Hurt and Assault (I.P.C., Sections 319, 324, 325, 326)

(a) Hurt (Section 319 IPC)

In this case, at night accused uttered a piercing shout and pointed a pistol towards the victim. Due to this she collapsed for nervous shock and was seriously ill for some time. The Court held that accused is guilty for causing hurt to her as it is an infirmity within the meaning of section 319 particularly when it caused temporary mental impairment or hysteria or terror; *Jashanmal Jhamatmal* v. *Brahmanand Sarupanand,* AIR 1944 Sind 19.

In this case, accused used to make telephone calls to victim at night. When women picked up the receiver, he would normally remain silent. Occasionally he indulged in heavy breathing. This resulted in neurotic disorders by the complainants. The Court held accused guilty for causing bodily injury to victims; *R.* v. *Ireland* v. *Burstow,* (1997) 4 All ER 225 (HL).

In this case, appellant punched a woman in the face while she was holding her 12 month-old child, due to which the child fell, hitting his head on the floor. The Court held him guilty for causing hurt to a child and dismissed the appeal. The Court held that in case of assault and battery, direct physical contact of the assailant with the victim is not required. But in this case, the movement by which the woman had lost hold of the child was entirely and immediately the result of appellant's action to punching her; *Haystead* v. *Chief Constable of Derbyshire,* (2000) 3 All ER 890 (QBD).

(b) Grievous Hurt (Section 324, 325, 326 IPC)

In this case, the Apex Court held that expression *"any instrument which, used as a weapon of offence, is likely to cause death"* should be construed with reference to the nature of the instrument and not the manner of its use. In other words, it means a dangerous weapon. In absence of pleading before trial Court about the weapon not being dangerous weapon, nature of charge held by courts below cannot be interfered with; *Nanda Gopalan* v. *State of Kerala,* 2015 (3) Crimes 55 (SC).

This was a case of assault where it was alleged that grievous hurt was caused by sticks. However there was no evidence on record to show that the sticks used were of a lethal type and something like a sharp blade or sharp point were attached to them. The Bombay High Court held that some evidence is necessary to prove that the sticks were of a lethal type and something like a sharp blade or sharp point were attached to them to prove that stick was an instrument which, used as a weapon of offence, is likely to cause death; *Jagannath* v. *State of Maharashtra,*1994 Mh LJ 1857.

In this case, grievous injury caused was the facture of base of second metacarpal bone of left hand and it was alleged that injury was caused when petitioners were quarrelling with brother of complainant and when complainant arrived and intervened. On the evidence on record, petitioners were convicted under section 325/34, IPC and were sentenced to six months imprisonment. Sessions Court in appeal upheld conviction but modified sentence to three months imprisonment with fine. In revision, the High Court convicted the petitioners under section 335/34, IPC and sentence reduced to period already undergone which was 14 days with fine by holding that petitioners could not be said to have caused grievous injury voluntarily but it was caused on provocation given by complainant; *Ghasiram* v. *State of Chhattisgarh,* 2011 (3) Crimes 672 (Chhatt).

In this case, injury sustained by the complainant was incised wound with slightly ragged margin of 2" x 1/8" x 1/8" vertically placed on 4" above the left eye. It was alleged by prosecution that said injury was caused by sharp cutting weapon. As to the nature of injury, the Court held that it cannot be termed as grievous in absence of further evidence to show that it had put injured to 20 or more days of severe pain or that on account of it he was unable to pursue his ordinary work; *Sapneswar Naik* v. *State of Orissa*, 1994 Cr LJ 204 (NOC) (Orissa).

Other Cases on Hurt, Grievous Hurt and Assault

1. *Parvesh* v. *State of Uttar Pradesh*, 1982 Cri LJ 1821 (1828) (All): It was held by the Allahabad High Court that, *"when the occurrence took place about 8 years ago, and the victim did not receive any visible injury from the slaps, conviction under section 323, I.P.C. was not justified."*

2. *State of Uttar Pradesh* v. *Nathu*, 2002 (8) JT 223: The Apex Court has held that, *"Non explanation of injuries by the prosecution suffered by the accused in the incident shows that certain facts have been suppressed. This makes the proseuction story doubtful and accused cannot be convicted under section 323, I.P.C."*

3. *Chhabilal C. Pardhi* v. *State of Maharashtra*, 2005 (1) Mh LJ 376 (Bom): The case of the prosecution was that the injuries were caused by means of a stick. However the prosecution did not produce the weapon used in the commission of the offence before the trial Court. Also there was no evidence on record whether the weapon used by the applicants/accused was a weapon which can be used for shooting, stabbing etc., which if used as a weapon of offence, is likely to caused death. In such circumstances the Bombay High Court set aside the conviction.

4. *Pradeep Krishna Mashelkar* v. *State*, 2005 All MR (Cri) 3038 (Bombay High Court, Panji Bench): In this case injuries were caused due to sulphuric acid. According to medical evidence injuries were superficial in nature. The Court held that, *"Each and every scar whether permanent or not cannot amount to disfigurement of face. It is the Court that must decide whether injury is simple or grievous and medical evidence will only describe the facts and not classify the hurt. As the witness/injured was in hospital for five days, his case was not covered either by clauses sixthly or eighthly of section 320, I.P.C. and hence conviction under section 326 had to be scaled down to section 324, I.P.C."*

5. *Ram Singh* v. *State of Haryana*, 1998 All MR (Cri.) 1081 (SC): In this case accused was tried for the offence punishable under sections 324, 325, I.P.C. It was alleged that the accused caused grievous hurt to the complainant. However, eye witness vaguely stated of accused assaulting victim but did not explain as to how the incident started or how injuries were caused. No injury by sharp-edged weapon was found on the person of victim. The Apex Court set aside the conviction holding that false implication of accused is probable on the particular facts and circumstances of the case.

6. *State of Madhya Pradesh* v. *Pillu*, 1983 (1) Crimes 621 (MP): It has been held by the Court that medical evidence is not necessary for proving offence of causing hurt under section 323 of I.P.C.

7. *Abani K. Debnath* v. *State of Tripura,* AIR 2006 SC 518: Where simple hurt was caused by bamboo stick and doctor also opined that all injuries are simple in nature, conviction is justified under section 323, I.P.C.

8. *D. Challaiah* v. *State of Andhra Pradesh,* AIR 1978 SC 1441: Where the assault on the public servant was the sequel of a private quarrel which took place between the complainant and the accused on the preceding day when the complainant was returning from the office, had no real nexus or casual connection or consequential relation with the performance of his duty as a public servant, and there was not even a scintilla of evidence from which it could be reasonably inferred that the intent of the accused assailant was to prevent or deter the complainant from the discharge of his duty as such public servant, the offence of the accused did not fall under section 332 but under section 323, I.P.C.

9. *Jagdish Prasad* v. *State,* AIR 1979 SC 1510: 1979 Cri LJ 1125: The Apex Court has held that unless there is a finding recorded by the Court that the injury has been caused by a dangerous weapon of the nature specified in section 324, conviction under this section cannot be recorded. The Court further held that where there was no eye witness to prove that the accused had inflicted any knife blow on deceased, the knife which was snatched from the accused did not contain any blood stains, circumstances proved in the case were incompatible with the innocence of the accused, the accused was acquitted of the charge under section 324.

10. *Mustafa Sheikh* v. *Lalchand Sheikh,* 1985 Cri LJ 1183 (Cal) (DB): Where the incised wound did not cause fracture nor cause severe bodily pain for a period of 20 days and the hurt was not grievous, the accused was convicted under section 324, I.P.C. and not under section 326, I.P.C.

11. *Dalapati Majhi* v. *State,* 1982 Cri LJ (NOC) 134 Orissa: Where the accused dragged the victim as a result of which victim fell down and received grievous hurt, the accused did not intend to cause grievous hurt or did an act with the knowledge that his act was likely to cause hurt or grievous hurt, the victim received grievous hurt by fall, then the accused could not be convicted under section 325, I.P.C.

12. *Sheelam Prabhakar* v. *State of Andhra Pradesh,* 2005 (3) Crimes 400: In this case appellant No. 2 was convicted for the offence punishable under section 326 read with 34 I.P.C. It was alleged that deceased was attacked by appellant No. 1 with an iron double on head which resulted in death of deceased. However evidence was laid that appellant caught hold of deceased when appellant No. 2 attacked her. The Court held this part of evidence to be an improvement during trial and benefit of doubt was given to appellant.

Anwar-Ul-Haq v. *State of Uttar Pradesh,* 2005 All MR (Cri) 2253 (SC): Expression *"an instrument, which used as a weapon of offence, is likely to cause death"* in section 324, IPC when read in the light of marginal note to section 324 means dangerous weapon which if used by the offender is likely to cause death.

Sreekumar v. *State of Kerala,* 2010 (1) Crimes 484 (Ker): Expression *"is likely to cause death"* in section 326, IPC is attributable to instrument which is used as weapon of offence and not to grievous hurt.

(iv) Cruelty (I.P.C., 498A)

In this case, Apex Court held that for the purpose of section 498A, harassment simpliciter is not cruelty. It is only when harassment is committed for the purpose of coercing a women or any other person related to her to meet an unlawful demand for property etc., that it amounts to cruelty punishable under section 498A; *State of Andhra Pradesh* v. *M. Madhusudhan Rao,* 2009 All MR (Cri) 547 (SC): 2009 ACR 118: 2009 (2) CRJ 517 (SC).

In this case, question arose as to whether a girl friend or a concubine can be regarded as relative of the accused. The Apex Court held that a girl friend or even a concubine would not be a relative of the accused within the meaning of section 498A. The word 'relative' brings within its preview a status and such a status must be conferred either by blood or marriage or adoption. However, if the woman concerned is regarded as wife and not as a mere mistress, she can be considered to be a wife and consequently as the relative of the husband. Proof of a legal marriage in the rigid sense is unnecessary for establishing an offence under section 498A, IPC; *U. Suvetha* v. *State,* 2009 (2) Crimes 357 (SC): 2009 (6) CRJ 209 (SC).

In this case, the Apex Court laid down the law regarding the applicability of the provisions of section 498A. The Apex Court held that for the provisions of section 498A to be applicable, consequences of cruelty which are likely to drive a woman to commit suicide or to cause grave injury or danger to life, limb or health, whether mental or physical of the woman are required to be established by the prosecution; *Rajendran* v. *State,* 2009 (1) Crimes 135 (SC).

In this case [*Giridhar Shankar Tawade* v. *State of Maharashtra,* (2002) 5 SCC 177: 2002 (4) Mh LJ 5 (SC)], the Apex Court laid down the law as regards what constitutes cruelty. In this case it was alleged that married woman succumbed to burn injuries in her nuptial home due to harassment which was in connection with demand for dowry. However there was absence of evidence regarding *"grave injury or danger to life, limb or health"* of the woman as contemplated under clause (a) of the explanation to section 498A. Therefore *Explanation (a)* is not attracted. Further the Court held that in absence of evidence regarding demand for dowry, harassment by itself would not constitute cruelty within the meaning *Explanation (b)* to section 498 A. The accused was acquitted as cruelty was not made out.

Recently, the Apex Court felt the need for serious re-look at entire provision by Parliament. The Apex Court held that it is the social responsibility and obligation of Bar and Bench to maintain social fibre of family life. Genuine cases of dowry harassment are a matter of serious concern but exaggerated version of small incidents should not be reflected in the criminal complaint. The Court further held that allegations should be scrutinised with great care and circumspection, especially against husband's relatives who were living in different cities and never visited or rarely visited the matrimonial home of the complainant; *Preeti Gupta* v. *State of Jharkhand,* AIR 2010 SC 3363: (2010) 7 SCC 667.

Other Cases on Cruelty (I.P.C., 498A)

1. *Ravindra Pyarelal Bidlan* v. *State of Maharashtra,* 1993 Cri LJ 3019 (Bom): The Bombay High Court has held that, *"Mere harassment or mere demand for property, etc., is not cruelty within the meaning of Explanation (b) of section 498A, I.P.C...... Reasonable nexus between cruelty and suicide must be established by the prosecution. Mere proof of cruelty or suicide is not enough."*

2. *Tapan Pal* v. *State of West Bengal,* 1992 Cri LJ 1017 (Cal): Where the deceased was asked to part with her jewellery and valuables for marriage of her sister-in-law and matter was not pressed further on her refusal and further there was no harassment or coercion by her in-laws, it was held that it does not amount to cruelty.

3. *Bhagwan* v. *State of Maharashtra,* 2000 (4) Mh LJ 410: The Bombay High Court has held that, *"Mere harassment does not amount to cruelty....... It must further be established that the beating or harassment was with a view to force the wife to commit suicide."*

Ganpat D. Garje v. *State of Maharashtra,* 2012 All MR (Cri) 1255: In this case, quarrels and incidents of ill-treatment suffered by victim from accused persons were on account of victim's desire to stay separately from joint family. The Court held that this does not constitute wilful conduct of accused persons which was likely to drive victim to commit suicide.

Laxman Ram Mane v. *State of Maharashtra,* 2011 All SCR 550: The Apex Court held that an illicit relationship of a married man with another woman would clearly amount to cruelty. Even assuming that it does not amount to cruelty, it could still be used as a piece of evidence of harassment and misbehaviour of the appellant towards the deceased.

K.R. Soorachari v. *State of Karnataka,* 2005 (3) B Cr C 419 (SC): Where evidence on record disclosed that appellant-husband of deceased was suspecting chastity and this was the cause for alleged harassment, it was held that appellant is not guilty of offence under section 498 A of IPC.

State of Maharashtra v. *Ibrahim K. Kazi,* 2003 All MR (Cri) 1259: In this case, the Court held that mere demand of Rs. 10,000 by accused for starting business unrelated to alleged beating and denial of food to wife does not attract section 498A.

(v) Forgery

In this case, Dr. Vimla purchased a car in the name of her minor daughter Nalini aged about 6 months. The price of the car was paid by her. The transfer of the car was notified in the name of Nalini to the Motor Registration Authority. The insurance policy already issued was transferred in the name of Nalini after the proposal form was signed by Dr. Vimla. Subsequently, Dr. Vimla filed two claims on the ground that the car met with accident. She signed the claim forms as Nalini. She also signed the receipts acknowledging the payment of compensation money as Nalini. Dr. Vimla and her husband were prosecuted under sections 120B, 419, 467 and 468 of the IPC. Both the accused were acquitted by the Sessions Judge. The State went in appeal and the High Court convicted Dr. Vimla under sections 467 and 468 of the IPC. Dr. Vimla filed special leave before the Apex Court. In appeal, the Apex Court held that the appellant was not guilty of the offence under sections 467 and 468 of the IPC. She was certainly guilty of deceit because though her name was Vimla, she signed in all the relevant papers as Nalini and made the Insurance Company believe that her name was Nalini, but the said deceit did not either secure to her advantage or cause any non-economic loss or injury to the Insurance Company. The charge did not disclose any such advantage or injury nor was there any evidence to prove the same. The entire transaction was that of Dr. Vimla and it was only put through in the name of her minor daughter. Nalini was in fact either a *Benamidar* for Dr. Vimla or her name was used for luck or other sentimental considerations. The Insurance Company would not have acted differently even if the car stood in the name of Dr. Vimla. The Apex Court further held that the definition of 'false document' is a part of the definition of 'forgery' and both must be read together. The expression 'fraud' involves two elements, deceit and injury to the person deceived. Injury is something other than economic loss, that is, deprivation of property, whether movable or immovable or of money and it will include any harm whatever cause to any person in body, mind, reputation or such others. A benefit or advantage to the deceiver, will almost always cause loss or detriment to the deceived. Even in those rare cases where there is a benefit or advantage to the deceiver, but no corresponding loss to the deceived, the second condition is satisfied (*i.e.*, making of such a document with an intention to commit fraud or that fraud may be committed); *Dr. Vimla* v. *Delhi Administration*, (1963) Supp 2 SCR 585.

In this case, the first appellant was tried for the offence of forging a valuable security punishable under section 467 of I.P.C. and for the offence of falsely personating another and presenting a document for registration punishable under section 82(c) of the Indian Registration Act, 1908. The second appellant was charged with abetment of these offences. The offence under the Indian Penal Code was tried with a jury and the offence under the Indian Registration Act was tried without a jury. The jury by a majority of 4 to 3 returned a verdict of guilty. The trial Judge rejected the verdict on the ground that there was *"absolutely no reliable evidence"* and referred the case to the High Court under section 307, Cr.P.C. (old Code of 1898). The trial judge also acquitted the accused of the offence under the Registration Act. No appeal was preferred against the order of acquittal. The High Court came to the conclusion that there was sufficient evidence to establish against the appellants the offence under the Penal Code. It was contended on behalf of the appellants that the trial Court having acquitted the appellants of the offence under the Indian Registration Act and no appeal having been preferred against the order, it was not competent to the High Court to rely on the evidence tendered to prove the offence under section 82 of the Registration Act for the purpose of convicting the appellants of the offence under the Indian Penal Code. Dismissing the appeal, the *Constitution Bench* of the Apex Court held, *"that an item of evidence may corroborate charges for more offences than one, and acquittal of the accused for one such offence will not render that item of evidence inadmissible in assessing the criminality of the accused for another offence corroborated thereby. The question in such a case is not one of admissibility but of weight to be given to that evidence"; Sekendar Sheikh* v. *State of West Bengal*, (1964) 1 SCR 852.

In this case, the Apex Court held that mere alteration of document does not make it a forged document. Alteration must be for some gain or for some objective; *Parminder Kaur* v. *State of Uttar Pradesh*, AIR 2010 SC 840.

(vi) Cheating

In this case, the Apex Court held that there has to be a dishonest intention from the very beginning which is *sine qua non* to hold accused guilty for commission of offence of cheating; *Joseph Salvaraj* v. *State of Gujarat*, 2011 All SCR 1601.

This was a case where the petitioner, a member of forward community filed a complaint in the Court against the respondents for offences under sections 415, 419, 420 read with section 34, I.P.C. It was alleged that he was induced to marry respondent No. 4 on the misrepresentation that the respondents belonged to forward community and on this misrepresentation he married respondent No. 4; and had he known that the respondents were members of Scheduled Tribe, which fact, it was alleged, came to his notice after the marriage, he would not have married respondent No. 4. During the investigation the respondents filed a petition under section 482, Cr.P.C. The High Court quashed the proceedings principally on the ground that section 415, I.P.C. relates to property, which, in the instant case was not involved, and, therefore, the F.I.R. was liable to be quashed. Aggrieved, the petitioner filed the present petition for special leave to appeal. The Apex Court while dismissing the petition, held that, *"The High Court was not correct in its interpretation of provisions contained under section 415, I.P.C. While the first part of the definition of 'cheating' relates to property; the second part need not necessarily related to property and speaks of deception which must be intended not only to do or omit to do something but also to cause damage or harm to complainant in body, mind, reputation or property. Thus, so far as the second part of section 415 is concerned, it is the doing of an act or omission to do an act by the complainant as a result of intentional inducement by the accused, which is material. Such inducement should result in the doing of an act or omission to do an act as a result of which the person concerned should have suffered or was likely to suffer damage or harm in body, mind, reputation or property. That is to say, in the first part, inducement must be dishonest or fraudulent. In the second part, the inducement should be intentional."* The Apex Court further observed that, *"the petitioner himself is a Scientist at the Centre for DNA Finger Printing and Diagnostics, Hyderabad which is a prestigious Institution of the Country. In this capacity, he can reasonably presumed to be aware of the bio-diversity at the Cellular and Molecular level amongst human beings without the 'caste' having any role in the field of Human Biotechnology"; G.V. Rao* v. *L.H.V. Prasad*, (2000) 2 SCR 123: AIR 2000 SC 2474.

In *M/s. Medchl Chemicals and Pharma Pvt. Ltd.* v. *M/s. Biological E. Ltd.*, (2000) 1 SCR 1169, the Apex Court held that, *"In order to attract the provisions of sections 418 and 420, I.P.C., the guilty intent at the time of making the promise is a requirement and an essential ingredient thereto and subsequent failure to fulfil the promise by itself would not attract the provisions of sections 418 or 420.* Mens rea *is one of the essential ingredients of the offence of cheating under section 420."*

The brief facts of the case [*State of Madhya Pradesh* v. *Mir Basit Ali Khan*, (1971) Supp SCR 125] were that the respondents organised a money circulation scheme and for alleged cheating and misrepresentation in connection therewith they were convicted by the Sessions Judge, Bhopal under section 120B and section 420 of I.P.C.. The High Court however acquitted them. The State of Madhya Pradesh by special leave appealed to the Supreme Court. Dismissing the appeal, the three Judge Bench of the Apex Court held that, " .... *there was an element of speculation in money circulation schemes, but those who ran them could not be held guilty of cheating unless there was misrepresentation or dishonest concealment of facts. It could not be said in the present case that the respondents had deceived the public and thereby induced it to contribute money to the scheme.*"

In this case, accused obtained advance loan against stock in trade of business by representing that business in question was free from all encumbrances. Later it was found that property in question was encumbered property. He was convicted by the lower Court. In appeal, while setting aside conviction, the Apex Court held that a mere representation which is neither claimed nor alleged to be dishonest or fraudulent, does not attract the charge of cheating only because the complainant parts with his money on the basis thereof; *Abdul Fazal Siddiqui* v. *Fatehchand Hirawat*, (1996) Supp 4 SCR 807.

The Apex Court in *Hridaya Rangan* v. *State of Bihar*, (2000) 2 SCR 859, has explained the distinction between mere breach of contract and the offence of cheating as under: "*the distinction between mere breach of contract and the offence of cheating is a fine one. It depends upon the intention of the accused at the time of inducement which may be judged by his subsequent conduct. But the subsequent conduct is not the sole test. Mere breach of contract cannot give rise to criminal prosecution for cheating unless fraudulent of dishonest intention is shown at the time when the offence is said to have been committed.*"

This is one of the classic examples of corporate fraud where within 9 months of the huge investment made in Iridium, it applied for bankruptcy protection under chapter 11 of the U.S. Bankruptcy Code and later Iridium was sold for a paltry sum of U.S. $ 25 Million. In this case, original complainant/appellant filed complaint case before Judicial Magistrate. He issued process. This order was challenged before High Court who quashed the said complaint. In appeal, the Apex Court held that corporate houses and companies can no longer claim immunity from criminal prosecution on ground that they are incapable of possessing necessary *mens rea*. *Mens rea* is attributed to Corporations on principle of *alter ego* of company. .... Complainant must prove that inducement has been caused by deception exercised by accused. Deception is necessary ingredient under sections 415, 420/120B. Non-disclosure of relevant information would also be treated as a misrepresentation of facts leading to deception. The Court further held that where prospectus invited investments for large and successful companies and misleading statements were made withholding vital facts causing wrongful damage to investors, it amount to cheating; *Iridium India Telecom Ltd.* v. *Motorola Incorporated.*, AIR 2011 SC 20: 2011 All MR (Cri) 989 (SC).

In this case, FIR was registered against the accused under sections 420, 506, IPC. It is the case of complainant that accused persons even after accepting substantial amount denied execution of sale deed and thereby cheated him. The investigation officer in his affidavit stated that not only accused person denied execution of sale deed but also hurled abuses and threatened complainant of dire consequences. The Apex Court held that prosecution cannot be quashed only on ground that dispute between parties is property dispute; *Kamlesh Kumari* v. *State of Uttar Pradesh,* 2015 All MR (Cri) 3295 (SC).

(vii) Criminal Breach of Trust and Misappropriation

While explaining the requirements of law regarding section 409, the Apex Court held that an act of breach of trust simpliciter involves a civil wrong of which the person wronged may seek his redress for damages in a civil Court but a breach of trust with *mens rea* gives rise to a criminal prosecution as well. The element of dishonest intention is therefore an essential element to constitute the offence of criminal breach of trust. The Court further held that it is for the same reason, the submission that as nobody ultimately suffered any loss, an offence under section 409 of the IPC was not made out, cannot be accepted. A Bank or Financial Institution may not suffer ultimate loss but if the money has been allowed to be used by another person illegally for illegal purposes, the ingredients of section 405 of the IPC would get attracted. A case involving temporary embezzlement also attracts the ingredients of section 405 of the IPC...... When a person allows others to misappropriate the property entrusted to him, that also amounts to criminal breach of trust; *R. Venkatakrishnan* v. *C.B.I.,* 2010 All SCR 15.

In this case [*Anil Saran* v. *State of Bihar,* (1995) Supp 3 SCR 58] a partnership firm, consisting of three partners viz. the appellant, the second respondent and one A, entered into an agreement with the first accused for exhibition of a film owned by the firm. Under the terms of agreement, the film along with the sale proceeds was to be returned after exhibition. On failure of the first accused to do so, the second respondent filed a complaint before the Chief Judicial Magistrate, Patna that the first accused in collusion with the appellant and the first partner of the firm stealthily and illegally misappropriated the collections and dishonestly made wrongful gain for themselves and caused wrongful loss to the complainant and the partnership firm. The Chief Judicial Magistrate examined the complainant and transferred the case to Judicial Magistrate-II who examined the witnesses and issued process under sections 406 and 420 of I.P.C.. The appellant's application under section 482 of Cr.P.C. was dismissed by the High Court on the ground that the complaint prima facie disclosed commission of the alleged offences. Dismissing the appeal, the Apex Court held that, *"partnership firm is not a legal entity but a legal mode of doing business by all the partners. Until the firm is dissolved as per law and the accounts settled, all the partners have dominion in common over the property and funds of the firm. Only after the settlement of the accounts and allotment of respective share, the partner becomes owner of his share. However, criminal breach of trust under section 406 of I.P.C. is not in respect of the property belonging to the partnership firm, but is an offence committed by a person in respect of the property which has been specially entrusted to such a person under a special contract and he holds that property in fiduciary capacity under special contract. If he misappropriates the same, it is an offence. In the instant case, it is not the case of the complainant that the appellant and the other accused were entrusted with dominion of the property of the firm in their capacity as partners of the complainant firm. Under these circumstances, it cannot be said that the imputations alleged against the appellants have been done in his capacity as a partner of the firm. Whether the offence has been made out, whether he is liable and what are the defences open to him are not matters at this stage for consideration. It is for the Magistrate to proceed with the trial and to deal with according to law."*

In this case [*Jiwan Das* v. *State of Haryana*, (1999) 1 SCR 922] according to the prosecution, *J* and *M*, employees of Government Heat Treatment Centre, were authorised to bring a certain quantity of light diesel oil from Indian Oil Corporation (IOC). For that purpose a bank draft and an authority letter were given to *J* which were deposited in the IOC office. *M* took delivery of the diesel oil and in token they had not only signed on the cash memo but also on the register itself. Senior Technical Officer, Government Heat Treatment Centre and Depot Manager, IOC in their oral evidence, confirmed that *M* took delivery of the diesel oil. However, on actual measurement the diesel oil was found to be deficient by 4300 litres. Subsequently, *J* give an undertaking that he would make up the deficiency. Disposing of the appeals, the Apex Court held that, *"To bring home a charge under section 409 of I.P.C., what is necessary to be proved is that the accused is a public servant and in such capacity he was entrusted with the property in question or with dominion over it and that he committed criminal breach of trust in respect of it. The prosecution must strictly prove the necessary elements constituted in the offence. It is true that prosecution need not prove the actual mode of misappropriation and once entrustment of or dominion over the property is established, then it would be for the accused to explain as to how the property was dealt with. .... Mere fact was that* J *was given the bank draft and authority letter to take delivery of diesel oil does not amount to entrustment of diesel oil to* J *or that he had dominion over the same. Even the subsequent undertaking given by* J *to make up the deficiency cannot amount to a confession or admission of guilt on the part of* J *. Hence, conviction of* J *under section 409, I.P.C. cannot be sustained. However, in view of oral and documentary evidence* M *is rightly held to be guilty of embezzlement of 4300 litres of diesel oil. Therefore, his conviction under section 409, I.P.C is upheld."*

In this case [*Cheekolu Nagaiah* v. *State of Andhra Pradesh*, 2005 All MR (Cri) Journal 189 (AP)] accused was acting as an agent of M/s. Tamilnadu Enterprises, who introduce the money circulation scheme. The accused allegedly collected money and sent to M/s. Tamilnadu Enterprises and the complainant was given a gift as per the scheme. The complainant filed a private complaint before the Court of Judicial Magistrate under sections 406, 409, 418, 419 and 420 of I.P.C. The accused filed a petition under section 482, Cr.P.C. before the High Court for quashing the complaint. While allowing the petition and dismissing the complaint, the Andhra Pradesh High Court held that, *"If members enrolled by complainant did not receive gifts as per scheme, accused cannot be said to have caused damage or harm to property of complainant...... The complaint does not fall within the definition of 'cheating' as contained in section 415 of I.P.C."*

The facts of the case are: the appellant was the Chairman of an autonomous co-operative society under the control and supervision of the State Government.

On receipt of complaints about the financial management of the Society, the Registrar of the Co-operative Societies appointed a special auditor to audit the Society's accounts. On the basis of the audit report a chargesheet was filed against all the accused for entering into a conspiracy to commit criminal breach of trust. The conspiracy charge having failed, all the accused except one were acquitted by the Sessions Judge. On appeal by the State, the High Court convicted the appellant in respect of three items, namely, purchase of fertilisers involving two transactions and missing of certain oil engines, on the ground that as Chairman of the Managing Committee he must be held to be vicariously liable for any order given or misappropriation committed by the other accused. Allowing the appeal, the Apex Court held that, *"There was not justification for the High Court to interfere with the appellant's acquittal. The case against the appellant had not been proved beyond reasonable doubt and he was wrongly convicted by the High Court. ..... In a case where there was serious defalcation of the properties, unless the prosecution proved that there was a close cohesion and collusion between all the accused which formed the subject matter of a conspiracy, it would be difficult to prove the charges against the appellant. The charge of conspiracy having failed, the most material and integral part of the prosecution story against the appellant disappear. .... In a criminal case of such serious nature* mens rea *cannot be excluded. Once the charge of conspiracy has failed the onus lay on the prosecution to prove affirmatively that the appellant was directely and personally connected with acts or omissions pertaining to the items purchased. ...... In the absence of a charge of conspiracy the mere fact that the appellant happened to be the Chairman of the Committee would not make him liable in a vicarious sence. There is no evidence either direct or circumstantial to show that apart from approving the purchase of fertilisers he knew that the firms from which the fertilisers were purchased did not exist"*; *Jethsur Surangbhai* v. *State of Gujarat*, (1984) 1 SCR 797.

In this case, the Court held that every offence of criminal breach of trust involves a civil wrong in respect of which complainant may seek his redressal for damages in the civil Court but every breach of trust in absence of *mens rea* cannot legally justify a criminal prosecution; *M/s. Tiwari Enterprises* v. *State of Bihar*, 2008 (5) CRJ 128 (Pat).

In this case, the Court held that word 'dishonestly' connotes an act done with intention to cause wrongful gain to person committing act or wrongful loss to another. Further, for offences under sections 403 and 406 to be established, there must be a pleading in the complaint to indicate that the property which has been wrongfully gained has been put to petitioners own use. In absence of such pleading, complaint is not maintainable; *Sesa Goa Ltd.* v. *State of Maharashtra*, 2009 All MR (Cri) 321.

In this case, petitioners/complainants claimed that they having worked as teachers in a school for some years resigned. They demanded their original testimonials to the management. When complaint was lodged, police declined to register FIR. The Court held that management has *prima facie* committed offence of criminal breach of trust; *A. John Paul* v. *State*, 2013 (1) Crimes 200 (Mad).

Where it was alleged that mother-in-law had taken all gifts/cash given by invitees, the Apex Court held that prima facie case was made out against mother in law under section 406 IPC; *Bhaskar Lal Sharma* v. *Monica*, 2010 All SCR 1407.

In this case, accused was charged for forging bills and misappropriating amount. However, the allegations of forging bills and receipts were not found true. Further, accused deposited the amount alleged to be misappropriated before the start of investigation. In such facts and circumstances, the Apex Court held that charge under section 409 of the IPC is not sustainable; *Narendra Pratap Narain Singh* v. *State of Uttar Pradesh*, 1991 Cr LJ 1816 (SC).

(viii) Theft (Section 379 of I.P.C.)

The essential ingredients of the offence of theft are—

(a) Removal of property of a person out of his possession;

(b) The removal must be dishonest;

(c) The property must be movable property;

(d) The removal must be without the consent of the owner of the property;

(e) The removal must be in order to the taking of the property.

To constitute theft the loss caused need not be permanent. Even temporary dispossession, though the person taking the property intended to restore it, may constitute theft. *Illustrations* (b) and (1) of section 378 of the IPC clearly show that a temporary deprivation of another person of his property may cause wrongful loss to him; *Pyare Lal Bhargava* v. *State of Rajasthan*, (1963) Supp 1 SCR 689.

Explaining the law regarding theft, the Apex Court held that it is an essential ingredients of the offence of theft that the movable property which was the subject matter of theft should have been moved out of the possession of any person without his consent. This could be possible only if the person moving the same had taken it out of the possession of the person concerned and transferred it to his own possession for the purpose of taking it dishonestly. Therefore, transfer of possession of the property, however transient is an essential ingredient of an offence of theft. In this particular case, it was permissible for the prosecution to establish, either that the accused were found to be in possession of the railway property , or that they were proved to have been in possession thereof; *State of Maharashtra* v. *Vishwanath Tukaram Umale*, (1980) 1 SCR 190.

Facts of this case are: appellants K.N. Mehra and M.Z. Phillips were cadets on training in Indian Air Force Academy, Jodhpur. On the day of incident appellants took off, not a Dakota, but a Harvard H.T. 822 and they landed at a place in Pakistan about 100 miles away from the Indo-Pak border. They were brought to India and arrested. Both were convicted under section 379 and were sentenced to 18 months imprisonment with fine of Rs. 750. The convicting and sentence was confirmed by Sessions Judge and the High Court. In appeal, the Apex Court held that as the flight was unauthorised there could be no consent, and as it was unlawful at the outset, in the circumstances of the case, and the appellant obtained a temporary use of the aircraft for his own purposes and deprived the Government of its use, there was a dishonest intention, and consequently the flight constituted a theft of the aircraft. The Court further held that a temporary retention of property by a person wrongfully gaining thereby or a temporary keeping out of property from the person legally entitled thereto, may amount to theft under section 378 of the IPC, and in this respect the offence differs from *larceny* in English Law which contemplates permanent gain or loss; *K.N. Mehra* v. *State of Rajasthan,* (1957) SCR 623.

In *Vindo Samuel* v. *Delhi Administration,* AIR 1991 SC 465: 1991 Cri LJ 3359 (SC), it was alleged that the accused snatched gold chain of a woman travelling in bus and was arrested on the spot after some chase. But the gold chain was not recovered from her possession. While acquitting the accused the Apex Court held that, *"Merely because soon after the incident the accused was seen running or walking briskly though might arise suspicion, it could not be said that the accused was the culprit."*

In *Chandi Kumar Das Karmakar* v. *Abazidhar Roy,* AIR 1965 SC 585: 1965 (1) Cri LJ 496, the Apex Court held that, *"Where the removal of a movable property is in assertion of a bona fide claim of right, the act does not constitute theft, although it my amount to a civil injury."*

In *Ram Ekbal Rai* v. *Jaldhari Pandey,* AIR 1972 SC 949: 1972 Cri LJ 584, the accused was convicted for the offence of theft of crop. *"However, the question of possession of land and crop on the date of incident was not proved beyond controversy and due attention was not paid to the evidence on record resulting in mis-judgement of the respective positions of the parties. The Apex Court set aside the conviction and sentenced under section 379 of I.P.C."*

In this case, the Apex Court held that where a *bona fide* claim of right exists, it can be a good defence to a prosecution for theft. An act does not amount to theft, unless there be not only no legal right but no appearance or colour of a legal right; *Suvvari Sanyasi Apparao* v. *Boddepalli Lakshminarayana,* (1962) Supp 1 SCR 8.

(ix) Unnatural Offences (Section 377, IPC)

The ingredients of the offence under section 377 are: (i) The accused had carnal intercourse with a man, woman or animal; (ii) Such intercourse was unnatural; (iii) The accused did the act voluntarily; (iv) There was penetration.

As the charge under this section is difficult to refute, evidence in support of the charge must be convincing; *Emperor* v. *Sain Dass,* AIR 1926 Lahore 375: 27 Cr LJ 593.

Where doctor did not find any external injury over the private parts of the accused and no semen was detected on the underwear, it was held that prosecution case is doubtful; *Kishan Lal* v. *State,* 1991 Cr LJ 742 (Del) (DB).

Where FIR was filed after a month of the date of incident and were medical evidence did not corroborate prosecution case, the Apex Court held that conviction is unsustainable; *Gowrishankar Swamigalu* v. *State of Karnataka,* AIR 2008 SC 2349.

In this case, the High Court set aside the conviction on the ground that evidence of doctor and CFSL report did not prove penile penetration into anus of deceased and sexual intercourse by accused; *Shahul Hamid* v. *State of Goa,* 2014 All MR (Cri) 2297.

(B) Certain Trials of Summons Cases Instituted on Police Report (Summary Trials)

(i) Outraging Modesty of Woman (I.P.C., 354)

In this case [*State of Punjab* v. *Major Singh*, AIR 1967 SC 63] it was alleged that the respondent/accused had caused injuries to the vagina of a 7½ months old child by fingering. The trial Court held him guilty for causing hurt under section 323 of I.P.C. In appeal, the Apex Court while holding the respondent/accused guilty under section 354 of I.P.C. and negativing the argument advanced on behalf of the respondent/accused, held that *"the question is whether section 354 speaks of outraging the modesty of a woman and at first blush seems to require that the outrage must be felt by the victim herself. But such an interpretation would leave out of the perview of the section assaults not only on girls of tender age but on even grown up women when such a woman is sleeping and did not wake up or is under anesthesia or stupor or is an idiot. It may also perhaps under certain circumstances, exclude a case where the woman is of depraved moral character. Could it be said that the legislature intended that the doing of any act to or in the presence of any women which according to the common notions of mankind is suggestive of sex, would be outside this section unless the woman herself felt that it outraged her modesty? Again, if the sole test to be applied is the woman's reaction to a particular act, would it not be a variable test depending upon the sensitivity or the upbringing of the woman? .... The test of woman's individual reaction to the act of the accused is not relevant. ...... [W]hen any act done to or in the presence of a woman is clearly suggestive of sex according to the common notions of mankind that act must fall within the mischief of this section. ..... The act of Major Singh in interfering with the vagina of the child was deliberate and he must be deemed to have intended to outrage her modesty."*

This was a case [*Rupan Deol Bajaj* v. *K.P.S. Gill*, (1995) Supp 4 SCR 237] where it was alleged that one evening, appellant accompanied by her husband had gone to the residence of a colleague of theirs, in response to an invitation for dinner. There were 20-25 couples present including the respondent/accused, who had come without his wife, and some other senior Government officers. The ladies were sitting segregated in a large semi-circle and the gentleman in another large semi-circle with the groups facing each other. The respondent/accused walked across to the circle of ladies and joined them occupying a vacant chair about five to six chairs to the left where the appellant was sitting. Slowly all the ladies sitting to the right and left of him started going into the house. The respondent/accused called out to the appellant and said that she should come and sit next to him as he wanted to talk to her. Responding to his request when the appellant went to sit in a chair next to him, the respondent/accused suddenly pulled the chair close to his chair. Realising something was wrong she went back to sit with the ladies. After about 10 minutes respondent/accused came and stood in front of her so close that his legs were four inches from her knees. He then by an action with the crook of his finger asked her to 'get up immediately' and come along with him. When she strongly objected to his behaviour he repeated his earlier command. She tried to leave the place but could not as he had blocked her way. When she draw her chair back and turned backwards he slapped her on the posterior in the full presence of the ladies and gents. She lodged report alleging commission of offence under sections 341, 342, 352, 354 and 509, I.P.C. On the basis of the report, F.I.R. was registered and investigation was taken up. The respondent/accused moved the High Court filing a petition under section 482, Cr.P.C. for quashing the F.I.R. The High Court quashed both the F.I.R. and the complaint. Hence she filed appeal to the Supreme Court. While allowing the appeal , the Apex Court held that, *"The ultimate test for ascertaining whether modesty has been outraged is the action of the offender such as could be perceived as one which is capable of shocking the sense of decency of a woman. When the above test is applied to the present case, keeping in view the total fact situation, it cannot but be held that, the alleged act of Mr. Gill in slapping Mrs. Bajaj on her posterior amounted to ' outraging of her modesty' for it was not only an affront to the normal sense of feminine decency but also an affront to the dignity of the lady – "sexual overtones" or not, not withstanding...... The sequence of events narrated by the appellant indicated that the slapping was the final to the earlier overtures of respondant, which considered together, indicated that he had the requisite culpable intention. Even if he had no such intention he must be attributed with such knowledge, as the alleged act was committed by him in the presence of a gathering comprising the elite of the society........ There was nothing in the F.I.R. to indicate that the indecent act was committed by him accidently or by mistake or it was a slip. Apart from the offence under section 354, I.P.C., an offence under section 509, I.P.C. had also been made out on the allegations contained in the F.I.R. as the words used and gestures made by respondent accused were intended to insult the modesty of the appellant."*

In this case, it was alleged by prosecution that accused assaulted informant intending to outrage her modesty and caused hurt to her. The informant stated in FIR that accused lifted and thrown her on ground while in evidence before Court she stated that accused twisted her left arm and pushed her on ground. In such facts and circumstances, the Court held that merely touching woman's body unintentionally would not amount to an offence punishable under section 354; *Hanumandas Pandurang Raut* v. *State of Maharashtra,* 2012 All MR (Cri) 1527 (Bom).

In this case, victim alleged that accused pressed her breast and torn her blouse. PW 1 and PW 2 accompanied her but did not notice the same and did not state this fact to police. The Court held that proof of assault or criminal force itself does not prove offence under section 354 unless there is proof of intention or knowledge. When criminal force or assault by accused is disbelieved, then it is not necessary to examine intention part of the offence; *Sopanrao K Jadhao* v. *State of Maharashtra,* 2014 All MR (Cri) 3942.

Other Cases on Outraging Modesty of Woman (I.P.C., 354)

1. *Pandurang Sitaram Bhagwat* v. *State of Maharashtra* , 2005 (1) Crimes 104 (SC): The Apex Court held that, *"approach that a lady would not put her character at stake may not be wrong but cannot be applied universally in a case under section 354, I.P.C."*

2. *Sailhendra Nath* v. *Aswini,* 1988 Cri LJ 343 (Cal) (DB): The Division Bench of the Calcutta High Court has held that, *"Intention is not the sole criterion of the offence under section 345, I.P.C. and an offence under section 354, I.P.C. can also be*

committed by the person assaulting or using criminal force to any woman, if he knows that by such acts the modesty of the woman is likely to be affected. Knowledge and intention are things of the mind and cannot be demonstrated like physical objects. The existence of such knowledge or intention or otherwise should be gathered from various circumstances in which and upon whom the alleged offence under section 354, I.P.C. is said to have committed."

3. *Ram Das* v. *State of West Bengal*, AIR 1954 SC 611: The Apex Court held that, *"In order to prove a case under section 354, it is not enough that the woman was pushed or given beatings. The prosecution has to prove that the push or the beatings were given with intent to outrage the woman's modesty or with the knowledge that it would be outraged."*

4. *Sadananda* v. *State of Assam*, 1972 Cri LJ 658 (Assam): It has been held that, *"where the girl is a consenting and willing party, there can be no outrage of the woman's modesty under section 354, I.P.C."*

(ii) Wrongful Restraints and Confinement

In this case [*Rupan Deol Bajaj* v. *Kanwar Pal Singh Gill*, (1995) Supp 4 SCR 237] the appellant lodged a complaint alleging commission of offences under sections 341, 342, 352, 354 and 509 of I.P.C. by the respondent/accused who was the Director General of Police Punjab at a dinner party. Treating that complaint as the first information report a case was registered and investigation was taken up. It was alleged by the complainant/appellant that the accused/respondent stood in front of her in such a manner that she had to move backward. The respondent/accused moved the High Court by filing a petition under section 482, Cr.P.C. for quashing the F.I.R. As regards the offence of wrongful restraint the Apex Court held that , " .... *So far as the offence under section 341, I.P.C. is concerned, the only allegation relating to the same is that Mr. Gill stood in front of Mrs. Bajaj in such a manner that she had to move backward. From such an act alone it cannot be said that he 'wrongfully restrained' her within the meaning of section 339, I.P.C. to make him liable under section 341, I.P.C."*

Where accused restrained the complainant in a *bona fide* belief that he has right to property, it was held that he cannot be convicted; *Kalidas Raha* v. *Deodhari Mistri*, AIR 1925 Cal 1214.

In this case, petitioner and others were chargesheeted on allegations that they as school children assembled under leadership of applicant No. 1 at National Highway as a consequence of which movement of traffic was disrupted and they dispersed only with intervention of SDM. Agitation was because administration failed to repair the road. In view of the facts and circumstances of the case and evidence on record, the Court held that no offence is made out under sections 147 & 341 of IPC; *Himanshu Negi* v. *State of Uttarakhand*, 2015 (2) Crimes 407 (Uttaranchal) (SN).

(iii) Rash Driving or Riding on a Public Way (I.P.C., Sections 279, 304A)

Acts beyond control of accused, error in judgment, parking of vehicle on wrong side of the road, mechanical defects in vehicle, unmarked speed breakers, non-display of sign boards and traffic signals, engineering defects in the approaching roads, etc. are some of the causes of accident. Recent studies carried out by researchers show that one in five driving errors was a result of driver's distraction which included braking suddenly, failing to see road signs and taking wrong turns.

Defence may use the above causes for bringing probabilities on record during cross-examination.

This case relates to tragedy at Uphaar Cinema Hall at Delhi on 13th June, 1997. The Hon'ble Apex Court upheld the conviction of the accused persons and held that *causa causans* for the tragedy is the faulty structure and absence of safety majors in cinema hall which led to death of 59 persons. Victims did not die of burn injuries. But they died because they could not exit the premises, construction of which was violative of building plan. The Apex Court explained the meaning of rashness, negligence and criminal negligence as—(a) Rashness – "Rashness" means acting with consciousness that a mischievous and illegal consequences may follow but hoping it will not. Imputability arises from acting despite consciousness. (b) Negligence – "Negligence" signifies breach of a duty to do something which a reasonably prudent man would have done under the circumstances. Essence lies in neglect of care. Existence of duty to care is first and foremost ingredients whereas breach of such duty and the consequences of it, are other two ingredients. c) Gross Negligence – Negligence in criminal law is distinct from negligence in civil action. Difference is only in the degree of proof. Negligence constitutes an offence punishable under section 304A only if the same is proved to be gross; *Sushil Ansal* v. *State through CBI,* 2014 All SCR 1162.

The facts of the case are: the appellant while driving a bus on a narrow road with deep ditches on both sides, a child suddenly attempts to cross the road. The appellant swerved the bus to right but child comes under the wheels and he is crushed to death. In appeal against conviction, the Apex Court while acquitting the appellant held that a grave error of judgement, particularly one apparent as such in the light of after events, is not wilful misconduct if the person responsible thought he was acting in the best interest of the passengers. In this case, the accused had swerved the vehicle to extreme right side of the road, not only to avoid collision with the ill-fated child but also to avoid the risk of the vehicle falling into deep ditches on either side of the road, with the resultant possibility of the greater harm to the passengers in the bus; *Syad Akbar* v. *State of Karnataka,* (1980) 1 SCR 95.

In this case, accident occurred when the truck going ahead was suddenly halted, which compelled the driver of the offending vehicle to apply his brakes, with a result of overturning of vehicle as it was heavily loaded. The Apex Court while acquitting the appellant held that if the appellant had not applied the brakes, his truck would have dashed against the truck going ahead; *Shivanna* v. *State of Karnataka,* 2010 (6) CRJ 119 (SC).

In this case, accused-driver stopped the bus at bus-stop. One passenger after alighting from bus went to its roof top for unloading his luggage. As the driver was not aware about said passenger, he started bus due to which passenger fell down and got injured. During trial conductor was not examined and even no evidence was led to show that the accused was negligent. In such facts and circumstances, the apex Court acquitted the appellant; *Braham Dass* v. *State of Himachal Pradesh,* AIR 2009 SC 3181.

In this case, investigation officer did not collect evidence of pedestrian and the passengers in the bus. He did not take photographs of the position of the vehicle, the electric pole, and the position of the victim, but had produced a most unsatisfactory rough sketch. There was no evidence of relevant factors such as the height of the karb, the state of the traffic on the road, the condition of the brakes, and of the probable speed of the bus which could have been ascertained by measuring the tyre marks on the road. In view of the said evidence, the Apex Court acquitted the appellant; *Nageshwar Shrikrishna Choube* v. *State of Maharashtra,* (1973) 2 SCR 377.

In this case the accused was charged under section 304A of I.P.C. While dealing with the appeal, the Orissa High Court held that, *"Death must be the direct result of rash and negligent act and act must be the cause without the intervention of another's negligence. It must be the* causa causas. *It is not enough that it may have been the* causa sine qua non; [*Krushan Chandra Ojha* v. *State of Orissa,* 1972 Cri. LJ 1404 (Orissa)].

The facts of the case reported in (1984) 25 Del LT 233 (235) were that while the bus was negotiating a turn, the deceased boy came towards the bus with the intention of boarding it and in the process was struck against leg by the left side of the bus and died in the hospital. It was held that the driver was not guilty under section 279, I.P.C. as the bus having right hand drive, the driver would not see what happened in rear.

It has been held by the Bombay High Court in *Madhukar Venkatesh Kulkarni* v. *State of Maharashtra,* 1983 (1) Bom CR 307, that unless a passenger is conversant with the driving, it is difficult to rely on the evidence of such a passenger to determine whether the bus was driven at a fast speed or otherwise.

Where pedestrian suddenly crossed road from west to east without taking note of the approaching bus, it was held that driver is not guilty of negligence; [*Bashir Ahmed* v. *Gulam Qadir* AIR 1972 SC 231 and *M. Narayan Rao* v. *G. Venkata Reddy,* AIR 1972 SC 221].

(iv) Bombay Prohibition Act (25 of 1949)

In this case [*Arjun Shankar Kumbhar* v. *State of Maharashtra,* 1997 (3) Mh LJ 282 (Bom)] accused, a conductor of ST Bus was convicted under section 85(1) of the Act. It was alleged that the accused was found sitting on conductor's seat under the influence of alcohol. The Bombay High Court set aside the conviction and sentence of the accused under section 85(1) of the Act on the ground that there was no evidence to show that the accused was behaving in a disorderly manner under influence of liquor and that the prosecution did not examine any passenger.

In *Popatlal M. Shah* v. *State of Maharashtra,* 1977 Mh LJ 855 the Bombay High Court has held that, *"merely proving giving abuses under influence of alcohol without details of abuses or disorderly behaviour is not sufficient to convict a person under section 85(1) of the Act."*

This was a case [*Bhagwanbhai Dhulabai Jadhav* v. *State of Maharashtra,* 1963 Mh LJ 134 (SC)] where the accused was convicted under section 65(a) of the Act for possessing bottles of foreign liquor which were seized from luggage compartment in car. The Apex Court set aside the conviction on the ground that there was no evidence on record that the liquor was imported.

(C) Summary Trials

(i) The Negotiable Instruments Act, 1881

Before a person is prosecuted for the offence punishable under section 138 of the Act, the following mandatory requirements have to be complied with: (a) The cheque has been presented to the bank within a period of three months from the date on which it is drawn or within the period of its validity, whichever is earlier. (b) The payee or the holder in due course of the cheque, as the case may be, makes a demand for the payment of the said of money by giving a notice, in writing, to the drawer of the cheque, within 30 days of the receipt of information by him from the bank regarding the return of the cheque as unpaid, and (c) The drawer of such cheque fails to make the payment of the said amount of money to the payee or, as the case may be, to the holder in due course of the cheque, within fifteen days of the receipt of the said notice.

Important provisions relating to trial of dishonour of cheque cases are as under:

(i) All the offences under Chapter XVII shall be tried by the Magistrate summarily and provisions of sections 262 to 265, Cr.P.C. shall apply. [Section 143(1)]

(ii) The trial of a case shall be continued from day to day until its conclusion. [Section 143(2)]

(iii) Every trial shall be concluded within 6 months from the date of filing of the complaint. [Section 143(3)]

Payee has a right to represent cheque to bank any number of time within period of its validity and complaint can be launched on the basis of second or any subsequent dishonour of cheque. However it has been held by the Apex Court in *Sadanandan Bhadran* v. *Madhavan Sunil Kumar,* AIR 1998 SC 3043, that, *"Cause of action arises and can arise only once. Payee can present cheque any number of times during the period of its validity. On each presentation and its dishonour, a fresh right, and not cause of action, accrues in his favour."*

In *M/s. Dalmia Cement Ltd.* v. *M/s. Galaxi Traders & Agencies Ltd.,* AIR 2001 SC 676, the Apex Court held that, *"cause of action for filing complaint arises from date of receipt of notice demanding payment."*

It has been held by the Apex Court in *K. Bhaskaran* v. *Sankaran,* AIR 1999 SC 3762, that, *"offence under section 138 is complete on failure of drawer to pay cheque amount within 15 days from the date of giving notice. Period of 15 days commences from the date when accused receives notice or refuses to accept it or disclaims it."*

Though it is necessary to file complaint within one month of the date on which the cause of action arises under clause (c) of the proviso to section 138, the complaint filed before expiry of notice period contemplated by section 138 (c), cannot be dismissed as premature; [*Narsing Das Tapadia* v. *Gowardhan Das Partani*, AIR 2000 SC 2946].

It has been held by the Apex Court in *M/s. Saketh India Ltd.* v. *M/s. India Securities Ltd.*, AIR 1999 SC 1090, that, *"Period of one month for filing complaint will be reckoned from the day on which period of 15 days from the date of receipt of notice by drawer, expires."*

As far as burden of proof is concerned, the Apex Court in *Kali Ram* v. *State of Himachal Pradesh*, 1973 (2) SCC 808 has held that the burden of proving the guilt of the accused is upon the prosecution. There are certain cases in which statutory presumptions arise regarding the guilt of the accused, but the burden even in those cases is upon the prosecution to prove the existence of facts which have to be present before the presumption can be drawn. If some material is brought on the record consistent with the innocence with the accused which may reasonably be true, even though it is not positively proved to be true, the accused would be entitled to acquittal.

In *Krishna Janardhan Bhat* v. *Dattatraya G. Hegde*, 2008 AIR SCW 738: 2008 All MR (Cri) 1164 (SC): 2008 Mh LJ 354 (SC), the Apex Court held that the presumption available in dishonour of cheque cases that the cheque has been drawn in discharge of some debt or liability does not extend to existence of such liability. The accused can prove that in fact there was no legally recoverable liability in reality. Statue mandates raising of presumption but it stops at that. Other important principles of legal jurisprudence, namely, presumption of innocence as human rights and the doctrine of reverse burden introduced by section 138 should be delicately balanced. Court must ensure that application of presumption does not lead to injustice or mistaken conviction. [**Note:** This case has been partly overruled by *Rangappa* v. *Sri Mohan*, AIR 2010 SC 1898: 2010 (3) Crimes 40 (SC): 2010 All SCR 1349. In this case the Apex Court held that presumption mandated by section 139 does indeed include the existence of a legally enforceable debt or liability. To that extent, the impugned observations in *Krishna Janardhan Bhat's* case may not be correct.]

In this case, question arose as to whether cognizance of an offence punishable under section 138 can be taken on the basis of a complaint filed before the expiry of the period of 15 days stipulated in the notice required to be served upon the drawer of the cheque in terms of section 138(c) of the Act. Due to difference of opinion between the Judges, this matter has been referred to larger Bench; *Yogendra Pratap Singh* v. *Savitri Pandey*, 2012 (2) Crimes 214 (SC).

In this case, the Bombay High Court held that for the purpose of issuing process under section 200, Cr.P.C., it is open to the Magistrate to rely upon the verification in the form of affidavit filed by the complainant in support of the complaint under section 138, NI Act and the Magistrate is not obliged to call upon the complainant to remain present before the court, not to examine the complainant or his witnesses upon oath for taking decision as to whether or not to issue process on the complaint; *Rajesh Bhalchandra Chalke* v. *M/s. Emco Dynatorq Pvt. Ltd.,* decided on 7th December, 2010, Bombay High Court (FB).

In this case, the Apex Court held that examination of complainant on solemn affirmation under section 200, Cr.P.C. is done away by section 145, NI Act. Therefore complainant is entitled to give evidence on affidavit. The affidavit has to be read in evidence in any enquiry, trial or other proceeding under Cr.P.C. Taking cognizance without examining complainant on solemn affirmation is not illegal; *K.S. Joseph* v. *Phillips Carbon Black Ltd.,* 2016 (3) Crimes 118 (SC).

Other Cases on The Negotiable Instruments Act, 1881

1. *Lalan Prasad* v. *State of Jharkhand,* 2004 Cri LJ 3622 (Jhar): AIR 2004 Jhar 2417: The Court has held that, if there is no subsisting liability of debt on the date of issue of the cheque, provision of section 138 are not attracted.

2. *Bhikajibhai R. Makwana* v. *State of Gujarat,* 2002 All MR (Cri) Journal 1: The Court has held that where there was no privity of contract between accused and complainant and no existing or future liability of debt on accused, no case is made out by the complainant under section 138 of the Act.

3. *M/s. MMTC Ltd.* v. *M/s. Medchl Chemicals,* 2002 All MR (Cri) 230 (SC): The Apex Court held that, it is for the defendant/accused to disprove the presumption under section 139 of the Act that there was no subsisting debt or liability.

4. *Dhanvantrai B. Desai* v. *State of Maharashtra,* AIR 1964 SC 575: The Apex Court held that, *"Unless the contrary is proved"* makes it clear that the presumption has to be rebutted by proof and not by a bare explanation which is merely plausible. (*i.e.,* reasonable and probable).

5. *A. Bhoosanrao* v. *Purushothamdas Pantani,* 1994 (4) Banking Law Journal (AP) 405: The Court has held that, *"the burden to prove that it is a legally enforceable liability rests on the complainant and he has to prove the same."*

6. *Modi Cements Ltd.* v. *Kuchil Kumar Nandi,* 1998 (3) SCC 249: The Apex Court has held that "stop payment" instructions to the bank does not preclude an action under section 138 of the Act. (**Note:** Observations in *K.K. Sidarathan* v. *T.P. Praveena Chandran,* 1996 (4) Crimes 102 (SC): 1996(6) SCC 369: 1997 (1) Mh LJ 1 (SC) were disapproved by a three Judge Bench in *Modi Cement's* case *i.e., supra*).

7. *Goa Plast (P) Ltd.* v. *Chico Ursula D'Souza,* AIR 2004 SC 408: (2004) 2 SCC 235: The Apex Court held that where drawer issued notice to the drawee or to the bank for stoppage of the payment, it will not preclude an action under section 138 of the Act because once the cheque is issued by the drawer, a presumption under section 13 must follow.

8. *M/s. Electronics Trade and Technology Development Corporation Ltd.* v. *M/s. Indian Technologists and Engineers (Electricals) Pvt. Ltd.,* AIR 1996 SC 2339: 1996 (3) Crimes 82 (SC): 1996 Cri LJ 1692 (SC): 1996 (2) Bom CR 150 (SC): Where the notice is issued to payee "not to present" the cheque for encashment but payee presents the cheque, it was held that, no offence is made out under section 138 of the Act.

9. *Ramchandran* v. *K. Dineshan*, 2005 All MR (Cri) Journal 117 (Ker): If amount once written is corrected without the knowledge and consent of maker of the cheque, that amounts to material alteration and no criminal liability can be fastened on the accused under section 138 of the Act.

10. *Avon Organics, Hyderabad Ltd.* v. *Poineer Products Ltd.*, 2003 All MR (Cri) Journal 105 (AP): The A.P. High Court held that, *"filing up amount portion and date as per the choice of the complainant is material alteration and accused cannot be held guilty for the offence punishable under section 138 of N.I. Act."*

11. *Taher N. Khanbati* v. *M/s. Vinayak Enterprises, Sikunderabad*, 1995 Cri LJ 560 (AP): Where a blank cheque was given as a security for loan and the same was presented for encashment, it was held that, this does not amount to giving cheque voluntarily and therefore no offence is made out.

12. *A. Bhushan Rao* v. *Purushottam Pantani*, 1998 Cri LJ 906: Where the amount of cheque is exorbitant then it is the duty of the complainant to prove that he indeed paid the said amount to accused and that he had the capacity to pay the same.

13. *Abdul Rahim* v. *U.P.K. Mohammed Haneefa*, 2004 (3) All India Criminal Law Reporter (Mad) 714: Where there was doubt as regards the capacity of the complainant to advance hand loan of Rs. 60,000 to accused, the accused was acquitted.

14. *K. Devadas Shettiy* v. *Dr. J.R. Pais*, 1998 All MR (Cri) Journal 28 (Karn): The Court has held that, *"Where complaint was filed beyond one month from the date of cause of action, delay cannot be condoned under section 5 of the limitation Act."*

15. *M/s. SIL Import, USA* v. *M/s. Exim Aides Silk Exporters, Banglore*, 1999 Cri LJ 2276 (SC): 1999 (2) All MR (Cri) 588 (SC): The Apex Court held that, *"If no complaint is filed within one month after expiry of 15 days, complaint is not tenable."*

16. *J. Parmeswarudu* v. *K. Krishna*, 2005 All MR (Cri) Journal 287 (AP): The Andhra Pradesh High Court has held that, *"Complainant is required to prove that complaint is filed within time."*

17. *P.K. Koya Moideen* v. *Hariharan*, 1996 Cri LJ 3153: 1996 (4) Crimes 434: The Court has held that, a person to be *"a holder in due course"*, he must come into possession of the instrument for consideration. If this is not proved, complaint is no maintainable.

18. *C. Antoni* v. *K.G. Raghavan Niar*, AIR 2003 SC 182: Where the complainant failed to establish the advancement of money to the drawer of cheque, it was held that, no offence is made out under section 138 of the Act and accused was acquitted.

19. *P. Narsimha Reddy* v. *D.L. Narsimha Rao.*, 2004 All MR (Cri) Journal 98 (AP): Where complainant did not adduce any documentary evidence to show that impugned cheque related to a legally enforceable debt, it was held that no offence is made out under section 138 of the Act.

20. *Sumant Sethi* v. *Ajay K. Churiwar*, AIR 2000 SC 828: The Apex Court held that, drawer of cheque is absolved from criminal liability if he pays

cheque amount to the payee. But regarding other incidental claims, civil suit is necessary.

21. *M/s. Sathavahana Ispat Ltd.* v. *Umesh Sharma,* 2007 (6) All MR (Journal) 3: 2007 (4) CRJ 528 (Karn): The Court held that a cheque issued in respect of future liability would not attract prosecution under section 138. However, the vendor's right to recover the amount in a Civil Court will not get affected.

22. *I.C.D.S.* v. *Beemna Shabeer,* AIR 2002 SC 3014: 2002 Cri LJ 3925 (SC): The Apex Court held that section 138 is not attracted where the cheque issued by the guarantor was dishonoured.

(ii) Prevention of Food Adulteration Act, 1954

The cases under this Act are technical in nature and require study of Chemistry, Pharmacology, etc. Therefore young advocates are advised to go through the basics and get acquainted with the principle involved in a particular case.

As far as the cases under this Act are concerned the act imposes stringent punishments for the violation of the said Act and Rules. Even mere fall in standard of the sample of any food article prescribed under Prevention of Food Adulteration Rules, 1955 is made punishable under the Act. *Mens rea* is not an essential ingredient for the offences punishable under the Act.

In *State of Kerala* v. *Alaserry Mohammed,* (1978) 2 SCR 820, the Constitution Bench of the Apex Court held that, *"The report of the Public Analyst under section 13 of the Act has got a great sanctity for protecting the general public and their health against use and consumption of adulterated food. On the other hand, it has great significance and importance for the protection of a citizen, as he can be convicted under the Act only on its basis, under section 16(1)(a)(ii) of the Act, because unless and untill the report of the Public Analyst is demolished, shaken or becomes doubtful, it is final and conclusive evidence of the facts stated therein, under section 13(5) of the Act."*

However, in *State of Himachal Pradesh* v. *Jai Lal,* 1999 (2) All MR (Cri) 1790 (SC), the Apex Court has held that, *"in order to bring the evidence of a witness as that of an expert, it has to be shown that he has made special study of the subject or acquired a special experience therein. ...... Credibility of expert's evidence depends on the reason stated in support of his conclusion and the data and materials furnished which form the basis of his conclusions....... Report submitted by an expert does not go in evidence automatically. Expert is to be examined in Court and has to face cross examination."* Same view has been taken by the Bombay High in *Mohd. Mansoori* v. *State of Maharshtra,* 2003 All MR (Cri) 506 (Bom), where it has been held by the Bombay High Court that, *"Prosecution is obliged to bring such evidence on record to convince a Court that such witness can be called as an expert in real sense."*

It has been held by the Bombay High Court in *Narayan Rajaram Wani* v. *State of Maharashtra,* 1978 Mh LJ 679, that, *"Where Food Inspector is unable to enlighten Court on material points, accused has the right to ask Court to summon Public Analyst to submit himself for cross-examination....... section 13 of the Act is not complete Code."*

Where there was contradiction in report of Public Analyst and Central Food Laboratory, it was held that, *"Report of Director of Central Food Laboratory annuls or replaces the report of Public Analyst and it gains finality...... If a State declares a fact final then no party can give evidence to disprove it. This is import of section 4 of the Evidence Act;"* [*Calcutta Municipal Corporation* v. *Pawan K. Saraf*, (1999) 1 SCR 74].

Other Cases under Prevention of Food Adulteration Act, 1954

1. *M.S. Bisaldar* v. *Radhe Shayam R. Agrawal*, 1981 Cri LJ (NOC) 102 (Guj): Where the prosecution did not examine the peon who cleaned the bottles in which samples of food articles were taken by the Food Inspector, it was held that, accused is entitled to benefit of doubt.

2. *M. Mohammad* v. *State of Andhra Pradesh*, 1978 Cri LJ. (NOC) 123 (AP): The Andhra Pradesh High Court has held that, *"provision of rule 14 of P.F.A. Rules 1955 regarding use of dry and clean bottles is mandatory. Its compliance must be proved by positive evidence."*

3. *State of Maharashtra* v. *Abbas Ismail Shaikh*, 1998 All MR (Cri) 1604 (Bom) (DB): Where the oil sample was not shown to be taken in clean bottle and there was absence of independent *pancha*, it was held that accused is entitled to benefit of doubt.

4. *State of Maharashtra* v. *Maganlal H. Tambodia*, 1983 Cri LJ 1148 (Bom): Where Food Inspector did not receive training of three months as required by rule, it was held that proceedings based on his report and investigation is not competent.

5. *Pimpri Chinchwad Nagar Palika* v. *Giriraj C. Sharma*, 1998 All MR (Cri) 1347 (Bom): The Bombay High Court has held that, *"it is mandatory to deliver the report of Public Analyst by Regd. Post or through person within ten days of the launching of prosecution. .... Non-compliance with rule 9A entitles the accused to be acquitted."*

6. *State of Maharashtra* v. *Parshuram Dattatraya Dabke*, 2000 All MR (Cri) 871 (Bom) (DB): Where the report of Public Analyst was sent to the accused seven days after filing case, it was held *"that delay is violative of rule 9A and accused is entitled to benefit of doubt."*

7. *State of Orissa* v. *Gauranga Sahu*, 2003 (2) All MR (Cri) 1371 (SC): The Apex Court held that, *"forwarding of Public Analyst report to accused is a mandatory obligation .... Not only despatch but service of copy of report upon accused person must be established by prosecution."*

8. *State of Maharashtra* v. *Hirji Dhanji Shah*, 1998 (2) All MR (Cri) 994 (Bom): The Bombay High Court has held that, *"order granting consent to prosecute accused must mention in what way food is adulterated either in nature or substance or in quality. .... Consenting authority has to mention about opinion of analyst.... Absence of these matters show lack of application of mind and hence consent is vitiated."*

9. *State of Maharashtra* v. *Mohiddin G. Chougule*, 2001 (2) All MR (Cri) 1533 (Bom): Where fact of stirring of milk was neither mentioned in complaint nor in *panchanama*, it was held that statement of Food Inspector for the first time in court that the milk was stirred before taking the sample is not credible.

10. *Kashmiri Lal* v. *State of Punjab,* 1993 Cri LJ 3820 (P&H): The Punjab and Haryana High Court set aside the conviction on the ground that sample of Ghee was analysed after about one month from its seizure and that prosecution failed to establish that deterioration was not caused due to exposure of sample to light or air moisture or that precautions were taken to avoid deterioration of sample.

(D) Complaints to Magistrate (Private complaint Cases)

If police does not register F.I.R. on the complaint/report lodged by a person for one or the other reason, he has remedy in law to file complaints before the concerned Magistrate. The procedure for filing such complaints is given in Chapter XV of Cr.P.C.

The Apex Court has held that examination of all witnesses in complaint is not a condition precedent for taking cognizance and issue of process against the persons named as accused in the complaint; *Shivjee Singh* v. *Nagendra Tiwary,* 2010 (6) CRJ 461 (SC).

Where accused was residing outside the territorial jurisdiction of the competent Court, the Bombay High Court held that postponement of issuance of process is not mandatory in all such cases. If the materials before Court make out a prima facie case, process can be issued without postponement; *ASR Systems Pvt. Ltd.* v. *Kimberly Clark Hygiene Products,* 2012 All MR (Cri) 557.

It has been held by the Apex Court that issuance of summons by Magistrate under section 204(1)(b) of Cr.P.C. to accused on a private complaint after committal of case to Sessions Court is illegal; *Jile Singh* v. *State of Uttar Pradesh,* (2012) 3 SCC 383.

In this case, the Bombay High Court held that where complaint filed before Magistrate is in respect of offence triable exclusively by Court of Sessions, it is obligatory for Magistrate to call upon complainant to produced all his witnesses and examine them on oath. Proviso to section 202(2), Cr.P.C. is mandatory; *Laxmanlal* v. *JMFC Khamgaon,* 1975 Mh LJ (Note 17).

In this case, the Court held that filing of list of witnesses with the complaint is not mandatory. Failure to file a list of witnesses is curable defect; *Herculano Coelho* v. *Antonia P. Dias,* 2009 All MR (Cri) 2349.

In this case, the Apex Court held that the process of enquiry under section 200, Cr.P.C. is not a decorative piece of legislation but is of great relevance and value to the complainant as well as the accused; *Vasanti Dubey* v. *State of Madhya Pradesh,* 2013 All SCR 638.

Where complaint alleges commission of offence under section 498A and also under section 494 of IPC, Court can take cognizance thereon even on a police report; *Ushaben* v. *Kishorbhai Chunilal Talpade,* 2012 All MR (Cri) 2088 (SC).

Where complainant after his conviction for negligent driving complained that offence was committed by some other person, the Apex Court held that it is for him to file complaint under section 200, Cr.P.C. and produce relevant material. The Apex Court quashed and set aside the order of conviction and directing fresh investigation passed by the High Court; *N.R. Govindaraji* v. *S. Venkatachalam,* 2002 All MR (Cri) 237 (SC).

As far as these cases are concerned, even second complaint is maintainable as has been held by the Apex Court in *Jatinder Singh* v. *Ranjit Kaur,* AIR 2001 SC 784. In this case, the Apex Court held that *"if the dismissal of the complaint was not on merit but on default of the complainant to be present, there is no bar in the complainant moving the magistrate again with a second complaint on the same facts. But if the dismissal of the complaint under section 203 of the Code was on merits the position could be different. ..... There is no provision in the Code or in any other statute which debars a complainant from preferring a second complaint on the same allegations if the first complaint did not result in a conviction or acquittal or even discharge...... However, when a Magistrate conducts an inquiry under section 202 of the Code and dismisses the complaint on merits, a second complaint on the same facts cannot be made unless there are very exceptional circumstances. Even so, a second complaint is permissible depending upon how the complaint happened to be dismissed at the first instance."*

CHAPTER XXX

STATEMENT OF ACCUSED

(SECTION 313 CRIMINAL PROCEDURE CODE)

Section 313, Cr.P.C. embodies fundamental principle of *'Audi Alteram Partem'* and provisions of this section are considered to be mandatory. It casts a duty on the Court to afford an opportunity to the accused to explain the incriminating material and circumstances against him. The examination of the accused under section 313 of Cr.P.C is not a mere formality and it is a procedural safeguard for an accused. The Apex Court has held this provision to be mandatory in nature; [*State of Uttar Pradesh* v. *Mohd. Iqram,* AIR 2011 SC 2296].

Highlighting the importance and evidentiary value of the statement of accused recorded under section 342 (Old Code), the Apex Court held that the statement of accused can also be a powerful and impressive weapon of defence in the hands of an innocent man. This means that statement must be treated like any other piece of evidence coming from the mouth of a witness and matters in favour of the accused must be viewed with as much deference and given as much weight as matters which tell against him anymore. Because of the presumption of innocence in his favour even when he is not in a position to prove the truth of his story, his version should be accepted if it is reasonable and accords with probabilities unless the prosecution can prove beyond reasonable doubt that it is false; *Hate Singh Bhagat Singh* v. *State of Madhya Bharat,* AIR 1953 SC 648.

In this case, the Apex Court while interpreting the provisions of section 313, Cr.P.C. observed that while clause (a) of section 313(1) is optional, clause (b) is mandatory. Failure of trial Court to comply with the mandate of the law cannot automatically ensure to the benefit of accused. Failure of trial Court to question accused on any incriminating circumstance would not *ipso facto* vitiate the trial, unless accused is materially prejudiced thereby. Accused should also show that such prejudice has occasioned failure of justice to him. The Court further held that issue of non-compliance of section 313 raised before Appellate Court cannot automatically result in acquittal of accused. Appellate Court can also put those incriminating circumstances to counsel of the accused and his answers would be deemed to be answers of the accused. The trial Court and Appellate Court are bound to put such questions to accused or his counsel. Where accused shows prejudice to him due to non-compliance of the provisions of section 313, Cr.P.C., Appellate Court, under section 386, Cr.P.C., can remand the case for examination under section 313 or order re-trial of the case from the stage at which the prosecution was closed; *Nar Singh* v. *State of Haryana,* 2014 (4) Crimes 252 (SC).

Court has discretion to dispense with the physical presence of an accused during such questioning only in summons cases. In all other cases it is incumbent on the Court to question the accused personally after closing prosecution evidence. The Court further held that an accused is entitled to put in written statement under sections 243(1), 247 and 233(2) of Cr.P.C.; [*Inspector of Customs* v. *Yash Pal,* 2009 (2) Crimes 108 (SC)].

However, in *Chandu Lal Chandrakar* v. *Puran Mal,* 1988 (Supp) SCC 570: AIR 1988 SC 2163, the Apex Court granted personal exemption to the accused in view of the accused's statement before the Apex Court that he would not make any statement under section 313 of the Code and would not raise any question of prejudice, if any, caused to him due to non-examination.

In *Basavaraj R. Patil* v. *State of Karnataka,* (2000) 8 SCC 740, the Apex Court held that *"If the accused makes an application to the Court praying that he may be allowed to answer the questions without making his physical presence in Court, the Court can allow such request provided that such application is accompanied by an affidavit .... The accused should affix his signature on all the sheets of the answered questionnaire and return the same to Court."*

The Apex Court has held that exemption from personal attendance statutorily given in summons cases can be extended to other cases if it works hardship on accused and the Court laid down the procedure for the same; [*Keya Mukherjee* v. *Magma Leasing Ltd.,* AIR 2008 SC 1807].

In *State of Madhya Pradesh* v. *Shyam Sunder Trivedi.* (1995) Supp I SCR 44, where the Trial Court did not put incriminating material appearing in the prosecution evidence against certain accused who were charged for an offence under section 201, I.P.C., the Apex Court set aside the conviction on the ground that no opportunity was offered to them to explain those circumstances and serious prejudice has been caused to them.

It has been held by the Apex Court in *Swapan Patra* v. *State of West Bengal,* (1999) 9 SCC 245, that a false answer offered by the accused in examination under section 313 offers an explanation as additional link in the chain of circumstantial evidence. Similarly in *State of Maharashtra* v. *Suresh* (2000) 1 SCC 471, the Apex Court has held that, *"a false answer can only be counted as providing a missing link for completing the chain."*

In *Joseph S/o Kooveli Poulo* v. *State of Kerala,* (2000) 3 SCR 729, a three-Judge Bench of the Apex Court has held that, *"total denial of all the incriminating circumstances by appellant accused provided missing link in the chain of circumstances to connect the appellant with the crime."* However in *Padala Veera Reddy* v. *State of Andhra Pradesh,* AIR 1990 SC 79, a three-Judge Bench of the Apex Court in particular facts and circumstances of the case held that, *"Though explanation offered by the accused was false, this unacceptable explanation would not lead to any irresistible inference that the accused alone should have committed the murder."*

In *Mohan Singh* v. *Prem Singh,* AIR 2002 SC 3582, the Apex Court held that, *"Statement made by accused under section 313 can lend credence to the evidence led by prosecution but it cannot be made the sole basis of conviction."*

It should be remembered that if the accused in his examination confesses to the commission of the offence charged, the Court can convict him. [*Narayan Singh* v. *State of Punjab*, (1963) 3 SCR 678: 1964 (1) Cri LJ 730]. The Law propounded by the Apex Court in *Narayan Singh's* case *(supra)* has been followed in *State of Maharashtra* v. *Sukhdeo Singh*, AIR 1992 SC 2100.

Recently the Division Bench of the Bombay High Court has held that, *"The statement made by the accused in his statement under section 313 of Cr.P.C. is not evidence but the same can be taken into consideration if it corroborates either the prosecution or the defence evidence;"* [*State of Maharashtra* v. *Ajay* alias *Rameshwar Raghuram*, 2006 All MR (Cri) 1999].

In this case, the Apex Court held that the circumstances which are not put to the accused in his examination under section 313, cannot be used against him and must be excluded from consideration. The said statement cannot be treated as evidence within the meaning of section 3 of the Evidence Act, as the accused cannot be cross-examined with reference to such statement; *Sujit Biswas* v. *State of Assam*, (2013) 12 SCC 406: 2013 All SCR 2153.

In this case, the Apex Court held that accused cannot be compelled to make a statement to the questions asked by the Court. The option lies with the accused to maintain silence coupled with simpliciter denial or in the alternative to explain his version and reasons for his alleged involvement in the commission of crime; *Manu Sao* v. *State of Bihar*, (2010) 12 SCC 310.

In this case, the Apex Court held that the accused has right to maintain silence during his examination under section 313, Cr.P.C. In such cases, Court can draw adverse inference against the accused with reference to facts and circumstances of the case; *Nagesh* v. *State of Karnataka*, 2012 All SCR 1882.

In this case, the Apex Court held that in a case resting on circumstantial evidence, explanation given by the accused under section 313 of Cr.P.C. about circumstances appearing against him, has to be considered for determining whether chain of circumstance is complete; *Munish Mubar* v. *State of Haryana*, AIR 2013 SC 912.

In this case, the Apex Court held that it is the duty of the accused to explain the incriminating circumstance proved against him while making a statement under section 313, Cr.P.C. Keeping silent and not furnishing any explanation for such circumstance is an additional link in the chain of circumstances to sustain the charges against him; *Neel Kumar @ Anil Kumar* v. *State of Haryana*, 2012 All MR (Cri) 2069 (SC).

In this case, the Apex Court held that opportunity should be provided to accused to state his case during his examination under section 313, Cr.P.C. Once accused opts to give answers and in fact, puts forward his own defence, then accused is bound by such statement and Court is at liberty to examine it in the light of evidence produced on record; *Bable @ Gurdeep Singh* v. *State of Chhattisgarh*, 2012 All MR (Cri) 2744 (SC).

In this case, the Apex Court held that a pleader cannot represent the accused for the purpose of section 342 (Old Code) which is presently section 313, Cr.P.C.; *Bibhuti Bhusan Das Gupta* v. *State of West Bengal*, AIR 1969 SC 381.

CHAPTER XXXI
EVIDENCE FOR DEFENCE

(SECTION 243 CR.P.C.)

The accused has the right to lead evidence in support of his defence or to rebut the evidence led by the prosecution. Where there is no clinching evidence against the accused, there is no need to lead evidence in rebuttal. However, where there is evidence against the accused, it is advisable to lead some evidence in rebuttal. It has been held by the Apex Court in *Haripada Dey* v. *State of West Bengal*, AIR 1956 SC 757, that, *"Where the prosecution has established its case, the accused must lead evidence to substantiate his defence; on failure, he should thank himself."*

In this case, accused stated in his statement recorded under section 313 of Cr.P.C. that he does not want to adduce any evidence. However, application was filed by accused later on, stating that they want to adduce evidence. But this application was rejected by the Court. The Allahabad High Court held that in session trial, after the prosecution evidence is recorded and the statement of the accused is also recorded, an order should be passed under section 232 of Cr.P.C. If accused is not acquitted, only then the accused should be called upon to enter into his defence and adduce any evidence he may have in support thereof as provided under section 233 of Cr.P.C.; *Pintu* v. *State of Uttar Pradesh,* 2002 (4) Crimes 379 (All): 2002 Cri LJ 2241 (All).

In this case, the Bombay High Court held that procedure of calling upon accused to enter his defence is not mandatory. Hence, non-compliance of provisions of sections 232 and 233, Cr.P.C. would not *ipso facto* vitiate proceedings; *State of Maharashtra* v. *Raju Jagdish Paswan,* 2013 All MR (Cri) 1431.

The names of the defence witnesses proposed to be examined can be given during examination of accused under section 313 of Cr.P.C. or a separate list can be filed.

Where the Special Judge refused to summon the six defence witnesses mentioned in list of witnesses filed by the accused/appellant, the Apex Court held that the trial is vitiated as it denied the fullest opportunity to defend himself; *Habeeb Mohammad* v. *State of Hyderabad,* AIR 1954 SC 51: (1954) SCR 475.

However, in *Arivazhagan* v. *State,* (2000) 2 SCR 155: 2000 SCC (Cri) 638, the Apex Court held that *"It is the duty of the Court to short list such proceedings. If the Court feels that the list is intended only to delay the proceedings, the Court is well within its powers to disallow even the whole of it."*

CHAPTER XXXII

ORAL ARGUMENTS

(SECTION 314 CR.P.C.)

After the evidence is led by both the parties, the stage is fixed for hearing and after the prosecution is heard, the defence has the right to oral argument. Even written notes of argument can be filed setting forth concisely and under distinct headings, the argument in support of his case. It is advisable to file written notes of argument even if oral argument is addressed.

The Bombay High Court has directed that in all trials by Courts of Session the presiding Judge shall record briefly, in writing, in English, the substance of the arguments of the public prosecutor and the lawyer for the defence, if any, and the notes so made shall be included as exhibits in the papers of the case. [Paragraph 3(1) of Chapter 4 of Criminal Manual]

CHAPTER XXXIII
JUDGMENTS

SYNOPSIS

(A) Sentence in Cases of Conviction of Several Offences at One Trial (Section 31, Cr.P.C.) and Sentence on Offender Already Sentenced for Another Offence (Section 427, Cr.P.C.)

(B) Suspension of Sentence: (Cr.P.C. Section 389)

(C) Obligation to Hear Accused on Question of Sentence (Section 235(2), Cr.P.C.)

(D) Plea Bargaining

The Apex Court in *Anil Rai* v. *State of Bihar*, AIR 2001 SC 3173: 2001 (2) All MR (Cri) 1930 (SC), has held that, *"Justice withheld is worst than justice denied"* and directed the subordinate Courts to deliver judgments without delay and the delay in pronouncement of judgment should not be beyond two months of conclusion of arguments in any case.

In *Som Mittal* v. *Government of Karnataka*, 2008 AIR SCW 1640, the Apex Court has directed the Courts to desist from making general observations, recommendations or directions which are alien to the dispute before it. Courts should only deal with the subject-matter of the case and issues involved therein. If necessary, Court may notify the parties so that they can put forth their views on such issue.

In *Mukhtiar Singh* v. *State of Punjab*, AIR 1995 SC 686, the Apex Court has held that if the judgment does not disclose as to what was argued before it on behalf of the prosecution and defence, but judgment contains only the conclusions and nothing more, such judgment cannot be sustained.

In this case, the Apex Court has directed all the Courts to pronounce judgment in open Court immediately after the conclusion of trial within six weeks or two months; *Anil Rai* v. *State of Bihar*, (2001) 7 SCC 318.

In this case, the Bombay High Court has issued directions as regards pronouncing of judgments. These are:

(a) Judgment should be pronounced within a period of three months from the date of conclusion of the arguments.

(b) In miscellaneous application and/or all other matters, order shall not be delayed beyond a period of 2 months from the date of conclusion of arguments.

(c) The practice of *quasi*-judicial authorities to communicate the decision to the parties after reserving the order should be discontinued forthwith.

(d) Certified copy of the judgment or order should be made available to the parties, if applied for, not later than 7 days and not later than 2 days if the copy is applied for on urgent basis.

(e) The Judicial Officers concerned shall also be liable for disciplinary action by the High Court and the State Government, as the case may be, for their persistent failure to comply with these directions; *Pradeep K.R. Sangodkar* v. *State of Goa*, 2007 (1) AIR Bom R 80.

In *Gurucharan* v. *State*, 2010 Cri LJ 3339, the Delhi High Court has held that in offences entailing extreme penalty of imprisonment for life or death, it is expected that every point urged would be dealt with by razor sharp precision and sound logical reasoning and not on the *ipse dixit* of a Judge.

Even paragraph 43(4) of Chapter 6 of Criminal Manual issued by the Honourable Bombay High Court mandates that the points that arise for decision should be dealt with one by one, marshalling the evidence for and against considering the arguments, and giving a clear finding on each point.

On the day appointed for judgment, the defence counsel must come prepared to argue on the point of sentence if the accused is held guilty for the offence charged against him. The defence lawyer must try to endeavour to convince the Court to give benefit of provisions of the Probation of Offenders Act, 1958 or provisions of section 360 of Cr.P.C. The defence lawyer must come prepared with the rulings of the High Courts or Supreme Courts which would support his cause. If the Court does not grant the benefit of the provisions of the Probation of Offenders Act, 1958 or provisions of section 360 of Cr.P.C. and imposes punishment and penalty, the defence must be prepared to pay the amount of fine and offer surety for the release with the application for suspension of sentence.

The provisions of section 428 of Cr.P.C. are mandatory in nature and accused is entitled to get the set off against the term of imprisonment imposed on him, (*i.e.*, the period of detention undergone by him during the investigation, inquiry or trial of the same case and before the date of such conviction).

In *Bhagirath* v. *Delhi Administration*, (1985) 3 SCR 743, the Apex Court held that even the persons sentenced to imprisonment for life are entitled to set-off their under-trial period of detention against their sentence.

(A) Sentence in Cases of Conviction of Several Offences at One Trial (Section 31, Cr.P.C.) and Sentence on Offender Already Sentenced for Another Offence (Section 427, Cr.P.C.)

In this case, the Apex Court held that ambit of section 31, Cr.P.C. is wide and it not only covers single transaction constituting two or more offences but also offences arising out of two or more transactions. Whether or not to exercise such power depends upon nature of offence and fact and circumstances of each case. It cannot be laid down as a general proposition that normal rule is consecutive sentences and exception is to order concurrent sentence; *O.M. Cherian @ Thankachan* v. *State of Kerala*, 2015 All SCR 282.

Where accused is sentenced to conviction of several offences including one that of life imprisonment at one trial, consecutive sentence cannot be imposed in view of proviso to section 31(2), Cr.P.C. And therefore, the Court directed the sentences to run concurrently; *Duryodhan Rout* v. *State of Orissa*, 2014 All SCR 2601.

Where the transaction relating to the offences is not the same or the facts constituting the two offences are quite different, consecutive sentences may be imposed; *Mohommed Akhtar Hussain* v. *Assistant Collector of Customs, Ahmedabad*, AIR 1988 SC 2143.

Where the Court has imposed sentence of imprisonment in default of payment of fine, there is no prohibition in law to order the default sentences also to run concurrently either under section 30 or 31 of Cr.P.C.; *M. Balasubramanian* v. *State*, 2012 (2) Crimes 401 (Mad).

Where complaints relate to cases involving dishonour of cheques issued by borrower towards repayment of loan arising out of single transaction, Court can exercise discretion for the benefit of the convict in such complaints for ordering concurrent running of the sentences; *V.K. Bansal* v. *State of Haryana*, 2013 (6) Mh LJ 107 (SC).

In this case, the trial Court imposed sentences on accused in one trial for offences under section 381 of IPC and section 52 of Post Office Act, for the offence of theft by post-office employee. The Apex Court held that sentences should run concurrently and such directions can be passed by the Appellate Court by invoking section 31 of Cr.P.C., it being in nature of consequential on and incidental to affirmance of conviction; *Nagaraja Rao* v. *CBI*, 2015 Cri LJ 1458 (SC).

(B) Suspension of Sentence: (Cr.P.C. Section 389)

In this case, the Apex Court held that section 389(1) of the Code confers power on the appellate Court to stay the operation of the order of conviction. If the order of conviction is to result in some disqualification of the type mentioned in section 267 of the Companies Act, we see no reason why we should give a narrow meaning to section 389(1) of the Code to debar the Court from granting an order to that effect in a fit case. The appeal under section 374 is essentially against the order of conviction because the order of sentence is merely consequential thereto; albeit even the order of sentence can be independently challenged if it is harsh and disproportionate to the established guilt. Therefore, when an appeal is preferred under section 374 of the Code the appeal is against both the conviction and sentence and, therefore, there is no reason to place a narrow interpretation on section 389(1) of the Code not to extend it to an order of conviction. In a fit case, if the High Court feels satisfied that the order of conviction needs to be suspended or stayed so that the convicted person does not suffer from a certain disqualification provided for in any other statute, it may exercise the power because otherwise the damage done cannot be undone. But, while granting a stay or suspension of the order of conviction the Court must examine the pros and cons and if it feels satisfied that a case is made out for grant of such an order, it may do so and in so doing it may, if it considers it appropriate, impose such conditions as are considered appropriate to protect the interest of the concerned; *Rama Narang* v. *Ramesh Narang*, (1995) 2 SCC 513.

The correct law as regards the suspension of sentence is the one rendered by the Apex Court in *Bhagwan Rama Shinde Gosai* v. *State of Gujarat*, (1999) 4 SCC 421, where the Apex Court held that, *"When a convicted person is sentenced to fixed period of sentence and when he files appeal under any statutory right, suspension of sentence can be considered by the appellant Court liberally unless there are exceptional circumstances."*

In *Kiran Kumar* v. *State of Madhya Pradesh,* 2002 (1) All MR (Cri) 473 (SC), where appeal was filed against conviction under sections 450, 376 and 506, I.P.C. and the appeal was pending, the Apex Court held that *"Sentence ought to be suspended during the pendency of appeal in absence of exceptional reasons for not doing so."*

Recently, the Full Bench of the Karnataka High Court in *Virabasayya P. Hallur* v. *State of Karnataka,* 2003 All MR (Cri) Journal 128, has held that *"unless accused has a right of appeal in law under the Code of Criminal Procedure or the Constitution of India, he is not entitled for suspension of sentence or bail. .... Where the Court has no power to suspend the sentence and grant bail under section 389(3) of Cr.P.C., it has no inherent power to grant bail in exercise of its power under section 482 of the Code."*

In *Navjot Singh Sidhu* v. *State of Punjab,* 2007 (1) Crimes 279 (SC): 2007 All SCR 617: 2007 (3) CRJ 591 (SC), the Apex Court held that, *"person seeking stay should specifically draw attention of the Court to consequences if conviction is not stayed. ...... Stay can be resorted to in rare cases depending upon special facts of a case."* The Court further held that, *"where the execution of sentence is stayed the conviction continues to operate. But where the conviction itself is stayed the effect is that the conviction will not be operative from the date of stay."*

However, the Apex Court refused to suspend the conviction of the accused convicted under Prevention of Corruption Act, 1988. The Honourable Apex Court held that *"conviction cannot be suspended in view of monstrous dimension of corruption cases in India"*; *K.C. Sareen* v. *CBI, Chandigarh,* (2001) 6 SCC 584: 2001 All MR (Cri) 2160 (SC).

In this case, the Apex Court expressed its displeasure at the order of High Court which suspended the sentence in a case of corruption. The Apex Court held that High Court should not have passed the order of suspension of sentence in a case involving corruption. The Court reminded the courts that corruption is a human rights violation in itself, as it leads to systematic economic crimes; *State of Maharashtra* v. *Balkrishna D. Kumbhar,* 2012 (4) Bom CR (Cri) 828 (SC): 2013 All SCR 163.

In this case, the Court stayed the conviction mainly on ground that it is coming in respondent film actor's way to travel abroad. However, no finding was recorded by the Court that if conviction is not stayed, irreparable harm/ irreversible consequences or injustice would be caused to respondents. The Apex Court set aside the impugned order of the High Court and remitted the case to the High Court to be decided afresh; *State of Rajasthan* v. *Salman Salim Khan,* 2015 All SCR 1221.

In this case, the Apex Court held that the possibility or otherwise of early hearing of the appeal is one of the relevant circumstances to consider suspension of sentence. Suspension of sentence can be considered by the appellate Court liberally unless there is exceptional circumstances which would not justify it.

Sentence can be suspended till the disposal of appeal; *Angana* v. *State of Rajasthan*, 2009 (1) Crimes 320 (SC).

In this case, the Apex Court held that sentence would generally be not suspended by Court in serious offences like murder; *Sidharth Vashisht @ Manu Sharma* v. *State (NCT of Delhi)*, (2008) 5 SCC 230.

It should be remembered that the Court dismissing appeal is not empowered to suspend the sentence or grant bail in any form after its decision in appeal, to enable the accused to approach the High Court in revision application; *Dilip R. Umare* v. *State of Maharashtra*, 1996 (2) Mh LJ 1004 (Bom).

In this case, the Patna High Court has held that interim suspension of sentence can be granted on humanitarian grounds; *Chandra Shekhar Bharti* v. *State of Bihar*, 2014 Cri LJ 2953 (Pat) (DB).

(C) Obligation to Hear Accused on Question of Sentence (Section 235(2), Cr.P.C.)

Hearing is obligatory at the sentencing stage. The purpose behind the same is to give an opportunity to accused to place all relevant materials and facts before the Court. In *Bachan Singh* v. *State of Punjab*, AIR 1980 SC 898: 1980 Cri LJ 636, the Apex Court held that, *"If a request for opportunity to produce evidence in made by either the prosecution or the accused, or by both, the Judge should give the party or parties concerned an opportunity of producing evidence or material relating to various factors bearing on question of sentence."*

However, the earlier view taken by the Apex Court in *Santa Singh* v. *State of Punjab*, (1976) 4 SCC 190: 1977 Mh LJ 1 (SC) and *Allaudin Mian* v. *State of Bihar*, AIR 1989 SC 1456: (1989) 3 SCC 5, regarding adjourning the matter to future date to hear the accused on the question of sentence has not been followed by the Apex Court in *Ram Deo Chauhan* alias *Raj Nath Chauhan* v. *State of Assam*, AIR 2001 SC 2231. The three-Judge Bench of the Apex Court in *Ram Deo Chauhan's* case has explained the legal position as follows:

(i) When the conviction is under section 302, IPC (with or without the aid of section 34 or 149 or 120B of IPC), if the Sessions Judge does not propose to impose death penalty on the convicted person, it is unnecessary to proceed to hear the accused on the question of sentence. Section 235(2) of the Code will not be violated if the sentence of life imprisonment is awarded for that offence without hearing the accused on the question of sentence.

(ii) In all other cases the accused must be given sufficient opportunity of hearing on the question of sentence.

(iii) The normal rule is that after pronouncing the verdict of guilty, the hearing should be made on the same day and the sentence shall also be pronounced on the same day.

(iv) In cases where the Judge feels or if the accused demands more time for hearing on the question of sentence (especially when the Judge propose to impose death penalty) the proviso to section 309(2) is not a bar for affording such time.

(v) For any reason the Court is inclined to adjourn the case after pronouncing the verdict of guilty in grave offences, the convicted person shall be committed to jail till the verdict on the sentence is pronounced. Further detention will depend upon the process of law.

In this case, the Apex Court held that when accused files a plea of bargaining and pleads guilty, complainant or victim must be heard before deciding on guilty plea of the accused; *Giriraj Prasad Meena* v. *State of Rajasthan*, (2014) 13 SCC 674.

Where the provisions of section 235(2), Cr.P.C. are not complied with, the appellate Court can either send back the case to the Sessions Court for complying with section 235(2), Cr.P.C. so as to enable the accused to adduce materials; or, in order to avoid delay, the appellate Court may by itself give an opportunity to the parties in terms of section 235(2), Cr.P.C. to produce the materials they wish to adduce instead of sending the matter back to the trial Court for hearing on sentence. In the present case, the Apex Court asked/allowed the counsel appearing for the appellants to file affidavits/materials on the question of sentence; *Mukesh* v. *State (NCT of Delhi)*, 2017 ALL MR (Cri) 2448 (SC).

(D) Plea Bargaining

Hitherto, the law which prevailed was that bargain on question of sentence was not permissible. In *State of Uttar Pradesh* v. *Chandrika*, AIR 2000 SC 164, the Apex Court held that, *"Mere acceptance or admission of guilt is no ground to reduce sentence. Concept of plea bargaining is against public policy under criminal justice system."* The same view has been taken by the Apex Court in *State of Uttar Pradesh* v. *Nasruddin*, AIR 2000 SC 3573.

However, plea bargaining has been legalised by the Parliament of India by inserting new Chapter XXI-A (sections 265A to 265L) by The Criminal Law (Amendment) Act, 2005 (Act Number 2 of 2006). This Act has received the assent of the President of India on 11th January, 2006.

In *Guerrero Lugo Elvia Grissel* v. *State of Maharastra*, 2012 Mh LJ 369, the Bombay High Court held that trial Court has no discretion to award sentence other than 1/4th of the punishment provided for or extendable, as the case may be, for the offence in question in cases covered by clause (d) of section 265E of Cr.P.C.

CHAPTER XXXIV
PENOLOGY

SYNOPSIS

In this chapter, the Judicial approach in sentencing has been given, which would enable the defence to convince the Court to take lenient view and soften the judicial conscience.

The fundamental principle in imposing punishment is that 'fouler the crime greater the punishment'. However, punishment must be proportionate with the crime charged. This is called the *Doctrine of Proportionality or Principle of Just Desert* which has been explained by the Apex Court in *Lehna* v. *State of Haryana*, (2002) 1 SCR 377, as under: *"The principle of proportion between crime and punishment is a principle of Just Desert that serves as the foundation of every criminal sentence that is justifiable. As a principle of criminal justice, it is hardly less familiar or less important than the principle that only the guilty ought to be punished. Indeed, the requirement that punishment not be disproportionately great, which is a corollary of Just Desert, is dictated by the same principle that does not allow punishment of the innocent, for any punishment in excess of what is deserved for the criminal conduct is punishment without guilt. ..... Punishment ought always to fit the crime; yet in practice sentences are determined largely by other considerations. Sometimes, it is the correctional needs of the perpetrator that are offered to justify a sentence; sometimes, the desirability of keeping him out of circulation, and sometimes even the traffic results of his crime. Inevitably, these considerations cause a departure from just desert as the basis of punishment and create cases of apparent injustice that are serious and widespread. Uniformly disproportionate punishment has some very undesirable practical consequences."*

Ordinarily, the legislative sentencing policy as laid in some special Acts where the parliamentary intent has been expressed in unequivocal terms should be applied. Sentence of less than the minimum period prescribed by the Parliament may be imposed only in exceptional cases; *Harendra Nath Chakraborty* v. *State of West Bengal*, 2009 All MR (Cri) 2477 (SC).

There are different theories of punishment. These are: (i) Deterrent theory (ii) Preventive theory (iii) Retributive theory (iv) Reformative theory.

The application of the one or the other theory of punishment depends on facts and circumstances of each particular case. The approach of the Courts regarding imposing punishment can be understood from the following cases:

The Apex Court has observed that crime is a pathological aberration, that criminal can ordinarily be redeemed, that State has to rehabilitate rather than avenge. The sub-cultural that leads to anti-social behaviour has to be countered not by undue cruelty but by re-culturisation. Therefore, the focus of interest in penology is the individual, and the goal is salvaging him for society. The infliction of harsh and savage punishment is thus a relic of past and the regressive times. The human today views sentencing as a process of reshaping a person who has deteriorated into criminality and the modern community has primary stake in the rehabilitation of the offender as a means of social defence. We, therefore, consider a therapeutic rather than an *in terrorem* outlook, should prevail in our criminal courts, since brutal incarceration of the person merely produces laceration of his mind. In the words of George Bernard Shaw: 'if you are to punish a man retributively, you must injure him. If you are to reform him, you must improve him and, men are not improved by injuries.' *Mohammad Giasuddin* v. *State of Andhra Pradesh,* (1977) 3 SCC 287.

In this case, the appellant who was 22 years old was convicted by the Court for raping the wife of his cousin. The High Court confirmed the conviction and sentence. In appeal, the Apex Court, while reducing the sentence, observed that a hypersexed *homo sapiens* cannot be habilitated by humiliating or harsh treatment, but that is precisely the perversion of unreformed jail justice which some criminologists has described as the crime of punishment. ..... In-prison treatment must, therefore, be geared to psychic healing, release of stresses, restoration of self- respect and cultural normalisation, apart from training to adapt oneself to the life outside. The functional failure of our pachydermic prison projects, exacerbated by its tension and trauma on the one hand and the reverse ethos inside on the other, deserve judicial cognizance. .... Given correctional courses through meditational therapy and other measures, his erotic aberration may wither away. ..... One major method in securing this goal is to keep alive the family tie of the person in prison so that he may not deteriorate into a non-person; *Phul Singh* v. *State of Haryana,* (1980) 1 SCR 589.

The Apex Court has observed that one of the principle purposes of punitive deprivation of liberty, constitutionally sanctioned, is decriminalisation of the criminal and restoration of his dignity, self-esteem and good citizenship, so that when the man emerges from the forbidden gates he becomes as socially useful individual.....Long prison terms do not humanise or habilitate but debase and promote recidivism. Life imprisonment means languishing in prison for years and years. Such induration of the soul induced by indefinite incarceration hardens the inmates, not softens their responses; *Dharmbir* v. *State of Uttar Pradesh,* (1980) 1 SCR 1.

In this case, the Apex Court observed that the Court has responsibility to see that punishment serves social defence which is the validation of deprivation of citizen's liberty. Correctional treatment with a rehabilitative orientation, is an imperative of modern penology which has abandoned *jus talionis*. A hospital setting and a humanitarian ethos must pervade our prisons if the retributive theory , which is but vengeance in disguise, is to disappear and deterrence as a punitive objective gains success not through the hardening practice of inhumanity inflicted on prisoners but by reformation and healing whereby the creative potential of the prisoner is unfolded. These values have their roots in Article 19 which sanctions deprivation of freedoms provided they render a reasonable service to social defence, public order and security of the State; *Lingala Vijayakumar* v. *Public Prosecutor, Andhra Pradesh,* (1979) 1 SCR 2.

In this case, the Apex Court observed that social defence is the criminological foundation of punishment. In the instant case, the trial Judge has confused between correctional approach to prison treatment and nominal punishment verging on decriminalisation of serious social offences. The first is basic and the second pathetic. The Court, which ignores the grave injury to society implicit in economic crimes by the upper-berth mafia, ill serves social justice. Soft sentencing justice is gross injustice where many innocents are the potential victims. ...... Coddling is not correctional any more than torture is deterrent. While iatrogenic prison terms are bad because they dehumanise, it is functional failure and judicial pathology to hold out a benignly self-defeating non-sentence to deviants who endanger the morals and morale, the health and wealth of society; *M.H. Hoskot* v. *State of Maharashtra,* (1979) 1 SCR 192.

Reminding the Bar and the Bench of their duties in the administration of justice, the Apex Court observed that to jail an accused is mechanical farewell to the finer sentencing sensitivity of the Judge of salvaging a redeemable man by non-institutionalised treatment. Sentencing legality is violated when the Judge shirks. And the Bar is often alien to correctional alternatives and concentrates its ammunition on culpability and extenuatory scaling down of imprisonment. Calling pre-sentence investigation reports, bestowal of intelligent care on the choice between institutional and non-institutional disposition like probation, conditional release and such community methods must form part of innovative sentences. But this should be based on careful study of the convict and his potentiality for reform; not guess-work, nor insensitive assessments. The Court further observed that the close nexus between violence and alcohol is a call to the State in every criminal investigation to identify the role of alcohol in the commission of the offence and in every prisoner's treatment to provide for anti-alcoholic therapy. To fail here is vicarious guilt of the State to society; *Dilbag Singh* v. *State of Punjab,* (1979) 2 SCR 1134.

In this case, the appellant was 12 years old at the time of incident. He along with his to elder brothers was convicted by trial Court under section 302 read with section 34, IPC. The High Court converted conviction from section 302 to one under section 326 read with section 34, IPC. While dismissing the appeal, the Apex Court observed that man is a rational being, and law is a system of behavioural cybernetics where noetic niceties, if pressed too far, may defeat its societal efficacy. ..... When a crime is committed by the concerted action of a plurality of persons, the degree of criminality may vary, depending not only on the injurious sequel but also on the part played and the circumstances present, a personalised approach with reference to each participant has to be made regarding the circumstances of involvement, his *doli capax*, age and expectation of consequences. ..... The ultimate desideratum of most sentences is to make an offender a non-offender. The Indian legal system must be sensitized by juvenile justice; *Hiralal Mallick* v. *State of Bihar*, (1978) 1 SCR 301.

In *Maru Ram* v. *Union of India*, (1981) 1 SCR 1196, the Constitution Bench observed that correctional strategy is integral to social defence which is the final justification for punishment of the criminal. And since personal injury can never psychically heal, it is obdurate obscurantism for any legislative criminologists to reject the potential for prisoner re-socialisation from the calculus of reformative remission and timely release. .... Alienation of our judicial system from our cultural quintessence, thanks to the hang-over of the colonial pass, may be the pathological root of the brute penology which confuses between crime and criminal. Torturing the latter to terminate the former is not promotional of human dignity and fair legal process.

The Apex Court has held that law should adopt corrective machinery or deterrence, based on factual matrix. By deft modulation, sentencing process be stern where it should be, and tempered with mercy, where it warrants to be. Undue sympathy to impose inadequate sentence would do more harm to the justice system; *State of Karnataka* v. *Raju*, AIR 2007 SC 3225.

The Bombay High Court in *Hanmantappa Murtyappa Vijapure* v. *State of Maharashtra*, 2004 All MR (Cri) 2117, set aside the conviction of the accused on the ground that sanctioning authority did not consider the fact whether departmental enquiry was just and proper in the circumstances of the case looking to triviality of the amount by applying the 'doctrine of triviality'.

This was a case of *E.K. Chandrasenan* v. *State of Kerala*, (1995) 1 SCR 277, where 70 persons died after having consumed liquor from the shops and sub-shops which were catered by the firm "Bee Vee Liquors" and 24 persons lost eyesight permanently. The Sessions Judge acquitted accused 5 to 8 and 10 of all the charges whereas accused No. 1 to 3 and 9 were convicted under section 120B and section 328 as well as sections 107, 109 and 272 Read with section 34, IPC. The Kerala High Court dismissed the appeals of accused No. 1 to 3 and 9. Accused 1 to 3 and 10 filed appeals before the Supreme Court. It was contended on behalf of accused No. 9 that his advance age is a mitigating circumstance and therefore benefit be given to him. As regards this contention, the Apex Court held that, "*So far as accused 9 is concerned, as to the advance age this was a mitigating circumstance, there exists an aggravating circumstance as well, the same being that it was this accused who was the prime mover, as would be apparent from the facts on record. Thus, the age factor has been neutralised by the active role played by this accused in the conspiracy. Therefore sentence imposed on accused No. 9 is enhanced to life imprisonment.*"

In *Smt. Mathri* v. *State of Punjab*, AIR 1964 SC 986, the incident occurred on land when some persons had gone there for taking delivery of possession with warrants which have ceased to be executable after expiry of date fixed for execution. As regards to some woman accused who were convicted, the Apex Court held that, *"No specific role is assigned to some woman accused. They did not take a leading role but come into the field when their menfolk came out – partly to save their fields and partly to save their menfolk. Therefore, sentence of woman accused reduced to the period of imprisonment already undergone."*

As regards the penological approach while dealing with a case under Contempt of Court, the Apex Court observed that, *"whether or not a person has obtained a definite advantage in making a false statement is immaterial in deciding whether the person has committed contempt of Court. However, it is a relevant factor for imposing the quantum of punishment;" Murray & Co.* v. *Ashok Kumar Newatia,* (2000) 1 SCR 367.

This was a case of *Jethmal Kothari* v. *State of Rajasthan,* 1987 Cri LJ 764, where the accused was convicted and sentenced to pay a fine of Rs. 2500 and in default of payment of fine to undergo 9 months rigorous imprisonment under the Prevention of Corruption Act but the State did not file any appeal for enhancement of punishment. The Honourable High Court observed that, *"in such a case the imposition of fine only is ridiculous. It protects, abates and encourages socio-economic crimes against the society and State, by Judicial process and brings judiciary in contempt of people .... However, there is no appeal from the side of the State, which again tantamounts to State's protective umbrella to such antisocial activities and unspoken, unwritten, undetected conspiracy to help accused indirectly."* Further, the Court directed Chief Secretary to enquire why State has not filed appeal for enhancement and take suitable action against erring officers as it smells of corruption in protecting corruption even after detecting corruption and directed to submit report within 6 months to Court.

The Constitution Bench of the Apex Court in *Bachan Singh* v. *State of Punjab,* (1983) 1 SCR 145, has held that, *"Penological goals also do not justify the imposition of death penalty for the offence of murder. The prevailing standards of human decency are also incompatible with death penalty. The standards of human decency with reference to which the proportionality of the punishment to the offence is required to be judged vary from society to society depending on the cultural and spiritual tradition of the society, its history, philosophy and its sense of moral and ethical values. .... It is obvious from the provision enacted in section 354(3) of the Cr.P.C. that death sentence is legislatively regarded as disproportionate and excessive in most cases of murder and it is only in exceptional cases that it can at all be contended that death sentence is proportionate to the offence of murder. .... Death penalty cannot be regarded as proportionate to the offence of murder, merely because the murder is brutal, heinous or shocking."*

In *Machhi Singh* v. *State of Punjab,* (1983) 3 SCR 413, the Apex Court held that *"the extreme penalty of death need not be inflicted except in gravest cases of extreme culpability. .... Life imprisonment is the rule and death sentence is an exception......... A balance sheet of aggravating and mitigating circumstances has to be drawn up and in doing so the mitigating circumstances has to be accorded full weightage and a just balance has to be struck between the aggravating and the mitigating circumstances before the option is exercised."*

In this case of *Ram Deo Chauhan* alias *Raj Nath Chauhan* v. *State of Assam,* AIR 2001 SC 2231, death sentence was upheld by two-Judges but one Judge allowed the review petition and altered the sentence of death to imprisonment for life. As regards the remedy open to petitioner/accused and the effect of such judgement the Apex Court held that *"the accused will not be remediless. .... If any motion is made in terms of sections 432, 433 and 433A of the Code and/or Article 72 or Article 161 of the Constitution as the case may be, the same may be appropriately dealt with and benefit may be given to him."*

(A) Sentencing in Dowry Death Cases

In this case, the Apex Court held that word 'may' in section 304B, IPC has to be interpreted to mean that it is not mandatory to award life imprisonment in each and every case. Life imprisonment should be awarded in rare cases. However, sentence should not be less than 7 years; *Hari Om* v. *State of Haryana,* 2015 (2) Crimes 156 (SC).

(B) Sentencing in Rape Cases

In this case, the Apex Court held that in absence of adequate and special reasons, recourse to proviso to section 376(2), IPC cannot be taken in a casual manner; *Bavo @ Manubhai A. Thakore* v. *State of Gujarat,* 2012 All SCR 827.

In this case, the Apex Court held that ground of compromise with victim, long pendency of trial or fact that victim is married and settled in life, cannot be construed as special factors for reduction of sentence. Proviso to section 376(2), IPC being an exception clause, requires strict interpretation; *Shimbhu* v. *State of Haryana,* 2013 All MR (Cri) 3306 (SC).

In this case, the Apex Court held that for heinous crimes like rape, there cannot be different standards for illiterate labourers from rural areas, as far as quantum of sentence is concerned; *State of Madhya Pradesh* v. *Bhagwat,* 2006 (2) Crimes 254 (SC).

(C) Sentencing in Honour Killing Cases

In this case, the Apex Court held that honour killing comes within the category of rarest of rare cases and deserves death penalty. The Apex Court warned the potential offenders who are planning to perpetrate honour killing should know that the gallows await them; *Bhagwan Dass* v. *State (NCT of Delhi),* AIR 2011 SC 1863.

(D) Sentencing in Fake Encounter Cases

In this case, the Apex Court held that fake encounters are nothing but cold blooded, brutal murders by persons who are supposed to uphold law. They must be given death sentence, treating it as a rarest of rare case; *Prakash Kadam* v. *Ramprasad V. Gupta,* 2011 All SCR 1402.

(E) Sentencing in Rash and Negligent Driving Cases

In this case, the Apex Court held that where a person is convicted for rash and negligent driving, sentence should be stringent. The Court further directed the policy makers to scrutinise, re-look and re-visit sentencing policy in section 304A, IPC; *State of Punjab* v. *Saurabh Bakshi,* 2015 Cri LJ 2459 (SC).

In this case, order of the High Court reducing sentence of imprisonment to period already undergone was held to be erroneous and the same was set aside by the Apex Court. The Apex Court held that one of the prime considerations in such cases should be deterrence; *State of Punjab* v. *Balwinder Singh*, 2012 All MR (Cri) 717 (SC).

(F) Sentencing in Corruption Cases

In this case, the Apex Court held that where a person is convicted under Prevention of Corruption Act, 1988, judicial discretion is restricted in imposing punishment. Theory of reformation of conduct has no significance in such matters. Only relevant object of punishment in such cases, is denunciation and deterrence; *Shanti Lal Meena* v. *State (NCT of Delhi) through CBI*, 2015 All SCR 2858.

In this case, accused was convicted for demanding and accepting money from complainant before operation of patient. It was pleaded on behalf of the convict doctor that he is on the verge of retirement and he suffered agony of investigation since 2007 and therefore proceedings be quashed. The Apex Court refused to quash the proceedings and held that if mercy is shown in such cases at this stage, it may send wrong signal in society because rampant corruption is seen in every walk of life; *State of Rajasthan* v. *Dr. Rajkumar Agarwal*, 2012 All MR (Cri) 3001 (SC).

(G) Sentencing in Cases of Criminal Breach of Trust

In this case, the Apex Court held that Court cannot take lenient view in awarding sentence on ground of sympathy or delay, particularly, if it relates to distribution of essential commodities under scheme of Government intended to benefit public at large; *Sadhupati N. Rao* v. *State of Andhra Pradesh*, 2012 All MR (Cri) 3034 (SC).

(H) Sentencing in Cases under Essential Commodities Act, 1955

In this case, the Apex Court held that the benefit of probation cannot be granted to offenders indulging in illegal sale in violation of section 7 of The Essential Commodities Act, 1955; *Sunil Kumar* v. *State of Haryana*, AIR 2012 SC 1754: 2012 Cri LJ 2093 (SC).

(I) Sentencing in Economic Crimes

In this case, the Apex Court held that white collar crimes should be viewed sternly for they involve wrongful appropriation of public funds and no leniency should be shown to the offenders; *Ram Narain Poply* v. *CBI*, AIR 2003 SC 2748.

(J) Sentencing in Cases of Kidnapping for Ransom

In this case, the Apex Court held that kidnapping for ransom is a crime which calls for a deterrent punishment. Fact that kidnapping had not resulted in death of victim, is irrelevant; *Akram Khan* v. *State of West Bengal*, AIR 2012 SC 308.

Other Cases on Penology

1. *Reddy Sampath Kumar* v. *State of Andhra Pradesh*, AIR 2005 SC 3478: Where the accused doctor (who was convicted for imprisonment of life) made his father-in-law and mother-in-law and their three minor children

believe that they were suffering from AIDS when it was not so and killed them by giving poisonous injection under the pretext of giving treatment, the Apex Court directed that, *"accused shall not get benefit of remission granted on auspicious occasion either granted by state or by the Government of India."*

2. *Dalbir Singh* v. *State of Haryana,* AIR 2000 SC 1677: (2000) 3 SCR 1000: The Apex Court held that, *"the benefit of probation under Probation of Offenders Act (20 of 1958) shall not be extended to persons convicted of offences of causing death by rash and negligent driving."*
3. *State* v. *Vishwanath Naik,* 2005 All MR (Cri) 2671: Where the truck dashed against scooter but the accident took place due to negligent driving of the scooterist while crossing main road without precaution , the Bombay High Court dismissed the appeal for enhancement of sentence filed by State on the ground that it is the duty of the person crossing an internal road to be more cautious as there is always a heavy traffic on the main road. The High Court imposed a sentence of fine of Rs. 1000 under section 279, I.P.C and Rs. 2000 under section 304A, IPC and held that it would meet the ends of justice.
4. *Shree Vijaykumar* v. *State by Inspector of Police, Kanyakumari,* 2005 (3) Crimes 55 (SC): In this case it was alleged that second appellant picked up a lighted Kerosene lamp from his shop and threw it on the deceased. They were tried for the offences punishable under sections 302/34, 304 Part II and were convicted by the trial Court for the offence under section 302/34, IPC. However, there was no satisfactory evidence to establish that it was petrol or kerosene or such other highly inflammable liquid. The Apex Court held that, *"A-1 can only be convicted under section 323, IPC for causing hurt to the deceased by hitting him with a bottle."*
5. *State of Madhya Pradesh* v. *Saleem* alias *Chamaru,* 2005 All MR (Cri) 2533 (SC): Where the sentence was reduced to custodial sentence of 6 months 23 days that was already undergone on the ground that accused were illiterate and belonging to lower income group and were of 23 years of age, the Apex Court held the reduction of sentence to be improper.
6. *State of Maharashtra* v. *Rashid Babubhai Mulani,* 2006 (1) AIR Bom R 800: The Bombay High Court reduced the sentence from one year to four months on the grounds that incident is 19 years old, accused came from poor background with family to support and was hardly 32 years old at the time of incident.
7. *Bhagwan Singh* v. *State of Madhya Pradesh,* AIR 2003 SC 1088: The Apex Court held that the accused should not be awarded punishment of imprisonment for life or extreme penalty of death where the case entirely rests on the sole testimony of a child witness and further held that adequate corroboration should be looked from other evidence to the testimony of child.
8. *Ram Pujan* v. *State of Uttar Pradesh,* AIR 1973 SC 2418: 1973 Cri LJ 1612: The Apex Court held that, *"the fact of compromise can be taken into account*

in determining the quantum of sentence even though the offence is a non-compoundable one."

9. *Ram Pal* v. *State of Uttar Pradesh,* 2003 AIR SCW 3792: The Apex Court held that, *"While in a given case death penalty may be appropriate sentence even for a single murder, it would not necessarily mean that in every case of multiple murders death penalty has to be the normal punishment."*
10. *State of Maharashtra* v. *Chimanlal,* 2005 All MR (Cri.) 80 (Bom): Where the adulterated food article was not found injurious to health and accused/ respondent was the retailer and not the manufacturer, the Bombay High maintained TRC but fine was enhanced to Rs. 1000.
11. *Santhosh Kumar* v. *Municipal Corporation,* 2000 All MR (Cri) 1239 (SC): Where only marginal deficiency in constituents of Groundnut oil was found but no foreign substance was detected, the Apex Court held that, *"the accused is entitled to benefit of commutation of sentence under section 433 of Cr.P.C."*
12. *Gian Chand* v. *M/s. Malwa Traders,* 1995 (4) Crimes 300 (P&H): Where the accused paid entire amount to the complainant in a case under Negotiable Instruments Act, benefit of section 360 of Cr.P.C. was given to him and was released on probation of good conduct on his executing a personal bond to a sum of Rs. 10,000 with a surety of the like amount.
13. *Pradeep Chandran* v. *Nimmi Velappan,* 1994 Cri LJ 2768: 1994 (3) Crimes 1027 (Ker): Where accused tendered payment of whole amount twice in front of Court but the complainant refused to accept amount, the Court while holding that no offence is made out held that, *"The accused must be deemed to have discharged his obligation and creditor is bound to accept the tender."*
14. *Ranjeesh Agrawal* v. *Amit J. Bhalla,* AIR 2001 SC 518: 2001 All MR (Cri) 1508 (SC): The Apex Court held that, *"If accused deposit the amount of cheque, lenient view regarding punishment can be taken."*
15. *Sumant Sethi* v. *Ajay K. Churiwar* , AIR 2000 SC 828: The Apex Court held that, *"Drawer is absolved from criminal liability if he pays the cheque amount. ...... Regarding other incidental claims, civil suit is necessary."*
16. *Rattan Singh* v. *State of Punjab,* (1980) 1 SCR 846: The Apex Court held that when the punishment is for driving offences, the State should attach a course for better driving together with a livelier sense of responsibility and in the cases of men with poor families, the State may consider occasional parole and reformatory course.
17. *Mulla* v. *State of Uttar Pradesh,* 2010 All SCR 823: (2010) 3 SCC 508: The Apex Court held that in cases of murder, socio-economic factors leading to crime must be taken note of. They may not dilute guilt but they may amount to mitigating circumstances. Criminal who commits crime due to his socio-economic backwardness is most likely to reform.
18. *Gurdip Singh* v. *State of Punjab,* AIR 1971 SC 2240: The Apex Court held that death sentence should not be awarded when there is some

probability of the deceased offering some kind of provocation.

19. *Santosh Kumar Shantibhushan Beriyar* v. *State of Maharashtra,* (2009) 6 SCC 498: The Apex Court held that quality of evidence is also a relevant factor in the sentencing analysis.
20. *Prakash Kadam* v. *Ramprasad V. Gupta,* 2011 All SCR 1402: The Apex Court held that fake encounters are nothing but cold blooded, brutal murders by persons who are supposed to uphold law. They must be given death sentence, treating it as a rarest or rare case.
21. *Bhagwan Dass* v. *State (NCT of Delhi),* AIR 2011 SC 1863: Honour killing comes within category of rarest of rare cases deserving death punishment. All persons who are planning to perpetrate honour killing should know that the gallows await them.

Probation of Offenders Act, 1958

In this case *Jugal Kishor Prasad* v. *State of Bihar,* (1973) 1 SCR 875, question arose as to whether the accused who was below 21 years of age and was convicted for an offence under section 326 read with section 140, I.P.C. to three years imprisonment can invoke the benefit of section 6 of the Probation of Offenders Act, 1958. The Apex Court answered the question as: *"The Act was enacted with a view to provide for the release of offenders of certain categories on probation or after due admonition with object of preventing the conversion of youthful offenders of less than 21 years age into obdurate criminals as a result of their association with hardened criminals of mature age in the jail. Where, however, the offence for which a person has been convicted is of a serious nature punishable with imprisonment for life, or is one of those specified in section 18 of the Act, the benefit of the Act would not be available. .... In this case, the appellant, on being convicted for the offence under section 149, I.P.C., was liable to be punished with imprisonment of life. Therefore, he would not be entitled to the benefit of section 6 of the Act. To hold otherwise would be treating the words 'but not with imprisonment for life' in the section, as otiose, contrary to rules of construction. ...... The fact that imprisonment for a lesser term can also be awarded for the offence would not take it out of the category of offences punishable with imprisonment for life."*

It has been held by the Bombay High Court in *State of Maharashtra* v. *Bodya,* 1979 Mh LJ Note 6, that *"while calling for a report from Probation Officer is obligatory under section 6(2), it is not so under section 4(2) of the Act though it is essential that such a report should ordinarily be called even under section 4(2) of the Act."*

In *Mohd. Aziz Mohd. Nasir* v. *State of Maharashtra,* AIR 1976 SC 730: 1976 SCC (Cri) 148: (1976) 1 SCC 657: (1976) 1 SCR 663, the accused who was below 21 years of age was convicted by the trial Court for the offence punishable under section 379 read with section 34, IPC for the theft of two sarees. While setting aside the sentence of imprisonment and giving benefit of section 6 of the Act, the Apex Court held that, *"Section 6 of the Act lays down an injunction not to impose a sentence of imprisonment on a person who is under 21 years of age. This inhibition on the powers of Court to impose a sentence applies not only at the stage of trial but also at the stage of High Court or any other Court when the case comes before it in appeal or revision. .... In the instant case the appellant was below 21 years of age and he was at one time a well-known child film actor and won several awards for acting in films. Subsequently he fell in bad company and took to evil ways. The offence of theft of two sarees, though it could not be lightly ignored, was of a minor character and this was the first offence of the appellant. It cannot be said that it would not be desirable to deal with the appellant under section 3 or section 4 of the Act."*

Where the accused, who was 20 years of age, was convicted for the offence punishable under sections 452, 397, IPC to seven years imprisonment but the report of Probation Officer showed that accused belongs to a middle class respectable family, the Apex Court gave benefit of the Act and his sentence was suspended; *Masarullah* v. *State of Tamil Nadu,* AIR 1983 SC 654: 1983 Cri LJ 1043: 1983 SCC (Cri) 84.

In *Daljit Singh* v. *State of Punjab through Secretary, Home Affairs,* 2006 (3) Crimes 162 (SC), the Apex Court held that where the provisions of the Probation of Offenders Act, 1958 are applicable, the employment of section 360 of Cr.P.C. is not to be made. .... by virtue of section 8(1) of the General Clauses Act, where the provisions of the Act have been brought into force, the provisions of section 360 of the Code are wholly inapplicable."

The Rajasthan High Court in *Ghasi Ram* v. *State of Rajasthan,* 2006 (3) Crimes 152, has held that the provisions of section 361 of Cr.P.C. are mandatory in nature and if the case of the accused is such which could have been dealt with under the provisions of section 360, Cr.P.C., or under the provisions of the Probation of Offenders Act, 1958, then for not dealing the case of the accused under the aforesaid provisions, the Court shall record 'special reasons' .... So far as the 'special reasons' within the meaning of section 361 of Cr.P.C. are concerned, they not only relate to the circumstances in which the offence was committed but also relate to the character, antecedents and age of the accused."

Other Cases on the Probation of Offenders Act, 1958

1. *Surendra Kumar* v. *State of Rajasthan,* AIR 1979 SC 1048: (1979) 4 SCC 718: 1980 SCC (Cri) 158: Where an offence is punishable with fine or with imprisonment with a term of seven years or less and the accused is below the age of 21 years at the time of commission of offence, he is entitled to avail the benefit of section 360 of Cr.P.C.
2. *Hansa* v. *State of Punjab,* AIR 1977 SC 1991: 1977 SCC (Cri) 550: (1977) 3 SCC 575: In this case the appellant was convicted for one year under section 325, IPC. The facts show that the occurrence took place between the parties on the quarrel of the children. The Apex Court directed to release the appellant on probation having regard to the circumstances of the case and the nature of the offence and also the character of the offender.
3. *Aitha Chander Rao* v. *State of Andhra Pradesh,* 1981 SCC (Cri) 637: Where the Session Judge had found that there was some amount of contributory negligence on the part of the appellant, it was held that it is a fit case in which the appellant may be released on probation.
4. *Om Prakash* v. *State of Madhya Pradesh,* AIR 1982 SC 783: 1982 SCC (Cri) 702: (1982) 3 SCC 224: Where the appellant was convicted under section

323, IPC, the Apex Court held that it would meet the ends of justice if the appellants are not sent to jail but are released on probation under section 360(1), Cr.P.C.

5. *N.M. Parthasarathy* v. *State by SPE,* AIR 1992 SC 988: (1992) 2 SCC 198: Where the appellant's Counsel placed before the Court documents showing several achievements of the appellant in the industrial field since his conviction, the Apex Court released the appellant on probation.
6. *Rajbir* v. *State of Haryana,* AIR 2000 SC 3472: (1999) 9 SCC 200: Where the accused was convicted for the offence punishable under The Prevention of Food Adulteration Act and he was below 18 years of age on the date of the commission of offence, the Apex Court held that the appellant is entitled to the benefit of section 20AA of The Prevention of Food Adulteration Act read with section 360 of the Criminal Procedure Code. The Apex Court released the appellant on probation for a period of one year.
7. *Jagat Pal Singh* v. *State of Haryana,* AIR 2000 SC 3622: 1999 SCC (Cri) 1313: Where the appellants were convicted under sections 323, 452, 506 read with section 34, IPC and were sentenced to three months' simple imprisonment, the Apex Court held that the Courts should have taken note of provision of Probation of Offenders Act or section 360, Cr.P.C. The Apex Court directed that instead of sentencing them to imprisonment, the accused persons be released on probation after exhibiting a bond before the Magistrate for keeping good behaviour and peace for a period of six months.
8. *Musakhan* v. *State of Maharashtra,* AIR 1976 SC 2566: 1977 SCC (Cri) 164: (1977) 1 SCC 733: The Apex Court released the accused/appellant on probation as the charge under section 395, IPC failed.
9. *Kuldip Singh* v. *State of Punjab,* 1994 Cri LJ 2201 (SC): In this case the appellant was convicted for the offence punishable under section 307/34, IPC. But the Apex Court released the appellant on probation on the ground that he gave only one blow on shoulder which caused simple injury.
10. *MCD* v. *State of Delhi* , 2005 All MR (Cri) 2294 (SC): The Apex Court held that release of accused on probation without giving opportunity to file conduct report is not legal.
11. *Shyam Lal Verma* v. *CBI,* (2014) 15 SCC 340: Accused is not entitled to get the benefit of probation for offences having mandatory minimum imprisonment.
12. *State of Himachal Pradesh* v. *Dharam Pal,* (2004) 9 SCC 681: Merely because the maximum punishment for offence is life imprisonment ,benefit of probation cannot be denied.

Juvenile Justice (Care and Protection of Children) Act, 2000

To avail the benefit of the provisions of the Act, the material factor to be taken into consideration is the age of juvenile and question often arises as to the reckoning of age of juvenile. Some of the Courts held that the reckoning date of a juvenile is the date of production before Court while some of the Courts held that it is the date of an offence. But this controversy has been resolved by the Constitution Bench of the Apex Court in *Pratap Singh* v. *State of Jharkhand,* AIR 2005 SC 2731: (2005) 1 Crimes 286 (SC): 2005 All MR (Cri) 2258 (SC), wherein the Apex Court held that, *"The reckoning date for the determination of the age of the juvenile is the date of an offence and not the date when he is produced before the authority or in Court. .... The 2000 Act would be applicable in a pending proceeding in any Court/authority initiated under the 1986 Act and is pending when the 2000 Act came into force and the person had not completed 18 years of age as on 1-4-2001."*

In *Rajinder Chandra* v. *State of Chhattisgarh,* 2002 All MR (Cri) 713 (SC), the Apex Court held that, *"where two views are possible about the age in border line cases, a view which is in favour of holding the accused to be juvenile should be adopted. Hyper-technical approach should be avoided."*

In this case, City Police Commissioner filed a petition before Delhi High Court against the order of Central Administrative Tribunal (CAT) which dismissed his order cancelling the candidature of the respondent for the post of Sub-Inspector in Delhi Police because of his criminal past when he was a juvenile. It was contended by the petitioner that the respondent juvenile was involved in a case of murder and conspiracy and such a candidate had no place in a disciplined force and law-enforcing agency like police. Repelling the contention of the petitioner, the Delhi High Court in a landmark judgment has held that even where a juvenile is found to have committed an offence, he shall not suffer any disqualification and even the records of his criminal past should be obliterated after a period of time and should not be allowed to stand in the way of his future life; *Commissioner of Police* v. *Vijay Kumar Malik,* W.P.(C) 3306/2012, decided on 29-5-2012.

CHAPTER XXXV
VICTIMOLOGY

SYNOPSIS

(A) Compensation to Victims (Cr.P.C. 357)

(B) Compensation for Accusation Without Reasonable Cause (Cr.P.C. Section 250)

Victimology is the study of why certain people are victims of crime and how lifestyles affect the chances that a certain person will fall victim to a crime. The field of victimology covers a wide number of discipline including sociology, psychology, criminal justice, law and advocacy.

There are certain provisions under which compensation can be awarded to the victims of crime. These are:

(A) Compensation to Victims (Cr.P.C. 357)

When a Court imposes a sentence, of which fine does not form a part, the Court may, when passing judgment, order the accused person to pay, by way of compensation, such amount as may be specified in the order to the person who has been suffered any loss or injury by reason of the act for which the accused person has be so sentenced. The law regarding the compensation to be paid to the victims of crime has been propounded by the Apex Court in *Hari Singh* v. *Sukhbir Singh*, 1988 (4) SCC 551, where the Court observed that, *"The power under section 357 is a measure of responding appropriately to crime as well as reconciling the victim with the offender. It is, to some extent, a re-compensatory measure to rehabilitate to an extent the beleaguered victims of the crime, a modern constructive approach to crimes, a step forward in our criminal justice system....... The quantum of compensation may be determined by taking into account the nature of crime, the justness of the claim by the victim and the ability of the accused to pay. .... The payment may also vary depending upon the acts of each accused. Reasonable period for payment of compensation, if necessary by instalments, may also be given."*

In this case *Mangilal* v. *State of Madhya Pradesh*, 2004 SAR (Cri) 239 (SC), High Court only fixed a compensation of Rs. 30,000 on the appellant out of the seven convicted persons. It was contended that the High Court did not give any opportunity of hearing to the appellant. In appeal, the Apex Court held that, *"The power of the Court to award compensation to victims under section 357, Cr.P.C. is not ancillary to other sentences but is in addition thereto. If it is found that compensation should be ordered to be paid, then while arriving at the quantum to be paid, Courts are obliged to keep into account the capacity of the accused to pay the compensation besides taking into consideration also the nature of the crime in each case. Even if a statute is silent and there are no positive words in the Act or Rules made thereunder, there could be nothing wrong in spelling out the need to hear the parties whose rights and interests are likely to be affected. Procedure is mainly grounded on principles of natural justice. Principles of natural justice do not supplant the law but supplement it. Opportunity has to be granted before directing payment of compensation under section 357(4) of Cr.P.C. ...... The principles of natural justice has many facets – two of them are: notice of the case to be met, and opportunity to explain."*

In this case, the Apex Court held that in awarding compensation it is necessary for the Court to decide whether the case is a fit one in which compensation has to be awarded. If it is found that compensation should be paid, then the capacity of the accused to pay a compensation has to be determined. In directing compensation, the object is to collect the fine and pay it to the person who has suffered the loss. The purpose will not be served if the accused is not able to pay the fine or compensation for imposing a default sentence for non-payment of fine would not achieve the object. If the accused is in a position to pay the compensation to the injured or his dependent to which they are entitled to, there could be no reason for the Court not directing such compensation. When a person, who caused injury due to negligence or is made vicariously liable is bound to pay compensation it is only appropriate to direct payment by the accused who is guilty of causing an injury with the necessary *mens rea* to pay compensation for the person who has suffered injury; *Sarwan Singh* v. *State of Punjab,* AIR 1978 SC 1525: 1978 Cri LJ 1598: (1979)1 SCR 383.

In this case, the Apex Court held that the Court should not first consider what compensation ought to be awarded to the heirs of the deceased and then impose a fine which is higher than the compensation. It is the duty of the Court to take into account the nature of the crime, the injury suffered, the justness of the claim for compensation, the capacity of the accused to pay and other relevant circumstances in fixing the amount of fine or compensation; *Palaniappa Gounder* v. *State of Tamil Nadu,* (1977) 3 SCR 132.

In *Nandkumar Krishnarao Navgire* v. *Jananath Laxman Kushalkar,* 1998 (2) Mh LJ 594 (SC), the Apex Court held that *"where in a case instituted on complaint or upon information given to a police officer or to a Magistrate, the accused is discharged or acquitted and the Magistrate by whom the case is heard is of opinion that there was no reasonable ground for making the accusation, on being satisfied that there was no reasonable ground for making the accusation, he can make an order for payment of compensation by such complainant or informant to the accused. ...... The Magistrate, initiating proceedings under section 250 of Cr.P.C., should conclude proceedings and pass final orders..... However, his successor cannot continue the proceedings initiated by his predecessor under section 250 of Cr.P.C."*

In *Kalpana d/o Nilaram Harinkhede* v. *State of Maharashtra,* 1999 (3) Mh LJ 483 (Bom), accused was prosecuted under section 354 read with section 34 of I.P.C. but he was discharged for non-prosecution. Petitioner/victim filed petition under Articles 226 and 227 and section 482 of Cr.P.C. for quashing the order of discharge. However the said petition was dismissed. Thereafter, the petitioner filed review application. Allowing the petitioner's claim for compensation from State, the Bombay High Court held that *"dismissal of petition filed under Articles 226 and 227 and section 482 of Cr.P.C. does not deprive the petitioner to press for compensation in review application. .... Petitioner/victim of the crime is entitled to compensation from State."*

In this case, accused persons were found guilty of kidnapping for ransom and committing murder of father and son. Application was filed by *de facto* complainant for compensation to family members of deceased but the said application was dismissed without any reason. The Apex Court held that State Government is liable to pay compensation to family of deceased. The Court directed to pay interim compensation of Rs. 10,00,000 to the family of victim; *Suresh* v. *State of Haryana,* 2015 All SCR 216.

In this case, the Apex Court held that it is the duty of the Court on taking cognizance of a criminal case, to ascertain whether there is tangible material to show commission of crime, whether the victim is identifiable and whether the victim of crime needs immediate financial relief. On being satisfied on an application or on its own motion, the Court ought to direct grant of interim compensation subject to final compensation being determined later. Such duty continues at every stage of a criminal case where compensation ought to be given and has not been given irrespective of the application by the victim; *Suresh* v. *State of Harayana,* AIR 2015 SC 518: 2015 Cr LJ 661: 2015 (3) Mh LJ (Cri) 565 (SC): (2015) 2 SCC 227: 2015 All SCR 216: 2014 AIR SCW 6810.

In this case, due to negligence of accused, deceased sustained electric shock and died. The Apex Court held that heirs of deceased are entitled to compensation of Rs. 5,00,000. However, considering financial constraints of accused, court imposed liability on accused to pay Rs. 2,00,000 and rest of the amount was directed to be paid by the State. If accused failed to pay, entire amount shall be paid by the State; *State of Madhya Pradesh* v. *Mehtaab,* 2015 All MR (Cri) 1233 (SC).

In this case, the Full Bench of Delhi High Court held that law of intestacy bear no necessary relation to kind of rights granted to victim simpliciter under section 372, Cr.P.C. "Legal Heirs" who are included within the definition of the term 'victim' cannot exclude those who actually fall within definition of 'victim' by virtue of emotional harm suffered, such as father or siblings of a deceased victim or other categories of persons (based on proximity). It is impermissible for an appellate Court to shut out an appeal by a legal heir based only on her/his not being an immediate heir, or being lower down in heirarchy *vis-a-vis* entitlement to the crime victim's estate. The Court further held that Cr.P.C. section 372, Proviso (as amended by Act 5 of 2009) is prospective; *Ram Phal* v. *State,* 2015 Cri LJ 3220 (Del).

(B) Compensation for Accusation Without Reasonable Cause (Cr.P.C. Section 250)

In this case, the Apex Court held that where complainant prosecutes criminal case knowing well that dispute is of civil nature, may be liable under section 250, Cr.P.C. to give compensation to accused; *ARCI* v. *Nimra Cerglass Technics (P) Ltd.,* 2015 (4) Crimes 86 (SC).

CHAPTER XXXVI
APPEAL, REVISION AND REVIEW

SYNOPSIS

1. Criminal Appeals: (Sections 374 to 389 of Cr.P.C.)

The Criminal appeals should be filed within the period of limitation prescribed in the second division of The Schedule to The Limitation Act, 1963.

(A) No Appeal to Lie Unless Otherwise Provided (Cr.P.C. Section 372)

No appeal shall lie from any judgment or order of a Criminal Court except as provided for by this Code or by any other law for the time being in force:

> Provided that the victim shall have right to prefer an appeal against any order passed by the Court acquitting the accused or convicting for a lesser offence or imposing inadequate compensation, and such appeal shall lie to the Court to which an appeal ordinarily lies against the order of conviction of such Court.

In this case, the Apex Court held that even if the victim is not a complainant, he has a right to appeal under the proviso to section 372 of Cr.P.C., but he has to seek leave of the Court; *Satyapal Singh* v. *State of Madhya Pradesh*, 2015 (4) Mh LJ (Cri) 219 SC.

In this case, the Full Bench of the Madras High Court has held that victim in a private complaint case has statutory right of appeal within the limits prescribed under section 372, Cr.P.C. He can file appeal after obtaining leave to appeal under section 378(4) of Cr.P.C.; *S. Ganpathy* v. *N. Senthilvel*, 2016 All MR (Cri) Journal 492 (Mad).

(B) Appeals from Conviction (Cr.P.C., Section 374)

(1) Any person convicted on a trial held by a Metropolitan Magistrate or Assistant Sessions Judge or Magistrate of the First Class or of the Second Class, or sentenced under section 325 or in respect of whom an order has been made or a sentence has been passed under section 360 by any Magistrate, may appeal to the Court of Session. [Section 374(3)]

(2) Any person convicted on a trial held by a Sessions Judge or an Additional Sessions Judge or on a trial held by any other Court in which a sentence of imprisonment for more than seven years has been passed against him or against any other person convicted at the same trial, may appeal to High Court. [Section 374(2)]

(3) Any person convicted on a trial held by a High Court in its extraordinary original criminal jurisdiction may appeal to the Supreme Court. [Section 374(1)]

In this case, Full Bench of the Gujarat High Court has laid down the procedure to be followed where the appeal is filed against conviction and the convict is absconding. The Court held that if advocate for the convict is present and ready to proceed with the appeal, Court has to decide the same on merits and deliver reasoned judgment even if convict is absconding. However, if advocate is also absent and convict could not be traced despite all possible efforts made by the Court and showing total disrespect to orders of the Court, Court can exercise inherent powers under section 482, Cr.P.C. and dismiss the appeal; *Niraj D. Shukla* v. *State of Gujarat*, 2016 All MR (Cri) Journal 73 (Guj).

Where the Court released the accused by giving him the benefit of sections 3 and 4 of the Probation of Offenders Act, 1958, the Apex Court in *Prithvi Raj* v. *Kamlesh Kumar*, 2004 All MR (Cri) 3139 (SC) held that complainant can file appeal questioning propriety of release order passed under sections 3 and 4 of the Act .... right to file appeal cannot be confined to convicted persons or to the state.

(C) Appeal by the State Government Against Sentence (Cr.P.C., Section 377)

(1) Save as otherwise provided in sub-section (2) the State Government may, in any case of conviction on a trial held by any Court other that a High Court, direct the Public Prosecutor to present an appeal against the sentence on the ground of its inadequacy—(a) to the Court of Session, if the sentence is passed by the Magistrate; and (b) to the High Court, if the sentence is passed by any other Court.

(2) If such conviction is in a case in which the offence has been investigated by the Delhi Special Police Establishment, constituted under the Delhi Special Police Establishment Act, 1946 (25 of 1946), or by any other agency empowered to make investigation into an offence under any Central Act other than this Code, the Central Government may also direct the Public Prosecutor to present an appeal against the sentence on the ground of its inadequacy—(a) to the Court of Session, if the sentence is passed by the Magistrate; and (b) to the High Court, if the sentence is passed by any other Court.

(3) When an appeal has been filed against the sentence on the ground of its inadequacy, the Court of Session or, as the case may be, the High Court shall not enhanced the sentence except after giving to the accused a reasonable opportunity of showing cause against such enhancement and while showing cause, the accused may plead for his acquittal or for the reduction of the sentence.

In an appeal filed by the State for enhancement of sentence, the High Court did not permit accused to argue for acquittal. The Apex Court set aside the order of High Court and remitted the matter back to it for deciding it afresh. The Apex Court held that accused has a right to be heard for acquittal even in case of appeal filed by the state for enhancement of sentence; *Arun B. Nirmal* v. *State of Maharashtra,* 2006 (4) Crimes 347 (SC).

(D) Appeal in Case of Acquittal (Cr.P.C., Section 378)

(1) Save as otherwise provided in sub-section (2), and subject to the provisions of sub-sections (3) & (5),—(a) The District Magistrate may, in any case, direct the Public Prosecutor to present an appeal to the Court of Sessions from an order of acquittal passed by a Magistrate in respect of a cognizable and non-bailable offence; (b) the State Government may, in any case, direct the Public Prosecutor to present an appeal to the High Court from an original or appellate order of an acquittal passed by any Court other than a High Court not being an order under clause (a) or an order of acquittal passed by the Court of Session in revision.

(2) If such an order of acquittal is passed in any case in which the offence has been investigated by the Delhi Special Police Establishment constituted under Delhi Special Police Establishment Act, 1946 (25 of 1946) or by any other agency empowered to make investigation into an offence under any Central Act other than this Court, the Central Government may, subject to the provisions of sub-section (3), also direct the Public Prosecutor to present an appeal—(a) to the Court of Session, from an order of acquittal passed by a Magistrate in respect of a cognizable and non-bailable offence; (b) to the High Court, from an original or appellate order of an acquittal passed by any Court other than a High Court not being an order under clause (a) or an order of acquittal passed by the Court of Session in revision.

(3) No appeal to the High Court under sub-section (1) or sub-section (2) shall be entertained except with the leave of the High Court.

(4) If such an order of acquittal is passed in any case instituted upon complaint and the High Court, on an application made to it by the complainant in this behalf, grants special leave to appeal from the order of acquittal, the complainant may present such an appeal to the High Court.

(5) No application under sub-section (4) for the grant of special leave to appeal from an order of acquittal shall be entertained by the High Court after the expiry of six months, where the complainant is a public servant, and sixty days in every other case, computed from the date of that order of acquittal.

(6) If in any case, the application under sub-section 4 for the grant of special leave to appeal from an order of acquittal is refused, no appeal from that order of acquittal shall lie under sub-section (1) or under sub-section (2).

(i) Appeal Against Acquittal in State Cases

Where cognizance of the offence was taken upon police report under section 190(1)(b) of Cr.P.C., it was held that *"State alone could file an appeal ..... setting aside order of acquittal by High Court in appeal filed by complainant is not proper;" Jagbir* v. *State of Punjab,* AIR 1998 SC 3130: 1998 Cri LJ 4588 (SC).

Where police case and private case were tried together and appeal against acquittal was filed by the complainant, it was held that *"appeal will only be maintainable if preferred by the state government. ...... complainant has no right to file appeal;" Khetra Bagi* v. *State of Orissa,* AIR 1970 SC 272: 1970 Cri LJ 369 (SC): (1970) 1 SCR 880.

In this case, the Apex Court held that it is obligatory on the High Court to consider and identify the error in the decision of the trial Court and then decide whether the error is gross enough to warrant interference; *Chandrappa* v. *State of Karnataka,* (2007) 4 SCC 415: 2007 All SCR 961.

In this case, the Apex Court held that proviso to section 372, Cr.P.C. confers statutory right on victim or his/her legal heirs and others to prefer an appeal from trial Court Judgment and order. However, this cannot override the substantive provision of section 372 which requires that appeal shall be filed in accordance with section 378(3). Thus, the father of the victim, being victim under section 2(wa) could prefer an appeal against acquittal of the accused persons, but after obtaining leave of the High Court; *Satya Pal Singh* v. *State of Madhya Pradesh,* 2015 AIR SCW 6251: 2015 All SCR 3523: 2015 (4) Crimes 124 (SC).

In this case, where the appeal was filed against the order of acquittal, the Apex Court held that appellate Court may reverse the order and direct that further inquiry be carried out or that the accused be retried or committed for trial. Even the appellate Court is competent to find him guilty and pass sentence on him. Only in case of death references, Court is under obligation to decide an appeal on merits, regardless of whether or not an appeal has been preferred by the convict; *Surya Baksh Singh* v. *State of Uttar Pradesh,* 2014 All SCR 644.

Where appellants and their pleader are absent on the day of hearing of appeal, Court is not bound to adjourn the case. The Code envisages disposal of appeal on merits after perusal and scrutiny of record. Hence, dismissal of appeal for non-prosecution simplicitor, is not justifed; *Bani Singh* v. *State of Uttar Pradesh,* AIR 1996 SC 2439: (1996) 4 SCC 720.

In this case, the Apex Court held that High Court must indicate reasons for refusal to grant leave. Since refusal has the effect of foreclosing right of appeal once for all, there is need to record reasons; *Khumbha Ram* v. *State of Rajasthan,* 2015 All MR (Cri) 4533 (SC).

(ii) Appeal Against Acquittal in Complaint Cases

In a complaint case under Prevention of Food Adulteration Act where accused is acquitted, complainant can challenge the order of acquittal by filing application for special leave in High Court and not in Sessions Court; *Subhash Chand* v. *State (Delhi Administration)*, AIR 2013 SC 395: (2013) 2 SCC 17: 2013 ALL SCR 908: 2013 (2) Mh LJ (Cri) 8 (SC).

(E) Appeal Against Death Penatly and Death Reference

Out of 196 countries in the world, 37 countries legally validated it, whereas 103 countries have abrogated *de jure* and 50 *de facto*. Rest of the 6 countries have abolished it for ordinary crimes but handling it for exceptional circumstances. United Kingdom has prohibited death penalty under Article 2 of the Charter of Fundamental Rights of the European Union. South Africa and Europe have abolished death penalty. *The Constitution Bench of 11 judges of the Supreme Court of South Africa has held the death penalty to be unconstitutional as the capital punishment was inconsistent with the commitment to human rights expressed in the Interim Constitution; [**State* v. *Makwanyane*, (1995) ZACC 3: 1995 (3) SA 391 (CC): 1995 (6) BCLR 665 (CC): (1996) 2 CHRLD 164: 1995 (2) SACR 1 (CC).

But executions are common in China, India, USA and Indonesia. In 2016, India voted against UN resolution on death penalty.

The 35th Report of Law Commission of India confirmed execution of at least 1,410 death row prisoners between 1953 and 1963. Public Union for Civil Liberties carried out research regarding death penalty and it located records of 1,422 executions in the decade from 1953 to 1963 alone. Readers are advised to read a report published by Amnesty International in 2008 titled *"Lethal Lottery: The Death Penalty In India"*. This is a well documented research which shows that provision of death penalty should be erased from the statute book keeping in view the international standards of human rights and dignity.

In this case, Harbans Singh, Kashmira Singh and Jeeta Singh were convicted by Additional Sessions Judge, Pilibhit on 1st May, 1975 for the murders of three persons and sentenced to death. On 20th October, 1975, the High Court of Allahabad affirmed the judgment of the trial Court in Criminal Appeal No. 1080 of 1975. As Jeeta Singh did not file any review petition or clemency petition, he was executed on 6th October, 1981. However, Division Bench of Supreme Court commuted Kashmira Singh's sentence of death into imprisonment for life. Harbans Singh's special leave petition was dismissed by Division Bench of Supreme Court on 16th October, 1978 and his petition for clemency to the President of India for commutation of his sentence was dismissed on 22nd August, 1981. His review petition was also dismissed by Supreme Court on 9th May, 1980 and his execution was fixed on 6th October, 1981. The execution of the death sentence of Harbans Singh was stayed by the Apex Court until the decision of President as the Bench recommended the President of India to commute the death sentence imposed upon him. The Apex Court observed that: *"The course which this case has taken makes a sad reading. Three persons were sentenced to death by a common judgment and, regretfully, each one has eventually met with a different fate. One of those three persons, Jeeta Singh, who did not file any review petition or writ petition in this Court was executed on 6th October, 1981. The other person, Kashmira Singh, succeed in having his death sentence commuted into life imprisonment. The petitioner was to be hanged on the same day on which Jeeta Singh was executed, but, fortunately he filed this writ petition on which we passed an order staying the execution of his death sentence."* Justice A.N. Sen observed that: *"it would be a sheer travesty of justice if for the same offence the petitioner had to pay the extreme penalty of death while the death sentence imposed on the co-accused, for the same offence had been commuted to imprisonment for life"*; *Harbans Singh* v. *State of Uttar Pradesh,* (1982) 3 SCR 235.

Lack of uniformity in awarding death sentence has been severely criticised by eminent jurists and academicians. In fact, the Apex Court itself has admitted the said fact. In one of the judgments, the Apex Court observed that: The inability of Criminal Justice System to deal with all major crimes equally effectively and the want of uniformity in the sentencing process by the Court lead to a marked imbalance in the end results. On the one hand there appears a small band of cases in which the murder convict is sent to the gallows on confirmation of his death penalty by this Court and on the other hand there is a much wider area of cases in which the offender committing murder of a similar or a far more revolting kind is spared his life due to lack of consistency by the Court in giving punishments or worse the offender is allowed to slip away unpunished on account of the deficiencies in the Criminal Justice System. Thus the overall larger picture gets asymmetric and lop-sided and presents a poor reflection of the system of criminal administration of justice. This situation is a matter of concern for this Court and needs to be remedied. (In view of other larger issues also, the Apex Court did not confirm the death sentence.); *Swami Shraddanand @ Murali Manohar Mishra* v. *State of Karnataka,* 2008 All SCR 2381.

Provisions contained in sections 366 to 371 of Cr.P.C. deal with submission of death sentences for confirmation.

When the Court of Sessions passes a sentence of death, the proceedings shall be submitted to the High Court, and the sentence shall not be executed unless it is confirmed by the High Court. [Section 366, Cr.P.C.]

While pointing out the duty of the High Court hearing confirmation proceeding of death sentence, the Apex Court held that a duty is cast upon the High Court to examine the nature and the manner in which the offence was committed, the *mens rea* if any, of the culprit, the plight of the victim as noted by the trial Court, the diabolic manner in which the offence was alleged to have been performed, the ill-effects it had on the victim as well as the society at large, the mind-set of the culprit *vis-a-vis* the public interest, the conduct of the convict immediately after the commission of the offence and thereafter, the past history of the culprit, the magnitude of the crime and also the consequences it had on the dependants or the custodians of the victim. There should be very wide range of consideration to be made by the High Court dealing with the reference in order to ensure that the ultimate outcome of the reference would instill confidence in the minds of peace-loving citizens and also achieve the object of acting as a deterrent for others from indulging in such crimes. The High Court must refer to the special reasons found by the Sessions Court for inclusion of the case in the rarest of rare category. The High Court has to see whether there is presence or absence of special reasons; *Kunal Majumdar* v. *State of Rajasthan*, (2012) 9 SCC 320: 2012 All MR (Cri) 3764 (SC).

In this case, the Apex Court enumerated the mandatory requirements as regards the consideration of death reference by High Court which are as follows:

(i) Death Reference shall be heard by a Bench of minimum two Judges. The Chief justice being the master of roster is free to constitute a Bench of more Judges.

(ii) On any point having a bearing on the guilt or innocence of the convicted person, for which there is no clarity, the High Court may,

(a) conduct a further inquiry;

(b) take additional evidence;

(c) get the inquiry conducted or additional evidence taken by the Sessions Court.

(iii) On the basis also of the inquiry or additional evidence, if any, the High Court may,

(a) confirm the death sentence; however, in case the convict has filed an appeal, the same has to be disposed of before passing the order of confirmation ; and , no order of confirmation shall be passed until the period allowed for filing an appeal has expired.

(b) pass any other sentence;

(c) annul conviction;

(d) convict the accused of any offence which the Court of Sessions would or could have convicted him.

(iv) Amend the charges.

(v) Order fresh trial on charges already framed or on amended charges.

(vi) May acquit the accused.

(vii) In case the Bench is equally divided in opinion, their opinions shall be laid before a third Judge of that Court and the decision will depend on the opinion of the third Judge.

(viii) If the third Judge before whom the opinions have been placed is of opinion that the matter should be heard by a larger Bench of Judges, the reference has to be heard by a larger Bench, in view of the requirement under section 392 of Cr.P.C.; *State of Rajasthan* v. *Jamil Khan*, 2013 All SCR 3396.

In this case, the Apex Court held that where the Sessions Court has submitted the death reference for confirmation, the High Court has to consider the entire evidence afresh and to arrive at its independent finding with regard to the guilt of the accused; *Ambalam* v. *State of Tamil Nadu*, AIR 1977 SC 2046: 1977 Cri LJ 1736: (1977) 4 SCC 603.

In this case, the Apex Court held that High Court has to first satisfy itself that conviction is right. Then the High Court should consider as to what sentence should be awarded independent of view expressed by the Sessions Judge. The confirmation of death sentence should not be based only on precedents or aggravating facts of any other case. High Court has to come to independent conclusion after considering proceedings in all respects; *Mohinder Singh* v. *State of Punjab*, AIR 2013 SC 3622.

When the conviction is for an offence punishable with death or, in the alternative, with imprisonment for life or imprisonment for a term of years, the judgment shall state the reasons for the sentence awarded, and, in the case of sentence of death, the special reasons for such sentence. [Section 354(3), Cr.P.C.]

The following principles emerge as regards awarding or non-awarding of death penalty:

(a) The death penalty is awarded in rarest of rare case where aggravating circumstances outweigh the mitigating factors. Where the probability that the accused can be reformed and rehabilitated is held as one of the mitigating circumstances, the State should, by evidence prove that the accused does not satisfy these conditions meaning thereby that the accused is not likely to be reformed; *Bachhan Singh* v. *State of Punjab*, (1980) 2 SCC 684.

(b) The Court must play a pro-active role to record all relevant information at this stage. Some of the information relating to crime can be culled out from the phase prior to sentencing hearing. This information would include aspects relating to the nature, motive and impact of crime, culpability of convict etc. Quality of evidence is also a relevant factor. For instance, extent of reliance on circumstantial evidence or child witness plays an important role in the sentencing analysis. Life imprisonment is the rule and death punishment is an exception; *Santosh Kumar Shantibhushan Beriyar* v.*State of Maharashtra*, 2009 (6) SCC 498.

(c) Where a case falls just short of rarest of rare category, the Court can convert death sentence into an imprisonment for life. The Court can sentence accused to imprisonment for rest of his life or term exceeding 14 years without remission; *Swami Shraddanand @ Murali Manohar Mishra* v. *State of Karnataka*, 2008 All SCR 2381.

(d) Poverty, socio-economic, psychic compulsions, undeserved adversities in life are some of the mitigating factors to be considered, in addition to those indicated in "*Bachhan Singh's* case and *Machhi's* case". The individually inconclusive and cumulatively marginal facts and circumstances tend towards awarding lesser sentence of life imprisonment; *Sunil D. Gaikwad* v. *State of Maharashtra*, 2013 (4) Crimes 119 (SC).

(e) There is a need to balance aggravating and mitigating circumstances. Factors like nature, motive and impact of crime, culpability, quality of evidence, socio-economic circumstances, impossibility of rehabilitation need to be weighed properly before affirming death sentence. In this case, the Apex Court observed that there exists circumstances such as there being no criminal antecedents of accused and entire case resting on circumstantial evidence including extra-judicial confession which contribute to uncertainty in "culpability calculus" and therefore death sentence is commuted to life imprisonment; *Kalu Khan* v. *State of Rajasthan*, 2015 (3) Crimes 1 (SC): 2015 All SCR 1817.

(f) Socio-economic factors might not dilute guilt, but they may amount to mitigating factor *i.e.*, the ability of the guilty to reform. It may not be misplaced to note that a criminal who commits crime due to his economic backwardness is most likely to reform. His ability to reform, amounts to a mitigating factor in cases of death penalty; *Mulla* v. *State of Uttar Pradesh*, 2010 (3) SCC 508: 2010 All SCR 823.

(g) A balance-sheet of the aggravating and mitigating circumstances has to be drawn up and further to accord full weightage to the mitigating circumstances and then to strike just balance between the aggravating and mitigating circumstances before the option is exercised; *Suhil Murmu* v. *State of Jharkhand*, AIR 2004 SC 394.

(h) Court is required to maintain a link between contemporary community values and penal system. Scope of determining the standardsis never precise. Courts must draw it from evolving standards of public morality and consciousness; *Shabnam* v. *State of Uttar Pradesh*, 2015 All SCR 2774.

(i) The condition of providing special reasons for awarding death penalty is not to be construed linguistically but it is to satisfy the basic features of a reasoning supporting and making award of death penalty unquestionable. The constant nagging would have to be taken as a mitigating circumstance in the commission of the crime; *State of Maharashtra* v. *Goraksha A Adsul*, AIR 2011 SC 2689.

(j) Inordinate delay in execution of death penalty is a ground to convert death penalty into imprisonment for life; *Vivian Rodrick* v. *State of West Bengal*, (1971) 3 SCR 546.

(k) Inordinate delay in disposal of mercy petition is a supervening circumstance for commutation of death sentence into life imprisonment; *V. Sriharan @ Murugan* v. *Union of India*, 2014 All SCR 1297.

(l) Prosecution is not expected to prove its case with absolute certainty. Proof is required to be beyond reasonable doubt. However, even after being convinced of guilt of accused beyond reasonable doubt, court can carry in its mind a "residual doubt" which is a mitigating circumstance favouring the accused at least upon the question to death sentence. In this case, the Apex Court observed that there remained residual doubt as to whether appellant alone could have executed the crime single handedly. Therefore, death penalty is converted to life imprisonment; *Ashok Debbarma* v. *State of Tripura*, 2014 All MR (Cri) 1521 (SC).

(m) In this case, the Apex Court held that the offence is brutal but the brutality alone would not justify death sentence in this case. The evidence on record shows that the appellant suspected her fidelity and the murder was the result of this possessiveness. Murder was the outcome of strained personal relationship. It was not an offence against the society. Further, no evidence was led by the State to indicate that he is likely to revert to such crimes in future. Therefore death sentence is commuted to life imprisonment; *Sushil Sharma* v. *State (NCT of Delhi)*, 2013 (4) Crimes 131 (SC).

(n) While awarding death sentence, the tests to be applied are "crime test", "criminal test" and the R-R Test and not "balancing test". To award death sentence, the "crime test" has to be fully satisfied, that is 100% and "criminal test" 0%, that is no mitigating circumstance favouring the accused. If there is any circumstance favouring the accused, like lack of intention to commit the crime, possibility of reformation, young age of the accused, not a menace to the society, no previous track record etc., the "criminal test" may favour the accused to avoid the capital punishment. Even if both the tests are satisfied that is aggravating circumstances to the fullest extent and no mitigating circumstance favouring the accused, still we have to apply finally the Rarest of Rare case Test (R-R test). R-R test depends upon the perception of the society that is "society centric" and not "Judge centric" that is, whether the society will approve the awarding of death sentence to certain types of crimes or not. While applying that test, the Court has to look into variety of factors like society's abhorrence, extreme indignation and antipathy to certain types of crimes like sexual assault and murder of minor girls, intellectually challenged, suffering from physical disability, old and infirm, women with those disabilities etc.; *Shankar Kisanrao Khade* v. *State of Maharashtra*, 2013 (5) SCC 546.

(F) Criminal Appeals to Supreme Court (Order XX of The Supreme Court Rules, 2013)

1. Every criminal appeal in which a certificate of the nature referred to in clause (1) of Article 132 or sub-clause (c) of clause (1) of Article 134 has been granted under Article 134A of the Constitution, shall be lodged in the Court within sixty days from the date of the certificate granted by the High Court, and every appeal under Articles 134(a) and (b) of the Constitution or under any other provision of law within sixty days from the date of the Judgement, final order or sentence appealed from:

Provided that in computing the period, the time requisite for obtaining a copy of the Judgment or order appealed from, and where the appeal is on a certificate, of the certificate, and the order granting the certificate shall be excluded:

Provided further that the Court may, for sufficient cause shown extend the time.

2. (1) The memorandum of appeal shall be in the form of a petition. It shall state succinctly and briefly, and as far as possible, in a chronological order, the principal steps in the proceedings from its commencement till its conclusion in the High Court.

(2) The petition of appeal shall be accompanied by a certified copy of the Judgement or order appealed from and in the case of an appeal on a certificate also of the certificate granted by the High Court, and of the order granting the said certificate. In appeals falling under any of the categories enumerated in sub-rule (1) of rule 5, however, in addition to the documents mentioned above, a certified copy (or uncertified copy if such copy is affirmed to be true copy upon affidavit) of the Judgement or order of the Court immediately below shall also be filed before the appeal is listed for hearing *ex parte*. At least 7 copies of the aforesaid document shall be filed in the Registry.

3. Where the appellant has been sentenced to a term of imprisonment, the petition of appeal shall State whether the appellant has surrendered and if he has surrendered then the appellant shall, by way of proof of such surrender, file the certified copy of the order of the Court in which he has surrendered or a certificate of the competent officer of the Jail in which he is undergoing the sentence. A mere attestation of the signatures on the *Vakalatnama* from the Jail authorities shall not be considered as sufficient proof of surrender. Where the appellant has not surrendered to the sentence, the petition of appeal shall not be accepted by the Registry unless it is accompanied by an application for seeking exemption from surrendering. Where the petition of appeal is accompanied by an application for exemption from surrendering, that application alone shall be posted for hearing/orders before the Court in the first instance.

4. Where the appellant is in Jail, he may present his petition of appeal and the documents mentioned in rule 2 including any written argument which he may desire to advance to the officer-in-charge of the jail, who shall forthwith forward the same to the Registrar of the Court.

5. (1) The petition of appeal shall be registered and numbered as soon as it is found to be in order. Each of the following categories of appeals, on being registered, shall be put for hearing *ex parte* before the Court, which may either dismiss it summarily or direct issue of notice to all necessary parties, or may make such orders, as the circumstances of the case may require, namely:

(a) an appeal from any judgment, final order or sentence in a criminal proceeding of a High Court summarily dismissing the appeal or the matter, as the case may be, before it;

(b) an appeal on a certificate granted by the High Court under Article 134A of the Constitution being a certificate of the nature referred to in clause (1) of Article 132 or sub-clause (c) of clause (1) of Article 134 of the Constitution or under any other provision of law is the High Court has not recorded the reasons or the grounds for granting the certificate.

(c) an appeal under clause (b) of sub-section (1) of section 19 of the Contempt of Courts Act, 1971 (70 of 1971).

(2) On the registration of the appeal and in the appeals falling under sub-rule (1) as soon as notice is directed to be issued, the Registrar shall send a copy of the petition of appeal and the accompanying papers, if any, to the High Court or the Tribunal concerned; and shall cause notice of the appeal to be given, where the appeal is by a convicted person to the Attorney General for India or

to the Advocate-General or the Government Advocate of the State concerned, or to both as the case may require, and in cases where the appeal is by the Government to the accused and in cases under sections 341(1) of the Code of Criminal Procedure, 1973 to the respondent.

6. The respondent may enter appearance in the Court within thirty days of the service of the notice of lodgement of the petition of appeal on him.

In case of concurrent findings of facts by the Courts below, the Supreme Court is not required to reassess the evidence. Further, an argument on a point of fact which did not prevail with the Courts below, cannot be availed by the appellants in Supreme Court; *Ram Chander* v. *State of Haryana,* 2017 (1) Crimes 12 (SC).

In *Mayuram Subramanian Srinivasan* v. *CBI,* 2006 (3) Crimes 131 (SC), the Apex Court has held that criminal appeal cannot be posted unless proof of surrender has been furnished by appellant who has been convicted. Requirement of Order XXI, rule 13A are mandatory in nature and have to be complied with except when an order is passed for exemption from surrender.

Where appeal was filed by the State under Article 136 of the Constitution challenging the sentence to period already undergone in a rape case, the Apex Court held that *"in effect, it is an appeal for enhancement of sentence. Though section 377(3)of Cr.P.C. is not in terms applicable to an appeal before Supreme Court, Court can permit respondent-accused to argue for an acquittal by adopting analogous provisions of section 377(3) of Cr.P.C."*; [vide *State of Rajasthan* v. *Kishanlal,* 2002 All MR (Cri) 1596 (SC).]

The facts of the case are: A dacoity was committed in village Jafrapur at about 9.00 p.m. The inmates of the house raised alarm. A large crowd gathered at the gate and lit a fire to add to the moonlight to enable recognition of the dacoits who opened fire and murdered three members of the family. The accused were of neighbourhood and admittedly inimical to the family of the deceased but apart from three inmates of the house, an inimical neighbour and another person, no independent witness from the crowd was examined by the prosecution. The accused were tried and convicted by the Sessions Court under section 396 and in the alternative under section 302/149, I.P.C., and sentenced to death. They were also convicted under sections 148, 395 and 324/149, I.P.C. and variously sentenced. The High Court affirmed the conviction and sentence. On appeal by special leave, a three-Judge Bench of the Apex Court while acquitting the appellants' of all the charges, agreed that the crimes were established, but doubted the appellants' participation in the same. The Court further held that ordinarily this Court does not re-appreciate the evidence in an appeal under Article 136 will not stand in the way of going into the whole matter once again in such an unusual case. This Court will not deny protection under Article 136 when there is a pervading sense of judicial unsafety in relying upon the evidence for the purpose of conviction; *Ram Lakhan Singh* v. *State of Uttar Pradesh,* (1978) 1 SCR 125.

Recently, the Apex Court has held that in an appeal under Article 136, re-appreciation of evidence is permissible only if trial Court is shown to have committed an error of law or procedure and conclusions arrived at are perverse; [*Radha Mohan Singh* v. *State of Uttar Pradesh*, AIR 2006 SC 951.]

Where the High Court maintained conviction, the Apex Court, in appeal, acquitted some accused persons on the ground that prosecution failed to prove its case beyond doubt. In such circumstances, the Apex Court held that remaining co-accused who were not before the Court and whose Special Leave Petition was earlier dismissed for default, are also entitled to the benefit of acquittal; *Mohinder Singh* v. *State of Punjab*, AIR 2003 SC 4399.

The Supreme Court could entertain appeals against the judgments of acquittal by the High Court at the instance of a private party also. Where a judgment of acquittal by the High Court has led to serious miscarriage of justice, this Court cannot refrain from doing its duty and abstain from interfering with it on the ground that a private party, and not the State, has invoked the Court's jurisdiction; *Arunachalam* v. *P.S.R. Sadhanantham*, (1979) 3 SCR 482.

2. Revision (Cr.P.C. 397 to 401)

Criminal revision must be filed within 90 days from the date of order as per Article 131 of The Limitation Act, 1963. However it should be remembered that revision against interlocutory order is not maintainable.

In this case the Apex Court held that, the revisional jurisdiction conferred on the High Court is not to be lightly exercised when it is invoked by a private complainant against an order of acquittal, against which the Government has right of appeal. It could be exercised only in exceptional cases where the interests of public justice require interference for the correction of a manifest illegality or the prevention of a gross miscarriage of justice. This jurisdiction is not ordinarily invoked or used merely because the lower Court has taken a wrong view of the law or misappreciated the evidence on the record; *D. Stephens* v. *Nosibolla*, (1951) SCR 284.

Where the order of acquittal was set aside by the High Court in revision and a retrial was directed, the Apex Court laid down certain guidelines. It held that the High Court would be justified in interfering in cases such as (i) where the trial court has wrongly shut out evidence sought to be adduced by the prosecution, (ii) where the appeal court had wrongly held evidence admitted by the trial court to be inadmissible, (iii) where material evidence has been overlooked either by the trial court or the court of appeal or, (iv) where the acquittal was based on a compounding of the offence not permitted by law and cases similar to the above. The Apex Court further held that it was open to a High Court in revision and at the instance of a private party to set aside an order of acquittal although the state might not have appealed. But such jurisdiction should be exercised only in exceptional cases, as where a glaring defect in the procedure or a manifest error of law leading to a flagrant miscarriage of justice has taken place; *K. Chinnaswamy Reddy* v. *State of Andhra Pradesh*, (1963) 3 SCR 412: AIR 1962 SC 1788.

Revision under section 397 is not maintainable against an interlocutory order. The expression 'interlocutory order' has not been defined in the Code of Criminal Procedure. The position in law is that the expression, as used in section 397(2), has been used in a restricted sense and merely denotes orders purely of an interim or temporary in nature which do not decide or touch the important rights or liabilities of the parties. An order rejecting the plea of the accused on a point which when accepted will conclude the particular proceeding is not an interlocutory order. It has to be given a liberal construction in favour of the accused. The revisional power of the Court could be attracted if the order was not purely interlocutory but intermediate or quasi final. An order directing issuance of process is not purely interlocutory. On the other hand, it must be held to be intermediate or *quasi* final and, therefore, the revisional jurisdiction under section 397 could be exercised against the same; *Rajendra K.S. Pande* v. *Uttam*, (1999) 1 SCR 580: AIR 1999 SC 2028.

In this case, the Apex Court held that sub-section (3) bars second revision so as to avoid frivolous litigation. However, in a special case High Court can entertain petition under section 482, Cr.P.C. Section 397(3) does not completely bar to approach High Court from decision of Sessions Judge; *Shakuntala Devi* v. *Chamru Mahto*, 2009 All MR (Cri) 1535 SC.

In *K. Pandurangan* v. *S.R.R. Vehisamy*, AIR 2003 SC 3318: 2003 (4) Crimes 96 (SC): 2003 Cri LJ 4964 (SC): 2003 (3) All MR (Cri) 2362, the Apex Court held that revision against aquittal filed by a complainant is maintainable.

The Apex Court in *Krishan* v. *Krishnaveni*, AIR 1997 SC 987, has held that second revision to High Court is maintainable and prohibition under section 397(3) of Cr.P.C. is not applicable when State seeks revision under section 401 of Cr.P.C.. High Court can entertain it in case of grave miscarriage of justice or abuse of process of court, etc., by exercising inherent powers and supervisory powers under sections 482 and 483 of Cr.P.C. respectively.

Sessions Judge has jurisdiction to entertain revision against an order of acquittal; *Milon Chandra* v. *Shiv Prasad Chakravarty*, 2003 Cri LJ 3845 (Gau).

In this case, the Apex Court held that order of Magistrate directing issuance of summons is not purely interlocutory but *quasi* final. Therefore, revision against it is maintainable; *Om Kumar Dhankar* v. *State of Haryana*, 2012 All MR (Cri) 1358 (SC).

In this case, the Apex Court held that persons who are arraigned as accused in complaint, have right to be heard in revision petition; *Manharibhai M. Kakadia* v. *Shailesbhai M. Patel*, 2012 All MR (Cri) 4105 (SC).

3. Review Petitions (Articles 132 and 134 of the Constitution)

Procedure of filing Review Petitions before the Apex Court is regulated by Order XLVII of The Supreme Courts Rules, 2013. These rules are given below:

1. The Court may review its judgment or order, but no application of review will be entertained in a criminal proceeding, except on the ground of an error apparent on the face of the record.

   The application for review shall be accompanied by a certificate of the Advocate on Record certifying that it is the first application for review and is based on the grounds admissible under the rules.

2. An application for review shall be by a petition and shall be filed within 30 days from the date of the judgment or order sought to be reviewed. It shall set out clearly the grounds for review.
3. Unless otherwise ordered by the Court an application for review shall be disposed of by circulation without any oral arguments, but the petitioner may supplement his petition by additional written arguments. The Court may either dismiss the petition or direct notice to the opposite party. An application for review shall as far as practicable be circulated to the same Judge or Bench of Judges that delivered the judgment or order sought to be reviewed.
4. Where on an application for review the Court reverses or modifies its former decision in the case on the ground of mistake of law or fact, the Court, may, if it thinks fit in the interests of justice to do so, direct the refund to the petitioner of the Court-fee paid on the application in whole or in part, as it may think fit.
5. Where an application for review of any judgment and order has been made and disposed of, no further application for review shall be entertained in the same matter.

In *Sheela Kr. Roy* v. *Secretary M/O Defence,* 2007 All MR (Cri) 2663 (SC), the Apex Court held that fairness and reasonableness in the action of the State whether in a criminal proceeding or otherwise is the hallmark of Article 14 of the Constitution of India. The doctrine of proportionality is one of the grounds on the basis whereof the power of judicial review could be exercised.

The Constitution Bench of the Apex Court in *P.N. Iswara* v. *Registrar, Supreme Court of India,* AIR 1980 SC 808: (1980) 4 SCC 680 has considered the scope of the review jurisdiction and held that *"the rule, on its face, affords a wider set of grounds for review of orders in civil proceedings, but limits the ground* vis-a-vis *criminal proceedings to 'errors apparent on the face of the record.' If at all, the concern of the law to avoid judicial error should be heightened when life or liberty is in peril since civil penalties are often less traumatic. So, it is reasonable to assume the the framers of the rules could not have intended a restrictive review over criminal orders or judgments. It is likely to be the other way about. Supposing an accused is sentenced to death by the Supreme Court and the 'deceased' shows up in Court and the Court discovers the tragic treachery of the recorded testimony, is the Court helpless to review and set aside the sentence of hanging? We think not. The power to review is in Article 137 and it is equally wide in all proceedings. The rule merely canalises the flow from the reservoir of power. The stream cannot stifle the source. Moreover, the dynamics of interpretation depend on the demand of the context and the lexical limits of the test. Here 'record' means any material which is already on record or may, with the permission of the Court, be brought on record. If justice summons the judges to allow a vital material in, it becomes part of the record; and if apparent error is there, corrections becomes necessitous."*

In *Ms. Savita Kumari* v. *Union of India* , 1993 Cri LJ 1590 (SC), review petition was filed under Article 137 of the Constitution and plea of self defence was raised. The Apex Court held that error of substantial nature can be reviewed. Plea of self defence can be examined in review petition if the Court is satisfied that it is probable. In peculiar facts and circumstances of the case, the Apex Court ordered to issue notice without limiting review to any specific point.

In this case, the Apex Court held that review of order is expressly barred under the Code of Criminal Procedure, 1973. Therefore, Court should not exercise its inherent power to reconsider the matter and record a conflicting decision unless there had been change in circumstances of case; *State of Punjab* v. *Davinder Pal Singh Bhullar,* AIR 2012 SC 364.

In this case, the Constitution Bench held that the law laid down in this judgment, *viz.*, the right of a limited oral hearing in review petitions where death sentence is given, shall be applicable only in pending review petitions and such petitions filed in future. It will also apply where a review petition is already dismissed but the death sentence is not executed so far. In such cases, the petitioners can apply for the reopening of the review petition within one month from the date of this judgment. However, in those cases where even a curative petition is dismissed, it would not be proper to reopen such matters; *Mohd. Arif @ Asfaq* v. *The Registrar, Supreme Court of India,* 2014 All SCR 3231.

4. Curative Petitions: [Order XLVIII of The Supreme Court Rules, 2013 w.e.f. 19th August, 2014]

As regards the question whether an aggrieved person is entitled to any relief against a final judgment/order of this Court, after dismissal of review petition, either under Article 32 of the Constitution or otherwise, the Constitution Bench held that a final judgment/order passed by this Court cannot be assailed in an application under Article 32 of the Constitution of India by an aggrieved person whether he was a party to the case or not. The jurisdiction of the Supreme Court under Article 32 of the Constitution cannot be invoked to challenge the validity of a final judgment/order passed by this Court after exhausting the remedy of review under Article 137 of the Constitution read with Order XI, rule 1 of the Supreme Court Rules, 1966. However, the Supreme Court to prevent abuse of its process and to cure a gross miscarriage of justice, may reconsider its judgments in exercise of its inherent powers. A petitioner is entitled to relief *ex debito justitiae* if he establishes: (i) that he was not a party to the *lis* but the judgment adversely affected his interests or, if he was a party to the *lis*, he was not served with notice of the proceedings and the matter proceeded as if he had notice and (ii) where in the proceedings a learned Judge failed to disclose his connection with the subject-matter or the parties giving scope for an apprehension of bias and the judgment adversely affects the petitioner. The petitioner, in the curative petition, shall aver specifically that the grounds mentioned therein had been taken in the review petition and that it is was dismissed by circulation. The curative petition shall contain a certification by a Senior Advocate with regard to the fulfilment of the above requirements; *Rupa Ashok Hurra* v. *Ashok Hurra,* AIR 2002 SC 1771: 2002 AIR SCW 1730: (2002) 4 SCC 388.

In this case, the appellant filed writ petition under Article 32 of the Constitution seeking modification of death sentence into life imprisonment on the ground that accused was juvenile at the time of commission of offence. However, death sentence was confirmed by the Apex Court in appeal and his review petition was also dismissed. Accused filed school certificate showing date of birth as additional evidence along with writ petition. Appellant's plea was that though two certificate issued by school authorities were filed along with memorandum of appeal, they were not brought to notice of Bench at the time of hearing of appeal. The Apex Court held that relief sought by accused cannot be granted in writ petition. Proper remedy is to file curative petition as per procedure indicated in *Rupa Ashok Hurra* case; *Zakarius Lakra* v. *Union of India,* 2005 AIR SCW 1047: 2005 (2) SCALE 166: AIR 2005 SC 1560.

In this case, the Apex Court held that curative petition can be filed in exceptional and rarest of rare case and except when very strong reasons exist; *Sumer* v. *State of Uttar Pradesh,* 2005 (3) Crimes 250 (SC).

The Constitution Bench dismissed Curative Petition filed after lapse of 14 years without any explanation in *Bhopal Gas Tragedy* case; *C.B.I.* v. *Keshub Mahindra,* 2011 All MR (Cri) 2337 (SC).

After the decision in *Rupa Hurra's* case, the Apex Court has framed rules regarding the filing of Curative Petition before it. These rules are given below:

1. Curative Petitions shall be governed by Judgment of the Court dated 10th April, 2002 delivered in the case of *Rupa Ashok Hurra* v. *Ashok Hurra,* Writ Petition (C) No 509 of 1997.
2. (1) The petitioner, in the Curative Petition, shall aver specifically that the grounds mentioned therein had been taken in the Review Petition and that it was dismissed by circulation.

   (2) A Curative Petition shall be accompanied by a certificate of the Senior Advocate that the petition meets the requirement delineated in the above case.

   (3) A Curative Petition shall be accompanied by a certificate of the Advocate on Record to the effect that it is the first Curative Petition in the impugned matter.
3. The Curative Petition shall be filed within reasonable time from the date of Judgment or Order passed in the Review Petition.
4. (1) The Curative Petition shall be first circulated to a Bench of the three senior-most judges and the judges who passed the judgment complained of, if available.

   (2) Unless otherwise ordered by the Court, a Curative Petition shall be disposed of by circulation without any oral arguments but the petitioner may supplement his petition by additional written arguments.

   (3) If the Bench before which a Curative Petition was circulated concludes by a majority that the matter needs hearing then it shall be listed before the same Bench, as far as possible.

   (4) If the Court, at any stage, comes to the conclusion that the petition is without any merit and vexatious, it may impose exemplary costs on the petitioner

5. Clemency or Mercy Petitions

(i) Powers of President (Article 72 of the Constitution)

In *Maru Ram* v. *Union of India,* AIR 1980 SC 2147: (1981) 1 SCR 1196, the Constitution Bench of the Apex Court held that the power under Articles 72 and 161 of the Constitution can be exercised by the Central and State Governments, not by the President or Governor on their own. The advice of the appropriate Government binds the Head of the State. Considerations for exercise of power under Articles 72/161 may be myriad and their occasions protean, and are left to the appropriate Government, but no consideration nor occasion can be wholly irrelevant, irrational, discriminatory or *mala fide*. On in these rare cases will the Court examine the exercise.

The Scope of Article 72 has been considered by the Apex Court in *Kuljit Singh* alias *Ranga* v. *Lt. Governor of Delhi,* (1982) 3 SCR 58. In this case the Apex Court held that undoubtedly, the President has the power in an appropriate case to commute any sentence imposed by a Court into a lesser sentence. But the question as to whether the case is appropriate for the exercise of the power conferred by Article 72 depends upon the facts and circumstances of each particular case. The power conferred by Article 72 can be used only for the purpose of reducing the sentence, not for enhancing it.

In this case, a three-Judge Bench held that delay in disposal of mercy petitions violates fundamental right of death convicts. Undue delay in deciding mercy petition entitles the condemned prisoner to approach Supreme Court under Article 32 of the Constitution and if it is found that there has been undue delay in deciding the mercy petition, the Court can commute death penalty to imprisonment for life. The Court observed that power of pardon under Article 72 or 161 of the Constitution is a constitutional duty. It is neither a matter of grace nor a privilege but an important responsibility vested in highest authority. It is to be exercised in the aid of justice and on the advice of Council of Ministers. Power under Articles 72 and 161 is *per se* above judicial review but the manner of exercise of such power is certainly subject to judicial review. The Court issued following guidelines regarding confinement, legal aid, mercy petitions and final execution of death sentence; *Shakrughan Chauhan* v. *Union of India,* 2014 All SCR 896.

(ii) Powers of Governor (Article 161 of the Constitution)

The Apex Court in *Dhananjoy Chatterjee* alias *Dhana* v. *State of West Bengal,* 2004 All MR (Cri) 2185 (SC) has held that order passed by Governor in mercy petition is subject to judicial review.

CHAPTER XXXVII
SUSPENSION, REMISSION AND COMMUTATION OF SENTENCES

(SECTIONS 432 TO 435 CR.P.C.)

The law as regards the right of prisoner to get remission has been propounded by the Constitution Bench of the Apex Court in *Gopal Vinayak Godse* v. *The State of Maharashtra,* (1961) 3 SCR 441. The petitioner had filed a petition under Article 32 of the Constitution for and order in the nature of *habeas corpus* claiming that he has justly served his sentence and should, therefore, be released. The petitioner was convicted in 1949 and sentenced to transportation for life. He earned remission of 2963 days and adding this to the term of imprisonment actually served by the petitioner the aggregate exceeded 20 years and therefore he contended that his further detention in jail was illegal and prayed for being set at liberty. Dismissing the petition, the Constitution Bench held that, *"The petitioner had not yet acquired any right to be released. A sentence of transportation for life could be undergone by a prisoner by way of rigorous imprisonment for life in a designated prison in India. Section 53A of the IPC, introduced by the Code of Criminal Procedure (Amendment) Act, 1955, provided that any person sentenced to transportation for life before the Amendment Act would be treated as sentenced torigorous imprisonment for life. A prisoner sentenced to life imprisonment was bound to serve the remainder of his life in prison unless the sentence was commuted or remitted by the appropriate authority. Such a sentence could not be equated with any fixed term. The rules framed under the Prisons Act entitled such a prisoner to earn remissions but such remissions were to be taken into account only towards the end of the term."*

In *Maru Ram* v. *Union of India,* (1981) 1 SCR 1196, the *Constitution Bench* of the Apex Court held that imprisonment for life lasts until the last breath and whatever the length of remissions earned, the prisoner can claim release only if the remaining sentence is remitted by Government. The fasciculur of clauses (Sections 432, 433 and 433A), read as a package, makes it clear that while the Code does confer wide powers of remission and commutation of sentences, it emphatically intends to carve out an extreme category from the broad generosity of such executive power. The *non obstante,* in terms, excludes section 432 and the whole mandate of the rest of the section necessarily subjects the operation of section 433(a) to a serious restriction. This embargo directs that commutation in such cases shall not reduce the actual duration of imprisonment below 14 years. Section 433A does declare emphatically an imperative intent to keep imprisoned for at list 14 years those who fall within the sinister categories spelt out in the operative part of section 433A. However, section 433A does not forbid parole or other release within the 14 year span. The power under Articles 72 and 161 of the Constitution can be exercised by the Central and the State Governments, and not by the President or Governor on their own. The advice of the appropriate Government binds the Head of the State.

The Constitution Bench of the Apex Court in *Smt. Triveniben* v. *State of Gujarat,* (1989) 1 SCR 509, has considered the question of commutation of sentences due to long delay in execution of sentences. The Constitution Bench held that the delay which could be considered while considering the question of commutation of sentence of death into one of life imprisonment could only be from the date the judgment by the Apex Court is pronounced ie when the judicial process has come to an end? While considering the question of delay after the final verdict is pronounced, the time spent on petitions for review and repeated mercy petitions at the instance of the convicted person himself however shall not be considered. The only delay which would be material for consideration will be the delay in disposal of the mercy petitions or delays occurring at the instance of the Executive. The question of improvement in the conduct of the prisoner after the final verdict also cannot be considered for coming to the conclusion whether the sentence could be altered on that ground also.

In *Ramdeo Chauhan* alias *Raj Nath Chauhan* v. *State of Assam,* AIR 2001 SC 2231, K.T. Thomas, Justice did not agree with the majority view and delivered his separate dissenting judgment. While delivering the judgment Justice Thomas observed in paragraph No. 23 (page No. 2239) that the doctors estimates of age is not a sturdy substitute for proof as it is only his opinion. But such opinion of an expert cannot be sidelined in the realm where we grope in the dark to find out what would possibly have been the age of a citizen for the purpose of affording him a constitutional protection. In the absence of all other acceptable materials, if such opinion points to a reasonable possibility regarding the range of his age it has certainly to be considered. When the possibility of the petitioner having been a juvenile on relevant date cannot be excluded from the conclusion by adopting such reasonable standards, the interdict contained in section 22(1) of the Juvenile Act cannot be bypassed for awarding death penalty to the petitioner so long as the death penalty is permitted to survive Article 21 only if the lesser alternative can be foreclosed unquestionably. In other words, if the age of the petitioner cannot be held to be unquestionably above 16 on the relevant date its corollary is that the lesser sentence also cannot unquestionably be foreclosed and with this observation the learned Justice allowed the review petition and altered the sentence of death to imprisonment for life. As to the effect of conclusion arrived at by Justice Thomas, the majority of the Justices observed that the accused is not remediless and held that if any motion is made in terms of sections 432, 433 and 433A of the Code and/or Article 72 or Article 161 of the Constitution as the case be, the same may be appropriately dealt with. It goes without saying that at the relevant stage, the factors which have weighed with my learned brother Mr. Justice Thomas can be duly taken note of in the context of section 432(2) of the Code.

The Constitution Bench has settled the controversy as regards remission and commutation of death sentences in the following case. The Court held that:

(i) Life imprisonment only means the entirety of life unless it is curtailed by remission validly granted either under sections 432, 433 of CrPC or under Article 72 and 161 of the Constitution.

(ii) Remission under section 432, CrPC is distinct from remission earned on the basis of Prison Rules for good behaviour. Unless remission is granted under section 432, there would be no scope to count the earned remission as per Prison Rule.

(iii) When judiciary imposes punishment for life imprisonment with condition that no remission shall be granted for 20, 30 or any number of years, in such a case, constitutional power of remission under Articles 72 and 161 will always remained untouched ie exercisable. However, statutory remission under sections 432 and 433 of CrPC cannot nullify the judicial pronouncement. Such statutory power under the Code of Criminal Procedure will revive as soon as the stipulated sentence is undergone.

(iv) View expressed by Supreme Court in *Swami Shraddhanand (2) @ Murali Manohar Mishrav. State of Karnataka* 2008 All SCR 2381: (2008) 13 SCC 767, is fully justified. Further, Court derives its power to determine appropriate punishment from penal provisions themselves.

(v) The power to modify death penalty into imprisonment for life lies only with High Court or Supreme Court and no other Court in the Country.

(vi) Commutation of sentence into life imprisonment by Supreme Court in exercise of its jurisdiction under Article 32 is independent of power of remission by State under the Constitution, as well as, the Statute. Power of remission always vests with State Executive and Court at best can only give a direction to consider any claim for remission and cannot grant any remission to provide for premature release.

(vii) There is every scope and ambit for Appropriate Government to grant remission under sections 432, 433, CrPC even if such consideration was earlier made under Article 72 or 161. As far as implication of Article 32 is concerned, it is not for Court to exercise said power and it is always left to be decided by Appropriate Government, even if someone approaches Supreme Court under Article 32.

(viii) For the purpose of remission of sentence when power of Union and State is co-extensive, the Court held that every case is to be tested keeping in mind the prescription of section 432(7) of CrPC and section 55A of IPC.

(ix) Power under section 432(1) of CrPC cannot be invoked *suo motu*. It can only be initiated on an application of the persons convicted as provided under section 432(2), CrPC.

(x) While considering remission of sentence, opinion of Presiding Judge convicting the offender under section 432(2) of CrPC is mandatory.

(xi) Where the State Government intends to remit the sentence in situations covered by sub-clauses (a) to (c) of section 435(1) of CrPC, the process of "consultation" has to be taken as requirement of "concurrence".

(xii) Tests laid down to determine power of remission in respect of matters falling within concurrent list and whether Union would have primacy over States; *Union of India* v. *V. Sriharan @ Murugan*, 2016 All SCR (Cri) 1.

CHAPTER XXXVIII
MISCELLANEOUS PROCEEDINGS

SYNOPSIS

(1) Order for Maintenance of Wives, Children and Parents – (Chapter IX of Cr.P.C.)

Provisions of section 125 are intended to protect the weaker section of the society such as children, deserted wives and neglected parents. A person claiming maintenance has to prove that:—(i) he/she is unable to maintain himself/herself, or (ii) he/she has been deserted, or neglected and (iii) the person from whom the maintenance is claimed has sufficient means. On proof of such things, the Court may grant maintenance to the aggrieved person. The claimant can claim interim maintenance pending final disposal of the application but the applicant should satisfy the Court that there exists a *prima facie* case for making such an order. However, it should be remembered that the applicant should file affidavit stating the grounds in support of the claim.

It has been held by the Apex Court in *Smt. Savitri Rawat* v. *Govind Rawat,* AIR 1986 SC 984: 1986 Cri LJ 41: (1985) Supp 3 SCR 615 that, *"the Magistrate may, however, insist upon an affidavit being filed by or on behalf of the applicant concerned .... Such an order may also be made in an appropriate* ex parte *pending service of notice of the application subject to any modification or even an order of cancellation that may be passed after the respondent is heard. If the allegations in the application or the affidavit are not true, it is always open to the person against whom such an order is made to show that the order is unsustainable."*

In *Nanak Chand* v. *Chandra Kishore,* AIR 1970 SC 446: 170 Cri LJ 522, the Apex Court held that the meaning of word 'child' appearing in section 125 of the Cr.P.C. is not limited to minor a child . Helpless children, who though major, unable to support themselves because of their imbecility or deformity or other handicaps are entitled to maintenance under section 125.

While interpreting the word "his" in clause (d) of section 125(1), Cr.P.C. the Apex Court in *Vijaya Manohar Arbat* v. *Kashirao Rajarao Sawai,* AIR 1987 SC 1100 has held that it includes both male and female children and therefore married daughter is liable to maintain her parents.

In *Padmaja Sharma* v. *Ratan Lal Sharma,* (2000) 2 SCR 621 the Apex Court has held that a minor child can claim a maintenance from his or her father or mother. It is the obligation of father and mother both to maintain the child.

The Apex Court has interpreted the expression "wife" as legally wedded wife. Therefore it has been held that marriage of woman with a man already having living spouse as per Hindu rites is complete nullity and she is not entitled to maintenance. [*Smt. Yamunabai Anantrao Adhao* v. *Ananatrao Adhao,* AIR 1988 SC 644: 1988 Cri LJ 793 (SC)]. Same view has been taken by the Apex Court in *Savitaben Somabhai Bhatiya* v. *State of Gujarat,* (2005) 2 Crimes 1 (SC): 2005 All MR (Cri) 1309 (SC).

The Constitution Bench of the Apex Court in *Mohd. Ahmed Khan* v. *Shah Bano Begum,* (1985) 3 SCR 844, has held that, *"a divorced Muslim woman so long as she has not married, is a wife for the purpose of section 125 of Cr.P.C. A divorced Muslim woman is entitled to apply for maintenance under section 125 of Cr.P.C....... 'Mahr' is not the amount payable by the husband to the wife on divorce and therefore, does not fall within the meaning of section 127(3)(b) of Cr.P.C."*

Where Muslim husband contracted second marriage or took mistress, it was held that, *"first wife is entitled to claim maintenance and separate residence. Contention that husband can marry again under Personal Law is immaterial....... Since offer to take back first wife is not accompanied with offer to set-up separate residence, it is not a bona fide offer;"* [*Subanu* alias *Saira Banu* v. *A.M. Abdul Gafoor,* AIR 1987, SC 1103].

It has been held by the Apex Court in *Dwarika Prasad* v. *Bidyut Prava Dixit,* AIR 1999 SC 3348 that in proceedings under section 125 of Cr.P.C. strict proof of performance of marriage is not required. It is sufficient if claimant *prima facie* satisfies the Court that the claimant and her husband lived as husband and wife. .... Performance of essential ceremonies need not also be proved.

In *Kirtikant D. Vadodaria* v. *State of Gujarat,* (1996) Supp 2 SCR 45 held that *"Expression 'mother' in section 125(1)(d) meant only real or natural mother and did not include step-mother who was distinct and separate entity. She could not be equated with natural mother who gave birth to the child....... An adoptive mother may, however, be included in the expression 'mother'. However, having regard to social object of section 125, Cr.P.C., childless step-mother could claim maintenance from her step-son provided she was a widow or her husband, if living, was incapable or maintaining her."*

In *Rajathi* v. *C. Ganesan,* (1999) 3 SCR 1047, the Apex Court held that, *"Trial Court is to take prima facie view of the matter and is not required to go into the matrimonial disputes between the parties in detail. .... Expression 'unable to maintain herself' would mean the means available to the wife while she was living with her husband and would not take within itself the efforts made by the wife after the desertion to survive somehow. Section 125 of the Code is enacted on the premise that it is the obligation of the husband to maintain his wife, children and parents. It will, therefore, for him to show that he has no sufficient menans to discharge his obligation and that he did not neglect or refuse to maintain them or any one of them. ...... Even though the wife was unable to prove that husband has remarried, yet the fact remained that the husband was living with another woman. That would entitle the wife to live separately and would amount to neglect or refusal by the husband to maintain her. Statement of the wife that she is unable to maintain herself would be enough and it would be for the husband to prove otherwise."*

In this case, the Apex Court held that where maintenance petition is filed by a major daughter even if she does not fall in one of the exceptions mentioned in section 125(1)(c), it would be still maintainable on a combine reading of both section 125, Cr.P.C. and section 20(3) of Hindu Adoptions and Maintenance Act, 1956; *Jagdish Jugtawat* v. *Manju Lata*, (2002) 5 SCC 422.

Othere Cases on Maintenance and Recovery

1. *K. Vimala* v. *K. Veeraswamy*, (1991) 1 SCR 904: Where the husband pleaded that his marriage is void on account of subsistence of his earlier marriage, the Apex Court held that, *"The Court should insist on strict proof of earlier marriage. ...... Insurance nomination and entry in identity card are not conclusive of subsistence of earlier marriage."*
2. *Popat Kashinath Bodke* v. *Kamalabai Popat Bodke*, 2003 All MR (Cri) 868 (Bom): 2003 (2) Mh LJ 608: Where agreement (*farkatnama*) executed by spouses clearly heralding their intention to live separately by mutual consent and which declared that after the said deed they were not to have relations as husband and wife as they are divorcing each other by customary system, it was held that wife in not entitled to maintenance. [However, opposite view has been taken by the Bombay High Court in *Tejaswini Anandrao Tayade* v. *Chandrakan Shirsat*, 2005 All MR (Cri) 2173].
3. *Sirajmohmedkhan* v. *Hafizunnisa*, (1982) 1 SCR 695: It has been held by the Apex Court that, *"Where it is proved to the satisfaction of the Court that a husband is impotent and is unable to discharge his marital obligations, this would amount to both legal and mental cruelty which would undoubtedly be a just ground as contemplated by the proviso for the wife's refusal to live with her husband and the wife would be entitled to maintenance from her husband according to his means."*
4. *Vinod* v. *Chhaya*, 2002 (4) Mh LJ 937 (Bom): Where husband did not pay interim maintenance to wife, Family Court cannot strike out defence of applicant husband as Civil Procedure Code has no application and proceedings would be governed by Criminal Procedure Code.
5. *Rejendra Kumar Pradhan* v. *Smt. Pramila Pradhan*, 1994 (1) Crimes 715 (Orissa): It has been held that in normal course issuance of distress warrants under section 125(3) is a condition precedent for exercise of the power to sentence but in a case distress warrants may not be insisted upon if Court is satisfied that such an exercise would be futile.
6. *Sharadchandra Chandrashekhar Satbhai* v. *Indubai Sharad Satbhai*, 80 Bom LR 69: The Division Bench of the Bombay High Court has held that where husband obtained decree for judicial separation on the ground of desertion by wife, wife is not entitled to apply under section 125 of the Code and is not entitled to maintenance.

7. *Kamla Samalprasad Pal* v. *Samalprasad Charanlal Pal,* 2005 All MR (Cri) 1958 (Bom): It has been held by the Bombay High Court that unless wife proves refusal and neglect on part of her husband to maintain her, she would not be entitled to claim a maintenance.
8. *Chaya* v. *K.G. Channappa Gowda,* 1993 Cri LJ 767 (Kant): Where the illegitimate child claimed maintenance and the paternity of child was totally denied by alleged father, it was held that evidence of mother cannot be accepted without proper corroboration.
9. *Sangita* v. *Arun,* 1984 Cri LJ 1524 (Bom): Where the wife left the matrimonial home of her own and alleged that her husband had neglected and refused to maintain her, it was held that she is not entitled to maintenance.
10. *Noor Jehen* v. *State of Maharashtra,* 1995 (1) Mh LJ 250 (Bom): It has been held by the Bombay High Court that right of a Muslim minor child to claim maintenance under section 125 of Cr.P.C. is neither taken away by section 3(b) of Muslim Women (Protection of Rights on Divorce) Act, 1986 nor is such right confined to claiming maintenance only upto the attainment of age of two years of child.
11. *Indu* v. *Sumanbai,* 1996 (2) Mh LJ 817 (Bom): It has been held that both legitimate and illegitimate minor children are entitled to claim maintenance from father.
12. *Shambu Nath Jiswal* v. *Smt. Anjana,* 1990 (3) Crimes 269 (Cal): It has been held that, *"what is the actual income of husband is a question of fact. Such question of fact is such which is in the special knowledge of the said husband. Therefore burden is on such husband to prove his income."*
13. *Gopal Krishna* v. *Mohd. Hazi,* AIR 1968 SC 1413: (1968) 3 SCR 862: The Apex Court held that, *"it is the duty of the husband to produce all the relevant documents in support of his income and all the relevant evidence which were in his possession. When he failed to do so, the Trial Court would be justified in drawing adverse inference against him."*
14. *Begum Subanu* v. *A.M. Abdul Gaffar,* AIR 1987 1103: The Apex Court held that, *"the personal income of the wife is very relevant for the purpose of calculating her maintenance allowance."*
15. *Shahada Khatoon* v. *Amjad Ali,* 1999 (3) Mh LJ 290 (SC): It has been held by the Apex Court that, *"Magistrate cannot order imprisonment of husband for more than one month. .... For breach or non-compliance with the order of the Magistrate the wife can approach the Magistrate again for similar relief."*
16. *K. Nithiyanandan* v. *B. Radhamani,* 1980 Cri LJ 1191 (Ker): The Kerala High Court has held that, *"Sentencing defaulter husband straightway to term of imprisonment is improper. Modes of realisation amount under section 421, Cr.P.C. should be followed before passing sentence."*
17. *Pandharinath Jadhav* v. *Savitribai Jadhav,* 2000 (1) Mh LJ 408 (Bom): It has been held that, *"the right of mother to claim maintenance from her son born from her first husband is not lost particularly after death of her second husband even though she has remarried."*

18. *Mahendra Kumar R. Gaikwad* v. *Gulabhai R. Gaikwad,* 2000 (2) Mh LJ 378 (Bom): It has been held by the Bombay High Court that, *"mother can claim maintenance from any one son or both of them. Choice is given to her. ...... She can claim maintenance from son even though her husband is living/ alive."*
19. *Kedari S. Shinde* v. *State of Maharashtra,* 1993 Bom Criminal Cases 282 (Bom): It has been held by the Bombay High Court that, *"there is not limitation for presentation of maintenance application . Silence for some years by such woman will not take away the right to claim maintenance."*
20. *Bhagwat* v. *Baburao,* 1994 Mh LJ 202 (Bom): It has been held by the Bombay High Court that recovery of maintenance allowance can be effected by attachment of the salary payable to the husband.

(2) Search for Persons Wrongfully Confined – (Cr.P.C. Section 97)

Section 97 of Cr.P.C. provide that if any District Magistrate, Sub-Divisional Magistrate or Magistrate of the first class has reason to believe that any person is confined under such circumstances that the confinement amounts to an offence, he may issue a search-warrant, and the person to whom such warrant is directed may search for the person so confined; and such search shall be made in accordance therewith, and the person, if found, shall be immediately taken before a Magistrate, who shall make such an order as in the circumstances of the case seems proper.

Bare reading of the section reveals that the confinement of a person must amount to an offence punishable under Indian Penal Code or any other Act in order to attract the said section. It should be remembered that the application under section 97, Cr.P.C. should be supported with proper affidavit stating the reasons and grounds for filing the application.

*Where father forcibly removed child from the mother's custody, it was held that, *"it amounts to wrongful confinement. Act of father also attracts sections 329, 340 of I.P.C. and therefore provision of section 97, Cr.P.C. are attracted........ Mother has right of custody of male child till he completes 7 years, in preference to father....... Application by mother under section 97 of Cr.P.C. cannot be said to be not maintainable in view of alternative remedy under Guardians and Wards Act, 1890. Welfare of child is paramount consideration in such cases."* [**Zahirul Hassan* v. *State of Uttar Pradesh,* 1988 Cri LJ 230 (All)]. However contrary view has taken by the Bombay High Court in *Anil s/o Baburao Angalwar* v. *St. Cyuthia Benard Samuel w/o Anil Baburao Angalwar,* 2007 All MR (Cri) 1611. In this case husband took away child from its mother and detained in his custody. The Hon'ble Court held that it does not amount to confinement and search warrant cannot be issued for its production?

In *S. Rama Iyer* v. *K.V. Natraja Iyer,* AIR 1948 Mad 294, the Madras High Court has held that, *"Since the minor (13 years old) was incapable of forming any opinion, his detention even if he remains in the custody of the maternal grandfather of his free will must be deemed to be illegal as against a person who is better entitled in law to take his custody."* This case has been approved by the Apex Court in *Gohar Begum* v. *Suggi* alias *Nazma Begum,* AIR 1960 SC 93.

In *Dushyant Somal* v. *Sushma Somal,* AIR 1981 SC 1026, the Apex Court has held that, *"Availability of alternate remedy under the Guardians and Wards Act is no ground to deny custody under section 97 of Cr.P.C."*

(3) Order for Custody and Disposal of Property – (Chapter XXXIV of Cr.P.C.; Section 451 to 459)

Order for custody (*Suprutnama*) of property can be made by the Criminal Courts at various stages of trial such as during any inquiry or trial, at the conclusion of trial and when seizure of property is reported to a Magistrate by any police officer but such property is not produced before a Criminal Court during inquiry or trial.

In *Sunderbhai Ambalal Desai* v. *State of Gujarat,* 2003 All MR (Cri) 363 (SC), the Apex Court while giving detailed directions for the disposal of property pending trial, held that, *"powers under section 451 of Cr.P.C. should be exercised expeditiously and judiciously. Court should pass appropriate orders immediately. ...... Articles are not be kept for a long time at police station, in any case, for not more than fifteen days to one month."*

In *Ram Prakash Sharma* v. *State of Haryana,* AIR 1978 SC 1282: 1978 Cri LJ 1120, the Apex Court has held that, *"the Court has power to dispose of property seized by the police but not yet produced before the Court. But it does not mean that the Court must always release such property to the person from whom the property has been recovered, especially when the stage of the case is in suspicion, the investigation is not over and charge-sheet has not been laid. The Court has to be circumspect in such a situation before releasing the property. The question of release has to be decided on its own merits in each case and the discretion of the Court has to be exercised after due consideration of the interests of justice including the prospective necessity of the production of the seized articles at the time of the trial. If the release of the property seized will in any manner affect or prejudice the course of justice at the time of the trial, it will be wise discretion to reject the claim for return."*

In this case [*Dadaji* v. *State of Maharashtra,* 1977 Mh LJ (Note No. 85) (Bom)] applicant was discharged for the offences punishable under sections 379 and 411 of IPC. But accused-respondent No. 2 was convicted. The trial court returned the property to the applicant on *Supratnama*. In appeal respondent No. 3-complainant compounded the offence and therefore Court acquitted accused-respondent No. 2 but ordered return of property to respondent No. 3-complainant. The Bombay High Court set aside the order and held that property should be allowed to be in possession of the applicant from whom the property was seized by the police.

In this case [*Kishan Pandurang Kagde* v. *Baldeo Singh Gian Singh,* 1977 Mh LJ 656 (Bom) (DB)] the Trial Magistrate passed an order for custody of vehicle in favour of accused during trial on the ground that registration of the vehicle stood in his name. However, the documents on record showed that prima facie ownership of the motor vehicle and possession thereof had both passed to the complainant who alleged theft of the vehicle by the transferor. In such circumstances the Bombay High Court set aside the order of Trial Court and directed that custody of motor vehicle be given to complainant and not to accused. The Court observed that *"the transfer of ownership does not flow from and does not depend on transfer of registration. The transfer of ownership takes place from the date of sale and not from the date on which name of transferee is recorded."*

Other Cases on Order for Custody and Disposal of Property

1. *Ashok Leyland Finance Ltd.* v. *State of Maharashtra,* 2005 All MR (Cri) 3052 (Bom): Where the vehicle was purchased under Hire-Purchase agreement, financer is the real owner and therefore financer is entitled to custody of vehicle.
2. *State of Madhya Pradesh* v. *Rameshwar Rathod,* AIR 1990 SC 1849: 1990 Cri LJ 1756: The Apex Court has held that, *"The jurisdiction of the Criminal Courts to pass orders for return of the vehicles is not affected by the Amendment Act 30 of 1974 made in Essential Commodities Act, 1955."*
3. *Nawalkishor Gowardhandasji Rathi* v. *State of Maharashtra,* 2006 (1) AIR Bom R 36 (DB): Where the vehicle was seized while transporting wild animals and offence was registered under Wild Life (Protection) Act (53 of 1972) and where application for release of vehicle by owner of vehicle even before charge-sheet was filed, it was held that, *"application is not maintainable at such premature stage."*
4. *Inter Continental Agencies Pvt. Ltd.* v. *Aminchand Khanna,* AIR 1980 SC 951: 1980 Cri LJ 689: The Apex Court held that, *"If the seized property is not traceable or cannot be delievered, the Court should direct the culprit party to pay the value of the property to the person entitled to it."*
5. *State Bank of India* v. *Rajendra Kumar Singh,* AIR 1969 SC 401: 1969 Cri LJ 659: The Apex Court held that, *"though the Criminal Procedure Code is silent and does not expressly require issuance of any notice, there is in the eye of law a necessary implication that the parties adversely affected should be heard before the Court makes an order of return of the seized property....... Where no notice is issued, order of return of property is vitiated."*
6. *N. Madhavan* v. *State of Kerala,* AIR 1979 SC 1829: 1979 Cri LJ 1197: The Apex Court set aside the order of confiscation of gun as opportunity of hearing was not given to the accused. The Court observed that, *"One well-recognised principle is that when after an inquiry or trial the accused is discharged or acquitted, the Court should normally restore the property, which is produced before it or which is in the custody of the Court, to the person from whose custody it was taken. Departure from this rule of practice is not to be lightly made when there is no dispute or doubt as in the instant case, that the property was seized from the custody of such accused and belong to him."*
7. *Haribhau Dhondiba Chavan* v. *Balkrushna B. Ballal,* 1987 Mh LJ 340: 1987 Mh LR 921: (1987) 89 Bom LR 197: Custody of vehicle should be given to registered owner during pendency of trial.
8. *Suraj Mohan* v. *State of Gujarat,* AIR 1967 Guj 126: The Gujarat High Court has held that, *"though police did not report seizure to Court, still Magistrate can pass order for release."*
9. *Milind* v. *State of Maharashtra,* 2003 (2) Mh LJ 735 (Bom): Where vehicle was seized from the possession of accused and who claimed that he was

transferee and owner of the same, it was held that accused is entitled to interim custody of motorcycle though complainant was erstwhile registered owner of the vehicle.

10. *Virendra Kumar J. Handa* v. *Dilawar Khan*, 1991 Mh LJ 1371: 1992 Cri LJ 2476: It has been held that the custody of the vehicle should be handed over to the person making out superior title notwithstanding that registration of the vehicle stood in the name of another.

11. *Jaganath Shirsat* v. *State of Maharashtra*, 2000 (2) Mh LJ 605: The Bombay High Court has held that, *"The Magistrate is required to consider the better right to possess the property. He is not required to decide the question of title."*

12. *Kamlesh J. Yadav* v. *State of Maharashtra*, 1997 (1) Mh LJ 198 (Bom): The Bombay High Court has held that, *"Section 52(2) of Forest Act, 1927 has no applicability to pre-conviction stage. ...... If a report is not made/sent to concerned authorised officer under section 61A of the Act, then the trial Magistrate has the jurisdiction to released the seized articles and vehicles on Supratnama."*

13. *Patel K. Venidas* v. *Kacharaji N. Thakore*, 1983 Cri LJ NOC 24 (Guj): It was a case of theft of gold ornaments wherein accused was convicted of admission. Facts showed that the ornaments sold by accused were melted by purchaser. In such circumstances, the Gujarat High Court held that, *"Owner of gold ornaments is not entitled to muddemal under section 452(5) of Cr.P.C. as no link was established between melted gold and the ornaments alleged to be stolen."*

14. *State of Maharashtra* v. *Manishkumar Babulal Biyani*, 1998 All MR (Cri) 89 (Bom): Where LPG cylinders were seized by police under Essential Commodities Act, 1955 and confiscation proceedings were not pending before Collector or State Government, the Bombay High Court held that, *"Criminal Court is not barred from exercising jurisdiction under section 457 read with section 451 of Cr.P.C."*

15. *State of Karnataka* v. *Krishnan*, AIR 2000 SC 2729: Where property was seized for the commission of offence under Forest Act, 1927, the Apex Court held that, *"Liberal approach in release of seized property is uncalled for. Vehicle seized shall not normally be returned to party till culmination of all proceedings in respect of said offence."*

16. *Deputy Commissioner, Daxin Kanada* v. *Rudolph Farnandis*, AIR 2000 SC 1132: Where the vehicle is seized under Essential Commodities Act (10 of 1955) and Court decides to impose fine in lieu of confiscation, the Apex Court held that, *"fine should be determined on the basis of market price of the vehicle. Fine amount should not exceed the market price of the vehicle on the date of seizure."*

17. *State of Gujarat* v. *Nareshbhai*, 1988 (3) Crimes 546 (Guj) (DB): The Gujarat High Court has held that, *"purchaser of the stolen articles would not get any title over the property inspite of the fact that he had purchased it* bona fide

by paying full market price. .... Since no inquiry under section 452, Cr.P.C. was made before passing the order of return of gold articles to the goldsmith (purchaser), order of the trial Court is illegal."

18. *Kailash Prasad Yadav* v. *State of Jharkhand,* 2007 All SCR 1376: In this case vehicle was confiscated under Essential Commodities Act, 1955 and Public Distribution system (Control) Order, 2001. The Apex Court held that *"valid seizure is a* sine qua non *for passing an order of confiscation."*

19. *Ravindra Tayade* v. *State of Maharashtra,* 2007 All MR (Cri) 3108: Where vehicle was seized under the provisions of Wild Life (Protection) Act, 1972, the Hon'ble Court held that *"Seized vehicle would become the property of the State Government only when after the trial relevant accused are held guilty for the offences charged and vehicles are proved to have been used in commission of offences."*

20. *State of Uttar Pradesh* v. *Lalloo Singh,* 2007 All MR (Cri) 2076 (SC): Where property was seized under the provisions of Wild Life (Protection) Act, 1972, the Hon'ble Apex Court held that *"Magistrate has power to give interim custody of the property. But intimation should be given to the Chief Wild Life Wardon or authorised officer."*

CHAPTER XXXIX
QUESTION AND ANSWERS

In this chapter, the topics which could not be covered in forgoing chapters are given in the form of question of answers.

1. **Whether process once issued can be recalled or reviewed by a Court?**

   Ans: No.

   [Please Read:—(i) *Adalat Prasad* v. *Rooplal Jindal,* 2004 All MR (Cri) 3131 (SC), (ii) *Subramanium Sethuraman* v. *State of Maharashtra,* 2004 (4) Crimes 78 (SC), (iii) *Bindeshwari Prasad Singh* v. *Kali Singh,* (1977) 1 SCR 125.]

2. **Whether Court can dispense with personal attendance of accused persons liberally?**

   Ans: Yes.

   [Please Read:—(i) *Maneka Sanjay Gandhi* v. *Rani Jethmalani,* (1979) 2 SCR 378, (ii) *Mr. Bhaskar Sen* v. *State of Maharashtra.,* 2004 All MR (Cri) 2889 (Bom). (iii) *M/s. Bhaskar Industries Ltd.* v. *M/s. Bhiwani Denim & Apparels Ltd.,* 2001 All MR (Cri) 1961 (SC). (iv) *S.V. Muzumdar* v. *Gujarat State Fertilizer Company Ltd.,* 2005 AllMR (Cri) 1581 (SC). (v) *Chockalingam* v. *Swastik Filaments Pvt. Ltd.,* 2003 Cri LJ 2500 (Mad)].

3. **Whether Court can allow compounding of a non-compoundable offence which is not covered by Table I or Table II of section 320 of Cr.P.C.?**

   Ans: No.

   [Please Read:—(i) *Bankat* v. *State of Maharashtra,* 2005 (2) Mh LJ 707 (SC)].

   Note:—Where a criminal prosecution and a Civil Suit have been filed, compromise in civil suits amounts to compounding of offence for all intents and purposes; [vide: *C.B.I.* v. *Duncans Agro Industries Ltd.,* 1996 (3) CCR 68 (SC)].

4. **Which proceedings should be stayed where there is simultaneous prosecution of civil and criminal proceedings regarding the same matter?**

   Ans: Civil Proceeding should be stayed.

   [Please Read:—*M.S. Sheriff* v. *State of Madras,* 1954 SCR 1144].

5. **Whether a officer-in-charge of a police station is duty bound to register a case on the basis of information disclosing cognizable offence?**

   Ans: Yes.

   [Please Read:—*Ramesh Kumari* v. *State (NCT of Delhi),* AIR 2006 SC 1322: 2006 (1) Crimes 229 (SC)].

6. Whether charge can be alternatively framed?

Ans: Yes.

[Please Read:—(i) *Dalbir Singh* v. *State of Uttar Pradesh,* AIR 2004 SC 1990. (ii) *Kisan* v. *State of Maharashtra,* 2007 Cri LJ 130 (Bom)].

7. Whether in absence of a charge under section 34 of I.P.C., conviction can be maintained under section 34?

Ans: Yes.

[Please Read:—(i) *Willie (William Slaney)* v. *State of Madhya Pradesh,* AIR 1956 SC 116].

8. Whether *locus standi* of the complainant is a *sine qua non* for filing a complaint?

Ans: No.

[Please Read:—*A.R. Antulay* v. *R.S. Nayak,* (1984) 2 SCR 914].

9. Whether sanction is required for the prosecution of an MLA?

Ans: No.

[Please Read: *R.S. Nayak* v. *A.R. Antulay,* (1984) 2 SCR 495].

10. Whether a second complaint can be filed after dismissal of a first complaint?

Ans: Yes.

[Please Read:—(i) *Pramatha Nath Taluqdar* v. *Saroj Ranjan Sarkar,* (1962) Supp 22 SCR 297. (ii) *Major General A.S. Gauraya* v. *S.N. Thakur* (1986) 2 SCR 771].

11. Whether accused can avail the benefit of proviso to sub-section (2) of section 167, Cr.P.C. at a later stage of the proceeding without filing an application for bail when right accrued to him?

Ans: No.

[Please Read:—*Dr. Bipin Shantilal Panchal* v. *State of Gujarat,* III (1996) CCR 103 (SC)].

12. Whether a juristic person or artificial person like Corporation can be prosecuted for criminal offence?

Ans: Yes.

[Please Read:—*Asst. Commissioner* v. *Velliappa Textiles Ltd.,* 2003 AIR SCW 5647].

13. Whether evidence of witness can be recorded by video-conferencing in presence of accused and/or his pleader?

Ans: Yes.

[Please Read:—*State of Maharashtra* v. *Dr. Praful B. Desai,* 2003 (2) Mh LJ 868 (SC)].

14. Whether certified copies of the documents which are not exhibited can be issued?

Ans: Yes.

[Please Read:—*K.R. Sengottuvelu* v. *Karuppa Naicker,* AIR 2006 Mad 11: 2006 (2) Civ LJ 464 (Mad)].

15. Whether Court fee is required to be paid on an application filed for taking objection on record during trial?

Ans: No.

[Please Read:—*Manoramabai* v. *Satyabhamabai,* 1968 Mh LJ 608 (Bom)].

16. Whether identification of an accused person by photo is admissible in evidence?

Ans: Yes.

[Please Read:—*Umar Abdul Sakoor Sorathiya* v. *Intelligence Officer, Narcotics Control Bureu,* AIR 1999 SC 2562: 1999 Cri LJ 3972].

17. Whether Magistrate can allow accused to make even first appearance through counsel before executing bail bonds?

Ans: Yes

[Please Read:—*V.S. Reddy* v. *M/s. Excel Glasses Ltd.,* 2012 (1) Crimes 160 (Ker) (SN)].

18. Whether presence of accused before Court is necessary for cancellation of non-bailable warrant?

Ans: No.

[Please Read:—*Prem Cashew Industries* v. *Zen Pareo,* 2001 All MR (Cri) Journal 33 (Del)].

19. Whether certified copies of judicial proceedings against accused by third party are relevant in a criminal trial against accused?

Ans: Yes.

[Please Read:—*Shaikh Abdul Rahim* v. *State of Maharashtra,* 2008 All MR (Cri) 1017].

20. Whether positive evidence of good antecedents of accused is relevant in a criminal trial?

Ans: Yes.

[Please Read:—*Mohan Singh* v. *State of Haryana,* (1995) 2 SCR 610].

21. Whether evidence of general reputation and general disposition is relevant in a criminal proceeding?

Ans: Yes.

[Please Read:—*Sardar Sardul Singh Caveeshar* v. *State of Maharashtra,* (1964) 2 SCR 378].

22. Whether second protest petition is maintainable?

Ans: Yes. (However, in exceptional circumstances).

[Please Read:—*Shiv Shankar Singh* v. *State of Bihar,* 2012 (1) Crimes 16 (SC): 2012 All MR (Cri) 354 SC].

23. Can a statement made by one accused in FIR, be used against other accused?

Ans: No.

[Please Read:—*Faddi* v. *State of Madhya Pradesh,* (1964) 6 SCR 312] and [*Bandla Ramaiah* v. *State of Andhra Pradesh,* 1996 Cri LJ 4463: 1997 SCC (Cri) 128].

24. Whether accused can be charged simultaneously for the offence punishable under sections 304 Part II and 338, IPC?

Ans: Yes.

[Please Read:—*Alister A. Pareira* v. *State of Maharashtra,* 2012 (1) Crimes 76(SC)].

25. Whether Magistrate is entitled to question accused under section 313, Cr.P.C. for a second time when case had reached final judgement stage?

Ans: Yes.

[Please Read:—*M/s. Chennai Covai Logistics* v. *S. Egyasamy,* 2011 (3) Crimes 59 (Mad)].

26. Whether a witness could appear before a Magistrate directly to get his statement recorded and whether Judicial Magistrate was duty bound to take his statement under section 164, Cr.P.C.?

Ans: Yes.

[Please Read:—*Mahabir Singh* v. *State of Haryana.,* AIR 2001 SC 2503].

27. Whether defence is entitled to place materials before Court at the time of framing of charge?

Ans: Yes. (Only in some of the rare and exceptional cases)

[Please Read:—*Rukmini Narvekar* v. *Vijaya Satardekar,* AIR 2009 SC 1013: 2009 Cri LJ 822 (SC): (2008) 14 SCC 1].

28. Whether a document procured by improper or even illegal means is admissible in evidence?

Ans: Yes.

[Please Read:—*Magraj Patodia* v. *R.K. Birla,* AIR 1971 SC 1295].

29. Whether actual presence of person who is intended to be annoyed is necessary for the offence of criminal trespass?

Ans: No.

[Please Read:—*Rash Behari Chatterjee* v. *Fagu Shaw,* (1970) 1 SCR 425].

30. Whether Court has power to direct investigation officer to include a person as an accused in the case while the investigation is pending?

Ans: No.

[Please Read:—*Director, CBI* v. *Niyamavedi.,* 1995 Cri LJ 2917 (SC)].

31. Whether decisions of Civil Courts are binding on criminal Courts?

Ans: Yes. (However, converse is not true)

[**Please Read:**—*M/s. Karamchand Ganga Prasad* v. *Union of India,* AIR 1971 SC 1244].

32. Whether accused can be convicted on evidence partly recorded by one Judge or Magistrate and partly by another in summary trial case?

Ans: No.

[**Please Read:**—*Ajoy Kumar Poddar* v. *State of Bihar,* 2010 (1) Crimes 471 (Pat)].

33. Whether a person could be discharged before trial commenced by giving notice of offence under section 251, Cr.P.C.?

Ans: No.

[**Please Read:**—*M/s. Asian Fans & Appliances Co. Pvt. Ltd.* v. *M/s. Usaka Industrial Components Pvt. Ltd.,* 2010 (1) Crimes 138 (Del)].

34. Whether Magistrate can direct investigation officer to incorporate the provisions of Atrocities Act and investigate the case in an application under section 156(3), Cr.P.C.?

Ans: No.

[**Please Read:**—*Balchandran* v. *State of Kerala,* 2010 (1) Crimes 552 (Ker) (SN)].

35. Whether defence taken by one accused can be treated as evidence against his co-accused?

Ans: No.

[**Please Read:**—*Satyavir Singh Rathi* v. *State through CBI,* 2011 All SCR 1474].

36. Whether an accused has right to cross-examine the approver who is examined under section 306(4) of Cr.P.C. by Magistrate at pre-committal stage?

Ans: No.

[**Please Read:**—*Ranadhir Basu* v. *State West Bengal,* (2000) 3 SCC 161].

37. Whether accused is required to be produced in Court along with the Chargesheet?

Ans: No.

[**Please Read:**—*State of Uttar Pradesh* v. *Anil Kumar Sharma,* 2015 (4) Crimes 166 (SC).]

38. Whether second complaint on the same facts is maintainable where the earlier complaint was decided on the basis of insufficient material?

Ans: Yes.

[**Please Read:**—*Shiv Shankar Singh* v. *State of Bihar,* 2012 AIAR (Criminal) 13 (SC)].

39. Whether Magistrate can issue summons on a private complaint in respect of the same case under section 204 of Cr.P.C. against new person after committal of case?

Ans: No

[Please Read:—*Jile Singh* v. *State of Uttar Pradesh*, 2012 AIAR (Criminal) 120 (SC): (2012) 3 SCC 383].

40. Whether accused persons can seek production of evidence filed in another case?

Ans: Yes.

[Please Read:—*Kamal A.M. Vakil* v. *State of Maharashtra*, 2013 All MR (Cri) 401].

41. Whether the High Court, in exercise of its jurisdiction under Article 226, can direct the CBI to investigate a cognizable offence, which is alleged to have been taken place within the territorial jurisdiction of a State, without the consent of the State Government?

Ans: Yes.

[Please Read:—*State of West Bengal* v. *The Committee for Protection of Democratic Rights, West Bengal*, 2010 (2) All MR 941 (SC) (CB)].

42. Whether a person summoned as accused pursuant to an order passed by a Court in exercise of power conferred by section 319, Cr.P.C., can be tried for the offence for which he is summoned even after the conclusion of the trial where in such an order of summoning was passed?

Ans: Yes.

[Please Read:—*Shashi Kant Singh* v. *Tarkeshwar Singh*, 2002 Cri LJ 2806 (SC)].

43. Whether in a summary proceeding Magistrate can rely on evidence recorded by his predecessor and acquit the accused?

Ans: No.

[Please Read:—*Nitinbhai S. Shah* v. *Manubhai M. Panchal*, AIR 2011 SC 3076].

44. Whether Court can look into the documents filed by the accused which are beyond suspicion and doubt at the stage of issue of process?

Ans: Yes.

[Please Read:—*Harshendra Kumar D.* v. *Rebatilata Koley*, (2011) 3 SCC 351].

45. Can a second wife file complaint under section 498A, IPC?

Ans: No.

[Please Read:—*Shivacharan Lal Verma* v. *State of Madhya Pradesh*, 2002 (2) Crimes 177 (SC)].

Note: *Reema Aggarwal* v. *Anupam*, AIR 2004 SC 1419 is *per incuriam* in view of the above decision.

46. Whether a Sessions Court or High Court while deciding a revision is required mandatorily to issue notice to opposite side who has not been summoned to stand trial?

Ans: Yes.

[**Please Read**:—*Hindustan Domestic Oil & Gas Co. Ltd.* v. *State,* 2013 (3) Crimes 382 (Del)]

47. **Whether Court can convict an accused for the offence punishable under section 304 Part I read with section 109, IPC where no charge under section 109, IPC was framed and accused was originally charged under section 302 read with 34, IPC?**

Ans: No.

[**Please Read**:—*Babu @ Balasubramaniam* v. *State of Tamil Nadu,* 2013 (3) Crimes 312 (SC)].

48. **Whether Special Judge under the SC & ST (Prevention of Atrocities) Act, 1989 can take cognizance of the offence directly on the basis of chargesheet filed before it though accused was not committed in terms of section 193 of the Code?**

Ans: Yes.

[**Please Read**:—*Rattiram* v. *State of Madhya Pradesh,* 2012 (2) Crimes 123 (SC): 2012 All SCR 1594].

49. **Whether a criminal prosecution can continue against a dead person?**

Ans: No.

[**Please Read**:—*U Subhadramma* v. *State of Andhra Pradesh,* (2016) 7 SCC 796].

50. **Whether Court can order return of private complaint filed for offence of theft of electricity holding that the same was filed without adopting prescribed procedure under section 135(1) of the Electricity Act, 2003?**

Ans: No.

[**Please Read**:—*M.P. Madhya Kshetra Vidyut Vitran Co. Ltd.* v. *Ramswaroop Kushwah,* 2015 (2) Crimes 446 (MP)].

51. **Whether a non-public servant can be prosecuted along with public servant for abetment of commission of offence under Prevention of Corruption Act, 1988?**

Ans: Yes.

[**Please Read**:—*P. Nallammal* v. *State,* (1996) 6 Supreme Today 516].

52. **Whether postponement of issue of process under section 202 of CrPC is mandatory?**

Ans: Yes.

[**Please Read**:—*Uday Shankar Awasthi* v. *State of Uttar Pradesh,* 2013 (6) LJ SOFT (SC) 296].

CHAPTER XL
LATIN WORDS AND PHRASES

In this chapter, meaning of Latin words and phrases are given:

1. ***actus reus*** – means deeds forbidden by law [*'actus'* means a deed whereas *'reus'* means forbidden by law].
2. ***mens rea*** – means some blameworthy mental condition, whether constituted by intention of knowledge or otherwise, the absence of which on any particular occasion, negatives the contention of a crime.
3. ***alibi*** – means elsewhere.
4. ***actus non facit ruem, nisi mens sit rea*** – means there can be no crime without a guilty mind (*i.e.*, the intent and act must both concur to constitute the crime).
5. ***actus curiae neminem gravabit*** – means an act of Court shall prejudice no man.
6. ***corpus delicti*** – means the body of a crime; the body, substance or foundation of an offence.
7. ***contemporanea expositio est optima est fortissima in lege*** – means a contemporaneous exposition is the best and most powerful exposition in law. [This doctrine relates to the field of interepretation of statutes. It has no application while interpreting provisions of Criminal Procedure Code.]
8. ***doli capax*** – means capable of crime.
9. ***doli incapax*** – means incapable of crime.
10. ***Falsus in uno, falsus in omnibus*** – means false in one thing, false in all. (However it should be noted that this maxim has not received acceptance in India).
11. ***nolle prosequi*** – means to be unwilling to prosecute.
12. ***nemo in propria causa judex, esse debet*** – means no one ought to be a judge in his own cause.
13. ***nemo inpropria causa testis esse debet*** – means no one ought to be a witness in his own cause.
14. ***nemo debet esse judex in propria causa*** – means no one should be a judge in his own cause.
15. ***nemo debets prodere ipsum*** – means the right against self-incrimination.

16. ***nemo debet is vexari, si constat curiae quod sit pro una et eadem causa*** – means no man ought to be twice put to trouble, if it appears to the court that it is for one and the same cause.
17. ***nemo tenetur prodere seipsum*** – means no one is obliged to criminate himself.
18. ***nemo tenetur seipsum accusare*** – means no man can be compelled to criminate himself.
19. ***per incuriam*** – means through inadvertance or through want of care.
20. ***qui approbat non reprobat*** – means he who approbates does not reprobate (*i.e.*, he cannot both accept and reject the same thing).
21. ***quid pro quo*** – (the literal meaning of the phrase is 'one for the other'); the giving of one thing of value for another thing of value; (rare) blunder made by using or putting one thing for another.
22. ***res gestae*** – means things done, or liberally speaking, the facts of the transaction; acts, declarations and incidents accompanying or explaining the fact in issue or which are deemed to constitute the fact in issue; facts so connected with a fact in issue as to form part of the same transaction.
23. ***res integra*** – means a point not covered by the authority of a decided case, so that a judge may decide it upon principle alone.
24. ***res nova*** – means a matter not yet decided.
25. ***res ipsa loquitur*** – means the thing speaks for itself. (a phrase used in actions for injury by negligence where no proof of negligence is required beyond the accident itself, which is such as necessarily to involve negligence).
26. ***sine qua non*** – means necessary condition.
27. ***status quo*** – means the existing state of things at any given date.
28. ***stare decisis*** – means to abide by authorities or cases already adjudicated upon.
29. ***vicarious liability*** – means liability incurred for others.

    [*Example*:—Corporation is liable for criminal acts of its directors and agents; State is liable for the criminal acts of its employees].
30. ***Rule Nisi*** – It is a Court order that does not have any force unless a particular condition is met. One the condition is met, the ruling becomes a decree absolute (rule absolute), and is binding.

CHAPTER XLI
PRECEDENTS

Precedent is an authority only for what it actually decides and not for what may remotely or even logically follows from it. Decision on question not argued cannot constitute a precedent. It has been held by the Apex Court in *Delhi Municipal Corporation* v. *Gujman Kaur,* AIR 1989 SC 38, that, *"direction by Supreme Court to Municipal Corporation in earlier case, to construct stalls for pavement squatters passed on consent of parties is not binding on subsequent judges. High Court should not follow it as precedent."*

Precedents lead to certainty of law, and therefore are important from the practical point of view. A Court is bound by the decisions of all Courts superior to it. In *Bishnu Ram Borah* v. *Parag Saikia,* (1984) 1 SCR 825 the Apex Court held that *"Judgments and orders of High Courts are binding and must be obeyed by all inferior Courts and Tribunals subject to their supervisory jurisdiction."*

In *Union of India* v. *Raghubir Singh,* (1989) 3 SCR 316 the Constitution Bench of the Apex Court while answering 'whether decision of the Division Bench rendered earlier in point of time is binding on subsequent Division Bench comprised of equal number of Judges or of more Judges?' held that *"a pronouncement of law by a Division Bench of Supreme Court is binding on a Division Bench of the same or a smaller number of Judges, and in order that such decision be binding, it is not necessary that it should be a decision rendered by the full Court or a Constitution Bench of the Court. For the purpose of imparting certainity and endowing due authority, decisions of this Court in the future should be rendered by Division Benches of at least three Judges unless for compelling reasons that is not conveniently possible."* Another Constitution Bench of the Apex Court in *Chandra Prakash* v. *State of Uttar Pradesh,* (2002) 2 SCR 913 has also held that *"when there is a conflict between Judgements of three-Judge Bench and two-Judge Bench, it is imperative for two-Judge Bench to follow decision of three-Judge Bench."*

To understand the importance of precedent and its practical application to cases, few examples are given below:

In *Deena* alias *Deendayal* v. *Union of India,* AIR 1983 SC 1155, the Apex Court has explained the judicial precedents as: *"any case, even a* locus classicus, *is an authority for what it decides. It is permissible to extend the ration of a decision to cases involving identical situations, factual and legal, but care must be taken to see that, this is not done mechanically, that is, without a close examination of the rationale of the decision which is cited as a precedent."*

In *Ram Prasad Sarma* v. *Manikumar Subba,* AIR 2003 SC 51, the Apex Court held that there is not precedent on facts. It is the legal proposition flowing from judgment which has binding effect.

The Apex Court in *Gangadhar Behera* v. *State of Orissa,* AIR 2002 SC 3633 has given a note of caution regarding precedential applications by observing that there is always peril in treating words of a judgment as though they are words in a legislative enactment. It is to be remembered that judicial utterances are made in the settings of the facts of a particular case. Circumstantial flexibility, one additional or different fact may make a world of difference between conclusions in two cases.

Justice V.R. Krishna Iyyer has explained the concept of application of precedent to cases as follows: *"The facts and circumstances often vary from case to case, the crime situation and myriad psychic factors, social conditions and people's life-styles may fluctuate, and so, rules of prudence relevant in one fact -situation may be inept in another. The agrument that regardless of the specific circumstances of a crime and criminal milieu, some strands of probative reasoning which appealed to a Bench in one reported decision must mechanically be extended to other cases cannot be accepted."* [*Rafiq* v. *State of Uttar Pradesh,* (1981) 1 SCR 402].

In *Union of India* v. *Dhanwanti Devi,* (1996) Supp 5 SCR 32 the Apex Court held that essence in a decision was its ratio which was binding and not every observation found therein. Every judgment must be read as applicable to particular facts proved. A precedent by long recognition matured into rule of *stare decisis.*

Other Cases on Precedents

1. *Punjab National Bank* v. *R.L. Vaid,* 2004 All MR (Cri) 3423 (SC): The Apex Court held that *"case should not be decided by citing a precedent without indicating its relevance to facts in issue in the case on hand. Treating words of judgment as if they are words in legislative enactment is not proper."*
2. *Rudrappa R. Jainpur* v. *State of Karnataka,* 2004 All MR (Cri) 2800 (SC): The Apex Court held that *"mere similarity of facts in one case cannot be used to determine a conclusion of fact in another. Each case must rests on its own facts."*
3. *Forasol* v. *ONGC,* (1984) 1 SCR 526: The Apex Court held that *"English decisions are not binding on Indian Court but have high persuasive value."*
4. *BSES Ltd.* v. *Fenner India Ltd.,* 2006 (4) All MR (SC) 5: The Apex Court held that *"When law in India is clear, settled and without any deviation whatsoever, there is no occasion to rely upon foreign case law."*
5. *Mishrimal Jethmal Oswal* v. *The Municipal Council of Lonavala,* 2006 (3) All MR 18 (Bom) (DB): The Division Bench of Bombay High Court has held that, *"Law laid down by Supreme Court in criminal case would apply equally to any other cases or even to Public Interest Litigation filed under Article 226 of the Constitution of India."*

CHAPTER XLII
INTERPRETATION OF STATUTES

SYNOPSIS

One of the important functions of the higher judiciary is to interpret the laws passed by the legislature. If any rule, provision, ordinance or law passed by the legislature is *ultra vires* the Constitution of India, the higher judiciary has struck it down as being unconstitutional. However Lord Denning has given a note of caution by saying that *"a Judge must not alter the material of which it is woven, but he can and should iron out the creases."* Few cases are given below to let the readers know the process of interpretation of statutes—

> It is well-settled rule of law that words and terms of criminal enactments have to be construed strictly and in favour of subject as far as possible giving meaning in common parlance. However modern trend seems to be that the penal statutes which deal with crimes of aggravated nature should be more strictly construed.

Question often arises as to whether a particular provision of a statute is mandatory or directory and Courts have to deal with this aspect of law. A provision is not mandatory unless non-compliance with it is made penal. On the contrary a directory provision gives no discretion and is intended to be obeyed, but a failure to obey it does not render a thing duly done in disobedience of it a nullity. The Apex Court in *Mannalal Khetan* v. *Kedar Nath Khetan,* (1977) 2 SCR 190 has laid down the following tests for finding out when a provision is mandatory or directory: *"The purpose for which the provision has been made, its nature, the intention of the legislature in making the provision, the general inconvenience or injustice which may result to the persons for reading the provision one way or the other, the relation of the particular provision to other provisions dealing with the same subject and the language of the provision. Prohibition and negative words can rarely be directory. Negative, prohibitory and exclusive words are indicative of the legislative intent when the statute in mandatory."*

(a) Use of Articles 'the' and 'a'

Article 'the' is generally used to specify or particularise a thing. The Apex Court while interpreting the meaning of article 'the' used in section 138 of the Negotiable Instruments Act, 1881 held that the use of the words 'a bank' and 'the bank' in the section is indicator of the intention of the legislature. The former is indirect article and the latter is prefixed by direct article. If the Legislature intended to have the same meanings for 'the bank', there was no cause or occasion for mentioning it distinctly and differently by using two different articles. It is worth noticing that the word 'banker' in section 3 of the Act is pre-fixed by the indefinite article 'a' and the word 'bank' where the cheque is intended to be presented under section 138 is pre-fixed by the definite article 'the'. The same section permits a person to issue a cheque on an account maintained by him with 'a bank' and make him liable for criminal prosecution if it is returned by 'the bank' unpaid. The payment of the cheque is contemplated by 'the bank' meaning thereby where the person issuing the cheque has an account. 'The' is the word used before nouns with a specifying or particularising effect opposed to the indefinite or generalising force of 'a' or 'an'. It determines what particular thing is meant; 'The' is always mentioned to denote particular thing or a person. "The" would, therefore, refer implicitly to a specified bank and not any bank. 'The bank' referred to in clause (a) to the proviso to section 138 of the Act would mean the drawee-bank on which the cheque is drawn and not all banks where the cheque is presented for collection including the bank of the payee, in whose favour the cheque is issued; [*Shri Ishar Alloyes Steels Ltd.* v. *Jayaswals NECO Ltd.*, AIR 2001 SC 1161].

(b) Use of 'Shall' or 'Shall and May'; 'Must and Should'

The word 'shall' is ordinarily mandatory but it is sometimes not so interpreted if the context or the intention otherwise demands; [*Sainik Motors* v. *State of Rajasthan*, AIR 1961 SC 1480].

In *Labour Commissioner, Madhya Pradesh* v. *Burhanpur Tapti Mill*, AIR 1964 SC 1687 the Apex Court held that the use of the word 'shall' with respect to one matter and use of word 'may' in the respect of another matter in the same section of a statute, will normally lead to the conclusion that the word 'shall' imposes an obligation, whereas the word 'may' confers a discretionary power.

In *Mohan Singh* v. *International Airport Authority of India*, (1997) 9 SCC 132 the Apex Court held that *"if an object of the enactment is defeated by holding the same directory, it should be construed as mandatory whereas if by holding it mandatory serious general inconvenience will be created to innocent persons of general public without much furthering the object of the enactment, the same should be considered as directory."*

In *State of Uttar Pradesh* v. *Jogendra Singh*, AIR 1963 SC 1618 the Apex Court held that *"the word 'may' may also be used in the sense of 'shall' or 'must' by the legislature while conferring power on high dignitary. When the context shows that the power is coupled with an obligation, the word 'may' which denotes discretion should be construed to mean a command."*

(c) Negative Words

Though negative words are clearly prohibitory and are ordinarily used as a legislative device to make a statute imperative, there are certain exception to this principle. In *Lila Gupta* v. *Laxmi Narain*, AIR 1978 SC 1351, the Apex

Court has held that *"though directions relating to solemnization of marriage has been given in negative words, the same is directory as the enactment did not provide further consequences that the marriage in breach of those directions shall be invalid."*

(d) Construction of a "proviso" to a Section or Clause in an Enactment

As a general rule, a proviso is added to an enactment to qualify or create an exception to what is in the enactment, and ordinarily, a proviso is not interpreted as stating a general rule. A proviso is normally used to remove special cases from the general enactment and provide for them specially.

In *Dattatraya Govind Mahajan* v. *State of Maharashtra,* (1977) 2 SCR 790 the Constitution Bench of the Apex Court held that *"it is an elementary rule of construction that a statutary provision must always be interpreted in a manner which would suppress the mischief and advance the remedy and carry out the object and purpose of the legislation. .... It is true that the orthodox function of an explanation is to explain the meaning and effect of the main provision to which it is an explanation and to clear up any doubt or ambiguity in it, but ultimately it is the intention of the legislature which is paramount and mere use of a label cannot control or deflect such intention. .... It is true that the proper function of a proviso is to except or qualify something enacted in the substantive clause, which, but for the proviso would be within that clause. The question is one of interpretation of the proviso and there is no rule that the proviso must always be restricted to the ambit of the main enactment. .... Every fundamental right, from the point of view of the individual, gives a right and from the stand point of the State is a restraint. Whether the manner of expression used is in positive terms or negatively, whether the statutory technique of a proviso, saving clause, exception or explanation, is used or a direct interdict is imposed, the substantive content is what matters. .... It is absolutely plain that in the context setting and purpose of a provision even a proviso may function as an independent clause."*

(e) *Non-Obstante* Clause

The expression *'non-obstante'* means notwithstanding. A clause beginning with *"notwithstanding anything contained in this Act or in some particular provision in the Act or in some particular Act or in any law for the time being in force"* is called *non-obstante* clause. Generally *non-obstante* clause is considered to prevail over other provisions of the same statute or provisions of any other Act. Thus, it has overriding effect. In case of any discrepancy between *non-obstante* clause and other provisions, *non-obstante* clause would prevail over other clauses. However it has been held by the Apex Court in *R.S. Raghunath* v. *State of Karnataka,* AIR 1992 SC 81 that *"a special enactment or rule cannot be held to be overridden by a later general enactment or simply because the later opens up with a* non-obstante *clause. There should be clear inconsistency between the two before giving an overriding effect to the* non-obstante *clause."*

While construing *non-obstante* clause in section 433A of Cr.P.C. and the savings provision in section 5 of Cr.P.C., the Constitution Bench of the Apex Court in *Maru Ram* v. *Union of India,* (1981) 1 SCR 1196 has held that the fasciculus of clauses (sections 432, 433 and 433A of Cr.P.C.), read as a package, makes it clear that while the Code does confer wide powers of remission and commutation of sentences, it emphatically intends to carve out an extreme category from the broad generosity of such executive power. The *non-obstante* clause, in terms, excludes section 432 and whole mandate of the rest of the section necessarily subjects the operation of section 433(a) to a serious restriction. It is elementary that a *non-obstante* tail should not wag a statutory dog. A *non-obstante* clause cannot whittle down the wide import of the principal part. The enacting part is clear and the *non-obstante* clause cannot cut down its scope. To read down section 433A to give overriding effect to the Remission Rules of the State would render the purposeful exercise a ludicrous futility. If 'Laws suffer from the disease of Language', Courts must cure the patient, not to kill him. "Notwithstanding" the "notwithstanding ...." in section 433 A, the Remission Rules and like provisions stand excluded so far as "lifers" punished for capital offences are concerned.

(f) Marginal Notes

Marginal Notes are inserted at the side of the sections in an Act and express the effect of the sections. In the interpretation of a statute, marginal notes are not used because most of these notes are inserted by the draftsman and not by the legislators and not even under the instructions of the legislators. However, there are exceptions to this principle. For example, in *Bhagirath* v. *Delhi Administration,* (1985) 3 SCR 743 the Apex Court while construing the marginal note of section 428, Cr.P.C. held that *"marginal notes are now legislative and not editorial exercises. .... The marginal note of section 428 of Cr.P.C. shows that the object of the legislature in enacting the particular provision was to provide that 'the period of detention undergone by the accused' should be 'set off against the sentence of imprisonment' imposed upon him. There are no words of limitation either in the section or in its marginal note which would justify restricting the plain and natural meaning of the word 'term' so as to comprehend only sentences which are imposed for a fixed or ascertainable period."*

(g) *Illustration*

While interpreting *Illustration* (b) to section 106 of the Evidence Act, the Apex Court in *Shambhu Nath Mehra* v. *The State of Ajmer,* (1956) SCR 199 held that *"the word 'especially' means facts that are pre-eminently or exceptionally within his knowledge. We recognise that an illustration does not exhaust the full content of the section which it illustrates but equally it can neither curtail nor expand its ambit; and if knowledge of certain facts is as much available to the prosecution, should it choose to exercise due diligence, as to the accused, the fact cannot be said to be 'especially' within the knowledge of the accused. .... The section cannot be used to undermine the well established rule of law that, save in a very exceptional class of case, the burden is on the prosecution and it never shifts. .... Illustration (b) is only an illustration and must be read subject to the section itself and cannot travel beyond it."*

(h) Conjunctive or Disjunctive Words

In *Ishwar Singh Bindra* v. *State of Uttar Pradesh,* AIR 1968 SC 1540 the Apex Court held that the word 'or' is normally disjunctive and 'and' is normally conjunctive but at times they are read as *vice versa* to give effect to the manifest intention of the Legislature as disclosed from the context.

In *State of Bombay* v. *RMD Chamar Baugwala,* AIR 1957 SC 699 while dealing with section 2(d)(i) of the Bombay Lotteries and Prize Competition Control and

Tax Act, 1948 , the Supreme Court read 'or' as 'and' to give effect to the clear intention of the legislature as expressed in the Act read as a whole.

(i) Preamble

Like the long title of a statute, the preamble of a statue is also a part of the Act and is an admissible aid to construction. It is not an enacting part but it is expected to express the scope, object and purpose of the Act more comprehensively than the long title.

In *Sita Devi* v. *State of Bihar*, 1995 Supp (1) SCC 670 the Apex Court held that *"the role of preamble in interpretation cannot be curtailed or restricted. Preamble can be an aid in construing a provision when the provision is ambiguous."*

However in *L.D.A.* v. *M.K. Gupta*, (1994) 1 SCC 243: AIR 1994 SC 787 the Apex Court held that a preamble can afford useful assistance to ascertain legislative intention but cannot control the plain meaning of a provision.

(j) Headings

Headings are of two kinds, those prefixed to a section and those prefixed to a group or set of sections. It is now well settled that the headings can be referred to in construing an Act of the Legislature.

In *Bhinka* v. *Charan Singh*, AIR 1959 SC 960 the Apex Court held that the headings prefixed to sections or set of sections in some modern statutes are regarded as preambles to those sections. They cannot control the plain words of the statute but they may explain ambiguous words.

(k) Punctuation

Punctuation is not much useful for the purposes of construction and it has been held to be a minor element in the construction of a statute. However, it has been held that if the statute in question is found to be carefully punctuated, it may be resorted to for purposes of construction particularly with respect to modern statute.

In *Mohd. Shabbir* v. *State of Maharashtra*, AIR 1979 SC 564: (1979) 1 SCC 568 the Apex Court while construing section 27 of the Drugs and Cosmetics Act, 1940 held that the presence of comma after 'manufactures for sale' and 'sells' and absence of any comma after 'stocks' indicates that mere stocking is not an offence within the meaning of the section. Only stocking for sale could amount to offence and not mere stocking.

(l) Defination Clauses

The object of a definition clause is to avoid the necessity of frequent repetitions in describing all the subject-matter to which the word or expression so defined is intended to apply.

In *K.V. Muthu* v. *Angamuthu Ammal*, AIR 1997 SC 628: (1997) 2 SCC 53 the Apex Court while interpreting a definition clause held that it has to be borne in mind that the interpretation placed on it should not only be not repugnant to the context, it should also be such as would aid the achievement of the purpose which is sought to be served by the Act. A construction which would defeat or was likely to defeat the purpose of the Act has to be ignored and not accepted.

(m) *Explanation*

An explanation is appended to a section to explain the meaning of words contained in the section. The explanation is to be limited to the purpose for which it was created and should not be extended beyond the legitimate field. The explanation creates a legal fiction and these fictions are created only for definite purpose.

In *S. Sundaram* v. *V.R. Pattabhiraman,* AIR 1985 SC 582 the Apex Court held that An explanation added to a statutory provision is not a substantive provision in any sense of the terms but as the plain meaning of the word itself shows it is merely meant to explain or clarify certain ambiguities which may have crept in the statutory provision.

CHAPTER XLIII
LEGAL WEBSITES

In this chapter certain legal websites are given below which would help the readers in accessing the same:

(A) Supreme Court of India

1. **http://www.Supremecourtofindia.nic.in/.** – This website relates to the constitution of the Court, its jurisdiction, rules, judges, calendar, etc.
2. **Cause Lists: (http://causelists.nic.in)** – All the cause lists are available on the internet and it is possible to locate the case through the name of either party or through the case number.
3. **Case Status: (http://www.courtnic.nic.in)** – This website can be accessed through the internet to ascertain the status of pending as well as disposed cases. The status can be accessed through the case number, title and advocate's name or lower case details.
4. **Daily Orders: (http://www.courtnic.nic.in)** – Daily orders passed by the Court are available on the internet within 24 hours. However, such orders, if downloaded through the internet, cannot be used as certified copies ....
5. **Judgements: (http://www.judis.nic.in)** – On this website, the complete text of all reported judgment of the Supreme Court from 1950 till date are available. Judgments can be accessed through the party name, advocate's name, and date of judgment and also through free text search with enables the user to retrieve all the judgments on particular subject. The Registry has also claimed that judgments are available on the site within 24 hours of their being delivered in the Court.
6. **E-kiosks** – E-kiosks have been installed in the Supreme Court premises in order to enable the litigants an advocates to have access to computerized information, without actually owning a computer.
7. **Interactive Voice Response System** (I.V.R.S.) – Interactive Voice Response System has been installed in the Court thereby enabling a person to know the position of his case on telephone without using the internet. The telephone number of I.V.R.S. is 011-24357276.

   (**Note:** Supreme Court permits filing of petitions online).

SUBJECT INDEX

•••